BOOK
OF 1000
FAMILY
GAMES

Reader's Digest

BOOK
OF 1000
FAMILY
GAMES

The Reader's Digest Association, Inc., Pleasantville, New York
The Reader's Digest Association (Canada) Ltd., Montreal

CONTENTS

INTRODUCTION

This treasury of family games is designed to create a rich source of fun for readers. It places at your fingertips all the necessary information about games of every sort. Here are games for youngsters, for teen-agers, for adults; games to be played by every member of the family, regardless of age; games that are robustly athletic and games that depend more on quick wits than on strength or physical agility. Here are teaching and learning activities, pastimes for rainy days, diversions to lighten the hours spent traveling and games for quiet moments by a campfire. In the pages that follow, you will find many old favorites in addition to a number of new games. But even for the most familiar activities, the rules and strategies of play are clearly and comprehensively explained.

For young children tumbling into the world of playmates and happy times, this book holds a wealth of good fun. It helps young parents to recall the favorite games of their youth; then provides them with point-by-point instructions that they can explain to their children.

Adults and teen-agers will turn to this book's pages seeking the rules to a long forgotten card game, or perhaps to gather some ideas for an evening's entertainment with friends. The book is bound for family travel. Not only does it offer fun and entertainment on the way, it's a portable recreation center while you picnic, camp or relax during the evenings at the summer cottage.

The book will help Dad set up a family badminton court or place Junior's basketball hoop at just the right playing height. And Mom will find it especially helpful when one of the youngsters is convalescing—or on rainy days when "there's nothing to do."

The photographs and diagrams in these pages were given special attention so that each illustration works with the text, showing and telling how the game is played. Another unique feature: Like recipes in a cookbook, all games on these pages have been tried and tested according to the instructions provided.

Game rules in this book have been gleaned from experts: recreational directors, teachers, official rulebooks and professional sports associations. Rules for children's games came mostly from experience, and the history of many of these games can be traced back to the early Greeks. A game called *Ostrakindra,* for example, was played by the children of Athens many centuries before the coming of Christ. Today it is still a favorite, and known in this country as *Crows and Cranes* (p. 21). Games have traditionally played an important role in teaching young people the rules of fair play and good citizenship. It seems natural that this should apply to our generation, particularly if games played within the home serve to strengthen family ties.

Games You Make Yourself, which begins on page 368, describes imaginative new toys and games that can be put together in a matter of minutes from such common household items as toothpicks, paper plates, plastic spoons and straws.

If there is a scout leader or teacher in your family, here is a veritable "tool book." Special instructions for working with groups together with a 27-page index make this especially valuable for organized activities. A key to this usefulness is the unique *Games at a Glance* tables beginning on page 399. The tables will help anyone planning an occasion where games will be played: a family outing at the beach, a house party for teen-agers, a child's birthday party or an informal get-together for adults. Tables give various choices for each of these situations. The indexes at the back of the book are designed for ready reference. A comprehensive index lists every game in the book, alphabetically by title. This is followed by more than a score of specialized indexes in which games are grouped together according to type. With pinpoint reference features, with more than 1000 games to choose from and with illustrations and diagrams to clarify points of play, 1000 FAMILY GAMES will provide every member of your family with a lifetime of fun.

The Editors

Games For Children

SECTION I

To Grow On

*He's safe!—for the moment, at least. By stooping, the little boy evades
a tag, but by counting to three, his pursuer can force him to move in* Stoop Tag.

CHAPTER 1

Games of Action and Agility

This chapter of action-packed games is intended for children ranging from pre-school age to 12 years old. Each game encourages alertness and teaches some basic physical skill; all are fun and exciting. Owing to the amount of activity involved, most of these activities are best suited to outdoor play, although many of them can be adapted to a playroom. Most games are preceded by recommendations for the number of players, age levels and, where necessary, items of special equipment. Equipment substitutions can be made in most instances.

Many of the games in the section will be familiar to most children, as they have probably played them in school or at other group functions. Generally, children 8 to 12 years old will often be able to supervise their own play. Younger children, however, should have some leadership, either from an adult or an older child who will see that the game rules are properly explained and that the teams are evenly matched. The group leader should also act as referee and encourage fair play.

The first group consists of tag games—all of which share a common characteristic: Someone is always chasing someone else. These games are good for working off children's excess energy and are especially suitable for opening activities for parties, outings, or Cub and Brownie meetings.

Numerals indicate the number of players. Spelled-out numbers suggest suitable age levels.

Stoop Tag

● *6 to 15* ● *Six to nine*

FORMATION: Players scatter freely around the field, which is at least 30 by 40 feet.
ACTION: One player is chosen as chaser. The chaser may tag any opponent who is not in a stooped position (knees bent close to the ground). A tagged player becomes the new chaser. Children usually enjoy the excitement of being chased and do not stay in the stooped position too long, but if one does, the chaser may stand within three or four feet of that child and count to three. If the player does not move, he is considered tagged and becomes the new chaser during the next round of play.
VARIATIONS: In *Hindu Tag* a child is safe so long as he is in a kneeling position with his forehead touching the ground. *Tree Tag* requires that a player be touching a tree or shrub to remain safe. In one version of this game only

one player can be touching a single tree at any time, and if a second player seeks safety there the first one is displaced and is exposed to tagging as he looks for a new refuge. *Metal Tag* is usually played on playgrounds or other places with metal fences. A player is safe so long as he is touching metal. In all of these games a chaser may force an opponent from safety by counting to three.

Shadow Tag

● *6 to 15* ● *Six to nine*

FORMATION: Players scatter around a playing area measuring at least 15 by 20 feet. This is a game for a bright sunny day, as the players must cast distinct shadows.

ACTION: One player is chosen shadow chaser. To make a tag he steps on any other runner's shadow. When a tag is made, the shadow chaser joins the runners while the tagged player takes over as the new shadow chaser. At any time the shadow chaser may call out: "Shadows cross over!" All runners sprint to the corner of the

play area farthest from where they were standing. This gives the shadow chaser a real opportunity to make a tag. The game has no winner and it goes on until the players lose interest.

Red Rover

● *8 to 20* ● *Seven to ten*

FORMATION: Two goal lines are marked 30 or 40 feet apart. The players divide into two groups (one behind each goal) except for one child, who is the caller and stands in the center.

ACTION: The caller shouts: "Red Rover, Red Rover, send [the name of a player] over!" The child called runs to the opposite goal, and the caller chases him, trying to make a tag before the runner reaches safety. If the caller makes his tag the runner is imprisoned in the rover's den, an area on the sidelines. Again the caller asks for a player and the action is repeated. The third and final call, however, is: "Red Rover, Red Rover, send all of them over!" All players now try to cross to the opposite side while the caller tags as many as he can. The number of prisoners taken in the three rounds constitutes the caller's score. The game goes on until all players have had their chance at being caller, and the player with the highest score wins.

VARIATION: In *Hill Dill* two goal lines are marked, about 35 feet apart. Half the players stand behind one, and half behind the other. The player picked to be caller stands in the center. The caller shouts: "Hill Dill, come over the hill, or else I'll catch you standing still!" At this, each group of players runs toward the opposite goal while the caller chases them. Those children tagged then help the caller tag the others. The game goes on in this manner until all the children have been caught by the caller. The last child to be tagged is the winner, and he gets to be the new caller when the game begins again.

Exchange Tag

● *8 to 25* ● *Seven to ten*

FORMATION: Indoors, children sit on chairs arranged in a large circle about 20 to 25 feet in diameter. Outdoors, they form a circle sitting on the ground. The player picked to be the chaser stands in the center.

ACTION: The chaser calls out the names of any two players, who try to change places in the circle. While they are running the chaser tries to tag one. If the chaser succeeds, he changes roles with his opponent. If the children do not all know each other's names, numbers may be assigned to the players and taped to their shirts. The chaser calls out any two numbers and the corresponding players try to cross over.

Bear in the Cage

● *8 to 12* ● *Seven to ten*

FORMATION: One child, the bear, is in a cage formed by all the other players (hunters), who join hands to enclose him.

ACTION: The bear tries to force his way out of the cage by stepping over, crawling under, or breaking through his captors' arms. The hunters keep their hands joined and move their bodies back and forth to prevent the bear's escape. They may not, however, directly hold their captive. When the bear finally does escape, the hunters pursue him. The first hunter to make the tag becomes the new bear and the game starts again.

VARIATION: In *Prison Break* two circles are formed and each team sends one of its members

Off and away! A small bear leaps for freedom through the bars of his cage. The group of hunters will quickly give chase in an effort to tag him.

to be a prisoner in the other circle. The first player to break out scores a point for his own team, which then sends over a new prisoner. The winning team is the one with more points after ten minutes of play.

Bronco Tag

● *10 to 30*   ● *Eight to twelve*

FORMATION: All but two players pair up and scatter around the playing field, at least 40 feet square. Each pair becomes a bronco, with one player in front (the head) and the second in back (the tail) with arms around the partner's waist. The other two players become the runner and the chaser.

ACTION: The chaser gives the runner a head start and then pursues him. If a tag is made, the two exchange roles. At any time, the runner may join a bronco by clasping the waist of the bronco's tail. The tail thus becomes the new head and the old head is displaced and becomes the new runner. Broncos may buck and dodge to prevent the runner from joining them, but they may not push a runner away.

Fox and Geese

● *8 to 12*   ● *Six to twenty*

FORMATION: A circle, about 35 feet in diameter, is marked on the ground with equally spaced spokes radiating out from the hub. One player—the fox—stands on the hub, the others—the geese—spread out at random on the rim and along the spokes of the giant wheel. This game is highly suitable for winter play because the wheel and its spokes are very easily drawn in the snow. Children can create the proper design merely by dragging a shovel along a flat snowy space.

ACTION: The fox chases the geese. Both fox and geese run only along the spokes and rim of the circle. When the fox tags a goose, the tagged player becomes the fox's helper in running down the other geese. The last goose to be caught is the winner, and that boy or girl becomes the fox for the next round of play.

Skip Tag

● *8 to 25*   ● *Six to ten*

FORMATION: One player is the skipper; the others form a large circle and face the center. The skipper stands outside the circle.

ACTION: The skipper skips around the circle, moving to the right. He touches the shoulder of any player and continues to skip, followed by the one he has tagged. The two players skip around the circle racing for the open spot. If the skipper reaches it first he fills the spot and his opponent becomes the new skipper.

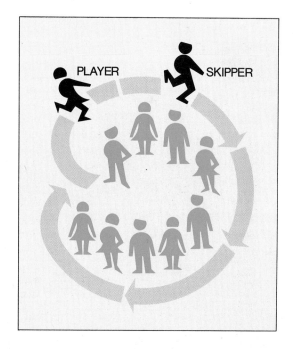

VARIATION: *Hop, Walk,* or *Run Tag* is played in the same way except that the tagger hops, walks, or runs around the circle instead of skipping.

Goose and Gander

● *4 to 10*   ● *Six to ten*

FORMATION: All players but one are geese. They form a single line, each player with his hands on the waist of the child in front of him. The other player is the gander.

ACTION: The object is for the gander to tag the last goose in line. To prevent this, the head goose moves around, swinging the line from side to side and using his arms to block the gander. The head goose may not, however, hold the gander. When the gander finally succeeds in tagging the last goose, he then joins the line at the end, and the head goose becomes the new gander.

VARIATION: *Hook On* is for larger groups numbering as many as 40 or so. All players but one form up into lines with four or five players in each. The one player who is the runner moves from line to line trying to hook on to the back of any column, as in *Goose and Gander.*

Back to Back
● *9 to 25* ● *Seven to ten*

FORMATION: One player is chosen to be the runner. He stands in the middle of a playing area while the others pair up and scatter around a play area at least 40 feet square. Each player stands back-to-back with his partner, their elbows hooked.

ACTION: The runner calls out: "Everybody change!" At this, all players leave their partners, and seek new partners with whom to lock arms. While this is going on, the runner seeks a partner for himself. If he succeeds, the player left over becomes the new runner and the game is repeated. There is no scoring and the game continues as long as everybody remains interested.

An agile mother goose swings her brood of goslings away from the gander, who turns on speed as he tries to tag the last gosling in the line.

Flying Dutchmen

● *10 to 20* ● *Six to ten*

FORMATION: Players divide into couples and form a circle facing in, each couple holding hands. Two players, however, are chosen the flying Dutchmen, and they stand, hand in hand, outside the circle.

ACTION: The flying Dutchmen walk (or run, skip, hop, depending upon the rules established) to the left (clockwise) around the circle. When the Dutchmen touch another couple, that pair steps outside the circle and moves around it to the right (counter-clockwise). Each couple tries to reach the empty place in the circle first. The two who lose become flying Dutchmen for the next round.

Two Deep

● *10 to 25* ● *Six to eight*

FORMATION: All but two players—the runner and the chaser—form a circle at least 25 feet in diameter, facing in. The runner and the chaser

now take up positions outside the circle a few feet apart.

ACTION: On signal, the chaser pursues the runner, attempting to tag him. If the chaser succeeds, the two exchange roles. At any time the runner may reach safety by entering the circle and stepping in front of a player, who then becomes the new runner. Because of continuing changes in roles, with new runners and chasers being made every minute or so, the game moves along rapidly.

VARIATION: In *Three Deep* the circle consists of an inner and an outer ring. The runner who enters the circle stands in front of a pair, making the circle "three deep" at that particular spot, and the player on the outside now becomes the game's new runner.

Have You Seen My Sheep?

● *10 to 20* ● *Six to nine*

FORMATION: Players stand in a circle, with one—the shepherd—standing outside.

ACTION: The shepherd walks around the outside of the ring, stops anywhere, and taps a player on the shoulder. The shepherd asks: "Have you seen my sheep?" The player replies: "How was he dressed?" The shepherd describes the clothing of another player and when the child being questioned recognizes that player, he answers: "Your missing sheep is Johnny [or Jane or Mary]." On being identified, the sheep bolts from the circle and races around the outside, pursued by the player who made the identification. If the sheep can get back in place before being tagged, he becomes the shepherd for the next round. If he is tagged, his pursuer is the new shepherd.

Chinese Tag

● *8 to 25* ● *Six to nine*

FORMATION: Players scatter around the play area with one child chosen to be the chaser.

ACTION: The chaser tries to tag any other player. When he does so, that player becomes the new chaser. While running, the chaser must keep one hand on the spot where he was tagged. An object of the game is to tag an opponent on the foot, the knee, or some other spot that is difficult to hold, forcing the chaser to hop or limp, instead of run, while going in pursuit of the others.

VARIATIONS: In *Reverse Tag* everyone, including the chaser, must run backward at all times. *Reverse Chinese Tag* combines the two games, with everyone running backward, but with the chaser also holding on to the spot on his body where he was tagged.

Run Around the Circle

● *10 to 25* ● *Six to eight*

FORMATION: Players form a fairly large circle with all of them facing in. One player, chosen to be the runner, stands within the ring.

RUNNER

ACTION: The runner moves around the inside of the circle and then stands between any two players. These two leave the circle and race around the outside, running in opposite directions. The one who returns first to their starting point fills the remaining vacant place. The other then becomes the new runner and the game is repeated for another round.

Elbow Tag

● *10 to 30* ● *Nine to twelve*

FORMATION: Players—all but two—divide into couples and scatter around the play area, each child having one elbow linked with his partner's. The remaining two players are the chaser and the runner.

ACTION: The chaser tries to tag the runner, who may seek safety at any time by hooking his own elbow on to one member of a couple—the other member immediately becoming the new runner. When a chaser tags a runner, the two reverse roles for a new round of play.

Red Light

● *6 to 20* ● *Six to ten*

FORMATION: One player is chosen light-keeper and stands on a line about 25 feet from the others with his back turned toward them.

ACTION: The light-keeper closes his eyes, counts to ten, calls out "Red Light," and then turns around. While the light-keeper counts, the other players advance, but when they hear "Red Light" they all stop. If the light-keeper sees anyone move he calls out the offender's name and that player returns to the base line. The action is repeated until one player gets within touching distance of the light-keeper. On being tagged, the light-keeper chases the tagger back toward the base line. If the light-keeper catches the tagger, he retains the position for the next round; if not, the tagger becomes the new light-keeper.

Hide and Seek

● *4 to 20* ● *Six to ten*

FORMATION: One child is chosen the seeker. He closes his eyes and counts aloud to ten or twenty while the others hide behind such objects as trees, bushes, benches, and trellises.

ACTION: The seeker finishes counting and calls out: "Ready or not, here I come!" The seeker then begins to search for the hidden players. The first one found becomes the new seeker.

VARIATIONS: In *I Spy,* when the seeker spots a hider, he calls out: "I spy Joseph [or Janet or Doris, etc.]." The two then race to home base (which can be a tree trunk, a bare patch of ground, a cellar door, etc.), and if the seeker reaches home first, he makes the hider a prisoner and forces him to help seek out the other players. The action continues, with seekers eventually outnumbering hiders, until all hiders are caught. If a hider reaches home base before the seeker, however, that hider need not change sides. After all hiders have been caught or have come in safe, a new seeker is chosen for the next round—usually it is the first child to have been made prisoner. In *Prisoner's Base,* the rules of *I Spy* apply, except that all prisoners can be freed to hide again if one of the players can dart from his hiding place, touch each prisoner, and escape without being himself caught by the seeker.

Squirrel in the Tree
● *14 to 35* ● *Eight to twelve*

FORMATION: All players, except for two, form into groups of three. Two members of each group join hands and they become a tree; the third member stands between them and is a squirrel. One of the two players left over is a hound, the other boy or girl acts the part of a running squirrel.

ACTION: On signal the running squirrel, with the hound in hot pursuit, seeks safety by finding a tree. The running squirrel may duck under the joined hands of a tree, to displace the squirrel already there, who becomes the new runner. When a hound finally tags a squirrel, their roles reverse. After every three or four minutes of play, the game can be halted while the squirrels change roles with the trees. In this way, everyone has a chance to take part in the action.

Missed! A hound (far right) just misses tagging a squirrel who takes shelter in a "tree" to displace another squirrel who runs off to escape the hound.

Chain Tag

- *8 to 20*   - *Eight to twelve*

FORMATION: One player is chosen the chain maker; the others scatter about the area.
ACTION: The chain maker chases the others. When he tags one, they join hands to form a two-link chain. Together they chase the other players, and when a third is tagged he too joins the chain. Thus the chain continues to grow, but it must stay together, and only the links on the two ends may make a tag. The last player to remain free of the chain wins the game and becomes the chain maker for the next round.

Toss the Cap

- *10 to 20*   - *Six to ten*
- *A baseball-type cap*

FORMATION: Boys and girls divide into two equal-size teams that stand facing each other on lines about five feet apart. One player, the cap tosser, stands between the teams. About 20 feet behind each team is a base line.
ACTION: One team is designated the "ups," the other, the "downs." The cap tosser throws his cap in the air. If it falls right-side up, the ups turn and run toward their base line with the downs chasing them. If the cap falls upside down, then the downs run toward their base line with the ups in pursuit. When a player is tagged, he joins the opposing team and the game continues until one team has no players left. Alternatively, the team with more players after ten minutes of play wins.

Fox and Farmer

- *8 to 20*   - *Six to eight*

FORMATION: This game is suitable for indoors and out. One player is chosen the fox, another, the farmer. All the rest form a circle facing in, with their arms outstretched and hands resting on one another's shoulders.
ACTION: On signal, the farmer begins to chase

the fox. To escape the farmer, the fox takes any route around the circle, weaving in and out among the players. The farmer must follow the fox's exact route. If the fox is tagged, the farmer chooses one of the players in the circle to become a new farmer while he becomes the fox for the next round. Should the fox elude the farmer for three minutes, time is called while a new fox and a new farmer are chosen, and then play resumes.

Crows and Cranes

- *10 to 30*   - *Eight to twelve*

FORMATION: The players are divided into two equal lines, one called crows and the other called cranes. They stand about five feet apart, facing each other, on opposite sides of a center line. Behind each group of players, and about 25 feet away, is a goal line.

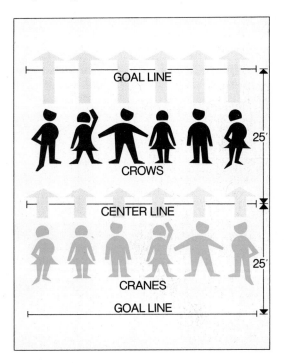

ACTION: When the game leader calls out "Crows!" that group turns and runs toward its own goal line with the cranes in pursuit. Any crow tagged before crossing the line joins the other side. The action continues with the leader giving each side a fairly even number of chances to catch their opponents—although he varies the order of calling them, to keep them alert. He may also tease them by calling "Crrrr—" before saying the complete word, or even calling words like "Cracker" or "Creep" from time to time.

Fish and Net

- *12 to 25*   - *Seven to ten*

FORMATION: Five players are chosen to be the net, while the others are fish who scatter about the playing area, which is at least 40 by 50 feet. ACTION: The children who form the net join hands in a line. The game leader calls out: "Swim, fish, swim." At this, the players who make up the net move about the playing area with hands still joined and try to capture as many fish as possible by surrounding them. The fish, of course, are running from the net. Fish who are caught become part of the net and the game continues until all the fish have been caught. When the game is repeated, the last five fish to have been caught become the new net.

Trades

- *8 to 20*   - *Seven to ten*

FORMATION: Players divide into two teams and stand behind two goal lines about 40 feet apart. ACTION: The players in Team 1 select some sort of occupation which can be demonstrated. They march to within five feet of Team 2, and exchange the following phrases:

Team 1: "Here we come."
Team 2: "Where from?"
Team 1: "From Chicago [or Montreal or Los Angeles, etc.]."
Team 2: "What's your trade?"

The players in Team 1 then show their occupation. If, for example, they were carpenters, they would all pretend to hammer, saw, and plane. As soon as a member of Team 2 guesses their

trade and calls it out correctly, the players in Team 1 run toward their goal line, chased by Team 2. Those who are tagged before crossing the goal become part of Team 2. Then the game is played in reverse, with Team 2 picking a trade, and Team 1 doing the chasing. After several turns, the team with the greater number of players remaining is the winner.

Last Couple Out

- *9 to 25*   - *Eight to twelve*

FORMATION: Players form two columns with all players facing front. One child, however, is the caller and stands three or four yards in front of the lines and between them with back turned to the other players.

CALLER

ACTION: The caller shouts: "Last couple out!" At this, the two players at the rear of the lines run forward and try to touch hands with each other in front of the caller. The caller, as soon as he sees them, tries to tag one before they touch. If he cannot, the caller chases either player back to his line. If the runner can elude the caller and make it back to the head of the line from which he came, the runner is safe. If tagged, however, the runner becomes the new caller and the old caller replaces him at the head of the proper line.

Steal the Bacon

- *8 to 20*   • *Eight to twelve*
- *Large handkerchief or Indian club or plastic bottle*

FORMATION: The group is divided into two equal teams. Each team stands on a line facing the other with about 20 feet between them.

Players on each line are numbered (1, 2, 3, 4, etc.), with the corresponding numbers diagonally opposite each other. A large handkerchief or some other object is placed in the center, between the lines.

ACTION: The leader calls out a number, and the players with that number run forward. They race for the handkerchief, and the one who gets it tries to reach his own goal line before he is tagged by his opponent. If he makes it, his team wins one point. If he is tagged, the other side wins a point. If players take too long to make their move the leader may count to five. If neither player tries to "steal the bacon" within this time limit, they go back to their places and a new number is called. The first team to reach a set number of points, usually 21, wins.

With her opponent off balance, a girl reaches to Steal the Bacon. *Then she will try to reach her teammates (rear line) before she can be tagged.*

Streets and Alleys

- *15 to 60*   - *Seven to twelve*

FORMATION: Boys and girls form parallel lines of about six players each. The children in each row hold hands with arms extended. When the players are facing front, the aisles between rows are called "streets." When they turn to the right, to form new rows, the aisles are called "alleys." Three players are not part of the rows: one is the runner, another the chaser, and the third, the caller, who stands in front of the rows. As the game begins, all players are facing front and each holds hands with his two neighbors.

ACTION: On signal, the chaser pursues the runner down the streets. At any time, the caller may shout, "alleys!" and the players turn to the right and take the hands of their new neighbors. At this, the runner and chaser must change their direction to run down the new aisles. When the caller shouts, "streets!" the players turn forward again and the direction of the chase is once more reversed. As neither the runner nor the chaser may run through or duck under clasped hands, the direction of the chase changes every time the caller gives a new command. A round ends when the chaser tags the runner, or after three minutes of play. For the next round, the chaser becomes the runner, the runner the caller, and the caller replaces one of the players in the lines, who becomes the new chaser.

VARIATION: *Running Up the Alleys* is a simple form of *Streets and Alleys.* The formation is the same, with the players forming rows of four or five players apiece. However, once the rows are formed, they remain the same. There is a runner and a chaser, the latter pursuing the former up and down the alleys. Both the runner and the chaser can move only in the alleys, or, when reaching the last alley on either side, they can skirt around the outside of that last row before re-entering the alleys. When a chaser tags a runner, they switch roles for a round, and then the game leader chooses a new runner and chaser.

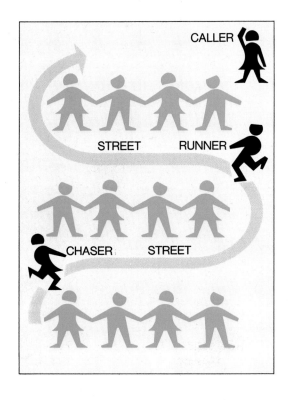

Dodge-Ball Games

Another popular type of children's game is the *Dodge-Ball* group. In these, the basic idea is to eliminate other players by hitting them with a ball. The ball should be an eight-inch rubber playground ball, or a volleyball, and "fair" hits are below the waist. Younger children find *Dodge-Ball* games very exciting, and they are often among the most lively and enjoyable contests in any get-together.

Numerals indicate the number of players. Spelled-out numbers suggest suitable age levels.

Team Dodge Ball

- *12 to 30* - *Eight to twelve*
- *Playground ball*

FORMATION: Two teams of equal size stand on opposite sides of a center line dividing the play area, which is at least 30 by 50 feet.

ACTION: The leader rolls the ball down the center line, and the first player to retrieve it starts the action. The idea is to eliminate players on the opposite team by hitting them below the waist with the ball. Any child who is hit, or who steps across the center line, goes to the sidelines. There are two ways to score the game: the team that has the most players left after a set period of time (three to five minutes) is the winner; or the team that manages to completely eliminate its opponents wins. If there are enough players and a very large playing area, more than one ball may be used.

VARIATION: In *Bombardment,* the players begin by standing on their own base line, while several balls are placed on the center line. At a signal, they all run forward to get as many balls as they can, and throw them at their opponents. If a player catches the ball on a fly, it does not count as a hit. The game goes on until all players on one side have been eliminated.

Circle Dodge Ball

- *8 to 15* - *Eight to twelve*
- *Playground ball*

FORMATION: All players but the dodger stand on or outside the rim of a circle about 25 feet in diameter. The dodger stands in the center.

ACTION: The players on the rim try to hit the dodger with the ball. They may not move within the circle itself when they throw, and a fair hit is below the waist. The player who hits the

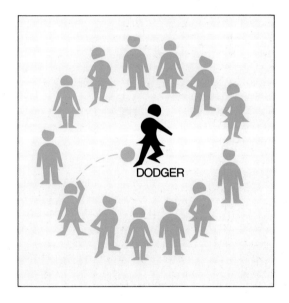

dodger exchanges roles with him. In this game, the leader's job is to make sure that the ball is not monopolized by a few players. After each throw, he passes the ball on to the next player.

Elimination Dodge Ball

- *10 to 20* - *Eight to twelve*
- *Playground ball*

FORMATION: Half the players stand in the center of a circle—about 25 feet across—formed by the others.

ACTION: Players on the rim throw the ball and try to hit those in the center below the waist. When a child is hit, he joins the players on the outside of the circle. The last player to be hit wins the game.

VARIATION: In *Squat Dodge Ball* when a player in the center is hit he squats and remains in that position. The other players in the center continue to dodge throws. When all in the center have been hit, their side is "out," and they exchange places with the circle players to repeat the game.

Indian Club Bombardment

- *12 to 30* • *Eight to twelve*
- *Indian clubs or large plastic bottles; four playground balls*

FORMATION: Two teams of equal size stand on opposite sides of a center line. Each team has a goal line five yards behind the center line. Four Indian clubs or cardboard or plastic gallon bottles are placed, each about a yard apart, on the two goal lines.

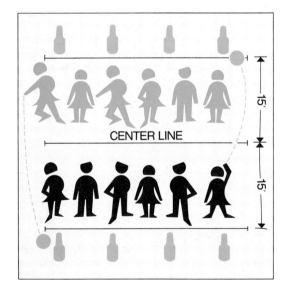

ACTION: Each team tries to knock down its opponents' clubs, while protecting its own. Players may pass the ball from one to another

to get in position for good throws. They may not step across the center line. There are two ways to score the game: the first team to knock down all its opponents' clubs is the winner; or a team receives one point each time it knocks down a club (the clubs are put up again at once), and the team with more points after five minutes is the winner.

Spud

- *6 to 15* • *Eight to twelve*
- *Playground ball*

FORMATION: All players get a number, and one is chosen the caller. The others form a circle about 15 feet in diameter, and the caller stands in the center with a ball.

ACTION: The caller shouts out a number and throws the ball high in the air; the player with that number retrieves it. While the ball is being retrieved, all other players scatter, but when the ball has been caught, the ball holder calls out "spud!" This is the signal for everyone to stand stock still, and the ball holder searches out an easy target and throws the ball at him. The target player may duck or swerve in place to avoid being hit but may not move his feet. If the target player is hit, he is penalized with "one spud," and becomes the new caller. If the target is missed, the player who threw the ball gets the penalty and is the new caller. A player who is "spudded" three times is out of the game, and the last player to be eliminated wins.

Train Dodge Ball

- *10 to 25* • *Eight to twelve*
- *Playground ball*

FORMATION: Four players in the center of a circle stand in single file, each with hands around the player in front; this is the train. The player at the head of the line is the engine; the one in back, the caboose. All the other players stand around the rim, about 20 feet in diameter.

ACTION: The rim players try to hit the caboose

below the belt line with the ball. The engine tries to protect the caboose by batting or kicking the ball away (he is the only one in the train who can do this), and by swinging the train

around to shield him. When the caboose is hit, the player who threw the ball becomes the engine; the old engine is now the first car; the first car moves to the second car position; the second car becomes the new caboose, and the old caboose replaces the new engine on the circle's rim. The engine who protects a caboose for the longest period is considered the winner.

Ball Pass

- *5 to 15* - *Seven to eleven*
- *Playground ball*

FORMATION: One player is the rover, and he has the ball. The others stand on bases scattered around a playing area at least 50 by 60 feet.
ACTION: Players on the bases try to change places with each other without being hit by the ball. They gesture to each other to cross over. When they cross, the rover tries to hit them below the waist with the ball. If the rover makes a hit, he takes the place of the player hit, and that player becomes the new rover. The rover

may also step on any vacant base that a player has left, and the player who cannot find a base becomes the rover. Players keep score on the number of times they have exchanged bases, and the one with the highest number of successful runs after a set period of time (ten or fifteen minutes) is the winner.

Free Zone, End Zone

- *12 to 40* - *Ten to twelve*
- *Playground ball*

FORMATION: Two teams of equal size stand on opposite sides of a center line. On each side of the line, and about 20 feet behind it, is a goal line. The areas between center line and goal lines are the free zones; the areas behind the goal lines are end zones.
ACTION: This game differs from most *Dodge ball*

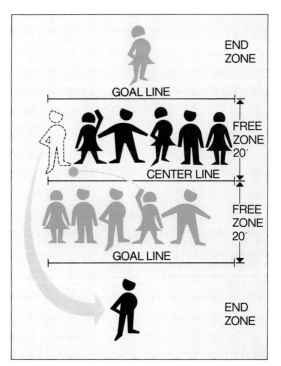

events in that players who are hit are not entirely eliminated. They go to the end zone behind the opposition and from there can continue to play should the ball come their way. Therefore, free-zone players must protect themselves from the rear as well as the front. But the object of the game is to get as many opponents behind one's own end zone as possible. The game begins with players trying to hit members of the opposing team below the waist with a ball on the fly. When a player is hit he goes to the opposing team's end zone, and though he may attack from there, should he get the ball, he may not move in front of the goal line. If, during the action, a player catches the ball on the fly, the thrower goes to the opposition's end zone. If the thrower was already there, the ball catcher can point out any member of the opposing team and send him to the end zone. Should one team lose all its free-zone players, the game automatically ends; otherwise it ends after ten minutes, and the winning team is the one with more players remaining in its free zone.

VARIATION: A less complex version of this game is *End Dodge Ball.* Players hit are not eliminated; they go to their own end zone and continue to play from there. They are forced to throw a much greater distance to make a hit and may not relay the ball to a teammate in the free zone. The game ends after ten minutes, and the team with more players in its free zone wins.

Relays and Novelty Races

In a relay, teams race against each other with each player taking his turn. The first team to complete the action wins. As the following selection shows, many relays require contestants to assume humorously awkward positions, while others challenge players to execute difficult maneuvers, and some demand a high order of teamwork. Most of these relays can also be played as novelty races among individuals or pairs when the group is too small to be divided into teams large enough to make exciting relays.

Numerals indicate the number of players. Spelled-out numbers suggest suitable age levels.

Simple Relay

● *8 to 30* ● *Five to seven*

FORMATION: Players divide into teams of between four and eight contestants. Each team lines up in single file behind a goal line (the starting line), the columns side by side. About 30 feet down field, directly opposite the goal line, is the turning line.

ACTION: On signal, the first player in each file runs down field to the turning line, touches it with his foot, and then runs back to his goal line and tags the number-two runner, who is now at the front of the column. The number-two runner repeats the action, touching the third runner as he returns. Each player moves to the back of his column after completing his run. The game can be scored in two ways: each race can be considered separately, with a team scoring a point for each win; or the team that is the

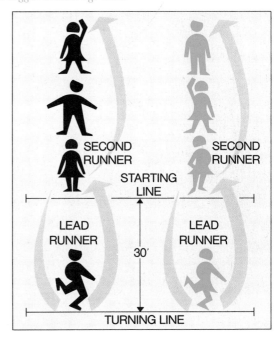

first to complete a full round of races—the lead runner being once more in the lead position—wins the contest.

Couple Hobble Relay

- *12 to 40* - *Seven to eleven*

FORMATION: Teams line up in pairs behind the starting line. A turning line is marked 30 feet away. The lead players stand side by side. Each places an arm around the partner's waist and lifts the knee of his outside leg as close as possible to the chest, gripping the knee with the free hand.

ACTION: On signal, each lead pair hops toward the turning line and back. The lead pair is immediately followed by the second pair—and so on until the cycle is finished. The column that completes the action first wins the *Couple Hobble Relay.*

One couple (right) approaches the turning line, while the other pair, having reached it, hops back toward their teammates in Couple Hobble Relay.

Crab Relay

● *8 to 30*   ● *Eight to twelve*

FORMATION: Teams line up in columns behind the starting line. Because crab relays are difficult to perform, the turning line should be only about 15 feet from the starting line. The first player in each line stands with his back to the starting line, squats, and reaches backward so that his hands are on the ground.
ACTION: On signal, the lead players race backward, traveling on heels and palms, to the turning line. They cross it and return in the same way. Each player in the lines repeats the action, traveling in this crab-like fashion. The first team in which all players have raced wins.

Bunny Hop Relay

● *8 to 30*   ● *Six to eight*

FORMATION: Teams line up in single files, four or five to a team. The turning and starting lines are about 15 feet apart.
ACTION: Each player races in turn to the turning line and back. He must do it by taking the "bunny hop" position: squatting, holding his arms around his knees, and jumping along.

Kangaroo Relay

● *8 to 30*   ● *Seven to twelve*
● *Playground balls or beanbags or balloons*

FORMATION: Teams form columns. The turning line is 20 feet from the starting line. Each lead player holds a rubber playground ball or similar object. It might be a balloon, a block of wood, or a beanbag, but it should be the same object for all of the teams.
ACTION: On signal, the lead player places the object between his knees and jumps along, feet together, toward the turning line. He may not hold the object in place with his hands. If the object falls, he must pick it up, place it between his knees, and start again from that spot. The first team to complete the action wins.

Crooked Walk Relay

● *8 to 30*   ● *Eight to twelve*

FORMATION: Teams form in two columns with starting and turning lines about 30 feet apart.
ACTION: The lead player on each team steps forward as far as possible on the right foot, and crosses the left foot behind it. He then crosses the right foot behind the left, placing the left forward, and keeps moving in this zigzag, "crooked walk," manner, until reaching the turning line. He may come back the same way, or may simply have to run back to his line—depending upon the rules previously established—to touch the next player and have the relay continue.

Bag Pile Relay

● *16 to 30*   ● *Seven to eleven*
● *About 20 beanbags*

FORMATION: Boys and girls form into two lines of equal numbers. Each team has half the beanbags at the foot of its line.
ACTION: Beanbags are passed swiftly from the backs of the lines to their fronts. Players at the heads pile up the bags with only the bottom bag touching the ground. Should the bags fall over, the player stacking them rearranges them, causing the passing of bags to halt while the stack is rebuilt. The first team to stack all its beanbags wins the round, and the best out of five rounds takes the game.
VARIATION: *Clothespin Pile Relay* is played in the same way but it is much more difficult because the clothespins are neither passed nor stacked as easily as beanbags.

Sack Race

● *8 to 50*   ● *Eight to twelve*   ● *Large sacks*

FORMATION: Players line up in columns by a starting line, about 30 feet from a turning line. Each lead player has a large sack, such as a potato or grain sack.

Covered from neck to toe by a grocery-store potato sack, this little kangaroo practices hopping for a Sack Race.

ACTION: At the signal, each lead player climbs into his sack, and holding its open end up around his waist, jumps to the turning line and back to touch the next player and give him the sack. The first team to have all players complete the action wins.

Crawling Relay

● *8 to 30* ● *Eight to twelve*

FORMATION: Contestants divide into two or more teams, each team standing in single file behind a starting line. A turning line is marked off at a distance of about 30 feet. This line may be painted on the flooring with washable poster paint if the relay is being held indoors. If held outdoors, the line may be chalked on the grass, or a cord may be stretched close to the ground and fastened between two stakes.

ACTION: On signal, the lead player on each team gets down on his hands and knees and begins to crawl toward the turning line. On reaching that line, he crawls back to the starting line and touches off the next player on his team, who repeats the action. The first team to have had all of its members perform the action wins the relay.

VARIATION: In the *Crawling-Running Relay* the action is the same, except that after crawling to the turning line, each player may rise and run back to the starting line.

Heel Relay

● *8 to 30* ● *Seven to twelve*

FORMATION: Players divide into equal-size teams of four or more players each. The members of each team form a single file behind a starting line and face a turning line about 30 feet away.

ACTION: On signal, the lead players begin moving toward the turning line, each player walking only on his heels. Upon reaching the turning line the players return, in the same manner, to the starting line and touch off the No. 2 players on their respective teams. The relay continues until one team, the winner, has had each player successfully perform the action. In general, no more than three teams should compete, because this relay requires that the game leader keep a careful eye on all contestants, making sure that none touches his toes to the ground. A player who commits this foul is sent back to the starting line and must begin his turn again.

Triple Squat Relay

- *8 to 30* - *Eight to twelve*

FORMATION: Teams form into files; there is no turning line.

ACTION: Each child squats in place. They are about two feet apart. The first player in each line stands up at the starting signal, turns to his right and runs clockwise once around his line. When he gets back to place, he does three squats, or deep-knee bends quickly, counting them out loud. Each player in turn repeats the action, and the first team to complete it wins.

Bounce Ball Relay

- *8 to 30* - *Seven to eleven* - *Basketball*

FORMATION: Players line up in equal teams on a starting line that should be about 30 feet away from a wall. A "throwing line" is marked, about ten feet from the wall. Each lead player has a basketball. (Younger players will find a playground ball or volleyball easier to handle.)

ACTION: On signal, the lead players run to the throwing line, throw the balls against the wall, and catch them on the first bounce. A player who fails to retrieve his ball in this manner repeats the action. The player then runs with the ball back to his team and gives it to the next player in line. The first team to complete the action wins.

VARIATION: In *Dribble Relay* players dribble the basketball up to the throwing line and back.

Over and Under Relay

- *8 to 30* - *Nine to twelve*
- *Playground ball*

FORMATION: Teams line up in columns. Each lead player holds a volleyball or basketball.

ACTION: The first player passes the ball over his head to the player behind, who then passes the ball between his legs to the next player. The action continues in this manner, with the ball passing "over and under" until it reaches the last player, who runs with the ball to the front of the line and begins the action again. The first team to have its lead player back in the lead position wins.

VARIATIONS: In *Archball* players simply pass the ball back over their heads. In *Tunnelball* they pass it back between their legs.

Dizzy Izzy Relay

- *8 to 30* - *Eight to twelve*
- *Baseball bats or broom handles*

FORMATION: Players line up in equal teams behind a starting line; there is a turning line about 30 feet away. Each lead player has a baseball bat or broom handle which is about three feet long.

ACTION: On signal, each lead player runs forward to the turning line. There, he places one end of the stick on the ground and, holding it upright, puts his forehead down on the upper end. In this position the player runs around the bat three times, then runs back to the starting line. The next player repeats the action. Running around the bat makes players dizzy, and the trip back from the turning line is usually not so straight as the trip toward it. The first team to complete the action wins.

Figure-Eight Relay

- *8 to 30* - *Eight to twelve*
- *Indian clubs or cardboard milk cartons*

FORMATION: Columns form on a starting line. About 30 feet from the line, and in front of each team, groups of three Indian clubs (or milk cartons) are placed on the ground in single-file formation. Each club is about five feet behind the preceding club.

ACTION: On signal, the lead player in each line runs to the clubs and passes to the right of the first club, the left of the second, and the right of the third. Then he weaves back through them in the same manner as if forming a figure eight with an extra loop. The first team in which all members have completed the pattern wins. If

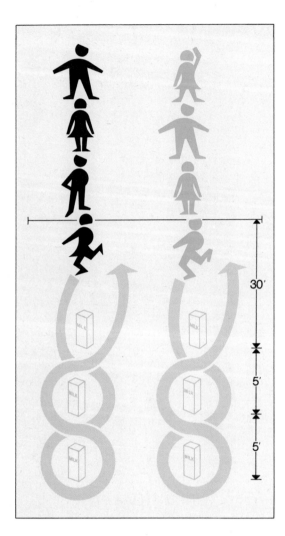

the spoon with the egg (or ball) on it crosswise in his mouth and on signal runs to the turning line and back. The lead player passes the spoon by hand to the second player, who puts the spoon in his mouth and repeats the action. The action goes on until all players have had a turn, and the winning team is the one that completes the relay first. If a player drops the egg, it is picked up and placed back on the spoon before the player can continue to run.

Potato Race

- *8 to 30* - *Eight to twelve*
- *Potatoes, spoons*

FORMATION: Players form columns behind a starting line, 15 feet distant from a turning line. Potatoes, in groups of three, are placed on the turning line, each group of potatoes in front of one of the teams. The lead player on each team has a large spoon.
ACTION: The first player on each team runs forward and scoops up one potato with the spoon—without touching the potato with a hand or foot. The player runs back with the potato on the spoon and places the potato on the ground at the starting line and returns for the second potato and then for the third. When all potatoes are at the starting line, the lead player passes the spoon to the second contestant, who returns the potatoes, one by one, to their original position on the turning line. The relay continues until every player has had a chance to move the potatoes back or forth, and the first team to complete the action wins. If this relay is played by six- and seven-year-olds, the rules can be bent to allow the children to pick up the potatoes with their hands and place them on their spoons.

Soccer Relay

- *6 to 30* - *Seven to eleven* - *Soccer balls*

FORMATION: Players form columns behind a starting line. A turning line is marked about 30 feet away. The first player on each team has a ball.

a club falls, the player stops and sets it up in place before continuing his sprint back to the starting line.

Egg Race

- *8 to 30* - *Eight to twelve*
- *Hard-boiled eggs or Ping-Pong balls; spoons*

FORMATION: Boys and girls form columns of four or five players each. The lead player on each team has a hard-boiled egg (or a Ping-Pong ball) on a spoon. The turning line is about 15 feet from the starting line.
ACTION: The lead player on each team places

ACTION: Each lead player dribbles the ball, soccer-style (using the side of his foot only), to the turning line and back across the starting line. The ball is brought to the next player in line; he does not leave his position to get it. The first team to complete the action wins.

Circle Relay

- *12 to 36*   • *Six to eight*
- *Playground balls*

FORMATION: Players divide into two or more teams of equal number. Each team forms a circle. One player on each team has a ball.

ACTION: On signal, the player with the ball runs to the right around the outside of his circle and back to his starting place. He gives the ball to the player on his right. This player repeats the action. The game continues until all the children have run. The first team to complete the action wins.

VARIATION: Older children may prefer *Dribble Circle Relay,* in which they dribble the ball, basketball-style, around the circle.

Tug-Along Relay

- *12 to 26*   • *Seven to twelve*

FORMATION: Players divide into equal-size teams, and team members form two-player partnerships. Teams line up, double file with partners side by side, behind a starting line. They face a turning line 30 feet away.

ACTION: On signal, the first pairs in each team join their inside hands and run toward the turning line. One partner leads the other, pulling him along. At the game leader's signal, the two partners change position; the one in front moving to the rear. During the action—to the turning line and back to the starting line—the game leader calls for a position change three or four times. If either partner is in the wrong position, or if one does not lag behind the other, the pair returns to the starting line to begin their run anew. The first team to complete the action wins the relay.

Wheelbarrow Relay

- *12 to 40*   • *Eight to twelve*

FORMATION: Players form columns behind the starting line. A turning line is marked about 20 feet away. Each team divides its members into pairs.

ACTION: The first pair in each team takes the wheelbarrow position. One player places hands on the ground and stretches legs straight out. The partner stands between the outstretched legs, holding them firmly at the ankle and lifting them to waist height. On signal, each lead pair races forward to the turning line, the front player traveling on his hands, and the other guiding him like a wheelbarrow. At the turning line, they reverse positions and race back to the starting line, to touch off the next pair, which has been waiting in wheelbarrow position.

Back-to-Back Relay

- *12 to 40*   • *Seven to eleven*

FORMATION: Teams line up in pairs behind the starting line. The turning line is marked about 20 feet away.

ACTION: The first pair in each team stands back-to-back, hooking both elbows firmly. At the starting signal, each lead pair races toward the turning line. They travel with one player moving forward and the other backward. After crossing the turning line and returning to the starting line in the same manner, they are followed by the next pair. The first team to complete the cycle is the winner.

Hobble Relay

- *8 to 30*   • *Seven to twelve*

FORMATION: Children line up in equal-size teams on the starting line, with the turning line about 20 feet away. The first player on each team lifts his left knee to his chest and holds it there with his right hand.

ACTION: On signal, the first player hops forward, in his starting posture, to the turning line. Then he hops back on his left foot, with his right knee held up. Each player does this in turn, and the first team to complete the action wins.

VARIATION: In *Hop Relay,* each child hops to the turning line on one foot, returns on the other. The runner need not hold up a knee.

Horse and Rider

● *12 to 30* ● *Ten to twelve*

FORMATION: Players form into equal-size teams behind a starting line and each team divides into pairs of children who are equally matched for size. A turning line is marked 30 feet away.

ACTION: The lead pair on each team takes a horse-and-rider position. The "rider" climbs on the "horse's" back, with knees locked around the horse's waist and hands on the horse's shoulders. At a starting signal each "horse and rider" race toward the turning line. There they reverse roles and race back to the starting line. The first team to have all its players complete the action is the winner. For younger children, it may be best to mark the turning line only 15 or 20 feet away.

They're off! Jockeys and thoroughbreds lurch from the starting line in a Horse and Rider *relay. At the turning line, horses and riders switch roles.*

Shuttle Relay

- *12 to 40* • *Seven to nine*

FORMATION: Players divide into equal-size teams of at least six players each. Two parallel lines, about 30 feet apart, are marked off for each team. The teams now divide—half the players taking up positions behind each line in single-file columns. Each half faces its teammates behind the other line.

ACTION: The lead player on each team runs across to the opposite line and touches the first player there and then moves to the back of that line. The player who was touched sprints to the opposite side, tags the first player in line there and takes a position at the rear of that line. This

action continues until all players are back in their original positions, and the team that completes the relay first wins.

VARIATIONS: *Shuttle Relay* can be played as *Crab Shuttle Relay, Hobble Shuttle Relay,* or *Crooked Walk Shuttle Relay* by having the contestants take the various positions that are described in detail on pages 29 and 30.

Jump-the-Stick Relay

- *12 to 40* • *Nine to twelve*
- *Lengths of wood*

FORMATION: Players form columns and stand behind the starting line. The first two players hold a stick about two feet long by its ends and take up positions one on either side of the starting line.

ACTION: Holding the stick close to the ground, the first two players run down the length of their column. Each player in the line must jump over the stick as it reaches him. When the two players with the stick reach the foot of the line, the first player lets go of the stick and takes his place in the back of the line. The second player runs back to the head of the line and teams up with the third. Together they repeat the action, and then the third player teams up with the fourth and so on until all players in a team have run with the stick. The first team to finish is the winner.

Ball Return Relay

- *12 to 30* • *Seven to nine*
- *Playground balls*

FORMATION: Players divide into equal-size teams and stand in columns behind a starting line. A second line (the throw line) is marked about 20 feet away, parallel to the starting line. Each lead player has a ball.

ACTION: Each lead player runs to the throw line and turns and throws the ball to the next player on his team. That player catches the ball and then runs to the throw line. He turns, throws the ball to the third player, and so the game

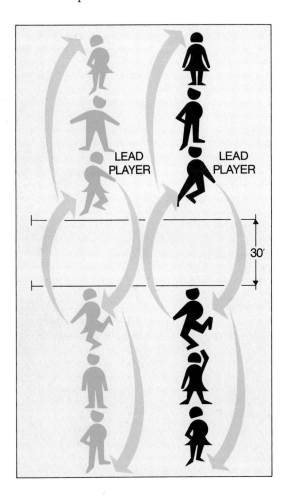

LEAD PLAYER · LEAD PLAYER · 30'

continues. If a catcher drops the ball, he retrieves it and returns to the starting line before running down field. The first team to move all players to the throw line wins. The distance between the lines may be increased when the game is played by older children.

VARIATIONS: In *Roll Return Relay* the ball is rolled from the throw line. In *Bounce Return Relay* the child on the starting line catches the ball on one bounce. If it is caught on the fly or after more than one bounce, it is returned to the thrower, who bounces it again.

Three-Legged Race

- *12 to 40*   ● *Eight to twelve*
- *Lengths of rope*

FORMATION: Players form columns and stand behind the starting line in pairs. Each pair of players has their inside legs tied together at the ankle, with a belt or piece of rope or a handkerchief will do.

ACTION: On signal, each lead pair races forward toward the turning line, about 30 feet away, and back. They touch off the second pair, and each pair in turn must complete the action. The first team to have all its players complete the *Three-Legged Race* is the winner.

Fetch and Carry Relay

- *12 to 30*   ● *Seven to nine*   ● *Beanbags*

FORMATION: Players form columns of equal numbers behind a starting line. Each lead player has a beanbag. A circle is drawn on the ground about 30 feet in front of each team.

ACTION: On signal the lead player runs forward and puts the beanbag in the circle, then runs back and touches the next player and moves to the back of the line. That second player runs forward, picks up the beanbag, and brings it back, giving it to the next player. The action is continued until all the players have run, and the first team to have the lead player back in the lead position wins.

Racing the Ball

- *12 to 24*   ● *Ten to twelve*
- *Playground ball*

FORMATION: The players divide into two equal-size teams. One team forms a circle, with the players standing about three feet apart, facing in. The other team stands in a straight line, facing toward the circle. One player in the circle holds the ball.

ACTION: The ball is bounce-passed (moved on one bounce) around the circle from player to player. If it is dropped, it is picked up, with the player returning to his place in the circle before passing it on. The ball travels around the circle as many times as there are players on the

team. As the action starts, the first player in the line runs forward and around the circle. When he gets back to place, he touches the second player, who performs the same action. The first team to complete its action—for the circle, bounce-passing the ball around as many times as there are players; for the line, having each player run in turn once around the circle—is proclaimed the winner. When the game is completed, the two teams reverse roles and play is resumed as before.

Human Caterpillar

- *12 to 30* - *Nine to twelve*

FORMATION: Players divide into two or more equal-size columns on a starting line, with players separated by about three feet. The first player stands with his feet wide apart; the next bends over in a leap-frog position. Positions alternate in this way, down each line.
ACTION: On signal, the last player in each line crawls under the legs of the player in front of him, vaults over the next player, crawls under the next, and so on, until he has reached the head of the line. Then the player now at the foot of the line repeats the action, always starting by going under the player in front of him. Thus players alternate their positions, first standing up, and then bending over. The team that completes the action first—so all the players are back in their original places—wins.

Simple Ball Games

Many of the games that follow are for children from five to eight years old. Like all the games in this book, they are primarily for enjoyment, but each helps the child develop fundamental skills with a ball—aiming, throwing, catching, bouncing, dribbling—skills that are essential for the more demanding activities of later childhood and adolescence.

Numerals indicate the number of players. Spelled-out numbers suggest suitable age levels.

Indian Club Bowling

- *8 to 20* - *Seven to twelve*
- *Two playground balls; ten Indian clubs or milk cartons*

FORMATION: Players divide into two teams and line up behind a starting line, with another parallel line drawn 20 feet away. Behind the second line, five Indian clubs or milk cartons are placed about two feet apart, in front of each of the teams.
ACTION: The first player on each team has a ball and rolls it, trying to knock down a club or carton. He then runs up, gets the ball, and throws it to the next player in his line. The first remains behind the Indian clubs to retrieve the ball. The other players take turns bowling, until they have knocked down all the clubs. The first team to knock down its five clubs wins.
VARIATION: In *One Club Bowling,* two teams (or individuals) take turns bowling at the same club, placed about 25 feet away. Each time the club is knocked down, that team makes a point. The team with the higher score after five minutes, or the first team to reach a set number of hits—such as ten—wins.

Leader's Choice

- *6 to 8* • *Five to seven* • *Variety of balls*

FORMATION: Players stand in a line, facing one child who is the leader. He has several balls of different types: a basketball, rubber playground ball, tennis ball, etc.

ACTION: The leader selects one of the balls and throws it with a bounce pass (on one bounce) to each of the children in the line, in turn. Each child catches it and returns it to the leader in the same way. When the leader has thrown to the entire line, he goes to the left end of the line, and the player at the right end becomes the new leader. Each new leader picks the ball he wishes to play with. This game is not a competitive one; it helps children learn the skill of throwing and catching different kinds of balls.

Wide Awake

- *6 to 15* • *Five to seven*
- *Playground ball*

FORMATION: The players stand about four feet apart in a circle, facing the center.

ACTION: A playground ball or volleyball is thrown from one child to the next around the circle. If a child makes a "bad" throw (one that is too poorly aimed to be caught) or fails to catch a "good" throw, he is eliminated. The one who remains in the game the longest is the winner. The game leader must decide which throws were "bad" and which were "good." The game may also be played by giving any player who makes a "bad" throw or fails to catch a "good" one a penalty point. After ten to fifteen minutes, the child with the fewest points wins.

Count the Passes

- *12 to 20* • *Five to eight*
- *Two playground balls*

FORMATION: Players standing five feet apart form two equal-size circles. Each team has a rubber playground ball.

ACTION: Each team begins to pass the ball in turn from player to player. The purpose of the game is to pass it as many times as possible within a set period of time, such as two or three minutes. A dropped or missed throw does not count. When the time is up, each team tells its score, and the winning team is given a point.

VARIATION: In *Variety Passes* a different type of throw is used in each two-minute round. The adult game leader calls for a chest pass, overhand throw, two-hand underhand pass, or bounce pass. Each round has a winner, and the team with most "round-wins" triumphs.

Keep Away Touch Ball

- *6 to 20* • *Eight to twelve*
- *Playground ball*

FORMATION: Players form a circle facing the center, and stand about five feet apart. One player is in the center.

ACTION: The circle players pass a ball rapidly from person to person, moving in any direction around or across the circle. Meanwhile, the player in the center tries to block or catch the ball. When he does, the last person to have handled the ball goes to the center.

Bucket Ball

- *6 to 10* • *Six to nine* • *Playground ball*

FORMATION: Children form a circle about 20 feet in diameter. In the center of each circle is a waste basket or plastic pail—the "bucket." One player has the ball.

ACTION: Each player takes his turn trying to throw the ball into the bucket from his place in the circle. He may try to throw it in on the fly or on a bounce. If he hits the bucket, he gets one point; if he gets the ball in, he gets two. After each player has had five chances, the one with the highest score is the winner.

VARIATION: In *Team Bucket Ball,* played with larger groups, players form into two, three, or four circles, with a bucket and a ball for each. The action is the same, but the teams compete for the highest score within a set period of time—eight to ten minutes.

Indian Club Guard

- *6 to 20*   • *Eight to twelve*
- *Indian clubs or milk cartons; playground ball*

FORMATION: Players form a circle about 25 feet in diameter. One player stands in the center, guarding a small triangle of Indian clubs or milk cartons which are placed there, about three feet apart.

ACTION: Players on the rim try to knock the Indian clubs down by throwing, bouncing, or rolling the ball. The player in the center may catch the ball directly and throw it back, or block it with his hands. The others can pass the ball around to get an open shot at the target. All throws are taken from the circle's rim. The game leader times how long it takes players to knock down all the clubs. Each child has a turn in the center, and the winner is the one who protected the clubs for the longest time.

Sky-High Ball

- *4 to 20*   • *Seven to ten*   • *Playground ball*

FORMATION: Players divide into two equal teams and scatter around a playing area that is about 30 feet square.

ACTION: A player on Team 1 throws the ball at least ten feet in the air and within the playing area. If a member of Team 2 catches it, he scores one point for his side. If not, the throwing team scores. Then a member of the second team throws it, and this continues until all the players have had a turn. The team with the greater number of points after 15 minutes of play wins.

Keep It Up

- *8 to 25*   • *Nine to twelve*
- *Two volleyballs*

FORMATION: Players divide into two equal teams. They stand in separate circles, with players about one or two feet apart from their neighbors. Each team has a ball.

ACTION: On signal, one player on each team tosses the ball in the air. The members of his team try to keep it in play by hitting it with both hands. It may not be caught or held. The team keeping it up for the longer time wins one point. The game may be repeated several times, and the team with the higher total score is the winner.

Center Stride Ball

- *8 to 15*   • *Seven to ten*   • *Playground ball*

FORMATION: Players form a circle and take "stride" position (standing so their feet are well apart, touching neighbors' feet on each side). One player, however, stands in the center, holding a ball.

ACTION: The center man tries to throw or roll the ball so it escapes to the outside, either between a player's legs, or between two players. If the ball passes over the players' shoulders, the throw does not count. Players on the rim, who keep their feet fixed to the ground in "stride" position, use their hands to block the ball, or hit it back into the middle. If the ball goes through a player's feet, that player changes position with the center man. If the ball goes between two players, the one on the left is considered responsible, and he moves to the center.

Center Ball

● *8 to 15*   ● *Six to eight*   ● *Playground ball*

FORMATION: One player, holding the ball, stands in the center of a circle which has been formed by the others.

ACTION: The ball holder throws the ball to any other player who catches it, moves to the center, places the ball on the ground, and then chases the ball thrower. The ball thrower runs through the opening in the circle left by his pursuer, and runs around the outside until he reaches the opening again, and then back into the circle to touch the ball. If his pursuer tags him before he can touch the ball, the pursuer becomes the new thrower and the game proceeds as before. If the pursuer fails to make the tag, the thrower continues in his position until he is caught. The game leader should not allow one child to be the thrower for too long a time, so that other players may have a chance.

Keep Away

● *8 to 20*   ● *Seven to ten*   ● *Playground ball*

FORMATION: Players are divided into equal-size teams, scattered over the same playing area at least 40 by 60 feet. For identification, members of one team should wear handkerchiefs tied around their arms.

ACTION: One team has a ball. On signal, it is passed from player to player, while the other team tries to intercept it. Scoring is not vital, but the game leader may time each team on how long it can retain control of the ball. The action is very lively, though tripping, holding, pushing, or other rough play is not permitted. The game leader can call fouls and put a player temporarily on the sidelines. If a ball is thrown out of bounds, the team that last touched it is responsible, and the other team puts it in play. The game may last from 15 to 20 minutes depending on the vigor of the players.

Lead-up Games to Team Sports

The games involve basic athletic skills such as throwing, catching, kicking, and running. In most cases the activities are simplified forms of such popular team sports as *Volleyball, Basketball, Soccer, Baseball, Softball,* and *Football.* Young children enjoy these games, and begin to learn the tactics and rules that will be useful when they actually play the sports themselves. Where other than standard backyard facilities are needed, such information is given.

Numerals indicate the number of players. Spelled-out numbers suggest suitable age levels.

Catch Ball

● *6 to 12*   ● *Eight to eleven*   ● *Volleyball*

FORMATION: Two parallel lines are marked about 15 or 20 feet apart. All the players but one stand behind one line. The lone player stands behind the other. He is the server.

ACTION: The server tosses a volleyball up with one hand, and hits it with the other, sending it into the group of players. If one of them catches it without a bounce, he becomes the next server. If not, the server continues until he has hit a ball that is caught.

Net Ball

● *8 to 24*   ● *Eight to twelve*
● *Volleyball and net*

FORMATION: Players divide into two equal teams. They stand on either side of a six-foot-high volleyball net in the center of a play area about 20 by 40 feet.

ACTION: A player on one team throws the ball over the net into his opponents' area. If one of the players on that team catches it, he must immediately throw it back from the place at which he caught it. This action is continued.

If the ball hits the ground within the play area, the team which threw it is given one point. If a team throws it out of bounds or into the net, the opposing team is given one point. The team with the most points after five or ten minutes of play wins the game.

Circle Serve

● *6 to 12*   ● *Eight to eleven*   ● *Volleyball*

FORMATION: Players stand in a small circle, eight to ten feet in diameter, facing in.
ACTION: The player with the ball points to a player across the circle, bounces the ball once, and serves it to him. This player catches the serve, bounces it once, and serves it to another player. The action is continued in this manner, with players who fail to serve accurately, or to catch the ball, given a penalty point. The player with the fewest points after ten minutes is the winner. The serve is normally done with the flat of the hand and an underhand or sidearm motion.

Circle Pass

● *8 to 15*   ● *Eight to twelve*   ● *Volleyball*

FORMATION: Players, spaced three feet apart, form a circle about 32 feet in diameter. One player is in the center and holds a volleyball.
ACTION: The center player volley-passes the ball (hitting it with both hands with a pushing action) to any player in the circle. That player catches the ball and volley-passes it back to the center player, who passes it to the next player and so on until each player in the circle has had a turn. The game may be played as an elimination contest, in which those missing the ball drop out, or as a relay between two groups who race to complete the action.
VARIATION: In *Circle Volley Bounce,* one player in the circle has the ball. He calls out the name of another, bounces the ball once, and serves it to the named player. If the serve is a good one, the called player receives it, either on the fly or on one bounce and, without holding the ball, bats it with his hand to yet another player whose name he has called. In this way each player tries to pass the ball to someone else. The game leader decides when a ball has been hit out of reach of a called player or when a called player has failed to hit a properly volleyed ball. When a player makes an error, he drops out and the action resumes with a new serve. Eventually only two players remain, and they bat the ball back and forth until one commits an error. His opponent then becomes the winner, and a new round of play can begin.

One-Bounce Volleyball

● *12 to 16*   ● *Ten to twelve*
● *Volleyball and net*

FORMATION: Players divide into two teams on volleyball court about 20 by 40 feet, with a center net about six feet high.
ACTION: The first player on the serving team serves the ball from behind his back line. If it crosses the net, an opposing player lets it bounce once before returning it. This is kept up until

a player fails to return the ball, or hits it out of bounds. If the serving team wins the exchange, it gets a point and keeps the serve. If it loses, the opposing team gets the ball and has a turn to serve and win points. The server is given two chances to hit a fair serve. The ball is always hit with the open hand, and no player may hit the ball twice in a row. Only one bounce is allowed before the ball is returned.

Five Tries

- *8 to 12* • *Eight to ten*
- *Playground, gymnasium, or backyard basketball court* • *Two basketballs*

FORMATION: Players divide into two teams. Each team stands in single file behind the free-throw line on a basketball court, facing a backboard. The first player in line holds a basketball. The last player on each team stands under the basket. ACTION: On signal, the first players on both teams begin to shoot. They continue from the free-throw line until one of them makes a basket, or until each has had five tries. The player under the basket retrieves the ball and passes it back. The first player to make a goal scores one point for his team. When this happens—or if both shooters have had five tries without scoring—the first players become retrievers, the second players move up to the throw line, and the former retrievers go to the rear of the line to wait their turn to shoot. The team with the higher score, after all players have had a turn, wins.

VARIATION: In *Basket Shot Relay,* each player shoots until he makes a basket and then goes to the back of the line. The first team to bring its lead man back into the lead position wins.

Twenty-One

- *4 to 6*   - *Nine to twelve*
- *Playground, gymnasium, or backyard basketball court*   - *Basketball*

FORMATION: Players line up at the free-throw line, facing the basket.
ACTION: The object of the game is to score exactly 21 points, by making basketball shots in the following way: Each player takes a turn, consisting of three successive throws at the basket. The first shot is made from the free-throw line, and scores five points, if made. The next two shots are made from wherever the ball is recovered. The second basket is worth three points, and the third is worth one. When the first player has taken his three shots, the next player takes a turn, and so on. The game goes on until one player gets 21 points. If, however, a player makes more than 21 points, his score goes back to zero and he must start the game all over again.
VARIATION: A simpler form of this game is *Twenty-One Plus,* which is scored in exactly the same way except that the winning player is the first to make 21 points or more.

Freeze-Out

- *6 to 8*   - *Ten to twelve*
- *Playground, gymnasium, or backyard basketball court*   - *Basketball*

FORMATION: Players determine the order of shooting. Then the first player stands any place on the basketball court.
ACTION: The lead player takes a shot at the basket. If he makes the basket, the player after him shoots from exactly the same spot and must also make the basket or else he is "frozen-out" (eliminated from the game). If the second player does make the basket, then the third stands in the same spot for a shot, and so on. Whenever a player is frozen-out, the next player can choose a new shooting position and need not make a basket to remain in the game. The winner is the last player to remain in the game.

Hot Ball

- *6 to 12*   - *Six to eight*   - *Soccer ball*

FORMATION: Children stand in a circle, facing in. One player has a soccer ball on the ground in front of him.
ACTION: The child with the ball calls: "The ball is hot!" He kicks it across the circle, hitting it with the inside of his foot, soccer-style. Other players continue to kick the ball quickly, the idea being that it is so "hot" that they must get rid of it at once or it will burn them. This goes on, until the ball escapes from the circle. Then a new player begins the action again. This game is cooperative rather than competitive. All players work together to keep the ball moving inside the circle. Children will usually continue to enjoy this game for about ten minutes.

Free Ball

- *4 to 8*   - *Six to eight*   - *Soccer ball*

FORMATION: One player (the caller) has the ball and stands about 30 feet away from the others, who are lined up facing the caller.
ACTION: The caller shouts the name of any other player and kicks the ball soccer-style (with the side of the foot) in that player's direction. The called player stops the ball with his foot and returns the kick; another player is called on, and the action is repeated until all have kicked the ball back once.
The caller then shouts: "Free Ball!" and kicks the ball in the general direction of the others, who scramble to receive it. The player who retrieves the ball, holding it over his head to prove his possession, will call the action for another round of play. The player who holds the caller's position most often in a ten-minute period wins.

Soccer Keep-Away

- *6 to 12*   - *Eight to ten*   - *Soccer ball*

FORMATION: Players divide into two teams and scatter over a playing area of about 30 by 40 feet. Members of one team wear armbands for identification.

ACTION: The purpose of the game is to keep control of the ball. A toss of a coin decides which team shall have the ball when the game begins, and its members dribble the ball with their feet or kick it back and forth among themselves to keep control. Using only feet, heads, or bodies, the opposition tries to intercept passes or steal the ball. A period lasts seven minutes, and the game leader keeps time to determine which team has held the ball longer.

Soccer Tag

● *6 to 15* ● *Seven to ten* ● *Soccer ball*

FORMATION: Players scatter around an area which is at least 25 feet square. Three players are chosen as kickers. They wear armbands or sashes to identify them.

ACTION: The kickers kick the ball around the area, trying to hit any of the other players beneath the waist. Any player who is hit becomes a kicker. The game continues until all players but one have been hit. The survivor becomes a kicker for the next game, and picks two others to help him. A hit scored above the waist does not count.

Bat Ball

● *8 to 20* ● *Seven to ten* ● *Playground ball*

FORMATION: There are two bases 30 to 40 feet apart. The players divide into two teams: one at bat behind home plate, the other in the field behind the long base.

ACTION: The lead-off batter stands at home plate and hits the ball into the field with fist or open palm. To score one run, the batter dashes to the long base and back to home plate without stopping. The batter is out if he hits a fly ball that is caught, or if a fielder hits him below the waist with the ball before he reaches home. A fielder may relay the ball to a teammate, who may then try to hit the runner with it. When the team at bat has had three outs, it changes

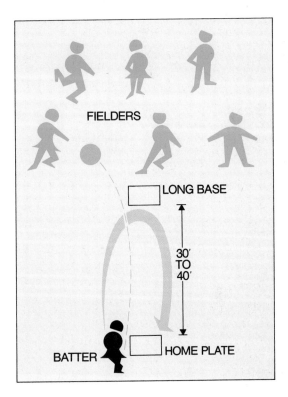

places with the team in the field. After four innings, the team with the higher score wins.

One Old Cat

● *8 to 12* ● *Seven to eleven* ● *Playground*
● *Softball and bat*

FORMATION: There are three bases: home plate, pitcher's box, and first base. One player is chosen to be the pitcher, one the catcher, one the batter, and the rest are in the field.

ACTION: One player comes to bat. The pitcher throws the ball underhand. There are no balls or called strikes: the batter swings at all good pitches. After hitting the ball, the batter runs to first base and back to home plate without stopping. The batter is out if he swings for three strikes, if he hits a fly ball which is caught, or if a fielder throws the ball to the catcher who touches it to the plate before the batter reaches home. If the batter reaches home safely, he scores one point and continues to bat until he is put out. Then he goes into the field, and the other players all move up one position. The pitcher becomes the catcher, and the catcher becomes batter. If some players are not able to pitch the ball accurately, the game leader may do this, with the rotations skipping the pitcher.

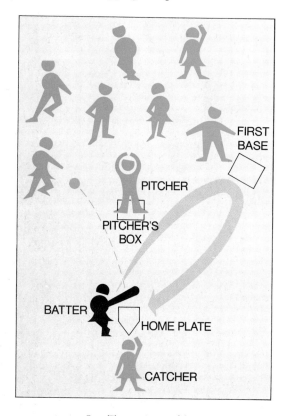

FIRST BASE

PITCHER

PITCHER'S BOX

BATTER

HOME PLATE

CATCHER

VARIATION: In *Team One Old Cat* the same layout is used and there are six to ten players per team. The fielding team has a catcher, pitcher, first baseman, and fielders. When the first batter hits the ball, he can run to first and on to home or elect to remain on first and hope that succeeding batters will drive him in. Each time a batter crosses home plate he scores a run for his team. A batter is out if he swings for three strikes, if he hits a fly ball that is caught, if he reaches first base after the ball has been received from the field by the first baseman, if he is tagged on the base path by a fielder with the ball, or if he reaches home plate after the ball has been received by the catcher.

Fly's Out

● *6 to 10* ● *Eight to twelve* ● *Playground*
● *Softball and bat*

FORMATION: One player is at bat, and the rest of the players in the field. There are no bases.
ACTION: The batter tosses the ball into the air and hits it into the field. If a fielder catches the ball on the fly, he becomes the batter, and the first batter goes into the field. If a grounder is hit, the player who fields the ball remains in position and roles the ball toward the bat, which the batter lays flat on the ground. If the ball misses the bat, or if it hits it and then is caught on the fly by the batter (who stands behind the bat), the batter keeps his place. If it hits the bat and falls to the ground without being caught, the fielder who rolled it becomes the new batter. No score is kept: the challenge lies in hitting, fielding, and trying to remain at bat.

Run Around the Team

● *12 to 20* ● *Ten to twelve*
● *Playground ball*

FORMATION: Players form two equal-size teams. One lines up in a column behind home plate; the other scatters in the field about 40 feet long. There are no bases.
ACTION: The first player hits the ball into the field with open hand or fist. Then he runs around the other members of his team, who are lined up in single file. Meanwhile, the players in the field line up, with legs apart, behind the player who caught the ball. The catcher rolls the ball through his legs and the others pass it back the same way. When the last player in the line gets the ball, he holds it up and shouts "Stop!" At this signal, the batter stops running around his team. The offense gets one point if the batter has gone three times around. If "Stop!" is called before the batter has gone three times around, no points are scored. After three players have had turns hitting, the teams change sides. The winning team is the one with the most points after five innings.

Three Times Round

- *12 to 24*   - *Five to seven*
- *Playground ball*

FORMATION: Players divide into two or more teams of equal numbers. Each team forms a circle. One player on each team has a ball.

ACTION: The lead player passes the ball, using both hands, to the player on his right. The second player gives it to the third, and so on until it has gone completely around the circle. When the ball reaches the first player again, he bounces it on the ground once and calls out, "One time round!" and passes the ball on. This action is repeated by each player, until the ball reaches the first player, who bounces it twice and calls, "Two times round!" The third and last time he bounces the ball three times and calls, "Three times round!" The first team to complete the circle sits on the ground to show it has won the game.

The winners in a game of Three Times Round *sit in their places while their team leader exuberantly holds their ball high as a sign of victory.*

Long Base Kick Ball

● *8 to 20*   ● *Seven to ten*   ● *Playground*
● *Playground ball*

FORMATION: The field has a home plate and a long base, about 30 feet apart. The players divide into two equal teams, with one team at bat and the other in the field, the players scattered behind the long base.

ACTION: The first player stands at the plate and kicks the ball into the field. He tries to run to the long base and back to home plate before the fielders can throw the ball back to the catcher. If he succeeds, he scores one point for his side. The batter is out if a fly ball is caught or if the ball is returned to the catcher before he reaches home plate. After each player on the kicking team has had a turn, the teams change places. The team with the higher score after two or three innings have been played wins the ball game.

Kick Ball

● *16 to 20*   ● *Ten to twelve*   ● *Playground*
● *Playground ball*

FORMATION: A field is laid out like a softball diamond, with bases about 30 feet apart. The players are divided into two equal-size teams—fielders and batters. The fielders are assigned to the various positions as in a regulation *Softball* or *Baseball* game.

ACTION: The game is played just like *Softball* or *Baseball*, except that the player "at bat" kicks a ball which is rolled toward him by the pitcher. The scoring is just as in *Softball*, and the following rules apply: a batter is out if he strikes out (three missed kicks, or four fouls), if he is thrown out before he reaches a base or is tagged on the base paths, if he kicks a fly ball which is caught, or if he is caught attempting to steal. The kicking team is allowed three outs and then the teams change places. The team with the higher score after five innings is declared to be the winner.

VARIATIONS: *Batter's Choice* is similar to *Kick Ball,* except that the player "at bat" throws the ball into the field instead of kicking it. To score a run for his team, he runs all the way around the bases to home. The batter does not stop on a base and wait to be driven in. The fielders put the batter out by catching a fly ball or by getting the ball to any base before the batter can reach it. However, fielders cannot throw the ball directly to any base but must throw it in order—to first, second, third, and home—before the runner is out. *Beat Ball* combines *Kick Ball* and *Batter's Choice.* The pitcher rolls a ball to the kicker, who kicks it into the field. The kicker tries to run completely around the bases before the ball can be thrown from base to base and relayed to home. If the kicker is successful he scores one point for his team. The kicker is out if a fly ball is caught or if the ball beats the kicker to any base. When the kicking team has three outs, it moves into the field and the members of the receiving team take over as the kickers. The team that has scored the most runs after five innings is declared to be the winner of the game.

Kick and Run

● *10 to 20*   ● *Six to eight*   ● *Playground*
● *Playground ball*

FORMATION: Players divide into two equal-size teams. One team is selected to be the kickers, while the other is in the field. A miniature baseball field is laid out, with the bases about 30 feet apart.

ACTION: The first player at bat places the ball on home plate and kicks it into the field. He tries to run completely around the bases before the ball can be recovered and thrown back to home plate. When the ball reaches home plate, the catcher yells "Stop!" The batter gets a point for every base he reached before this call. If he reached first base, he gets one point; if he reached second, he gets two points, and so on. Each player on the kicking team gets a turn, then the teams reverse roles. After one complete inning, the team that makes the higher score wins the game.

Punt and Catch

- *10 to 20* - *Ten to twelve* - *Playground*
- *Playground ball*

FORMATION: Players form two equal teams and each stands behind a goal line. The goal lines are from 30 to 50 feet apart, depending upon the age and kicking ability of the players composing the two teams.

ACTION: The first player on one team punts a ball from behind the goal line toward the other team's goal line. If the ball crosses the other team's goal line without being caught, one point is scored for the kicker's team. If it fails to go over the goal line, or if it is caught on the fly, the receiver's team gets one point. After the first player on the kicking team has had a turn, the ball is given to a player on the second team to punt. The game continues until all the players have had a turn at punting the ball. The team with the higher score becomes the winner of the game.

Broken Field Run

- *3 to 20* - *Ten to twelve* - *Playground*
- *Stopwatch*

FORMATION: The game leader sets up an obstacle course—made up of garbage cans or similar markers—along a 30-yard track. Players line up single file behind a starting line.

ACTION: On signal, the first player runs down the course, circling around the obstacles, each in its turn. Upon reaching the turning line, 30 yards away, he returns back down the track, circling the obstacles in reverse order. When the first contestant has completed the run, the second moves out, then the third, and so on. Each contestant is timed by the game leader, and the one to complete the course in the shortest time wins the race.

VARIATION: When many contestants are on hand, a *Broken Field Elimination* may be staged. Three or four runners compete at once, and the winners meet in several semifinal races. Then the semifinal winners run in a final.

Touchdown

- *12 to 30* - *Ten to twelve* - *Playground*
- *Playground ball*

FORMATION: Players form two teams. All but three from each stand in a play area about 40 feet square, each team on its side of a center line. The extra players are placed in a goal area behind the opponents' home territory.

ACTION: One team begins by trying to pass the ball over the heads of its opponents to one of its goal players. The opposing players try to intercept the ball, but they are not allowed to step over into the other team's territory. Players may not run with the ball, but they may pass it from one player to another in their own territory. A team may continue to throw as long as it keeps the ball. One point is scored each time a pass is completed to a goalie, and the scoring team retains the ball after scoring. The defensive team moves to the offense only when it intercepts a pass. A game lasts 15 minutes, and the adult leader sees to it that the team in the lead does not try to freeze the ball.

Stunts and Simple Contests

The following games involve simple physical performance stunts or "self-testing" activities. Some can be done by just one child at a time, others by two children cooperating with each other, and still others as a contest between two children. These stunts require no special equipment or mats, and most can be performed on a rug in a basement playroom as well as on the grass in the backyard.

Numerals indicate the number of players. Spelled-out numbers suggest suitable age levels.

Distance Beanbag Throw

● *2 to 10*   ● *Five to seven*   ● *Beanbags*

Several children line up on a throwing line. Each player, in turn, throws a beanbag in the same direction, and then goes and stands by it. The winner is the child who throws the farthest.

Five Jumps

● *4 to 8*   ● *Five to seven*

Several children stand with their toes on a starting line. On signal, all jump forward five times. This may be played as a contest, with the child farthest from the starting line the winner; it may be done individually, with each child marking the point he reached with a piece of chalk or a small object before returning to the starting line. The child then tries again to improve his distance.

Cross the Creek

● *4 to 12*   ● *Five to nine*

The "creek" is formed by stretching two lengths of string in parallel lines about two feet apart. Children line up along one of the lines and take turns jumping or leaping across to the opposite line. After all the children have crossed, the "creek" is widened by three or four inches. Again they take turns crossing it. When a child fails to make it across, he sits down. The "creek" is continually widened until only one child—the winner—is able to cross it.

VARIATION: *Beneath the Bar* is similar to *Cross*

the Creek, as it offers a challenge which gradually becomes more difficult as the game progresses. Children line up in pairs to walk under a crossbar held by two players. After the whole group has walked under the bar, it is lowered a few inches. Again, the children walk under in pairs. After a while, the bar becomes so low that, in order to pass under, the children must crawl. If either player in a pair touches the crossbar or lets go of his partner's hand, the couple is eliminated. The last pair to pass beneath the bar successfully wins.

Chinese Get-Up

● *Eight to ten*

Two children sit on the floor back-to-back, with their arms locked together at the elbows. While keeping arms locked, they try to stand up to-

Halfway up from a sitting position, two boys try to stand upright to complete the Chinese Get-up *stunt.*

gether. This is a difficult feat of balance, and should be done gradually. When several pairs are playing, the couple to stand first wins.

VARIATION: In *Tailor Stand* players sit on the floor in a cross-legged position, with arms folded on their chests. On signal, they try to rise slowly to a standing position, without uncrossing their arms or legs. Any player who accomplishes this then tries to sit down again in the same way.

Coffee Grinder

● *Eight to twelve*

While in a squatting position, each player places his right hand on the floor, with the palm flat and the arm stiff. The child then extends both

In game sessions involving eight- and nine-year-olds, the adult leader might well overlook the rule that the body be kept absolutely straight.

Bear Dance

● *Eight to twelve*

Children take a squatting position with arms folded in front for balance. Each puts weight on the left foot, thrusts the right foot straight forward. Still squatting, each brings the right foot back and thrusts the left foot forward. This is done quickly, several times in a row, with the back kept straight at all times. Children may do this dance by facing a partner, joining hands, and starting together with the right foot. The

The Coffee Grinder *turns round, as this young lady, pivoting on one arm, describes a circle with her feet.*

These boys step out smartly to an American beat while doing the Bear Dance, *a favorite stunt among Russians.*

legs out straight to his left side. Keeping the body as straight as possible and using his right arm as a pivot, he walks around in a clockwise circle. This may then be repeated, counterclockwise, using the left arm as a pivot. The first player to complete the action successfully wins.

Bear Dance can easily be made into a contest; the last player (or couple) to lose balance wins. As this stunt is derived from a traditional Russian dance step, fast-paced Russian folk music—played either on a piano or phonograph—adds considerable enjoyment to the exercise.

Crab Walk

● *Six to ten*

The children begin in a squatting position. Each child leans back and places hands flat on the floor. In this position, back to the floor, and head and body in a straight line, the child moves about in a crab-like manner. This stunt may be used in races or relays (see p. 30).

Human Rocker

● *Seven to ten*

Each child lies down on his stomach on a mat or soft grass. Gripping his ankles with his hands,

It's tough to be a Human Rocker, *but it's good fun too, and great exercise for arm, leg and stomach muscles.*

the child throws the head back and raises the chest. This rounds the entire body, and the child can rock back and forth from knees to chest.

Mule Kick

● *Five to seven*

Each child crouches, palms flat on the floor, knees bent, weight on the toes. On signal, the players kick out their legs behind them, mule fashion, one leg at a time or both legs at once. As they kick they bray. The leader selects the child who makes the best mule and gives him a set of long paper ears.

Duck Walk

● *Five to seven*

Each child squats down and grasps his ankles with his hands. In this position the child walks along rapidly, an action which looks very much like the waddle of a duck. In a contest, the child who maintains this walk longest (or farthest) is the winner.

Wringing the Dishrag

● *Five to eight*

Children take partners and face each other holding hands. The trick is for each child to turn completely around without letting go of his partner's hands. By raising one pair of joined hands and turning to that side, the children are back to back. The turn is completed by raising the other pair of hands and turning under them. The secret is to hold hands loosely and turn quickly.

Wheelbarrow Walk

● *Six to ten*

This stunt is done in pairs. One child crouches, with hands flat on the floor in front of him and legs straight back behind him. The other child stands between his partner's legs and grips them firmly at the ankle. Lifting his partner's legs to waist height, he raises the lower part of the child's body up into the air. In this position, the first child "drives" the second child around like a human wheelbarrow. This stunt can be part of a relay (see p. 34).

Measuring Worm

● *Eight to ten*

Children lie on the floor, face down, and then raise themselves so that their arms are perpendicular to the floor, their bodies rigid and their legs fully extended behind. Keeping their hands in place, they take very small steps forward until their feet reach or come close to their hands. The body is held firmly and the legs are kept straight. From this position, the hands are then moved slowly forward until the body has straightened out again in the original position. Both actions are repeated several times without stopping. This stunt, which resembles the movements of a measuring worm, requires limberness and strength.

Frog Handstand

● *Nine to eleven*

Each child squats so that the hands are flat on the floor, with arms inside the thighs, and elbows pressed hard against the inside of the knees. Leaning forward slowly, to take the weight of the body onto the arms and hands, the child lifts feet from the floor and holds this position for several seconds before returning to the original position. When this stunt is used in a contest among several players, the winner is the contestant who manages to keep his legs up in the air the longest period of time. The champion may be awarded a medal in the shape of a frog, which the game leader has cut from green construction paper.

A balancing act! It looks simple, but one false move and the stunt man can go tumbling head over heels.

Contests of Strength

The following are a number of simple contests which are performed by two boys or two girls ranged against each other, or by a whole group, divided into two equal teams. The stunts involve some degree of combativeness or physical aggression, and caution should be employed to make sure that the opponents are of approximately the same age and strength. Although boys particularly enjoy testing their strength and determination against each other, there is no reason why girls should not be included as well. In general, however, girls should be matched only with other girls. Most of these activities can be played either as simple two-man contests or as elimination events with the winners of each round meeting in the next, until only one contestant remains.

Spelled-out numbers suggest suitable age levels.

Rooster Fight

● *Eight to twelve*

Within a circle about eight or twelve feet in diameter, two players take a squatting position, with arms crossed in front of their chests. The object is for each child to try to force his opponent out of the circle, or to make him lose balance and fall, or to make him touch a hand to the ground. Players may butt, push, and shove with their bodies but the crouching position is maintained throughout the contest. Because bouncing in a crouched posture is very tiring, children should compete for only three minutes before being replaced by two other opponents.

Indian Wrestle

- *Ten to twelve*

Two contestants lie on their backs, side by side, with heads in opposite directions so that their right legs are adjacent. They hook right arms at the elbow, and at the leader's count each raises the right leg three times. The third time, they lock legs, and each tries to overpower the other by forcing the opponent's back off the floor. The contestant who succeeds at this, while keeping his own back on the floor, is the winner.

Crisscross Wrestle

- *Eight to twelve*

Two contestants are on their knees facing each other, an arm's length apart. Each contestant thrusts out his arms in front of him in a crisscross fashion. Player A grips the left shoulder of Player B with his left hand, then grips the right shoulder of Player B with his right hand. Player B follows the same procedure. Once the signal to start is given, each contestant tugs and pulls in an effort to make his opponent lose balance and topple off his knees. Because of the crossing formation of the arms, this is no easy feat, and a novel contest is certain to ensue. When there is a number of players, winners of each contest meet in elimination matches.

Indian Hand Wrestle

- *Ten to twelve*

Two players stand side by side, facing in opposite directions with feet apart in a stride position. Each player puts his right foot slightly forward so that it touches the outside edge of his opponent's right foot. With elbows bent, they grip right hands and try to force each other off balance. Using the right hand only, each may pull and twist to try to accomplish this goal. The player who moves either foot or touches the ground with any part of his body other than his foot loses the contest.

Cane Fight

- *Eight to twelve*

Both children have a cane apiece (broomsticks or lengths of doweling will do). The canes are crossed on the inside and each player grips his cane at both ends. The players face each other with canes crossed overhead and each tries to force the other to release his grip by twisting, pulling, and pushing the canes. Only the arms are used in this contest, and such tactics as tripping and shoving or pushing with the body are against the rules. If neither player has let go after two minutes, the contest is a draw.

Distance Boxing

- *Eight to twelve*

The contestants stand on sturdy low wooden boxes or stools, which have been placed five or six feet apart. Each is given a long stick with a boxing glove tied on to one end. Each player grips the stick at the opposite end and, on signal, tries to force his opponent off his box. This is done by thrusting and pushing; players may not swing their sticks. The first player to force his opponent off the box is the winner. A contest lasts two minutes.

Tug of War

- *Seven to twelve*

Players divide into two equal teams. A line is drawn down the center of the playing area, and a strong rope, long enough to be gripped by all the players, is placed across the center line. With the center line between them, both teams line up and grip the rope. On signal, each team pulls on its end of the rope and tries to force the opposition's lead player across the center line. The first team to accomplish this is the winner.

VARIATION: In *Two-Man Tug of War* the same rules apply except that each player tries to pull his opponent across the center line.

Strength or team spirit? A good Tug of War *tests both—if the teams are evenly matched. A cloth wrapped round the rope helps prevent rope burns.*

Street, Sidewalk and Park Games

Children who live in cities are often at a disadvantage in terms of play space, which, because of population congestion, may be at a premium. Nonetheless, through the ages, youngsters have devised a variety of active games suitable for limited areas or city parks. Although the games and contests that follow are often most popular among city and suburban youngsters, they are certainly suitable for their country cousins as well. The place of play is much less important than the games themselves. Wherever the games are played the fun remains the same.

Numerals indicate the number of players. Spelled-out numbers suggest suitable age levels.

Ten and Out Hopscotch

● *2 to 10* ● *Seven to ten*

FORMATION: A rectangular diagram, about four feet wide and ten feet long is drawn on a flat, paved surface. The diagram is rounded at one end and is divided into eleven spaces—marked 1 through 10 and "out."

ACTION: The first contestant stands on the edge of the diagram at the baseline in front of space 1 and tosses a small stone—the puck—into that space. Then he hops on one foot into the space, stands there, bends over—while still on one foot—picks up the puck and hops out again. Having performed this successfully, he tosses the puck into space 2 and repeats the action. The player continues until he fouls out—by failing to toss the puck into the proper space, by hopping on a line or by losing his balance and putting his other foot down. When a foul occurs, the next player takes his turn, and so on. When every player has had a turn, the first contestant goes again, starting with the space where he failed last time around. The first player to complete the course—that is, the player to reach the area marked "out" and return to the baseline—wins the contest.

VARIATIONS: In *Ten Spaces* the first player throws his stone into successive sections and proceeds as in *Ten and Out,* except that when he makes a foul his stone remains in the last square he reached. The next player begins, tossing his puck into square 1, then 2, and so forth, skipping the space in which an opposition player's puck rests, and in hopping, must leap over that space. The first player to complete the course—or to come closest to completing the course—wins. In *Hopscotch* games, as in many other street activities, the rules vary widely from city to city, and even from neighborhood to neighborhood. The two versions described here are good starter games for children who are unfamiliar with this traditional activity.

Pogo Stick Race

● *3 to 6* ● *Nine to Twelve* ● *Pogo Sticks*

FORMATION: The Pogo stick is undoubtedly one of the strangest devices of locomotion ever invented. It is a spring-operated stick on which the rider stands, supported by two footrests. As he presses down on the stick, the spring retracts and then bounds the rider forward, in a leap not unlike that of a kangaroo. Pogo sticks—which require a good sense of balance to ride—can be bought at many toy and sporting-goods stores for under $10. In the *Pogo Stick Race,* contestants stand at a starting line and face a turning line 20 yards away.

ACTION: On signal, each youngster mounts his Pogo stick and begins hopping forward. On reaching the turning line, he makes the turn while still on the stick and bounds back to the starting line. The first player to return to the starting line wins the race. Should a player place a foot on the ground or fall off his Pogo stick,

he must remount before continuing.

VARIATIONS: In *Pogo Stick Relay,* the rules of the *Pogo Stick Race* apply except that players form into teams and line up single file behind the starting line. On signal, the first player on each team mounts his Pogo stick and hops to the turning line and back again. On crossing the starting line he gives his Pogo stick to the next player, who repeats the action. The first team to have all players complete the action wins. In the *Backward Pogo Race* players stand at a starting line with their backs to the turning line, drawn 10 feet away. Each contestant bounces backward to the turning line and backward to the starting line again. This contest can also be the *Backward Pogo Relay* with teams competing.

Perfect Pogo stick form is demonstrated by the youngster in the foreground. For best results, Pogo sticks should be operated on a hardtop surface.

Bicycle Race

- 2 to 10   • Eight to twelve   • Bicycles
- Playground or hard-surface track

FORMATION: Children line up beside their bicycles at a starting line and, depending on the size of the area, a finish line is marked off 50 or 100 or 200 yards away.

ACTION: On signal, contestants mount their bicycles and head for the finish line. The first player to cross the line wins the race. A player who loses his balance and falls is out of the race, as is a player who attempts to interfere with the progress of an opponent.

VARIATIONS: In *Bicycle Relay,* teams stand in single file behind the starting line. There is one bicycle to a team, and when a player completes the course, he turns over his bicycle to the next teammate. The first team to complete the course wins. In a *Zigzag Bicycle Race* obstacles such as benches and barrels are set up in a zigzag pattern along the course, and the players weave in and out between the obstacles. For safety's sake, no more than three contestants at a time should participate. When there are more players, separate heats may be run, with the winners of the heats meeting in elimination contests. The race can also be run against the clock, with each contestant making a solo run and the one completing the course in the fastest time winning. In the *Slow Race* the object is to complete the course in the slowest possible time without falling off the bicycle, or riding out of the boundaries of a lane that is at most four feet wide. In *Jump the Net* a line is strung across the course midway between the start and finish line. On approaching the "net," the player dismounts from his bicycle, lifts it over the line, and then continues. The player to complete the course in the fastest time wins. In the *Newsboy Contest* a line of barrels is set up along one edge of the course and each contestant is given a rolled-up newspaper for each barrel. One at a time the contestants ride along a line six feet from the line of barrels and parallel to it. As each player passes by the barrels he tosses the newspapers, trying to get one into each barrel.

Roller-Skating Race

- 3 to 12   • Eight to twelve   • Roller skates
- Extensive paved surface

FORMATION: Youngsters stand behind a starting line, with a finish line marked anywhere from 50 to 200 yards away, depending on the space available. Relatively small areas can be effectively doubled or tripled by having the contestants skate to a turning line then back to the starting line three or four times.

ACTION: On signal, skaters move out from the starting line and, staying in lane so there will be no interference, skate as fast as possible to the finish line—or to the turning line and back to the starting line. The winner is the skater who completes the course first.

VARIATIONS: *Backward Speed Race* is just like the regular race, except that the players skate backward. Because this is quite difficult, the course is usually short. In the *Coast for Distance* a starting line is drawn 50 or 60 feet behind the coasting line. Players skate to the coasting line, building up as much speed as possible, and then coast. The player who coasts farthest beyond the line wins. In the *Single-Skate Race* players wear only one skate each. They glide on the foot with the skate and push with the other foot. The first player to complete a 50- or 60-yard course wins. Potatoes are scattered over the course for the *Skating Potato Race.* On the way to the turning line, skaters stop to pick up potatoes and then skate back from the turning line as fast as possible. Each player gets one point for each potato he brings back, and the first player to complete the course gets an additional three points. The contestant with the highest point total wins. In the *Roller-Skate Tug of War,* players divide into two equal-size teams with each team standing single file on opposite sides of a line. Wearing roller skates, each team takes one end of a strong rope. On signal, each tries to pull the opposition completely over the dividing line. Because it is hard to get traction while wearing skates, the action is lively, with players scrambling to keep their balance and pull the rope at the same time.

Games from Many Lands

Most North Americans know that many of the sports we play originated on distant shores. *Badminton,* for example, came from India, *Bowling* from Holland, *Tennis* from medieval France and *Golf* from Scotland. The same is true of many of the simpler games that require little special equipment. The children of ancient Athens were playing varieties of *Tag* and *Hide-and-Seek* more than 20 centuries ago. The following games from many lands will probably prove exciting to North American youngsters also.

Numerals indicate the number of players. Spelled-out numbers suggest suitable age levels.

Hit the Coin

- *3 to 12* - *Six to twelve*
- *A coin, a broomstick*

FORMATION: In this Brazilian game, one end of the broomstick is hammered into the ground and a coin is balanced on the other end. A circle about 36 inches in diameter is drawn around the broomstick. Children form a second circle five feet from the pole.

ACTION: Youngsters take turns tossing small stones at the coin, trying to knock it off the pole. If a child succeeds in knocking the coin from its place, and it falls within the inner circle, the boy or girl gets one point; if the coin falls beyond the inner circle, the child gets two points. Each time the coin is hit it is replaced. After each child has had five turns, scores are added. The one with the highest total wins.

Hana, Hana, Hana, Kuchi

- *6 to 12* - *Five to eight*

FORMATION: In this Japanese game, children form a circle with one player in the middle.

ACTION: The child in the middle taps his nose three times and then his mouth once, and says *"Hana, hana, hana, kuchi,"* (nose, nose, nose, mouth). The children forming the circle follow his lead, touching their noses and mouths as he does. The second time he repeats the phrase, the center player may touch any features in any order, regardless of the words he is saying. The children on the rim try to follow the center player's actions rather than his words.

Inzema

- *6 to 20* - *Eight to twelve*
- *Broomsticks, a playground ball*

FORMATION: This African game, common to numerous tribes, had a serious purpose; teaching small boys to throw spears with accuracy, thus preparing them for their roles as hunters. Youngsters, each with a broomstick, stand next to one another along a line scratched in the ground or chalked on a hardtop surface. In front of the line, and about 10 feet to one side, stands the game leader. He has a playground ball. In Africa, a gourd and spears would be used.

ACTION: The game leader rolls the ball in front of him. Each youngster tries to hit the ball with his broomstick as it rolls by. Those who succeed remain to play a second round, but this time the ball is rolled faster and from a greater distance, perhaps 15 feet from the line. The game goes on in this way until only one child is left, and he is declared chief huntsman of the tribe.

Pole Tag

- *8 to 20* - *Seven to eleven*
- *A pole, approximately 12 feet long*

FORMATION: In this Burmese game all children but one stand astride the pole laid on the ground. The other player, the chaser, stands a few feet away. A playing area, about 20 feet square, is marked off.

ACTION: On signal, the chaser tries to tag one of the other players, who scatter within the playing area. They may evade him by crossing over the pole while the chaser must always go around it. Children may not leave the playing area to avoid being tagged, however. When the chaser catches an opponent, he leads his captive back to the pole (in Burma, the chaser rides piggyback on his captive), and the two change roles as everyone assembles at the pole for a new round of play.

Tug and Pull

- *6 to 20* - *Nine to twelve*
- *Lengths of strong rope*

FORMATION: In this adaptation of a traditional German contest, players pair off, kneel to the ground and face each other across a dividing line. A short length of rope, perhaps eight feet long, is wound around their waists.
ACTION: On signal, each player pulls with his body and tries to drag his opponent across the dividing line. A player may move backward, but may not rise from his knees or touch the rope with his hands. The winners of the first round pair off for another round, after which the winners pair off again, until only two players are matched in the finals, the winner of which is the *Tug and Pull* champion.

Stykes

- *5 to 12* - *Nine to twelve*
- *Two bricks; one stick a yard long, another eight inches long*

FORMATION: This centuries-old Danish game remains one of the most popular in that Scandinavian nation. All players but one form a small circle. The lone player, the batter, stands in the center. He places the two bricks on the ground, four or five inches apart, and then puts the short stick across them.
ACTION: The batter takes the long stick, puts one end on the ground under the short stick, and then, holding the other end in his hand, snaps the long stick up to send the short one flying in the air. The rim players try to catch the short stick before it falls. If a player makes the catch, the batter then puts the long stick

across the two bricks, and his opponent throws the short stick, trying to knock the longer one off the bricks. If the thrower succeeds, he and the batter change places for the next round of play. If not, the thrower gets a second chance to replace the batter by trying to throw the short stick so that it lands between the bricks. If the thrower fails in this, the batter gets a chance to score. Again he snaps the long stick under the short one, trying to hit the short stick as great a distance as possible. Players on the rim do not try to intercept it. When the short stick lands, the batter measures the distance it has gone and gets one point for each yard it has traveled. The game goes on until each player has had three turns at bat, and the one with the highest score wins.

Mount Ball

- *10 to 20* - *Ten to twelve* - *Volleyball*

FORMATION: This game was popular among the children of ancient Greece and is played by the boys of that nation today. Boys pair off into teams, one boy in each pair mounting the shoulders of his partner who steadies him by locking arms around his lower legs. Holding this position, the pairs form into a circle, all players facing in.
ACTION: The mounted players toss a volleyball (the Greeks in ancient times used a bull's bladder blown tight and covered with leather) back and forth across the circle. If a player makes a bad throw or fails to catch a good one (matters for the game leader to decide), his pair gets a penalty point. The pair with the fewest points at the end of 10 minutes of play wins. For the second round of play, the players reverse roles: Players who have been sitting on top become the supports.

Maika Bowling

- *4 to 8* - *Eight to twelve*
- *Two sticks, shuffleboard discs*

FORMATION: The people of Polynesia have enjoyed this variation of *Bowling* for centuries.

Two sticks are driven into the ground several inches apart, and each contestant in turn stands at a bowling line about 15 yards from the sticks. Players each have a *maika* stone (a flat disc carved from lava). North American players may substitute shuffleboard discs.

ACTION: Players take turns. Each tries to roll his disc between the sticks. A point is given for each good roll, and the high scorer in 10 rolls wins.

Loulou

● *2 to 20*   ● *Eight to twelve*

FORMATION: In this Polynesian contest, players pair off, with each member of a pair facing the other. They hook their right forefingers together.

ACTION: On signal, each player pulls with his own forefinger against that of his opponent. The object is to force the opponent to straighten out his forefinger or let go altogether. The contest can be played as an elimination, with the winners of each round meeting in the next. The two best players meet in the finals. The winner becomes the *Loulou* champion.

Scorpion's Sting

● *5 to 12*   ● *Six to ten*

FORMATION: In this game from India, children scatter around a small play area, perhaps eight by ten feet. One child is chosen the scorpion.

ACTION: On signal the scorpion, who crawls on all fours, tries to tag one of the players. A tag is made with a raised leg. The fun of the game is teasing the scorpion by moving in very close to touch his head or arms while trying to escape the "stinger." When the scorpion makes a tag, he changes roles with his victim.

In Scorpion's Sting, *one player, by moving in close, almost comes to grief, as the scorpion reaches with his foot and barely misses his fast-stepping prey.*

Two small Shoe Hunt *contestants are still searching for their shoes in the box while their playmates are already racing to lace up theirs.*

CHAPTER 2

Indoor and Outdoor Animated Fun

This chapter offers a wide selection of group games, stunts, mixers, relays, and novelty contests which are suitable for children's parties and fun sessions. All may be played indoors as well as out, and are generally less boisterous than the activities described in the preceding chapter. Most can be played with as few as four or five boys and girls or as many as twenty to twenty-five. As many of these games are suitable for children of both sexes ranging in age from five to twelve, it is often unnecessary to classify the activities according to age. In those cases, however, where a game is particularly appropriate for younger or for older children, such information is given. Although many of these games are educational, the youngsters will be having enough fun so that they won't even realize they're learning while playing.

Numerals indicate the number of players. Spelled-out numbers suggest suitable age levels.

Shoe Hunt

● *Five to eight*   ● *Cardboard box*

Each child takes off both shoes and places them in a large cardboard box in the center of the room. While the leader mixes up the shoes together in the box, the children form a large circle around it. On signal, they all run forward, find their own shoes, and put them on. The first child to come to the leader with his shoes on, and tied or buckled, wins the game. For five- and six-year-olds the requirement of tying shoes may be waived.

Hide the Clock

● *Portable clock*

All the players leave the room while the leader hides a loudly ticking clock. (An electric clock will not do because its cord will give it away, and because it is too quiet.) On signal, the children return to the room and search for the clock. The first child to find it is the winner and is given the privilege of hiding the clock the next time.

Peanut Hunt

● *Peanuts; dishes or cups*

The leader hides unshelled peanuts in every possible nook and corner of the room—under cushions, in drawers, behind doors and curtains, in ash trays, and on top of books, etc. Each child has a dish or a cup and sets out in search of the hidden peanuts. The players may hunt as individuals or divide up into small teams. The game ends after the search has continued for five minutes, and the player or the team with the most peanuts is the winner. This game may also be played outdoors, by scattering peanuts over a backyard or other play area.

Circle Peanut Hunt

● *Blindfolds; peanuts or beanbags; paper bags*

A large circle (about 20 feet in diameter) is marked out on the floor, and the peanuts or beanbags are scattered about inside the circle. Three or four children step into the circle. Each is blindfolded and has a paper bag. On signal, the children get down on their hands and knees and grope for the peanuts or beanbags. After three minutes, they remove their blindfolds and a count is made to see who has collected the most. This game can be played with any small objects in place of peanuts or beanbags, such as bottle caps, wrapped candy, etc.

VARIATION: In *Peanut Derby* four or five children are selected. They assemble at a starting line. On the floor, in front of each player, is a peanut. On signal, each player gets down on his hands and knees and pushes his peanut across the room to a finish line—using his nose only. A player who touches a peanut with any other part of his body is disqualified. When there are many players, several heats can be run to determine the peanut-pushing champion.

Groping in the dark, these players scramble for beanbags in Circle Peanut Hunt.
The player who collects the most bags in three minutes takes the prize.

Hidden Treasure

- *Any small common object*

The leader takes a small object—a short pencil or pen, a matchstick, a marble, a lollypop, etc.—and shows it to all the players. Then the players leave the room, and the leader hides the object in some location where it can be seen without the children having to lift or disturb other objects. On signal, the boys and girls come back in and search for the object. As soon as any child sees it, he whispers to the leader its location and then quietly takes a seat without telling any of the other players where the object is. The game comes to an end when all of the children have finally found the object and are seated.

VARIATIONS: In *Magic Music,* one child is sent out of the room, while the others hide the object somewhere in the room in plain sight. The first child returns and looks for the object, while the others hum a song—softly when he is at a distance from the object, and more loudly when he approaches it. With the help of this "magic music" the child usually finds the hidden treasure very quickly. In *Hot or Cold,* one player leaves the room, while the others decide on some action which he must perform. This may be as easy as picking up or touching any object in the room, or may involve his doing something either with the object or with other players. He might be expected to turn a light on and off, change a record, untie someone's shoelace, shake someone's hand, etc. When the first player comes back into the room, the others all begin to sing a familiar song they have selected. They sing softly at first. Whenever the first player moves close to the spot where he is expected to perform his action, the group sings louder. When he moves away, the singing becomes quieter. In this way, by indicating whether he is "hot" or "cold," they help him find the object or person involved in the action he must perform, and also help him as he tries different actions. When he finally succeeds in performing the required task, the whole group sings out at top volume.

I See Blue

One child secretly selects an object in the room or in the immediate vicinity and writes down its name on a slip of paper, which is given to the game leader. The object should be visible to all players. The child who has chosen the object gives the others a color clue, saying, "I see blue" (or whatever the color of the object actually is). One at a time, the players try to identify the object. It may be a piece of furniture, a section of a picture on the wall, something seen through a window, or any player's article of clothing. The first child to guess the object selects a new object for the other players to guess.

Observation

- *15 or 20 small household objects*

A number of varied objects are placed on a table. They may include such items as a pencil, a knife, a salt shaker, a sneaker, a glass, a marble, an eraser, and an ash tray. Children stand around the table for one or two minutes and try to memorize the objects. Then the objects are covered with a sheet, and the children write down as many as they can remember. After three or four minutes, time is called and the lists are turned over to the leader. The young player who has written correctly the greatest number of objects is the winner.

Baby-Picture Contest

- *Baby pictures of players*

Each child is asked to bring a picture of himself as a baby. The pictures are numbered and tacked or taped to the wall. Children try to guess the correct name to go with each numbered picture and write the names on a piece of paper. After three to five minutes the game leader collects the lists, and the player who has succeeded in correctly identifying the most baby photographs wins the game.

How Many Beans?

● *Jar or bottle filled with beans, marbles, or pebbles*

Before the children come into the room, the leader fills a large glass bottle or other transparent container with beans, marbles, large pebbles, or similar objects. Only the leader knows how many objects are in the container. After examining the container carefully, the children guess how many beans or marbles, etc., are in the container and write their estimates along with their names on a slip of paper. After all the slips are in (this may be at any time during a party or game session) the leader calls for quiet and announces the correct number of objects. The child whose estimate came closest is crowned the champion guesser and may be awarded a small appropriate prize such as a handful of jelly beans.

Find the Bell

● *Small bell*

One player stands with eyes closed in the center of a circle formed by the others. The center player counts aloud to 20. At the same time, the other players pass a small bell around the circle, ringing it as it travels. When the counter reaches 20, all the players on the rim put their hands behind their backs. The child in the center opens his eyes and tries to guess who has the bell. The counter has three guesses; if he guesses correctly, the player who held the bell comes into the center. If not, the counter closes his eyes, counts to 20 and the game continues as before. No child should be permitted to remain in the center of the circle for more than two or three turns.

Look, See, Look

This game is best played in a room with many different objects in it. One player secretly selects some object that is visible and says: "Look, see, look."

The other players ask: "What do we look for?" The first child replies: "The letter C," or whatever is the first letter of the object. Children take turns in guessing the name of the object. The first young player to successfully identify the mysterious object now selects a new object and the game is repeated.

Card Hunt

● *Set of blank cards (5 for each player)*

The object of the game is for each player to collect five cards of any one number—five ones, five twos, five threes, etc. Using blank file cards, the game leader puts a number on one side, leaving the other side blank. If, for example, there are six children playing, the numbers will go from one to six, five cards to each number. The leader then shuffles the cards and deals them out to the children, who then make "blind trades" with each other as each tries to assemble a complete set of one number. The first to do so wins.

Blind Man's Buff

● *Blindfold*

Children are scattered around a playing area. One child is blindfolded and is turned around in place three times. The "blind man" then goes searching for the other children, who are not allowed to move their feet, but may twist their bodies around to escape his touch. When the blind man does find another player, he touches his face and clothing and tries to identify him. If the blind man guesses correctly, the player whose name he guesses becomes the next blind man. If not, the blind man must catch someone else and try again.

VARIATIONS: In *Circle the Blind Man* the players walk in a circle around the blind man until he claps his hands three times. The players stop walking and the blind man points toward the rim of the circle. The player closest to the spot where he points enters the circle, and the blind man chases him. If the player is caught within two minutes, he becomes the blind man; if not, the blind man tries again. In *Blind Man's Staff,* players walk in a circle around the blind man, who holds a stick long enough to reach from the center of the circle to its rim. Players stop walking when the blind man points his staff toward the rim of the circle. The player nearest the stick takes hold of it and the blind man says, "Who's there?" In a disguised voice the player says, "It's me." If the blind man guesses the player's name, they exchange places; if not, the blind man takes another turn.

In *Seated Blind Man's Buff* all the players except the blind man sit on chairs in a tight circle. The blind man sits on the lap of a player and tries to identify him without touching any part of his body. The player whose lap the blind man sits on usually giggles. This helps the blind man guess who it is. If the blind man guesses correctly, he trades places with the seated player. If the blind man does not guess correctly he takes another turn. If, after three turns, he has still not made a correct identification, the game leader chooses another player to be blind man.

Squatting to fool their blindfolded playmate, these youngsters playing Blind Man's Buff *may twist in place to avoid being tagged, but not run away.*

Up, Jenkins

● *A 25-cent piece; a table*

Two teams sit on opposite sides of a table. (A long picnic table would be most suitable.) The players on one side are given a 25-cent piece, which they pass back and forth among themselves under the table. When the captain of the other team says, "Up, Jenkins," the children on the team with the quarter hold their clenched fists up high. Then he says, "Down, Jenkins," and they bring their hands down sharply on the table, palms flat, trying to keep the coin hidden. The players on the other team consult and try to agree on who has the quarter under his hand. This is partly guessing, but it also requires keen observation of the players' expressions and acute hearing to identify the source of the clinking sound made by the coin against the table. Each time a team guesses correctly, it gets one point. The action alternates back and forth: A team has the coin one time, and tries to guess who has the coin the next time. The team which has accumulated the most points after five minutes of playing time has elapsed wins the game.

Animal Pairs

● *Animal pictures from magazines*

This is a mixer game which pairs off children, helping them get acquainted and forming partnerships for some of the games to come. In this mixer the game leader cuts pictures of animals out of magazines and then cuts each picture in half. Each child is given half a picture and then, on signal, all scurry about to find their partners— which is done by matching halves to form a whole animal.

VARIATIONS: In *Animal Calls* each child is given a slip of paper with the name of an animal on it. Two of each animal are given out. These must be animals with familiar calls, such as donkey (bray), dog (bark), wolf (howl), pig (grunt), etc. On signal, players make the sound of the animal named on their slips and, at the same time, listen for the other child who is making the same sound. When the two find each other, they remain partners for the next activity. *Song Titles* is another mixer, this one most suitable for dividing children into small groups, rather than pairs. Children are given slips of paper with the titles of songs that would be familiar to all. The children go around the room singing their songs, joining together with others carrying the same tune. When all the groups have formed, each sings its respective song in turn to entertain the others.

Ring on a String

● *Long piece of string; ring*

Players sit in a circle holding a string which goes around the entire circle. A ring is on this string; it is moved along the string from player to player in either direction. One player stands in the center. As the ring moves around the circle, that child closes his eyes and counts slowly to ten. Then the child in the center opens his eyes and guesses which child has the ring, tapping that player on the hand. If he guesses correctly, the two players switch roles. After three incorrect guesses, the game leader chooses another child to stand in the center and the game continues as before.

Poison Penny

● *Penny or other small object; record player, whistle, or bell*

Children sit or stand in a circle. As music is played on a record player, a penny is passed around the circle from player to player. When the music stops, the child who is holding the penny is eliminated. The game is played until only one child remains. If no music is available, the leader may strike a drum, ring a bell, or blow a whistle to stop the action. Large groups may be divided into two or more circles. This game makes for lively action as the concern of each player is to get rid of the penny just as fast as possible.

Missing Child

● *12 to 20*   ● *Blindfold*

One player stands blindfolded in the center of the room. All the other children change places, except that one of their number quietly leaves the room. The blindfold is then taken off the child in the center, and he is given one minute to name the missing player. If he guesses right, the missing child is blindfolded. If not, the guesser takes another turn in the center.

Fox, Gun, Hunter

Players divide into two teams. Each team goes into a huddle and decides to be one of three things: a fox, a gun, or a hunter. Each of these is superior to one of the others and inferior to another: The fox outranks the hunter, the hunter outranks the gun, and the gun outranks the fox. If a team has chosen to be the fox, all members put their hands on their ears and bark; if a gun, all take aim and shout "Bang!"; if a hunter, all cross their arms and shout "Hey!" After selecting their roles, the two teams face each other and, on signal, advance, each team acting in the manner of the character it has chosen. The team with the superior role wins a point. If both teams have chosen the same role, neither wins. The game is repeated, with new roles chosen, until one team has won five points.

Guess My Name

Before the game begins, the leader cuts out a number of pictures of well-known comic strip characters. Then, without letting the children see the pictures, he pins one to each child's back. The children circulate around, and ask each other questions to try to identify the character they are representing. Any question may be asked except the direct one, "Who am I?" The first player to guess his character is the winner, but the game continues until all or most of the players have guessed who they are.

Add an Action

Children sit in a small circle. One child begins by performing some simple physical action, such as clapping hands, stamping a foot, waving an arm in a circular motion, etc. The player on his right must perform this action, and then add a different one of his own. The next player on the right must perform both of these actions in the correct sequence, and then add yet another. The game continues in this manner, and children who cannot remember the previous actions, or the sequence in which they should be performed, drop out. The last player to perform all the actions in the right sequence is the winner of the contest. The more players who take part in this game, the more difficult and funnier this contest becomes.

Yes or No

● *Dried beans*

The players are given ten or fifteen beans apiece and are told to ask each other questions on any subject. Any player who answers with a "yes" or "no" anywhere in the reply must pay the questioner with a bean. Sounds or gestures equivalent to "yes" or "no," like "uh-huh," or "nope," or shaking the head cause the loss of a bean. The game continues for five minutes, with a great hubbub of conversation, as children try to win beans from each other. At the end of the game, a general counting takes place and the child with the most beans is declared the winner of the game.

VARIATION: In *Odd or Even* players are divided into pairs, each member having about 40 beans. One member takes any number from his stockpile, puts them in a fist and asks his opponent, "Odd or even?" The opponent guesses, and if he is correct he gets the beans from the questioner; if incorrect, he turns over that number from his own pile to his opponent. After five minutes of play, the player who has been most successful in collecting beans is declared the winner.

Meet My Friend

This game is usually played at the beginning of a party where the children do not know each other well. Each child is asked to find out the name of another child, where he lives, where he goes to school, and other facts. Then each child, in turn, rises and introduces his new friend to the entire group, telling what he has learned about him. To insure that everyone is introduced, the players sit in a circle and interview and introduce the player to their right.

Indian Chief

● *Four to eight*

One child is chosen to be the scout and goes out of the room. The other players, who are sitting in a circle, choose one of their number to be the Indian chief. The Indian chief leads the other players in a series of physical actions, such as clapping, stamping, waving, or nodding heads. The scout enters the room and stands in the center of the circle. As the circle players continue to change from action to action, the scout tries to find the Indian chief. The scout is given three guesses. If he is successful, the Indian chief becomes the new scout and leaves the room. If not, the old scout goes, out again, or another child takes his place.

Stop Laughing

● *Chairs, playground ball*

Children sit in chairs in a semicircle. One player faces them holding a playground ball. On a signal, this child throws the ball into the air, lets it bounce once, and then catches it. While the ball is in the air, the other players laugh loudly and continuously. They are completely silent, however, before the ball is thrown and after it is caught. Any player who laughs at these times is eliminated. The throwing is repeated again and again, until only one player—the one who laughs on signal only—remains in the game as the winner.

Color Call

● *Six to eight*   ● *Beanbag*

Children form a circle with one player in the center. The child in the center throws the beanbag to a player on the rim and calls out a color. The player who catches the beanbag responds by naming an object of the color called and then throws the beanbag back to the center player while calling a new color. Now the boy or girl in the center must name an appropriate object. The game goes on in this manner with colors repeated, if necessary; but objects may not be repeated. When a player on the rim fails to catch the beanbag or cannot name an object of the color called, he is eliminated. When the child in the center drops the beanbag or answers incorrectly, he leaves the game and his questioner moves to the center. The game continues until only one player remains. This player becomes the winner. A ball may be substituted for a beanbag if desired. This has a tendency to speed up the game, as a ball is a bit harder to catch and results in players being eliminated faster.

Stay Sober

Children form two teams and stand facing each other. The children on the first team are given one minute to make anyone laugh on the opposite team. They may make faces, gestures, funny or teasing remarks, but they are not allowed to touch the players on the opposite team. Then the action is reversed, and members of the second team try to make the children on the first team laugh. Any child who laughs must leave the line. The team with the most remaining players after several turns is the winner.

VARIATIONS: In *Giggle Belly* children lie on the floor in a line. Each rests his head on the next child's stomach. On signal, the first player says, "Ha!" the next says, "Ha, Ha!" and the third, "Ha, Ha, Ha!" and so on. Rarely does this continue beyond the fifth child, for by that time, all of the youngsters are convulsed by laughter. In *Silly Telegram,* a number of humorous telegrams are written ahead of time. The children form into two lines facing each other. Player No. 1 on team A gives his telegram to player No. 1 on team B. The player who receives the telegram reads it in a loud voice. If he succeeds in orally delivering the message to the assembled players without laughing, his team scores a point. If he fails, the other team gets the point. Successive telegrams are delivered in this manner, first from one side, then the other. The side with more points after all telegrams have been delivered wins the *Silly Telegram* contest. The telegrams are pure nonsense, such as, "Telegram for Miss Sweet Susie Swann, South Street, Salem. Send seven special spinach sandwiches to Sassy Sally's sister. (Signed) Slippery Sammy Smith." Or, "Telegram for Lassie. We are dispatching a shipment of our best fleas. Guaranteed to be up to scratch. (Signed) Puss in Boots."

Only a tickle—and that's against the rules—will make the straight-faced players on the right laugh. Oblivious to antics, they Stay Sober *to win.*

Bird, Beast, Fish

Players sit in a circle, with one child (the caller) in the center. The caller points to any other child and says, "Bird, beast, fish—Fish!" or "Bird, beast, fish—Bird!" By the count of ten, that child must then name a fish (or bird) not previously mentioned. If successful he sits in the center of the circle. If not, the same child remains in the center, calling on a different child to name a specific animal. The game becomes more difficult as many different creatures are named by the contestants.

VARIATION: In *Earth, Air, Fire, and Water* the child in the center picks someone in the circle and calls out one of the following: "Earth," "Air," "Fire," or "Water." By the count of ten, the child called upon must name a creature, not already named, that walks on the ground, flies in the air, or swims in the water. If "Fire" is called, nothing is said. If the child in the circle answers correctly before the count of ten, he goes into the center and becomes the new caller. If not, the old caller retains his role for another round of play and challenges the others once more.

Fizz

● *Eight to twelve*

This game is based on the multiplication table for five. Players sit in a circle and count from left to right, starting with the number one. When the number five or any multiple of five comes up, the word "Fizz" is called out instead. The first player would begin by calling out "One!" The next would call "Two!" The game continues with "Three!" "Four!" "Fizz!" "Six!" "Seven!" "Eight!" "Nine!" "Fizz!" and so on. The game may also be played having the child who says "Fizz!" quickly stand up and sit down. If the circle gets as far as the number 55 ("Fizz-fizz!") the player bobs up and down twice. Any player who hesitates too long or who incorrectly calls out "Fizz!" or a number is given a penalty point and the game starts all over again. After about ten minutes of play the child with the fewest number of penalty points is the Fizz champion.

VARIATIONS: In *Buzz* any number which has a seven in it, or which is a multiple of seven (like 14 or 21), requires that the player whose turn it is call out "Buzz!" In addition, whenever "Buzz!" is called, the direction of the number calling is reversed. If the game progresses into the 70s, the counting changes to "Buzz-one," "Buzz-two," and so on. Whenever a player makes a mistake, he gets one penalty point and starts the game from the beginning again. In *Fizz-Buzz* any five or multiple of five calls for a "Fizz!" Any seven or multiple of seven calls for a "Buzz!" and a change of direction in the number calling. A number that is a multiple of both five and seven, like 35, would call for "Fizz-buzz!" to be called out, followed by a change of direction.

Prince of Paris

● *Eight to twelve*

Children sit in a circle and each is given a number. One player begins by saying: "The Prince of Paris has lost his hat. Have you found it, number eight, sir?" (Any other number might be used, of course.)

The child whose number is eight replies: "Who, sir? I, sir?"

The dialogue continues: "Yes, sir, you, sir!"

"No, sir, not I, sir!"

"Who then, sir?"

Number eight then identifies another player by number. For example he might answer with: "Number three, sir."

The player whose number is three begins the dialogue anew with: "Who sir, I sir?"

Number eight now replies with the same words his questioner used before. And so the game goes on, with the player being questioned becoming the new questioner when a round ends. Whenever a player makes a mistake by failing to reply or by saying the wrong word, he gets a penalty point. The child with the fewest points after ten or fifteen minutes of play is declared to be the winner of the game.

Who Is It?

One player leaves the room. On returning, he is told that the others have selected one of the children in the room and that he must guess who it is. He tries to find out by asking one question at a time of each child in the circle. The questions may ask anything about the mysterious player, except "Who is he?" The answers may be only "Yes," "No," or "I don't know." As the questioning continues, the player in the center gets more and more puzzled by what seem to be contradictory or confusing replies. The reason is that the members of the group have not picked a single player, but instead each player is thinking of, and describing, the player on his own right. The game continues until the player in the center guesses the secret. If, after five minutes, he does not guess the secret, or if he gives up, the others tell him about the trick.

Willie, Willie

Children sit in a circle. The game leader is in the center and demonstrates an action he challenges the others to repeat exactly. He holds his right hand up so that all can see it and with his left index finger he points to each finger of the right hand, starting with the pinky. As he points he says: "Willie, Willie, Willie, Willie." Each "Willie" is said as the index finger points to another finger on the other hand. "Whoops" comes as the left index finger is run down from the right index finger and back up to the top of the thumb. Then the action is reversed, with "Willie" repeated as the left index finger points to the thumb, and "Whoops" repeated as the left index finger moves from the thumb to the right index finger. Finally the action is completed—or so it seems—as the left index finger moves down the right hand, ending on the right pinky with a last "Willie." Upon finishing the demonstration, the game leader asks the players to repeat it. Many will apparently do it correctly, but will be told they have not. The players must do two things to get the

LEFT HAND POINTS

RIGHT HAND

WILLIE WILLIE WILLIE WILLIE WHOOPS

NOW CLAMP BOTH HANDS IN LAP

RIGHT HAND

WILLIE WILLIE WILLIE WILLIE WHOOPS WILLIE

action exactly right: First they use the left hand for pointing while the right one remains stationary; Second, when they have completed the action, they must clasp their hands and place them in their laps. The game leader does this when demonstrating the stunt, but only the most observant children, usually after five or six tries, will have noticed.

Guess the Proverb

● *Seven to twelve*

Children divide into two teams and sit in rows facing each other. Each team picks a familiar proverb, such as "Haste makes waste," or "A rolling stone gathers no moss." Each player of the team is given one word of the proverb his team has chosen. (The same word may be given to more than one child, depending on the number of players.) On signal, all the children on one team shout their words loudly in unison and the players on the opposite team try to guess the proverb. When the second team has succeeded, they call out their words, and the first team tries to guess their proverb.

The Ocean Is Calm

Children sit in chairs scattered around a room. Without telling the others what he has chosen, each child picks the name of some creature that lives in the ocean. One player is picked to be the fisherman. He stands and says: "The ocean is calm." Walking around the room, he calls out the names of various fish or other sea creatures: "Sharks!" "Eels!" "Clams!" "Salmon!" "Squid!" "Sea turtles!" "Codfish!" and so on. When a player hears the name of his creature, he gets up and walks behind the fisherman, calling out the names of other sea creatures. When most of the players have been called out of their seats, the fisherman shouts: "The ocean is stormy!" At this, all the children—those still sitting and those already caught—must find new seats. The last child to find a seat becomes the new fisherman.

One Less

● *Small household objects*

The players line up side by side behind a starting line. About ten feet away are piled a number of objects, such as pencils, erasers, items of clothing, etc. There should be one less object than the number of children. On signal, the youngsters run forward and try to grab an object. The child who does not get an object is eliminated. The game continues, with the leader taking away one object each time. Thus the number of players becomes smaller and smaller. The last remaining child wins the game.

Musical Chairs
(also called *Going to Jerusalem*)

● *Chairs; piano or record player*

A number of chairs—one less than the number of players—are placed side by side but facing in alternate directions. On signal, the players walk counterclockwise (to the right) around the chairs to the accompaniment of a piano or music from a record player. When the music stops, every child tries to find a seat. The boy or girl who cannot get a seat drops out of the game and a new round begins, again with one less chair than the number of players. The game continues until there are only two children competing for one chair—the player who sits in it when the music stops wins the game.

Magic Carpets

● *Newspapers or pieces of cardboard; piano or record player*

A number of newspapers or large sheets of cardboard (as many as there are players) are scattered around on the floor. After the music starts and players march around the floor single file to the right, the leader removes one sheet of paper. When the music stops, each player must find a sheet of paper to stand on. The one child who cannot find a "magic carpet" is eliminated. This action is repeated, until only one child—the winner—remains in the game. **VARIATION:** In *Prison,* a wide rectangle is marked across the floor with chalk. This is the "prison." As music is played, contestants either singly or in pairs walk around the floor in a circle, passing through the prison each time around. When the music stops, any child or pair caught in the "prison" is eliminated. This is repeated until only one child—or one pair—is left.

Musical Madness

● *Whistle; piano or record player*

Players form a large circle and march around to the right as music plays. When the music stops, the leader blows a whistle two, three, or four times. If he blows the whistle four times, children must immediately form circles of four members each. If he blows the whistle three times, each circle must have three children, etc. Any player unable to join an appropriate circle is eliminated. The game is continued until only one set of winners remains in the game.

Simon Says

● *Four to ten*

One child is Simon. He faces the other players and commands them in certain actions, such as: "Clap hands!" "Jump in place!" "Bow!" "Touch your head!" "Touch your toes!" "Pull your left ear, then your right!"

As Simon gives each command, he performs the action himself, and each child instantly imitates the action—but only if the command has been preceded by the words: "Simon says!" If Simon has not said: "Simon says," the players ignore the command and do nothing. A child who ignores a command with "Simon says," or performs an action that was not preceded by these words, is eliminated from the line. To make the game more difficult, Simon may try to trick the players by giving a rapid string of commands with "Simon says" and then suddenly giving a command without the phrase. The last child to remain in the game is the winner. With four- or five-year-olds playing the game, it is usually wise to have the adult game leader assume the role of Simon.

One slip-up and you're out, in Simon Says. *Each player must listen closely to Simon's commands to avoid having to sit out part of the game.*

Dog and Bone

● *Chairs; a book; a blindfold*

Boys and girls sit on chairs arranged in a semi-circle. One child, the dog, sits blindfolded on the floor about 15 feet in front of the others. Beside the dog is a book; this is the bone. The game leader points to a child in the group, who then tries to creep or crawl silently up to the bone and bring it back to his place without being heard by the dog. If the dog hears a player creeping up, he points in the direction of the sound and if his pointing is reasonably accurate (a matter for the leader to decide), the dog keeps his role for another round. If not, and the thief gets back to his chair without being discovered, the thief becomes the dog for the next round of the game.

Squirrel and Nut

● *A peanut*

Boys and girls sit in a 20-foot-diameter circle. They have their heads down, eyes closed, and their hands cupped in front of them. One player, the squirrel, walks quietly around the inside of the circle. The squirrel holds a peanut which

he drops into the hands of one of the players. The player who gets the nut jumps up and chases the squirrel once around the inside of the circle back to the empty spot. If the squirrel gets back first and sits down without being tagged, the player who received the nut becomes the new squirrel. If not, the old squirrel must give the nut to someone else and try again.

Fish-Net Scramble

● *Chairs*

The players sit on chairs in a circle with one player, the fisherman, in the center. The fisherman gives each of the others the name of a fish: "trout," "salmon," "herring," "guppy," etc. He then calls out the names of any two fish. The two children with these names quickly exchange places while the fisherman tries to get one of their seats. Of the three, whoever does not find a seat becomes the fisherman for the next round. At any time, the fisherman may call out "Fish net scramble!" and all the players scramble for new seats.

VARIATION: In *Fruit Basket,* children sit in a circle with one player in the center. The center player assigns the name of a popular fruit to various circle players. (Some become pears, some apples, some peaches, etc.) He calls out "All apples change places with all pears," or a similar phrase. While the two groups scramble to change places, he tries to get one of the seats that has been vacated. The center player may also call out the name of several kinds of fruits at once, making it easier for him to get a seat. If "Fruit basket upset!" is called out, all the children in the circle must change seats.

Apple-Paring Contest

● *Nine to twelve*   ● *Apple peelers; apples*

Each boy and girl has an apple peeler and an apple. On signal all the players begin to peel their apples. The winner is the child who ends up with the longest unbroken piece of apple peel after two minutes.

Pretzel

● *Eight to twelve*

One player volunteers to leave the room. The others join hands in a circle, and *without* letting go, form themselves into a complicated, twisted mass of bodies. This is done by maneuvering about—raising arms and ducking under, lifting feet over joined hands, climbing over or under each other. The players are drawn closer together until finally they become a tight knot, with heads, arms, and feet protruding in different directions. The child outside comes back and tries to unravel this human pretzel. He tries to return it to a circle shape without loosening any of the players' hands. This may be performed as a competitive race between two teams.

It would take a Pretzel *unbender to straighten this gang without unlinking their hands. But that's the challenge the boy in stripes is facing.*

Reuben and Rachel

● *A blindfold*

Two players, a boy and a girl, are chosen to be Reuben and Rachel. They stand in the center of a circle of players. To begin, Reuben is blindfolded. He calls out, "Rachel," and the girl must immediately answer, "Here, Reuben." With only the sound of her voice to guide him, Reuben tries to catch and tag Rachel. If he succeeds, the roles are reversed; Rachel is blindfolded and tries to catch Reuben. The two players should keep calling and answering each other rapidly, so the blindfolded player has a chance of catching the other player.

VARIATION: In *Tin Can* the player who is being chased rattles a tin can partly filled with small stones or beans. The blindfolded player pursues the rattling sound in trying to tag the other player. After a tag the two players switch roles for another round.

Community Sneeze

The leader sits facing the players and divides them into three separate groups. The group on the left practices saying, then shouting, the word "Hishee"; the center group practices the word "Hashee," and the group on the right practices the word "Hoshee." Then, on signal, all three groups shout their word at once. The result sounds amazingly like a giant sneeze. The leader smiles and says, "Bless you!"

VARIATION: In *Barnyard Chorus* the leader has each child in the group take the name of a barnyard animal whose sound can be easily recognized: cows, horses, ducks, chickens, dogs, pigs, etc. If the group is large, more than one child may be given a particular name. Then, on signal, all the players give the cries of their animals as loudly as possible. This kind of group stunt is usually a little more amusing if the leader explains at the beginning that with the group's help, he is going to create an authentic scene of nature. When they make the mass noise—which can be deafening—he says, "Welcome to the barnyard!"

Hare and Hound

● *Blindfolds*

Two blindfolded children stand on one side of a large table from which everything has been cleared. One player is the hare; the other is the hound. The hound tries to catch the hare. As the two move around, they must keep their hands on the table. Those watching should be as quiet as possible, so the players will have a chance to hear each other. When the hare is finally caught, the two players reverse roles or two new players are chosen to play the game.

Balloon Basketball

● *Newspaper; balloon*

There are two equal teams, with at least three or four children on a side. A newspaper is taped to the wall on either end of the room. These two pieces of paper serve as the baskets. To start the game one member of each team moves to the center. The leader hits the balloon in the air and each player tries to hit it, with his hand or arm, toward his teammates. The object of the game is for each team to try to bat the balloon toward the other team's "basket." If the balloon touches the paper a goal is scored. After about five minutes of play the team with more goals is the winner.

VARIATION: In *Pop the Balloon* a goalie stands under each basket with a pin. As the balloon nears the basket, the goalie can either bat it, swat it, or pop it with his pin. This makes it much harder to score.

Hat Head Duel

● *Two blindfolds; two balloons; two paper hats*

Two players with paper hats on their heads stand in the center of the room. They are blindfolded and each is given a balloon. On signal, each player tries to knock the paper hat off his opponent's head by swinging his balloon. To help them locate each other, one player must keep calling out "Here!" and the other "There!" The first player to knock off his opponent's hat is declared the winner.

VARIATION: In *Hat in the Ring* the children form a circle. Each child wears a paper hat. In the center of the circle is a large ring marked on the floor. On signal, one child takes off his hat and throws it toward the center, trying to make it land in the ring. The first player is quickly followed by a second who does the same, and so on until every player on the circle has thrown his hat toward the ring. No one may move from his position on the outer circle while throwing. As paper hats are light in weight, the chances are that not many of them will land inside the ring. But the owners of the ones that do will be the winners. There may be a runoff of the successful children so that a champion

Blindfolded and armed with long balloons, two swordsmen in Hat Head Duel *swing roundhouse style as each tries to knock off the other's hat.*

can be established. It is wise to experiment beforehand as to just how far a paper hat may be expected to travel when thrown, for a game that has no successful player—and therefore no winner—is bound to prove extremely disappointing to everyone concerned.

Swat

● *Newspaper; tape or cord*

All children sit in a circle of chairs, facing in. A very loosely rolled-up newspaper, tied with cord or bound with tape, is placed on a chair or stool in the circle's center. The game leader chooses one player to leave his seat and move to the center. On signal, the child takes the newspaper and walks around the inside of the circle. Suddenly he stops and hits another child across the legs with the paper. The swatter then

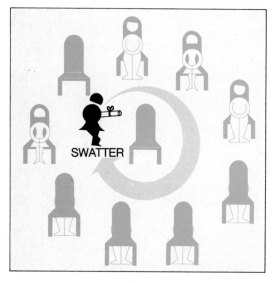

SWATTER

puts the paper back in its place in the circle's center and returns to his own seat. He moves quickly, trying to return to place before his victim can grab the paper and return the blow. If the swatter succeeds in eluding the pursuer, he holds his position for another round of play. However, by the rules of the game, if he is hit, the chaser becomes the swatter for the next round of *Swat*.

Broom Hockey

● *Eight to twelve*   ● *Two brooms; a rag*

Children divide into two teams and stand in lines facing each other on opposite sides of the room. To serve as goal markers, two chairs are placed about four feet apart at the ends of each

line. A rag and two brooms, with their handles facing the goals, are placed on the floor in the center of the room. Each team numbers off so that the number-one players are diagonally opposite each other. The leader calls out a number, and the player on each team with the corresponding number runs forward and picks up the broom belonging to his team. Both players try to sweep or push the rag in the center of the room into the opposite goal. The action is similar to hockey and some care should be taken to curb too enthusiastic behavior on the part of the players. The first player to score a goal wins a point for his team. When a goal is scored, the rag and brooms are put back in the center of the room and new numbers are called. After ten minutes the team with the highest score is the winner.

Novelty Contests

These contests make use of simple items that are usually available around a home, such as beans, potatoes, bottle tops, articles of clothing, toothpicks, tin cans, candles, pieces of fruit, etc. They may be played separately, or as part of an overall "carnival" of games, in which large numbers of players take part.

Spelled-out numbers suggest suitable age levels.

Balloon-Blowing Contest

● *Balloons*

The players have deflated balloons. On signal, they begin to blow them up. The winner is the player who makes his balloon the biggest within three minutes. Any boy or girl who breaks a balloon, however, must drop out of the contest.

Potato-Spearing Contest

● *Nine to twelve*　● *Forks; potatoes*

Each player has a large uncooked potato and a fork. At a signal they all throw their potatoes into the air and try to spear them with a fork as they come down. They receive one point for each successful spearing. Individual players may compete against each other, the highest score winning after five tries. Players should each have an area of about five feet square in which to move. If the children stand too close, they might spear one another instead of the potato.

Pie-Eating Contest

● *Pies; paper plates*

Children kneel on the floor in a circle, with their hands behind their backs. A paper plate with a quarter of a pie is placed on the floor in front of each. On signal, the boys and girls lean forward and eat the pie as quickly as they can. The first child to eat all the pie and pick up the empty paper plate with his teeth is the winner. It's a good idea to spread newspapers on the floor and cover each player's front with a large towel. Blueberry and cherry make the best pies for these contests; they taste good, go down easily, and lend color to the contestants!

VARIATIONS: In the *Ice Cream Contest* two blindfolded children lie flat on the floor, with their faces close together. They each have a dish of chocolate ice cream and a tablespoon, and, at a signal, they try to feed each other. Here too it makes good sense to have plenty of newspapers on the floor and towels on the players. For a *Cereal-Eating Contest* players divide into several teams of two children each. They sit cross-legged on the floor facing each other with a large bowl of dry cereal between them. Each child is given a large spoon and, on signal, they start to feed each other. The first team to finish all the cereal wins. Blindfolds may be used in this game.

Coin in the Desert

● *Coins; cornflakes; paper plates*

Boys and girls stand in front of a table with their hands tied behind their backs. In front of each player is a paper plate on which is a coin hidden in a heap of cornflakes. On signal each player tries to dig the coin out of the cornflakes with his teeth. The first player to lift his head with the coin between his teeth is the winner. Before using the coins, they should be boiled to make them germ-free.

Peanut Jab

● *Shelled peanuts; toothpicks*

Peanuts are strewn about within a large circle marked out on the floor. Several players come into the circle, each holding two toothpicks and a small paper bag. On signal, the players try to lift, chopstick style, as many peanuts as they can with their toothpicks and drop them into their paper bags. When all the peanuts have been gathered, the player with the greatest number wins the game.

Shoot Out the Candle

- *Eight to twelve*   - *Candles; water pistols*

Because this game involves fire, it is essential that an adult be in constant attendance. A lighted candle rests on a plate or tray about six or eight feet away from a line of players. Boys and girls on the shooting line take turns trying to shoot out the flame with a water pistol. If a player succeeds, he wins one point, and the candle is relighted for the next player. The game may also be played by setting up several candles in a row. A point is given for each candle shot out using only one pistol-load of water. Winners may be given a "marksmanship award" at the end of the contest.

Broom Lacrosse

- *Eight to twelve*   - *Broomsticks; quoits*

Children divide into pairs. One child per pair has a quoit—a piece of heavy rope taped together at its ends to form a circle about six inches in diameter. Both children, however, have a broomstick cut to a length of about three feet. The children face each other and stand about six feet apart. The child with the quoit tosses it underhand toward his rival, who tries to spear it with his stick. Then the receiver returns the throw in the same manner. The child who makes the greatest number of catches within three minutes is the winner. The game leader decides when a throw is too wild to be caught, and such throws are repeated. When a large number of children are playing, this game can be played as an elimination contest, with the winners of each round meeting for the next until only one player remains.

VARIATION: In *Chair Ring Toss* a four-legged chair is placed upside down, supported, with its legs upright, by the seat of another chair. Each player has five quoits and stands about ten feet from the chair. Tossing the quoits underhand, the players take turns trying to ring the legs. Each ringer counts five points, and if a quoit lands on the seat the toss is worth one point. Should a player ring all four legs during his five chances, he receives a bonus of 20 points. The boy or girl with the most points after every player has had a turn wins the game. Should the scoring be low, the distance players stand from their target can be reduced to about six feet or even less.

Hammer Contest

- *Eight to twelve*
- *Hammer; nails; a piece of lumber*

The game leader drives one nail per player into a piece of softwood (such as pine) lumber. The nails are driven in just far enough to secure them. Each contestant takes a turn trying to drive his nail all the way into the wood, and the one who can do this with the fewest hammer blows wins the game. This contest should be well supervised, as accidents can easily happen if some of the players become overly excited.

Money Throwaway

- *A large dishpan; a saucer; a handful of pennies*

The dishpan is half filled with water and the saucer carefully placed on the surface so that it floats. Children line up at a throwing line, three feet from the dishpan. Each child has five pennies and is instructed to toss the coins, one at a time, at the floating saucer. Players try to throw each penny so that it stays on the saucer and doesn't slide or bounce off. Each coin that stays in the saucer scores a point for the thrower. Being able to keep a tossed penny in the saucer is difficult as the coin either bounces off or slides off the saucer. After a number of children have played the game, it may be necessary to recover the pennies from the bottom of the dishpan and dry them off before starting the game anew. Also, the saucer will need to be dried from time to time and then refloated. In the majority of games such as this one, where water is used, it is a good idea to cover the floor with a plastic sheet, or at least have plenty of newspapers under and around the dishpan. The player who manages to get the greatest number of coins to remain in the saucer wins the game. Other flat objects, such as bottle tops or metal washers, may be used instead of the coins if a sufficient number of pennies are not available.

Speed Shaving

● *Can of shaving cream; "shaving" implements*

Players divide into teams of two. Using a pressure foam dispenser, one player per team covers the lower part of his partner's face with foamy shaving cream. Then, using a wooden tongue depressor, a spoon, or a bladeless razor, one player on each team "shaves" his partner's face clean. The action is repeated with the other partner doing the shaving. The first team finished is declared the winner.

Holding bladeless razors, two apprentice barbers race to shave their clients clean while other customers await their turns during a Speed Shaving *contest.*

In the Hat

- *Seven to twelve*
- *One or two decks of playing cards; a hat*

Boys and girls, each with ten playing cards, form a circle about 20 feet in diameter. In the center of the circle is a hat that rests upside down. Players, standing on the rim, try to flip their cards into the hat. The game may be scored so that a card that lands in the hat is worth two points, and one that lands on the brim or leans against the hat is worth one. The winner is the player with the most points after all cards have been tossed.

Bottle Tenpins

- *Seven to twelve*
- *Ten plastic or cardboard bottles; a playground ball*

The plastic or cardboard bottles are set up in a triangular pattern, like bowling pins. The players stand behind a line about 15 feet away and try to knock down the bottles by rolling a playground ball. If a player knocks them all down the first time, he gets ten points, plus a bonus of five for the "strike." If not, he is allowed a second try, and his score is the total number of pins knocked down. Children may play against each other as individuals or compete as teams.

Drop-the-Beanbag Relay

- *Two beanbags*

Boys and girls divide into relay teams that line up in single file. The lead player on each team has a beanbag. On signal, he raises the beanbag over his head and, without turning, lets it drop behind him. The next player picks up the beanbag and repeats the action. The first team to complete the action is the winner. If there is an equal number of boys and girls present, the game can be made into an exciting contest between the sexes.

Apple Ducking

- *Large washtub; apples*

Children gather around a large tub of water, in which several apples have been placed. Players compete (either one at a time, or all at once) to see who can get one of the floating apples out of the water without using his hands. To do this, they plunge their heads right into the water and try to bite the apple. If all the children duck at the same time, the winner is the first to get an apple, and the runner-up is the second. If the children take turns, to determine the winner they should be timed with a watch that has a second hand. A stopwatch would be even better. In a game of this kind it is advisable to have a number of towels on hand to dry off the contestants. Also, keep a mop nearby, as invariably some water is going to be spilled on the floor.

Hanging Apples

- *String; darning needles; apples*

Thread a large darning needle with strong string and run the string through a button. Then, when the button is secured to one end of the string, run the needle through an apple so that its bottom rests on the button. Repeat this with several apples and then hang them from the ceiling or an overhead beam or fixture so that they dangle at about the height of each player's chin. Boys and girls line up in front of the apples with their hands behind their backs. On signal, each child tries to eat the apple in front of him, using only his teeth to seize it. This may be difficult, particularly if the apples are large. After a minute or so of futile effort, the leader might point out that if the players start an apple swinging back and forth like a pendulum, and then meet it with a strong bite, it is possible to get a toothhold on the apple.

VARIATION: In *Apple Turnover*, the apple is threaded in the same way as described above. The string has a loop large enough to go over a child's head. Two children, on their hands and

Just a bite and the boy is a winner in Hanging Apples.
The rules say he may not touch the apple with a hand.

Hit the Deck

● *Two decks of playing cards; two cardboard hat boxes or similar containers; two tables*

The children form into two teams of not more than 13 players each. They line up facing each other from either side of the room. In between the teams are two card tables. On each table is a cardboard box. There is a deck of cards in each box. The cards have been shuffled thoroughly, then dumped into the boxes in complete disarray. On a signal from the game leader, the first child in each line hurries to his team's box. His object is to paw through the playing cards until he finds a king. When he does, he quickly removes it and runs to a corner of the room. There he places the king face up on the floor and hurries back to his teammates. He touches the next child in line. This player now runs to the team's box and hunts for a queen of any suit. On finding it, he too, takes it to the same corner, places it face up beside the king and returns to the line. The third player now goes into action. He must find a jack and follow the same procedure as his teammates before him. The game continues with each succeeding player on both sides hunting for, and finding, the next card in sequence—regardless of suit. The first team to put down a complete run from king to ace (the low card) wins the contest. If there should be too few children to make up two teams of 13 each, the game may still be played by removing all the kings if there are just 12 players per team; or by removing the queens also, if there are 11, and so on until there are just enough cards in each box for each team.
VARIATION: In *Find the Suit,* the game is played in the same manner except that the players of each team are instructed to find not just any king or queen, and so on, but ones of a special suit, such as hearts. The other players must follow suit throughout the entire sequence. This complicates the search and prolongs the game somewhat, but adds to the suspense. Other variations may be played as the leader calls for poker hands such as a full house, a straight, a straight flush and so on.

knees, face each other. Each child has an apple on the string hanging down from his neck and swinging freely like a pendant. On signal, the children advance toward each other and each endeavors to get his teeth into the apple hanging from his opponent's neck. The child who succeeds in getting the most bites after an agreed upon interval of time has passed wins the duel. Contestants are required to remain on their hands and knees throughout the game.

Bucket Brigade

- *Seven to twelve*
- *Miscellaneous household objects*

Players form two teams behind a starting line. At the turning line, about 15 feet away, there is a pile of objects for each team. These piles may include such things as old hats, books, tablewear, pencils, etc. On signal the lead players run to the turning line. Each picks up an object and runs back to the starting line. The lead players pass on their objects to the second players, who in turn pass them down the line while the lead players take their places at the rear of their lines. When an object reaches the end of the line it is placed on the floor. As soon as the second players pass on the objects given them, they too run to the turning line, pick up one item apiece and run back to pass on their objects. As each player completes the action, he goes to the end of his line. The game ends when one team has picked up all its objects and rebuilt the pile behind the starting line.

Retrieving Contest

- *Paper clips; wire hangers; a pan*

The game leader empties a boxful of paper clips into a large pan of water. Players kneel around the pan, and each is given a straightened-out wire coathanger, on which a small hook has been bent at one end. On signal, the players try to pull out the paper clips with the hook. When all the clips have been retrieved, the player with the most clips is declared the winner.

Lemon Race

- *Lemons; table knives*

Boys and girls line up, evenly spaced, behind one line drawn on the floor, and face another line about 15 feet across the room. Each player is given a lemon and a table knife. Touching the lemons with their knives only, players roll them to the turning line and back again. The first player to complete the action is the winner.

If the contest is played as a relay, the first team to finish wins. Apples or potatoes may be substituted for lemons, and toothpicks for knives.
VARIATION: In *Balloon Fanning,* boys and girls stand behind the first line holding balloons and shirt cardboards. On signal, each places his balloon on the floor and, using his cardboard, begins to fan it toward the line across the room. The first boy or girl to fan his balloon to the turning line and back wins the race. Players do not touch the balloons; it is the breeze from the fan that drives them. This contest may also be played as a relay race.

Stepping-Stone Race

- *Shirt cardboards*

Players line up behind a starting line about 15 feet away from a turning line. Each player has two shirt cardboards; these are the stepping

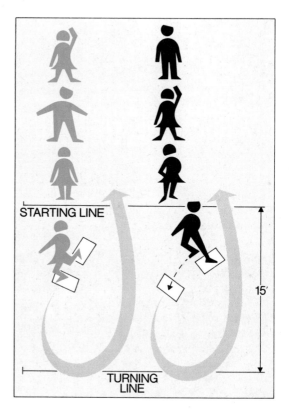

STARTING LINE

TURNING LINE

15'

stones. On signal, each player places his cardboards on the ground, one in front of the other, and places one foot on the front cardboard and another foot on the rear cardboard. To move toward the turning line, he picks up the rear cardboard, moves it in front of the other, and then steps forward. In this manner, boys and girls continue to move until one, the winner, has reached the turning line and returned to the starting line. This race can be performed as a contest among individuals or as a team relay. **VARIATION:** In *Sir Walter Raleigh,* players divide into pairs. On signal, one player in each pair crouches and moves the cardboards forward; the other walks only on the cardboards, lifting his foot, and placing it down again when a cardboard is placed in a forward position. Each pair travels to the turning line and back, after which the roles are reversed. The first pair of players (or the first team, if the game is being played as a relay) to complete the action wins the race.

Toothpick Pass

● *Nine to twelve*   ● *Toothpicks; two cherries*

Players divide into two equal teams and line up as in a relay race. Each of the players has a toothpick, and the two lead players have maraschino cherries on their picks. At a signal, the first players run forward to a turning line (about 15 feet away) and back again. Then they transfer their cherries to the toothpicks of the second players. (They may not use their hands in the transfer—only the toothpick.) The second players repeat the action, and the relay continues until one team, the winner, completes the round.

VARIATION: *Cherry Pass* is even more difficult to perform. Players grip the toothpicks tightly with their front teeth and, as in *Toothpick Pass,* the cherry must be transferred directly—the use of hands is not allowed. When a cherry drops to the floor, however, a player may pick it up by hand, but then only to put it once more on his own toothpick. When the game is played by 11- and 12-year-olds—or by teen-agers and adults—even this concession can be dispensed

with. A player who drops a cherry may not continue the action until he has speared the fruit and lifted it off the floor without using his hands and with his toothpick still gripped by his teeth.

Pass-the-Orange Relay

● *Two oranges*

Players divide into two teams and sit side by side on the floor facing the opposite team. The first player in each line has an orange. At the signal, he places the orange on top of his feet, which are close together and extended straight forward. Then, using only his feet, he transfers the orange to the top of the next player's feet. The orange is thus passed down the line and back again. If the orange drops to the floor, the last player to have possession of it must pick it up with his feet before continuing the action. The first team to finish wins the race.

Forehead Fruit Relay

● *Eight to twelve*   ● *Two oranges*

Players divide into two teams, and the teams divide into pairs. Both teams line up behind a starting line. The first two players on each team face each other and place an orange between their foreheads. Holding it firmly forehead to forehead and without using their hands, they run to a turning line and back. If they drop the orange en route they stop and replace it between their foreheads before continuing the race. When they return to the starting line they may use their hands to set the orange between the foreheads of the next two in line. The race continues in this manner until one team completes the relay and wins the game.

Head Balance Relay

● *Seven to twelve*   ● *Paper cups*

Players divide into equal teams and line up behind a starting line. The first player on each team has a paper cup which he places on top of his head. On signal, he walks or runs to the turning line while balancing the cup on his head. If the cup falls the runner replaces it before continuing the race. The winning team is the first one finished. Books, apples, beanbags, etc., may be substituted for the cups.

Knife and Peanut Race

- *Seven to twelve* - *Peanuts; table knives*

Players form in two teams behind the starting line. Each player holds a dull table knife. The lead players place a peanut on the blades of their knives. On signal, they walk or run to the turning line and back, balancing the peanut. On returning to the starting line, they transfer the peanut to the knife of the next player without using their hands. The team that completes the action first wins the relay.

Cracker-Barrel Race

- *Eight to twelve* - *Two chairs; soda crackers*

Players divide into two relay teams and line up behind a starting line. About 15 feet away, in front of each team, is a chair. The game leader stands between the chairs. On signal, the lead players run to the chairs, sit down, and are given two salted soda crackers each. They race to eat the crackers and then whistle audibly. Having whistled, they run back to their lines and touch off the next players. The first team to complete the action wins.

Coat and Hat Relay

- *Five to seven* - *Two coats and two hats*

Players divide into two relay teams, and each team is given one coat and one hat. At the starting signal, the first player on each team puts on the hat and the coat, which he must button completely. Then he takes off the coat and hat and passes them to the next player in his line. The first team to have each player in the line dressed and undressed wins.

Raisin Relay

- *Eight to twelve*
- *Two bowls; raisins; toothpicks*

Boys and girls form into two relay teams. Every player has a toothpick. The first player in each line has a small bowl of raisins. On signal he turns and, with his toothpick, spears three raisins, which he feeds to the next player. Then the second player takes the bowl, turns, and feeds the next player three raisins in the same way. Finally, the last player must bring the bowl to the head of the line and feed the first player three raisins. The first team to complete the action wins the race.

Button-Sewing Relay

- *Nine to twelve* - *Buttons; needles; thread*

Boys and girls divide into two teams and sit on the floor in two lines. Each player has a button, and the first player in each line has a needle and a large piece of cloth. On signal, the first player threads the needle and sews his button securely onto the piece of cloth. When he is finished, he knots the thread and passes the needle and the cloth to the next player in line. This action is repeated until all the players on the team have sewn their buttons to the cloth. The first team to finish is the winner. The game leader decides when a button has been securely sewn.

Broom, Potato, Plate Relay

- *Eight to twelve*
- *Two whisk brooms; two potatoes; two paper plates; two chairs; string*

Players divide into teams behind a starting line. A turning line, about 15 feet away, is marked by two chairs, one for each team. The first player on each team has a potato, a small whisk broom with a string attached, and an unbreakable plate. On signal each lead player places the plate on top of his head, puts the potato between his knees, and winds the string of the whisk broom

*Tough luck comes near the finish line for this disappointed racer who drops
the potato from between his knees during a* Broom, Potato, Plate Relay.

around his finger. Then, twirling the broom, each makes his way to the turning line, around the chair, and back to the starting line to touch off the next player. If any object drops, the player must pick it up and replace it before moving on. The first team to complete the action wins the relay.

Ring-on-the-String Relay

- *Two rings; two lengths of string*

Before the game begins, two rings are threaded on two long pieces of string, one ring to each length. The ends of each string are then knotted, resulting in two large loops. The players are now divided into two teams with each team forming a circle. The players are permitted to stand or sit. A loop of string, which the players hold in their hands, is given to each group. One player on each team holds the ring. On signal, the rings are sent around the circle of string, passing from one player to another. The greater the speed in forwarding the ring the better, as the first team that manages to successfully pass the ring around the circle three times becomes the winner. A metal washer or a spool of thread may be used as a substitute for a ring.

VARIATION: In *Doughnut on the String,* the game is basically the same as above, with one exception—instead of a ring being threaded on the string, a doughnut is used. When the signal to begin is given, the doughnut is passed around the circle. Great care should be taken, particularly if the doughnut is very fresh, as it may crumble and break apart before completing the circuit three times. The team whose doughnut unfortunately happens to fall apart loses the game. Each of the members of the winning team may be given a doughnut as a prize.

Hit the Penny

- *A penny; a rubber ball*

Two players stand facing each other on parallel lines six to eight feet apart. A penny is placed on the floor midway between the two lines. The players bounce a rubber ball back and forth to each other, and try to hit the penny. Each time a player does he scores one point. The first player to score five points wins that round of the game. Other rounds may follow.

VARIATION: In *Target Cards,* a deck of cards is spread out on the floor between the two players, each card face up and each placed apart from others so that no two cards touch or overlap. The first player announces the suit he wants, say spades. He then throws the rubber ball, trying to hit the lowest card, the ace of spades. If he does so, he next tries to bounce the ball on the two of spades, then the three, and so on until the king of spades is reached. If he fails to hit the card next in sequence, the ball is given to the other player. The opponent, in turn, announces his suit of cards, say diamonds, and proceeds in a like manner. The game may be played with the king becoming the first target and on down to the ace. The first player to hit, in the prescribed order, every card of his selected suit wins the game.

Bottle-Top Toss

- *Seven to twelve*   • *Five bottle tops*

A target of five interlocking circles, each about ten inches in diameter, is drawn on the floor. The circles are numbered as shown in the diagram. (If it is not convenient to draw on the floor, the circles may be drawn on a large sheet of poster paper and laid flat on the floor.) The players stand on a line about 12 feet away and, taking turns, each tosses the five bottle tops, one at a time, toward the target. A player gets the appropriate number of points for each top that lands in an area. If the top lands on the line between two areas, the player gets the higher score. The player with the most points wins.

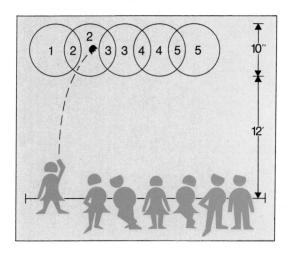

VARIATION: In *Mystery Toss,* the same equipment is used as described above. However, the numbers which are lettered within each circle are covered over with pieces of tape so that the player tossing the bottle tops has no idea of the value of the circle he may be aiming for. All he can do is hope for the best. The leader has a master chart showing the values of each circle. He keeps score, and when each player has had his turn, the scores are added up. The highest score wins.

Double-Bounce Contest

- *Seven to twelve*   • *Wastebasket; rubber ball*

A wastepaper basket is placed against a wall and a line is marked on the floor about ten feet away. From behind this line, the first player throws a rubber ball so that it bounces once on the floor and then lands in the basket. One point is given for each basket. Each player is given five tries. The highest score wins.

Washday Race

- *Clothesline; two shirts, two pairs of socks, two pairs of shorts; eight clothespins*

Players divide into relay teams and stand behind a starting line. A clothesline is stretched across a turning line about 15 feet away. The first player on each team is given a shirt, a pair of shorts, two socks, and four clothespins. On signal, he runs and hangs each of these articles on the clothesline. Then he races back and touches off the second player who runs up to the clothesline, takes down the clothing, and brings them back to his team. The action is repeated, and the team that finishes first wins.

Fanning Football

- *Seven to twelve*
- *Shirt cardboards; a Ping-Pong ball*

Goal lines are marked near opposite ends of a room, and two teams of children stand in strategic positions between the goal markers. No player may move more than three feet from his assigned place. Each boy or girl has a shirt cardboard (the fan), and a Ping-Pong ball (the football) is thrown into the center zone. Using their cardboards as fans, players try to move the ball, from teammate to teammate, toward the opposing goal. The ball may only be fanned, not hit, and when it is sent over a goal, the scoring team gets six points for its touchdown. Should a player hit the ball by mistake, his team is penalized one point. A touchdown scored by

a hit does not count. After ten minutes of play, the team with the higher score wins.

Funnel Ball

- *Seven to twelve*
- *Rubber ball; funnel*

Children line up behind a line drawn ten feet away from the wall. The first child has a small rubber ball and a kitchen funnel. He throws the ball so that it bounces once, hits the wall, and bounces again. The object is to catch the ball on the rebound with the funnel—without stepping over the line. Each player has five tries, and the child with the most catches wins.

Tin-Can Stilt Race

- *Tin cans; lengths of rope*

Stilts are made by punching holes in large tin cans on their sides, near the tops. A length of heavy cord is run through these holes and tied at the end inside the can. Players step onto the stilts and grip the cord firmly. The first two players stand behind a starting line. On signal, the players walk up to the turning line, which is about 15 feet away, and back. If they fall off their stilts they must get back up before continuing the race. This contest may be performed as an individual race or as a team relay.

Medley Relay

- *Seven to twelve*
- *Two beanbags; two jump ropes; two rubber balls*

Players divide into two teams and stand behind a starting line. At a turning line, about 15 feet away, are three items for each team: a jump rope, a beanbag, and a rubber playground ball. On signal, the first player runs up to the turning line. He takes the jump rope and jumps ten times with it, then tosses the beanbag in the air and catches it ten times, and finally bounces the playground ball on the floor ten times. The player runs back to his team to touch off the next player, who repeats the sequence. The first team to complete the actions wins.

The Quiet Olympics

Occasions often arise when a group of children must be entertained inside a house or in a backyard where noise must be kept to a minimum. The answer to such a situation may well be the *Quiet Olympics,* a group of novelty contests very loosely based upon track and field events.

Discus Throw

Players are given paper plates and line up at one end of the room; a small square is marked off at the other end. The leader demonstrates how to throw a discus, with the hand flat and the wrist turned out. Each player is given three tries to throw his plate in the square. The contestant who comes closest to a bull's-eye wins.

Javelin Throw

A small circle is drawn on the floor. One player stands in the circle, turns around two or three times, and hurls a toothpick toward a line about ten feet away. Each player has three throws, and his longest throw is marked. The player who throws the farthest is the winner.

Shot-Put

A large paper shopping bag or balloon is blown up and tied tightly at the end. Each player stands on a line and throws this improvised shot for distance. No matter how hard it is thrown, it will never go more than a few yards. The winning shot is determined by using a tape measure to the nearest quarter-inch.

Reverse Discus Throw

A player stands with a mirror in his hand, with his back to a large hoop that has been hung from a ceiling light fixture or beam. Using the mirror to take aim, the player throws a Ping-Pong ball or beanbag back over his shoulder toward the hoop. Each player has five tries, and for every ball or bag that goes through the hoop he gets a point. The winner is the player with the most points.

Running Broad Jump

The players line up, and each one smiles as broadly as he can. The leader measures the width of each smile with a ruler or tape measure. The boy or girl with the broadest grin is the winner of the event.

Mile Walk

Players line up at one end of the room. On signal they race across the room and back by placing the heel of one foot against the toe of the other at every step. The first player to complete two lengths of the room wins.

Mile Run

The game leader gives each child a pencil and a piece of paper with a column of figures on it. The first boy or girl to add up correctly the figures, which come to 5,280—the number of feet in a mile—wins.

High Jump

Each contestant takes a deep breath and whistles. The contestant who holds one note for the longest time is the high-jump champion.

Forty-Four-Yard Dash

Each player is given a threaded needle—a large blunt-pointed one of the sort used in elementary school sewing projects. Players also have a patch about three or four inches wide, and a large piece of cloth. On signal, the players begin to sew the patch to the cloth. The first player to finish the job of sewing by using exactly 44 stitches—no more, no less—wins the contest and becomes the sew-and-sew champion.

High Dive

Each player is given ten corks and a glass filled with water. He puts the glass on the floor, and with an arm outstretched and kept shoulder high he tries to drop the corks one at a time into the glass. The boy or girl who manages to get the greatest number of corks into the glass of water becomes the winner of the high-dive contest. (If young children find this contest too difficult, the game leader may substitute a large bowl for the glass.)

Four-Man Relay

Players divide into teams of four players each. Each team has four small paper cups and a large bottle of soda. On signal, the first player on each team opens his bottle, fills his cup, and drinks the soda. The cup must be completely empty, so that when it is tipped upside down no liquid spills out. The bottle is passed to the next player and the process repeated. The first team to finish the bottle of soda wins.

Fifty-Yard Medley

Each player has a straw, a spoon, and a large bowl filled with water. During the first ten seconds, counted off by the leader, the players use their straws to drink the water. During the second ten seconds, only spoons are used. Then, on signal, the players drink the water directly from the bowls. The first one to finish the water wins the *Fifty-Yard Medley*. (If this contest is played indoors, the floor should be covered with plastic or oilcloth.)

"Water-logged" is the word for these 50-Yard Medley racers. Step one had them drinking through straws; two calls for spooning and three for bottoms-up.

Contests of Skill and Dexterity

Over the centuries, children have enjoyed competing with one another in games that require considerable manual dexterity. Among the oldest forms of these contests are games played with jacks. Contests with Yo-Yos, however, are of much more recent vintage. By now, more than four decades have passed since Yo-Yos first appeared, and their continuing popularity indicates that Yo-Yo contests will remain a favorite childhood activity for years to come.

Numerals indicate the number of players. Spelled-out numbers suggest suitable age levels.

Jacks

● *2 to 8* ● *Six to twelve*

Jacks is a centuries-old pastime but still very popular. Originally played with small stones, multipronged metal jacks are now used with plastic jacks also available. Six jacks, a small rubber ball and a level surface are needed to play. While performing the many variations of the game a player must not touch any jacks except those specified. If a player does not perform a stunt correctly, he forfeits his turn and when his turn comes around again, he begins with the stunt he previously could not do. Only when he is successful does he tackle, in order, the harder tricks. In *Jacks,* the player to complete all the stunts wins.

The basic *Jacks* contest is called the *Baby Game.* The first player starts his turn by scattering the jacks on the playing surface with a single movement of his right (or left) hand. Using the same hand throughout, the player tosses the ball in the air, picks up one or more jacks and catches the ball, allowing it to bounce once. This is done in the following order. "Ones": When the ball is tossed, the youngster picks up one jack as specified above. The jack is transferred to the other hand, and the action is repeated until all the jacks have been picked up, one by one. "Twos": Now the jacks are picked up two at a time. "Threes": The jacks are picked up by threes. "Fours": The player picks up four jacks and then two, or two jacks and then four. "Fives": The player picks up five jacks and then one, or vice versa. "Sixes": All jacks are picked up at once.

VARIATIONS: In *Downs and Ups,* a player holds all six jacks and the ball in his playing hand. He tosses the ball up, scatters the jacks, and catches the ball before it bounces. Then the action is reversed. With the jacks already scattered, the ball is tossed, the jacks picked up and the ball caught before it bounces.

In *Eggs in Basket,* the player scatters the jacks. Using only one hand, he tosses the ball and picks up one jack. He transfers the jack to his other hand—the basket—and catches the ball on one bounce. In this manner he picks up all the jacks, one by one; by twos, threes, and so on, as in the *Baby Game.*

In *Crack the Eggs* a player scatters the jacks, then using one hand, he tosses the ball up, picks up one jack, taps it on the floor (to "crack the egg") and catches the ball on one bounce. The action is repeated by ones, twos, threes, etc.

In *Sweeps* the jacks are scattered, the player tosses the ball, sweeps the jacks, one at a time to his side before picking them up. The ball can bounce once before the action is completed. The game goes on by twos, threes, etc.

In *Pigs in the Pen,* the player forms an open-ended "pen" with the thumb and forefinger of his non-throwing hand. He places the pen on the floor, and, between tossing the ball and catching it on one bounce, sweeps the jacks, one by one, into the pen. The player repeats this action for all the ones, then twos, and so on. *Pigs Over the Fence* is played in the same way, except that the non-throwing hand—the fence—is placed on edge on the playing surface. Between the toss and the catch, the jacks are put over the fence.

Yo-Yo Contests

- *1 to 20* • *Seven to twelve*

Despite differences in size and color, Yo-Yos are all pretty much the same, being two round pieces of wood or plastic, joined together by a short axle to which one end of a two- or three-foot string is attached. If the string end is embedded in the axle, the Yo-Yo is of the standard type, which allows for only one kind of action. The loose end of the string is looped around a player's forefinger and, when the Yo-Yo is thrown sharply down or forward, it unwinds along the length of the string and then immediately winds itself up again, returning to the player's hand. If, however, the string is loosely looped around the axle, it is a stunt Yo-Yo, permitting numerous variations on the basic action. It is the stunt Yo-Yo that is needed to perform the tricks described here, all of which require considerable practice to master. Once youngsters become proficient in these tricks, they can compete among themselves to see who can keep them going the longest.

Once flicked down, the Yo-Yo spins, or Sleeps, at the end of its string. When spinning slows, player will raise Yo-Yo on the string.

The *Sleeper Contest* employs the easiest Yo-Yo stunt. With a flick of the wrist, the Yo-Yo is thrown downward. When it reaches the end of its string, it begins to spin—"sleep"—as the string remains fully extended. When the spinning motion slows down, the player jerks his wrist up slightly, and the Yo-Yo climbs up its string into the youngster's hand. Players compete to see who can keep a Yo-Yo sleeping for the longest time.

In the *Forward Pass,* a player's arm rests loosely by his side, the palm of his hand facing in. His arm is then brought up sharply in a forward motion and the Yo-Yo is released, sending it out to the end of its string. As it returns the

In Forward Pass, *the girl's palm is down as she throws the Yo-Yo out from her body. She'll turn her palm up to receive returning Yo-Yo.*

hand is turned palm up to receive it. The player who "throws" the most forward passes without stopping wins the contest.

To perform Over the Falls, *the girl first throws a* Forward Pass, *then lets the Yo-Yo drop straight down into a* Sleeper *stunt.*

Over the Falls combines the *Sleeper* and *Forward Pass* stunts. It begins like the *Forward Pass,* but when the Yo-Yo returns, the player, instead of catching it, turns his hand and lets it fall straight down, where it sleeps. When the sleeping motion begins to flag, the player brings the Yo-Yo up and repeats the action. In a contest, the youngster who performs this double trick the greatest number of times wins.

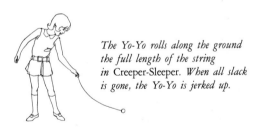

The Yo-Yo rolls along the ground the full length of the string in Creeper-Sleeper. *When all slack is gone, the Yo-Yo is jerked up.*

In the *Creeper-Sleeper,* a youngster throws a fast *Sleeper.* When the Yo-Yo is fully extended on its string, the player lowers his hand close to the ground to allow the Yo-Yo to travel forward, moving out the full length of the string. The player then jerks the string sharply upward, the Yo-Yo returns to his hand and the youngster repeats the action. The player who can keep this up the longest wins the contest.

CHAPTER 3

Teaching and Learning Games

Many games serve a dual purpose: Besides being fun, they are very helpful to children with their schoolwork. In this chapter you will find numerous activities that help sharpen a child's skills in English, addition, subtraction, social studies, geography and science. A selection of spelling and vocabulary-building games begins the chapter.

Numerals indicate the number of players. Spelled-out numbers suggest suitable age levels.

Word Pyramid

● *2 to 4*   ● *Six to eight*

Boys and girls copy the pyramid design onto a sheet of paper. On signal each child must fill in the spaces horizontally with words that fit the number of boxes—a two-letter word for the first row, a three-letter word for the next row, and so on. The first child to complete the game

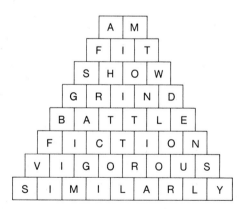

wins. To make the game a vocabulary-building project, the winner may be asked to give the meaning of each word in the pyramid.

Word Hunt

● *2 to 30*   ● *Six to eight*

Players are given a fairly long word—such as *lieutenant*—which they print at the top of a sheet of paper; the word should contain at least two or three vowels. On signal each player writes down as many three-letter words as he can think of, using only letters which are found in the key word. Because young children have a limited vocabulary, it may be best to allow proper names, plurals or verb forms ending in "s," slang terms, or other odd words they may know. The winner is the child who writes down the most three-letter words in five minutes.

VARIATION: In *Advanced Word Hunt,* a game for eight- to twelve-year-olds, boys and girls are each given a sheet of paper with a long word written on it. On signal each child writes down as many words (each must have at least five letters) as he can form, using only the letters found in the key word. No letter can be repeated more times in any word than it appears in the key word. The game continues for five minutes, after which the child with the most words wins. Proper names, plurals, or verb forms ending in "s" are not acceptable.

Spelling Bee

- *10 to 20* - *Seven to twelve*

Children form two equal teams and sit or stand in lines facing each other. The leader reads a spelling word, and the first player on Team 1 tries to spell the word. If he is successful, his team gets a point and the first player on the other team gets a new word to spell. However, if the lead player on Team 1 cannot spell the word, the first player on Team 2 has a chance to spell it and get a point for his team. The leader then goes on to the second child in line, and so on. After a child has had a chance at spelling, he goes to the end of the line, and the other players move up one position. When all the children on each team have had their chance, the team having more points is declared the winner. Words should be drawn from an appropriate spelling list for the age level of the players.

Card Spelling Bee

- *10 to 30* - *Eight to ten*

Boys and girls divide into two or more equal teams, and line up behind a starting line. On a table about ten feet away are piles of cards, one card pile for each team. There are 26 cards in each pile and on each card is printed a large-sized letter of the alphabet. The cards in each pile are well shuffled. The leader calls out a word consisting of four or five letters, such as *horse, rain,* or *peach.* The lead child in each line now runs up and searches in his pile of cards for the first letter of the announced word. When he finds it, he races back to his team and stands facing his teammates, holding his card across his chest. The next child runs up and tries to find the next letter of the word, and so on. The first team to spell the word correctly wins one point. The cards are then replaced in the various piles and reshuffled. The children who have spelled the word go to the foot of their lines. The leader calls out another word and new children run up to find the letters. The first team

to get a set number of points, perhaps five or six, wins the game. The game leader or teacher should be careful not to choose words containing double letters, such as *rabbit,* or *apple,* as each pile of cards contains only one copy of each letter of the alphabet with no duplications.

Word-Making Race

- *10 to 30* - *Seven to ten*

Children divide into two or more teams. Each player has a card with a letter on it. All teams have the same letters. Using these letters, the players make up words (at least three letters long), and one player on each team lists these words on a piece of paper. After five minutes, the team with the greatest number of correctly spelled words wins the contest.

Synonyms

- *2 to 30* - *Eight to twelve*

The game leader reads a list of words which the boys and girls copy onto a piece of paper. On signal the players write a synonym next to each word. Any word that is reasonably similar in meaning to the original word may be accepted as a synonym. For instance, synonyms for the word, *tow,* could include *pull, yank, tug, draw, haul, drag, slide.* At the end of the game, players count the letters in their synonyms, and add up the total number of letters. The child with the highest total of letters, not words, wins the game. **VARIATIONS:** In *Word Synonyms,* a game for eleven- and twelve-year-olds, each player tries to think up as many synonyms for each word on the list as he can. The player with the largest number of acceptable synonyms wins the game. *Team Synonyms* is played in much the same way, except that boys and girls divide into equal teams, each team having the same list of words. Team members privately consult with each other for five minutes and then hand their team list of synonyms to the game leader for judging. The team with the highest total of acceptable synonyms wins.

Categories

● *2 to 30* ● *Eleven to twelve*

Players are given pencil and paper. Each draws a chart that has five or six rows of boxes across and up-and-down the paper. Categories are then selected by the players or presented by the leader; examples might include names of trees, flowers, cities, states, countries, colors, automobiles, sports stars, etc. One category is written at the top of each vertical row. A five- or six-letter word is printed vertically, in the left hand column. On signal each player tries to print a word

	CARS	TREES	CITIES	FOODS	STATES
H					
O					
U					
S					
E					
S					

in each box. Horizontally, the words must begin with the same letter as the word on the left; vertically they must fit the proper categories above. After five minutes, each player calls out the words he has written under each category heading. Any correct entry which no one else has written is worth two points. Duplicate entries are worth one point. The player with the highest total score wins the game.

VARIATIONS: In *Team Categories,* players form into two teams and the members of each consult among themselves on the words to be written in the boxes. After five minutes the two charts are compared and the team with the higher point total wins. In *Exchange Categories,* players sit in a circle, and each makes up a table, using a key word and categories of his own choosing. Contestants then pass their puzzles to the neighbor on the right. The first player to fill in completely his assigned category puzzle wins the contest.

Blackboard Obstacle Relay

● *8 to 20* ● *Seven to twelve*

Children divide into two equal teams and stand behind a line about 15 feet from a blackboard. The game leader calls out a word for spelling and the first child in each line hops up to the blackboard, writes the word, and hops back to the end of the line. The first child to complete the action wins a point for his team, provided he has spelled the word correctly. After each child has had a turn, the team with the most points wins the race. The leader may vary the action, by having the children travel to and from the blackboard by skipping, jumping, turning in circles, walking backward, or even crawling on all fours.

Begin-and-End Race

● *2 to 30* ● *Eight to twelve*

Two children, chalk in hand, stand at a blackboard (or pads in hand, sit on chairs). On signal they write all the words they can think of that begin and end with the letters called out by the game leader. The letters, for example, might be "t" for the beginning and "l" for the end. In this case, among the words that most players would write would be "tell," "tall," "tail," and "till." The player who writes the most words (correctly spelled) after three minutes of play wins. The game can be played as a contest for two children or as a competition among teams. If it is played by teams, the winner of each round scores a point. After all the boys and girls have had a chance, the team (or individual) with the most points wins.

Boat Race

● *Eight to eleven*

Each child cuts out a simple boat model from cardboard. The game leader writes a number of beginning consonant blends—such as "ch," "st," "bl," "sc," and "gr"—horizontally across the top of a blackboard or a large sheet of paper taped to a wall. Two children go to the board and

BL	CH	ST	SC
BLUE BLOW	CHILD CHIN	STOP	

tape their boats beneath the first consonant blend. On signal, they start writing words beginning with the blends; each time a correct word is written the boy or girl moves his boat on to the next blend. The first child to write a word for each blend becomes the winner of the contest.

Matching Words

● *2 to 10* ● *Eight to twelve*

Two children stand at the blackboard. The leader reads out a familiar word. The first child to write a word on the board that is generally paired with that word wins a point. There are dozens of sets of matching words which may be used, such as: "salt and pepper," "bacon and eggs," "bread and butter," and "night and day." This may be played as a contest between individuals or teams.

Sentence Relay

● *10 to 20* ● *Eight to twelve*

Boys and girls divide into two teams and line up behind a starting line about five feet away from a blackboard. On signal the first player on each team runs up and writes a word on the blackboard to begin a sentence. The next player in line runs up and writes a second word. The action continues until all the players have contributed one word to the sentence. The last player on each team reads over what has been written and makes any necessary corrections. The first team to complete a sentence—which must be at least five words long—is the winner.

Making Sentences

● *2 to 30* ● *Nine to twelve*

The game leader writes a list of 15 familiar words (including articles, nouns, and verbs) on a blackboard. Using only these words, the players try to think of as many sentences as they can and write them on a piece of paper. After five minutes, the player with the greatest number of complete sentences is the winner. To permit flexibility, children should be allowed to use other forms of the verbs on the board.

Building Words

● *2 to 30* ● *Nine to twelve*

The leader or teacher writes several three-letter words on the blackboard. Players copy these words onto paper, one word to a line. On signal each tries to build other words out of these base words by adding single letters, prefixes, or suffixes. Some examples are: *Ran*—Bran, Grant, Rant, Cranberry, Rancid; *Bar*—Barb, Barber, Bargain, Barley. After five minutes, time is called, and the player with the most words wins the contest. This game may also be played in teams, using only one base word for each team and having each player in turn run up to the board to write a new word from the base word.

Games with Shapes and Numbers

As children learn to distinguish between shapes and to count, simple games may be used to help them increase their powers of observation and to understand the processes of arithmetic. Later, when their skills become more acute, the games themselves can become more complicated and challenging.

Numerals indicate the number of players. Spelled-out numbers suggest suitable age levels.

Jigsaw Shapes

● *2 to 30*   ● *Four to six*

The game leader makes up a set of cardboard squares, rectangles, triangles, etc., and cuts them into two or three pieces each. Each shape should be a different color, so that children know which

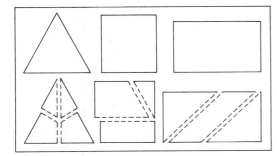

pieces should fit together. On signal the players try to fit the pieces together into the original shape. Boys and girls may also be directed to make up their own set of "jigsaw" shapes, and then have other children try to put them back together again.

How Big?

● *2 to 30*   ● *Five to seven*

This game helps improve the child's sense of shape and relative size, and sharpens his awareness of the environment. Players are each given a pencil and paper and asked to draw the following things:
A circle the size of a quarter.
A line the length of a new pencil.
A rectangle the size of a playing card.
A rectangle the size of a regular book of matches.

A rectangle the size of a postage stamp.
A line the length of a fork.
If the object in question is something that sometimes appears in different sizes, such as a postage stamp, an example may be shown to the children just for a moment. Boys and girls are given four minutes to draw the objects as they visualize them. Then each child shows his drawings, and they are measured and compared for accuracy with the actual size of the objects listed. The child with the greatest number of fairly accurate pictures is the winner.

Magic Square

● *2 to 30*   ● *Eight to twelve*

Children draw a large square, three to six inches wide, and then divide this into nine smaller squares. Each player fills in the small squares with the numbers 1, 2, 3, 4, 5, 6, 7, 8, and 9, with one number in each square. The trick

8	3	4
1	5	9
6	7	2

is to place the numbers so that the total of each column or row of numbers (vertical, horizontal, and diagonal) is 15. After a while, if none of the players is able to figure out the placement, the leader may give the clue that the number in the center is 5 and that each set of outside numbers at the end of each vertical, horizontal, and diagonal row adds up to ten. Using these clues, the children will soon find the answer.

Magic Circles

● *2 to 30* ● *Nine to twelve*

Children draw nine small circles on a piece of paper, three circles to a row. They then must write the nine even numbers from 2 to 18 (2, 4, 6, 8, 10, 12, 14, 16, and 18) in the circles.

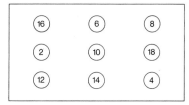

The numbers must be placed in such a way that any three circles in a line will add up to a total of 30. The secret that makes this puzzler easy to crack is that the figure 10 must be placed in the center circle. Once the children have figured this out, placing the other numbers correctly will be easy. However, if the young players do not come up with the correct solution after some time has passed, they may be given the number 10 clue and allowed to proceed in filling in the other numbers in the surrounding circles to complete the puzzle.

Target Arithmetic

● *2 to 10* ● *Six to twelve*

The game leader draws a large target of four or five concentric circles on the blackboard. An arithmetic problem is written in each circle, with the simplest problem in the center and the more difficult problems in the outer circles. Players stand behind a line, eight to ten feet away from the blackboard, and take turns throwing a ball of clay at the target. The thrower must then solve the problem written in the circle in which the ball of clay has landed. He gets one point for answering the problem correctly. Once the problem is solved, the leader erases it and writes another problem of similar difficulty in that circle. After each player has had several turns, the player with the most points is the winner.

Stop the Tiger

● *2 to 10* ● *Six to twelve*

On a blackboard, the game leader draws a lamb tied to a post with five ropes, an angry tiger creeping up to attack the lamb, and five fences which the tiger must cross to get to the lamb.

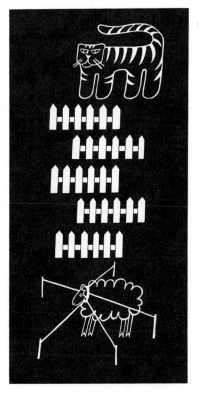

Children divide into two teams, the lambs and the tigers. In turn, players from each team answer arithmetic problems put to them by the leader. When a "lamb" answers a problem correctly, he may erase one of the ropes tying the lamb to the post. When a "tiger" answers correctly, he may erase one of the fences between the tiger and the lamb. The purpose of the game is twofold: the lamb tries to get rid of the ropes and escape; the tiger tries to jump the fences and capture the lamb. Whichever team accomplishes its goal first wins the game. This game may also be played using spelling, geography, reading, or science problems.

Blackboard Football

● *2 to 10*   ● *Nine to twelve*

Players divide into two teams and each takes the name of a football team. On the board the game leader draws a replica of a football field with ten-yard dividers and a ball on the fifty-yard

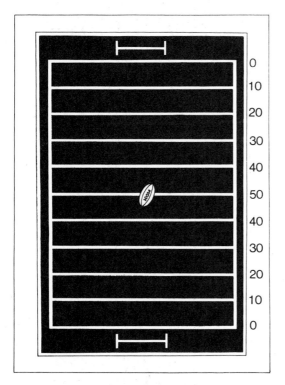

line. The leader also writes questions on slips of paper for the players to answer. The questions are put into three piles: simple problems—worth ten yards; moderate problems—worth twenty yards; and difficult problems—worth thirty yards. To put the ball into play, the first player on one team asks for a question from one of the piles. A team is allowed three turns (downs) to score a touchdown—worth six points. If they score a touchdown, the other team takes the ball on the fifty-yard line. If they give a wrong answer, or use up three downs without scoring, the other team takes over the ball. The team with the higher score after ten minutes of play wins the game. *Blackboard Football* can also be

played by only two players. Each represents a team, and each takes three questions per turn. Otherwise, the same rules apply as in the team form of the game.

Arithmetic Tictactoe

● *2 to 6*   ● *Six to twelve*

The game leader draws a tictactoe diagram on the blackboard. Children divide into two teams. One team is the X team, and the other is the O team. In turn, players from each team answer arithmetic problems posed by the leader. When a player answers a question correctly, he writes an X or an O in one of the squares. If he gets the answer wrong, however, he cannot write anything. The first team to get an uninterrupted row horizontally, vertically, or diagonally wins the contest.

Blackboard Number Relay

● *10 to 20*   ● *Eight to ten*

Players divide into two equal teams and stand behind a line about 15 feet from the blackboard. On signal each lead player runs up to the blackboard and writes a two- or three-digit number. Then the second players follow, putting their two- or three-digit numbers below those of the lead players. The action continues in this way until the last players have their turn. Instead of putting down new numbers, the last players add up the lists. The first team to finish adding and have the correct total is the winner.

Guess a Size

● *2 to 20*   ● *Eight to twelve*

The game leader holds up various objects, one by one for a moment each, and asks the players to write down a particular measurement for each item. The leader might ask, for example, the circumference of a tennis ball, the length of a book, the cubic capacity of a box, or the number of pints a pitcher would hold. When all the items have been shown, each child reports on his guesses. The player who comes closest to the correct answer for each object gets a point, and the contestant with the most points wins. Two teams can also compete, with team members conferring on each item before giving an answer. The team that comes closest for each item is awarded one point, and the team with the highest score is declared the winner.

Number Relay

● *8 to 20*   ● *Nine to twelve*

Players divide into two equal-sized teams. Members of each team stand in single file at a starting line. Each team faces a turning line about 20 feet away. On the turning line are two shoe boxes, one for each team. Every player has a folded card with a mathematical problem (an algebra equation, numbers to add, long division, etc.). Player No. 1 on Team A has the same problem to solve as player No. 1 on Team B. Player 2 on Team A has the same problem as player 2 on Team B, and so on. A player may not open his card and begin solving his problem until his turn comes up. On signal, the first two players open their cards and each, with a pencil, solves his problem. As soon as a player finishes his assignment, he passes his pencil to the next player in line, who begins to work on his own problem. The player who has solved his problem runs to the shoe box and puts his card inside and then runs to the back of his line. A team gets three points for finishing first and five points for each correct answer. The team with more points wins the relay. This game can also be played as a contest among individuals, each player receiving the same three or four mathematical problems. Scoring is as above.

Mystery Shape

● *6 to 12*   ● *Five to twelve*

This game is played in a room filled with many objects. One player is asked to leave the room. The others sit in a circle on the floor and choose an object that the absent player will try to identify, when he is called back, by asking questions about its size and shape. Any object in the room may be chosen (a vase, rug, record player, letter opener, candle, etc.) except items of clothing. (When the game is played by young children, the objects should be simple and familiar.) When the chosen player returns, he is allowed to ask up to 15 questions about the mystery object's size or shape. Questions such as "Is it round? Is it a geometric shape? Is it larger than two cubic feet? Does it have both straight and curved lines?" are all acceptable. When a player has guessed the object's identity or used up his 15 questions, another contestant and another object are chosen. The game goes on in this manner until all players have had a chance at guessing. Those who guessed correctly may play elimination rounds until only one, the champion guesser, remains.

Draw a Shape

● *2 to 10*   ● *Eight to twelve*

The game leader blindfolds all players and places a piece of paper, a pencil and two cardboard cutout shapes in front of each. These shapes may be of any design, but it is wise to keep them relatively simple. While blindfolded, the players

are given one minute to feel the two cutouts. Then the game leader collects the shapes and takes off the blindfolds. The players try to draw from memory the two shapes they have just felt. After two minutes, the player whose drawings most resemble the cutouts is declared the winner.

Games Based on Geography

Geography can be a very exciting subject for children. The following games not only test what they already have learned about the subject but also provide motivation to learn more about the world around them.

Spelled-out numbers suggest suitable age levels.

Jumbled Cities

● *Eight to twelve*

Players divide into two equal teams and sit in groups on opposite sides of the room. The leader gives each team a sheet of paper on which the names of ten well-known cities in North America and Europe have been written with the letters scrambled. Examples are:

GOACHIC	CHICAGO
WEN ROYK	NEW YORK
NETROLAM	MONTREAL
ONTROTO	TORONTO
DOLNON	LONDON
SIRPA	PARIS

At a signal the teams huddle together and try to figure out the names of the cities. As they unscramble each group of letters, one child on each of the teams writes the correct city on the sheet of paper. The first team to figure out all the cities and then write them on paper wins the game.

Know Your Capitals

● *Nine to twelve*

The game leader makes up a list of various nations with three cities for each nation. One city is the capital city of that nation. He reads the list, and the players (individually or in teams) write down the correct name of that country's capital, taken from one of the three cities given. Examples:

ITALY:	Rome, Florence, Venice.
JAPAN:	Tokyo, Kyoto, Yokahama.
POLAND:	Warsaw, Krakow, Lodz.
INDIA:	Calcutta, New Delhi, Madras.

After 15 or 20 nations and cities have been read out, the correct answers are given. The individual or team with the most correct answers is the winner.

VARIATIONS: For *Guess the Capital* a more advanced knowledge of geography is required. The game is played in the same way except that only the names of countries are read out. The players supply the appropriate capitals from knowledge rather than from a listing of multiple choices. The same method is followed in another variation called *Know The Provinces*. The names of Canadian provinces are read out, say Alberta, Prince Edward Island, Quebec, etc. and the players supply the provincial capitals, Edmonton, Charlottetown, Quebec, etc.

Circle Geography

● *Eight to twelve*

Players sit or stand in a circle. One child begins by naming a geographical location (city, state, province, or country). The next player to the right in the circle names another location which begins with the last letter of the previous location. Example:

First player:	"ALABAMA."
Second player:	"ABERDEEN."
Third player:	"NEW BRUNSWICK."
Fourth player:	"KENYA."

If a player cannot give a correct answer within 30 seconds, he gets one penalty point. The player with the fewest points after five minutes is the winner. It's a good idea to keep a world atlas or some similar type of a reference book handy to verify places and to settle arguments in a game such as this one.

Simple Science Projects

There are many basic scientific and technological principles that children can learn while playing. The following projects—all of which can be done at home with ordinary materials found in or near the house—exhibit the workings of nature. In addition, they are fun—providing surprises, suspense, and amusement.

Spelled-out numbers suggest suitable age levels.

Nature's Earth Mixer

- *Six to twelve*
- *Glass jar; sand; leaf mold; earthworms*

The purpose of this experiment is to show how soil is enriched through natural processes. About two inches of clean white sand is put into a glass jar. The sand is then covered with a three-inch layer of well-rotted leaf mold, and, finally, several earthworms are placed in the jar. The jar is then covered and every day water is sprinkled into it to keep the contents moist. After about two weeks the children will discover that the earthworms have thoroughly mixed the leaf mold in with the sand, enriching the soil with organic matter so that it can nourish plant life.

Soil Conservation

- *Six to twelve* • *Cake tins; dirt; water*

By working with this easily constructed model, children may see for themselves the importance of proper plowing in order to prevent soil erosion during heavy rainfalls. Two large cake tins are filled with mounds of dirt and are then placed side by side on a table. Following the procedure done in actual contour plowing, several grooves are run horizontally around one of the mounds. Then, vertical grooves are scratched into the dirt of the other mound. Everyone is advised to watch closely as water is now sprinkled over both of the mounds. It very quickly becomes apparent to the children that the mound with the horizontal grooves retains more water and loses far less soil through the run-off of water than does the mound with the vertical furrows.

A Homemade Telephone

- *Six to twelve*
- *Two coffee cans; a length of thin wire*

While a coffee-can telephone is great fun to make, it also serves a practical purpose in that it shows that wire conducts sounds. A small hole is punched in the bottom of each can, and one end of a ten-foot length of wire is inserted into each hole. The wire is secured by knots on the inside of the cans. Two children stand at opposite ends of a room, stretching the wire tightly.

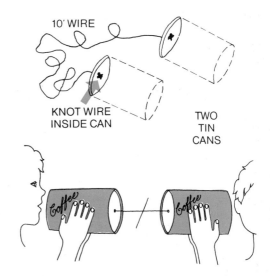

10' WIRE

KNOT WIRE
INSIDE CAN

TWO
TIN
CANS

One talks very softly into one can while the other holds an ear to the other. The children discover that even a whispered remark can be heard in this way, thanks to the taut wire that conducts the sound. The point can be proven by letting the wire go slack; the voice will then not be heard.

Jar That Won't Stay Dry

- *Six to twelve*   - *A glass jar*

To prove that there is always moisture in the air, a jar is filled with ice cubes and tightly covered. After a few minutes, the outside of the jar becomes wet. Even after the jar is dried off with a cloth, it quickly becomes wet again. The secret is that when the bits of moisture in the air touch the outside of the cold glass jar, they "condense" or join together in little drops of water. This is why dew forms on the cool grass in the early morning before the sun warms up the ground and makes the moisture disappear.

Colored Celery

- *Six to twelve*   - *Water coloring; celery*

This experiment demonstrates that plants and trees take in water from the ground. Children place a stalk of celery (with the leaves up) in a large glass of colored water. After a few hours, the stalk and leaves of the celery will be lined with the color. This is because the celery, even though picked, is still alive, and its sap tubes draw the liquid up from the glass.

Hot and Cold

- *Six to twelve*
- *Two mixing bowls; two balloons; a soda bottle*

This experiment demonstrates the effect of heating and cooling on air, illustrating the general principle that heat causes matter to expand, while cold makes it contract. One mixing bowl is filled with ice water and the other with very hot water. A deflated balloon is fitted over the neck of the bottle, and the bottle is placed in the bowl of hot water. Before long, the balloon will begin to inflate just as if it were being blown up. The reason is that as the bottle heats up, the heated air inside expands into the balloon. In contrast, when the bottle with the now-inflated balloon is placed in the cold water, the air inside contracts and the balloon deflates.

A Homemade Xylophone

- *Six to twelve*
- *Identical soda bottles (or water glasses); a spoon*

Eight identical soda bottles are lined up on a table and a different amount of water is poured in each (the most water is put in the bottle on the far right and lesser amounts in each bottle to the left). When the children hit the bottles

with spoons, they discover that each one makes a ringing sound at a different pitch according to the water level in the bottle. By varying the amount of water in the bottles, children will even be able to create a scale of whole notes, and by adding more bottles with different levels of water they will produce sharps and flats as well. In this way, a bottle xylophone can be built and simple tunes can be played on it.

Air to Burn

- *Six to twelve*
- *Three candles; three jars (pint, quart, and gallon)*

This simple demonstration shows that fire consumes oxygen and when the oxygen is gone the fire goes out. Because the experiment does involve fire, an adult should always be on hand. Three candles of the same size are lit, and one jar is placed over each. Boys and girls will discover that the candle in the pint jar goes out in a very short time, the flame in the quart lasts about twice as long, and the flame in the gallon burns approximately eight times as long as the one in the smallest jar.

CHAPTER 4

Games for Creative Play

Here is a variety of games based on music, drama, and art. These activities
offer a different kind of challenge and interest from those described
in earlier chapters. Although these games are primarily for children,
most of the ones suitable for 12-year-olds can be easily adapted for teen-agers
and adults. Drama games form the first grouping in this chapter.

Numerals indicate the number of players. Spelled-out numbers suggest suitable age levels.

A Noun That Rhymes

● *2 to 12* ● *Six to twelve*

A boy or girl says, "I'm thinking of a one-
syllable noun that rhymes with—." For example,
he might say that it rhymed with "row," and
be thinking of the word "snow." One at a time,
the other members of the group try to guess
and act out the correct word. They pick words
that rhyme with "row," such as "toe," "hoe,"
"throw," or "show." Each time a word is acted
out, the leader must guess it, and then say
whether or not it is his secret word. The player
who is successful in guessing and acting out the
secret word now becomes the leader. He thinks
of another word and gives the rhyming clue to
the other players, and the game continues.

Guessing Professions

● *6 to 20* ● *Six to twelve*

Children divide into two or three teams. One
player from each team comes up to the game
leader, who whispers the name of a profession
to them. The representatives run back to their
groups and, without making a sound, try to act

out the professions. (It is best to pick such
professions as "doctor," "baseball player," "automobile driver," or "carpenter," which can
easily be pantomimed, rather than nonvisual
occupations such as "computer programmer" or
"insurance salesman.") The first team to guess
the profession receives one point. The game
continues and new players are given other professions to act out for their teams. After several
minutes of play, the team with the most points
wins the contest.

Guess the Creature

● *6 to 20* ● *Six to twelve*

One player from each team is given the name
of a creature to act out. If it is a bird, they
return to their teams with arms waving as if
they were flying. If it is a beast, they return
crawling on all fours. If it is a fish, they return
with a swimming movement. Then, without
making a sound, each actor pantomimes the
specific creature for his team. He may nod his
head affirmatively or negatively to show the
group whether they are "hot" or "cold" in their
guessing. When the team has guessed the exact
creature—if a child has to act out "gorilla," for

example, it is not enough for the team to guess the word "ape"—the actor runs back to the leader and is awarded one point for his team. The game continues with new players acting out different creatures. After everyone has had a chance to act, the team with more points is declared the winner.

Skeleton Stories

● *6 to 20*   ● *Eight to twelve*

Children divide into two or more teams. Each team makes up, or is given, a one-line plot for which they make up a skit. The plots should be very simple, as in the following examples: "You are suddenly transported to a totally unfamiliar city and you set about trying to find your way home."
"You find a magic charm that gives you any three wishes."
"A little man with a greenish face and pointed ears pops out of some bushes and asks you to take a ride in his space ship."
In acting out these plots, the players are allowed to speak.

Going to California

● *6 to 14*   ● *Eight to twelve*

Players sit in a circle. One child begins by saying, "I'm going to California, and I'm taking a—." Instead of saying the name of the object, he pantomimes its use. It may be a comb, a tennis racquet, an auto, a guitar, or any other familiar article. The next player to his right repeats the phrase, pantomimes the first article shown, and then pantomimes a second object. The action continues, with each player in turn showing all the objects as they have been shown before and then adding a new object and pantomime of his own. Since the objects must be shown in the correct order with the same pantomimes as used before, the game becomes rather difficult after six or eight players have had a turn. The last player to be able to show all the objects correctly is the winner.

Hidden Adverb

● *8 to 20*   ● *Six to twelve*

One child is chosen to leave the room. When he is out of hearing range, the other players select a "hidden" adverb. When the first child comes back into the room, he asks the other players to perform in the manner suggested by the adverb. He might ask one player to show how he would eat pie, in the manner of the adverb. He might ask another to show how he would play baseball, or dance, or read a book, or drive a car—always as suggested by the hidden adverb. After several such pantomimes, he tries to guess the adverb. He is allowed three tries: if he guesses correctly, the last person to pantomime leaves the room; if not, the same child may leave the room again or the group may select another child to guess a new adverb. When playing this game, children should be encouraged to pick familiar adverbs which give a clear picture, such as "slowly," "angrily," or "happily." If the game is being played with young children, the meaning of the word "adverb" must be explained, and examples given.

Prop Plays

● *5 to 20*   ● *Six to twelve*

The leader prepares a large paper bag for each team. Each bag contains a number of props, such as a fork, a flashlight, a ring, a pipe, a tie, a coin, etc. As soon as each team receives its bag of props, it opens the bag and examines the objects inside. Then the members of each team huddle together and prepare a little play or skit making use of all of the props. After each team has finished rehearsing, it performs the skit for the other groups. A prize may be awarded for the most original skit.
VARIATION: In *Treasure Hunt Dramatics,* each team collects ten different objects and prepares a skit using all ten objects meaningfully. Each team acts out their skit for the leader, who may give a prize for the play he considers to be the most original.

A little girl digs down in the bag for an object while her teammates for Prop Plays *examine the items they will use in an improvised skit.*

Other Dramatic Activities

Other dramatic activities involve children making their own puppets and then putting on original playlets, using these same puppets as characters.

Numerals indicate the number of players. Spelled-out numbers suggest suitable age levels.

Peanut-shell Puppets

● *2 to 6* ● *Four to eight* ● *Peanuts; items for decorating*

Children cut peanut shells in half so that they fit over their forefingers. Then, using bits of cloth, toothpicks, or beads, they decorate the outside of the shells to look like pirates, cow-

Easy to make and manipulate, a whole cast of tiny Peanut-shell Puppets fits on the fingers of a puppeteer.

boys, or other characters. Young children will need help in doing this. To put on a play, two or three children may portray different characters, or one child may fit shells on more than one finger of his hand and have a one-man show.

Paper-bag Puppets

● *2 to 6* ● *Four to eight* ● *Rags, items for decorating*

Children cut holes in a brown paper bag to represent the puppet's eyes and mouth. They may paste pieces of colored paper on the bag or paint with poster paint to create the nose,

ears, eyebrows, and hair. The child puts his hand into the paper bag puppet and ties it around his wrist with a rubber band or string. To stage a puppet show, the children kneel behind a table, which has been draped with a sheet, and hold their puppets up over the table top.

Handkerchief Puppets

● *2 to 6* ● *Four to eight* ● *Kerchiefs; thumbtacks*

A knot is tied in the corner of a large colorful scarf or kerchief. The child places his forefinger in the knot, making it the head of his puppet.

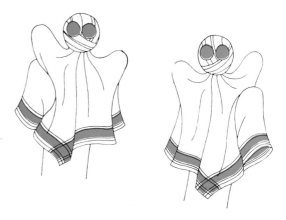

A child's hand directs the movements of this ghostly puppet, quickly made with a kerchief and two thumbtacks.

He then wraps the kerchief around his hand, with part of it fastened around the thumb and part around the middle finger. These two fingers become the arms of the puppet. Two large colored thumbtacks may be placed in the knot, to represent the puppet's eyes. This type of puppet permits a child to use his hand freely.

Potato Puppets

- *2 to 6* • *Four to eight* • *Potatoes; items for decorating*

A hole about two inches deep is cut in one end of each potato so that a finger may be inserted to manipulate the puppet. A face is made on the potato side, using raisins, thumbtacks, and pasted paper. Cotton or wool is fine for hair and beards, and scraps of cloth can be turned into fancy hats. By putting a finger in the hole and draping a handkerchief around the hand, a child now is ready for the show to begin.

Puppet Theaters

Children may simply hide behind a table or chair to put on a puppet play, but for a somewhat more impressive stage a cardboard carton may be used. The top flaps are taped shut to make a roof for the stage, and the front end, facing the audience, is cut away. The bottom six inches of the back of the box are cut away, so that children can put their puppets up through the opening. The "theater" is placed on a table so that the back section extends beyond the table's edge. A sheet or blanket is hung in front of the table to hide the puppeteers in back. The lights in the room may be turned out, and flashlights or a lamp may be used to light up the stage. When planning plays, children may act out stories they have read in books, portray their favorite television characters, or even make up their own characters and stories.

Shadow Theater

Both the front and back of a cardboard carton are completely cut away. A piece of old sheet is fixed tightly across the front of the carton with tacks, tape, staples, or pins. A bright light is placed behind the sheet to create a shadow effect. The "shadow theater" is placed on a table and a blanket is hung in front of the table. Children hold up their puppets from below, moving them around and speaking for them. Puppets with arms should be used for this type of play in order to create interesting shadows.

A world of wondrous laughter exists within this cutaway cardboard box where puppets cavort, directed by their masters hiding behind the table.

How to Make
Ball Puppets

Putting on a puppet show is great fun for children in the primary grades. It is doubly fun when youngsters construct their own puppets and make up a play to act out with these homemade characters. Among the many varieties of puppets that a young child can make, the ball figures shown here are among the easiest to construct and manipulate.

All that is needed for this project is a supply of tennis-size, hollow rubber balls (preferably light-colored), a pair of scissors, some watercolor or poster paints, two paint brushes (one narrow width, one medium width) and a vivid imagination. Even a very young child—with a little help—will be able to turn out an original, funny-faced hand puppet in about half an hour's time. An entire cast of characters can be completed in the space of an afternoon, with only one or two children doing all the labor. Should the children decide to have more characters than there are balls, they may paint a different face on each side of the ball or, during the production, they may use the same face for different characters—changing their voices to indicate each of the roles.

When the puppets are completed, the youngster slips an index finger, representing the character's neck, into the hole at the base of the head and he uses the other fingers to depict the puppet's arms and body. After practicing a while, children invariably discover that they are able to perform a variety of movements with their puppets. Once this has been accomplished it is only a matter of making up a short play, setting up an instant puppet theater and collecting an audience of parents and playmates. Then the performance with the homemade ball puppets is ready to begin.

The audience is seated facing a doorway in a playroom or living room. An old sheet is stretched across the doorway and secured with masking tape. Behind the sheet, which is both stage and curtain, the puppeteer hides.

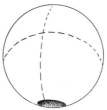

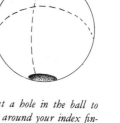

Cut a hole in the ball to fit around your index finger. With a pencil, divide the ball into quarters.

Sketch the face; eyes on the horizontal line, equidistant from the vertical; nose and mouth centered below.

To hold the ball, insert a roll of cardboard. With a pencil, finish the features. Turn the ball around and draw another face—different from the first.

Using a fine-tipped brush for small features and a medium brush for larger areas, color the puppets.

Telling a Story with Puppets

JUNIOR: *Hello, mother. How was your day?*
MOTHER: *Terrible! I'm afraid I'm not feeling well.*

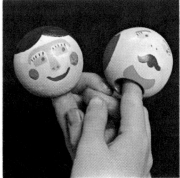

JUNIOR: *Why not lie down until father is home?*
MOTHER: *How can I? I haven't made dinner yet.*

JUNIOR: *Don't worry, mother, I'll make dinner.*
MOTHER: *(lying down) I feel better already.*

JUNIOR: *I'll make peanut butter sandwiches.*
MOTHER: *(sounding sicker) And what's for dessert?*

JUNIOR: *Plain peanut butter!*
MOTHER: *(sounding positively ill) Wonderful. Your father will love it.*

MOTHER: *(brightening a little) There's father now.*
JUNIOR: *I'd better get the dinner on the table.*

MOTHER: *Hello, Horace. How are you?*
FATHER: *Starving! I haven't eaten all day.*

MOTHER: *Junior made dinner. It's only peanut butter.*
FATHER: *(screaming) WHAT?*

MOTHER: *Ssh! He's very proud. Say something nice.*
FATHER: *You know what I feel like— peanut butter!*

Rhythm Activities

There are numerous games which develop rhythm or knowledge of sound. Younger children in particular enjoy rhythm-band activities, clapping games, and interpreting sounds. A selection of such activities is provided in this section.

Rhythm Band

● *4 to 7*   ● *Four to eight*

Using a variety of rhythm instruments, children can experiment with different rhythmic beats and create unusual sound effects. They can play as accompaniment to phonograph records or to a piano, or provide their own accompaniment to group singing and creative dancing. Rhythm instruments may include simple drums which may be played by hand or by softhead or regular drumsticks, rattles, bells, gongs, tone blocks, tambourines, and triangles. Such instruments may be purchased directly from musical supply stores or may be constructed by the children themselves. For example, a piece of inner tube stretched tightly over the top of a large can or wooden bucket or barrel makes a good drum. Heavy plastic or parchment may also be used for drum heads and tied tightly around the drum with cord. It helps to spray the drum head with shellac to make it stiffer and to give it a fuller tone. Rattles can be made by filling tin cans with dried beans or peas or with bottle caps. Wood scrapers can be constructed by covering rectangular pieces of wood with sandpaper. Rhythm sticks can be made by covering hardwood doweling with paint or wood sealer; when struck against each other, these provide a sharp, staccato rhythm. Gongs can be made by punching holes at the tops of metal pie tins or pot lids and suspending the tins by string from a bar.

Clapping Names

● *2 to 8*   ● *Four to six*

Children may practice clapping the rhythm of their names, in order to sharpen rhythmic awareness. For example, one child says, "My name is William Vandenberg. Wil-liam Van-den-berg." As he says it the second time, he claps the rhythm with his hands, or beats it on a drum. Each child in turn then claps or beats the rhythm to his or her own name.

Clapping Songs

● *3 to 12*   ● *Four to twelve*

One child begins by clapping the melodic rhythm of a familiar song or nursery rhyme that the other children would know. He does not say its name, and the others must guess by the beat the song he has in mind. A good example is *Three Blind Mice,* which has such a distinctive beat that other children should be able to recognize it after hearing just the first line. When a child has called out the correct name, he becomes the new clapper and beats out the rhythm of the first line of another nursery rhyme or song. Older children, teen-agers, and adults will also find this an amusing party game. In place of nursery rhymes, they may tap or clap the beat of popular songs, folk songs, or songs from TV commercials.

A Rhythm Band *might have these instruments (left to right):*
scrapers, a small drum, drumsticks, rattles, gongs and their sticks, and a large drum.

Copy the Beat

● *2 to 8* ● *Four to eight*

The leader distributes various rhythm instruments, one to each child. One child acts as the "composer" and beats out a short rhythmic passage of no more than 10 or 15 beats. Each child in turn must then reply by beating out the same message on his rhythm instrument. The composer changes the passage after everyone has answered. When they "get the message," the children return it to him. After the composer has played three or four passages and has been answered, he changes place with another child in the group. If a large drum is used to send the message, this may be moved around from child to child, so that each one has a turn as the composer.

Transportation

● *3 to 6* ● *Four to six*

Each child is given a rhythm instrument. In turn, each child uses his instrument to show the rhythm he feels is most typical of a particular type of transportation. The types of transportation that might be chosen include airplanes, trains, cars, boats, bicycles, and so forth. Children may supplement these sounds with creative movements that visually represent the particular mode of transportation. Thus, through beating out the rhythms and then through interpretive movements, they may show the different tempos and locomotion patterns of traveling on a raft on a river, a wheelbarrow, or a Pogo stick.

Barnyard Sounds

● *6 to 10* ● *Five to eight*

The instruments are placed in a box in the center of the room. In turn, each child goes to the box and selects an instrument (or instruments) that can show the rhythm of movement of a particular barnyard animal. For example, a heavy, deep-voiced drum might be used to show an old cow moving slowly around the barnyard. Rhythm sticks or wood blocks, struck sharply or in a moderate tempo might show how a pony trots around a pasture. Rapidly shaken maracas or tambourines might give the image of barnyard chickens frantically pecking at grain scattered on the ground. A toy trumpet may be employed to represent a rooster crowing at dawn. A prize may be given for the most realistic or original interpretation.

Machine Sounds

● *3 to 6* ● *Five to eight*

The rhythm instruments are placed in a box in the center of the room. Each child, in turn, goes up to the box and selects an instrument that he thinks best captures the sound and rhythm of a particular type of machine. The machines could range from steam shovels to bulldozers, piledrivers, compressed-air drills, lawn mowers, or sewing machines. After each child has had a turn representing a machine of his choice, all children may play their instruments simultaneously—still keeping the rhythm and sound of their particular machines.

Miscellaneous Sound Effects

● *4 to 12* ● *Six to ten*

Players divide into teams of two. The couples sit in a circle around a box of rhythm instruments. In advance, the leader makes up a list of distinctive sounds and writes them on slips of paper, so that every team receives a copy of the same sound each time. After the teams receive their first sound—for example, a thunderstorm— each couple, in turn, goes to the box and chooses rhythm instruments. Then, using the instruments, as well as feet and hands if they wish, the couples take turns "performing" the sound for the group. After every team has interpreted a particular sound, a prize may be given for the most accurate rendition.

Singing Games

Another familiar kind of children's play activity based on music is the ever-popular and ever-beloved singing game. While joining together in singing the words of the songs, the children perform a series of actions which tell a story or illustrate sections of the song. These singing games have been handed down from generation to generation with few or no changes. Although they are most suitable for children of preschool or kindergarten age, they can be carried on with children of almost any age bracket. Group singing may be used as a break during a hike, or as an interlude during an active game session. While children often sing on their own, an adult leader can best get the songs started and encourage participation. Musical accompaniment is desirable but not vital. Several of the best known action songs are presented below.

Numerals indicate the number of players. Spelled-out numbers suggest suitable age levels.

The Mulberry Bush

● *5 to 12*　● *Four to six*

FORMATION: Children form a large circle. No partners are needed.

ACTION: All join hands and walk around the circle to the right, with everyone singing the chorus:

> Here we go round the mulberry bush, the
> 　mulberry bush, the mulberry bush,
> Here we go round the mulberry bush, so
> 　early in the morning.

ACTION: Children then stop and face the center, and sing Verse 1, pantomiming the vigorous scrubbing of clothes. This is followed by the chorus again.

> *Verse 1*
> This is the way we wash our clothes, wash
> 　our clothes, wash our clothes,
> This is the way we wash our clothes, so
> 　early Monday morning.

ACTION: Children perform each of the verses in turn, while going through with the appropriate pantomime. Each verse is followed by the chorus and its action.

> *Verse 2*
> This is the way we mend our clothes . . .
> 　so early Tuesday morning.
> *Verse 3*
> This is the way we iron our clothes . . .
> 　so early Wednesday morning.
> *Verse 4*
> This is the way we sweep the floor . . .
> 　so early Thursday morning.
> *Verse 5*
> This is the way we scrub the floor . . .
> 　so early Friday morning.
> *Verse 6*
> This is the way we bake the bread . . .
> 　so early Saturday morning.
> *Verse 7*
> This is the way we go to church . . .
> 　so early Sunday morning.

Two Little Blackbirds

● *8 to 16* ● *Four to six*

FORMATION: Children form two concentric circles. The boys are on the inside, each facing a girl on the outside circle.

Verse

1. Two little blackbirds, sitting on a hill,
2. One named Jack and the other named Jill.
3. Fly away, Jack, and fly away, Jill.
4. Come back, Jack, and come back, Jill.

ACTION: During line 1, on the word "sitting," both partners quickly squat. In line 2, at the word "Jack," the boys spring up and clap hands once. At the word "Jill," the girls do the same. In line 3, the boys "fly away," waving their arms and traveling in a small circle away from their places. Then the girls do the same. In line 4, first the boys come back to their places, and then the girls do the same.

Two Little Blackbirds

Legs pumping and arms outstretched, these children "soar" like birds on the wing, as they act out one of the lines in the song Two Little Blackbirds.

Did You Ever See a Lassie?

● *5 to 12*   ● *Four to six*

FORMATION: Children form a large circle. No partners are needed. One child, the "lassie," (or "laddie," if it is a boy) is in the center.

Verse

1. Did you ever see a lassie, a lassie, a lassie,
2. Did you ever see a lassie go this way and that?
3. Go this way and that way, go this way and that way?
4. Did you ever see a lassie go this way and that?

ACTION: During lines 1 and 2, the children in the circle hold hands and sing, while the player in the center performs any action she (or he) wishes. This may be clapping hands, jumping or turning in place, skipping around, stamping feet, etc. During lines 3 and 4, all the children in the circle imitate exactly what the child in the center showed. At the end of the verse, the player in the center taps another child, who takes her place in the center and starts the game again.

All the children sing Did You Ever See a Laddie? *while the little boy in the center of the ring leads with actions that the others follow.*

Eentsy-Weentsy Spider

● *6 to 20*   ● *Four to eight*

FORMATION: Children take any position. In this song, the hands tell the story.

Verse

1. The eentsy-weentsy spider went up the waterspout.
2. Down came the rain, and washed the spider out.
3. Out came the sun, and dried up all the rain.
4. And the eentsy-weentsy spider went up the spout again.

ACTION: On the first line, children touch the forefinger of one hand to the thumb of the other and then turn the hands so the other thumb and forefinger touch. They do this several times, raising their hands higher and higher each time. On the second line, children shake their hands, moving them lower with each shake. At the beginning of the third line, children make a large circular sweeping motion with their arms and then hold out their hands, palms up, at the end of the line. On the fourth line, children repeat the climbing motion of the first line.

Children repeat the song three times. The first time, they sing the words and perform the actions. The second time, they hum the music and perform the actions. The third time, they perform the actions without making a sound.

Little Tom Tinker

● *3 to 12*   ● *Four to six*

Young children enjoy this lively action song. (The word "clinker" is slang for a red-hot coal which has fallen from a stove or locomotive.)

Verse

Little Tom Tinker got burned by a clinker

And he began to cry,
Ma! Ma!
What a poor fellow am I.

ACTION: The first time this is sung, everyone throws his hands up in the air twice, while singing "Ma! Ma!" The second time, everyone stands up twice, while singing "Ma! Ma!" The third time, everyone throws up his hands and stands, while singing "Ma! Ma!"

Hickory Dickory Dock

● *4 to 12*   ● *Four to six*

FORMATION: Children stand in a circle, with their hands joined.

Verse

1. Hickory, dickory, dock, the mouse ran up the clock.
2. The clock struck one, and down he'd run,
3. Hickory, dickory, dock.

ACTION: On line 1, children stamp their feet, left-right-left, on "hickory, dickory, dock," and walk to the left. On line 2, children clap hands on the word "one," join hands and walk to the right. One line 3, they stop and stamp left-right-left again on "hickory, dickory, dock."

Coming Round the Mountain

● *6 to 20*   ● *Six to twelve*

Verse

1. She'll be coming round the mountain when she comes.
2. She'll be coming round the mountain when she comes.
3. She'll be coming round the mountain,
4. She'll be coming round the mountain,
5. She'll be coming round the mountain when she comes.

ACTION: In this first verse, singers wave their hands above their heads and shout "Hi Babe!" after lines 1, 2, and 5. In the following two verses (sung in the same pattern), a different phrase is called out and a different action is performed, combining the phrase and the action as in the previous verse:

She'll be driving six white horses when she comes, ("Whoa back!" and pull back hard on the reins).

She'll be wearing red pajamas when she comes, ("Scratch, scratch!" and scratch backs of arms vigorously).

If You're Happy

● *3 to 12*   ● *Four to eight*

Verse

If you're happy and you know it, clap your
  hands (clap, clap)
If you're happy and you know it, clap your
  hands (clap, clap)
If you're happy and you know it, then your
  life will surely show it,
If you're happy and you know it, clap your

hands (clap, clap).

ACTION: At the end of the first, second, and
fourth lines, children clap their hands twice, as
indicated. In the succeeding verses, a different
action is given each time. These are: "stamp your
feet," "bow your head," "shut your eyes," "turn
around," and "wave goodbye." These words are
sung and the action is performed twice. At the
end of each verse, all the preceding actions are
said and *done* in order, before going on to the
next verse.

Where Is Thumbkin?
(To the tune of *Frère Jacques*)

● *3 to 12*   ● *Four to six*

A simple action song for younger children.

Verse	*Action*
Where is thumbkin?	Both hands are hidden behind
Where is thumbkin?	singer's back.
Here I am.	Right hand is brought out
Here I am.	in front, thumb pointing up. Left hand does the same.
How are you today, sir?	Right thumb "bows" four times.
Very well, I thank you.	Left thumb does the same.
Run away.	Right hand disappears behind back.
Run away.	So does left hand.

The Gallant Ship

● *8 to 16*   ● *Four to seven*

FORMATION: Children form two circles—one outside the other—and face the center.

Verse

1. Three times around went our gallant ship, and three times around went she,
2. Three times around went our gallant ship, and she sank to the bottom of the sea.
3. Haul her up, haul her up, came the word to the crew, haul her up, haul her up, cried they,
4. Haul her up, haul her up, came the word to the crew, and they worked very hard that day.

ACTION: On lines 1 and 2, the outer circle walks to the right, and the inner circle walks to the left. On the words "and she sank," the children in the inner circle sink slowly to the floor. On lines 3 and 4, the children in the outer circle try to bring the "gallant ship" up, by pretending to pull ropes and turn cranks or windlasses, etc. On the last phrase, "and they worked very hard that day," the inner circle slowly rises.

The More We Get Together

● *3 to 12*   ● *Four to twelve*

Verse

Oh, the more we get together, together, together,
Oh, the more we get together, the happier we'll be.

Chorus

For your friends are my friends,
And my friends are your friends,
Oh, the more we get together, the happier we'll be.

ACTION: During the verse, singers clap their hands together once, then clap their hands against their knees twice, to get a 1–2–3 rhythm. This is done in a steady rhythm beginning with the word *more* on the first line and ending on the word *be*. During the chorus, singers put their hands on each other's arms or shoulders and sway slowly to the rhythm of the music. On the last line of the song they repeat the 1–2–3 clapping action.

Musical Quizzes

The following games test musical knowledge and some involve participation in activities with musical accompaniment. Many of these games deal with "musical memory"—the ability to identify song melodies and titles. The songs selected should be those most likely to be known by the group playing the game. Younger children should be asked songs they are likely to have learned in school, camp, or club programs; older children might be quizzed on popular records.

Numerals indicate the number of players. Spelled-out numbers suggest suitable age levels.

Name the Tune

● *6 to 20* ● *Ten to twelve*

The leader plays a short strain from a group of pre-selected phonograph records. (Any record or part of a record in which the words of the singer might be a clue to the title of the melody should be avoided.) Players write down the name of each selection, next to a number assigned it, on a sheet of paper. The player with the highest number of correct answers wins. Contestants might also be asked to identify the composer by name in the case of classical music, or the person or group singing, in the case of popular music.

Musical Bingo

● *6 to 20* ● *Ten to twelve*

The game leader selects 20 to 25 phonograph records. He prepares a different Musical Bingo card for each player by drawing a Bingo diagram (nine boxes, with three rows of three boxes each) and writing the title of one of the records to be played in each box. Each player gets a card, listens to a portion of each record, and, on recognizing a strain of music from a record named on his Musical Bingo card, draws an X through that box. The first player to have three boxes crossed out in a row (vertically, horizontally, or diagonally) calls out "Musical Bingo!" and is declared the winner. Prizes may also be given to those players who finish in second or third place, or to the first contestant who fills in *all* of the boxes.

Play Another Note

● *10 to 20* ● *Eight to twelve*

Players divide into two teams—"A" and "B." The game leader begins by playing three or four notes from a fairly well-known song on a piano, harmonica, guitar, or some other instrument. Any contestant on either team who thinks he knows the title raises his hand, the game leader calling on the first one to volunteer. If that player guesses correctly, his team wins five points; otherwise the opposing team wins one. After an incorrect guess, any player from the opposition may, if he wishes, guess the tune. If he too is incorrect, his team loses the one point. If neither team guesses correctly, the game leader adds a note to the three or four he already played. The game goes on as before—with more notes added after each round—until the song title has been found. Then the game leader begins a new song and the action continues in this manner until one team—the winner—has amassed 21 points.

Continue Singing

● *12 to 20* ● *Eight to twelve*

Players divide into two teams. The leader sings the first line of a fairly well-known song and the lead player on one team must then sing the second line correctly. If he is successful, he wins five points for his team. If not, the first player on the opposing team may try. If a player is able to sing the melody, but cannot remember the correct words, he wins one point for his team. There is no penalty for a wrong answer. In this manner, players from each team take turns back and forth, with new songs. The team with the higher score is the winner.

VARIATION: In *Song Relay,* players sit in a circle. One person begins by standing and singing the first line of a popular song. This person then points to another player who must stand and sing the second line. He then points to another player who sings the third line, and so on. Whenever a player fails to pick up his cue and sing the correct line, he is eliminated from the game. The last player to survive is the winner.

Musical Hash

● *3 to 15* ● *Eight to twelve*

The leader prepares a list of familiar song titles, but with the letters of each word scrambled—for example: *Cajk nad Lilj* (*Jack and Jill*). A copy of the list is given to each player, and the first one to unscramble all the titles is the winner. It helps players if all the titles used are drawn from one particular category of song, such as old folk songs, Christmas carols, Mother Goose rhymes, and the like.

VARIATION: In *Team Musical Hash* the leader holds up large cards with one scrambled title written on each so that all the players can see them. Each card is held up for 30 seconds. The team to write out the most titles correctly wins the game.

Musical Neighbors

● *10 to 20* ● *Eight to twelve*

Players divide into two teams. Members of the first team are blindfolded and sit on chairs in a circle, leaving every other chair vacant. Members of the second team sit in the empty chairs, and, on signal, they sing a song previously agreed upon. Each member of the first team listens and tries to identify, by the sound of the voice, his neighbor to his immediate right or his immediate left. When any player identifies one of them, he may take off his blindfold and

join the singing. This goes on until every player has correctly identified one of his musical neighbors. Then the game is played again, with the two teams reversing roles.

VARIATION: In *How Many Singers?* members of one team are blindfolded and seated in chairs, their backs toward where the second team is grouped. A certain number of Team 2, no less than three and no more than six, begin to sing a song. After a minute or so, they stop and the first team is required to guess how many people were in the singing group. Only one team guess is permitted. If it should be right, the first team wins a point and the roles are reversed. Should the guess be wrong, Team 2 selects another group to sing a song. A time period can be fixed with the team with the higher number of points winning the game.

Musical Words

● *3 to 20* ● *Ten to twelve*

The leader prepares a list of definitions which describe everyday objects and happenings and have musical meanings as well. Individual players or teams then compete to see who can most quickly come up with the correct musical term that fits each definition. They may do this by trying, in turn, to name each word aloud, or by writing the definitions and terms in a list as the game is played. Examples:

Definitions	*Musical Terms*
A foot-policeman's route	Beat
Measures gas or water	Meter
After a steam-roller goes over it	Flat
Place for liquid refreshment	Bar
The object of playing in a game	Score
Comes from a pine tree	Pitch
A fish's outside	Scales
A nasty remark	Slur
Small-mouth or large-mouth	Bass
Tools should be kept this way	Sharp
Part of a sentence	Phrase
Open a locked door with this	Key
Before you cross the street	Pause

Drawing Games

In addition to play activities based on dramatics and music, children also enjoy games that involve drawing and painting. Although many such activities are individual projects, and are therefore included in Chapter Six—"Quiet Play for Quiet Times"—those described on the following pages do lend themselves to parties and game sessions. They are all easy to play and fast-paced, and the results of these artistic endeavors are usually quite funny.

Numerals indicate the number of players. Spelled-out numbers suggest suitable age levels.

Self-Portrait

● *4 to 20*   ● *Six to twelve*   ● *Drawing paper; transparent tape; colored chalk or poster paint and brush*

The leader gives each boy and girl a sheet of drawing paper and some strips of tape. Each child puts the paper in front of his face, and fixes it there with the tape. The leader then gives each player soft colored chalk or a paintbrush and container of paint. Without being able to see what they are doing, the players draw their own eyes, nose, mouth, eyebrows, chin, and other features. When all have finished their "self-portraits," they take the papers off and put them on display. The results are usually hilarious, with the various features scattered randomly all over the paper. Sometimes, however, a child will do a remarkably good job. The children take a vote to determine who has done the best drawing.

What Is It?

● *5 to 20*   ● *Six to twelve*   ● *Paper; chalk or crayon*

The leader gives each player a large sheet of paper, chalk or crayon, and a slip of paper with the name of an animal on it. On signal, each child carefully draws the animal assigned him on the sheet of paper. When all the drawings are complete, they are put up on the wall and numbered in consecutive order. Children copy the numbers and try to write the proper animal beside each number. After all have done this,

each drawing is correctly identified. The child who identified the greatest number of animals correctly is declared the winner. The child who drew the animal which was correctly identified by the most players may also be named a winner.

Blind Pig

● *6 to 20*   ● *Six to twelve*   ● *Paper; crayons*

Boys and girls are blindfolded and given paper and crayon. Each draws the outline of a pig without lifting the crayon from the paper. A player may, however, lift his crayon at the very end to draw the eye where he thinks it belongs. When everyone has finished, children take their blindfolds off and vote for the drawing they think is best.

Progressive Artists

● *5 to 20*   ● *Eight to twelve*   ● *Paper; pencils*

Players are given a large sheet of paper and a pencil. Each player begins by drawing a head (any age, either sex) at the top of his paper. He then folds over the sheet so that the head is hidden, but a bit of the neck still shows. At the leader's signal, all the players pass their folded papers to the next person on the right. Each player then draws the torso, including the arms, down to the waist and folds the paper over so that only the belt is showing. They pass the papers to the right again, and the next players draw from the belt to the knees. These players fold the drawings for the last time and pass them to the players on the right, who finish the drawings. The completed drawings are unfolded and put on display. Usually, the results are hilarious, partly because of the different drawing styles and varied items of clothing, and partly because a man's body may be attached to a girl's head, and so on. If the group is large, several circles of players can be formed—each circle doing its own series of drawings.

The Artist's Game

● *6 to 20*   ● *Ten to twelve*   ● *Paper; pencils*

Players divide into small teams of three or four and sit in clusters around the room facing the leader in the center. One player in each group has a piece of paper and a pencil. Each group sends an "artist" up to the leader, who shows them all a word he has printed on a piece of paper. It may be simple and direct, such as "dog," "house," or "automobile," or may be more abstract, such as "crime," "religion," or "happiness." The "artist" hurries back to his group and tries to draw a picture that conveys the meaning of the word. He may not write any letter or number, and may not make any sound at all. As the other players guess, the "artist" indicates with gestures whether they are "hot" or "cold." He keeps drawing, and they keep guessing—until finally someone guesses the word. The "artist" runs back to the leader to report to him. The first group to identify the word gets five points, the next three points, and the last one point. The game is played again, with a new "artist" from each group. After everyone has had a chance to draw the secret word, the scores are tallied, and the team with the highest total is the winner.

Initials

● *6 to 20*   ● *Eight to twelve*   ● *Paper; crayons*

Each boy and girl has a sheet of newsprint and a crayon. On signal, all print the initials of their first and last names. The two letters should cover a fairly large part of the sheets. Each child then does a drawing on the paper using his initials as a part of the design. When all the drawings are complete—and some will be quite ingenious— the players select the drawing which uses the letters in the cleverest way.

Profile Hunt

● *6 to 20*   ● *Five to twelve*   ● *Paper; pencils*

As boys and girls arrive at a party, they stand, one at a time, sideways in front of a strong light, which throws their shadows against a sheet of paper taped to the wall. The game leader out-

A light casts this girl's shadow on paper for sketching. Later the silhouette will be used in Profile Hunt.

lines the child's silhouette on the paper with a heavy black crayon or soft pencil. He numbers each sheet on the front and writes the name of the child on the back. Later in the day, all of the pictures are put up on the wall. Children try to guess the model for each profile and write down the number of each one next to the name of the child they think it represents. When everyone has had sufficient time to write down his guesses, the leader reads the correct names and numbers. The child with the highest number of correct identifications is the winner.

CHAPTER 5

Magic Tricks and Stunts

One of the most amusing types of activities is the magic trick or stunt, in which one player (the "magician") baffles an audience by performing a mysterious feat that simply can't be explained. In fact, such tricks are usually quite simple—once the secret is discovered. This chapter includes a variety of tricks that do not require special equipment or a high level of performing skill. Included are "mind-reading" stunts, card and coin tricks, optical stunts and illusions, mathematical puzzles, and a group of miscellaneous stunts.

Although these tricks are simple enough to be performed by adults, teenagers, and older children—and are thoroughly appreciated by young audiences—many do require a degree of manipulative skill and should be practiced beforehand. This is particularly true in the case of card, coin, and handkerchief tricks, in which some action must usually be hidden. Presentation is an important part of any trick's success. The performer should try to create the illusion that he really is doing something based on magical skill and knowledge. Smooth patter or accompanying talk can help to build this atmosphere and interest and baffle the audience. As a general rule, it is a good idea for the magician not to give away the secret of any magic stunt or trick. Particularly with the mind-reading stunts, the magician should insist that it is his magic power of concentration, rather than any pre-arranged signal, that is responsible for his successful performance. If the other players urge the magician to show a stunt again, it may be a good idea for him *not* to do so, if he feels they are likely to guess the secret. Instead, he may decide to show a similar trick—but one based on a different principle.

The first group of tricks involves the magician's claim that he is able to read the minds of others in the room. Usually he has an assistant planted in the group who provides the clues that will help the magician do the tricks.

Black Magic

THE TRICK: The magician and his assistant stand in front of the group. The magician says he will leave the room and when he returns he will be able to name any object that the audience selected. After a suitable absence, the magician returns and his assistant begins pointing to objects. When the correct object is indicated the magician identifies it.

THE SECRET: The assistant gives the magician the necessary clue. Before pointing to the correct object he points to one that is black or nearly black.

VARIATION: In *Red, White, and Blue,* the magician leaves the room three times, and three different objects are chosen for him to identify. The first time, the assistant points to the secret object after pointing to a red article; the next time after a white article; and the last time after a blue one.

Magic Spoon

● *A tablespoon or teaspoon*

THE TRICK: The magician boasts that he has a magic spoon which acts like a camera and can take a picture of anyone in the room. He also says that only he and his assistant can see the picture that appears on the bowl of the spoon. To prove these claims, the magician sends his assistant out of the room, and the audience selects one person to have his picture taken. The magician holds his spoon up before that child and makes believe he is taking a picture with it. Then he places the spoon on the floor and calls his assistant back in. The assistant glances at the spoon, picks it up, peers into the bowl and then identifies the correct boy or girl.

THE SECRET: When the magician puts the spoon back down on the floor, he points its handle in the general direction, though not directly at, the correct person. That is clue number one. In addition, the magician sits in exactly the same position as the chosen boy or girl. With these two clues, the assistant has no difficulty in se-

lecting the right person. If the magician has been chosen to take his own picture, he lets his assistant know this by means of a pre-arranged signal—he sits with his legs crossed and he points the spoon's handle directly at a door.

Mystic Ashes

● *A pencil; slips of paper; hat; matches; ashtray*

THE TRICK: The magician asks members of the audience to name some famous persons and he writes these names, one at a time, on slips of paper and puts them in a hat. He then asks a boy or girl to come forward and pick a slip out of the hat. The child is told to keep the slip folded. The magician puts the remaining slips in an ashtray and burns them. He studies the "mystic ashes," and after a while calls out the name of the person on the remaining slip. The player who has drawn that slip unfolds it and announces that the magician is right. As proof the slip is shown to the audience.

THE SECRET: When the magician is writing on the slips of paper, he does not write down all the names suggested, just the first one. Thus all the slips have the same name on them.

Silent Telepathy

THE TRICK: The magician tells the audience that while he is out of the room it is to choose one of its number. He then tells the group that he will identify that person by reading the thoughts of his assistant. The magician leaves while the audience chooses and then he returns. After staring intently at the assistant for a minute or so, as if he were indeed reading the assistant's mind, the magician makes the correct identification.

THE SECRET: Before the magician returns, the assistant crosses his legs with the toe of the upper foot pointing directly at the chosen person. When the magician enters the room he quickly glances at his assistant's foot and then pretends to be lost in contemplation before making the identification. This trick works best in a small group, so that the magician can be sure exactly where the foot is pointing. If the person chosen is sitting right next to the assistant, it may be hard to point a foot at him. In this case, the assistant leaves his legs uncrossed and crosses his arms instead, with the upper hand pointing directly at the person to be identified.

Legs

THE TRICK: When the magician leaves the room, his assistant tells the audience to select any object. Upon the magician's return, the assistant begins pointing to objects, each time asking if it is the selected one. Of course the magician says "no" until the right object is indicated.

THE SECRET: The first object the assistant points to contains the vital clue. If an object with legs is indicated by the assistant, then the magician knows that the correct article does have legs. The assistant then points to a number of articles without legs, such as ashtrays, lamps, or pictures, and when next he indicates an object with legs the magician knows that that is the correct object. If the group chose an article without legs, then the assistant reverses his procedure. First he points to an object without legs, then several with, and finally, the correct object.

Mystery Cities

THE TRICK: The magician leaves the room and boys and girls select a city for him to name. The magician's assistant is told the name of this city. When the magician returns, his assistant begins rattling off the names of various cities. To each of these the magician shakes his head, but when the right city is named, the magician immediately identifies it as such.

THE SECRET: If the audience has selected a one-word city, such as Paris or London, the assistant starts out naming several two-word cities, such as New York, New Orleans, San Francisco, etc. This is the clue the magician needs and he will identify the first one-word city after a string of two-word cities have been named. If, on the other hand, the audience has chosen a two-word city, the assistant will first name several one-word cities to give the magician the required clue.

Car

THE TRICK: With the magician and his assistant looking on, the group selects three objects and places them in a row on the floor. The magician leaves the room, and the group picks one of the three objects for him to guess. When the magician returns he immediately points to the correct article.

THE SECRET: The clue is in the phrase the assistant uses to call the magician back. It is based on the word "car." If the phrase begins with a C ("Come in!") the magician knows that the correct object is the one on the left. If it begins with an A ("All right!"), the object is the middle one. If it begins with an R ("Ready"), the chosen object is the one on the right.

VARIATIONS: In *Count the Letters* several objects are placed on the floor, one of them having been chosen as the secret object. When the magician returns to the room, the assistant points to the objects one by one and the magician selects the correct object. Again, the clue is in the first word the assistant says. If that word has one letter, as in "I think we're ready to start," then the first object the assistant points to is the one. If the word has two letters, as in "We can begin now," the second object pointed to is correct, and so on. In *Count the Words,* it is the number of words in the assistant's call that furnishes the clue. If he says, "Enter!" the first object he points to will be it. If he says, "Come in!" it will be the second object, and so on.

Hand in the Air

● *A blindfold*

THE TRICK: The magician is blindfolded and asks a volunteer to raise one of his hands. As the volunteer is holding up a hand, the magician gives him a series of instructions, such as, "Cross your legs," "Count aloud to 20," "Sing a verse of *I Been Workin' on the Railroad.*" Then the magician says, "Now lower your hand." As the volunteer does so, the magician takes off his blindfold, and examines the two hands of the volunteer, pointing to the hand that was held in the air.

THE SECRET: The magician can identify the hand held up because it will be somewhat paler than the other. When a hand is held high for 30 seconds or so, it loses blood and its color is slightly altered. While the difference is slight, it can be detected. The purpose of the series of instructions is merely to prolong the time that the hand is held up, so that it will lose a significant amount of blood.

Temple Magic

THE TRICK: When the magician leaves the room, the boys and girls pick a number from 1 to 10. The magician returns, stands behind his assistant, and places his hands lightly on the assistant's temples. After a few moments, the magician calls out the correct number.

THE SECRET: While the magician is holding his hands on his assistant's temples, the assistant is clenching his jaw the required number of times. This action cannot be seen by the audience, but the magician can easily feel the clenchings with his fingertips.

Mystical Numbers

THE TRICK: The magician leaves the room while the boys and girls pick a number from 1 to 20. When the magician comes back, the assistant calls out several numbers. When the correct one is called, the magician identifies it without any hesitation.

THE SECRET: The first number called by the assistant is the clue. If the assistant, for example, says, "Is it five?" the correct number will be the fifth one called. Another way of giving the clue—one that is harder to detect—is that a two-digit number is called first and the magician

adds up the digits to get the answer. For example, if the assistant calls out 14, the magician adds the 1 and the 4 to get 5; thus the fifth number called will be the correct one.

This Row and That Row

● *Books or magazines*

THE TRICK: Two rows of books are placed on the floor and the magician then leaves the room while the boys and girls choose the book to be identified. When the magician returns, his assistant begins pointing at the books one by one, with the magician shaking his head "no" until the assistant points to the correct book.

THE SECRET: The magician and his assistant had worked out the whole trick beforehand. The upper row is designated "this row"; the lower row, "that row." If the secret book is in the lower row, the assistant begins by pointing to the books in the upper row. As he points he asks "this book?" When he reaches the lower row he switches and asks for each, "that book?" But when he reaches the secret book, instead of saying "*that* book," as is proper for the lower row, he says "*this* book," giving the clue to the magician. When the secret book is in the upper row, he says "this book," for each until he reaches the one to be identified and then says "that book."

VARIATIONS: In *This One, That One,* the clue is much the same. Four books are laid out in a square formation. The book at the upper left has been predesignated "this," the one at the lower left, "that"; the book at upper right, "this one," and the book at lower right, "that one." When questioning the magician, the assistant uses any words but the correct ones except when he is pointing to the secret book. When pointing to the books, the assistant might say, "Could it be this one?" or "Could this be the book?" But if he is pointing to the secret book he uses the predesignated words. Thus if the secret book is the one on the upper right, the assistant will ask, "This one?" The trick *Nine Books* is performed in a similar manner, but the clue is given wordlessly. Nine books are arranged in three even rows with one selected as the secret book. When the magician returns to the room, the assistant points to various books. The clue is in the way he points to the first book. If, for example, he touches it on the upper-left-hand corner, he is telling the magician that the secret book is on the top row, left; if he touches it square in the middle, the book is in the center of the middle row, and so on.

The Hindu Cane

● *A cane or broomstick*

THE TRICK: While the magician is out of the room, the boys and girls pick a word for him to guess. When the magician returns, his assistant stands in front of him and taps out with his "Hindu cane" (an old cane or broomstick said to have magical powers) an apparently

meaningless pattern. As he taps, the assistant makes encouraging comments. Suddenly the magician looks up from deep contemplation and says, "The cane tells me the magical word is—" and then tells the correct word.

THE SECRET: Every vowel in the word is given by taps with the cane: one tap for A, two for E, three for I, four for O, five for U. Consonants, however, are given by the first letter of the first word in every sentence spoken by the assistant. Suppose the secret word is "music." The assistant might use the following signals:

"My feeling is that it may be difficult to communicate today." The letter M is thus given.

Five taps of the cane for the letter U.

"Somehow, I think you feel the cane talking." There's the letter S.

Three taps of the came indicates the letter I.

"Come now, I'm sure you're getting it," for the letter C.

Tricks and Puzzles with Numbers

Although these tricks are based on simple mathematical formulas, they never fail to baffle and amuse audiences. They may be presented before large groups or small, or even by a parent for the amusement of his own children. All require paper and pencils.

Loose Change

THE TRICK: The magician tells the audience that he can tell not only a volunteer's age but also how much loose change is in that child's pocket (provided it is less than one dollar).

THE FORMULA: A boy or girl is picked and told to write down the following:

His age:	10
Double it:	20
Add 5:	25
Multiply by 50:	1250
Subtract 365:	885
Add amount of change in pocket (65¢):	950

The magician asks for the last figure and then adds 115 to it. In this instance the result is 1065. The first two figures represent the child's age, the last two the amount of change in his pocket. No matter what the volunteer's age or the amount of change he has (under one dollar), the formula always works.

Number and Age

THE TRICK: The magician picks any volunteer from the group. He tells him that through the use of a magic mathematical formula, the magician will deduce both the volunteer's age and the last five digits of his telephone number.

THE FORMULA: The magician gives the volunteer a piece of paper and pencil and asks him to perform the following calculations. (Sample figures are being used.)

Telephone number (last five digits):	89858
Multiply by two:	179716
Add 5:	179721
Multiply by 50:	8986050
Add age:	8986061
Add 365:	8986426
Subtract 615:	8985811

The first five digits of the result are the last five digits of the volunteer's telephone number; the last two digits are his age. To add to the bafflement of the audience, the magician asks each volunteer for the number he has reached after adding 365. The final step—subtracting 615—the magician does by himself.

Your Age, Sir

THE TRICK: The magician asks for a volunteer from the audience. When a boy or girl comes forward the magician tells the child that he can guess the volunteer's age through the use of a secret mathematical formula.

THE FORMULA: The child is given a pencil and paper and is told to list the following:

His age:	11
Multiply by 3:	33
Add 6:	39
Divide by 3:	13

The magician then asks the child for the last figure and subtracts two; the result is the volunteer's age. It doesn't matter how old the volunteer is. The answer will be correct.

VARIATION: In *How Old Are You?* a volunteer's age is revealed through a different formula.

His age:	12
Double it:	24
Add 1:	25
Multiply by 5:	125
Add 5:	130
Multiply by 10:	1300

Now the magician asks the child for the answer. The magician subtracts 100 from this figure, giving him 1200. Then he drops the last two digits, and the result—12—is the child's age.

Reverse the Numbers

THE TRICK: The magician writes a number on a slip of paper and puts it in an envelope. He tells the audience that a volunteer can write any three-digit number in descending order—i.e., 831, not 138—on a piece of paper and through a magic formula the resulting figure will match the one in the envelope.

THE FORMULA: A boy or girl writes a number.

The number:	742
Subtract the reverse of that number:	247
First result:	495
Add reverse of result:	594
Final total:	1089

The number in the envelope is 1089, which is the figure always used in this trick. The formula will work so long as the number picked has three digits written in descending order.

Magic Numbers

THE TRICK: The magician writes a number down on a piece of paper and places it in an envelope. Then he picks a member of the audience and tells him that by using a formula based upon the volunteer's age, date of birth, and other information, the volunteer will reach a number-total the same as the number in the envelope.

THE FORMULA: This is a straight matter of addition, and sample figures follow:

Year of birth:	1960
Year entered school:	1965
Age:	11
Years in school (at the end of current calendar year):	6
Total:	3942

When the magician opens the envelope he takes out the paper on which he had earlier written the number 3942, exactly the same number reached by the volunteer. The secret is that the sum of the numbers above will always total twice the year in which the trick is performed. Thus, if the trick is performed in 1971, the number the magician writes down is 3942, and the total reached by the volunteer will be the same. This trick is best performed with relatively young school children who would be most unlikely to have missed a year of school—a circumstance that would throw off the whole formula.

Coin Tricks

There are many coin tricks that the beginning magician can use to entertain an audience. Some of these involve skillful manipulation, however, and must be practiced beforehand. Others involve no special skill at all except the ability to present them dramatically. All require different combinations of coins.

Make it Odd or Even

THE TRICK: The magician places a number of coins on a table top. He asks any player to take several coins in his hand and close his fist. Then the magician himself takes an odd number of coins and announces:

"I will add my coins to yours, and, if you now have an odd number of coins, mine will make the total even. If you have an even number, adding mine to it will make the total odd. I guarantee it!"

The player shows his coins, and the magician shows his. It turns out just as he promised it would.

THE SECRET: When the magician puts his coins on the table, they are, of course, an *odd* number. An odd number will always make an even number odd, or an odd number even. Although this trick is very simple, young boys and girls will rarely figure out the secret unless it is repeated several times.

The Vanishing Coin

THE TRICK: The magician places a coin in a wooden matchbox. He closes the box and shakes it to show that the coin is still there. When he opens the box, however, the coin has disappeared.

THE SECRET: This trick depends on advance preparation. The magician has cut a narrow slit in one end of the matchbox drawer, close to the bottom. When he shakes the box sideways, the coin rattles, proving it is still there. When he tilts the box slightly, with the slit down, the coin slides into his hand. A moment later he opens the box and it is empty.

Heads or Tails

THE TRICK: The magician tosses a coin into the air. He catches it in his right hand and slaps it on the back of his left hand. "Call it!" he says. "Heads or tails?" After a player guesses, the magician lifts his right hand to show that the coin has disappeared.

THE SECRET: This is a sleight-of-hand trick. While pretending to catch the coin in his right hand, the magician holds the hand with the fingers straight up and the back of the hand toward the other players. Instead of catching the coin, he lets it drop into his coat sleeve. Then he closes his right hand and pretends to slap the coin on the back of his left hand. This trick requires careful advance practice.

The Hidden Coin

THE TRICK: A volunteer puts a coin on the table, along with three small covers (tops of pill containers, soda-bottle caps, or Ping-Pong ball halves, for example). The magician turns his back while the player puts one of the covers over the coin and the others next to it. The magician turns around, recites an incantation, and passes his hand mysteriously over the containers several times in order to locate the coin. He then lifts one cover and reveals the coin hidden beneath it.

THE SECRET: The magician has previously affixed a short hair to the bottom of the coin with wax or glue. The hair is too small to be detected by the audience, but the magician is able to see it protruding from under the cover concealing the coin. His hand gestures are for show—and to help create an air of mystery—while he looks for the hair.

Impossible Total

THE TRICK: After closing his fist over an odd number of coins that add up to an even amount in value, the magician asks a member of the audience to guess whether the total he has is odd or even. No matter what the child says, the magician tells him, his answer will be wrong.

THE SECRET: The trick depends on how the magician defines total. If the boy or girl guesses odd, the magician opens his fist to reveal, say, a dime, a nickle and five pennies. Then he says: "Sorry, you're wrong. The total is 20 cents." If, on the other hand, the child guesses even, the magician counts the number of coins—a total of seven—and again the child is wrong. This trick, of course, only works with small children, and even they are very likely to catch on if the stunt is repeated.

How Far?

THE TRICK: The magician places two coins— about a foot or more apart—on a table, and puts another coin between them, but not exactly in the center. He asks the other players to judge which two coins are the farthest apart. Usually, they will pick the middle coin and either the end coin on the right or the left. Then the magician tells them that they've all guessed wrong. Using a ruler, he proves, beyond a doubt, that it is the two *end* coins that are the farthest apart.

THE SECRET: Of course it's all based on deliberately confusing the audience. By putting the center coin down last, the magician indicates that he is talking about the distance between the center and one of the two ends; but this is not what he said, as the audience realizes after it has been tricked.

Move the Coins

The magician takes two quarters and a nickel —or any three coins of any denominations— and places them in a row touching each other

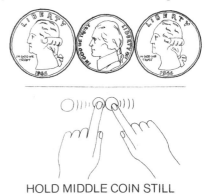

HOLD MIDDLE COIN STILL

with the nickel in the middle. The magician says he can move one of the quarters from its place on the end of the line and put it between the other two coins while observing the following rules:

1. The quarter on the left may be moved, but not directly touched.
2. The nickel in the middle may be touched, but not moved.
3. The quarter on the right may be both touched and moved.

THE SECRET: Following these rules, it would seem impossible to carry out the trick, but the magician shows how it can be accomplished. He puts the index finger of his left hand on the nickel, which may be touched. He puts the index finger of his right hand on the quarter on the right, which may be both touched and moved. He moves the quarter away slightly, then strikes the nickel with it sharply. He holds the nickel in place with his finger. The force of the blow will knock away the quarter on the left, which can be moved but not touched, just as in a *Croquet* game. Thus, the magician has created a space between the quarter on the left and the nickel, so that he can slide the other quarter around and place it between the two.

What Date Is It?

The magician tells one player to place a quarter—date-side up—on the table. After the other players have examined the coin, the same player places a piece of typing paper over it. Although he has not seen the coin, the magician claims he can tell its date, without lifting the paper from its place.

THE SECRET: By rubbing a well-sharpened pencil on the paper over the coin, the magician makes an impression of the coin on the paper, and he is able to read the date on the quarter without lifting the paper.

Take the Coin

THE TRICK: The magician holds a coin and switches it rapidly from hand to hand. Then he holds his clenched right hand forward and says "Take the coin," at the same time slapping it down on a wooden table. The sound of the coin hitting the table can be heard clearly. Yet when a player reaches forward to take it, the coin is not there.

THE SECRET: The magician has actually kept the coin in his left hand, which rests on the table at a distance from the right hand. When the right hand seems to slap the coin down, it is the left hand that actually clicks it against the table. The audience is not aware of his left hand at all, since their eyes are on his right hand at the time. They are astonished when the magician lifts his right hand and they see that the coin is not there.

Now You Have It

THE TRICK: The magician chooses a volunteer from the audience. The volunteer is given a coin—a dime or a penny—which he holds in the palm of his hand. The magician presses the child's palm firmly with his left thumb and, at the same time, closes the player's fingers over the coin with his right hand. The player is certain that the coin is still in his hand. When he opens his hand to prove it to the group, however, the coin is not there.

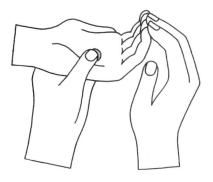

THE SECRET: First, the magician has placed a small piece of double-sided adhesive tape on the ball of his left thumb. When the tape is pressed to the coin, it adheres to it and lifts it away. Second, by pressing the coin into the player's palm, the magician creates a lingering physical effect. The player cannot actually feel that the coin has been taken away—and is extremely surprised when he sees it is missing.

Card Tricks

Everyone enjoys being baffled by tricks with playing cards. Here are several such tricks that can be performed without any particular sleight-of-hand ability. They should be performed with an air of professionalism, however, and the magician should learn to shuffle and deal cards smoothly. A complete deck of cards is needed for each trick.

The One-Way Pack

THE TRICK: The magician asks a volunteer to pick a card, look at it, and then return it to the deck. He then tells the group that he can identify the card chosen by the volunteer.

THE SECRET: The trick is based on the fact that some decks of cards have a one-way design on their backs—a picture of a flower or a landscape, etc.—instead of the usual symmetrical pattern. Using such a one-way deck, the magician first arranges the cards so that the pictures on their backs all face in the same direction. He then shuffles the cards without changing the direction and holds them out fan-like to any member of the audience. After a volunteer has picked a card, the magician unobtrusively turns the pack around so that when the card is replaced in the deck its picture on the back will be facing in the opposite direction from the others. Again the magician shuffles the deck and then, with a great show of concentration, searches for the secret card. It is easy to find, for the picture on its back will be facing one way and all the rest of the cards will face the other.

Color-Changing Deck

THE TRICK: The magician shows the players a deck of cards with the joker in front. He riffles the end of the pack with his thumb, so that the other players see only red cards. He then blows on the pack, and riffles it again. This time they see only black cards. He blows on the pack again, and riffles it once more. This time the cards are both red and black!

THE SECRET: The magician prepares the pack in advance, by separating the black cards from the red and then putting the deck together so that every odd card is black and every even card, red. The edges of the cards are not flush: the red cards protrude slightly at the top and the black cards protrude at the bottom. When the deck is first riffled, only the red cards show. Then, as the magician blows on the cards, he turns the pack around, so that only the black cards show when he riffles them. The last time he riffles the pack, he pushes all the cards together— this time exposing both colors. This trick demands dexterity and must be carefully practiced. When it is performed, the deck of cards must be held tightly.

The Falling Card

THE TRICK: A chosen card is shown to all members of the audience and then placed on the top of the deck. The magician cuts the deck, placing the top half on a table with his right hand, holding the bottom half in his left hand. The magician then throws the bottom half high in the air, thrusts out his right hand and catches the chosen card—presumed by all to be on the table—on the back of his right hand.

THE SECRET: The magician has some double-sided tape on the back of his right hand. As he puts the top half of the deck on the table, he presses his hand against the top card—the chosen card—so that it adheres to his hand. The audience, at this time, is distracted by the cards being thrown in the air, and the magician quickly thrusts his right hand out—palm side up to hide the chosen card—and makes believe he is going to catch one of the cards as it falls. As the cards are falling down and the children are following their course, the magician turns his hand, pretending to catch the chosen card, which is actually stuck to his hand.

Reverse the Card

THE TRICK: A member of the audience picks a card from a deck held out fan-shaped by the magician. The volunteer returns the card to any spot in the deck, after which the magician looks through the deck and quickly identifies the mystery card.

THE SECRET: The deck is rigged beforehand. The magician turns the bottom card so it is face up and all the others are face down. When he fans out the deck, he conceals the bottom card in his palm. After the volunteer selects a card, the magician quietly turns the deck over so that the bottom card is now on top, face down, all the others being face up. When the volunteer returns the card to the deck the only card he can see is the one on top and he places the mystery card back in the deck face down, for he thinks all the cards face in that direction. With flourishes of his hand and a constant patter of talk about the amazing nature of the trick, the magician looks through the deck, knowing that the first card he comes to—after the top card—that faces in the opposite direction from the others will be the mystery card.

Four Kings

THE TRICK: The magician shows the audience four kings, which he has sorted out of a deck of cards. He explains that he is going to scatter these kings throughout the deck, and then mysteriously bring them together again.

THE SECRET: Before holding up the four kings, the magician secretly places two other cards behind the second king from the left. He places all four kings on top of the deck (the cards are all face down). Then he takes the first king and puts it on the bottom of the deck; he takes the second card, which the audience believes is a king, and slips it into the middle of the deck, and he does the same with the third

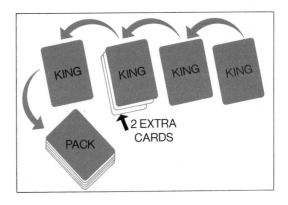

card. Then he says: "Ladies and gentlemen, you've all seen me scatter the kings in the deck of cards. One is at the top and one is at the bottom of the deck and two are somewhere in the middle. Is that right?"

When the others agree, he cuts the deck once, bringing the king at the bottom of the pack together with the three kings still on top. Then he turns the cards face up, fans them out, and, to everyone's surprise, shows all four kings together. This trick depends upon the magician's ability to keep the two cards well hidden behind the four kings at the beginning of the demonstration. It requires practice beforehand to be performed successfully.

Find the Card

THE TRICK: The magician picks 21 cards from a pack of 52, and deals them out face up into three packs of seven cards each. While the magician's back is turned, a volunteer chooses any one of these cards, shows it to the group and returns it anywhere in the same pile from which it came. The magician turns around and asks the volunteer which pack the chosen card is in. He then puts the three packs together and deals them again into three piles. He deals one card at a time to each pile until all 21 cards are dealt. Again, he asks the player who picked the original card to show him in which of the three piles his card appears. He puts the cards together, deals three piles again—one card at a time to each pile—and asks the player a last time which pile his card is in. This time, the magician points to the chosen card.

THE SECRET: Each time, before dealing out the cards, the magician puts the pile in which the chosen card appears between the other two piles. In this manner, after he has dealt out the piles three times, the card will turn out to be the middle card in whichever pile the volunteer points to as the correct one. All the magician has to do is go through this pile and hold up the fourth card.

Magic Packs

THE TRICK: The magician asks a volunteer to name any number between one and ten. He then goes through a deck of cards, and takes out all four cards of that number. This leaves 48 cards. He deals these cards into six piles of eight cards each. The magician then turns his back, or leaves the room, while the volunteer takes one card from near the center of any pile. He shows this card to the group, returns it to the top of the same pile, and stacks the six piles in any order that he wishes. The magician returns to the room and goes through the deck of 48 cards, turning each card face up. In a short time, he holds up the chosen card to the astonished audience.

THE SECRET: The deck has been stacked. In advance, the magician places six picture cards at the top of the deck and the other six picture cards at the bottom of the deck. As a result, when he deals out the six piles of eight cards each, the top and the bottom card of each pile will be a picture card. The card that the volunteer player picks from the center of a pile, therefore, will never be a picture card. When he returns this card to the top of one pile and places the piles one on top of another, this card must wind up *between* two picture cards. It is simple for the magician to find, since it is the *only* non-picture card between two picture cards.

Miscellaneous Tricks

There are many entertaining tricks and puzzles which make use of common household articles such as pieces of fruit, hard-boiled eggs, glasses, needles, handkerchiefs, checkers, strings, bottles, matchsticks, coins, and balls.

Disappearing Orange

● *An orange peel; an apple*

THE TRICK: The magician places an orange and a large colored handkerchief on the table, explaining that he is hungry and wants to eat an orange. He waves the handkerchief loosely in the air, to show that it does not conceal anything, and places it over the orange. Then he says: "Come to think of it, I'd really rather have an apple. But that's all right, because—" At this, he lifts up the handkerchief, crumples the cloth together and stuffs it in his pocket. Behold! Instead of an orange, an apple appears.

THE SECRET: Actually, the apple was there all the time, with a whole orange peel fitted around it. The orange is prepared by taking a thick-skinned navel orange and slitting the peel into four slices with a sharp knife, making certain to leave the rind joined at the top. In advance, the magician sets the peel over a small apple. The audience does not suspect because, from a distance, it is difficult to see the cuts in the skin. When the magician lifts the handkerchief, he squeezes off the orange peel, crumpling it together with the handkerchief, and places it out of sight in his pocket. All eyes are on the apple which has miraculously replaced the orange on the magician's table.

The Floating Needle

- *Candle wax; two needles; bowl; cloth*

THE TRICK: The magician drops a needle into a jar or bowl of water and, being metal, it sinks to the bottom. He wipes the needle off with a cloth and permits another player to drop it into the jar. The needle again sinks to the bottom. Then, he takes the needle out of the water, wipes it, and says a magic incantation. This time, when he puts it into the water, it floats!

THE SECRET: While wiping the needle the second time, the magician replaces it with a similar needle which has been rubbed against a candle and has a wax coating. With the wax on it, the needle will float. The magician keeps the waxed needle hidden in the cloth that is used to wipe the original; he must practice beforehand so that he can secretly switch the needles without being detected.

The Rising Egg

- *A hard-boiled egg; jar; pitcher; salt*

THE TRICK: The magician puts a hard-boiled egg into a glass jar holding about four inches of fresh water. The egg sinks directly to the bottom. He asks any member of the group to pour a little more water into the jar. This is done, but the egg remains on the bottom. Now the magician pours out some of the water, saying that *he* will pour in more water and command the egg to rise from the pitcher's bottom. He does this, mutters some mystic phrases, and the egg obeys him, rising slowly, as if on command, to the surface of the water.

THE SECRET: The pitcher from which the magician pours water the second time contains a strong solution of salt water. Its density makes the egg rise. In preparing for this trick, the magician should experiment until he knows exactly what amount of salt is needed to make the trick work. Also, because salt water appears slightly cloudy, he should use a tinted glass jar and pitcher to help conceal the trick from the audience.

VARIATION: In *The Educated Egg,* the magician shows his audience a hard-boiled egg, which, he explains, understands English and will follow his directions. He puts the egg into a glass jar filled with water and it begins to sink slowly. As the magician says magic words and commands it to stop, the egg slows up and then hangs suspended in the middle of the water. Then, the magician stirs the water with a wand, saying, "Now, egg, sink!" At once the egg obeys, dropping to the bottom of the jar. The secret is in the way the jar of water is prepared. In advance, the magician makes a strong solution of salt water filling the jar halfway. Then, using a small funnel, he adds fresh water, a little at a time, trying not to disturb the salt water. The water is now in two layers, with the fresh water on top. In the trick, the egg sinks through the fresh water and stops when it reaches the denser salt water. Stirring the water weakens the solution, and the egg sinks to the bottom.

Disappearing Pencil

- *A pencil; a handkerchief*

THE TRICK: The magician places a pencil under a handkerchief, holding it up so its shape can be seen. Suddenly, with the other hand, he pulls the handkerchief aside—and the pencil is gone.

THE SECRET: The magician points his forefinger up under the handkerchief, making the audience think it is the pencil, and at the same time he lets the pencil slip down his sleeve.

The Fireproof Handkerchief

- *A candle; a handkerchief*

THE TRICK: The magician—who in this case should be an adult—lights a candle, and then shows the group an ordinary handkerchief. He announces that he can pass the handkerchief slowly through the flame, and it will not burn or even smolder. Holding the handkerchief by the upper corners, he does this. Although an ordinary handkerchief would surely burn, this one does not.

THE SECRET: The handkerchief has been soaked in a strong solution of borax and water, which makes it almost fireproof. As in any trick involving flame, extreme care must be taken to prevent accidents.

The Tie That Binds

● *A large handkerchief*

THE TRICK: The magician takes a large colored handkerchief and wraps it around his left wrist, letting the ends cross. He places his right wrist over his left, with the fingers pointing towards the left elbow. He asks a volunteer to pull the ends of the handkerchief tight around his right wrist and tie a knot. The magician appears to be securely bound in the handkerchief, which is in a figure-eight shape. He turns his back and immediately is able to free himself.

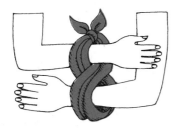

THE SECRET: The magician simply twists his right hand to the right and his left to the left, so that the fingers come toward each other. This movement unties the figure-eight binding and frees both his hands.

Tie the Knot

● *A large handkerchief*

THE TRICK: The magician spreads out a large handkerchief. He challenges any one to tie a knot in it by holding one corner of the handkerchief in one hand and the opposite corner in the other but not letting go of either corner during the knotting. When a few have tried and failed, the magician shows how it is done.

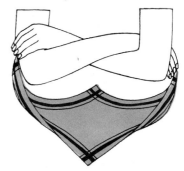

THE SECRET: He simply folds his arms across his chest, with one hand on top of one arm and one hand under the other arm. With his arms and hands in this position, he picks up the corners of the handkerchief. Then by uncrossing his arms and bringing his hands out to either side, he is able to make a knot in the handkerchief without letting go of either corner.

Dime in a Glass

● *Wine glass; dime; half dollar*

THE TRICK: The magician places a dime in a shallow, curved-bottom wine glass. He then places a half-dollar on top of the dime. He challenges any player to remove the dime *without* touching the half-dollar directly or turning the glass over. No one can figure out a way to do it. Then the magician blows sharply down the side of the glass, and the dime pops out.

THE SECRET: The magician's breath makes the half-dollar revolve at the bottom of the glass, hitting the dime and knocking it out. This will work only if the wine glass is the correct shape. The trick must be practiced beforehand.

Nickels and Pennies

THE TRICK: The magician lays out 12 coins—4 horizontal rows and 3 vertical rows. Nickels and pennies must be placed exactly as shown in Diagram 1. The magician challenges any player to see if he can make the first and third horizontal rows (from the top) all nickels and the second and fourth horizontal rows all pennies. After someone volunteers, the magician tells him that he may only directly touch one coin to change the rows.

THE SECRET: When the others have found the trick impossible to perform, the magician shows that it is really quite easy. He places his forefinger on the center coin of the top row (a penny) and slides it to the right around the other coins so it is just below the middle vertical

row of coins. Then, touching only that penny, he pushes the entire middle row up one place.

String Through the Neck

● *A piece of string*

THE TRICK: The magician takes a piece of string 36 inches long and makes a loop 18 inches long by knotting the ends together. He holds up the loop of string and explains that he is going to pass this cord right through his neck. He slips the string around his neck with the two ends of the loop stretched out in front of him. Using his thumbs, the magician draws each end taut, as far from his neck as possible but with the two ends of the loop very close together. He utters a magic word and pulls the loop sharply, apparently bringing it forward right through his neck. He is still holding the ends of the taut loop with his thumbs, but the whole string is now in front of him.

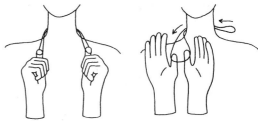

THE SECRET: When the magician brings his hands together in front, he secretly slides his right index finger into the right end of the loop and, still holding the left end with his left thumb, slips his right thumb through the left end of the loop. Then, all in one motion, he lets go of the right end completely and pulls the left end of the loop forward, straightening it out in front of him with both thumbs. It happens so quickly that the audience isn't sure what has occurred, but it looks as if the cord has gone through the magician's neck.

Captive Couples

● *Two lengths of cord*

THE TRICK: The magician takes a cord about three feet long and ties the ends around the two wrists of one volunteer. He takes a second cord of equal length, and ties one end to the wrist of another volunteer. He passes the free end of the second rope over and under the cord tying the first player's wrists, and then ties the free end to the second player's other wrist. The two players must free themselves without untying any knots, cutting the cords, or slipping them off their wrists. After assuming all kinds of contortions, they will probably give up. Then the magician shows them how it's done.

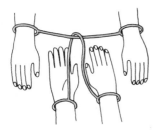

THE SECRET: One of the pair must take the cord of the other and pass it through the loop around one of his own wrists. He must pass it under the loop from the body side, and not entangle

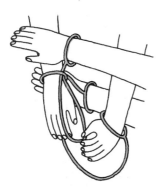

it with his own cord while passing it through the loop. Then he pulls this cord far enough through the loop so that he can slip it over his own hand. As soon as this is done, the cords are no longer linked with each other, and the two players are separated.

Checker Challenge

● *Checkers*

THE TRICK: The magician puts eight checkers in a row, red and black alternating. He chal-

lenges a volunteer to make four moves, using two checkers at a time, so that all the reds will be together and all the blacks will be together. When others have tried the stunt and failed, the magician shows them how this trick can be easily performed.

THE SECRET: The magician gives each checker a number from one to eight and assigns nine and ten to the two empty spaces on the right. Then he moves the checkers in this way: checkers two and three to spaces nine and ten; five and six to the places emptied by two and three; eight and nine to the places emptied by five and six; and one and two to the places emptied by eight and nine. He has moved all the checkers—making only four moves and moving two checkers each time—so that now the reds are on one side and the blacks are on the other.

Lifting Ten Matches

● *Wooden matches*

THE TRICK: The magician challenges any player to lay ten matches on the table in such a way that they can all be picked up at the same time, using only one other match. When the players have tried and failed, he shows them how the trick can be done.

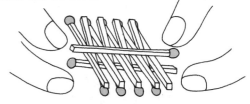

THE SECRET: He lays one match flat on the table, and lays nine other matches across this match. They alternate, pointing in opposite directions, and the center of each lies on top of the first match. Then he places one other match across the top of the nine matches, directly over the first match but pointing in the opposite direction. The magician uses the thumb and forefinger of both hands and, gripping the ends of the two parallel matches, he lifts all the matches at once. Thus, as claimed, he has used one match to lift ten matches.

Slippery Quarters

● *Two quarters; a glass*

THE TRICK: The magician places two quarters on opposite sides of the rim of a glass. He then challenges any player to try to remove them from the glass, using only the index finger and thumb of one hand and taking both quarters at the same time. After the volunteers have tried and failed, he shows how it can be done.

THE SECRET: He places his thumb over the coin on the left and his index finger over the one on the right. He carefully tilts the quarters over so they tip in an outward direction, at the same time pressing and holding them against the outer sides of the glass. Then, by squeezing, he moves the coins together along the outer edge of the rim, so that they drop into his hand. This trick demands practice.

Matchstick Puzzles

The following puzzles cannot be classified exactly as magic tricks, but they do require some pretty creative thinking to be performed successfully. In each case, the leader should show the beginning layout and explain the challenge. However, he should not let the players see the solution until each has tried to work it out. If a large box of kitchen matches is used, several players can work together in trying to solve these puzzles.

MATCHSTICK PUZZLE 1. Arrange 17 matches as shown in Diagram 1. Then remove five matches to make three squares (Diagram 2).

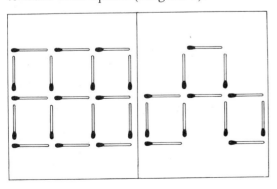

MATCHSTICK PUZZLE 2. Arrange 12 matches as shown in Diagram 1. Then move three matches, so that there are only three squares (Diagram 2). All 12 matches are still used.

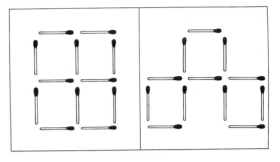

MATCHSTICK PUZZLE 3. Arrange 24 matches to make nine squares, as shown in Diagram 1. Take away eight matches and leave only two squares (Diagram 2).

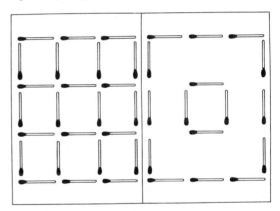

MATCHSTICK PUZZLE 4. Take six matchsticks of equal length and make four equilateral triangles.

The solution is to use three matches to make a base, and to construct a pyramid with the other three, as shown in the diagram.

MATCHSTICK PUZZLE 5. Using nine matchsticks, make three equal squares and two equal triangles, all connected. The solution is a tentlike structure illustrated in the diagram.

MATCHSTICK PUZZLE 6. Using eight matches, form two squares and four triangles as shown in the diagram.

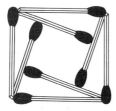

MATCHSTICK PUZZLE 7. Place six matchsticks parallel to one another, with a space between each as in Diagram 1. Then, without moving any of them, add five matches to make nine (Diagram 2).

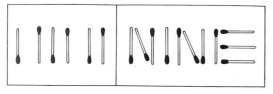

MATCHSTICK PUZZLE 8. Form three squares with 12 matches, as in Diagram 1. Then take away any two matches and rearrange the others to leave two (Diagram 2).

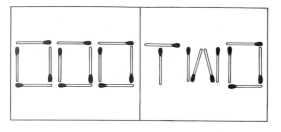

The Mysterious Ball

● *Small wooden ball; thumbtack; thread*

THE TRICK: The magician shows the group the palm of his hand, which is empty. But then he reaches up in the air, and a wooden ball suddenly appears at his finger tips.

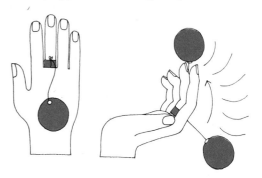

THE SECRET: A small tack is imbedded in the ball beforehand. One end of an inch-long thread is attached to the tack and the other end to a ring which the magician wears on his second finger. When he holds his palm up to the audience, the wooden ball hangs out of sight behind his hand. The magician throws his hand upward with a twisting motion, and the ball swings up so he can catch it on his fingertips. With a little practice, this is a very deceptive illusion.

Where Did It Go?

● *Small ball; handkerchief*

THE TRICK: The magician holds a small ball in his right hand. He then covers his hand with a large handkerchief, and invites other players to reach in under the handkerchief to make sure that the ball is still there. As soon as the last person has felt the ball, the magician whips away the handkerchief and the ball has disappeared. He covers his hand with the handkerchief again, and the other players reach under to make sure the ball is not there. After all the players have done this and agreed that his hand is empty, the magician again snatches away the cloth. This time he has the ball in his hand.

THE SECRET: The magician has a confederate, who is the last person to reach under the handkerchief each time. The first time, he takes the ball away. It is small enough to be hidden in his hand. The second time he replaces the ball. Of course, the other players do not know that he is in cahoots with the magician.

The Powerful Breath

● *Candle; bottles*

THE TRICK: The magician lights a candle and sets it behind a large bottle on a table. He blows against the bottle and the candle on the opposite side goes out. It looks as if the magician has blown directly through the solid bottle.

THE SECRET: If the bottle is round, the magician's breath divides into two air currents that go directly around it and join on the other side to blow out the candle. With practice, this trick may even be done with two or three bottles in a row.

The Strong Straw

● *A bottle; a straw*

THE TRICK: The magician challenges any player to lift an ordinary glass bottle using only a drinking straw. They try, but cannot. Then the magician shows how it can be done.

THE SECRET: He bends the straw near one end so a short section of it is doubled back, and the magician pushes this part of the straw into the bottle. The short section is forced against the side of the bottle, pointing up, and acts as a lever which holds the straw firmly in place when the bottle is lifted. The magician lifts the bottle by raising the long end of the straw.

The Stubborn Napkin

● *Paper napkin; glass of water*

THE TRICK: The magician tightly twists a paper napkin so that it resembles a rope. The magician then invites volunteers to try to tear the twisted napkin in half by pulling directly on the ends. They will not be successful, as most napkins are strong enough to resist this type of pressure. Then the magician takes the twisted napkin and he pulls it apart easily.

THE SECRET: While the others are trying the trick, the magician wets his hands in a glass of water. When he takes the napkin, he holds the center and twists it tighter. By moistening the center of the napkin, he weakens the paper, and it tears easily when he pulls the ends.

The Disappearing Ball

● *Small wooden ball; thumbtack; piece of elastic*

THE TRICK: The magician takes a small ball from his vest pocket and squeezes it between his hands. Suddenly, it disappears.

THE SECRET: There is a tack attached to the ball. Tied to the tack is a length of strong elastic, which runs back under the magician's vest and is looped to the side of his belt. When he shows the ball, he stands with his side toward the audience. When he releases the ball, it is pulled back under his vest by the elastic, which is hidden by his arm. For further camouflage, the elastic should be the same color as the vest. If the magician handles the ball quickly and cleverly, the audience will not be able to detect that it is attached, or even see how it disappears.

The Traveling Ball

● *Ping-Pong ball; black thread*

THE TRICK: The magician holds a small Ping-Pong ball up in the air, and suddenly it seems to travel mysteriously from one hand to the other.

THE SECRET: This trick is done by tying the ends of a black thread, 36 inches in length, to form a loop. The magician holds the loop taut with his forefingers, both hands stretched out as far as the loop will permit. This forms a narrow track along which the ball glides easily. A Ping-Pong ball works well with this trick because it is light in weight, and because its color makes it easily visible to the audience. From a distance, the black thread will not be seen. Considerable practice is needed for this trick.

The Trick Bridge

● *A piece of writing paper; three glasses*

THE TRICK: The magician takes a sheet of strong writing paper and places it over two glasses that are a few inches apart, forming a bridge between them. He tells the other players that he can place a glass upright on this bridge and challenges any other person in the room to try it first. When they do, they soon find out that the paper is not strong enough to hold the weight of the glass. Then the magician successfully performs the trick.

THE SECRET: He takes the same paper and folds it several times lengthwise, creating a pleatlike effect. This strengthens the sheet of paper considerably, and it is easily able to bear the weight of the glass. It's wise to use unbreakable plastic glasses for this trick.

Body Tricks

Sometimes magicians will work with equipment that is no more elaborate than a part of their own or someone else's body, in order to create puzzling effects. The following group of tricks illustrates this phenomenon.

Feeling No Pain

THE TRICK: The magician states to his audience that, as everyone knows, it is most painful to strike the knuckles of a hand against something hard such as the edge of a table. However, he continues, he will demonstrate how he can do that very thing and suffer no pain. Making a hand into a fist he lightly taps his knuckles against the edge of a nearby table. Then, he raises his arm high and brings his fist sweeping down, aimed at the table edge. The knuckles apparently hit the edge in a hard blow as the audience can hear the impact. Yet the magician appears to have suffered no pain.

THE SECRET: As the magician is swinging his fist at the table edge, he opens his hand so that his fingers are extended, just a fraction of a second before the table edge is reached. The finger tips, not the knuckles, hit the table in an almost painless blow. The fingers are immediately contracted into a fist again before the end of the downward sweep. The action is so swift that the audience is convinced that the magician has indeed cracked his knuckles hard without suffering any pain.

The Hypnotized Knee

THE TRICK: The magician announces that he will hypnotize a volunteer's knee so that he will not be able to move one leg in any direction.

THE SECRET: It's all a matter of how the volunteer is directed to stand. The magician places the child with his right side pressed firmly against the wall. He then challenges the volunteer to move his left leg without moving his right side from the wall. Try though he may, the volunteer cannot perform the feat.

Stay There

THE TRICK: "I will hypnotize a boy or girl so that he cannot move at all," says the magician. When a volunteer comes forward the magician seats him in a chair with his arms folded, his head thrown back and his feet extended. Then the magician lightly touches the volunteer's forehead with a finger and says, "You cannot rise! Stay there!" The volunteer tries to rise but cannot—until the magician removes his finger.

THE SECRET: The volunteer's position makes it

virtually impossible for him to rise, for in order to do so he must move his head forward and up. The pressure of the magician's finger prevents him from doing this. So long as the volunteer's arms are crossed and legs extended, he cannot exert any strength at all.

Paralyzed Fingers

THE TRICK: The magician tells the audience that he will paralyze two of the fingers of any volunteer so that they cannot move on their own. THE SECRET: When a volunteer approaches, the magician tells him to press the middle knuckles of one hand against the middle knuckles of the other. Then he says, "Now draw your hands apart," a motion the volunteer can easily perform. Next he has the volunteer move his knuckles together again and raise the ring fingers of both hands so that the tips are touching.

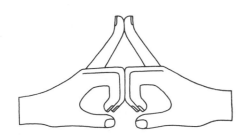

The magician then mutters some "mystical" mumbo jumbo to cast the hypnotic spell. Afterwards, he challenges the volunteer to move the two fingers apart without moving his hands in any way. The volunteer tries, but finds that he cannot move the fingers at all. No hypnosis is involved; it's just that the position of the hands makes it impossible for anyone to move these two fingers.

Removable Thumb

THE TRICK: The magician tells the audience that he is going to separate his own thumb into two halves and then put the pieces together again. THE SECRET: He holds his hands as in Diagram 1. Quickly he hides the visible thumb behind its

palm, as in Diagram 2, while at the same time bringing up his other thumb and crossing it under his index finger to reveal its tip. The illusion is that one thumb has been broken into two pieces. Then the magician reverses the ac-

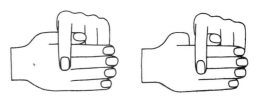

tion to "restore" his thumb to its original form. He repeats the trick quickly several times, in what seems to be sequence of instant thumb breaking and mending. The success of the trick depends on the manual dexterity of the magician and it should be practiced several times before a performance.

Magic Elevator

THE TRICK: A volunteer is seated in a straight chair. Four other volunteers, of about equal size, stand on either side of the seated one—two on a side—facing in. The magician says he will give the four standees power to lift the seated player out of the chair, each using only two fingers. The four are told to clasp their own hands together, leaving only the forefingers extended. Two of the four then put their forefingers under the seated one's knees; the other two put their forefingers under the armpits. At the command "Lift!" the seated one is easily raised into the air.
THE SECRET: Before the act of lifting, all five volunteers count together, "One, two three." After "one," and "two," they all take deep breaths, then expel. After the count of "three," each holds his breath. At this point, the four volunteers place their fingers under the seated player's knees and armpits. Still holding their breath, they lift. The trick works, but it will fail if anyone expels his breath before the seated person is returned to the chair.

A master builder with cards displays this feat of engineering expertise as he constructs a castle worthy of a knight of King Arthur's court.

CHAPTER 6

Quiet Play for Quiet Times

This chapter presents several different kinds of interesting activities
suitable for one or two participants in a limited indoor space. There are
frequent occasions when children are forced to be by themselves, or with only
one or two playmates. Such times may occur when the youngster is sick and
confined to his room or when rain keeps him from going outdoors or keeps
others from visiting him. The child who lives in an apartment without friends
of the same age nearby, or in a house that is at a distance from others,
has a real need for self-directed imaginative activities that he can play
by himself or with only one or two friends. The most desirable kinds of
play activities for young children are those in which they learn to
manipulate simple materials, to explore the environment, to express their
imagination and use their creativity. But, most of all, children should have
lively fun experiences—whether by themselves or with a few friends.

Spelled-out numbers suggest suitable age levels.

Play with Cards

● *Four to ten*

Building cities and palaces out of playing cards
can often keep a youngster busy for hours. Such
play, however, requires considerable manual
dexterity, and if a boy or a girl has not built
with cards before, it may be wise for a parent
to show the child just how the cards can be
balanced against each other. Because one false
move or even too hard breathing can cause an
elaborately constructed card palace to topple,
such projects require both patience and a will-
ingness to accept frustration. However, the rewards of seeing a deck or two of playing cards
transformed into an elaborate model city spread
across the playroom floor are often more than
worth the time and effort required.

Sand Play

● *Two to six*

Young children enjoy playing with sand either
at the beach or in a sand box or sand pile in
a backyard or playground. To begin with, children may simply want to fill pails with sand
and turn them over to build little mounds, or
let the sand run through their fingers or a
strainer. Later on, they may make pies and cakes,
and build roads and tunnels or town and country
scenes, in which they can place toy animals,
people, houses or cars and trucks. Pails, little
shovels and toy sets with molds, and even old
kitchen utensils lead children to more creative
projects with sand. Sand may be collected at the
beach, or coarse construction sand can be bought
at any lumberyard.

Play With Blocks

● *Two to six*

Pre-schoolers usually begin by simply pushing the blocks around, or by placing them on top of each other and then pushing them over, or putting them in different simple formations. Gradually, they begin to build hills, buildings, tunnels and even more complicated structures. Some blocks are rectangular-shaped chunks of wood or heavy cardboard. Solid wooden blocks, however, often come in different shapes, such as circles, semicircles, posts, squares, triangles and arches. These varied shapes permit four-, five- and six-year olds to experiment with interesting constructions. As a general rule, parents should not interfere in simple block-building projects,

beyond suggesting a type of construction project. Children left on their own will often come up with some highly imaginative building construction designs.

Water Play

● *Three to six*

The child should be dressed in a smock or waterproof apron. The kitchen or bathroom sink is filled with water. The child may sit on a high stool, or stand on a sturdy bench. If he is given water toys, or even such regular utensils as funnels, strainers, wooden spoons or pots and pans, he will probably be very happy to play on his own at the sink for a period from 20 minutes to half an hour.

Arts and Crafts Activities

Arts and crafts activities lend themselves well to "quiet times." The most enjoyable types of arts and crafts activities for young children include the following: playing with clay, crayon and chalk drawing, finger painting, easel painting, cutting and pasting paper, papier-mâché, printmaking and soap carving. As in all of children's creative activities, parents should not impose adult standards on artistic projects. Children should be praised and encouraged and should never be criticized because they have distorted form. Their personal observation of the environment and their individual expression of what they see are most important and should be stressed rather than the object's "aesthetic" quality from an adult point of view of the world.

Spelled-out numbers suggest suitable age levels.

Play with Clay

● *Three to twelve*

Young children greatly enjoy working with this type of material—soft enough to squeeze in their hands and mold into shapes. There are two types of clay—hardening and non-hardening—which are available in art and school-supply stores. Clay

may also be bought as dry powder. If it is mixed with water, it will keep soft and can be easily molded. If it is permitted to dry out, it becomes extremely hard. This is the type of clay that can be fired in a kiln after objects are molded. Non-hardening clay has an oil base; it never dries out and can be used again and again. This may be a disadvantage if children create objects that they would like to keep, since the clay is always fairly soft. This type of clay is most often used in schools and is found in most clay sets sold in stores. Since clay tends to be messy—especially wet clay—an oilcloth or plastic cloth should be placed on the surface being used, and children should wear a protective smock or other covering. (An old shower curtain works very well for this.)

At the beginning, young children just like to handle clay: they pound it on a table, squeeze it, flatten it out and roll it into long coils or round balls. A long coil of clay may become a "snake," a "banana," or a "carrot." A ball of clay may be an "apple" or "orange." Gradually, children begin to make a variety of objects which are more or less realistic, such as animals, people, houses and cars or trucks. They may wish to use large nails, toothpicks, or other utensils when making these clay objects.

Besides such objects, older children are often interested in making bowls or simple vases as a beginning form of pottery. At this stage, parents who are somewhat familiar with the craft of pottery might show the children how to build up coils of clay to construct the walls of a bowl or mug. However, for children under the age of nine it is still too early to master a complex method of making clay pots. At this point, the child should work almost entirely on his own, unconcerned with learning formal skills.

Crayon and Chalk Drawing

● *Three to six*

When starting to draw, very young children should be given large wax crayons (the type used in kindergarten), since smaller crayons tend to break in their grasp, and are more difficult to grip. If the parent peels the crayons before giving them out, children will soon learn that by using different parts of the crayon—the point, the flat end and the sides—they can create many varied effects. It is usually a mistake for parents to "teach" young children how to draw faces, animals or other objects in that it tends to discourage them from trying their own efforts.

Instead, the parent should simply encourage children to experiment with lines and scribbles and, possibly, show them how different textures, stippling effects or other patterns may be made with the crayon. Gradually, parents may show ways of drawing simple forms—such as circles, squares, spirals and zigzagging lines—and encourage the youngsters to try creating their own shapes. At first, children are not too aware of colors and are often satisfied with one or two crayons. After a while, they begin to use a fuller range of colors and learn to blend them.

Chalk may also be used for drawing by young children. It creates a somewhat crisper effect, and, though messier (particularly when it crumbles) should be part of children's early art experience. It may be used on a blackboard, if the child has one, or on rough paper.

Children should learn from the very beginning to put the crayons, chalk and paper away neatly and to tidy up the art area; also, just as grown-up artists would do, they should be allowed to hand their finished drawings around the room. The sides of refrigerators make good display areas.

Cutting and Pasting

● *Four to six*

Children enjoy cutting out pictures and pasting them onto sheets of paper or into a scrapbook. They may draw their own designs on colored paper and cut them out, or they may cut pictures from old magazines. As a safety precaution, young children should only be allowed to use blunt-edged scissors. By cutting out pictures of objects, people and interesting backgrounds, children may compose scenes that tell stories.

VARIATION: *The Collage,* in which miscellaneous odds and ends, or parts of other pictures, are pasted up in unusual patterns, is a more advanced kind of art project usually enjoyed by children over the age of five. Children may put together bits of old ribbons, aluminum foil, Christmas cards, fabric, dried leaves, flowers, shells, or just about anything else, to form imaginative collages.

Finger Painting

Finger paints and finger-painting paper (a sturdy stock with a smooth, glossy surface) are available at most art-supply stores, stationery shops and department stores. If, by some chance, you are unable to purchase the paper, smooth shelf paper or even oilcloth will prove a satisfactory substitute. Either a table or the floor will serve as a work area for finger painting.

Finger painting is one of the freest and most creative forms of early childhood art. Not only does it feel good to the child to move his fingers and palms around in the paint, but such maneuverings often result in strikingly good art.

Once the paper is in place and the children are in smocks, the fun begins. Using a cup of cold water, the child thoroughly wets the paper and applies a large blob of one of the colors of paint to the center of his paper. Then, using his fingers, palms and wrists, he spreads it evenly over the entire sheet of paper.

The child soon learns that by using only his hands, he is able to create many different kinds of lines and shapes—provided that the paper is moist enough. With his fingertips he can make thin spiraling or waving lines—one at a time or many together—as well as differently textured dots. By dragging the tips of his fingernails lightly over the paper, he can make fine,

For these youngsters Finger Painting *is a delightfully messy experiment with form and color. A dropcloth protects the floor from the paints.*

delicate lines. He can create heavy effects with the heel and sides of his hand. Because of the hard, glossy surface of the paper, the child can keep wiping out what has been done and starting over.

At first a boy or girl should work with only one or two basic colors, thus avoiding muddy effects. Gradually, more colors can be added, preferably one by one. Through experimentation, the child learns how to mix colors to achieve interesting hues and create fascinating patterns of form and color.

A great part of finger painting's appeal for children is its sloppiness. Digging right into wet, soft paint and pushing it freely around a sheet of paper with fingers, hands and wrists is a delightful experience for youngsters. But because it can be messy, it needs to be supervised. At first, the parent should stand by to explain how to apply the colors and to make sure that the paper is not wrinkled. When a painting is finished, the parent might demonstrate how to lift it carefully by the corners and place it on a newspaper to dry.

Easel Painting

● *Three to six*

An easel, or a large piece of plywood placed on a straight-backed kitchen chair, is set up in the center of the work area. (Since easel painting can be messy, the work area should be protected with old newspapers or sheets of plastic, and the "artist" should wear a smock or one of his father's old shirts.) Several pieces of sturdy paper, about 18" by 24" should be thumbtacked to the easel so the child can tear off each picture as he completes it.

Large-sized, inexpensive bristle brushes with long handles and ready-made poster paints in the primary colors may be used. Instead of pre-mixed poster paint, dry powdered pigment (available at art supply stores) may be mixed with water and placed in small glass jars with tightly fitting lids. The powdered pigment is

actually preferable for two reasons: it is much less expensive and, by mixing his own paints, a child learns how water affects hue. A water pan for cleaning brushes and a rag for wiping them should also be furnished.

In general, children should be discouraged from trying oil or water-color paints until they have first demonstrated their skill in handling brushes and poster paint at the easel.

Papier-Mâché

● *Six to twelve*

A piece of newspaper is torn up into long, narrow strips. The child soaks the strips thoroughly in a bowl or pail that contains a mixture of water and flour. The soak should be runny in consistency but still thick enough so that it is sticky. The strips are then placed, one at a time, upon a base until the child has the form he wants. If, for example, a hand-puppet were being made, the base might well be a small rubber ball with a hole for a finger cut into it. As the child builds up the form he molds a nose and ears and then, when the basic shape of the puppet head is completed, he allows it to dry. After the head has completely dried, the child can begin the painting of the construction with poster paints.

Papier-mâché can be molded over almost any base, including Styrofoam shapes, dolls, little toy animals or hardened clay objects. A wire clothes hanger or chicken wire may also be used as a base, by bending it into the required shape. In some instances a child will want to remove the base after the mache form has dried. This is easily accomplished by sawing through the papier-mâché, removing the base and then gluing the cut edges of the papier-mâché form together again. A mat knife will usually suffice for this task. Because of the sharpness of the knife, only an adult should use it. There is practically no limit to the variety of designs and objects that can be modeled in this simple way, and the very simplicity of the process makes this kind of sculpting particularly attractive to children.

Other Crafts Projects

Materials found around the home may be used in many ingenious crafts projects. Some adult supervision may be necessary for such projects, as they often involve cutting with a knife or sharp scissors and usually require a greater degree of manipulative skill than the more basic crafts projects previously described. Sculpture is one of the most popular activities of this type.

Spelled-out numbers suggest suitable age levels.

Coat-Hanger Mobiles

● *Eight to ten*

Children may improvise simple *stationary* mobiles by taking pieces of wire coat hangers and bending them into different shapes with a pair of pliers. The pieces of hanger are then imbedded in a base of clay. Lengths of thread, pieces of paper, buttons, beads or other small, light objects may be hung from the wires in an interesting pattern. *Hanging* mobiles can be made by hooking two or three coathangers together—attaching the top one to an overhead light fixture. The hangers may be wrapped with brightly colored ribbon to match the color scheme of the room, and metallic paper cutouts may be fixed to the various hanger levels with different lengths of white thread.

Potato Prints

● *Five to ten*

A large potato is cut in half, with a smooth, flat cut. The design that is to be put on the cut potato surface is first drawn on a sheet of paper and then copied onto the surface of the potato with a soft pencil. (If there are any letters or numbers in the design, they should be drawn in reverse, because the process of printing will then turn them on the right side.) The area of the potato around the design is then scraped out with a small knife so that the design that is to be printed will protrude up about one-quarter or one-eighth of an inch. Using a small

rubber roller, the raised area is covered with poster paint. A sheet of drawing paper is laid on the potato surface. When the back of the paper is rolled with a clean rubber roller, the design is transferred to the paper.

This type of block printing may be done by children as young as five or six with parental supervision. Older children (nine- or ten-year-olds) may do this project themselves.

Cereal-Box Sculpture

● *Five to eight*

A child may improvise an old *castle* by using a round oatmeal container. The top is removed and the bottom cut away. Then doorways, windows and battlements are cut where needed. The finished project, colored with poster paints

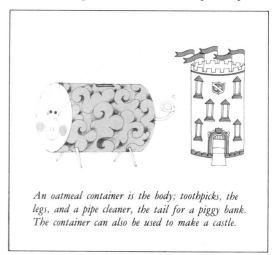

An oatmeal container is the body; toothpicks, the legs, and a pipe cleaner, the tail for a piggy bank. The container can also be used to make a castle.

and bedecked with streamers made of ribbon, is an extremely real-looking castle that can be used with toy knights and horses. Using the same kind of oatmeal container, a child can make a *piggy bank*. A slot big enough to admit pennies or nickels is cut in one side of the container. Toothpicks are fitted into the carton's opposite side for legs. A coiled pipe cleaner inserted at the back becomes the tail, and the piggy's face is drawn on in front. To make the piggy bank even more attractive, the oatmeal box may be covered with bright paper.

Chain of Figures

● *Five to nine*

A paper chain of figures is very easily made. A 12- to 14-inch long strip of paper is folded in half and then folded again twice more. The right- or left-hand side of a figure is then cut along the folded edge of the paper, making sure to leave at least one place connected. It is this linked portion of the figure that holds the entire strip together. When the paper is unfolded, it has been transformed into a long chain of figures. Once parents have demonstrated this project a few times, children should be able to do it themselves and may also learn to make chains of birds, animals, flowers or other simple objects.

Jigsaw Puzzles

● *Four to eight*

Children can make their own jigsaw puzzles with a sheet of cardboard and a large colored picture cut from a magazine. The picture is pasted on the sheet of cardboard with rubber cement. Lines are drawn on the back dividing the cardboard into irregularly-shaped pieces, making sure that each piece of the puzzle is different, so the pieces can only fit together in one way. The child then cuts along these lines.

Homemade Motorboat

● *Eight to twelve* ● *Coping saw*

The making of a rubber-band-driven motorboat is a beginning carpentry project. A coping saw is used to cut a pointed end, or prow, in the top of a cigar box or similar sheet of wood. From the other end, a section resembling an inverted U is cut out of the stern. A rubber band is now looped over the two ends and a small piece of wood, such as a stick from an ice cream bar, is inserted between the rubber strands to form a propeller. The propeller is twisted backwards several times to wind it up. When the boat is placed in a tub of water and the propeller released, the boat will surge forward.

A chain of charming figures can be created with a pair of scissors and a sheet of paper folded accordion-style. The method of cutting is described in the text.

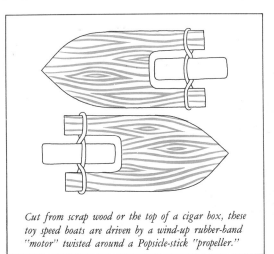

Cut from scrap wood or the top of a cigar box, these toy speed boats are driven by a wind-up rubber-band "motor" twisted around a Popsicle-stick "propeller."

Soap Sculpture

● *Eight to twelve*

One side of a cake of soap should be lightly scraped (using a small kitchen knife), so it is absolutely flat and smooth. It is best to use a large rectangular piece of white floating soap that is as fresh as possible. If the soap is too old, it will be dry and brittle; if it is a smaller oval or round shape, it will be difficult to work with. The object that is to be carved is drawn on a sheet of paper, and this outline is then copied on the smooth side of the cake of soap. The knife can be used to cut away large sections of soap and get the carving down to the approximate form that is desired. A nail file, an orange stick and similar small implements are used in rounding off the sculpture and in carving smaller details. When the soap sculpture is finished, it should be allowed to dry for a day or two and then be carefully polished with a paper napkin to develop an ivory-smooth and shiny surface.

Paper-and-Pencil Games and Puzzles

There are a number of activities requiring only a piece of paper and a pencil that are highly enjoyable pastimes for children who are shut in for one reason or another. A number of the puzzles and games that follow are essentially solitary activities. These, however, can be turned into contests when more than one child is available. Other activities require the participation of at least two players. All are quiet pastimes that challenge the mental prowess of children rather than their physical strength and stamina.

Spelled-out numbers suggest suitable age levels.

Dots and Squares

● *Seven to twelve*

A large rectangle of dots is drawn and laid out in rows. There should be at least twelve or fifteen rows in each direction. Two players take turns drawing lines which connect any two dots, either vertically or horizontally. The object of the game is for one player to complete as many small squares as he can, while trying to prevent his opponent from doing the same thing. Whenever a player sees a place in the diagram where three sides of a square have been completed, he may draw the fourth side and put his initial in the box. Whenever a player completes a square, he draws another line. Thus, when the diagram gets fairly well covered with lines, he may find that he is able to complete several squares without stopping. For his last line he may then have to draw the third side of a square, giving his opponent the chance to fill in some boxes. The trick of winning is to draw lines that will not give the opponent a chance to score. When all the lines have been drawn, the player with the most squares filled in and initialed is the winner.

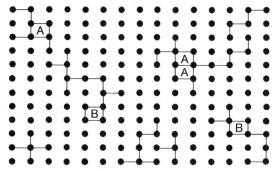

Tictactoe

● *Six to twelve*

A design is drawn, consisting of intersecting parallel lines. Players take turns drawing circles and crosses in the boxes. One player draws circles, and the other one draws crosses, or X's. They alternate until one player has succeeded in getting three circles or three X's in a row—either horizontally, vertically or diagonally. If a player does this, he gets one point. Usually, the game is played several times, and the child with the most points at the end is the winner. Since it is an advantage to go first, the player who lost the preceding game is usually permitted to make the first move.

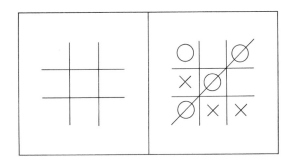

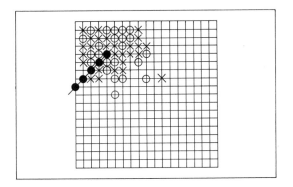

VARIATION: In *Gomuku,* a popular Japanese pastime, a playing grid is drawn with 19 vertical lines and 19 horizontal lines. One player chooses to use O's, and the other player chooses X's. They take turns drawing X's or O's on the intersections of the lines. The first player to get five X's or O's in a straight line is the winner.

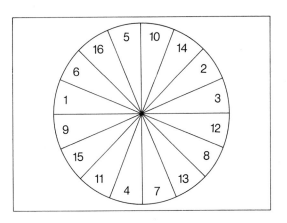

Roulette Wheel

● *Six to nine*

A large circle is drawn on a sheet of cardboard, using a compass or a piece of string tied around a pencil. The circle is divided into equal-sized segments and each segment is given a number. The circle is then fixed to a piece of plywood with a nail through the center. The center hole should be a little larger than the nail, so the "wheel" will spin easily. Then, with his eyes closed, the first player spins the wheel sharply. With his eyes still closed, he jabs a pencil down on the wheel. Opening his eyes, he writes his initial in the segment where the pencil landed. There are two ways of scoring the game: A player may get credit for the numerical value of the segment, and the first player to reach a set number of points is the winner. Or, the player who initials the most segments is the declared winner. In scoring this second way, a player receives a point only if his pencil lands in a segment that has not been initialed previously.

Name the States

● *Seven to ten*

On a map of the United States, several states with recognizable outlines—such as New York, California, Florida, Texas—are traced and numbered. They are then transferred onto a large sheet of paper in a random pattern. Two children compete (using separate sheets with the same states on each) to see who can correctly name the greatest number of states in the shortest time. Each correct identification is worth one point.

VARIATION: In *Name the Provinces,* outlines of several Canadian provinces are traced and numbered. The same rules as the ones above apply.

Find the Fort

● *Seven to ten*

A small square with an opening in one side is drawn in the center of a sheet of paper. The square is the fort, and the opening is its gate. The numbers from 1 to 15 are then scattered at random all around the paper, with a small

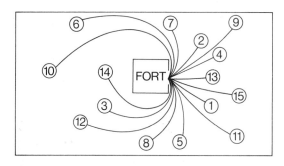

circle around each number. The numbers represent outlying settlements under attack. The object of the game is to draw a line from each settlement—beginning with number one and then number two, and so on—to the gate of the fort without touching or crossing the path from any other settlement. One penalty point is given for each trail crossed.

This game may be played singly or between two players. In the latter case, each player makes up a sheet for his opponent to solve. The player with the fewest penalty points when all settlements have been linked to the forts wins.

VARIATION: In *Pairing Numbers* a sheet is prepared with <u>two</u> sets of numbers from 1 to 15 scattered around it. No number should be near its paired number. The purpose of the game is

to draw a line from each number to its pair—starting with number one, then number two,

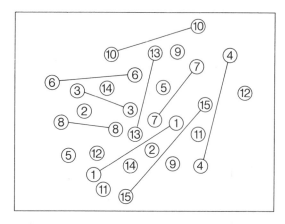

and so on—without crossing any other line. This game is generally played with two children taking turns drawing lines. The first player who is unable to draw a line connecting two numbers without crossing another, loses the contest.

Shortest Crossword Puzzle

● *Seven to ten*

THE TASK: A crossword puzzle is drawn, with four vertical and four horizontal squares. Players are given one clue—that the *down* clues all have the same answer—and five minutes to solve the puzzle. The definitions are as follows:
Across: 1) insects; 5) organs of sight; 6) to torment or tantalize; 7) comfort and relaxation.
Down: 1) what lions do; 2) what rats do; 3) what dogs do; 4) what mosquitoes do.

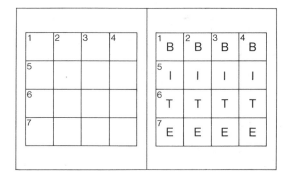

THE SOLUTION: The *across* answers are bees (B's), eyes (I's), tease (T's), and ease (E's). The *down* answers are all bite.

Hangman

● *Seven to eleven*

The "hangman" draws a gallows, or upside-down L, at the top of a piece of paper and writes the alphabet across the bottom. Then, he thinks of a word containing five or more letters and writes down as many dashes as the word has letters above the alphabet at the bottom of the page. The opponent tries to guess the word by

calling out one letter at a time. If he makes a correct guess, the hangman writes in the letter wherever it belongs in the word. If the opponent guesses a letter that is not in the word, the hangman draws a head below the gallows and also crosses out the letter in the alphabet, so it will not be guessed again.

Every time a correct letter is called, it is written in the word. Every time a wrong letter is called, a new section is added to the figure under the gallows. (They are added in ten stages in the following order: 1. the head; 2. the neck; 3. the body; 4. the two arms; 5. the two hands; 6. the two legs; 7. the two feet; 8. the nose, eyes and mouth; 9. the two ears; 10. the noose.) If the opponent guesses the word correctly before the entire figure can be drawn and the noose put in, he is the winner, and becomes the new hangman. If not, the hangman is the winner and he takes another turn.

Non-Stop Triangle

● *Seven to twelve*

THE TASK: Three small triangles are drawn within a large triangle, without going over any line more than once or lifting the pencil.

THE SOLUTION: Start at A, go down to B and then up to C. Draw line to D and then down to A. Go up to E, down to F and across to G. To complete the puzzle, go up to H, down to I and then across to A again.

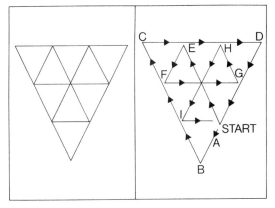

VARIATION: The *Non-Stop House* can also be drawn with only one line. Start at A and, without taking the pencil off the paper, follow the route shown, moving from letters A to I in alphabetical order.

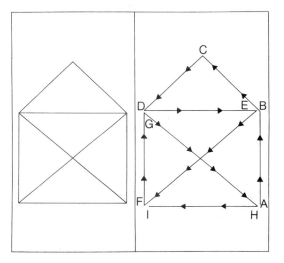

Letter Jigsaw

● *Four to seven*

A large letter is carefully drawn on a sheet of paper and then cut up into several smaller pieces. Two exact copies of the puzzle are prepared. Two children compete to see who can correctly re-assemble the letter in the shortest period of time. Several different letters may be prepared, with each letter jig-saw puzzle being a separate contest; the child who wins the most contests wins the entire game. For four- and five-year-olds, it is advisable to indicate on the puzzle pieces the letter of the alphabet to be formed.

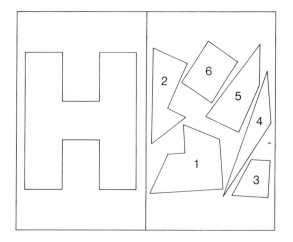

Hit Every Dot

● *Seven to twelve*

THE TASK: First a large square, subdivided into 16 smaller squares, is drawn with a dot in the center of each square. Players must then draw six straight lines, without lifting the pencil from the paper, that will pass through each of the 16 black dots.

THE SOLUTION: Start at A, go down to B and across to C. Go up to D, down to E. To finish, go across to F, and back up to G. Part of the secret is to let the lines travel outside of the diagram itself.

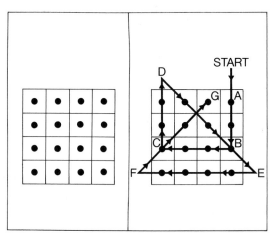

Rows of Twelve

● *Eight to twelve*

THE TASK: Seven circles are drawn. Players must fill in the circles with the numbers 1 to 7, so that each of the five rows of three circles (two horizontal, two diagonal, and one vertical) adds up to exactly 12. No number can be used in more than one circle and all seven numbers are used.

THE SOLUTION: The numbers in the two horizontal rows are 6, 1, 5 and 3, 7, 2. The numbers in the two diagonal rows are 6, 4, 2 and 5, 4, 3. The numbers in the one vertical row are 1, 4 and 7.

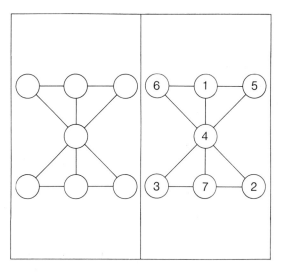

Card Games for Children

Cards are a popular form of quiet play for all ages, but there are many card games which, because of their simple rules, are especially appropriate for young children. Although card playing is primarily a mental form of recreation involving observation and logical thinking, many of the children's card games which follow demand quick physical action and actually become an exciting form of play.

Spelled-out numbers suggest suitable age levels.

Seven of a Kind

● *Six to ten*

THE DEAL: This game is played with three, four or five players. The deck is prepared according to the number of players: for three players, a deck of twenty-one cards with seven cards in each of three suits (hearts, diamonds, spades); for four players, a deck of twenty-eight cards with seven cards in each of the four suits; for five players, a deck of thirty-five cards with eight or nine cards in each of four suits. The deck is shuffled, and seven cards are dealt to each player.

THE PLAY: One at a time, each player passes a card to the player on his left, each player discarding those cards least likely to make him a winner.

THE SCORING: The first child to collect seven cards of one suit wins. While playing the game, children quickly learn to keep those cards that look as if they might develop into strong suits, while passing along cards from other suits.

Go Boom

● *Five to nine*

THE DEAL: Although this game works best with three or four players, it may be played successfully with two. Seven cards are dealt to each player. The remaining cards are placed in a pack face down on the table.

THE PLAY: The first player begins by putting one of his cards on the table, face up. The player on his left must play a card that matches it, either in value or in suit. For example, if the card is a six of diamonds, he must put down either a diamond or a six. If he cannot, he must draw from the pack until he finds a diamond or a six. Then the next player to the left puts down another matching card, and the game continues in this manner.

THE SCORING: The winner is the first player to get rid of all the cards in his hand. If no player has won by the time the last card in the pack has been drawn, the discards may be re-shuffled and the drawing continued until a boy or girl wins. Alternatively, the game can end when the last card from the pack is drawn, with the player holding the fewest cards declared the winner.

Go Fish

● *Five to nine*

THE DEAL: This game is played in groups of two to five players. If two or three children are playing, they are dealt seven cards apiece. If four or five children are playing, they are dealt five cards each. The remaining cards, the "Fish Pond," are placed face-down on the table.

THE OBJECT: Players try to build sets of four cards of a kind, such as four tens, four threes, four jacks, etc.

THE PLAY: After looking at his hand to determine which cards he should try to build up initially, the first player asks the player on his left for any cards of a particular number. For example, he might ask, "Do you have any fives?" or "Do you have any jacks?" If the player on the left has one or more of the card requested, he must give them to the first player. If he does not have the card in question, he says "Go Fish."

The first player then draws a card from the pack. If the card he picks up happens to be the card he requested, he shows it to the others, puts it in his hand, and asks the next player for another card. If the card he picks up is not the one he requested, he simply puts it in his hand, and the next player takes a turn. The action continues in this manner, with all of the players taking turns. Whenever a player has put together a set of four of a kind, he places it face-up on the table in front of him. He then takes an extra turn in asking for another card.

THE SCORING: The winner may be determined in two ways. In one form of the game, the first player to discard all of his cards, by building sets, is the winner. In a second form of the game after the Fish Pond has been used up, the player who has collected the most sets wins.

Pig
● *Six to eight*

THE DEAL: From three to six children are needed to play this game. A deck is prepared with four cards of a kind for each player. (If there are five players, the deck has twenty cards—four aces, four kings, four queens, four jacks and four tens.) The prepared deck is then shuffled and dealt, each player receiving four cards.

THE PLAY: Each player attempts to get four cards of a kind or to notice when some other player gets four of a kind in his hand. Each player looks at his own hand and, at a signal, passes an unwanted card, face down, to the player on his left. He in turn receives a card from the player on his right. This action continues until one player collects four cards of a kind. The successful player then stops passing and quickly puts his forefinger on his nose. As soon as another player notices, he stops passing and also puts his finger on his nose. The last child to realize what is happening and to put his finger on his nose is the "pig."

VARIATION: In *Donkey* any child who gets four of a kind, instead of placing his finger on his nose, simply places the cards face down on the table. As other players notice what he is doing, they do the same. The last player to put his cards on the table becomes the "donkey."

Slap Jack
● *Five to eight*

THE DEAL: Two or three children sit close together around a small table. A well-shuffled deck is placed face down on the table. In turn, each player takes a card from the deck and puts it face-up in another pile directly in front of him.

THE PLAY: Whenever a jack appears, all the children must clap their hands overhead two times, and then slap the jack. The child who does this first wins the jack and any other cards in the face-up pile underneath. The action continues until all the jacks have been taken. The child who captures the last jack also wins any cards that may be remaining in both the face-down and face-up deck.

THE SCORING: When all the cards are used up, players count their piles, and write their scores on a sheet of paper. After the game has been played three times, the player who has collected the most cards is the winner.

Concentration
● *Six to twelve*

THE DEAL: This game tests alertness and memory. The cards are placed face-down on the table.

THE PLAY: Each player, in turn, overturns two cards. If they are the same (two fives, two jacks, etc.) he keeps them, making a pile in front of him. He then is given a second turn. If he does not overturn a pair, he turns the cards face down, leaving them in the same spot. The next player to the left takes a turn and the action continues until all the cards have been collected.

THE SCORING: The trick of the game, of course, is to remember what cards were turned up and their position on the board. This becomes progressively easier as fewer cards are left. The winner is the player with the most cards.

Earl of Coventry

● *Six to ten*

THE DEAL: After the shuffle and cut, the cards are dealt, one at a time, until all cards are dealt out. Any number can participate, and hands need not be equal.

THE PLAY: The player to the dealer's left puts any card, face up, on the table, announcing, "There's as good an ace (or six, or jack, etc.) as can be." If the player to his left has a card of this same denomination, he lays it down, saying, "There's one as good as he." If he does not, the next player to the left has a chance to play. Going in order around the table, the holder of the third card plays it, saying, "There's the best of three." The holder of the fourth card then plays, announcing, "There's the Earl of Coventry." The player of the fourth card leads on the next turn. The play continues in order from the leader's left. The first player to get rid of his cards wins.

War

● *Six to twelve*

THE DEAL: Two players sit facing each other at a small table. One player shuffles the deck and deals out 26 cards to his opponent and 26 to himself, thus dividing the deck into halves.

THE PLAY: Both children turn their top cards over at the same time. The child with the high card takes both and puts them under his stack. (In this game the ace is low and the king is high.) If the two cards turned up are the same (two sixes or two queens, for example), "war" is declared. Each child then turns up one more card, and the player with the high card of that pair takes all four cards. If again the cards are the same, it's "double war," and two additional cards are turned up, with the player who has

the high card of the pair taking all three pairs and putting them at the bottom of his deck. The game goes on in this manner until one player has captured all the cards—which may take quite awhile.

VARIATION: In *Triple War* three players are each dealt 17 cards, and the odd card is discarded. On signal, the three children turn up their top cards, and the player with the high card takes in all three, placing them at the bottom of his deck. If all three cards turned up have the same value, the players wage war as above. If two cards match and the third card is higher, the boy or girl holding the latter wins all three. If the two matching cards are higher than the third, the players whose cards match wage war, the winner taking in all the cards including the third player's card.

Old Maid

● *Six to eleven*

THE DEAL: Three queens are removed from a deck of cards, and the remaining queen becomes the "old maid." Three, four or five players sit in a circle, and a boy or girl deals out all the cards, one by one. Because there are only 49 cards in the deck, one player will wind up with one extra card, or fewer cards, each time.

THE PLAY: Each child looks at his hand, takes out all pairs and puts them face-up in the center of the table. Then the player on the dealer's left holds out his hand, face-down, to the player on his left, who takes one card and puts it in his own hand. If that card makes a pair with one of his own cards, the child puts the two cards in the center along with the other pairs. The second player then turns to the next player on the left and the action is repeated. The game goes on in this manner until all pairs have been matched and discarded in the center. Because there is no queen to pair up with the old maid, that card will be the last one left.

THE SCORING: During the game the old maid will probably pass from hand to hand, but the loser is the player left with the solitary queen.

Marble Games

Although marble games are usually played outdoors on the pavement, they may also be played indoors. Here are some interesting marble games that can be played in a small area with a limited number of players. The generally approved method of shooting a marble is to kneel, hold the marble between the thumb and forefinger—with knuckles resting on the ground—and then propel the marble by flicking the thumb forward.

Numerals indicate the number of players. Spelled-out numbers suggest suitable age levels.

Piggy

● *2 to 6* ● *Five to eight*

FORMATION: A saucer is placed on the floor, and a "pitch" line is drawn about ten feet away. Each player is given five marbles.

ACTION: The players take turns shooting their marbles from the pitch line, trying to make them hit the saucer. After all the marbles have been shot in this way, the players again take turns shooting the marbles from where they rest. If a player succeeds in hitting the saucer, he continues to shoot. When he misses, the next player takes a turn. The first player to hit the saucer with all five of his marbles wins the game.

Ringers

● *2 to 6* ● *Six to twelve*

FORMATION: A circle—ten feet in diameter— is drawn in chalk on a wood, tile or cement floor. Two straight lines are also drawn tangent to the circle and opposite each other. One is the "lag" line, the other the "pitch" line. Thirteen marbles are placed, about three inches apart, in a cross formation in the center of the circle. Before the game begins the contestants determine the order of play by each kneeling in turn at the pitch line and shooting his shooter marble toward the lag line. The boy or girl whose shooter comes to rest closest to the lag line will take the first shot, the player whose shooter is the next closest is the second to play, and so on.

ACTION: The purpose of the game is to knock the marbles in the center cross out of the ring. The first player takes his shot and if he knocks one of the target marbles out, he shoots again. If, however, his shooter comes to rest either inside or outside the ring without knocking one of the target marbles out, the next player takes his turn. The second player repeats the action and may get a second turn if his shooter knocks a target marble out of the ring or if it knocks an opponent's shooter—that has come to rest inside the circle—out of the ring.

After the initial shot, a player makes subsequent shots from the point where his marble has come to rest, if the shooter is inside the circle. If it lands outside, the player may shoot from any point that is the same distance from the center as where the marble came to rest. The game continues until all the marbles in the cross are shot outside the ring. The winner is the player who hits the greatest number of marbles out of the circle.

Roll 'Em Through

● *2 to 6* ● *Six to twelve*

FORMATION: Five rectangular cutouts of different sizes are made along one side of a wooden cigar box, which is then placed on a smooth surface floor about 15 feet from .the pitch line. Each cutout has a point value from one, for the largest, to five, for the smallest.

ACTION: Players each have five marbles, and, taking turns, they kneel at the pitch line and try to shoot into the cutouts. The player who accumulates the highest number of points wins.

Marble Golf

● *2 to 6* ● *Six to twelve*

FORMATION: Nine checkers, or similar objects, are placed around the room to resemble a nine-hole golf course. Each checker has a number from 1 to 9. (The numbers are drawn in crayon and taped or glued on the checkers.) Some pieces of furniture may be used as obstacles or hazards.

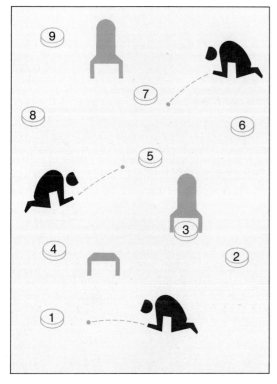

ACTION: The players each have one marble, and, starting from the same spot, they take turns shooting trying to hit the checkers in order. The game may be scored on a "hole-by-hole" basis; the player who hits the checker with the fewest shots wins a point for that hole. At the end of the game, the player with the most points is the winner. Another way of scoring is to keep a count of the total number of shots a player must take to complete the course—the low score for the nine-hole course winning the *Marble Golf* game.

Shooting the Ring

● *2 to 8* ● *Six to ten*

FORMATION: A circle about eight feet in diameter is drawn with chalk on a wood, tile or cement floor. Outdoors, a stick may be used to scratch out a circle on hard, bare ground. Each player lays one marble on the rim of the circle. The marbles are spaced evenly along the circumference. A shooting line is drawn two yards from the ring. Every player has a shooter, a jumbo-sized marble which cannot be lost during play.

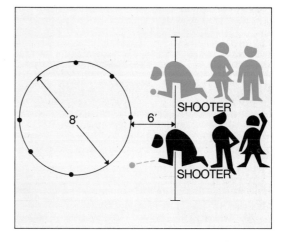

ACTION: Players first determine the order of turns by rolling their shooters from the line toward the center of the circle. The player whose shooter lands closest to the center of the ring takes the first turn; the player whose shot is next closest takes the second, and so on. The first player aims his shot from the shooting line. Subsequent shots are taken from the point where the marble stopped. The first player tries to hit one of the marbles on the circle's rim and knock it outside the circle. If he succeeds, and his shooter also falls outside the circle, he wins the marble he hit and continues to shoot. If he fails, he adds a marble from his own stock to the rim and relinquishes his turn to the next player. The game goes on in this manner until all marbles on the rim have been won, and the player who has accumulated the most marbles during the game is the winner of the contest.

Fun For Teens

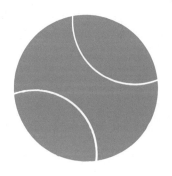

And Grownups

SECTION II

CHAPTER 7

How to Lead a Game Group

Games are great fun! That is the primary reason why they are played and why they have continued to survive in an era when there are so many other forms of leisure-time pursuits to claim our attention. Yet, unfortunately, certain games are not always fun for everyone concerned, and the game leader has the responsibility of trying to remedy this situation.

The nervous little boy, the overly plump little girl, the self-conscious or badly coordinated man or woman can be made miserably unhappy when forced into joining an activity that may bring attention to a real or imagined disability. It is the job of a game leader, whether he be a parent or a professional in the field, to be on the alert for such problems and to do something about them.

Creating an Atmosphere

The first mark of a successful game session—and it doesn't really matter whether that session is a small get-together of adults or a birthday party for six-year-olds—is an atmosphere of relaxation. In general, a good way to establish this atmosphere is with an informal mixer or icebreaker game. There are a number of such games described in Chapter Two (for children) and Chapter Eleven (for teenagers and adults).

The point of mixers and icebreakers is to put people into contact with one another in such a way that the usual fumblings over introductions are avoided. They give the shy person a frame of reference within which he can move to meet other people. In other words, the mixer takes the burden of responsibility for meeting people off the individual guest, because the act of meeting becomes a game in itself.

In most situations, a game leader will find that a good follow-up to the mixers are a few group contests. The mixers will cause the guests to mingle, but some may still feel a bit of tension. The group contests, in which mistakes are shared by a team rather than made the responsibility of an individual, may very well help relax the shy and uncertain guest. So long as the pressure to excel is kept muted, those who lack self-confidence are usually able to play with the same enthusiasm as the most self-assertive.

Problem Guests

In leading a game, the host, game leader or parent will sooner or later be confronted with rather serious personality problems from his guests. These occur more obviously in the young, but, they are far from rare among adults.

A typical personality problem is the one presented by the bad loser. If he is a child, he may put on so violent a tantrum as to disrupt the entire party. A similar case is that of the overexcitable child who, can turn ordinarily well-behaved youngsters into a pack of rampaging rioters. Finally, in this category falls the cheater: the youngster who believes that winning is all important and that cheating at a game is perfectly acceptable so long as he isn't caught.

These problems cannot be ignored by a game leader, because such personality traits can adversely affect all of the guests. In most cases, the bad loser and the over-excited child are so gripped by the enthusiasm of the moment that they are not really aware of what they are doing. The group leader, by swinging smoothly into another type of game—perhaps a quieter, non-competitive one, such as a group sing—can sooth injured feelings and quiet raucous emotions. It is *not* a good idea to try to quiet a children's party that is getting out of hand by immediately serving food. In an over-stimulated atmosphere, hot dogs, baked beans, potato salad and the like may easily turn into missiles thrown back and forth—thus making a bad situation ten times worse.

As for the boy or girl who cheats, the game leader must remember two things: The cheating must stop, and the offender is a child. Whatever the provocation, no one has the right to humiliate a small guest before his friends. During a game, the leader, in his capacity as a referee, can quietly point out that there has been an infraction of the rules; he can award a point to the child or team against which the offense was made. Usually, this is sufficient to put a cheater in his place. If a child continues to cheat, however, the game leader should await an opportune moment for a quiet "man-to-man" talk. The child should not be called out in the middle of the game—thus being made an object of derision; a short break between games usually affords a moment or two for a personal conversation. If all else fails, the game leader might point out to the consistent offender that a continuation of anti-social behavior means that he will not be invited again.

Handicapped Guests

The handicapped person, such as the stutterer, is in an extremely vulnerable situation and should be subtly protected by the game leader. Word or talk games are to be avoided if at all possible. In the case of the chubby youngster

who is unable to tag others in a chasing game, the leader should bend the rules in such a way that the child does not remain a chaser for more than a minute or two.

There is no game from *Hide-and-Seek* to *Baseball* with rules so inflexible that they cannot be modified to suit the abilities and desires of the participants. After all, a game exists for the players—not the players for the game. A parent, a host or a game leader should certainly remember that people—from the smallest children to the oldest adults—have different talents. No one will excel in every type of activity, but each person *will* excel in some type of activity! Thus, it is the game leader's job to make sure that there is a sufficient variety of activities so that every guest will have a real chance to display his individual talents. In short, the role of game leader clearly requires a combination of patience, tact, observation and skill in dealing with a wide variety of personality types. This is true whether the occasion is a child's birthday party, a Parent-Teacher Association get-together or a large community affair with a hundred or more in attendance.

Selecting the Games

The first task of the game leader in drawing up a schedule of activities is to consider the nature of the group and the circumstances under which the games are to be played. To do this, the game leader must be thoroughly familiar with the pertinent details in advance. Is the occasion a class picnic, a family party, a teen-ager's social? How many people are expected? Is the affair to be held outdoors in a backyard, at a playground, in a park or at the beach? Or will it be indoors in a playroom, a gymnasium or a church hall? Is there a record player available; are there balls and bats or other sports equipment? Once the leader has the answers to such questions, he can begin to select activities suitable to the group or the event. Of all the questions, the most important has to do with the age level of the participants.

THREE- TO FIVE-YEAR-OLDS: Up to the age of three or four or five, children are usually most interested in individual activities or small-group imaginative play—with toys, dolls, clay, sand, water and arts and crafts materials. Their capacity for organized games is very limited. Youngsters in nursery school and kindergarten, however, do enjoy simple singing games or action games, such as *Tag* and *Simon Says*.

SIX- TO NINE-YEAR-OLDS: In selecting activities for this age group, it is best to pick active group games with easily understandable rules: relays, tag and chasing games, circle ball games and other games described in Chapter One. Guessing and dramatic games, as well as stunts and simple novelty contests, are also suited to this age level. Because of the short attention span of youngsters in the primary grades, instructions should be kept brief. Usually boys and girls in this age group are willing to play the same games together, although some may balk if they are compelled to take partners of the opposite sex. Thus, it is best to keep a party or game session as informal as possible.

Children between the ages of six and nine are apt to become easily excited when they are over-stimulated. To maintain effective control of the group, it is important to pick games that do not encourage wildness or roughness. At the same time, games should be selected that give each child an opportunity to shine. Games like *Circle Relay, Bucket Ball* and *Red Light* are quite suitable.

TEN- TO TWELVE-YEAR-OLDS: Youngsters between the ages of ten and twelve are both physically and mentally equipped to tackle much more difficult games than their younger brothers and sisters. They are able to play all of the complicated or strenuous activities described in Chapter One. Their range of knowledge is also broader than younger children's, and they are able to grasp the point of mental games and respond to the challenge of quizzes or word games within their range of interest. Children in this age group are already reasonable beings and not nearly so likely to become overly excited as those just a year or two younger.

Although boys and girls in this age group tend to resist group activities with those of the opposite sex, under some circumstances, such as birthday parties, they are willing to take part in coed games. Pre-teen-agers are apt to be highly competitive and will throw themselves into games which involve either a physical or mental challenge. A number of games of this type should always be included.

TEEN-AGERS: In terms of physical ability, or the knowledge required to play any of the quizzes or mental games described in Chapters Eleven, Twelve and Thirteen, teenagers are comparable to adults. Special care should be taken, however, to avoid selecting games that they might resent as being too childish. Humorous stunts and novelty contests are likely to capture their interest. Teenagers usually resist adult leadership and supervision. When teen-age programs are planned, it is a good idea to have the young people themselves select the activities. However, it is important to have adult leadership available if it is needed and requested.

ADULTS: This group, particularly middle-aged married couples, are generally not too interested in physical recreational pursuits. Naturally, there are those who enjoy *Tennis, Badminton* and other vigorous outdoor activities; yet the majority of adults beyond 50 or so are much more receptive to quiet card games, social mixers or mental contests and stunts, such as *Twenty Questions*. Even so, it is possible, if done carefully, to lead a game session to fairly lively activities and to have adults take part with enjoyment. Lawn games, such as *Croquet,* where strategy plays a larger role than stamina and speed, are activities that can often stimulate and enliven an outdoor adult party.

OLDER ADULTS: In selecting games for much older persons, particularly "senior citizens" in their late sixties and beyond, a game leader should first think of the physical disabilities that many of the guests may have. It is true that many elderly persons continue to be physically active and strong for years past retirement age, yet every group in this age range has members who have heart trouble, poor eyesight, hearing impairment or some other ailment. Active stunts might lead to over-exertion or to the risk of slipping and injury. It is important to remember that an elderly man or woman may easily feel humiliated if it becomes apparent that he or she is no longer able to perform feats of physical exertion. Although games that require a slight degree of physical activity may be scheduled, even these should be arranged in such a way that a guest can quietly decline to participate.

Guessing games and similar stunts are, naturally, very much in order. Especially appealing to older adults are games which center on knowledge of the past, such as quizzes on history, political events or sports figures and stars of the entertainment world from a few decades back.

Teaching the Games

At any party, it is always a possibility that some of those present may be familiar with the game to be presented. But it is a good idea for the leader to review the game in advance so that he will be able to teach it if necessary. There is nothing quite so embarrassing for a host or game leader as to present an activity, only to realize that he isn't sure of the rules or how the game develops at a certain point. The host or game leader should go over the directions for the game carefully beforehand, and, if necessary, practice it with others present just to be sure he will be completely understood. If equipment should be needed, or a room set up in a special way, this should be attended to well in advance. The same thing applies if prizes are to be given: The game leader should make sure they are on hand and not forgotten in somebody's car trunk.

MOTIVATION: Before actually presenting the game itself, it is a good idea for the game leader to have the participants take whatever formation is needed—such as dividing into teams, sitting in chairs in a circle or having people volunteer to take part in a stunt. This is so that the game leader won't have to break into the explanation of the game itself in order to form teams, part-

ners or whatever. Once the stage is set, the game should be introduced in a manner to arouse interest and anticipation. Very often, it is helpful to have a practice round in which the players learn a game by playing it.

Generally, players should not be asked if they would like to play a particular game. Someone is very likely to shout "No!" or to suggest another game, resulting in confusion. The leader should always go ahead in a *positive* way to explain the game that he selects.

EXPLAINING THE GAME: As stated earlier, teaching the game should be done as rapidly and easily as possible. This depends, of course, on how complicated the game is, but every effort should be made to cut down on long-winded explanations. First of all, the leader must make sure that everyone understands the basic point, or purpose, of the game—without boring everyone by over-teaching. If it is a tag game, children should grasp the idea that it is the chaser's role to tag someone else and thus make that person the chaser. The basic action of a more or less complicated game may be demonstrated by having one team (if there are several) go through the motions of play, while the leader explains the action. Any special method of keeping score should also be clearly explained and demonstrated by the leader.

After the initial explanation, if it is a simple game, the players may be able to swing into action promptly without further comment from the leader. If, however, the game is more involved, the leader may have to stop it briefly, to explain a rule or to point out strategy that will quicken the pace or make it more fun for all concerned. Usually, however—once the explanation is given—the leader should stand back and let the players carry on by themselves.

ENDING THE GAME: When a game is played casually around a picnic table or while driving in a car, no one has to tell the players when to stop. That will happen naturally when the players become bored or tired. Such is not the case when a game is in progress among a larger group of people and in a more organized setting. It is sometimes necessary for the leader to bring the game to a halt. If he doesn't, the game may become a drag, with players dropping out because of sheer boredom. The leader should be alert to the level of interest of the group. When a game has been played through several times, he may sense that interest is beginning to die down and may suggest that the game be stopped or played through just once more. It is better to stop a game while the group is still actively enjoying it, so that their enthusiasm will be carried over to the next activity. Usually, the best way to end a game is to suggest that another be played; the leader must be prepared with a ready supply of games suited to that particular group.

The Group Leader

The most basic and vital ingredients of the truly effective leader include two elements: a warm and outgoing personality and a knowledge of the specific skills and methods of group leadership. People of any age naturally respond best to those in charge who are friendly and easy to know. Moreover, the group leader must have drive, enthusiasm and organizing ability.

In addition, he must have sufficient command of language to be able to communicate his enthusiasm for the games he proposes. Nothing falls flatter than suggestions by a game leader when it is apparent that he is not *really* all that keen on the activities he proposes. It is particularly important, when dealing with children, that game leaders strike a delicate balance between being excessively passive and overly domineering. Social psychologists who have studied different methods of group leadership of boys' clubs have discovered that passive, or "laissez-faire," leaders fail to get youngsters involved or to achieve a high level of morale and interest in participation. On the other hand, the dictatorial or authoritarian game leader often has considerable success in getting groups to function at a seemingly high level of enthusiasm. This, however, is sometimes more apparent than

real. Once the game leader turns his back, the group, without a strong authority figure to look up to, often disintegrates—with considerable bickering and absolutely no unity.

It is the democratic leader who is best prepared to help youngsters provide themselves with a healthy and enjoyable group experience and to bring out the highest level of participation, interest and constructive behavior. Such leaders help group members with advice, information and ideas; they are always ready to assist the group in solving problems or in settling definite limits beyond which the group must not go.

Democratic leaders are careful not to dominate every action of the group, or to have it look to them constantly for praise and rewards. When leading games, the leader should be careful to interfere only to clarify rules or make a decision that is absolutely necessary. He should help keep the action moving, encouraging all group members to take part and praising their efforts. At the same time, he should remain at a little distance from stage center. Under the guidance of these democratic leaders, groups tend to develop inner strengths and habits of self-discipline that are not achieved under either passive or dictatorial leadership.

Learning to Get Along

Competitive interaction through play, whether in games or in other kinds of recreational activity, has important contributions to make in a person's development. From the very beginning, man has engaged in rituals, sports and games that were apparently a very important part of his social life. During the period of Greece's classical glory, the Athenian philosopher, Plato, praised games as a useful means of teaching children and youth the laws of society and of raising them to become public-spirited and responsible citizens. In fact, Plato went so far as to recommend that game rules be made unalterable. He believed that if children were allowed to change the "laws" of play, they might, upon growing up, wish to change the laws of government.

BUILDING SELF-CONFIDENCE: Active sports help to develop in children a sense of fair play and of living up to the rules and of doing their very best to meet a challenge. Games also provide a way for children to gain confidence in their own abilities and a feeling of acceptance by others. For this to happen, leaders should be sure that children are not permitted to undergo failure consistently, or to become the butt of ridicule or antagonism from others.

It is natural for youngsters to form cliques of close friends, from which some children are excluded. Whenever possible, however, the leader should try to have the group atmosphere an accepting one, in which every child can feel that he is liked by the others. One way to accomplish this is to subtly encourage the youngster who is not part of the clique to participate in the group activities with added enthusiasm. The leader may express an extra quotient of praise for that child's efforts, but he should be careful not to overdo it. Too much praise for the "left-out" child may achieve just the opposite of the intended effect. The boy or girl's isolation could well be confirmed if the others think the child is a "teacher's pet."

BUILDING STRONG RELATIONSHIPS: Another value of games is that they provide an opportunity for people of different ages and backgrounds to share a common interest. Too often, Americans tend to become rigidly segregated along age lines. Several decades ago, families were much closer; they lived with as many as three or four generations under one roof. Living in small towns or on isolated farms, each family relied mostly on its own resources for both entertainment and subsistence. It was taken for granted that everyone in the family—regardless of age—shared common interests and concerns. Although such a tight family system may have been lacking in many respects, it did impart to all members—grandparents, parents, children, uncles, aunts and cousins—a sense of strength, support and cohesiveness that is often sadly missing in today's homes.

Frequently, the modern child has little meaningful contact with his parents—to say nothing of his grandparents and more distant relatives. He frequently breaks away at the earliest opportunity to join in the subculture of the teen-age world—a world often utterly hostile to adult influence. By the same token, parents, whose interests are remote from those of their children, sometimes react to teen-age rebellion either with an attitude of repression or permissiveness. In either case, the gap between generations is enlarged rather than closed.

Sharing recreational interests, such as games, obviously cannot provide a complete answer to such problems. However, when families enjoy themselves on vacations, in mutual hobbies, in making music, in craft projects or in competitive sports, it helps strengthen a bond of affection and mutual respect that can endure through the years. Similarly, when people of different ages and different racial and social backgrounds get together in community-sponsored programs, the gaps in understanding that separate one group from another sometimes disappear quickly. By breaking down reserve and helping people get to know each other as individuals—rather than merely as members of sometimes hostile groups—such recreational activities offer an invaluable means of building goodwill among people of diverse backgrounds and cementing relationships in organizations and community programs.

Considering Safety

Far too often, unfortunately, even experienced partygivers neglect one important element in their planning. They fail to ask themselves what protection they have, should a guest injure himself on their property. Even when extreme caution is taken, accidents happen—and accidents have a way of leading to long, embarrassing and expensive law suits. Happily, most homeowners carry personal liability insurance, and professional recreational associations are similarly covered. For an individual, such insurance is usually not prohibitively expensive, and, in addition to financial protection, it offers peace of mind. Anyone who does not have such a policy might well consider getting one.

Insured or not, anyone giving a party, especially for children, should have the activities well supervised. A backyard swimming pool, in particular, is a common site of accidents—often tragic ones. When the pool is being used, at least one adult—an expert swimmer—should be in constant attendance to supervise. When a pool is not being used, it should be separated from the children by a high fence and a securely locked gate. Similar precautions should be observed when a barbeque pit or outdoor fireplace is in use. Tools like power mowers and hedge clippers should be securely locked out of sight and the keys should be removed from any cars in the driveway. The investigative instincts of a child should never be underestimated: A key dangling from an ignition lock or a power mower left out in the open can often be just too strong a temptation to resist. Similarly, games that require the use of dangerous implements, like sharply pointed darts or penknives, should certainly be eliminated from any proceedings where small children are in attendance. It is a truth that if one takes the trouble to play a game safely and sanely, he will make himself safe from trouble.

Developing a Plan

In planning a party or social event in which games will be a major part of the program, two additional factors—balance and sequence—must be considered.

BALANCE: Whatever the nature of the group, the games presented should include many different types of activities. Some games should be physically active and should be balanced with quieter, mental games. Such a balance provides rest and helps avoid too much stimulation and over-excitement.

The social structure of games should also be varied. Some may be played between teams; others involve players as individuals. In some, the entire group may be massed against a single player, trying to keep him from discovering a secret—*Indian Chief,* in Chapter Two, for example. In others, such as *Hot or Cold* (also in Chapter Two), the group may actually help the player discover the secret. For some activities, particularly the mind-reading stunts and magic tricks explained in Chapter 5, the idea is for the game leader and an accomplice to both tantalize and entertain all of the guests, who, in turn, try to discover the secret behind the apparent magic powers displayed by their host. In still other games, like some of the informal dramatic activities in Chapters Four and Eleven, the element of competition is completely absent or subdued, being replaced by group cooperation. One mark of a really successful game session is that it incorporates as many different kinds of games as possible.

SEQUENCE: Another factor to be considered in planning a game session is the presentation of activities in a logical sequence. Unless all members of the group arrive simultaneously, or are already present for a while before the games begin, it is a good idea to start with an activity in which players may join, one at a time, as they enter. An example of such a game is *Guess My Name,* in Chapter Two.

It is a good idea to gradually move from such simple, unstructured games to others that may be more complicated or require more instruction. By the time everyone is present and involved in some simple activity, games involving teams and competitive action may be introduced.

Games should be blocked together in similar types, as far as the formation or group structure is concerned. This means that, instead of having players shifted from one kind of pattern to another, two or three quiet games may be played first with everyone sitting in a circle. Then another type of formation, such as having chairs drawn up in a block facing in one direction—for a magic stunt or action songs—may be introduced. When members of a group divide into teams, these teams may first be used for quizzes and then for action games.

CHAPTER 8

Game Sessions for Special Groups

If a party is being planned for a certain age, interest or specialized group, the host must consider the needs and limitations of those attending. He should select not only the most enjoyable games but also those that the guests are able to play easily. This chapter is concerned with the games that fit into special categories: the various age groups, the physically handicapped and the mentally retarded.

Pre-Teen
Game Session

Adults are often called on to plan a birthday party or game session for youngsters between the ages of nine and 13 in connection with school, church or other club activities. Assuming that the participants are all roughly about the same age—as in a class party or a program for Cubs, Brownies or Scouts—the following guidelines may be helpful.

First, the leader should recognize that children in this age bracket tend to be lively and alert. They also have a good sense of humor and are usually ready to join together in group activity. The activities most likely to be successful include active group games, novelty contests, social mixers and party stunts. Quiet games are not likely to go over as well. *Jacks, Hopscotch* or paper-and-pencil games may not be successful either, simply because they prohibit group participation.

MIXER-TYPE GAMES: To get things started, the host might begin with such icebreakers (described in Chapter Two) as *Yes or No, Odd or Even, Meet My Friend* or *Guess My Name.* These games do not require players to form teams and may be introduced quickly to the group with a minimum of explanation.

ACTIVE GROUP GAMES: Following this, a number of active group games might be presented—particularly if the party is being held outdoors. *Two Deep, Flying Dutchmen, Crows and Cranes* or *Streets and Alleys* (all found in Chapter One) fall into this category. Other active team games (also in Chapter One), like *Train Dodge Ball* or *Indian Club Bombardment,* would also be popular with children of this age.

QUIETER PARTY GAMES: If the party is being held indoors, it is wise to include some quieter group games, such as *Hidden Treasure, Hot and Cold, Observation* or *How Many Beans?*

NOVELTY CONTESTS: Pre-teen-age children enjoy *Pie Eating Contest, Speed Shaving, Hammer Contest, Shoot Out the Candle* and other such novelty activities. In playing games of this type, it is possible to plan a tournament where children move from event to event in small groups. Such rotation keeps interest high, with all the youngsters constantly participating in different activities. Simple prizes may be given to the winning teams.

Teen-Age
Game Session

As Chapter Seven points out, teen-age boys and girls are likely to resist adult supervision and advice and want to "do their own thing." While many adolescents avoid organized or structured activity, this is not true of the entire teen-age population. Great numbers of boys and girls belong to church or school clubs, scouting organizations, community centers and similar groups that sponsor social events on a fairly regular basis. Programs are usually most successful if they provide a variety of activities—rather than allow the teen-agers to just "hang around," listening to music, and eating refreshments.

It is a good idea to encourage members of this age group to plan their own parties and social events. Adult advisors may help the teenagers make arrangements or pitch in with ideas, but only if they are asked to do so. Generally, the club members themselves have the best judgment about what the overall group is likely to enjoy, but here are some suggestions for games (most of them described in Chapter 11) that would fit well into a teen-age social event of any type.

PARTY MIXERS: At an early point in the party, various mixers or simple dance contests, such as *Multiplication Dance, Balloon Grab* or *Backward Choice,* may be introduced. Elimination games, like *Heads or Tails, Siege* or *Statues,* provide humorous competition between dancing couples.

INACTIVE GROUP GAMES: If the group is not too large, participants might sit around in a circle to play word games. *Twenty Questions, Coffeepot* or *Ghost* are good examples. Games of observation or alertness, such as *Know the Ads, Feel* or *Smugglers and Inspectors,* are also popular, as are humorous stunts, like *Pat and Rub, Silly Milly, Likes and Dislikes, Midget Man* or *The Strength of Superman.*

QUIZZES AND CHARADES: If the members of the group are competitively minded, team quizzes dealing with topics of teen-age interest are apt to be extremely popular. Boys might compete against girls to heighten the level of team spirit. Similarly, the overall group may be divided into smaller numbers to play acting games, such as *Going to California, Hidden Adverb* or *Charades.*

NOVELTY CONTESTS: Although teen-agers tend to think of themselves as too sophisticated for childish kinds of activity, such novelty stunts and contests (described in Chapter Two) as *Apple Paring Contest, Pass the Orange* or *Cracker Barrel Race* will probably prompt enthusiastic participation. Finally, informal dancing is a useful activity in winding up a party of this type.

GROUP SINGING: Folk songs and songs learned at camp or school are likely to be known by most of the group, and they lend themselves to community singing better than do the currently popular "rock-and-roll" songs. Teen-agers also enjoy action songs (described in Chapter Four), like *Eentsy-Weentsy Spider* or *Coming Round the Mountain,* provided that such songs are led by one of their own members, rather than forced on them by an adult.

Adult Game Session

In general, whatever the theme, parties for adults tend to consist of eating, drinking, informal conversation and, sometimes, dancing. However, there are times when a large number of grown-ups are brought together, and no meal is planned or no cocktails are served. At such an occasion, there is a need for activities to provide sociability and help the group members mingle easily. Games of various types are useful at these times, and even presumably dignified adults are surprised to see how easy it is to relax and join in with others in informal contests and mixers.

As Chapter Seven points out, very strenuous or slapstick activities should be avoided in planning adult activities. However, many of the same icebreakers and get-acquainted games which teenagers enjoy playing (found in Chapter Eleven) may also be popular with adults.

BEGINNING MIXERS: When many adult couples are present who do not all know each other, such icebreakers as *Name Game, Name Bingo, Handshake Treasure* or *Scattered Proverbs* are useful to get the game session under way. If social dance music is available, either with a band or with a record player, dance mixers, like *Multiplication Dance, Pass the Hat* or *Lucky Number Dance,* help to break down the initial reserve.

If the group is a small one, almost any of the quiet party games described in Chapter Eleven—including paper-and-pencil games, quick-response games or games of alertness and observation—are of interest. If the group is large, with 40 or more people, such games usually do not work well. Instead, it is a good idea for the leader to present games or stunts in which he can challenge the entire group with a puzzle or stunt or in which some of the group members may compete while the others watch.

NOVELTY CONTESTS: Several teams, of four or five players each, might compete in such novelty contests as *Knife and Peanut Race, Coat and Hat Relay, Button Sewing Relay* or *Orange Relay,* while others watch and cheer them on.

MAGIC TRICKS: Such "magic" tricks as *Silent Telepathy* or *Magic Spoon* may also be shown to the overall group, with its members trying to figure out how the stunt is performed. Card tricks and coin tricks also make good entertainment. If a player is to mystify and entertain a large group, he should practice until he develops a skillful presentation.

One way of organizing a large group of adults in a game session is to have them divide into several smaller groups of 10 to 20 players each. If the program is held in a fairly large hall or auditorium with movable chairs, it is possible to be flexible in this way.

A volunteer leader is then assigned to each group, to play a sequence of games. A typical sequence for such a party or game session might fall into the following order:

1. Dancing and get-acquainted mixers for all.
2. Participants separate into smaller groups, to play social games or to develop group dramatic stunts.
3. Players sit in a large group, to see dramatic stunts presented, to watch baffling magic tricks or to witness some members of the group take part in amusing novelty contests.

4. Still sitting in larger group, all participants take part in community singing.
5. Refreshments are served, followed by social dancing for all to end the program in a relaxed mood.

Programs for Older Adults

Throughout the United States there are thousands of Golden Age Clubs or Senior Citizens' Centers, where men and women who are usually past retirement age meet one or more times a week for social activity. While such centers offer a variety of personal services for older persons—including health services, counseling and legal and housing aid—their main purpose is usually to provide recreational programs to make the lives of club members fuller and more enjoyable.

Often, men and women who are past retirement age no longer have strong family involvements. Living alone, usually on limited budgets, they cannot afford travel or expensive recreational pursuits. Therefore, for social companionship, they must depend heavily on activities provided by Golden Age Clubs, churches and temples, recreation departments, housing centers and similar agencies. These include arts and crafts, discussion groups, card playing, music, social dancing and service projects, through which club members may perform needed services for other aged people who are homebound or in hospitals.

QUIET GAMES: In planning game sessions for older persons in Senior Citizens' Centers, the characteristics of the members should be looked at carefully. The members of such groups usually range rather widely in age, with many persons in their 70s and 80s. Although they may be fairly mobile and independent, the majority of club members are likely to have some limitations in terms of sight, hearing or physical mobility. Therefore, the kinds of activities which are most suitable do not demand particularly good eyesight or hearing and do not require quick response. The activities should stress easygoing fun, thus making it possible for as many club members as possible to participate without becoming frustrated or embarrassed.

SOCIAL DANCING AND PARTY MIXERS: Dancing, which most older persons have done at one time or another in their lives, is usually of interest—particularly such dance forms as the foxtrot, waltz and two-step. Party mixers based on such dances, including *Multiplication Dance, Matching Mates, Change Partners* or *Lucky Number Dance,* help to make social dancing more appealing to older participants. Dance music from the Twenties or Thirties also adds to the occasion.

QUIZZES AND GUESSING GAMES: *Buzz, Fizz* or *Chain Word,* games requiring a quick response on the part of contestants, are not suitable for most older persons. However, guessing games, like *Twenty Questions* or *Animal, Vegetable or Mineral,* which oldsters can play at their own pace, are perfectly appropriate. Quizzes are also interesting to older persons, particularly if such quizzes deal with the period of their youth or middle age. Thus, quizzes about old movie stars or stage entertainers, sports teams and players or political events and fads of several decades ago have nostalgic appeal—testing the elderly on knowledge which they are likely to recall.

COMMUNITY SINGING: As with guessing games and quizzes, when community singing is done in a Golden Age Club, it makes sense to do old favorites, like *Let Me Call You Sweetheart, Bicycle Built for Two* or *Down By The Old Mill Stream.*

CARD PLAYING: Cards are popular in many Senior Citizens' centers, with members especially enjoying *Bridge, Hearts, Pinochle* and various forms of *Rummy.* In addition to being a favorite daily pastime for the aged, card playing may lend itself to a special cards tournament or to a round-robin contest.

STUNTS AND NOVELTY CONTESTS: All games for the elderly should be kept at an easygoing pace, without pressure to participate. It is very important to avoid doing childish activities or stunts that senior citizens may feel demean their dignity or suggest that they are in their "second childhood." Often it is a very good idea in program planning to have members of Golden Age Clubs themselves plan their own activities and take over their own leadership. The elderly are frequently the best judges of what their companions would enjoy.

Games for the Physically Handicapped

On many occasions adults and teenagers are called on to assist in leading recreation activities in hospitals, rehabilitation centers or community groups that serve physically handicapped children and youth.

The most common kind of handicap involves a physical limitation brought about either through an accident or injury, a birth defect or a progressive illness. Individuals may have cerebral palsy, brain injury that affects movement, or muscular dystrophy. They may be confined to a wheelchair or be on crutches, have limited use of hands or have poor hand-eye coordination. However, the physically handicapped child's need for recreation is as great as that of the normal child, and he enjoys the same kinds of activities. The problem then is to select or adapt activities which are suitable to such children and in which they can find a degree of success and a sense of personal accomplishment—as well as fun!

ACTIVE GROUP GAMES: Games like tag, relay or dodge ball usually are not suitable for the physically handicapped child because of his limited mobility. Also, the space available in a hospital ward or recreation room is frequently not large enough for such activities. Some such games might be played with adapted rules, and it certainly would be possible for children in wheelchairs or on crutches to take part in certain simple novelty races.

QUIETER GAMES: Games, involving hand-and-arm movement, which are played while sitting in a circle, like *Ring on a String, Add an Action, Poison Penny* or *Indian Chief,* are particularly appropriate.

NOVELTY STUNTS: Stunts which do not require mobility, like *Chair Ring Toss, Shoot Out the Candle, In the Hat* or *Bottle Tenpins,* can easily be played by this group.

CREATIVE ACTIVITIES: Dramatic games like *Going to California, Hidden Adverb, A Noun That Rhymes* or *Prop Plays,* are also well-suited to the handicapped. Those not severely restricted can also do creative work in the area of puppetry and arts and crafts. Drawing games, word games and tricks and puzzles with numbers, coins and cards are also popular with this group.

If their physical defect is such that it is difficult for them to grasp objects, it is possible to buy or make equipment that makes it easier for them to participate. For example, very large, thick playing cards are sometimes used with children who cannot grasp regular cards easily. Children who lack the ability to hold a paintbrush in their hands may use a brush strapped to their foot, or even held between their teeth.

What is most important is that the physically handicapped be given the *chance* to participate in play activities as normal children do. Often their need for personal expression and social involvement is so great that they are able to engage in games or creative pastimes that one might think would be literally impossible for them. Whenever one works with the physically handicapped, it is important not only to lead activities that they can carry on in a group setting, but to introduce the child to tasks and games requiring no leader—activities he can enjoy by himself, with a friend or two, or with members of his family.

Games for the Mentally Retarded

The mentally retarded child needs special care. Planning play programs for mentally retarded youngsters is quite different from planning activities with the physically handicapped. In many communities, public recreation departments or voluntary organizations offer recreation pro-grams, designed especially for retarded children and youth. Such groups may meet weekly or sometimes even every day, as in day camps provided for the retarded.

Directors of such special play programs have found that retarded children are able to engage in many of the same kinds of land sports, aquatic activities, team games, arts and crafts projects and music and dance activities that normal children enjoy. Indeed, a rich program of play activity is very important in making sure that retarded youngsters reach their full physical and mental potential. Too often, the fact that they are retarded is used as an excuse for not providing any sort of social activities for such handicapped children. As a rule, retarded children need the sort of stimuli and encouragement that will help them develop interests and skills and contribute to their overall healthy growth.

The primary difficulty of retarded children is in grasping complicated skills and ideas, and in understanding and using verbal communication as fully as normal children. Therefore endless patience is a prime requisite for the play leader.

The task in planning play activities for the mentally retarded is to select activities in which they can find success and satisfaction. It is necessary to pick activities which have simple rules, limited strategy and a minimum of required teaching. Each game should be explained slowly and clearly, and the leader should be prepared to repeat instructions, if necessary, to help children who are having difficulty understanding the actions or the rules.

ACTIVE GROUP GAMES: Many of the games described in Chapters One and Two are quite suitable for use with retarded children. As an example, games like *Hide and Seek, Back to Back* or *Keep Away Touch Ball* can be played with many educable or moderately retarded youngsters. On the other hand, a game like *Streets and Alleys,* which requires quick and uniform reaction to signals by the participants, or *Squirrel in the Tree,* in which children must be prepared to change roles rapidly, is certainly not suited for most retarded children.

STUNTS AND NOVELTY CONTESTS: Simple stunts and self-testing activities like *Bean Bag Throw, Five Jumps, Cross the Creek* or *Beneath the Bar* can also be used quite successfully. Relays like the *Bunny Hop Relay, Potato Race* or *Wheelbarrow Relay* can be played by educable, retarded children, provided that such games are carefully taught and patiently led. Other novelty contests, like *Balloon-Blowing Contest, Apple Ducking, Cereal Eating, Speed Shaving* or *Bottle Tenpins,* are popular with such groups.

QUIETER PARTY GAMES: *Shoe Hunt, Peanut Hunt, Hidden Treasure* or *Poison Penny* work very well with retarded children. In contrast, games involving number skills and quick mental or verbal responses, like *Fizz, Buzz* or the *Prince of Paris,* are almost always too difficult for retarded children.

It is important to select games in which the majority of players can carry on the activity and in which even the few who might be having difficulty with it can be successfully coached. Otherwise, the failure of one or two children to understand a game may ruin it for all the others—resulting in the group's frustration. In addition to the kinds of games mentioned in this chapter, action songs, rhythm band activities, singing games, drawing and arts and crafts are all suitable for use with retarded children.

Guides for Working with Special Groups

In planning game sessions with the special groups described in this chapter, a few general guide rules should be kept in mind. 1. The game leader should always make his plans in terms of the group with which he will be dealing—be it children of a particular age bracket or adults with a certain kind of disability. Age level and physical condition are the prime considerations in determining the kinds of games that should be of general interest and that the group will be able to play most successfully. 2. A tentative list of games should be planned that will take up more than the allotted time period to play.

The reason for this is that should a particular game prove too difficult or should the group appear not to enjoy it, the leader may cut it short and move on to a new one—rather than force any game on the participants. 3. If and when this happens, the leader should make a note of the game and remember not to play it again, especially with a similar group. On the other hand, if a certain game proves very successful and is played with obvious enjoyment, a note should be made of that fact so that the game may be repeated at other sessions. 4. When special supplies and equipment are needed for a game, arrangements should be made ahead of time. 5. It should never be assumed that everyone knows the directions and rules of a game—even an obviously popular one. The leader should go over the rules and directions before the game is begun, making the explanations clear but short. If there are questions from the players, they should be asked, and answered, ahead of time so that the actual playing of the game is not interrupted. 6. The leader should keep a sharp watch out for the first sign that interest in a game is beginning to lag. If such a thing happens, the game should be brought to a quick and smooth conclusion and a new one introduced. Conversely, if enthusiasm for playing a particular game is high, the leader may allow it to be continued for a short while longer than planned. Even so, it should be ended while interest is still keen. 7. The leader must be aware of the sensibilities of all the players—especially those with disabilities. Tact, politeness and warmth are essential qualities for the person leading a game session.

Apart from the kinds of general guides offered in this chapter, it is difficult to predict exactly which games will be most appealing to any given group. In part, the leader must learn by trial and error which activities are the most useful. In addition to learning from experience in this field, he should encourage participants to suggest games that they know and enjoy. If the leader is not familiar with these group-suggested games, he may ask the players to describe the games themselves, so that he can teach them to others in the future.

CHAPTER 9

Card and Table Games

Whether played for sheer amusement or as serious competition, card and table games are mentally stimulating leisure-time activities for adults and teen-agers around the world. Many of the card and table games popular today began in different form thousands of years ago and changed gradually with the passing of time. In fact, card and table games have engaged mankind in most known civilizations since the beginning of written history. The original purpose of card and table games was for teaching military strategy to fledgling warriors. *Chess* and *Backgammon,* with their symbolic men, were ways by which a competitor might learn to outsmart his rival on the field of battle. Playing cards demonstrated an even greater wealth of tactical maneuvers, with the four suits representing four separate armies.

Believed to have been first invented either in Pharaonic Egypt or Brahman India, card games first became popular among the ruling nobilities of the Orient. By the 12th century, card games were already providing amusement in royal courts as far apart as China and the Middle East. Present-day cards still show the signs of their noble origins in the face cards: king, queen and knave (jack). The four suits originally symbolized the four major classes contending for power in medieval Europe: the church and the clergy (hearts); the military forces (spades—swords); the merchants (diamonds—a stylized version of accounting tiles) and the civil officials (clubs— possibly derived from a three-leaf clover or a three-lobed archway).

Card games represent an enjoyable and wholesome form of recreation. They encourage alertness and observation. In the following pages a number of card games are explained. From the better-known (*Hearts, Draw Poker* and *Contract Bridge*) to the lesser-known (*Fan Tan, Red Dog* and *Lift Smoke*), regulations, strategy and rules of play are outlined clearly so that even the individual with "no card sense" can be a winner. A glossary of some of the most frequently used card terms begins the chapter.

Glossary of Card-Playing Terms

ANTE: In *Poker*, before dealing, the dealer may require every player to put one or more chips into the center of the table. Called the ante, these chips are the foundation for the pot.

BETTING: Many *Poker* and showdown games involve the risking of chips or other counters. This chapter explains the form of the betting for each game of this type.

BIDDING: Bidding is a key element in games such as *Contract Bridge* and *Auction Pinochle,* where the object of play is to take more tricks than an opponent. A player bases his bidding on the strength of his hand: His highest bid should not exceed his prediction of the number of tricks he can win in a particular hand. Bidding always takes place before the start of play, beginning with the dealer or the person to his left and going clockwise around the table. In some games there is but one bidding round; in others, the bidding keeps rotating around the table until no one elects to raise the last bid made by another player.

CALL: In *Poker,* a call is made when a player matches the amount bet by an opponent on his right; this allows him to stay in the game. A call on the final betting round means that he elects to play against the hands of his opponents in the showdown.

CONTRACT: In *Contract Bridge,* the partners who win the bidding are said to have established a contract. This means that they must take at least the number of tricks that they stated in their final bid.

CUT: After the shuffle, the dealer offers the deck to the person on his right for the cut. This person takes a top portion of the deck, numbering no fewer than five cards, and places it in a pack on the table toward the dealer. The dealer picks up the remaining section of the deck and places it on top of this pack—reuniting the deck. If anyone sees the bottom card of the reunited pack, a new cut may be called for.

DEAL: In most games, players draw (or cut) cards from the deck, with the drawer of the highest card winning the deal. After the shuffle and cut, a certain number of cards is distributed to each player by the dealer. The dealer always begins with the person to his left and proceeds clockwise around the board, ending with himself. In most games, the cards are distributed one at a time, face down, until each player, including the dealer, has a complete hand.

DECLARER: In *Contract Bridge,* the partner who is first to bid the suit of the contract is the declarer. He plays all the cards—his own hand and his partner's hand. Play opens with the person to the left of the declarer, who leads a card of his choice face up onto the table.

DUMMY: In *Contract Bridge,* the declarer's partner is the dummy. After the opening lead, he places his entire hand face up before him on the table. The dummy exposes his hand with the trump suit in a vertical line to the far right and the remaining suits in alternate vertical lines of contrasting color to the left of the trump suit. The declarer plays cards from the dummy whenever it is the dummy's turn to play. Also, whenever he takes a trick with a dummy card, he must lead from the dummy on the next trick.

HAND: The cards dealt to the player make up his hand. The term is also used in another way to denote the various successive rounds of any given game. For example, players speak of playing a few hands of a card game in the way a person might speak of playing a few innings of baseball or a few holes of golf. In this sense, when everyone in the game plays off all the cards he holds, a hand is said to be finished.

LEAD: The card played to open a trick is called the lead. In games such as *Contract Bridge* where there is bidding, the first lead is made by the person to the left of the winning bidder. In other games where tricks are played for, the first lead is the person seated to the left of the dealer—unless, as in *Hearts,* a special card is designated to open the play. The lead on successive tricks goes to the player who captures the previous trick.

MELD: In games such as *Bezique, Pinochle* and *Rummy,* players receive points for forming card combinations using the cards in their hands: for instance, in *Pinochle,* four kings and/or the jack of diamonds and queen of spades. These combinations must be shown on the table in order to count as points. They are referred to as melds, and the act of exposing them on the table is called melding.

OVERTRICK: In *Contract Bridge,* if a team takes more tricks than the number it bid, these extra tricks are called overtricks. Overtricks are scored as bonus points and do not count toward the actual winning of a game.

POT: In *Poker,* the pot is comprised of the chips bet by the players; it lies in the center of the table. In a pot-limit game, no bet or raise may be made that is larger than the amount in the pot at that time.

RUFF: In *Contract Bridge,* taking a trick by means of playing a trump card onto the suit that is led is called a ruff.

SEQUENCE: A sequence is a number of cards in numerical order. In *Poker,* sequences must consist of five cards—such as five, six, seven, eight and nine. They have one value if the cards are of varied suits and a higher value if of the same suit. The rules governing sequences vary from game to game and are set forth in the descriptions of the games that follow in this chapter.

SHOWDOWN: The showdown is common to most *Poker* games. It occurs when the players declare their holdings. The winner of the showdown is determined on the basis of the highest ranking hand. This happens in all cases after the final betting round is completed. Where all players, save one, drop from the game, the remaining player wins automatically and need not show his hand.

SHUFFLE: Before every new deal, and prior to the cut, the deck should be collected and thoroughly mixed—or shuffled.

SLUFF: When a player cannot follow the suit that is led and discards a card of any other suit except trump, it is called sluffing a card.

STOCK: The stock consists of the cards remaining in the deck after each player is dealt a full hand.

SUIT: A standard 52-card deck contains four suits—clubs, diamonds, hearts and spades. Each suit consists of 13 cards, ranging from the ace (high or low), king, queen, jack, ten, down to the four, three, two. To follow suit means to play a card of the same suit as the card that opens the trick.

TRICK: In games such as *Contract Bridge* where the purpose is to capture cards, the play falls into rounds called tricks. A trick consists of one card from each player. Thus, when four play, a trick contains four cards; when five play, five cards, etc. A trick opens with someone leading the first card; then each of the other players, moving to the left in a clockwise direction, play a card onto the trick in turn. In most games they must play a card of the same suit as the one led. Thus, if a jack of diamonds is led, the other players to the left must follow suit with a diamond. When all cards are played on the trick, the player of the card with the highest ranking denomination of the suit that is led takes in the cards and places them in his trick pack. As winner of the trick, he has the privilege of opening the next trick by playing any card from his hand face up onto the table. Again, the players to his left have to play a card of the same suit.

If a player does not hold cards of the suit that is led, he may play any card from his hand onto the trick. In games where there is a trump suit, he may play trump. With trump, he automatically wins the trick unless another player plays a higher trump card. Remember that when trump doesn't fall onto a trick, the highest ranking card of the suit that is led wins the trick—even though someone plays an ace of a different suit.

TRUMP: In some games, the top card of the stock is faced up to designate the trump suit. In other games, as in *Contract Bridge,* the winner of the bidding names trump. A card of the trump suit defeats any other card in the deck except a higher ranking trump. In *Contract Bridge,* one of the four suits may be trump, or, in a fifth category, the game may be played in no trump. When a contract is sealed in no trump, obviously no suit is designated as trump in the ensuing play for tricks.

VOID: If a player's hand contains no cards of one of the four suits, he has a void (blank) in that suit. In many games where there is a trump suit and players must follow suit, it is an obvious advantage to have a void in some suit. Whenever a particular suit is led and the player is void in that suit, he may play a trump card to capture the trick.

VULNERABLE: In *Contract Bridge,* a team that wins one game of 100 is vulnerable. Once vulnerable, the team is more severely penalized in the event that it fails to make its contract.

WILD CARDS: A wild card is a card that may be used to represent any other card in the deck. Many games employ wild cards. Usually, jokers, deuces (two's) and one-eyed jacks are designated wild cards, although in some games a variety of cards are wild.

Numerals indicate the number of players.

Bezique

● 2 ● *A prepared deck of 64 cards (each of the four suits represented by two each of the following: ace, king, queen, jack, ten, nine, eight, seven); scoring pad and pencil*

OBJECT: Each player tries to be first to score a total of 1,500 points.

RANKING OF CARDS: Ace (high), ten, king, queen, jack, nine, eight, seven (low).

PREPARATION: The cards are shuffled and cut. High card wins the cut for deal, according to the order of rank shown above.

DEAL: Starting with his opponent, the dealer gives out eight cards in groups of three, two and then three. (If the dealer makes any mistake in the deal, his opponent may immediately call for a new deal.) The remaining cards—"the

talon pack"—are placed face down on the table. The top card is faced up beside the talon pack to indicate the trump suit. If the trump card is a seven, the dealer receives ten points.

PLAY: The action is in two stages. In the first, beginning when the player opposite the dealer leads a card from his hand, the players draw a card from the top of the talon pack after every trick. The winner of the trick draws first. In this first stage of *Bezique,* the players need not follow suit during play and may trump at any time. As in most games where there is play for tricks, the highest card of the suit led wins, unless trumped—in which case, the highest trump card takes the trick.

At the same time, as this rather free form of play takes place, players may tally points through a device known as "melding"—that is, by laying certain valuable combinations of cards face up before them on the table. Only the winner of the trick just played may meld, and he does so before drawing from the talon pack. He may meld only one combination, retaining others for melding—one combination at a time—upon winning future tricks. Once a combination is melded and scored, it is left lying face up on the table. However, it is considered part of the player's hand, such that cards from the melds may be played directly from the board onto ensuing tricks. During this first stage, the players keep their trick piles face down on the table, but separated from the area where melds are laid down.

There are a number of various melds, each worth a certain number of points. The possible card combinations follow:

VALUE OF MELDS

Class I

A Marriage (king and queen, same suit) . . . .
. . . . 20 points
A Royal Marriage (king and queen of trumps)
. . . . 40 points
Trumps Sequence (Trumps — ace, ten, king, queen, jack) . . . . .250 points

Class II

Bezique (Jack of diamonds and queen of spades)
. . . . 40 points
Double Bezique (Both jacks of diamonds and
queens of spades) . . . . .500 points

Class III

Four Aces (any suit) . . . . .100 points
Four Kings (any suit) . . . . 80 points
Four Queens (any suit) . . . . 60 points
Four Jacks (any suit) . . . . 40 points

Other Scoring

Brisque (any ace or ten taken on tricks) . . . .
. . . . 10 points
Dix (any seven of trumps held in hand and
declared as a meld) . . . . 10 points
Last Trick. . . . . 10 points

Before drawing from the talon pack, the winner of a trick may meld one of the above combinations. The score is marked down in a running account and is totaled at the end of the hand. Frequently, the same card can be employed in more than one combination. This is true if those combinations fall into different classes, or if the second combination has a higher point value than the first within the same class. A Royal Marriage can, therefore, later be incorporated into a Trumps Sequence; a Trumps Sequence, on the other hand, cannot be broken apart to score a Royal Marriage once the Trumps Se-

quence is scored. Either partner in a Marriage or Royal Marriage may be combined with three others of its kind to make four of a kind under *Class III*. By the same token, the queen of spades that is partner in a Marriage may be combined with the jack of diamonds to score a Bezique under *Class II*. However, the same queen (or king) may appear in only one Marriage.

When a player holding a seven of trumps takes a trick using another trump card, he may exchange the seven for it and score a Dix (ten points). The player who holds, by chance, both trump sevens may score ten apiece. If the first such seven is already declared, the holder of the second seven need only show it when he takes a trick to score Dix—that is, he needn't place it on the table. A Dix counts as a combination, meaning no other cards may be melded at the same time. A person who by accident (or calculation) melds a false combination must subtract the value of the true combination from his score. Then his opponent may instruct him to lead any card of the false combination to begin the next play. If, however, the person in error hasn't yet taken a card from the talon pack, he may correct his mistake and suffer no penalty.

When the talon gets down to a single remaining card, the winner of the next trick takes it while the loser of the trick takes the trump indicator. With the talon gone, the second stage of play commences. Players pick up their combinations

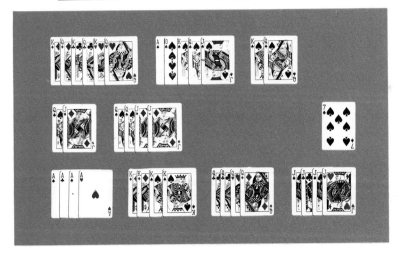

In Bezique, the players score points for these various combinations of cards, called melds. During the game, a player uses cards from his hand to form the melds face up on the table. The scoring is detailed above.

After play opens with the jack of clubs, the other players each follow with a club, as they must if their hands contain clubs. As the highest ranking club played, the ace takes this trick. A trick consists of one card from each player's hand.

By playing the trump seven (spades were named as trump) onto this heart trick when he holds no cards in hearts, the bottom player wins over the ace of hearts. In Bezique, a trump card defeats cards of other suits regardless of rank.

from the table, blending them into their hands. The winner of the last trick leads a card of his choice. *Hereafter, the players must follow suit. If void in the suit that is led, they must play trumps if they hold any trumps. Furthermore, a player must overcall wherever possible, that is, play a card of higher denomination than the card that is led.* Should two cards of the same rank fall on the same trick, the first one played wins the trick.

If a player neglects to overcall when he possesses a card that could take a trick, his opponent—on discovering the oversight—may require that the game be replayed from the point where the error was committed.

Note that for each ace and each ten taken during the tricks ten points is scored, as well as ten for the last trick. Thus the clever manipulation of play may result in a large point reward. The point totals are computed after each hand. A grand winning total can be set either at 1,000 or 1,500 points.

VARIATIONS: In *Three-Handed Bezique* a 96-card deck is prepared. To make up the pack, another 32 cards are added to the regular *Bezique* deck: an ace, ten, king, queen, jack, nine, eight and seven of each of the four suits—such that there are now three of every card. The winner of the trick draws first from the talon pack, melds and initiates the new round of play with a card led from his hand. *Triple Bezique* is valued at 1,500 points. A player who has already melded Bezique and/or Double Bezique may simply add the third pair of cards and win 1,500. The grand winning total can be set at 2,000 or 2,500 points.

In *Four-Handed Bezique* the deck consists of 128 cards, four each of the following: aces, tens, kings, queens, jacks, nines, eights and sevens. Generally, the game is not played with partners. However, if it is, the individual scores of the two-player teams are combined on the score pad. The Quadruple Bezique is worth 1,500 points, as is the Triple Bezique. Grand winning totals of 2,000 or 2,500 points may be set.

Black Jack (*Twenty-one*)

- 2 to 10 players   • A standard 52-card deck; plastic chips (or some other kind of counters, such as matchsticks)

OBJECT: Each player tries to draw a hand with a higher point total than the dealer's hand without exceeding 21 points.

RANKING OF CARDS: Ace, one or 11 (player's option); king, queen and jack, ten points each; the ten through the two, worth their numerical value.

PREPARATION: Cards are drawn from the top of the deck (or dealt out), the first player to receive an ace winning the deal. After the shuffle and cut, the dealer must bury the top card of the pack face up at the bottom of the deck. An ace, picture card or ten may not be buried;

Black Jack (left, above) and five cards under 21 (right) win double the bet. Averages favor not drawing to a hand of 17 or higher (middle).

they must be returned to the middle of the pack. If, after three tries, the dealer has not turned up a card that can be buried, he pays each player a counter, reshuffles and starts again. When he succeeds in burying a card, he may deal out the cards around the table.

DEAL: The dealer distributes the cards, one at a time, in a clockwise rotation from his left. He gives each player, including himself, two cards—the first one face down, the second up.

PLAY: Players should agree on table rules before the start of play, since the rules of play for this game vary considerably in different places. In some places, the rule is that players bet after examining only their first card, which is kept face down on the table; in other places, the rule is that bets are made on the basis of the first two cards dealt. Generally, a limit is placed upon the size of bets. Once placed, a bet cannot be altered—raised or lowered. Players place their counters directly before them on the table. The dealer does not bet, since he is acting as banker—paying off or winning the amount of each player's bet.

If any player draws an ace and a picture card for his first two cards, he turns his cards up and announces, "Black Jack" (21). In some circles, a ten and an ace are also counted as Black Jack. In most localities, the dealer cannot beat a Black Jack even with one of his own. A player is always paid double by the banker (dealer) for a Black Jack. This player then takes over the deal at the end of that round: shuffling, cutting,

Black Jack *dealer (hand above topped by queen) elects to call his opponents without drawing cards from the deck to add to his point total.*

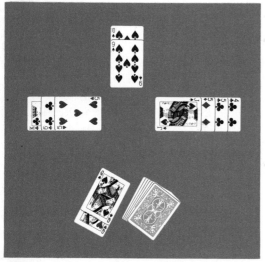

All cards are face up. With 20 points (two queens), dealer loses to 21 points (left), beating 19 (top) and hand over 21 points (right).

burying a card and acting as banker. If he wishes, however, he may sell the deal to the highest bidder. After the dealer has dealt everyone two cards, each player, beginning with the person on the dealer's left, has the option of drawing one or more additional cards to add to his point total. These cards are dealt face up, one at a time, and are called "hits." After each hit, the player decides whether to stand with his hand or ask for another hit. When a player decides he wants no more hits, the next person to his left may now ask for hits, and so on around the table. If he exceeds 21 points—that is, goes "bust"—he loses his bet to the dealer and folds his hand, which goes into the discard pile.

A player—other than the dealer—who receives paired cards in the first deal may turn up the face-down card and play, in effect, two hands. The person playing in this manner can receive hits on both cards from the dealer, the first hit on each card going face down. He plays each hand separately.

When the dealer has dealt hits to all players, he turns his two cards face up on the table, deciding whether or not to take any hits himself. If, for instance, he stops at 18, he collects the counters of those with scores of 18 and under, while paying off the bets of players with 19, 20 or 21 points. If the dealer goes over 21, he must pay off all players with point totals of 21 or less. If the dealer is dealt Black Jack (and no other player is), he declares this— immediately sweeping all bets from the board. Then all hands are discarded, and a new deal follows. (In some places, the dealer collects double from each player for a Black Jack; in others, he collects exactly the amount bet from each player for a Black Jack.)

Whereas the dealer usually is given the advantage of winning all ties (in some circles, even when Black Jack is involved), there are situations that automatically win for the player: One of these is Black Jack, as described above. Another, sometimes termed "Five Card Charlie," occurs where a player draws a hand of five cards totalling 21 points or less; it wins double the amount of the bet. A six-card hand under 21 wins triple the bet; seven cards, four times the bet, and so forth. The highest such progression would be the four aces (one point each), the four twos and three threes—11 cards totaling exactly 21 points; this would pay eight times the amount bet. The dealer is generally not permitted to "double up" or play combinations such as the Five Card Charlie. Such combinations are options available only to the other players as compensation for the dealer winning ties.

When, in the process of dealing, the dealer reaches the buried card at the bottom of the pack, he collects all discards from previous hands. Then follow the shuffle, the cut, the burying of a card and a new deal.

Canasta

- 2 to 6 • *Two standard 52-card decks (each with two jokers added) combined into one deck of 108 cards*

WILD CARDS: Four jokers; eight deuces (twos).

OBJECT: Players attempt to score 5,000 points before the opponent can do so (or, in a game of partners, before the opposing team can do so). They arrive at this point total by receiving bonus points and by making various melds. The largest of the melds is a Canasta. A Canasta may be Natural (consisting of seven cards of the same denomination) or Mixed (consisting of seven cards of the same denomination, but using one or more wild cards to represent cards in the combination).

PREPARATION: The deck is shuffled then cut to determine the deal, highest card winning. If a joker appears, the cut is repeated. If partners play, cards are drawn—the two highest cards playing together. Partners take alternate seats so that no two members of the same team play in consecutive order.

DEAL: After the shuffle and cut, the dealer distributes the cards face down, one at a time. He begins with the person to his left, dealing to himself last. With four players or more, each person receives 11 cards; with three players, 13 cards; with two players, 15 cards. (If, in the deal, a player receives a Red Three, he places it face up on the table and draws a replacement from the stock.) The remainder of the deck is faced down in the middle of the table as a stock, and the stock's top card is faced up on the table.

Should this card prove to be a Red Three, another card must be turned up from the top of the stock to cover it.

PLAY: The person on the dealer's left starts the action. He may draw the top, face-down card from the stock, or he may take the face-up card if he holds in his hand a pair of the same denomination as that card. (A Red Three, if drawn, must be placed on the table, but—unlike the deal—no replacement card is drawn.) Once he takes either card, he places a card—either the one just drawn or one from his hand—onto the discard pile, face up. The next person to the left has the same choice, and so on around the table in a clockwise direction.

Bonuses are given for a Red Three, four Red Threes, Natural Canasta (second from bottom) and Mixed Canasta (bottom, with wild cards).

If the top card of the discard pile is the same denomination as a pair in his hand, he may take the card for his hand or meld it immediately. A player's "initial meld" must total at least 50 points. This can be accomplished by melding two combinations on the same play: for example, three jacks (ten points each) and three eights (ten points each), for a total of 60 points—ten more than mandatory. The minimum limit might be reached with a single

A pair of queens in the hand takes the queen on discard pile. The discard queen could also be taken with one queen and wild two.

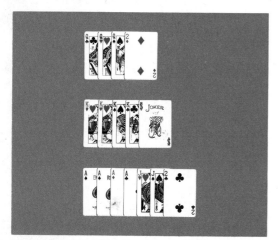

Minimum initial meld levels are attainable in various ways: for instance, the top meld is worth 50 points; middle, 90; bottom, 120.

combination, such as three nines (ten points each) and a deuce (20 points). Each meld must always consist of at least two natural cards of the denomination, and never more than three wild cards (jokers and deuces). Thus, for instance, a player could not legitimately attempt to meld an ace and two jokers, an eight and two deuces or two queens and four deuces, etc.

After the initial meld, a player, on his turn, may meld as little as one card at a time—adding a card or cards to one of his combinations. Partners are permitted to build upon one another's

combinations: To eliminate confusion, all team melds are kept in front of one partner.

If, at any time, a player is able to meld the top card in the discard pile, he may take all the cards that lay underneath it. In other words, once the initial meld is made, a player may draw the entire discard pile whenever he holds a pair of the same denomination as the top card (or one card of that denomination and a wild card), or when any of his melds match the top card. However, a wild card or a Black Three placed on top of the discard pile freezes the cards. The pile remains frozen until someone has a natural pair of the same denomination as the top card. The person who succeeds in unfreezing the discard pile in this manner takes the entire pile, including the top card.

After a player forms a Canasta—either Mixed (seven cards of the same denomination, but using one or more wild cards to represent one or more cards of the run) or Natural (seven cards of the same denomination)—he may choose to rid his hand of all cards and go out. At the conclusion of the hand all players (or teams) total their bonus points: that is, their points for Canastas, Red Threes, Going Out and for Going Out with a Concealed Hand. (A Red Three, or threes, only count as bonus if the initial meld is made.) Then each player counts up the point values of the individual cards in his melds. Hence, Canastas yield double mileage—first a bonus, then the points for individual cards comprising them. The exact point values for individual cards as well as for the various bonus-point situations follow:

POINTS FOR MELDED CARDS

Joker	50
Two	20
Ace	20
King, queen, jack, ten, nine or eight	10
Seven, six, five, four or black three	5

BONUS POINTS

Red Three
Separately	100
All Four	800

Mixed Canasta 300
Natural Canasta 500
Going Out .100
Going Out with Concealed Hand 200

If the game is being played with teams, a player must ask his partner for permission to go out. In some localities, the rule is that if one of the partners wishes to Go Out With a Concealed Hand—meaning that neither he nor his partner has yet melded anything—he may do so without asking permission. Of course, to Go Out With a Concealed Hand, he must hold a Canasta and another smaller combination so that the entire hand can be melded simultaneously.

Should the stock be used up before anybody can go out, the play continues with the players taking turns at drawing the face-up top card of the discard pile. If a player can meld this top card, he must do so. If the top card cannot be used by any of the players, the hand ends. Players must subtract the points still held in their hands from their melds and bonus points.

The grand winning total is 5,000 points. Once a player scores 1,500 or more points, the minimum limit for the initial meld rises to 90 points on the next deal. When a player's total score reaches 3,000 points, the initial meld must be at least 120 points. Thus the jokers—at 50 points—become more valuable assets as the game progresses. If, however, a player or team scores negative points—"goes into the hole"—on the hand, there is no initial meld requirement for the next hand.

Canfield

● 1 ● *A standard 52-card deck*

OBJECT: The player attempts to play the entire deck onto four foundation cards, by suit, in ascending sequence.

RANKING OF CARDS: Ace, low; king, high.

PREPARATION AND DEAL: The deck is shuffled. First, the player deals a "Misery Pile" of 13 cards face down; he then turns it right side up on the table to his left. He turns the next card in the deck face up, representing the first foundation card and determining the denomination of all four foundation cards. This first foundation card is placed face up at some distance beyond the Misery Pile. The player then deals out four cards, face up, forming the "Tableau" line and running horizontally in a line to the right of the Misery Pile. The rest of the deck is his stock.

PLAY: Any card in the Tableau of the same denomination as the first foundation card may automatically be moved up as the second, third or fourth foundation card and is replaced from the Misery Pile. Similarly, if the top card of the Misery Pile is of the same denomination as the first foundation card, it is moved into position above the Tableau as the second foundation card.

Throughout the game, the top card of the Misery Pile is playable either onto the foundation piles or Tableau piles wherever it fits into a sequence. The foundation sequences must build upward numerically in the appropriate suits; therefore, given a ten, the jack, queen, king, ace (low), two, three, four . . . and finally the nine of the corresponding suit would follow. In the Tableau, on the other hand, the sequence is descending and alternating between red and black. Whenever a foundation card appears, it

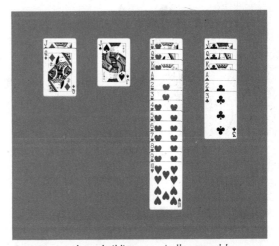

Sequences are shown building numerically upward by suit upon four jacks serving as the foundation cards in a typical Canfield game.

is moved up—as is any card that fits into the established foundation sequence.

Within the Tableau itself, individual cards may not be moved, except in the case where only two cards make up a stack: Here, the second card may be switched into place at the end of a sequence on another stack. However, an entire stack may be moved to another stack in the Tableau; this may be done where the first card of one stack fits sequentially onto the last card of some other stack—always observing the rule of contrasting colors. If a stack is moved in this manner, a vacancy is created in the Tableau stacks. The vacancy is filled with the top card of the Misery Pile or—if the latter is depleted—with a card from the stock.

As in *Patience,* players go through the stock three cards at a time. Where the top card of a group of three is playable, the second card may be played; if the second is playable, the third may be played. In different sections of the country, rules vary, as to how many times the player may thumb through the entire stock. Generally, a player is permitted to continue going through the stock, three cards at a time, until none of the exposed cards are playable.

Casino

- *2 to 4 (if 4, partners play)*
- *A standard 52-card deck; scoring pad and pencil*

OBJECT: Each player (or team) tries to score 21 points before any other player (or the other team) can do so.

RANKING OF CARDS: Ace (one), two, three, four, five . . . ten. Picture cards have no hierarchical ranking.

PREPARATION AND DEAL: The deck is shuffled and cut. Low card wins cut for deal. The dealer distributes the cards clockwise from his left, face down. He gives each player two cards at a time so that each player has four in his hand. He deals four cards face up onto the center of the table, and he sets aside the remaining cards face

down as a stock. After a hand is finished, the dealer again passes out cards from the stock, four per player. However, he does not deal the four cards to the center of the table. When the stock is depleted, the deal passes left for the next round.

PLAY: Play begins with the person to the dealer's left. If this player has a card in his hand that is the same denomination as one face up on the table, he may play this card—taking both the played card and the card from the table. If two or more cards of this same denomination are on the table, he may capture both of them (except in the case of picture cards, where only one may be taken in at a time). He may also capture combinations from the board. For instance, if he has a ten in his hand and a seven and three are on the table, he may take both these cards by playing the ten. If two such combinations (adding up to ten) are exposed on the table, both may be taken on the same play. Furthermore, should a ten lie on the table, it may be collected along with the combinations. A play that takes every card from the table is called a "Sweep"; a Sweep is a bonus point in the scoring.

If unable to make a play on turn, the player puts a card from his hand face up with the others on the table. When all players are out of cards, the deal is repeated using the stock. Cards are not dealt to the table, however, even if it is bare. The person making the last successful play on the final hand of the round claims all the cards remaining on the table. At the finish of a round, each player counts and sorts through his pack of cards gathered from the table. Points are awarded as follows:

Sweeps	1 point each
Aces	1 point each
Little Casino (deuce of spades)	1 point
Big Casino (ten of diamonds) . . .	2 points
Most Cards Captured	3 points
Most Spades Collected	1 point

More rounds are played until, at the close of a round, one player (or team of partners) scores 21 or more points, thus winning the game.

The player holding this Casino *hand (fanned cards) against the four cards dealt to the table uses his six to take the four and two.*

With this hand (fanned cards), the Casino *player may place his four upon the table's six, announcing that he is "building tens."*

STRATEGY: Various strategies are open to the player. One involves the building of combinations on the table. A player holding the ten may see a five and a four on the table. In addition to the ten he holds, he may possess an ace. Pairing the five and four on the table and placing his ace on the pile, he announces, "Building tens." On his next turn, he plays his ten and gathers in the combination. Similarly, if there were a nine on the table and an ace and ten

in his hand, he could do the same by placing his ace on the nine. He can only build in this way if *he can actually make the play on his next turn.* Meanwhile, before this player's turn comes up again, another player may steal the combination, providing he holds a ten in his hand.

Moreover, another player may raise the build. If one player announces that he is building sixes, the next person may raise the bid to an eight by placing a two in his hand on the combination. A strict rule of the game is that one cannot raise his own builds; that is, a player announcing that he is building eights *may not change his build* by adding yet another card on his next turn. He must play the eight and gather in the cards. The card that raises a build must come from a player's hand; builds are never raised using cards from the table.

To prevent other players from raising a build, a player may resort to a tactic known as the call. Suppose, for instance, that a five and a three lie on the table, and that a player holds a pair of eights. Making a pile of the five and three, he adds one of his eights and announces, "Eights—call!" Similarly, if an eight and a five are on the table, and a player holds an eight and a three, he may play his three onto the five, with the same effect—calling "Eights." Now, no other player can raise the build. However, even this tactic isn't foolproof, since someone else holding an eight in his hand may take in the cards.

VARIATIONS: *Spade Casino* differs from traditional *Casino* only with respect to the high premium placed upon the spade suit in scoring points. In addition to the point awards for Cards, Big Casino, Aces and Sweeps, Spade winnings carry the following values: jack of spades, two points; deuce of spades, two points; all other spades, one point each. Because 24 points or more may be won in each round, the grand game-winning total is generally set at 61.

In *Draw Casino* only the deal differs. After the initial deal—in which each player receives four cards, and four are dealt face up in the center of the table—the remaining cards are placed face down as stock. Following each play, a player draws a card from the top of the stock. Therefore players always have a full hand of four cards.

Clock Solitaire

● 1 ● *A standard 52-card deck*

OBJECT: The player tries to move every card of every denomination into correct clock position before all four kings are turned up.

RANKING OF CARDS: Ace (one), two, three, four . . . ten; jack (11); queen (12); king (13).

PREPARATION AND DEAL: After the shuffle, cards are dealt face down into 13 equal stacks of four cards each. Twelve stacks are arranged to represent the positions of the numerals of a clock. The 13th stack of four cards occupies the center point of the circle.

PLAY: The player begins by turning up the top card of the center stack. If this card proves to be a seven, he slides the seven face up *beneath* the pile of cards at the seven-o'clock position

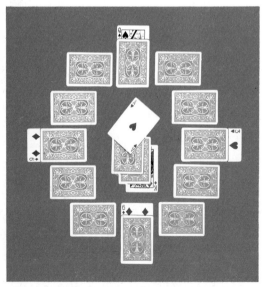

The ace turned up from the center pile goes under the pack at the one o'clock position in the "dial" of the Clock Solitaire *tableau.*

in the circle. Similarly, a jack would go under the 11-o'clock stack, a queen under the 12-o'clock pile. Whatever position the top center card belongs in, the player turns up the top card of that pile and treats it in the manner described—burying it face up at the bottom of the pile in the correct clock position. The top card of that pile is turned up, and the procedure is repeated around and about the circle. Whenever a king appears, it goes beneath the center stack; the top card is turned up and played just as any other card. When the fourth and final king is turned over, the game ends.

VARIATION: In *Multiple Clock Solitaire* any number can play. Each player has his own deck and plays on his own Tableau. A player collects one point for each card played prior to the appearance of the fourth king. The first player to make 100 points wins the competition.

Contract Bridge

● 4 (2 Teams) ● *Two standard 52-card decks; scoring pad and pencil*

OBJECT: Each player works with a partner to take "tricks" (one card from each player) and win points for his team. Each team tries to prevent the opposing team from doing the same.

RANKING OF SUITS: The suits are ranked in order from the lowest to the highest: clubs, diamonds, hearts, spades. Spades and hearts are major suits; diamonds and clubs, minor suits. In bidding and raising, the rank of the suits is always observed. For example, if a bid is one heart, the next bid must be two—if in hearts, clubs or diamonds.

RANKING OF CARDS: Ace (high); two, (low). Cards of the trump suit rank higher than other suits regardless of denomination.

SCORING HONORS: Prior to the opening of play, the teams record on the score pad above the score line, any points held in trump honors. The honors are the ace, king, queen, jack and ten of trump. If one player holds any four of them, he scores 100 points for his team; if all five, 150 points for his team. In a no-trumps situation, a partner holding all four aces scores 150 points.

PREPARATION: One of the decks is shuffled. Each person draws a card from anywhere in the deck. Those two players who draw the highest cards are paired as partners against the two others who draw the lowest cards. Partners take seats opposite one another across the table. The player who draws the highest ranked card (the ace of spades being highest) has the first deal. After shuffling, he offers the deck to his right for the cut. At the same time, his partner begins shuffling the extra deck for the next dealer.

DEAL: The dealer distributes the cards one at a time. He deals them face down in clockwise rotation, starting with the player on his left; each person receives 13 cards. At the end of the hand, the deal passes to the left. The new dealer uses the deck prepared by the partner of the previous dealer while his partner collects and prepares the cards from the concluded hand.

BIDDING: After the players receive and inspect their hands, arranging their cards by suit, they begin the bidding for the privilege of naming the trump suit. A bid implies a commitment to take a certain number of tricks over the "book"; six tricks constitute a book. Hence, a bid of one implies a commitment to take seven tricks; a bid of two, eight tricks. The highest possible bid —seven, for a Grand Slam—represents a contract for all 13 tricks, meaning that the opposition cannot take any tricks at all. A bid of six is called a Small Slam—a contract for 12 tricks. A player may raise a bid by his partner; he may also raise his own previous bid to a higher level if his opponents have kept the bidding going by their action. In raising and answering the bid, the ranks of the suits must be strictly observed. In other words, a one-club bid may be raised with a one bid in any of the three higher ranking suits (or obviously a bid of two clubs or more); a one-spade bid, however, requires the next person bidding to go up at least one unit (bid two) in any other suit. If bidding no trumps, a player may bid the same number as any suit previously bid—no trump outranking all suits.

These nine tricks are scored in Contract Bridge *as three. The first six (shown stepped) make up the "book," which carries no value.*

A team may take more than the number of tricks for which it bids. For each such extra trick (or "overtrick"), a team receives bonus points; however, only the number of tricks actually bid is scored toward the winning of any given game. The bonus points for overtricks and honor cards, together with penalty points for the failure to make the number of tricks bid, are written above the line on the score pad and totaled up at the end of the "rubber"—when one team wins two games out of three. To win a game, one team must score at least 100 points on contracted tricks alone before the other team can do so. After the book (which carries no value), each trick carries the following value: when clubs or diamonds are named trump, 20 points per trick; when hearts or spades are designated trump, 30 points per trick; when no trump is designated (that is, there is no trump suit in the play for tricks), 40 points for the first trick and 30 points per trick for all the others. Thus, in any hand, only the team that wins the bid and names trump scores points toward game. It is possible to win an entire game in just one hand of play, if the team carries the bidding up to the following levels or higher:

Four spades . . . . .120 points
Four hearts. . . . . .120 points
Five diamonds . . . . .100 points
Five clubs . . . . .100 points
Three no trump . . . . .100 points

Dealer (at bottom) opens with a bid of one club on the strength of his club honors and 19 points. Next to bid is player to left.

Common sense is the greatest aid in bidding. A player who holds no high ranking cards whatsoever should pass rather than enter an opening bid, since, on the strength of his hand, he cannot foresee his team's capturing a large number of tricks. Several methods of assessing the strength of a hand are popular. The simplest such system asks the player not to enter an opening bid except when his hand totals 13 or more points, according to the following scale:

Ace	4 points
King	3 points
Queen	2 points
Jack	1 point
Void (missing suit)	3 points
Singleton (only one card in a suit) . .	2 points
Doubleton (only two cards in a suit)	1 point

In cases where, because of insufficient points, everybody at the table declines to bid—that is, where all players pass—the hand is thrown in. A new hand is then dealt by the person to the left of the previous dealer.

The player to make the opening bid is the dealer. Generally, if his hand has fewer than 13 points, he would be wise to pass. However, should he hold seven or more cards of one suit, he may wish to enter a so-called "pre-emptive" bid (a bid of three) in that suit—thus signaling

his partner that he has a "long" suit. If, on the other hand, the opening bidder holds a very strong hand—for example, 21 points in top cards and a strong suit in hearts, namely the ace, king, ten, nine, eight and four—he would probably not limit himself to a bid of one heart. Instead, he would signal his great strength with a bid of two hearts; however, the person to his left (the next bidder) would very likely pass—so many of the available points being concentrated in the first hand. After this opponent makes his decision, the first bidder's partner gets a chance to bid. If the partner holds moderate strength in points—luckily, together with a few cards of the heart suit—he would want to signal this to his partner and, at the same time, keep the bidding going. (This is so that his partner can, if he chooses, raise the contract to the level of four hearts—giving them sufficient points to win a game in a single hand.) Thus, the second partner would very likely call out a bid of three hearts. The bid being this high, his opponent to the left (the next bidder) would probably pass. His partner—the original bidder of hearts—would answer his partner's three-heart bid with four, after which no one would bid further.

The above description is typical of a simple round of bidding. However, more complicated bidding often occurs. Frequently, both teams enter the bidding, each competing for the contract. One team, should it feel that the contracting team's bid is too high, may challenge the bid on the final round by "doubling"; the contracting team may "redouble" if it feels it can, indeed, make the original bid. Both of these are special penalty bonus situations detailed further along in this section.

The partner who first mentions the suit in which the contract is finally established is called the "declarer." (Since, in the above example, the contract is established in hearts, the opening bidder—who started with a bid of two hearts—is the declarer.) The declarer plays both hands for his team as described in the PLAY section below.

PLAY: The person to the left of the declarer opens the play for tricks. He does so by playing any card, face up, onto the center of the table. After this first card is played, the declarer's partner places his entire hand, face up, on the table before him for all to see. His hand is thereafter known as the "dummy." The declarer then reaches across the table and plays from the dummy any card of the same suit as the opening card of the trick. (If void of that suit in the dummy, the declarer may use a trump card, or any other card, from the dummy.) Continuing clockwise, the opponent on the dummy's left plays a card of the opening suit, and, finally, the declarer does the same. The highest ranking card of that suit wins the trick (four cards); the winner of the trick leads the first card of the next trick. Where any player holds no cards of the suit led (where he is void in that suit) he may play a card of the trump suit. A trump card beats any other card except a higher ranking denomination in trump; thus, for example if hearts are trump, a two of hearts played onto a trick otherwise consisting of the ace, king and ten of diamonds wins the trick.

One partner from each team collects all the tricks won by his team. When all 13 tricks are captured, the contracting team counts up how many tricks it has over book and enters its score according to the contract. Where the bidding team makes exactly the number of tricks for which they bid, the appropriate number of points is entered on the score pad beneath the game line. For instance, if four hearts are bid and the bidding team wins ten tricks, the partners make their bid—receiving 120 points. If five clubs are bid and 11 tricks taken, the bid is made—the score received being 100 points. In both examples, a full game is won. Hence, the winning team in each example now has one game against the necessary two for rubber—two games out of three. After the first game, a new game line is drawn horizontally across the score pad, and points for the second game are written below this line—with any prior points scored not counting for either team in this new game. In short, each game starts afresh.

If the bidding team fails to make the number of tricks for which it establishes a contract, it pays a penalty to the opposing team. The opposing team scores these points above the initial game line, according to the rates shown in the table below: For example, if three no trump is bid but only eight tricks are taken instead

According to Bridge *rules, this trick consists of a card from each player; declarer (bottom) also plays partner's hand—the dummy (top).*

Declarer trumps his opponent's club trick with a low diamond from dummy; if dummy had a club, then trump could not be played.

of the required nine, a 50-point penalty bonus is paid to the opposing team; if the bid is not made after being challenged by a double, a penalty of 100 points is paid to the doubling team; if redoubled by the bidding team, 200 points are awarded to the doubling team. After winning a game, a team is said to be "vulnerable," that is, they have to pay a special penalty should they fail to meet their contract in any future game. If the bidding team is vulnerable, is challenged with a double and then redoubles, the penalty for missing the contract by a single trick is 400 points.

As noted, such penalties, together with bonuses for overtricks and honors, are written above the initial game line and figure in the total point score at the conclusion of the rubber. The following international Scoring Table details in full the points receivable in *Contract Bridge:*

SCORING TABLE

Trick Score—Contract Made*

Each trick over book	♣Trump	♦Trump	♥Trump	♠Trump
Undoubled	20	20	30	30
Doubled	40	40	60	60
Redoubled	80	80	120	120

First trick over book	No Trump
Undoubled	40
Doubled	80
Redoubled	160
Each additional trick	
Undoubled	30
Doubled	60
Redoubled	120

Scored below line by declarer's side.

Penalties—Contract Not Made**

First undertrick	Not Vulnerable
Undoubled	50
Doubled	100
Redoubled	200
Each additional undertrick	
Undoubled	50
Doubled	200

	Redoubled	400
First undertrick		Vulnerable
Undoubled		100
Doubled		200
Redoubled		400
Each additional undertrick		
Undoubled		100
Doubled		300
Redoubled		600

***Scored above line by declarer's opponents.*

Bonuses—Tricks Above Contract†

Each overtrick	Not Vulnerable
Undoubled	Trick Value
Doubled	100
Redoubled	200

Each overtrick	Vulnerable
Undoubled	Trick Value
Doubled	200
Redoubled	400

† *Scored above line by declarer's side.*

Premium Score—Game and Rubber††

Making contract, doubled or redoubled	50
Bidding and making grand slam (all 13 tricks) vulnerable	1500
Bidding and making grand slam, not vulnerable	1000
Bidding and making small slam (12 tricks), vulnerable	750
Bidding and making small slam, not vulnerable	500
Winning rubber, two games to zero	700
Winning rubber, two games to one	500

†† *Scored above line by declarer's side.*

After the points for the hand are correctly scored, the cards are passed to the dealer's left and dealt for a new hand. Again, the bidding opens with the dealer, and it rotates to the left. Play continues in this fashion through as many hands as required until one team wins two games, at which time the rubber ends. At the close of the rubber, the scorekeeper totals up all the points listed for each team. Usually, but not always, the team that wins the rubber also comes out ahead in the final scoring—above and below the line. Cases to the contrary may occur where the opposing team scores, say, a Grand Slam (1000 points above the line) or collects a great number of penalty points above the line.

Cribbage

● *2* ● *A standard 52-card deck*

OBJECT: Players attempt to score 61 (or 121) points before their opponent can do so.

RANKING OF CARDS: King (high), queen, jack and ten all have a numerical value of ten; nine, nine; eight, eight etc. down to ace (low), which is valued at one.

PREPARATION AND DEAL: The cards are shuffled and cut. In the cut for deal, the lowest card wins. The dealer starts with his opponent and distributes six cards, face down, dealing one at a time. An error in the deal automatically results in two points for the dealer's opponent. The opponent, in this case, may demand a new deal if he hasn't yet looked at any of his cards; otherwise, the error is corrected either by drawing cards from the stock or returning cards to the stock. The loser of the first hand deals the second hand, and so on throughout the game.

Before starting play, each person discards two cards, face down, into a common pack. These four cards are kept on the table as the "Crib" until the close of play, at which time the dealer has the advantage of taking the Crib to use in forming combinations.

After creation of the Crib, the dealer's opponent cuts the stock. Reuniting the stock, the dealer turns up the top card—the "starter." Should this card prove to be a jack (His Heels in the scoring chart shown below), the dealer can automatically mark off two points for himself. At play's end, the starter will figure in the formation of combinations by both players.

SCORING: As soon as one of the scoring plays listed below appears, the person who makes it should score it immediately. After a player takes another turn, he cannot go back and tally points won on previous turns. A scoring table citing the various point-plays follows:

POINT-PLAYS

His Heels (a jack faced up as starter): 2

His Nobs (jack of starter's suit, counted with the hand or the Crib): 1

31, when reached exactly during play: 2

Nearest to 31, achieved on the last card put down during play: 1

15, when formed as a sum in the course of play: 2

15, when reached on the last card layed down during play (including the point for nearest to 31): 3

Pair, during a play, any card of the same denomination as the last card played and still face up on the table; when counted as part of the hand or Crib, any two cards of the same denomination: 2

Triplet, scored during play with a third card of the same denomination as a Pair lying face up on the table; scored when counting the hand or Crib as any three cards of the same denomination: 6

Four, scored during play with a fourth card of the same denomination as a Triplet, still showing face up, coming consecutively after the last card of the Triplet; scored when counting the hand or Crib as any four cards of the same denomination: 12

Sequence, or Run, scored during play with the third (or fourth or fifth, etc.) card played in a numerical series; the other cards of the Sequence must be lying face up on the table, although they need not necessarily be in strict sequential order. For each card: 1

Double Run of Three, scored only when counting up the hand or the Crib; this is a three-card Sequence with any card of the Sequence also paired: 8

Double Run of Four, as above, but with a four-card Sequence: 10

Triple Run, scored only when counting the hand or the Crib; this combination is a Triplet with two cards in Sequence, i.e., three threes, a four and a five: 15

Quadruple Run, scored only when counting the hand or the Crib; this is a combination of two Pairs and connected by a single card in

Sequence; i.e. a pair of twos, a three, a pair
of fours:. 16

Four-card flush, four cards of the same suit, in
hand only: 4

Five-card flush, four cards, in the hand or the
Crib, of the same suit as the starter: 5

PLAY: The dealer's opponent leads the first card,
playing it face up on the table directly before
him and announcing its numerical value. As
noted previously, picture cards have a value of
ten points, aces one point, and all other cards,
their denominational value.

After his opponent lays down a card, the dealer
does likewise—keeping the card face up, directly
in front of him. Then the dealer announces the
sum of the values of the two cards exposed so
far. Play continues alternating back and forth
between the two people in this way. If the first
card played is a ten, and the dealer then lays
down a five, he announces 15. In doing so, he
scores two points for himself, as shown in the
chart above. Suppose the dealer's opponent follows by playing a five himself. Announcing the
running sum as 20, he hastens to score two
points for himself for creating a Pair on the table
(the dealer's five being paired with his five).

At no time may the running tally of either
player exceed 31. If a player does not hold a
card that is playable, he is forced to announce
"Go"—a sign that his opponent may continue
and may play off all his playable cards one at
a time. He scores one point because Go is called.
Pairs, Triplets, Fours and Sequences—listed on
the aforementioned chart—are normally formed
alternately; when a Go is declared, however, the
requirement of alternation is suspended. Hence
such combinations may be built by the player
who is given the Go signal, so long as he does
not exceed 31 points.

If exactly 31 points are reached, the person
making the play receives two points. Where the
players run out of cards before the tally reaches
31, the person playing the last card receives one
point for nearest to 31. When the last card
makes a total of exactly 15, the player gets three
points: two for the 15 and one for nearest 31.

On those occasions where 31 is reached or where
both players are forced to announce Go for lack
of playable cards, *each person turns face down
those cards already played.* The tally reverts to
zero, and the player whose turn it is then begins
anew by playing a card from his hand. The play
then alternates as previously described.

Once all cards are played onto the table, each
person picks up his hand. A second round of
scoring now commences, based solely on the
players' respective ingenuity in recognizing
scoring combinations—a facility that grows
larger the more experienced players become with
the game. The dealer's opponent is first to
count; he treats the starter as though it were
part and parcel with his hand. Afterwards, the
dealer counts up his points: First, he tots up
the combinations he can make, using his hand
in combination with the starter; then he tallies
the points he finds in the Crib, including the
starter. (Remember, the Crib is always awarded
to the dealer.) Obviously, the dealer has the
advantage; however, the loser of the hand does
have the advantage of being the dealer for the
next hand. The scoring can be done with pencil
and paper, but a Cribbage Board greatly facilitates the process.

The Cribbage Board contains four rows of holes
with 30 holes per row. At either end of the
four rows are one or two game holes. The board
is laid on the table so that the game holes are
horizontal. Both players begin to score from the
same end of the board, moving away from the
game holes; they each use two rows of holes.
Each player is given two pegs to keep track of
his score, which he moves first along the outside
row of holes nearest him, then back up along
the inside row in the opposite direction. The
first score is marked by inserting a peg at the
appropriately numbered hole away from the
game hole. The second score is marked by inserting the second peg ahead of the first peg
the correct number of holes. On the third score,
the trailing peg (the first peg) is moved forward
ahead of the peg in front of it (the second peg).
This action continues until a peg reaches the
61st hole (unless a game of 121 is agreed on).

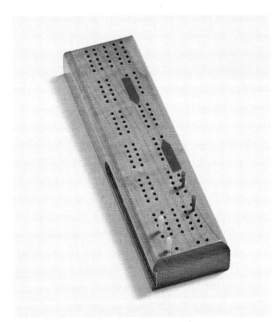

Cribbage *players keep score on this special board by moving pegs; first along the outside row of holes, then back along the inner row.*

When the winner hits 61 before his opponent reaches 31 (or 121 as against 91) the game is declared a "Lurch," and counts as two winning games for the victor.

VARIATIONS: In *Three-Handed Cribbage,* each person is dealt five cards and one card is dealt into the Crib. Each player also discards one card from his hand into the Crib—making a total of four cards per hand in the crib. After each hand the deal passes left. The rest of the game is the same as two-handed *Cribbage.* A three-handed scoring board is used.

In *Four-Handed Cribbage,* the deck is cut to decide on teams, the cutters of the two highest cards playing as partners against the two lowest. The lowest card wins the deal. Each person gets five cards on the deal—which proceeds clockwise, one card at a time, beginning with the player on the dealer's left. All players discard one card to form the Crib. The person on the dealer's left cuts the stock before the dealer faces up the starter. One player from each team is designated as scorer for his team. A regular scoring board is used; the scorer on each team records his score and his partner's score, jointly, with the same two pegs along the same row of holes. Game is 121 points, and the deal passes left after each hand.

Dunk in the Ocean

● *2 to 7* ● *A standard 52-card deck for each player*

OBJECT: Each player tries to play off 35 cards before any other player.

RANKING OF CARDS: Ace, low; king, high.

PREPARATION AND DEAL: Each player receives a 52-card deck and serves as his own dealer. Players deal 35 cards into five equal stacks, placed face up before them. The remaining 17 cards are kept face down in a stack called "the dunk stack." The first player is determined by drawing straws—pre-cut to various lengths.

PLAY: After every player's preparations are complete, the first player cries, "Dunk!" At this signal, each player quickly takes the top card from his own "dunk stack" and places it face up in the center of the table. Then each player builds rapidly on all of the center cards—picking cards from the tops of his five upturned stacks. He builds without regard to suit: For instance, an eight of clubs may be laid on a seven of diamonds; a nine of spades on the eight of clubs; a ten of hearts on the nine; a jack of clubs on the ten, etc. The sequence may also be built in descending order: six upon seven, five upon six, four upon three, etc. Turns need not be taken in any prescribed order—that is, players may lay a card on any pile whenever they see an opportunity. (In a case where two or more players put the same card on top of a pile, the first card that touches the pile remains.) When no one is able to make a play from the tops of his stacks, the center cards are removed to the side. When the table is cleared, the first player again cries "Dunk!" and the wild play begins anew. The first player to rid himself of all 35 cards in his face-up stacks is the winner.

Eights
(*Crazy Eights or Swedish Rummy*)
● *2 to 4*   ● *A standard 52-card deck*

OBJECT: Each player attempts to play off all cards in hand before any other player can do so.

RANKING OF CARDS: Eights are wild. Other cards have their face value: King, <u>high</u>; ace, <u>low</u>.

PREPARATION: The cards are shuffled and cut. When four play, they are divided into two teams of partners who sit opposite one another across the table. In the cut for deal, high card wins.

DEAL: The dealer distributes cards, one at a time, clockwise from his left. When two play, each receives seven cards; if there are three or four players, five cards. After the deal, the remaining cards are put face down on the table as a stock. The top card of the stock is then faced up as the "starter."

PLAY: The player on the dealer's left begins play by placing on top of the starter a card either of the same suit or of the same denomination. Thus, should the starter be the king of diamonds, any diamond or any other king can be played onto it. Since eights are wild cards, an eight may also be played. The player of the eight names the suit he wishes his card to represent. The denominational value of the eight is that of the card on which it has been laid—in this case a king.

In this fashion, play moves clockwise around the table. If a player has a card that can be played, he *must* play it. After making a successful play, a person may draw a single card from the top of the stock if he so chooses. When a player cannot make a play, he must draw from the stock until he pulls a card that is playable. Once the stock is depleted, anyone who cannot make a play forfeits his turn to the player on his left. Otherwise, the player (or team) to get rid of all cards first wins the hand. The winner collects points as follows: for each eight still held by opponents, 50 points; for each picture card, ten points; for each ace, one point; for

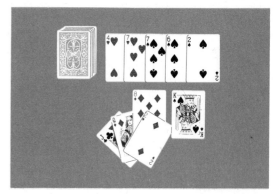

Here, the last card in the discard row is the deuce of spades. Another deuce, another spade or a wild eight may be played onto it.

all other cards, their numerical value. The grand winning total is generally set at 100 points. If the stock is depleted and no player can make a play, the game ends in a "block." The hands are then put face up on the table for inspection. The player (or team) with the lowest number of points left wins.

Fan Tan

● *2 to 6 (best with 3 to 6)*   ● *A standard 52-card deck*

OBJECT: Each player tries to discard all cards in his hand before any other player.

RANKING OF CARDS: Ace, <u>low</u>; king, <u>high</u>.

PREPARATION: If three, five or six people are to play, one or more cards of one suit are removed from the deck beforehand to make the deal come out even. The "end cards" are the ones removed; for example, the ace in a three-handed game, the ace and king in a five-handed game, the ace, two, king and queen in a six-handed game. The cards are shuffled and cut. In the cut for deal, the low card wins.

DEAL: The dealer distributes the cards clockwise, one at a time, starting with the player on his left.

PLAY: In *Fan Tan,* participants discard one card per play into 12 piles—four horizontal rows and three vertical columns. The horizontal rows each consist of a single suit. The card that opens play is the seven. The four sevens eventually will be aligned in the central vertical column.

At the start of play, the person on the dealer's left goes first, discarding a seven of some suit if he has one. Once a seven is on the table, players have the option of discarding another seven under it or of building piles on either side of the seven (or sevens) already on the table. (Remember that in *Fan Tan* a player *must* make a play if he has a card that can be played.) If the next player does not have another seven, the six of the same suit may be placed to the left of the first seven; the matching eight to its right. Then the remaining cards in the suit are discardable upon the six and the eight. Discards must follow strictly in numerical order: At left, beginning with the six, the order is descending—the five on top of the six, the four on top of the five, etc.—and at right, beginning with the eight, the order is ascending—the nine atop the eight, the ten atop the nine, etc. The

order of the suits played is determined only by the sequence of the sevens laid down—changeable from game to game.

In this way, play proceeds. The first player to rid his hand of all cards is the winner. When scoring under a point system, the winner of the hand collects one point for each card still held by the other players. Fifty (or some other mutually agreed-upon grand total) can be set as the ultimate winning score. If chips are used, a player pays one chip to the pot whenever he is unable to play a card. In addition to this pot, the winner collects a chip for each card still held by his opponents at the end of the hand.

VARIATION: In *Two-Handed Fan Tan* the same rules apply except that hands for three players are dealt, with the extra hand forming a pack placed face down on the table. When a player cannot make a play, he draws from the top of the pack, continuing to do so until the pack yields a playable card.

Gin Rummy

● 2 ● *A standard 52-card deck; scoring pad and pencil*

OBJECT: A player tries to arrange his hand into combinations before his opponent can do so.

RANKING OF CARDS: Ace (low); king (high). In counting, ace equals one; picture cards equal ten each; nine, nine; eight, eight, etc.

PREPARATION AND DEAL: The cards are shuffled and dealt. In the cut for deal, low card deals. The dealer, beginning with his opponent, distributes the cards, one at a time, face down. In the most popular form of the game, he deals 11 cards to his opponent and only ten to himself. He puts the remainder of the deck, face down, in the center of the table as the stock. The winner of a hand deals the next hand.

In Fan Tan, *columns are laid out as above with discards being placed on the sixes and eights in both numerical order and by following suit.*

PLAY: The dealer's opponent starts play by placing a card from his hand face up beside the stock (reducing the number of cards in his hand to ten). The dealer then either picks up the card laid down by his opponent or draws the top card from the stock. He discards one card, face up, onto the pile of discards forming beside the stock. Play alternates between the two people in this way. In drawing from the discard pile, only the top card may be taken and only this card should be visible.

As play proceeds, each person tries to arrange the cards in his hand into combinations. These are three of a kind, four of a kind or a numerical sequence of three or more cards of the same suit. If a player can arrange all his cards into combinations as he lays down his discard, he calls out, "Gin." Then he exposes his hand on the table, winning a bonus of 20 points. In addition, he receives points for every odd card held by his opponent according to denominational value. Game is 100 points.

A Gin hand is worth 20 points. It shows all cards in runs of at least three of the same denomination or in numerical sequence by suit.

A player need not wait for a perfect Gin before exposing his cards. At any time that his odd cards total ten points or less he may "knock"— that is, rap the table and expose his hand. When a player knocks, however, he is gambling that he holds fewer odd points than his opponent. If so, he takes the difference (with no bonus). When a player knocks, his opponent has the right to lay off odd cards onto his combinations. For example, suppose the dealer knocks with three kings; three jacks; four, five, six of diamonds and an odd ace. If dealer's opponent holds an odd king, an odd jack, and a seven and eight of diamonds, he may lay off all these cards onto the dealer's exposed hand—reducing greatly the odd points in his hand. Where the opponent's hand contains the same number (or

A player "knocks"—here with three odd points: an ace and deuce. He collects the difference between his odd points and his opponent's.

fewer) odd points, he takes a bonus of ten from the person who knocked, as well as the difference in points as described above.

In some sections of the country, equal hands of ten cards are dealt to each player. To begin the discard pile, the top card of the stock is faced up on the table. If this card proves to be a spade, the point totals for the hand are automatically doubled. Moreover, the denomination of the face-up card sets a limit for knocking: For instance, if it is a six, a player must hold six or less points in odd cards in order to knock.

VARIATIONS: In *Hollywood Gin,* three *Gin* games are played and scored concurrently—each game with a winning total of 100 points. In Game I, the first hand a player wins is scored under his name; the second hand he wins is scored both in Game I and Game II, and the third hand he wins is scored in all three games—as are any hands won by him thereafter. Thus, a player must score in the first game before he can score in the second game, and so forth. Generally, a bonus of 100 points is awarded to the player who "shuts out" (holds scoreless) his opponent in any given game. A bonus of 100 points may be given to the winner of the "rubber" (two games out of three).

In *Around the Corner,* the ace may be either low or high (whereas in *Gin Rummy* it is always low). In addition to ace, two, three and queen, king, ace, the aces may be used in around-the-corner sequences—such as, queen, king, ace, two, three, or king, ace, two. When one person knocks, the other may lay off cards as described for *Gin*. All the cards in the discard pile may be inspected at any time (whereas in *Gin* only the top card can be looked at). Odd aces in the hand are valued at 15 points. Game is set at 125 points.

Hearts

- *3 to 6* - *A standard 52-card deck; scoring pad and pencil*

OBJECT: Each player attempts to take in fewer points than the other players, or—more rarely—all the points.

RANKING OF CARDS: Ace, <u>high</u>; two, <u>low</u>. In scoring, all hearts have a value of one point each; queen of spades, 13 points; ten of diamonds, minus (−) ten.

PREPARATION AND DEAL: Cards are shuffled and cut. Cards are distributed one at a time in a clockwise rotation, beginning to the left of the dealer until the deck is dealt out evenly among the players. If any odd cards remain at the end of the deal, they are used to make a "kitty" face down on the table. The kitty is taken in by the winner of the first trick.

PASS: Each player arranges his hand, keeping it concealed from the other players. Each player passes three cards of his choosing face down to the player on his left.

PLAY: The two (deuce) of clubs opens play. The player holding the deuce in his hand plays it face up onto the table. Should the deuce be in the kitty, the three of clubs leads in its place. All players, in turn, follow suit—moving clockwise from the person who opens play. Where a player is able to follow suit, he must do so. Otherwise, he may "sluff" a card of another suit onto the trick. The highest card played of the original suit wins the trick. Since there is no trump, a heart or the queen of spades may be safely sluffed onto tricks in which a player is void of the suit. At the start of play, the pass can be used to create voids that will permit the sluffing of hearts and the queen of spades. Neither hearts nor the queen of spades may be

A four-handed Hearts game opens with the lead of the club deuce (left). The others must play clubs if able. The ace wins the trick.

The club deuce (right) opens play; the trick is taken by the club ace. The fourth player, without clubs, discards heart ace onto trick.

led until one or more hearts or spades is sluffed onto a trick. If play proceeds to a point where a person holds only hearts or the queen of spades, however, he may lead them even though they have not previously been broken in a sluff.

Play proceeds until the players hold no more cards. At the end of play, each person totals up his points as follows: for each heart, one point;

for the queen of spades, 13 points; for the ten of diamonds, minus ten points. When any one of the players reaches 50 points, the game ends, with the low scorer winning.

Generally speaking, players will avoid taking tricks that contain either hearts or the spade queen. However, a player holding many hearts and high cards in his hand may wish to "shoot the moon" by taking all 13 hearts and the spade queen—thereby winning minus 26 points. Anyone planning to shoot the moon is wise to control the first trick or tricks, since the kitty may conceal vital cards. Although worth minus ten, the ten of diamonds needn't be taken for a successful moon shot. Obviously, as soon as even one heart or the queen of spades falls to any other player, the possibility of shooting the moon no longer exists.

VARIATION: In *Two-Handed Hearts* each player is dealt 13 cards, with the remainder forming a face-down stock on the table. After each trick, players draw one card from the top of the stock—the winner of the previous trick having first draw. When the pack is depleted and the players empty their hands, the trick piles are inventoried and scored as in regular *Hearts*.

Lift Smoke

● *4 to 6*   ● *A standard 52-card deck*

OBJECT: Players attempt to retain cards when others have played out their hands.

RANKING OF CARDS: Ace, <u>high</u>; two, <u>low</u>.

PREPARATION AND DEAL: Cards are shuffled and dealt. High card wins the cut for deal. The dealer distributes the cards, one at a time, clockwise from his left until each person, including himself, has six cards (five cards in a five-handed game). The stock, made up of the remaining cards, is placed face down in the middle of the table. The dealer turns up the last card dealt to himself, indicating the trump suit.

PLAY: Play begins with the person on the dealer's left, who leads any card from his hand. Play

In Lift Smoke, *the trump suit is determined when the dealer faces up the final card dealt to himself; here diamonds become trump.*

moves clockwise, and the other players follow suit if possible. When unable to follow suit, a player *must trump*. If a player is void in the suit and void also in trumps, then he may sluff any card onto the trick. The highest card played of the suit led wins the trick if the trick is not trumped. Trump will win any trick. Where more than one trump card falls, the highest trump takes the trick. The winner of the trick draws a card from the top of the stock, then leads from his hand to open the next trick. *Only the winner of the trick may draw from the stock.* The winner of the game is the player who still holds a card or cards when the others have no cards left in their hands. In an end-game situation where two or three players have a single card which they play on a final trick, the person who takes this trick wins the game.

Patience

● *1*   ● *A standard 52-card deck*

OBJECT: Each player tries to build completely the four suits in ascending order on the four foundation aces.

RANKING OF CARDS: Ace, <u>low</u>; king, <u>high</u>.

PREPARATION AND DEAL: Of the many variations of *Patience,* the most widely played form is described here. After shuffling, the player deals a line of seven cards from left to right—the first card face up, the rest face down. Now he repeats the process, but skipping the first card: He places a card face up on the second card from the left and cards face down on the remaining piles.

Again, the deal is repeated—first card up, the remainder down—this time, beginning with pile number three. The deal continues until only one card remains, which is laid face up on the seventh pile. The resulting arrangement—the "Tableau"—is seven piles, each capped by a face-up card. The piles contain one, two, three, four, five, six and seven cards respectively—28 cards in all. The 24 remaining cards are put aside as a stock for later use.

PLAY: Because only the face-up cards can be manipulated, there are seven cards to work with at the outset. If the player is fortunate, one or more of these top cards will be aces. Aces are automatically moved to an area above the Tab-leau, where they serve as foundations for subsequent building. Given great luck, a two and three of the same suit as a foundation ace may be showing. All such matching top cards are transferred to the area above the Tableau: Ace, two, three . . . etc. by suit. When the top card of any pack is moved, the card under it may be turned over. If this card also proves playable, the next card down may be turned face up, and so forth.

The other type of play involves moving cards about within the Tableau itself. As noted, in the case of the foundation aces, the order of building is ascending. Inside the Tableau, however, the order of sequences is always descending:

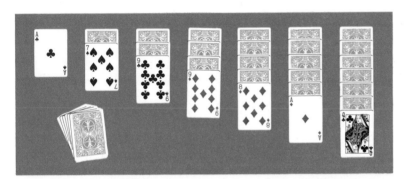

Before the start of play, the Patience Tableau contains 28 cards in seven piles of progressively larger size, each capped by a face-up card. The first pile consists of just one card, face up; the seventh, of six cards face down, one up.

After the Tableau is dealt, the remaining 24 cards are put aside as a stock to be turned up in threes. Above the Tableau, building upon aces takes place in upward numerical order by suit; within the Tableau, the building alternates between red cards and black, in downward order. As they are uncovered, face-down cards are turned up. On this play, the red three from the stock can go on the black four; then the red jack on the black queen and the red queen on the black king.

King, queen, jack, ten, nine . . . two. Furthermore, a red card must always be placed upon a black card, and vice versa. A variety of plays are possible. For example, if among the top cards, there are a black king and a red queen, the latter can at once be moved and laid upon the former. As a result of this switch, the face-down card at the top of the pack from which the queen was taken is now turned up.

Should it prove to be a black jack, it is played on the queen, and the next card under the jack is turned up. Elsewhere among the top cards may be a black eight and a red seven. The seven is shifted over onto the eight. A red nine may now appear in the turning of the top card from the seven's old pack. Should this happen, the black eight with its attached red seven are both moved over onto the nine. Should a black ten surface where the eight was, then the whole nine, eight, seven chain is moved onto the ten. When all the cards in a pack are played off, leaving an empty space, a king can be moved to fill the vacancy. Play proceeds within the Tableau in the above manner. As opportunities arise, cards can be moved up to build on the foundation aces. Such moves cannot be made from the middle of a chain, however. The card to be moved must either be last in a building-chain, or alone and face up at the top of a pack.

Frequently, a temporary impasse will occur in which no play seems possible. At such times, the player may resort to the stock of 24 cards previously set aside. The stock is thumbed through, three cards at a time. The first group of three cards is turned face up as a pack, and the top card is examined. If this card is playable, the second card in the group may also be used. Similarly, the third card is eligible for play if the second is played successfully. If the first card in the three-card pack is not playable, the player turns up the next pack of three. In this fashion, the player passes through his entire stock. If ever he goes all the way through the stock without a successful play resulting, the game automatically ends.

VARIATION: In *Double Patience,* there are two players and each tries to play the entire deck onto foundation aces before his opponent. The play differs from *Patience* in that the foundation aces are mutually held property. For instance, if one player moves an ace of hearts above his Tableau line, the other player may lay a two of hearts onto it, and so forth. A player may delay playing cards onto foundation aces if he wishes to temporarily block certain plays by his opponent. Where neither player plays off all his cards, the person with the fewest cards remaining in his Tableau and stockpile automatically becomes the winner.

Pinochle For Two

● *A double deck of 48 cards consisting of two each of the ace, king, queen, jack, ten and nine of each suit; scoring pad and pencil*

OBJECT: Each player attempts to score points by melding combinations and by taking tricks.

RANKING OF THE CARDS: Ace (high), ten, king, queen, jack, nine (low). In counting up the cards taken in tricks, ace equals 15, ten equals ten, king equals five, and the other cards count zero.

PREPARATION AND DEAL: The cards are shuffled and cut. In the cut for deal, the high card wins. Beginning with his opponent, the dealer distributes 12 cards in groups of four at a time to himself and his opponent. (An opponent may demand a new deal where the dealer makes a mistake.) He places the remaining cards face down in the center of the table as the "talon pack." The top card of the talon is faced up beside the talon to indicate the trump suit. If this card is a nine (Dix, or low trumps), the dealer automatically scores ten points.

PLAY: The action and the scoring is in two stages. The first stage of play begins with the dealer's opponent, who leads any card from his hand. The dealer then plays a card from his hand. Unless a trump card is played, the higher denomination of the suit that is led captures the trick. Should two cards of an equal rank (remembering there are doubles of each card in the deck) fall on the trick, the first card played wins the trick. (Because there are only two players, each trick consists of just two cards.) The tricks taken are kept in a face-down pile in front of each player. After every trick, the players draw a single card each from the top of the talon pack. The winner of the trick draws first. In this first stage of play, the players need not follow suit and may trump at any time.

As the first stage of play progresses, the players may score points by a device known as "melding"—that is, by placing certain combinations of cards face up before them on the table. Only the winner of the trick just finished may meld, and he does so before drawing a card from the talon pack. Only one combination may be melded, and any other combinations a player may hold are retained for melding on a later turn. Once a combination is melded and scored, it is left lying face up on the table. However, it is treated as part of the player's hand, in that melded cards may be played directly from the board onto following tricks.

The possible card combinations, and the values of the melds, are as follows:

VALUE OF MELDS

Class I

Marriage (king and queen of same suit) . . 20

Royal Marriage (king, queen of trumps) . . 40

Royal Sequence (ace, ten, king, queen, jack—all of trumps) 150

Class II

Pinochle (queen of spades and jack of diamonds) 30

Double Pinochle (both spade queens, both diamond jacks) 60

Class III

Four Aces (one of each suit) 100

Four Kings (one of each suit) 80

Four Queens (one of each suit) 60

Four Jacks (one of each suit) 40

Dix (nine of trumps), each 10

Frequently the same card will be used in more than one melded combination. This can be done if the combinations in which the card is used fall into different classes (as shown above), or if the second combination in which the card is used has a higher point value within the same class than the first combination. For instance, a Royal Marriage can later be incorporated into a Royal Sequence; a Royal Sequence, however, cannot be broken apart to score a Royal Marriage once the Royal Sequence is scored. Either partner in a Marriage or Royal Marriage may be combined with three others of its kind of different suits to make four of a kind under Class III. Similarly, the queen of spades in a Marriage may be combined with either jack of

In Pinochle, these various card combinations, called melds, carry special point bonuses. For instance, a king-queen of the same suit, a Marriage, is worth 20 points, the jack of diamonds-queen of spades, or Pinochle, 30 points. Full scoring of the three classes of melds is explained in the table above.

diamonds to score a Pinochle in *Class II.* However, the same queen or king may appear in only one Marriage. When a player holding a nine of trumps takes a trick using another trump card, he may exchange the nine for it, thus scoring a Dix (worth ten points). The player who by chance holds both trump nines may score ten for each. If the first nine is already declared, the second need only be shown in taking a trick to score Dix—that is, it needn't be placed on the table. Because a Dix counts as a combination, no other cards may be melded at the same time.

A person who melds a false combination must subtract the value of the true combination from his score. His opponent may then instruct him to lead any card of the false combination to begin the next trick. If, however, the person at fault hasn't yet drawn a card from the talon pack, he may correct his error without suffering a penalty.

When the talon pack gets down to a single remaining card, the winner of the next trick takes this card. The loser of the trick takes in the card faced up beside the talon pack as the trump indicator. Now, with the talon depleted, the second stage of play may begin immediately. Picking up their melded cards from the table, the players blend them into their hands. The winner of the last trick leads any card of his choice. From this point on, the players must follow suit. When void in the suit that is led, they must play a trump if they hold any trump cards in their hands. Furthermore, a player must overcall whenever possible, that is, play a card of higher denomination than the card that is led (when following suit). When a player cannot follow suit and also holds no trump cards, he may discard any card from his hand— regardless of suit or rank. If a player neglects to overcall, or does not follow suit when able to do so, his opponent—on discovering the oversight—may require that the game be replayed from the point at which the error was committed.

After all cards are played, the players go through their captured tricks, counting up points as follows—15 points for each ace contained in their tricks, ten points for each ten, five for each king and ten points for capturing the last trick of the hand. The trick points are added to the melded points. The cards are then gathered up, shuffled and cut for a new deal. The deal alternates after each hand, with the play and scoring proceeding as described above, until one of the players reaches 1,000 points—thus winning the game.

The rules governing *Pinochle* are not the same everywhere. For instance, different laws may control the bidding or the point count for aces, tens, kings and other cards captured in the play for tricks. Thus, when playing with a new group of acquaintances, it is wise to settle upon common ground rules before the start of play.

VARIATIONS: In *Three-Handed Pinochle* each player is dealt 16 cards. Beginning with the person to the dealer's left, players bid for the privilege of naming the trump suit. Bids are calculated on the basis of the points a player expects to win through melding and in the tricks. Each player is permitted only one bid; thus any person on his left may win the privilege of naming trumps by calling out a higher bid. The last to bid is the dealer.

After the bidding and the naming of trumps, each person exposes his melds—laying down all his combinations at once. The melds are the same as listed in the table under *Two-Handed Pinochle.* After the melds are duly recorded under each name, the melded cards are returned to the hand. Play opens with the bidder leading any card he likes. During the play, players are obliged to follow suit, overcalling where possible, and must play trumps when void in a suit—again trying to overcall.

In order to have his score count for melds, a player must take at least one trick following the melding. Where a player fails to make his bid, he is "set back." That is, the full amount of his bid is subtracted from his previous score, or, if he has no points, it is entered as a negative total. In one variety of *Auction Pinochle,* the person to the dealer's left is required to make a bid of at least 90 points. Should no other player bid, he is stuck with the bid himself. If he cannot make 90 points through melding and taking tricks, the amount of the bid is subtracted from his score. Game is 1,000 points.

In *Four-Handed Partners Pinochle* the deck is cut to determine partners (the two highest draws playing together). It is cut again to determine the deal, with the high card winning. Twelve cards are distributed to each player in groups of four, as in regular *Pinochle.* Bidding begins to the left of the dealer, with each player allowed only one bid. With the bid settled, the melds are shown—each team combining its points.

After the melds are restored to the hands, play begins with the person to the left of the dealer. If possible, a player must win any trick opened by his partner. Players must follow suit, but a person who is void need not trump if he does not wish. After each hand, the deal passes left. Game is 1,000 points.

Auction Pinochle Using A Widow is played with three players, each of whom receives 15 cards on the deal. Three cards are left that form the "Widow" which is kept face down on the table. Bidding begins with the person on the dealer's left, who generally is required to make a bid of not less than 150. The bidding proceeds clockwise around the table, in turn. It continues upward in increments of at least ten points, until no one is willing to go higher than the last bidder.

The last bidder turns up the Widow for the others to see, then takes these cards into his hand and declares trumps. Next, he discards three cards of his choosing, face down, to form the basis of his trick pile—in other words, he can count any points in these three cards with those taken later in the tricks. Only the person who has captured the bid may meld, and he melds all his combinations. After recording his scores for melds, he returns the exposed cards to his hand. The rules of play as described for *Three-Handed Pinochle* now apply, except that game is 1,500 points.

Following a nine-of-diamonds lead, other hands must play diamonds. The ace—the highest-ranking diamond played—wins this trick.

A nine of trump, here hearts, takes a trick in clubs. To trump a trick in Pinochle, *player can hold no cards of suit that is led.*

In *Auction Pinochle* there is a meld not usually seen in other forms of *Pinochle:* The Roundhouse, worth 240 points. A Roundhouse consists of a Marriage (a king and queen of the same suit) in each of the four suits. Where a Roundhouse is melded in combination with a Trumps Sequence, the Royal Marriage is lost—making the total value of the melds 350 points.

Poker

- *2 to 8*   - *A standard 52-card deck; plastic chips in white, red and blue*

OBJECT: There are literally scores of major games based on *Poker* and hundreds of minor ones that vary slightly from place to place. Nonetheless, all varieties of *Poker* share a number of common rules, and most share a common objective—to obtain a hand of higher rank than any other hand at the table.

RANKING OF CARDS: Ace (high); two (low). The ace may also be ranked below the two in building sequences such as ace, two, three, four, five. No ranking is given to the suits; all of them have equal weight.

RANKING OF HANDS: The highest natural hand (that is, without wild cards) is a Straight Flush—five cards in sequence of the same suit. Four of Kind—four cards of the same denomination—comes next, followed by a Full House—three of a kind and a pair. Then comes a Flush—five cards of the same suit but out of sequence—followed by a Straight—five cards in sequence but of varied suits. Three of a Kind

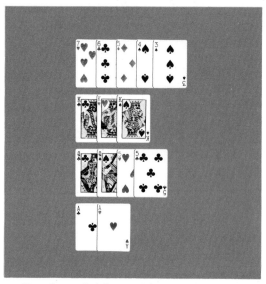

Ranking after a Flush is a Straight (top)— a sequence of five cards of mixed suits. Next is Three of a Kind; Two Pair; One Pair.

comes next, then Two Pair and One Pair. When no one has so much as a pair, the holder of the highest single card wins. Should two or more players hold similar hands—two Flushes, two Straights, etc.—the winner is the player holding the highest denomination cards. For instance, an ace-high Flush or an ace-high Straight beat a king-high Flush or Straight, respectively.

ODDS: *Poker* is a game of betting according to the odds. Although few players know the exact chances of drawing a particular hand, most experienced players can distinguish a strong from a weak hand. Shown below are the average winning hands for the six most popular types of *Poker* games:

Draw Poker (nothing wild) . . . . Pair of jacks
Five-Card Stud (nothing wild) . . Pair of kings
Seven-Card Stud (nothing wild) . . Three eights
Draw Poker (joker wild) . . . . . . Three eights
Draw Poker (deuces wild) . . . . Three aces
High-Low Draw Poker (nothing wild). High— pair of jacks; low—no pair, with the highest card a nine.

WILD GAMES: Many people like to play *Poker*

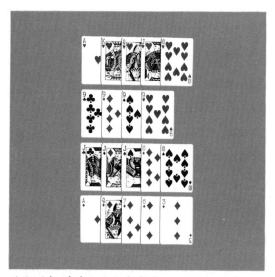

A Straight Flush (top) is the highest-ranking natural hand. The next highest is Four of a Kind, then comes a Full House, then a Flush.

with wild cards; that is, certain pre-designated cards that can be used to represent any other cards in the deck. The dealer of the hand, on naming the game that is to be played, announces which cards, if any, are wild for the game. For example, in a joker-wild game, the joker added to Four of a Kind yields Five of a Kind, a combination that will beat even a Straight Flush. In a deuces-wild game, a pair of two's added to any card produces Three of a Kind, as does one deuce added to One Pair, etc. One-eyed jacks are often named as wild cards, and certain games are played with special wild cards—such as threes and nines.

BANK: One player is named banker and has charge of the chips and he distributes them to all players. Traditionally, the blue chips are worth the most; the reds come next, and, finally, the whites. In a non-stakes game, monetary values may be ascribed to the chips, although no one actually buys them. An equal amount of chips is distributed to each player at the start of the game, and when the session is over the chips are merely turned in without money changing hands.

ANTE: Before a hand begins, players may be required to pay chips into a pool called the "ante." The ante is paid after the game is announced but before any cards are dealt. Generally the dealer names the amount of the ante, and the ante forms the basis of the pot for the ensuing game.

DEAL: There are numerous ways to determine who deals the first hand. One is to have the host deal each player a card, face up, with the person receiving the high card winning the opening deal. Another is to give the deal to the first player to draw a jack. The dealer distributes the cards, starting with the player on his left, clockwise around the table. The deal itself also moves clockwise after each hand.

BETTING: A limit (such as a blue chip or a red) can be set on the amount that may be bet (and on the amount of each raise). A limit may also be placed on the number of raises during any betting round. In a pot-limit game, no bet is permitted larger than the value of the pot at the time of the bet. Where table stakes operate, no player may bet more in a given hand than the number of chips exposed before him on the table at the hand's start. Should a player run out of chips, a side pot is made up of the chips contained in the pot at that point. This player may then remain in the game, but his winnings will be limited to the side pot. The other players continue their bets in the main pot. Thus, frequently, the chips bet in the course of a hand are divided among more than one winner.

In many *Poker* games, the betting begins with the person on the dealer's left and continues in strict clockwise rotation around the table. If the first player cannot bet—or chooses not to because his hand is weak—he announces that he "checks." Thus, the responsibility to bet passes to the player on his left, who also may either bet or choose not to—in which case the responsibility rotates leftward again. In some games, where everyone checks, the next card is received free. In other games, such as *Jacks-or-Better Draw Poker,* the hands are thrown in; there is another ante, and the deal passes left for a new hand.

When a player does bet, however, the others on his left are in turn required either to call ("see" or match the bet), raise or fold their hands (leave the game). Once a bet is raised, everyone next in turn must either call, raise the raise or fold their hands. Although a player may raise another person's bet or raise, he may not raise his own bet or raise. No bet, call or raise is valid until the chips backing it are actually put into the pot.

Draw Poker

ANTE: Before the hand is dealt, each player contributes an amount, designated by the dealer, to the pot. Often this will be an amount agreed upon by all players as a common ante for all games.

DEAL: Beginning with the person seated on his left, the dealer distributes the cards. He deals them one at a time, face down, until each player receives five cards.

In Draw Poker, *this player keeps pair of jacks, discarding three cards for which dealer gives replacements. (Hand is exposed to illustrate play.)*

BETTING—FIRST ROUND: After examining their cards, keeping them hidden from the others, the players begin the first betting round. The player on the dealer's left opens. Suppose that he holds a pair of jacks, plus three unmatched superfluous cards. In *Draw Poker,* a pair of jacks is a strong hand. Thus, instead of passing and making the player to his left responsible for placing the first bet, he decides to bet a white chip—the limit allowed him. The next player can call, by betting a white chip; raise, by betting a red chip or fold and leave the game. Let's suppose this player holds five cards of varied suits and denominations; because his hand is very weak, he folds. The third player on the dealer's left, with the same choices, also folds. The fourth—with a pair of eights—calls, and the fifth—with a pair of sevens—also calls. The dealer folds. At this stage, three players remain in the game, each having put a single white chip into the pot.

DRAW: Any player who bets (in this case, three players) may elect to improve his hand by drawing. He may discard some of his cards—face down—and request the dealer to give him an equal number off the top of the deck. Traditionally, each player may discard and draw up to three cards, but house rules can vary—permitting a draw of from one card to five.

BETTING—LAST ROUND: The opening bet is made by the player who opened the preceding round. After drawing three cards, the first player has a pair of jacks and a pair of aces—a very strong hand. He bets a white chip. Even though the second remaining player has not improved his hand at all with his draw of three cards, he decides to call the first player—putting a white chip into the pot. The last player—with three drawn cards, two of them queens—raises, putting a red chip into the pot. The first player must now make his decision. He puts into the pot the white chip owed, because of his opponent's raise, and an additional white chip. Thus, it will cost the second player a red chip (or two white ones) to stay in; he folds. The last player raises again, by putting a red chip into the pot. The game is now between two players—the one holding queens over sevens and the one with aces over jacks. Since both have strong hands, the raising goes on for several bets until one of them calls the other by declining to raise.

SHOWDOWN: When the raising stops, the player whose last bet is called must show his cards. If the other player has a better hand, he reveals his cards and takes in the pot; otherwise he folds his cards and yields the pot.

VARIATIONS: In *Jacks-or-Better* the rules of *Draw Poker* apply, except that an opening bet may not be made unless the player is holding a pair of jacks or a higher ranking hand. If no player can open, the dealer reshuffles the cards and deals again—everyone contributing a second ante equal to the first. This continues until a player can make an opening bet. *Progression* is similar, and on the first deal the opening better must have jacks or better. On the next deal, he must have queens or better; then kings; then aces. If, on the aces-or-better round no one opens, the necessary openers move down the scale from kings back to jacks. As the openers move up, so does the ante—doubling each time up to aces; as the openers get lower, the ante is halved each time down to jacks. In this way, a large pot may be built up even before the first round of betting begins. In *High-Low Draw,* each player, after making his draw from the deck, declares his hand as high or low. At the showdown, the pot is divided by the players with the highest and lowest hands. However, a player who calls "high," when his hand is actually the lowest, or vice versa, does not share in the pot when the showdown occurs.

WHISKEY POKER

As in *Draw Poker,* the dealer distributes five cards to each player, face down. In the process, he forms an extra hand—the "widow"—in a pack on his immediate right. After the deal, play begins with the person on the dealer's left. Should this player believe that his hand is strong enough to win a showdown against the others, he knocks at once on the board. The widow is faced up, and everyone—except the person knocking—is permitted, in turn, to draw any number of cards from the widow. Cards that are drawn from the widow are replaced with cards from the hand. A player may even exchange his entire hand for the widow. If a player does not wish to draw, he may simply pass. When all have had a turn drawing (or passing), the showdown takes place.

Generally, no one is so quick to knock, however. Usually, a player seeks to put off the showdown while trying to strengthen his hand. The play rotates clockwise. Should all pass on a given round, the dealer turns up the widow. Each player then passes or draws from the widow as he chooses, the play continuing until someone knocks. The knock is followed by the final round of drawing and the showdown. It should be remembered that the player who knocks may not draw from the widow.

Whiskey Poker is a high-only game—that is, the highest ranking hand wins the entire pot. As a rule, the pot is created by means of an ante prior to the deal. In some localities, the holder of the highest hand also receives an amount equal to that in the pot from the player with the lowest hand. In other places, there is no ante or pot; the lowest hand merely pays the highest a chip for every person in the game.

SHOTGUN

In *Shotgun* the cards are dealt as in *Draw Poker.* The first betting round comes after each player receives his first three cards from the dealer. The fourth and fifth cards are also followed by rounds of betting. At this stage, when everyone has a full five-card hand, each player may draw substitutions for as many cards as he wishes in his hand. After the draw, a final betting round ensues, followed by the showdown.

VARIATION: In *Double-Barreled Shotgun* the cards are dealt as in *Draw Poker.* After each player receives five cards, a betting round commences with the player seated on the dealer's left. Following the betting, players draw substitutions for discards. After the draw, each person arranges his hand and places it, face down, before him, in a pack. Players now simultaneously "roll"—face up—the cards of their pack, one card at a time. After each roll, a betting round ensues, beginning with the person exposing the highest ranking card or cards. In most areas, *Double-Barreled Shotgun* is played as a high-low game, with high and low hand declared before the final card is rolled.

SPIT IN THE OCEAN

DEAL: Beginning on his left and moving clockwise, the dealer distributes four cards, face down, one at a time to each player. After the deal, the dealer faces up the next card in the center of the table; this center card is shared in common by everybody as a wild card. The other three

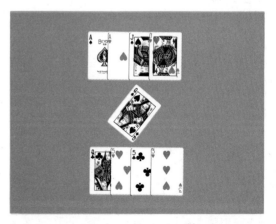

In Spit, *center card—here a queen—is wild and common to all hands. Other queens are also wild to give bottom hand (four fives) the edge.*

cards of its denomination are also wild cards.

BETTING: Generally, the dealer calls for an ante to start the pot. In some localities, only one betting round occurs—after all the cards, including the face-up center card, are dealt; after the one betting round there is a showdown—with the best poker hand taking the pot. In other places, a betting round follows each stage of the deal. After everyone receives the first card, the person to the left of the dealer either folds or bets, and the betting proceeds clockwise around the table, until everyone folds, bets, calls or raises. The center card is faced up after the fourth round of bets, and a final round of betting precedes the showdown.

In many places, *Spit in the Ocean* is played with a discard and draw. After all cards, including the face-up card in the center are dealt, a betting round commences with the player to the left of the dealer. After the betting, the players staying in the game may discard any or all of their cards and draw substitutions, face down. A second and final betting round ensues before the showdown.

VARIATION: In *The Wild Widow* each player is dealt four face-down cards. One card is then faced up in the center of the table, as a wild-card indicator. Any card of the same denomination in a player's hand is automatically wild. Immediately after the deal, a betting round commences. After the betting, those players remaining in the game receive a fifth card. At this point, a final betting round begins—again with the person nearest to the dealer's left—followed by the showdown.

ANACONDA

The dealer gives each player seven cards, face down. He distributes the cards, one at a time, beginning with the person on his left and moving in a clockwise rotation. An ante precedes the deal, and a single betting round follows the deal—both beginning with the person seated on the dealer's left.

After the close of the first round of betting, each player passes three cards of his choosing, face down, to the person on his left. The pass is made simultaneously by all players on a signal from the dealer. Following the pass, a second round of betting commences with the person to the dealer's left. After this, each player selects his five best cards and places them, face down, in a pack before him on the table.

On signal, each player then "rolls"—faces up on the board—the top card of his pack. When everyone has one card exposed on the table, a new round of betting opens—starting with the person showing the highest card. Then another card is simultaneously rolled by all players, and another round of betting follows, and so forth. The game can be played as a high-only game or as a high-low game. In the latter case, players must declare high or low hands at the end of the betting round when only one card remains, face down, in front of each person. This last card is then rolled for the showdown, and high and low hands divide the pot.

Stud Poker

DEAL: *Stud Poker* is the second major category of *Poker*. The chief difference from *Draw Poker* is that only the first card to each player is dealt face down; the other four are dealt face up.

BETTING: In *Stud Poker* the ante is not necessary. Betting begins after the first two cards are dealt and continues thereafter through the fifth card. When the first two cards are dealt, each player looks at his face-down card (the "hole card") to see what possibilities he has. The player with the highest face-up card must either bet or fold. If he folds, the player with the next best card bets or folds, and so on with the remaining players calling, raising or folding, in turn. When all players who do not fold finish betting, the third card is dealt, face up. Again the betting begins—the player with the highest face-up combination opening. The sequence is repeated after each card until five cards are dealt to each player. The last round of betting then follows, with four cards of each player's hand showing. The last round of betting is followed by the showdown, when each player reveals his hole card. The highest ranking *Poker* hand wins.

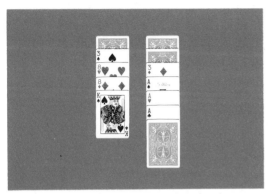

In Five-Card Stud (*left*) *first card is dealt face down, the rest, up. In* Seven-Card Stud *first two and last go down, middle four, up.*

VARIATION: In *Seven-Card Stud,* the first two cards are dealt face down; the next four, face up and the last card, face down. Betting begins after each player has three cards, and it continues on every card thereafter. Players base their bets on the best possible five-card combinations. After the last bet is placed, each chooses his best five cards from the seven for the showdown. *Six-Card Stud* is another variation of *Stud Poker,* in which each player is dealt the first card face down and the second face up. After everyone receives the second card, the player with the highest ranking card exposed on the board opens the betting. Every player—unless he folds— receives the next three cards face up. There is a betting round after each of these cards is received. The sixth, and final, card is dealt face down; it is followed by a last round of betting and the showdown—in which players use their best five cards. The game is usually played as a high-only game with wild cards—deuces or one-eyed jacks—or as a high-low game without wild cards. In *Eight-Card Stud* each player receives two cards face down and a third card face up. All aspects of the game thereafter are exactly like those of *Seven-Card Stud*—save that an eighth card is also dealt to the players, face down. As in *Seven-Card Stud* each player selects his best five cards for the showdown. The game can be played numerous ways: high-only with wild cards, *Low Hole Card Wild, High-Low Stud* and so forth.

HIGH-LOW STUD POKER

DEAL: As in regular *Five-Card Stud Poker,* the first card is dealt face down to each player, and the remaining four cards are dealt face up, until each player has five cards.

BETTING: As in regular *Stud,* the first round of betting starts after all players receive their second card. First to bet is the person showing the highest face-up card; he either bets or folds. Play continues with each player either folding, betting, calling or raising. After the first betting round is finished, each player remaining in the game receives his third card. Another round of betting then ensues, starting with the player showing the highest ranked face-up cards. After the fifth card is dealt and the final betting round is ended, each player remaining in the game announces, "high" or "low." Generally, this is done by all players simultaneously—by some device, such as concealing their fists beneath the table then unclenching them on the table at the same time. Players who hold a chip in their palms are declaring for high hand; those with no chip, for low hand. The pot is divided equally between low and high winner—with any odd chip usually going to the high hand.

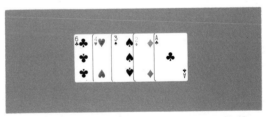

This lowest-ranking hand—or "perfect low"—claims half the pot in High-Low Stud Poker. *It consists of ace, 2, 3, 4, 6 of mixed suits.*

VARIATION: In *Seven-Card High-Low Stud Poker* seven cards are dealt, instead of five, with the first two cards and the seventh card face down. Betting begins after the third card is dealt, as in *High-Low Stud.* After the final betting round, players declare for high or low hand in the same way as in the five-card form of the game. (Once high or low is declared players may not change their declarations.) A player uses any five of the seven cards he possesses for his final hand. In *Seven-Card High-Low Stud,* it is possible to "go both ways"—that is, declare for both high and low hands. The player so doing may use any arrangement of the seven cards to form two different hands—one for high and the other for low. If he wins both, he takes the entire pot. However, if he loses either, he forfeits both.

LOW HOLE CARD WILD

The deal, the betting and other aspects of play are the same as for *Seven-Card Stud Poker.* However, the lower-ranking card of the two dealt face down to each player at the start of the game is automatically wild. If these cards—called the "hole cards"—are paired, the player holds two wild cards; moreover, any card received, face-up, of the same denomination as the low hole card is also wild.

In one popular variation, players have a choice on how they want the seventh card dealt. They may take it either face up or face down. A choice to take this card face up might typically be made where the player holds paired hole cards of a rather high denomination—for example, a pair of queens—and does not want to risk seeing them undercut by a lower denomination hole card at the end of the deal. In another widespread and popular variation of *Low Hole Card Wild,* a game called *Virginia-Chicago,* the person who holds the highest ranking hole card in spades may split the pot evenly with the winner of the hand.

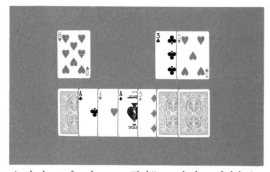

As the lowest face-down—or "hole"—card, three of clubs is wild. As all other threes held are wild, this hand yields five aces.

BASEBALL

The deal, the betting and the other aspects of play are like those described for *Seven-Card Stud Poker.* The game derives its name from the distinctive roles of the nines and threes—the number of innings and players and the number of outs and strikes, respectively, in actual *Baseball.* Nines and threes are wild cards. When a player receives a three face up, however, he must match the number of chips in the pot in order to remain in the game. Otherwise, if he cannot, he must fold his hand.

If a player is dealt a face-up four, he automatically receives another face-up card from the dealer. If he is dealt a four "in the hole" (face down) he turns it up, receiving a replacement from the dealer, face down. If a player wishes, these fours, as well as their replacement cards, may be figured into the final five-card hand. *Baseball* may be played as a <u>high-only</u> game or as a <u>high-low</u> game.

VARIATION: In *Night Baseball* seven face-down cards are dealt, one at a time, to each player, moving clockwise from the dealer's left. Keeping their hands concealed, players arrange them in any order they choose. They put them into a pack, which is placed, face down, on the table. The cards are then "rolled" (faced up) one at a time. Each player rolls simultaneously with the others. After each roll, a betting round follows—beginning with the person who exposes the highest card or cards. When a player shows a three, he must match the pot or fold his hand. Both threes and nines are wild. On facing up a four, a player receives an extra card, face up, from the dealer. The best five cards are used, with the final betting round coming after the roll of the last card. *Night Baseball* may be played either as a <u>high-only</u> or a <u>high-low</u> game.

RED AND BLACK

All aspects of the game are like *Stud Poker,* except for the method of determining the ranking of hands. Point values are ascribed to the cards as follows: aces, one point; picture cards and tens, ten points; other cards at face value—i.e., a nine, nine points; an eight, eight points, and so forth. Points in a red suit (hearts and diamonds) are positive; in a black suit (spades and clubs), negative. Thus, the points held in black must be subtracted from those held in red—with the highest plus point-total representing the highest ranking hand.

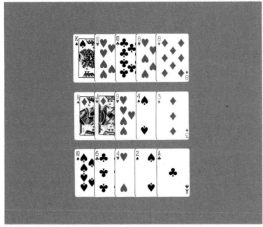

The middle hand, with 28 points, wins in this Red and Black *game. Holder has 32 plus points (red cards) and four minus points (black).*

Red and Black is also played as a high-low game. Aces may be counted either as one or fifteen—plus or minus, depending on color. Players declare high or low after the final betting round as detailed in the description of *High-Low Stud Poker*. In the event that no one holds a negative hand, the low hand is the one with the smallest plus point-total. Otherwise, the greatest negative total wins for the low hand.

Red Dog

- *2 to 8 players* • *A standard 52-card deck; plastic chips (or some other kind of counters, such as matchsticks)*

OBJECT: Players attempt to win in a showdown against the top card of a face-down stock.

RANKING OF CARDS: Ace (high), king, queen, jack, ten, nine . . . down to two (low).

PREPARATION: Low card wins the cut for deal.

Following the shuffle and cut, all players put one chip (or other counter) into a common pot in the center of the table. Should anyone win the entire pot, all players contribute another chip to make a new pot.

DEAL: The dealer distributes the cards, one at a time, clockwise from his left. He gives each player, himself included, five cards. The leftover cards are placed face down in full view of all players. This pile is a concealed stock against which each player, in turn, will conduct a game of showdown.

PLAY: The person to the left of the dealer has the first opportunity to bet against the top card of the stock, which is face down. To beat it, he must hold in his hand a card of higher denomination and of the same suit as that card. Since he doesn't see the card, however, he must gauge his probabilities for success solely on the strength of his own holdings. If his hand holds all four aces, obviously he is a sure winner. He will be able to top any card that may lie at the top of the stock. Conversely, if he holds four twos and a three, he is a certain loser. Two picture cards of different suits would give him about a fifty-fifty chance of winning.

Should he decide to pass, he throws his hand

Red Dog dealer turns up king of clubs from top of deck, beatable only by the ace of clubs. Bottom hand has club ace and its holder wins his bet.

into the "trash pile" (sometimes called the "deadwood"), paying one counter into the pot as a penalty. If he chooses to bet, however, he may risk any number of counters up to the total in the pot. Lost bets are added to the pot. Winnings are paid to the player from the counters in the pot at a number equal to the size of his bet.

Once the player decides his bet, the dealer turns up the top card of the stock. After the outcome is resolved, the player's full hand—as well as the overturned card from the stock—is thrown into the trash pile. The next player on the left then passes or bets. This continues around the table until everybody, dealer included, has a chance to play. The deal then passes left, and each player contributes one new counter to the pot. When the game is stopped, any chips remaining in the pot are divided equally among the players around the table.

Rummy

- 2 to 6   ● A standard 52-card deck; scoring pad and pencil

OBJECT: A player attempts to meld all the cards in his hand before any other player can do so.

RANKING OF CARDS: Ace (low), king (high)

PREPARATION: The cards are shuffled and cut. In the cut for deal, the low card wins: the next lowest gets first choice of seating position with respect to the dealer, and the third lowest, second choice of seat, etc.

DEAL: The dealer distributes the cards, one at a time. He deals in a clockwise rotation, beginning with the person on his left (or his opponent in a two-handed game). If two are playing, each person receives ten cards; if three play, seven; if four or more, six. After the deal, the remainder of the deck is placed, face down, in the center of the table as a stock; its top card is faced up beside it, beginning the discard pile.

PLAY: The player on the dealer's left begins play. He may draw either the top card from the stock

In Rummy, *combinations such as these—three or four of a kind and numerical sequences by suit—are melded, one combination per turn.*

or the face-up card beside the stock, according to his choosing. He adds this card to his hand, and he inspects his hand for combinations—three or more cards of the same denomination or a sequence of three or more cards in the same suit, such as the ace, two and three of hearts. Such combinations are melded onto the table face up before the player. In addition to these melds, a player may meld a single card onto his opponent's meld. A fourth jack, for example, might be played onto someone else's three jacks; a four or an eight of hearts onto his five, six, seven of that suit. Only a single meld of any type is permitted per turn.

Once the player lays down his meld—or realizes that he has no play—he must discard one card from his hand onto the discard pile. Each player, in turn, follows the above procedure, drawing either the top card from the stock or the top card from the discard pile. If, during a hand, the stock runs out, the discard pile is collected, shuffled, placed face down as a new stock and the top card turned up on the table beside it. Play continues in clockwise rotation.

When one player empties his hand by melding his last remaining cards (or by melding and discarding his last card), play stops. The winner of the hand receives points for all the cards still held by his opponents—picture cards counting ten, aces one and the other cards their face value. The score is marked on a pad, the cards reshuffled and the deal passes to the left for the next hand. Game is usually set at 150 points in this form of *Rummy*.

VARIATIONS: *Knock Rummy* differs from standard *Rummy* in that a player avoids melding until he thinks he can catch his opponents holding a higher sum of points than he holds in unmatched cards. Suppose, for instance, all cards in a player's hand, save an ace, can be melded; he holds only one unmatched point. After his draw and discard, he knocks on the table, exposing his hand for others to see. If no other player holds as few points, the person who knocks collects from each opponent the difference between their unmatched points and his. However, should someone else either have fewer points, or an equal number, that person wins the hand—collecting points from the others, as described above, and a bonus of ten points from the knocker as well. Scoring is done in double-entry fashion: That is, under the players' names, minus points are recorded in the amount that are lost to the winner of the hand, and the positive points collected by the victor are also recorded. All other aspects of the preparation, deal and play are like those of regular *Rummy*.

500 Rummy is much like regular *Rummy*, with two significant variations. First, a player may draw from the discard pile all the way down to an exposed card that he intends to meld in the same turn. He must take all the cards above it as well. Obviously, the discard pile must be arranged so that all cards are at least partly visible—best done by means of overlapping. Remember, *the card stopped at must be used as part of a meld in that same turn.* It need not necessarily be used to make a new combination. It may be added, instead, to a sequence or combination already melded by the player, or it may be added to match another player's meld. In the last case, the card is melded face up among the player's own exposed cards—not with the other player's melded cards.

In 500 Rummy, *a player wishing to make a meld with the king in the discard pile must also add all cards on top of the king to his hand.*

Thus, sequences can be continued by more than one player. For example, should someone meld a sequence of ace, two, three and four of hearts, someone else may meld the five, and still another person may lay down the six before himself, etc. (Sequences may also run in descending numerical order.) No card can be played, though, until after the appearance of the card immediately prior to it in the series. Besides being able to draw more than one card from the discard pile, the other big difference between *500 Rummy* and regular *Rummy* is that, in *500 Rummy*, points are awarded for the melds. A running account is kept on the score pad as players, in turn, lay down their meld. Each card of a combination

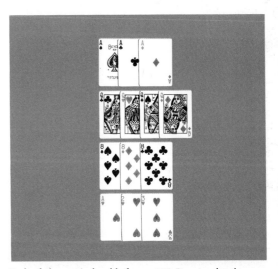

Each of these typical melds from a 500 Rummy *hand carries a point value of its own. Point values of melds are explained on page 222.*

is counted into the total as follows: ace is worth 15, unless melded in an ace, two, three sequence when it counts as one; picture cards are worth ten; all other cards usually are worth their denominational value (unless assigned a value of five to facilitate scoring). When ridding his hand of all cards a player calls out, "Rummy" and play stops. The others are caught with cards in their hands, for which he collects points as valued above. The players still holding cards must subtract these points from their accumulated melding points.

When the stock is gone, it can be reformed from the discard pile, as in regular *Rummy*. Another alternative is that play can continue, until no further melds are possible for anyone at the table. When a given hand ends, the deal passes left. Where more than four people play *500 Rummy,* a double deck of 104 cards is used—each person receiving nine cards on the deal. Where four or less play, one 52-card deck is used—with each person receiving seven cards in a four-handed game, eight cards in a three-handed game or nine cards when two play.

In *Michigan Rummy,* as in *500 Rummy,* points are tabulated for melded combinations. Also a player going out on a "Rummy" collects additional points from the others in the game, who subtract any points caught in the hand from their meld totals. The differences with respect to *500 Rummy* are twofold: A person may lay down as many melds as he wishes on any given turn; also, if a card is discarded that will play upon some meld exposed on the table, the first player who notices may call out, "Stop!" He may then pick up the card, play it and receive points—without regard to following in turn. All other aspects of the game are identical with *500 Rummy,* including the game-winning total of 500 points. After each hand is played and scored, the deal passes left.

Scorpion

● 1 ●   *A standard 52-card deck*

OBJECT: The player attempts to arrange the entire deck within the Tableau in descending order and by suits.

RANKING OF CARDS: Ace, <u>low</u>; king, <u>high</u>.

PREPARATION AND DEAL: The deck is shuffled. A row of seven cards is dealt onto the table—the first four cards face down and the last three face up. The second and third rows are dealt in the same way—four cards down and three cards up—the second row overlapping the first and the third overlapping the second. Then, four more rows of seven cards are dealt all face up, each row overlapping the previous row. Thus, the Tableau consists of seven horizontal rows

The tableau of Scorpion *is made up of 49 cards in rows of seven. The first three cards in the first four rows are face down, the others, face up. The three cards left over are the "Merci," played when an impasse occurs.*

of overlapping cards and seven vertical columns. There are 49 cards in all: 12 cards are face down; the rest are face up. The three leftover cards—the "Merci"—are put aside for use later in the game.

PLAY: There are no foundation cards, hence no building outside the Tableau itself. Building takes place with cards of the same suit, progressing in descending numerical order. A card may be moved from its position in the middle of a column onto the last card of any other vertical column where there is the next highest ranking card of its suit. All cards attached below it must go along. For example: The eight of spades is at the bottom of column one; the seven of spades is the third from the bottom in column six. The seven may be moved over onto the eight in column one—as long as the two cards below the seven are moved over as well.

When a face-down card is uncovered it is faced up and becomes part of the play. When an entire column is moved, the vacancy may be filled by moving in a king and any cards attached below the king.

If the player reaches an impasse, he deals out the Merci one card at a time onto the bottoms of the first three columns at the left. The player, in shifting groups of cards or single cards, tries to unite the suits in descending numerical sequences within the columns. If he can arrange all four suits in perfect sequence from the king down to the two, he wins the game. If not, he collects the cards, shuffles the deck and deals the cards again in the same manner—with seven horizontal rows and seven vertical columns.

Whist

- 4 (two Teams) • A standard 52-card deck; scoring pad and pencil

OBJECT: Each team tries to win more tricks than the opposing team.

RANKING OF CARDS: Ace (high); two (low). The ace, king, queen and jack of trumps are called "honors," and they are worth one point each in the initial scoring for each hand. In the play for tricks, cards of the trump suit rank higher than cards of other suits—regardless of denomination.

PREPARATION: The deck is cut once by each person. Those players cutting the two highest cards play as a team against those cutting the two lowest. Partners take seats opposite one another at the table. Then there is another cut of the deck to determine who has first deal, with the highest card winning. (Since trumps are determined later, ace is the highest card.) The cards are shuffled by the person who wins the cut—the dealer.

DEAL: The dealer offers the deck to the person to his right, who cuts the cards before the deal. The dealer then gives everyone 13 cards, face down. He distributes the cards, one at a time, in a clockwise rotation, starting with the person seated on his left. The dealer takes the final card that he has dealt to himself and turns it face up on the table. This card determines the trump suit. (For example, if the card is a diamond, then every card of the diamond suit becomes a trump.) After the completion of each hand, the deal passes to the left.

PLAY: Players arrange their hands by suits. They then score any trump honors before the start of the play for tricks. As noted above, the trump

In Whist, *dealer faces up final card dealt to himself to determine the trump suit. Ace, king, queen, jack of trump are called "honors."*

honors are the four picture cards of the trump suit. The players inspect their hands privately, then briefly expose, on the board, the honors—if any—which they hold. Where the honors are split evenly between the teams, no points are scored. When one team holds three of the honors and the other team just one, the former scores two points. Should either team hold all four honor cards in trump, that team scores four points.

After the honors are recorded on the score pad, the play for tricks begins. One player on each team is designated to collect all the tricks won by him and his partner. The person on the dealer's left plays first, placing a card from his hand, face up, in the center of the table. The others must now play onto this card, in turn, moving clockwise around the table. If they have a card of the suit that is led, they must play this card—or, if possessing more than one, any card in that suit. When every player is able to follow with cards in the suit led, the highest ranking card of the suit wins the trick. If a player is void of cards in the suit that is led, he may play a trump. He thus takes the trick—unless another person follows with a trump of higher denomination.

The winner of the trick leads any card from his hand to begin the play for the next trick, and so on, until all 13 tricks are captured (and every player's hand is empty). At the end of each hand, both teams count up their tricks. The first six tricks are called a "book"; no points are scored for book. For each trick thereafter, however, a team wins one point. In other words, a team will score one point for taking seven tricks, two points for eight tricks, three for nine and seven for all 13 tricks. The points scored for tricks are added to those recorded for honors. The cards are then collected, shuffled, cut and dealt again—by the person to the left of the former dealer. One hand follows upon another until one of the two teams scores seven or more points—thus winning the game.

VARIATION: In *Chinese Whist* each player is dealt six cards face down, followed by six face-up

As the highest-ranking card of the suit led, ace of clubs takes this trick. All players had clubs, thus no one could play a trump.

Six tricks, each with a card from every player, make book. With diamonds trump, the trick at bottom right is won by the eight of diamonds.

cards to cover them. Finally one card—the "playing card"—is dealt face down and held in hand. After the dealer names trump, the player to his left leads his playing card or a face-up card. The other players follow suit or trump. As soon as a face-up card is played, the face-down card beneath it must be faced up. The scoring for tricks is as in regular *Whist.*

Table Games

On all continents, archaeologists have unearthed many types of distinctively etched and polished pebbles believed to have been used in the "table-like" games of Stone Age peoples. Objects very similar to contemporary dice were found in the tombs of the Egyptian Pharaohs. These discoveries show that, since the very beginning, man has employed various objects to play games of shrewdness. The games that follow—requiring manipulative objects of some type and, often, a board—are the modern-day counterparts of these ancient mental contests.

Numerals indicate the number of players.

Backgammon and Acey Deucy

● *2* ● *A Backgammon board; 30 plastic or wood discs in two colors—usually 15 black and 15 either white or red; two pairs of dice; two dice cups*

OBJECT: A player tries to move all the men of his color off the board. He must move each man from his opponent's inner table, through his opponent's outer table, through his own outer table, to his inner table and then off the board before his opponent can do so.

PREPARATION: Players take seats opposite one another, with the board between them. Each person is situated behind 12 triangles or "points"; the "bar" divides the board vertically, so that six of a player's triangles lie on the left side of the bar and the other six on the right.

To determine the choice of color, each player casts a single die, high throw winning. The winner also gains the right to decide which side of the board, with respect to the bar, is to be named the "inner table" and which the "outer table."

Next, both players position their men—15 discs of the same color. As noted, 12 triangles, or points, form a row in front of each person. Mentally, each player numbers these points, starting with the one nearest the outside edge of his inner table. Hence, each person's territory consists of an inner table with points one through six and an outer table with points seven through 12—the bar dividing the two regions. The men are put onto the board as follows:

two on the opponent's one-point, which lies directly opposite the player's own one-point; five on the opponent's 12-point, directly across from the player's own 12-point; three onto the player's own eight-point and five onto his own six-point. Since each player places his men accordingly, the prepared board has the two colors arranged in a mirror image of one another, lined up within the triangles of the opposing one-, six-, eight-, and 12-points.

With a one and a two on the dice, red opens play in Backgammon by moving a man from opponent's one-point to opponent's four-point.

STARTING THROW: First move is decided by each player casting one die, high throw winning. The winner uses the die thrown by his opponent, together with his own die, to arrive at the count for his opening move.

PLAY: After the starting move, the players throw two dice apiece, alternating turns. A man may be moved forward in the proper direction (see OBJECT) onto any point that isn't occupied by two or more enemy soldiers. Any number of a player's own soldiers may be gathered on a point. In counting off the moves, the two dice are always viewed as being two separate and distinct throws. Thus, one man may be moved the number of spaces shown on one of the die while a second man is advanced the number on the other die. A player may also make both moves in a turn, using just one of his men and counting off each die separately. However, should the first die counted off bring the man onto a point held by two or more enemy men, the whole move is blocked. The player is then forced to use his turn in moving some other man or men. A person must play the full number of counts per throw, if he can do so in any way. In tight situations where only one of the two counts can be played, a person must play the higher of the two counts, if possible.

Unlike many other games, a throw of doubles does not grant the opportunity to cast the dice a second time; instead, the actual value of the throw is doubled. Hence, a throw of double fives would be treated as five, five, five, five. One or more men may be used to carry out these four counts. For instance, one man might be moved five points, a second man 15 points; or one man might be advanced ten points, and two other men five points apiece.

A single man located on a point is known as a "blot." If a player lands squarely on an opponent's blot at the end of a count for one or both dice, the blot is taken off the playing area and imprisoned on the bar. Then the person whose man is thus isolated must return that man into play from the bar before he may move any other man. To do this, he must obtain a throw—from one or both dice—that corresponds to a point from one up to six within his opponent's inner table not held by two or more of his opponent's soldiers. Should a player's man land upon an enemy's blot in coming off the bar, the enemy's blot now goes onto the bar.

Obviously, where a player's man is on the bar and every point inside his opponent's inner table is held by two or more enemy soldiers, he does not even get to throw the dice.

In enemy territory, a player moves his men in the direction going from his opponent's one-point toward his opponent's 12-point. At the opponent's 12-point, his men cross over into home territory and proceed in the reverse direction—from their own 12-point toward the one-point. Since a man may never be moved backwards, even to attack a blot, the two colors—or opposing armies—always head along opposite directions around the perimeter of the board.

Only after all 15 of a player's men enter his own inner table may he begin to remove men from the board—or "bear off" men. (If one of a player's men is on the bar, this man must be returned to play and reach his inner table before any other men can be borne off the board.) Suppose that all men are within the inner table and the player throws a four-two on the dice. He may bear off one man each from the four-point and the two-point. If, for reasons of strategy, he prefers not to remove men from these points, he may move men down from higher to lower points. For example, he may move one of his men from the six-point to the two-point and one from the five-point to the three-point. If he casts a number higher than any point on which men are resting, he may bear off men from the next lower point or points.

SCORING: The player who first bears off all his men is the winner. If a player can bear off all his men before his opponent manages to remove even one man, the game is recorded as a double victory—a Gammon. If a player bears off all his men before his opponent can bear off even one man and while one or more of his opponent's men is on the bar or trapped inside the winner's inner table, this is scored as a triple victory—a Backgammon.

VARIATION: In *Acey Deucy,* as in *Backgammon,* a player tries to move all his men onto the board, around the "points" (triangles) to his own inner table, and then off the board before his opponent.

PREPARATION: Players take seats opposite one another with the *Backgammon* board between them. Each player is situated behind 12 triangles, or "points." The "bar" divides the board vertically, so that six points lie in the area to the right of the bar and six more to the left of the bar. The players cast a single die each, and high throw names which side of the board, with respect to the bar, is to be the "inner table" and which the "outer table." In contrast to *Backgammon,* play commences with the board completely free of men. Each person keeps his men or stones together in a place off the board and enters them, according to the roll of the dice, into his opponent's inner table.

PLAY: After designating which sides of the board are the inner and outer tables, the player who wins the first cast of the dice opens play. To do so, he throws two dice from his own cup.

All men are off the board. A player enters his men into his opponent's inner table on the basis of his throw: For instance, if his count on one die is six and on the other die three, he may move one of his men onto his opponent's six-point and another onto his opponent's three-point. Thereafter, on succeeding rolls of the dice, he may either enter more men in the above manner or move the men already in play forward the appropriate number of points. From the place of entry on the opponent's inner table, a player's men progress toward the opponent's 12-point. From the 12-point a player may cross his men over into home territory and progress from the 12-point toward the one-point, just as in *Backgammon.* Once a player moves all his men into his inner table, he may begin to remove his men from the board—or "bear off"—a process fully described in the *Backgammon* section.

The dice are always counted as two separate throws. One man may move the number of dots shown on one of the die and then again move the number shown on the second die; on the other hand, one man may move the distance shown on one die while another man moves the number of points indicated on the second die. A man may not be moved onto a point held by two or more enemy men; however, any number of a player's own men may be gathered at a single point. Where the count of the die brings a player's man onto an enemy "blot"— one lone man on a point—the blot is removed to the bar. This is described in the *Backgammon* section, with the same stringent rules governing play for a person with a man on the bar as operate in *Backgammon.*

Thus, so far, *Acey Deucy* differs from *Backgammon* in that at the beginning of the game the men are situated off the board from where they enter into play according to the counts on the dice. There is another major variation, however—the one from which the game receives its name. When a player rolls one-two (*Acey Deucy*), he first executes the normal *Backgammon* moves for such a roll. Then, he has the privilege of calling out any doublet from one-one to six-six and moving any man or men as if he actually did throw this doublet on the dice. As in *Backgammon,* a doublet is counted four times instead of just two; thus double sixes means a series of moves as though four dice are thrown, coming up six, six, six, six. Using double sixes in this way, a single man could be entered first at the six-point on the opponent's inner table and then be moved three more times in moves of six points per move, to a player's own one-point. Alternatively, two men could each be moved six-points, two times apiece; four men, six each and so forth. Of course, in the process, no man can touch down at a point held by two or more enemy men. After the player throwing *Acey Deucy* executes his various moves, he throws the dice again and moves accordingly. If, however, he cannot use the initial roll of one-two in its entirety, he is not permitted to call out a doublet or roll the dice another time. A player who throws *Acey Deucy* need not call out a doublet that he can use in its entirety if some tight strategic situation makes him prefer a different call—say, in order to attack a blot. If he does not use the doublet in its entirety, however, he gives up the privilege of rolling the dice another time.

SCORING: The loser pays the winner one point for each man that he has left on the board, on the bar or not yet entered into play. Under one popular scoring variation, the loser counts the number of points remaining between each of his men left on the board and the bearing-off point—awarding the sum of these units to the winner. For a man on the bar or not yet entered into play, the loser must pay the winner 24 points.

Box Hockey

- 2 or 4   ● *A Box-Hockey box, including four special sticks and a wooden puck*

OBJECT: Each player (or team, if four are playing) attempts to score more points—or goals—than his opponent (or the opposing team). A player seeks to slap the wooden puck through the goal in his opponent's territory while defending his own goal from similar attempts by the opposition. Neither player may permanently block his goal with his stick in front of the slot.

PREPARATION: Before the game begins, the puck is placed on the notch on the top of the middle dividing partition. This partition divides the board into two compartments—each representing the home territory of a player (or team). At the far end of either compartment a slot in the back wall is the goal.

PLAY: The game opens with a "face-off" as in regular *Ice Hockey.* Each player (or one player from each team) performs the face-off. After tapping their sticks alternately on the floor and then together in the air above the puck three times each, both players attempt to strike the puck first—shooting it, of course, into the opposing player's compartment toward his goal.

Thereafter, the action may take either of two forms: The players may take alternate turns at hitting the puck, without any defensive interference from the opponent; or, the play can proceed fast and furious, with the players' swinging simultaneously at the puck. Whenever a player knocks the puck off the board (that is, when the puck jumps the side wall or back wall), a free shot is awarded to the opponent. This free shot can be taken from the starting notch or from anywhere in a player's home territory.

When teams play, one member of the team generally plays offense—that is, in the opposing team's compartment—while the other plays defense in home territory. The defense tries to send the puck sliding through one of the two slots in the base of the middle partition to his partner for a shot at the enemy goal.

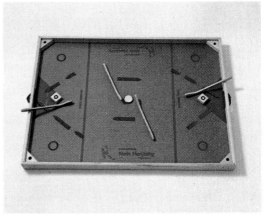

Box Hockey *board is set up for opening center face-off. Goalies may not block area between goal and wooden diamond with their sticks.*

Five points is usually set as the winning score. After each goal scored, the puck is returned to the center notch for a new face-off.

A *Box-Hockey* board can be made in a home workshop, using plywood or planking. The floor should be five feet long and 18 inches wide. The side walls and central dividing partition—which runs the width of the board along the midline—should be roughly three inches high all around. The central divider should contain two slots flush with the floor—each about three inches wide and two inches high, and placed flush with the side wall at the outside end of the slot. At each end of the board, a goal is cut: a slot in the center of the back wall, flush with the floor. *Hockey* sticks, of about 28 inches in length and of the same shape as regulation *Hockey* sticks, can be cut with a saw from pine planking. Finally, the puck, also made of wood, should be one and five-eighths inches in diameter and one-half inch thick.

Chess

● *2* ● *A chessboard; 32 chess men (or pieces) in two colors—generally, 16 black and 16 white*

OBJECT: Each player attempts to move men into positions from which they can capture enemy pieces and finally checkmate the opposing king—thereby winning the game. A king is checkmated when it is brought under attack by an opposing man and cannot be rescued—either by moving into an adjoining space free from attack or by using a man to block the attack.

PREPARATION: Sitting opposite one another across the table, the players place the board between them..The board must be situated so that a non-black (red or white) square lies in the righthand corner nearest each player. One of the players then takes a man of each color, concealing one in each fist. Next he presents both fists to his opponent, who taps one. When that fist is opened, the color of the piece inside becomes the opponent's color for the game, while the color of the second piece becomes the other player's color. White has first move in the game. The white player always sets down his men as follows: in the back row, the "queen" is placed on the white square in the vertical file to the left center of the player. The "king" is placed next to his queen on the black square in the other central file. To each side of the queen and king, a "bishop" (distinguished by his high bishop's headpiece), a "knight" (or horse) and a "rook" (or castle) are placed in that order. The queen's bishop, knight and rook are to her left; the king's bishop, knight and rook, to his right. The two rooks are on the back squares of the outside vertical files. Black does exactly the same except that, to start, the queen is placed on the black square in the central vertical file just to the right of the player. The king is placed on the white square to the left of his queen. Thus, the corresponding black and white pieces lie directly opposite each other on the same vertical file. With the back row thus filled, the remaining eight men (the "pawns") are set up on the squares of the second row.

MEN: Each of the above-described *Chess* men moves in a way different from the other men in the game. No two pieces may ever occupy the same square. One of a player's own men on a square blocks the movement of any of his other men to that square or past it (except for the knight, which may jump over friend and foe alike). When a player moves a man onto a square occupied by an enemy piece, the latter is considered captured and is removed from play.

These chessmen are arranged in their appropriate positions for the start of the game. The first move is always made by white, with players taking alternate turns. Note that with the board properly oriented, right-hand corner nearest each player is distinguished by a light-colored square.

The Pawn. Each pawn, on its first move, may go straight ahead either one or two spaces, unless blocked from doing so by another piece. After the first move, the pawn moves forward only one space at a time.

Pawn moves straight ahead one square except on its first move, when it may advance two, or in capturing men, when it moves diagonally.

The pawn is the only piece that cannot capture an opposing man lying in its path. However, the pawn may capture any man standing on either of the two squares diagonally ahead—in other words, to the left and right, just in front of it. To make the capture, the pawn is moved onto the square and the enemy piece is removed and taken off the board. A pawn may never move backwards and may move diagonally only when capturing.

If a player can slip one of his pawns into the enemy's back row, he may exchange it for any other piece of his color. Usually, this will be a queen; hence, the move is known as "queening the pawn." If a queen has not been captured, some other piece can be so designated, to give the player, in effect, two queens. Should an opposing pawn—by moving two spaces forward on the first move—attempt to pass a pawn that a player has moved into enemy territory, the opposing pawn may be captured automatically with a call of "en passant." The enemy pawn is merely removed from its square and replaced by the pawn that it tried to pass.

The Knight. The knight, or horse, enjoys a privilege that other *Chess* men are denied. It may jump over the top of any piece lying between it and its destination. Its moves are made in an L-shaped pattern. Traveling two squares sidewise along a row—or forward or backward along a file—it then hops one square to either side. The L-shaped pattern may also be thought of as going one space in the first direction, then two spaces to either side. However visualized, the patterns result in exactly the same range of targets for the knight. The knight, landing on any square occupied by an enemy piece, captures this piece and removes it from the board.

Knight, which jumps men, traces an L-pattern: two squares along a row or file, then one sidewise (or one straight ahead, then two sidewise).

The Bishop. The bishop may move along any diagonal path made up of squares of the same color as the square on which it rests at the start of the game. Thus, one bishop operates along the white diagonals, and the other along the black. The bishop may move as many spaces along a diagonal as desired. On future turns, it may change to a diagonal at right angles to its previous diagonal heading; so long as it remains on the diagonal of its color, it may reverse directions. An opposing piece that lies upon a bishop's diagonal may be captured by the bishop, who takes over the square of the piece that it captures.

Bishop moves along any diagonal path of the same color as its original square; thus each player has a "white" and a "black" bishop.

The most potent of chessmen, the queen moves any number of spaces forward or backward along a file, a row or a diagonal pathway.

The Rook. The rook may move any distance in a straight line—left or right, forward or backward—but never on a diagonal. Moreover, the rook may be used to capture an opposing man that lies anywhere along such a path at right angles to it.

to be resting at the time. The queen's prowess derives from its ability to move any number of spaces desired in any direction; thus, it can capture opposing men along any row, file or diagonal on which it rests.

The King. Like the pawn, the king moves only one space at a time. However, the king isn't restricted to straight-ahead movement. Rather, it can move a single space in any direction: forward, backward, diagonally or sidewise. Although a king may be used for capturing an

Rook moves any number of squares along a row or file— left or right, forward or backward—but it may never move on a diagonal heading.

The Queen. This is the most versatile and powerful of pieces. Like the king, the queen may move in any direction: straight ahead, backwards, sidewise or on a diagonal path of the same color as the square on which it happens

King moves one space at a time—forward or backward along a file, right or left along a row, or to any diagonally adjoining square.

opposing man on an adjoining square, it may not be placed in the path of the enemy—put into "check"—in the process. In fact, a king may never be moved into check, since it would be captured on the opponent's next move—thereby ending the game in defeat.

SPECIAL MOVES: Besides the moves of the individual pieces described above, there are certain special *Chess* moves which also must be learned.

Castling the King. Castling is a move to provide the king with a more protected position and is executed with the king and either of the two rooks if the pieces concerned have not yet been moved. Two pieces are thus moved simultaneously, but the play counts as only one move. First, a path along the back row between the king and rook must be cleared of all other men. With the way clear, the king is moved two squares toward the rook, at the same time as the rook is moved onto the square on the other side of the king. If the king—or any of the squares between the king and the rook—should be under attack, the move cannot be made.

Check and Checkmate. At various times during a game, a player's king may come under attack from enemy chessmen. At such times, the king is said to be in check. The king must be rescued from check if the player can move another piece into a blocking position between his king and the enemy man, or, if he can move the king itself to an adjoining space that doesn't lie in the open line of attack of an enemy piece. However, when the king cannot be rescued from an attack in the above ways, he is the victim of a checkmate. In other words, having no means of escape, he is captured—with the player masterminding the checkmate winning the game.

Stalemate. If a player's king, though not actually in check, cannot be moved without placing it in check and if the player has no other move, the king may not be moved at all according to the rules—since the king may never be moved into check. Thus, the game ends in a stalemate with neither player winning. A stalemate is a draw.

Draw. Players may agree to call a game a draw if both feel that a stage has been reached where neither can win. For instance, when just two kings remain on the board, neither player can win. Similarly, a player left with only a bishop and a king will not be able to checkmate his opponent and should accept a draw. Sometimes these situations can be forseen in advance and a draw agreed upon with several pieces still remaining in play. If a player repeats the same two moves 50 times in succession his opponent may call for a draw. This is called the "50-move rule." If a player moves all of his men left in the game into the same pattern of positions three times in succession, his opponent may call for a draw. In some cases, this supercedes the 50-move call.

CHESS ANNOTATION: Newspaper reports of *Chess* tournaments, as well as games played through the mails, are facilitated by a special type of annotation. In newspaper annotations, a castling move is noted as 0-0 when the move is made with the king's rook and as 0-0-0 when made with the queen's rook. An "X" means captures (or takes), as B x KP (bishop takes king's pawn). P-K4 translates as pawn to king four, or a first move of two spaces by the pawn in front of the king to the fourth square in the king's file. Kt-KB3 indicates a move by the knight on the king's side to the third square in the line in front of bishop next to the king (the king's bishop).

White gains checkmate: black can't block the bishop's attack on king; nor can king escape, as surrounding squares are also under attack.

One bishop is thus called the king's bishop; the other bishop is called the queen's bishop. Similarly, all the other major pieces are named either the king's or the queen's, depending on which side of the back row they are positioned. The pawns are named when necessary for the major pieces standing behind them. A file is named for the major piece that stands upon the first square of the file. The squares in the file are numbered beginning with one for the back row, two for the pawn row, etc. Thus white's queen eight is black's queen one and vice versa.

Checkers

● 2 ● A checkerboard with 24 checkers

OBJECT: The object of the game is for a player to move his 12 men across the board to his opponent's rear line in such a way that he either captures all or most of the opponent's 12 pieces or else successfully blocks them so that they cannot move.

PREPARATION AND PLAY: *Checkers* is played with a square board which is divided into 64 smaller squares—colored alternately dark and light. Each player is given a set of 12 checkers, or "men"; the sets are of contrasting colors such as black and red, black and white, etc. The two players sit on opposite sides of the board, with the board so placed that the corner square to each player's left is black. Both players line up their 12 checkers on the black squares of the three rows nearest to them. When all pieces are in place, the board's two center rows are empty.

The player with the dark checkers usually makes the first move. (As the sets of checkers are exchanged after every game, each player has an equal opportunity to lead off in succeeding games.) Moves are made diagonally on black squares only. The opening player moves one of his frontline men one space diagonally forward to an empty black square.

His opponent then counters by moving a frontline man in the same way. Play continues with

Black makes this opening move (arrow) in a game of Checkers. *Men advance diagonally one space per turn, staying on the dark squares.*

each player, in turn, endeavoring to move his men into his opponent's rear line.

During play, situations arise when one player is able to jump, and capture, one or more of his opponent's men. This occurs when a black square diagonally opposite one player's man is occupied by one of his opponent's men and when there is an open black square diagonally beyond the opponent's piece. The player may jump over the opponent's man, moving to the vacant square beyond, and remove the jumped

Red executes a double jump, removing two of black's men from the board. One of the objects of Checkers *is to capture enemy men by jumping.*

man from the board. One, two or more men may be jumped if they are positioned so that an empty black square is diagonally in front of each. Should a player overlook a possible jump, the opponent may require any other man moved to be replaced and the jump taken or he may remove the man failing to jump. Should two or more jumping opportunities present themselves at one time, the player must decide on one and be prepared to lose the second man to his opponent.

When a player is able to move one of his men into a black square on his opponent's back line, or "king row," this man becomes a "king." The opponent is obliged to crown a king by putting a checker of the same color (one of the captured men) on top. A king has special privileges in that it may be moved forward *or* backward diagonally and, in jumping, both

Player gains a king by moving man into foe's back row (single arrows). A king (crossed arrows) moves forward or backward diagonally.

ways in succession on the same jump. Also, the king does not have to take a jump, as does a regular man.

The game continues until one player captures all his opponent's men, removing them from the board, or traps them so that they cannot move. If neither player is able to move, the game ends in a draw. If only a few men remain on the board—appearing that neither

player can win—the two players may agree to allow a set number of moves, such as 20. If a game is not over after 20 moves, it is a draw.

Dice Twenty-one

● *2 to 6*   ● *One standard die; chips or other counters*

Each player, in turn, attempts to reach 21 exactly, or come as close to that number as possible without exceeding it—by means of successive rolls of the die. The score of a player's second roll is added to that of his first roll, that of the third roll added to the second roll and so forth. If a player exceeds 21, he pays a chip into the pot. Once a person ends his turn—say, at 19—he cannot later decide to take another turn with the die to amend his score.

The player who gets 21, or nearest to 21, wins the chips in the pot plus an additional chip from each person. Thus those players who exceed 21 end up paying double. If a tie occurs, the players involved stage a play-off to decide the winner.

Dominoes

● *2 to 9*   ● *A standard set of dominoes consisting of 28 dominoes ranging in denomination from the blank (zero) to the six*

OBJECT: There are many variations of *Dominoes,* but most games share a common objective—to try to rid the hand of all dominoes before an opponent (or opponents) can do so.

RANKING OF SUITS: In *Dominoes,* "suit" and number mean the same thing. There are seven doubles: the double blank, zero-zero; the double one, one-one; two-two; three-three; four-four; five-five and six-six. In addition, there are 21 dominoes with each end showing a different denomination: for instance, six-five; four-one; three-blank. A domino with two different numbers belongs to two suits: A six-five, for example, belongs to both the six suit and the five suit. A double—since both ends are the same—belongs to only one suit.

PREPARATION: The set of dominoes is faced down on the table and thoroughly mixed—a process like that of shuffling in a game of cards. Each player draws to determine who has the first play—high winning, with the double six being highest. An appropriate number of dominoes, or "bones," are then drawn by each player to form his hand; this number varies depending upon the specific game and the number of players in the game. The remaining dominoes are kept face down in what is known as the "boneyard," which is situated near at hand, but away from the center of the table. A player conceals his hand from opponents—generally by standing his dominoes on end directly in front of himself so that only he can see their values.

BLOCK DOMINOES

There are two players; each draws seven dominoes to form his hand. The boneyard cannot be resorted to thereafter and is moved off to the side of the table. The winner of the draw for first play takes any domino from his hand and places it face up in the center of the table. His opponent must follow suit; in other words, he must match with a number from his hand one of the ends of the domino on the board. For example, if the first domino is a five-five, any domino with a five at one end will do. Should the opponent hold, say, the five-one, he places it with the five end touching either end of the five-five. The first player then takes his

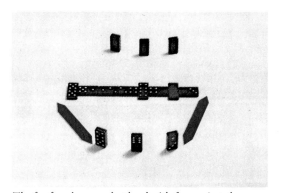

The five-four bone can be played with five against the double five (left arrow), or the one-three bone with threes touching (right).

second turn. Before him he sees two dominoes in a row; at one end of the row there is a five (the unplayed-upon end of the five-five) and at the other end there is a one. Hence, any domino with a five or a one at either end can now be played. Whenever a doublet is played (in this case, a five-five), the next player, if he has two dominoes with a five on one end, may play a domino on either end.

In the above fashion, the players alternate turns in building a row of dominoes across the table—the dominoes always linked by numbers of the same suit. If one player cannot follow suit, he calls out, "Go!" thus signaling his opponent to make another play. If the blocked player still cannot follow suit after this second play, he must again call "Go!" continuing to do so for as long as he is blocked.

When one player plays off all his dominoes the game ends. His opponent counts up the points on all the dominoes he still holds—the sum going to the winner as his score for that hand. In cases where both players are blocked, they each count up the points remaining in their hands. The person with the fewest points is winner and collects the difference in points between the two hands. Fifty is generally set as the grand game-winning total. After each hand, the players draw new hands of seven from the boneyard, and the loser of the previous hand begins play in the next game.

VARIATIONS: In *Draw Dominoes,* the player who finds himself blocked must continue to draw from the boneyard until he gets a playable domino. Two dominoes must stay in the boneyard; in other words, the drawing stops when only two bones remain in the yard. *Tiddley Wink* is played by six to nine people. To start, each player draws three dominoes ("bones") from the boneyard. No additional bones may be drawn after this initial draw. The first play is made by the person holding the highest doublet, the six-six being the highest. Afterwards, each player must follow suit or pass, as described in *Block Dominoes.* A play may be made only onto the last previous bone played. When a person plays a doublet, he may take another turn, if able to do so (this includes the starter). The game continues until one of the players rids himself of his three dominoes or play is blocked all around. The scoring is the same as in *Block Dominoes*.

ALL FIVES

This *Domino* game is best with two or three players but may be played with five. All aspects of the game with respect to the draw, the boneyard, the requirements to follow suit, and the draw from the boneyard when unable to follow suit are the same as described for *Block Dominoes*. However, even when he can follow suit, a player may, instead, pass his turn and draw one domino from the boneyard in order to improve his hand.

First play is made by the person holding the highest doublet—the six-six being highest—which he places face up in the center of the table. Should no one have a doublet, the players take turns drawing from the boneyard until someone receives one. At the start, in a two-player game, each person draws seven dominoes; when more than two play, each draws five.

All Fives differs from ordinary *Dominoes* in that points can be scored during the play. The initial doublet is built upon both at the ends and the sides, resulting in a cross formation with four ends, rather than the two of a simple horizontal

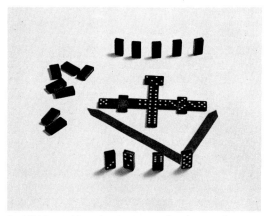

In All Fives, *either play (arrows) makes the outer bones in the four arms of the cross add up to 25—a number divisible by five.*

row. However, all doublets after the first may be built upon only at their sides. Should a player position a domino that makes the outside numbers in all four arms of the cross total a sum divisible by five—such as 15, 20, 25—he receives that number of points automatically. Of course, the rule governing the matching of suits in ordinary dominoes also applies in *All Fives*—i.e., a two can only be played on a two, a blank only adjoining a blank, a six only adjacent to a six and so forth.

As in *Block Dominoes,* the first player to rid himself of all dominoes in his hand collects all the points still held by his opponent—but rounded off to the nearest five. For instance, if an opponent holds 13, 14, 16 or 17 points, the score is written as 15. If the play is blocked, the low man subtracts his points from those of the high man—again rounding off his score to the nearest five. Points scored during play are added up with those received for ridding oneself of all dominoes. Generally, the game is 100 points, and the first player to attain this score wins the game. After the game, the dominoes are collected, faced down, mixed and a new hand is drawn.

SEBASTOPOL

There are four players, and each player draws seven dominoes (bones) from the boneyard. The opening play is made by the person holding the six-six. The person to his left is next in turn, and so on, clockwise around the table. After the six-six is set in place, the next four plays must also be of the six suit. A person not holding a domino of the six suit must pass his turn. The four plays are made end-to-end with the doublet and at right angles on either side of the doublet—such that the initial formation is a four-pronged cross consisting of six dominoes of the six suit.

Thereafter the game proceeds with the players following suit as in *Block Dominoes,* but building outward upon the four arms of the cross. A player who first rids his hand of dominoes collects from the other players all points remaining in their hands. If all players are blocked, the person with fewest points left in his hand collects the difference in points from each of his opponents.

BERGEN

This is best when played by two people, but it is a good game for three also. The first play is decided by a draw, with high winning—the double six being highest.

Each player starts with six dominoes (bones) drawn face down from the boneyard. When a player cannot follow suit (match a number) he must draw from the boneyard until able to play. When the boneyard gets down to two bones, no more bones may be drawn by anyone.

The dominoes are placed end-to-end on the table in a horizontal line. Inside this line, the doublets are positioned at right angles to the other dominoes. These inside doublets may only be played upon, horizontally, at their two sides—not at their ends. In *Bergen,* the purpose is to make the number at one end of the row match the number at the other end of the row. For doing this with a two-suit domino (different count at each end), the player receives two points. He receives three points if he accomplishes a match by using a doublet from his hand or if he can make a match against a doublet already at the opposite end of the row.

The first player to rid his hand of dominoes scores one point; or, should play be blocked for both people, the person with the fewest points remaining in his hand scores one point. In the latter case, though, the low man must not hold a doublet. If the high man holds no doublet while low hand does, the high man, instead of the low man, receives the one point. After each hand, the dominoes are mixed face down, and the draw commences for a new hand. The grand winning total is 15 points.

MATADOR

As in *Block Dominoes,* the entire set of dominoes (bones) is faced down on the table at the start of play. The players draw hands of seven bones each, if two are playing; five each, when more than two play. Normally, the player holding the

highest doublet—six-six being tops—opens play, placing the doublet face up in the center of the table as the foundation for a horizontal row.

In *Matador,* doublets are positioned end-to-end, and the other dominoes are placed at right angles to the horizontal line of doublets. Should no one hold a doublet, the highest two-suit domino (different unit at each end) is used instead to open play in a vertical formation.

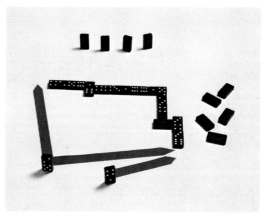

In Matador, *both dominoes are playable: the five-two bone is wild, and the one on the four-one bone may be played upon the six to make seven.*

Matador differs from other *Domino* games in that the object is not to match suits but, rather, to make adjoining denominations add up to the value of seven. Hence, to play upon a six-six, a player has to hold a bone one side of which is a one; in order to play upon a five, he has to have a bone showing a two, and so forth. The double blank (zero-zero) is regarded as wild and is playable upon any number whatsoever. Like the zero-zero, dominoes whose full face value is seven are regarded as wild—four-three, five-two and six-one—and may be played on any number. Thus, there are six wild men—or "Matadors"—in the game. Only the Matadors (or a zero-zero, representing a seven-seven) may be played on a blank.

If a player cannot make a sum of seven, he draws from the boneyard until receiving a domino that allows him to do so. However, the last two bones in the yard may not be taken. The first person to rid his hand of all dominoes wins the total number of points still held by his opponent. If the play is blocked all around, low man wins the difference in points still held by himself and his opponent or opponents.

Helma (*Chinese Checkers*)

● *2 to 6* ● *A Helma (or Chinese Checkers) board; 90 marbles in six colors, 15 of each color*

OBJECT: Each player tries to move all his marbles from one of the six points of the star into the opposite point of the star before any opponent can do so.

PREPARATION: Players choose colors. If two are playing, they take seats opposite one another. Each player positions 15 marbles of a single color into the point of the star in front of him— opposite his opponent's point. If three or more play, ten marbles are used instead of 15; these are grouped within any point of the star a player chooses.

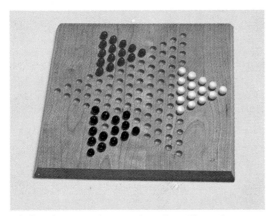

Black makes an opening move in Helma. *Players jump their own marbles as well as opponent's in race to put men in opposite star-point.*

PLAY: A draw of lots determines who plays first. Players take alternate turns. With three or more people, the turns move in a clockwise direction from the left of the person who goes first. A player may move only one of his marbles on each turn. Moreover, he may move this marble only one space forward into an open hole, unless a jump is possible. A player may jump any man in an adjoining hole—either his own marble or his opponent's—as long as the hole beyond is open. Multiple jumps may be executed when several marbles lie in alternate positions with open holes. A player may not move backwards —except in a series of multiple jumps which end ahead of the marble's starting point. The first player to get all his marbles into the star point opposite the one he starts in wins the game.

Parcheesi (*Parchisi*)

● *2 to 4* ● *A Parcheesi board; 16 discs in four colors, four of each color; one pair of dice dice cup for each player*

OBJECT: Each player attempts to get four discs into the center of the board before any other player can do so.

PREPARATION: Taking seats at a table, the players open the board, positioning it so that a circle of one of the four colors is before each player. Each player takes the four discs of the same color as his circle and places the discs into his circle. A single die is cast by each person, high throw winning the first move. If there is a tie, the die is cast again until the tie is broken.

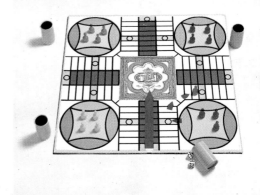

A five on one die lets red player move a man out. A six on the other advances man six spaces. Arrows point out pathway to home.

PLAY: The players take turns, rotating in a clockwise direction. On each of his turns, a player casts two dice from his cup. In order to move a disc, or "man," from the home circle, a five must be cast—not as the sum of two dice but as a whole number five showing on one die. When a five is thrown, a player may move one disc onto the colored space just next to his home base. If double fives are cast, two men may be moved out at the same time, one man moved out and then moved five spaces forward or some other man, already out, moved five spaces forward.

At any time during the game, when a player throws a doublet—such as a pair of fives or a pair of sixes—he moves his men the correct number of spaces forward and rolls the dice again. Under some rules, if a player casts three consecutive doubles, he pays a penalty. He is forced to return to the home circle whichever man of his is farthest around the board—at the same time passing the turn to his neighbor on the left.

The dice are played as two separate counts, as in *Backgammon*. In other words, where a player rolls a six and a four, he may move one man six spaces and another man four spaces.

No more than two men may be positioned on one space at the same time. Two men of the same color on the same space block passage past that point to any men coming up behind. As noted, a player may move two men per turn, each advancing the number of spaces shown on one of the die. In this way, should a player roll doubles, he may move two men into blocking position side-by-side. Where a block lies ahead and the number on the dice would carry any player's man up to the block or beyond the block, that player may not move his man forward even one space. For instance, if a block lies on a space four units ahead and the cast of the dice yields six, five or four, the player may not move the man at all. A player may not jump over his own roadblock (or an opponent's) until he (or his opponent) moves one or both of the men out of blocking position.

Where one man lies alone on a space, an opposing man landing squarely on that space sends the first man home. Thus, if an opponent's man lies four spaces ahead and a player casts a four on one die—or a combination on both die add up to exactly four—he moves up his man, replacing the opposing man and sending him back home. A man sent home in this way cannot re-enter the game until the player throws a five—as at the start of play. The blue-colored spaces that lie at strategic locations around the board are safe bases. A man placed on one of these spaces cannot be sent home, regardless of whether an opponent lands a man beside him.

After traveling around the rest of the board, a player's men enter the center of the board through the avenue just to the left of his home circle. Once inside this avenue, a player's men cannot be attacked by an opponent's men. Men are moved in the avenue just as they are around the rest of the board; however, no man can enter the inner circle unless the exact number of spaces necessary to do so appears on one of the die or as the sum of both dice. Hence, a man lying six spaces from the inner circle can move into the circle only if a six or some combination adding up to six is thrown. If a five is cast, a man can move up to the first space of the avenue. However, the only way this man can move into the inner circle is if a one shows up on a die on a subsequent turn; a two or some higher number does not allow a move into the inner circle.

The first player to move all his discs into the inner circle wins the game.

Poker Dice

● *5 to 7* ● *Five dice, either specially marked or regular dice; one dice cup*

If the special set of dice are used, each cube is sided with an ace, king, queen, jack, ten and nine. If ordinary dice are used, the one is considered to be the ace; the six, the king; the five, the queen; the four, the jack; the three, the ten; the two, the nine.

Each player, in turn, puts all five dice into the dice cup, shakes the dice and casts them onto the table. If dissatisfied with the first roll, a player may return the dice to the cup and throw them again. Should this second roll also seem unsatisfactory to him, he may cast the dice a third and final time. When a player decides to throw the dice again, he cancels out the previous throw, thus making the last throw his hand—not the best throw of the three.

The hands are ranked as follows: five of a kind; four of a kind; full house; straight; three of a kind; two pair; one pair; high card. Since there are no suits, there can be no flushes or straight flushes. (See description of each hand in *Poker* on p. 212.) Where two or more players have hands that tie, they roll the dice again to break the tie. The player with the highest hand wins the game.

Roulette

- *Any number over 1 (best with 5 or more)*
- *A Roulette wheel with small metal ball; plastic chips or some other kind of counters; printed betting "layout" for convenience of players*

OBJECT: Players attempt, on the basis of chance, to win a bet against the bank that some number, combination of numbers or color will come up as the result of the spin of the wheel.

PREPARATION: The *Roulette* wheel is situated at the center of the table or at one end of the table, in full view of all players. Ahead of time, someone offers to act as banker. In casinos where the game is played for money, the players purchase their chips from the bank, hence each color chip—white, red and blue—has a specific monetary value. In a home game, by common agreement, all players draw an equal amount of chips from the bank at the start of the game. The betting layout (or layouts) should be conveniently situated around the table within easy reach of the players and in full view. Generally, in a home game the banker is in charge of the wheel and also acts as "croupier"—settling up

the bets for everyone betting prior to the next spin of the wheel.

PLAY: All betters examine the betting layout, decide upon their bet or bets, place their chip or chips upon the appropriate number, combination or color and await the spin of the wheel. After everybody places his bet, the banker gives the wheel a spin, dropping the ball into the groove on the wheel. At this point, no further bets may be placed and no one may alter his bet. When the wheel finally comes to rest, the ball lodges in one of the pockets at the edge. Depending upon the number (1-36; 0; 00) or color of the pocket where the ball stops, the bets are settled by the banker. He pays off the winners according to the odds—described below—and collects the chips of the losers from the table.

ODDS PAID BY BANK: The odds listed below are paid by the bank when a 36-number wheel with a zero (0), or a zero and a double zero (00), is used in the game:

A bet placed upon any single number when that number comes up (including the 0 or 00) . . . . 35 for 1
On the line between two numbers, when either number comes up . . . . 17 for 1
On the intersection of four numbers, when any of those numbers comes up . . . . . . 8 for 1
To the right or left of a row of three numbers (such as 31, 32 and 33) when any of the three numbers comes up . . . . 11 for 1
On the right or left end of the line horizontally separating two rows of three numbers (a six-number combination) . . . . 5 for 1
At the bottom of a vertical column of 12 numbers . . . . 2 for 1
On the line between two vertical columns of 12 numbers . . . . $\frac{1}{2}$ for 1
On the combination 1-12 . . . . 2 for 1
On the combination 13-24 . . . . 2 for 1
On the combination 25-36 . . . . 2 for 1
On the vertical dividing line between any two of the above three combinations . . . $\frac{1}{2}$ for 1
High (19-36) . . . . Even Money
Low (1-18) . . . . Even Money

A red odd number—23—comes up on the Roulette *wheel. On betting layout, all of the white chips are on winning combinations; others lose.*

Odd (1, 3, 5, 7, 9, etc. to 35) . . Even Money
Even (2, 4, 6, 8, 10, etc. to 36) . Even Money
Black (any black number) . . . . . Even Money
Red (any red number) . . . . Even Money

When the 0 (or 00) comes up, the bank pays off only for bets placed on it and takes all other chips except those placed on Even—which are set aside for a decision on the next spin of the wheel. If the ensuing roll comes up on an even number, the even player wins even money; if odd, the bank takes the chips.

A wheel with fewer than 36 numbers pays odds smaller than a 36-number wheel. For instance, a 33-number wheel pays 32 for 1 on a single number; a 30-number wheel, 29 for 1 and so forth. The combinations are scaled down proportionately, such that with a 30-number wheel, a two-number combination would pay 14 for 1. Even money payoffs, of course, are not affected.

Roulette sets are now available for home recreation and parties. In general, the more moderately priced sets have wheels smaller than those in casinos and a metal ball about the size of a small roller bearing. Excellent, easily read betting layouts usually come as part of the set.

Skittles

● *1 to 12* ● *A Skittles board; 12 pins; top and string; scoring pad and pencil*

OBJECT: Players try to knock down as many pins as possible by spinning the top.

PREPARATION: The pins are set up on the board—on the numbered marks in the compartments. The first player winds the string around the stem of the top and holds the top ready before the entrance portal at one end of the board.

PLAY: The player pulls sharply on the string—at the same time releasing the top. As the top goes careening through the entrance portal into the first compartment, it begins a path determined by its collisions with the pins and walls—perhaps detouring into a side compartment or possibly traveling on through other portals of the labyrinth. When the top's momentum is lost and it topples over, the point-values of the pins brought down by the spinning top are noted and the sum entered on the pad as the player's score. The game can be played with each contestant having five or ten tries, with the person accumulating the highest point-total as the winner.

At the starting hole on Skittles *board, the top awaits the pull of the cord that sends it careening through compartments, toppling pins.*

If a *Skittles* board can't be purchased locally, it can be constructed according to the following specifications: floorboard, 42 inches by 24 inches; side and end walls, as well as compartment partitions, five and one-half inches high. An entrance opening and compartment portals, each of about three inches breadth, are cut into the respective slats. If the pins are also fashioned at home, they should be roughly one inch in diameter and five inches tall—the top, one and three-fourths inches in diameter and three and five-eighths inches high.

Table Cricket (*Table Polo*)

● *2 to 8* ● *A Table-Cricket board and ball*

OBJECT: Each player tries to drive the ball through the opposing goal.

PREPARATION: One team lines up on one side of the board, and the opposing team lines up on the other side. There are eight paddle-rods stretched across the board—four of the handles of which are one one side. If there are four persons per team, each player controls one of the paddle-rods that run across the breadth of the board. If only two play, each player has to manipulate all four paddle-rods on his side of the board. Each team chooses to defend one of the two goals, located at either end of the board.

ACTION: The ball is dropped into the center of the board, and the players begin manipulating the paddle-rods. They try to drive the ball toward the opposing goal and, at the same time, to keep it away from their own goal. When the ball is driven into the opposing goal, the scoring-team receives one point. Five points may be established as the winning score. If the ball is driven off the table, it is returned; the play begins anew with a center drop.

If a *Table-Cricket* set cannot be purchased locally, one can be produced in a home carpentry shop. The board should be 40 inches long and 18 inches wide. The side walls should be four and one-half inches in height, with the end walls an inch or so high. The end walls each contain a central slot about three inches wide and three inches in height, set flush with the floor—serving as the goals.

Because making a complete *Table-Cricket* set may involve more carpentry than many people would care to engage in for this purpose, the game can be modified to dispense with the rods and their attached paddles. In this simpler form of the game, only two players may compete at any one time. Instead of manipulating paddles by turning rods, each player has an ice-cream stick which he uses to push the ball up and down the board. (If a small ball is not available, a marble will do nicely as a substitute.) Each contestant tries to block his opponent's shots, steal control of the ball and make goals. A player may use only the ice-cream stick to do so. Should a player touch the ball with his hand, his opponent gets a free shot at the goal from the center of the board. Each goal scored counts as one point, and the first player to make five goals wins.

CHAPTER 10

Planning a Party

Unlike the small family party which thrives on informality and spur-of-the-moment activities, the large party can be a disaster without sufficient planning. In planning a party of any size, it is a good idea to use a particular theme and to relate the invitations, decorations, refreshments and games to this theme. Care should be taken, however, that all of the party activities—and particularly the games—are suitable for the guests. The party planner should know the ages of the guests, their levels of sophistication and whether the group is mixed or all of one sex. What will work nicely for a group of 10-year-old boys may be "kid stuff" to a mixed group of 12-year-olds. By the same token, teen-agers may be baffled or bored by some of the activities that work well with adults.

The only meaningful way of judging whether or not a party is a success is for the host to ask himself, "Did all the guests have a good time?" If they did, it was a "fun party," and any invitations to parties the host may plan in the future will be well received. The one thing that marks all "fun parties"—whether the guests be adults, teen-agers or children— is a friendly, relaxed atmosphere. This is reflected in the easy way in which the guests mingle and take part in the various events. All of the party suggestions and games listed in this chapter aim toward this convivial atmosphere. Suitable activities, food and decorations are presented for a variety of parties and a variety of ages. In addition to the games in this chapter, many of the games elsewhere in the book may be adapted for a particular party.

Holidays, in addition to providing party themes, are in themselves ideal party times. All of the following holiday parties, listed chronologically, have suggestions for distinctive invitations, refreshments, decorations and games for all ages. While the holidays included are especially popular for parties, there are other holidays—like New Year's Day, Columbus Day and May Day—that, with a little planning and imagination, also lend themselves to parties.

Valentine's Day

● *February 14th*

THEME: This is an ideal occasion for a boy-girl party at almost any age level. The theme should be romantic and sentimental. Since red is the traditional *Valentine's Day* color, it should be used for invitations, refreshments and decorations and, whenever possible, for food.

INVITATIONS: Inexpensive valentines may be used, with a handwritten invitation written beneath the printed message, or red hearts may be cut from construction paper with the invitation written directly on them.

REFRESHMENTS: Red-colored punch or pink lemonade are in keeping with the holiday colors, and either one is simple to make. Small sandwiches, cut into heart shapes, make an attractive arrangement on a tray. An ice-cream cake, decorated with a heart or bow-and-arrow design—or a jello fruit salad, set into a large heart-shaped mold—makes a striking centerpiece on the serving table.

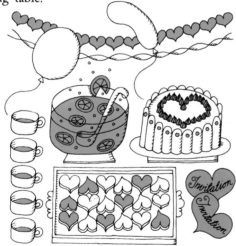

Refreshments for a Valentine's Day *party may include ice-cream cake, punch and cookies in the shape of hearts.*

DECORATIONS: Red and white crepe-paper streamers interspersed with red paper hearts can be hung from walls and ceilings. Red and white balloons, a display of valentines and cut-out Cupid silhouettes also add to the atmosphere.

GAMES: In *Matching Hearts* a number of hearts are made out of red construction paper, and each one is cut in two along a jagged line. No two hearts should be cut the same way. The right sides of the hearts are given to the girls and the left sides to the boys. On a signal, the girls and boys begin comparing heart-halves until each finds the half that fits with theirs exactly. Boys and girls with matching halves become partners for the next dance or game.

In *Sing a Love Song,* the names of a number of well-known old love songs, such as "Let Me Call You Sweetheart," are written in duplicate on a sheet of paper. The lists are cut so that the name of each song appears on two slips of paper. One set of slips is given to the girls; the other to the boys. On signal, all of the players begin to sing or hum their song while walking about to hear what the other players are singing or humming. When the girl and boy humming the same song find each other, they become partners for the next activity. Instead of love songs, more recent popular songs may be substituted for teen-agers.

In *Heart Darts* a number of hearts are cut out of red paper, and the name of a girl guest is written on one side of each. The hearts are then tacked to a large dartboard or a sheet of plywood, with the blank side face up. The boys line up and take turns aiming darts at the hearts. A heart is taken down after it is hit, and the dart-thrower takes the girl named as his partner.

Partner Quiz is played after one of the partner-matching games above. The girls and boys are separated, sent to opposite sides of the room and told to face the wall. Each person is then given a sheet of paper containing a list of questions about his or her partner—the person standing opposite. Questions might include:

How tall is your partner?
What color are his (her) eyes?
What street does he (she) live on?

In turn the boys (or the girls) call out the answer to each question. The player who answers most of the questions correctly—with the partner acting as judge—is the winner.

In *Hidden Heart* each player is given a large piece of red tissue paper. While holding the paper behind his or her back, each player must try to tear a heart shape out of the paper as accurately and as quickly as possible. When time is called, the player with the best facsimile of a heart gets a prize. (A small candy heart would be appropriate.)

In *Heart Hunt* a number of small, red, paper hearts—each with a number written on it—are placed around the room on shelves, tables, curtains and picture frames. There should be five times as many hearts as there are guests, and each number should appear on five hearts. At a signal, the players begin gathering all the hearts they can find, trying to collect five hearts with the same number. When all of the hearts are collected, the players may swap with one another until one player has five of a kind and becomes the winner.

In *Love Letters* each player is given a sheet of paper and a pencil. At the top of each boy's sheet are different combinations, such as John Alden to Priscilla, Romeo to Juliet or Adam to Eve. At the top of the girls' sheets are the same names reversed. The object is to write a short love letter in the style of the first person named to the second person. When the letters are completed, the appropriate couples are matched up, and read their letters aloud to each other. The couple whose letters receive the most applause wins.

In *Do-It-Yourself Valentines* red and white paper, paper lace, paste, scissors, crayons and colored pencils are laid out on a wide table, and each player is asked to make a valentine for his or her partner. The most original valentine wins a prize.

Washington's Birthday

- *February 22nd (celebrated on the preceding Monday)*

THEME: Red, white and blue decorations are appropriate as are hatchets and cherry trees.

INVITATIONS: A cut-out paper hatchet or a large cherry tree make ideal invitations.

Cherries appear as table decorations and in ice cream and pie at a traditional Washington's Birthday *celebration.*

REFRESHMENTS: "Patriotic sandwiches" may be made of three slices of white bread with fillings of cherry jam, cream cheese and blueberry jam. Dessert can be cherry pie, cherry ice cream or gingerbread topped with maraschino cherries.

DECORATIONS: Red, white and blue crepe-paper streamers are good decorations for doorways and windows. Walls can be decorated with clusters of cherries—formed by red cardboard circles and green paper stems, paper hatchets or a few copies of the original 13-star flag.

GAMES: In *Hatchet Relay* the players line up in two equal teams and stand side by side. About 15 feet in front of each team is a "cherry tree"—a thorny bush or some branches to which have been fastened an equal number of real or artificial cherries (or paper cutouts of cherries). The first player on each team is given a cardboard "hatchet." He must run up to his tree, pick a cherry, place it on his hatchet and return to his place before removing the cherry and passing the hatchet to the next player on his team. The relay continues until one team—the winner—picks all the cherries.

In *Throw the Silver Dollar* the "silver dollar" is prepared by cutting a circle from some light-weight material, such as cardboard or Styrofoam, and covering it with tinfoil. Players can take turns trying to throw it across a line labeled "Rappahannock River" seven or eight feet away. Since the dollar is quite light, it cannot be thrown far. Each player gets three tries, and the player whose dollar crosses the river, or comes closest to the river, wins.

In *Words from Washington,* each player or team is given paper and pencil and told to make as many words as possible of three letters or more from the word "Washington." There are quite a few possibilities, including: <u>wash</u>, <u>ton</u>, <u>washing</u>, <u>sing</u>, <u>tow</u>, <u>shin</u>, <u>swan</u>, <u>swing</u>, <u>was</u> and <u>stag</u>. There is a five-minute time limit, and the player or team with the greatest number of words wins.

In *Jumbled Presidents* the players divide into two or more teams. Each team is given a list of Presidents' names in which the letters have been jumbled—as in GINSHAWNOT for Washington or KOCSANJ for Jackson. The team to unjumble all the names first is the winner.

St. Patrick's Day

● *March 17th*

THEME: You don't have to be Irish to enjoy Ireland's national holiday, but some Irish songs and dances can help to set the proper mood. The important thing is to be sure that there is plenty of green, as *St. Patrick's Day* is traditionally the day for the "wearin' of the green."

INVITATIONS: Large shamrocks (three-leaf clovers), cut from green construction paper, or small green shamrocks pasted in the corners of white paper, make ideal invitations. The message should have a bit of Irish flavor. One way to "go Irish" is to change the family name by adding an "O" to the front of it; if it comes out "O'Smith," so much the funnier.

REFRESHMENTS: The traditional *St. Patrick's Day* dinner is corned beef and cabbage. However, anything with a touch of green in it is acceptable: for example, "pig sandwiches" of minced

ham and green relish or cream cheese sandwiches with bits of chopped peppers. A colorful *St. Patrick's Day* salad can be made by mixing well-chopped apple and cabbage in lime jello and setting the jello in a shamrock-shaped mold. Proper green desserts include: lime ices, pistachio ice cream or cake and cookies tinted with green vegetable dye.

DECORATIONS: The traditional symbols of *St. Patrick's Day* are harps, clay pipes, shillelaghs, shamrocks and funny Irish hats. All of these can be cut from green construction paper and used to decorate the room. Green crepe-paper streamers are useful, as are clusters of green balloons and small pots of paper shamrocks taped to wire stems. A single large green shamrock makes a fine centerpiece for the refreshment table.

Paper cutouts of harps, clay pipes, floppy Irish hats and shamrocks add notes of authenticity to a St. Patrick's party. Balloons also help make the occasion festive.

GAMES: In *Blarney Stone* a large stone is placed in the center of the room. Under it are placed a number of cards—one for each guest—with a long green string tied to each one. Each guest, in turn, pulls on a string and draws out a card on which has been written a brief, unfinished story. The player must read the story and make up an ending for it. An example might be: Pat and Mike were walking through the forest one day when a tiny leprechaun suddenly appeared before them. "I will grant each of you one wish," he said, "if you can count all of the shamrocks in the forest before nightfall." "That's impossible," said Pat. "No, it isn't," said Mike, with a twinkle in his eye. Then he ——. (The player finishes the story.)

In *Shillelagh Duel* the players are paired off and blindfolded. Each player is given a green cardboard hat to wear and a loosely rolled-up newspaper to use as a club. On signal, each player goes at his partner with his noisy but harmless club, trying to knock off his hat. The winners of each contest meet each other in the next round, and the elimination continues until only one player—the shillelagh champion—remains.

In *Praty Race* two teams compete against each other by carrying a praty (the Irish word for potato) on the flat of a dinner knife from the starting line to the finish line and back. The players may not touch the potato with their hands, except to place it back on the knife if it drops. The first team to have all of its members complete the relay wins.

In *Potato Hockey,* the players are divided into two teams of four or five players each. Each player is given a "hockey stick"—a wooden ruler, wooden mixing spoon or a short length of broom handle. A potato serves as the puck. The teams try to score goals by rolling the potato across the room and through the opposing team's goal (the legs of a designated chair). As in *Ice Hockey,* passing back and forth and interceptions are permitted.

In *Paddy's Jack Straws,* a number of small green candies or gumdrops are piled in a mound and placed in the center of a table; a small toy pig is placed on top of the mound. Players take turns seeing how many pieces of candy each one can take away from the pile before the pig tumbles down. The mound is rebuilt each time with the addition of more candy from a supply that the leader keeps handy. After every player has a turn, the one with the most candies wins the game—and the toy pig.

In *Irish Croquet,* a small croquet court is laid out on the floor, with wire clothes hangers bent and stuck into pieces of clay forming the wickets. Round potatoes are used for balls, and large wooden spoons for mallets. In general, the rules

Hangers—their ends stuck in clumps of clay—are wickets; spoons are mallets, and potatoes are balls, in Irish Croquet.

of *Croquet* (page 342) are used, although the leader may make whatever changes are needed to adapt the game to potatoes—which rarely roll in a straight line.

In *Shamrock,* the players are divided into teams, and each team is given a large cardboard chart with the letters S-H-A-M-R-O-C-K printed across the top. A long vertical line is drawn between each letter, and horizontal lines, about an inch apart, are drawn below the word. As many different categories as there are players are printed down the left-hand side of the chart.

	S	H	A	M	R	O	C	K
CARS								
FOODS								
NAMES								
STATES								
TOYS								

(Categories may include cars, foods, toys, countries or the last names of famous people.) If there are five categories (five players), there should be 40 boxes—five under each of the eight letters of Shamrock. At a signal from the leader, each team member tries to fill in the eight boxes of each category by using words beginning with the letter at the top of the chart. If the first category is food, appropriate entries might be: Salmon, Hash, Apples, Macaroni, Ravioli, Oranges, Carrots and Knockwurst. If a player can't think of a word, he can ask other members of his team for help; he also can assist other members of his team. At the end of a designated period of time—five to ten minutes—the leader collects the charts and checks the entries. The team that has filled in the most boxes with appropriate words is proclaimed the winner.

In *Who's Pat?* the leader makes up a series of questions which can be answered by one word containing Pat somewhere within it. Here are a few possibilities:

Who's Pat in a design? (Pattern)
Who's Pat playing a fatherly role? (Paternal)
Who's Pat in getting along well with people? (Compatible)

The words, and the questions that provide the clues, can be as simple or as difficult as the leader sees fit. Each player writes down his answers on paper. The winner is the person with the most correct answers. In case of a tie, the leader should have some more difficult Pat clues to determine the champion.

April Fool's Day

● *April 1st*

THEME: By tradition, *April Fool's Day* is a time of pranks and practical jokes. It is a fine occasion for a children's party with lots of surprises.

INVITATIONS: Cut-out figures of dunce caps or of jesters are appropriate. The message should be humorous and might contain a warning that the host is not responsible for any tricks played on the guests. It could also ask the guests to come prepared with their own tricks or practical jokes. A funny touch is to print the invitation backward, so that the receiver has to hold it up to a mirror to read it.

REFRESHMENTS: Simple refreshments, served buffet style, are suitable and also give the host a chance to play some tricks on his guests. An ordinary cake can be scooped out and filled with a mixture of gelatin, fruit and nuts, or a baked apple can be filled with tuna fish, or ham salad. A candy dish can contain real candies together with chocolate-covered pickles or olives, and delicious doughnuts (made of rings of cotton wool dipped in batter and fried like the real thing) can be mixed together with genuine ones on a serving platter.

A paper clown expresses the tone of an April Fool's *party. Other decorations include pictures hung upside down and streamers. Invitations are shaped like a dunce's cap.*

DECORATIONS: Crepe-paper streamers hung with colorful dunce caps or dancing jesters are attractive. Decorations should be full of surprises: Pictures can be hung upside down, for instance, and large posters of optical illusions may be pasted on doors and windows. Paper flowers, painted with garish colors in wild designs, may be placed in vases around the room. Furniture can be arranged in unusual patterns—with all the chairs facing walls, for example—or removed completely and replaced with outdoor lawn furniture or broken-down relics from the basement or attic. Nothing is too zany on *April Fool's Day*.

GAMES: Practical jokes and stunts are the order of the day, but here are a few appropriate games to play if things get too quiet.

In *Stubborn Gum,* each player is given a package of gum, or a roll of hard candy, and is told that there will be a race to see who can open his package first and pop a stick of gum or a piece of candy into his mouth. Just before the signal is given, the leader suddenly "remembers" that he has forgotten one thing. He then goes around with a roll of Scotch tape, fastening the thumb, forefinger and middle finger of the players' hands together. What appeared in the beginning to be an easy task now becomes a difficult—and quite hilarious—feat.

In *Backward Spelling Bee* players divide into two teams. The leader asks each person in turn—first from one team and then from the other to spell a word backward. As in a regular spelling bee, the shorter, easier words are given first; progressively difficult words are given as the game continues. Players who fail to correctly spell a word backward sit down. The last player left standing wins a point for his team.

In *Monkey* the players sit in a circle on the floor, and the leader places a large bag or bowl of peanuts in the center of the circle. The leader then announces that he will assign the names of different animals to the players, and that he will give the same animal name to two players. He goes on to explain that when he calls an animal, the two players assigned that animal are to race to the peanuts to see which one can remove a peanut first. After the explanation, the leader goes around the circle, whispering animal names into each player's ear. When finished, he calls out an animal (for example, "Elephants!") and two players race for the peanuts. He calls out other animal names and the same thing happens. Finally, however, he shouts out "Monkeys," and all of the remaining players dash forward—because the leader has previously assigned all of them the same name. The game is a good practical joke, and no one will be offended by it if played in the proper spirit.

Independence Day
● *July 4th*

THEME: Patriotism is the dominant theme; consequently, lots of red, white and blue should be used. Because the weather is generally favorable on the *Fourth of July,* an outdoor party can be planned.

INVITATIONS: These can be written on red, white and blue decorated paper; on a rectangle of red construction paper, rolled up and taped to look like a big firecracker, or on grey paper, cut in the outline of the Liberty Bell and trimmed in red, white and blue. The invitation should make clear what sort of party it is—indoors or out-

July Fourth *invitations—shaped like firecrackers, Liberty Bells or star-spangled maps of the United States— have party details written on their reverse sides.*

doors, picnic or barbecue style. In some parts of the country neighborhood parties are often held on *July Fourth,* and guests provide their own food. If everyone is supposed to "bring their own," the invitation should make this quite clear. The host usually supplies the liquid refreshments for this type of party.

REFRESHMENTS: The outdoor standbys—grilled frankfurters and hamburgers, heaping platters of baked beans and potato salad and plenty of soda and beer—are still the best bet for the *Fourth.* For children's parties, the holiday colors can be presented with red-colored punch; cake with red, white and blue frosting; servings of strawberry, vanilla and blueberry ice cream and red, white and blue frosted cookies—cut in the shape of the Liberty Bell.

DECORATIONS: Red, white and blue streamers add color to the party area, as do small American flags, cut-out figures of Liberty Bells, cocked hats and Minute Men. Where legally permitted, a display of fireworks is the customary way of concluding an evening party. Many places that do not permit fireworks do permit sparklers, which may be given out to the adult guests as an alternative.

GAMES: If the party is held outdoors during the day, almost any relay or active group game is suitable. The games listed here are particularly useful when the party is held indoors or at night.

In *Know Your Country* the players must listen to a song and identify a United States city, state or river named in its title. Some familiar examples include: "My Old Kentucky Home," "California, Here I Come," "Oklahoma" and "The Missouri Waltz." The leader should try to have someone play a number of such songs on a piano, accordion or other musical instrument. The winner is the player who can name the most places correctly.

In *Patriotic History* the leader selects questions about the American Revolution from standard history books. Questions may be difficult or easy, depending on the age and education of the guests. A few sample questions might include:

Who said, "Give me liberty or give me death"? (Patrick Henry)
Where was the "shot heard 'round the world" fired? (Concord, Massachusetts)
Who was the first President to live in the White House? (John Adams)
Which was the first state to join the original 13? (Vermont)

In *Give a Speech* each player is given a slip of paper on which are written ten different words. He is instructed to give a short patriotic speech using all of the words. Some of the words listed

should be fairly easy to utilize in such a speech, for instance "justice," "freedom" and "revolution." The other listed words should be far more difficult to use, like "percolate" and "chimpanzee," for example. As each player gives his speech, the leader checks off the words used. The player who uses all the words and has the funniest speech—determined by the applause of the audience—wins the "oratory contest."

Sparkler is played in the evening on a large, flat lawn and is beautiful to watch. Players divide into two teams and the first player on each team is given a lighted sparkler. At the starting signal, this player walks as quickly as he can to a predetermined spot at the lawn's edge, returns to the starting line and gives the lighted sparkler to the next player on his team. If the sparkler goes out, the player must return to the starting line, have it relit and begin the race again. The first team to complete the relay wins a prize.

Halloween

● *October 31st*

THEME: This autumn holiday is a favorite for parties built around witches, black cats, jack-o'-lanterns, skeletons, ghosts and a generally spooky atmosphere.

Cutouts of jack-o'-lanterns, witches on broomsticks and cats make spooky Halloween *party decorations and invitations.*

INVITATIONS: Any combination of orange and black paper with decorative cutouts of pumpkins or witches is suitable.

REFRESHMENTS: A "jack-o'-lantern salad" can be made by hollowing out apples, cutting faces into them and then stuffing the insides with fruit salad. For a "black cat sandwich," a circle of white bread is covered with cream cheese, and the figure of a cat's face is cut from a slice of brown bread and placed on top. A delicious "witches' brew" can be concocted by boiling cider with cinnamon, cloves and ginger root. The mixture is allowed to cool, and orange juice is added shortly before serving.

DECORATIONS: The traditional colors are orange and black, and these colors should be used throughout for crepe-paper streamers, real or paper pumpkins and for cutouts of witches, black cats or ghosts. Large cardboard skeletons, with moveable arms and legs, can be taped to walls and/or suspended from the ceiling. To create a spooky atmosphere for the party, lights should be dimmed. Candlelight is the best method of illumination, especially when the candles are flickering inside the grinning faces of jack-o'-lanterns.

GAMES: Two games traditionally associated with Halloween—*Apple Ducking* and *Hanging Apples*—are described elsewhere in this book. The games listed here are adaptations of other games, with the addition of special holiday touches.

Chamber of Horrors requires considerable preparation to be effective. The chamber can be set up either in the room where the party takes place, or in a nearby room. The room should be either completely dark or nearly so, with a rope line stretched across it serving as a guide for those passing through. Large tin cans are arranged about the room so that they will rattle and clank as unwary players stumble against them. Strips of wet cloth are hung from overhead to brush against players' faces. Hidden "ghosts" ring bells, moan, shriek, clutch the clothing of the player or touch his hand with an ice cube. Eerie effects can also be obtained by using ultraviolet light and special paints that glow in the dark. Care should be taken not to make any of the special effects in the chamber of horrors too gruesome or frightening, espe-

cially if the party is for young children.

In *Pin the Bone on the Skeleton* a cardboard skeleton is hung on a wall, and an arm or a leg is removed. In turn, each player is blindfolded and spun around. He is then given the missing part and is asked to pin it to the proper place on the skeleton. The player who returns the missing part closest to the actual spot on the body wins the contest.

In *Halloween Tenpins* ten apples, each speared on a tripod of three toothpicks, are set up in a triangular formation. The players form a line about ten feet from the apples, and each player gets three tries at knocking all of the apples over by rolling a small, round pumpkin. The player with the best score wins.

In *Pumpkin Necklace* the players are divided into teams of three or four. Each team is given a bowl of wet pumpkin seeds, a medium-sized needle and a long thread. On signal, each team begins stringing the pumpkin seeds on the thread. Each player threads three seeds before passing the needle and thread to the next player on his team. After five minutes, the team with the longest pumpkin-seed necklace is named the winner.

In *Black Cat* players divide into two teams and stand in lines a few feet apart on either side of the leader. The leader then reads aloud, from a prepared list, definitions of words beginning with the letters C-A-T. The players on the two teams compete to shout out the correct word for each definition. Some examples of definitions that could be used follow:

An ancient burial place (Catacomb)
A terrible misfortune (Catastrophe)
A large church (Cathedral)

The team that is quickest in providing the most correct answers wins the game.

In *Pumpkin Head Race* the players line up in teams of two behind a starting line. Each couple receives a small pumpkin which they place between their foreheads. On signal, all the couples attempt to cross the room and return without dropping the pumpkin. They may not use their hands, except to replace the pumpkin between their foreheads if it falls. The first team to complete the round trip wins the race.

Fortune Telling includes many kinds of "occult" games in which the leader dresses as a fortuneteller, or witch, to add to the effect. Included in this category are these interesting events: In *Hidden Omens* a coin, a thimble and a ring are hidden in a bowl of flour. Each player, in turn, dips his hand into the bowl and comes up with one of the objects. The fortuneteller tells the player that the coin signifies eventual wealth, the ring means imminent marriage and the thimble is a sign of bachelorhood. In *Food Fortunes* a piece of pork, a pickle, a marshmallow and a sweet pepper are hung at face level from strings attached to the ceiling. In turn, the fortuneteller blindfolds each player and leads him toward the strings. The player tries to bite at the first object that he feels. If he bites the pickle first, it means that he has a sour disposition; if he bites the marshmallow, a soft life is in store; if the red pepper, he will have a vigorous life and if the pork, he is a natural politician. The bitten omen is replaced while the next player is being blindfolded. In *Apple Fortune* the fortuneteller gives each player an apple and a paring knife, asking him to peel as long an unbroken piece of skin as he can. After doing this, the player turns around and tosses the apple peel over his shoulder toward the fortuneteller. The fortuneteller lets the peel fall to the floor before examining it to determine the letter of the alphabet it most resembles. He then announces that the letter will have some important meaning to the player very soon—that it is the first letter of a person or place that will play an important role in the player's life.

Thanksgiving Day

● *Fourth Thursday in November*

THEME: This is an occasion for family get-togethers and traditional turkey dinners. It is also a fine opportunity to give a party with an emphasis on autumn themes or the Pilgrims—the first people to celebrate *Thanksgiving*.

INVITATIONS: Cutouts of turkeys or Pilgrim hats, in autumn colors of red, orange and yellow make an appropriate background.

Pilgrim hats, turkeys, maple leaves and apples—all cut from construction paper—make appropriate invitations and decorations for a gala Thanksgiving Day *feast.*

REFRESHMENTS: If the party follows the big *Thanksgiving* dinner, chances are that nobody is going to be very hungry. Some leftover slices of turkey on a platter, with some sliced bread nearby for making a sandwich, should take care of whatever appetites remain. Pumpkin, apple and mince pies all suit the holiday mood, as do bowls of cranberry sauce or cranberry salad. Cider and doughnuts are old standbys.

DECORATIONS: The autumn colors should predominate, especially the deep red of apples, maple leaves and red-eared Indian corn—all of which make lovely *Thanksgiving* decorations. Large cardboard cutouts of turkeys and figures in Pilgrim costumes can be hung on the walls.

GAMES: In *Pilgrim Hat,* a tall, black Pilgrim hat is made of stiff cardboard. Players sit in a circle and pass the hat from head to head. The leader, meanwhile, counts off a predetermined amount of time—usually one minute—and then shouts "Stop." The person with the hat on his head is eliminated and the game begins again. The game continues until only one player remains; the winning player gets to keep the Pilgrim hat.

In *Candy Harvest* a clothesline is hung across the room so that it is slightly higher than the heads of the players. Pieces of candy are suspended from the clothesline, tied onto bits of thread. The players divide into two teams and line up about two feet away from the clothesline. On signal, the first player from each team clasps his hands behind his back and leans forward, trying to snap off one of the suspended candies with his teeth. When he succeeds, he hurries back to the end of his team's line, and the next player tries. The first team to complete the task successfully wins the game.

In *Turkey Trot* the players line up along one side of the room. Each player is given a drinking straw and a turkey feather (or a chicken feather, if turkey feathers are too hard to come by). On signal, players place their feathers on the floor and blow them across the room with the straw. The player who blows his feather across the room and over the finish line the fastest wins. As a variation, the game may be played as the *Turkey Trot Relay* by having each team propel a single feather back and forth across the floor.

In *Popcorn Feeding Contest* the players divide into couples—preferably a girl and a boy. All players are blindfolded, and one partner in each pair is given a large wooden spoon and a bowl of popcorn. On signal, they begin feeding popcorn to their partners with the wooden spoon. The pair with the first empty bowl wins. Since the action is usually fast, furious and messy, a broom should be kept handy.

In *Plymouth Rock* several large pieces of cardboard, cut in rock shapes, are scattered around the floor. If there are ten couples there should be nine rocks. Players take partners and, as in a regular dance, move about the floor. When the music stops, at a signal from the leader, the dancers must quickly step on one of the "rocks." Only one couple is allowed on each rock; the couple that cannot find a rock is eliminated. Before the music begins again, one of the rocks is removed. The elimination process continues until only one rock—and one couple—remains.

Christmas

● *December 25th*

THEME: Good fellowship and gift-giving are the order of the day. The former is symbolized by Santa Claus, the latter by the Christmas tree. *Christmas* is a favorite holiday for adult parties, including company, club and family affairs.

The spirit of Christmas *may be expressed with party invitations and decorations cut in the shape of bells, stars, wreaths, stockings, Santas and gaily wrapped presents.*

Needless to say, *Christmas* is the perfect time for a children's party.

INVITATIONS: Obvious shapes for invitations are Christmas trees, Santa Clauses, candles, stars, wreaths and bells. For more formal *Christmas* parties, white note paper invitations, decorated with these themes or with an attractive winter scene, may be used. At many *Christmas* parties, it is customary for the guests to bring inexpensive gifts for a "grab bag" from which each guest draws a gift. If a grab bag is planned, it should be stated in the invitation.

REFRESHMENTS: The traditional *Christmas* meal is baked ham, garnished with pineapple and cherries. A spiced fruitcake is in keeping with the holiday and goes very well with a couple of traditional drinks—mulled wine and hot apple cider.

DECORATIONS: Sprigs of holly, mistletoe and pine boughs should be plentifully displayed around the room. The best decoration of all is a prominent Christmas tree; it can be decorated in advance, or left bare for the guests to decorate as part of the party fun. If there is enough greenery about, little more is needed for house decoration. For children's parties, a cutout or two of Santa Claus and his reindeer may be used to cover any bare walls, and some bells and stars may be suspended from the ceiling for a festive holiday touch.

GAMES: In *Ring the Bell* a holly wreath is hung from a ceiling or doorway, and a small bell is suspended in the center of the wreath. The players—usually small children—line up six to eight feet away and try to hit the bell with cranberries or small cotton balls. Each player gets three turns, and the one with the most hits wins.

A variation is *Sock Target,* in which a large Christmas stocking is the target. The top of the stocking is held open with a wire hanger, and, in turn, the players try to toss pennies into it.

In *Santa's Helpers* two large, identical outlines of Santa Claus are cut from pieces of cardboard. One of the outlines is taped to a wall, while the other is cut up so that each player gets a piece of it—a nose, a beard, a belt buckle and so on. Each player, in turn, is blindfolded, and spun around several times. He then tries to pin his piece of Santa to the appropriate part of the Santa cutout on the wall. The player who comes closest wins a prize.

In *Snowball Relay* the players divide into two teams and line up behind a starting line at one end of the room. Each team is given a simulated snowball—either of cotton or Styrofoam—and a piece of cardboard. On signal, the first player on each team tries to move the ball across the floor and back by fanning it with cardboard. (A player may not touch the snowball with the cardboard or with his hands.) He then gives the cardboard to the next team member, who repeats the action. The game continues until all team members have completed the race. The first team to finish wins.

In *Threading Popcorn* a large supply of popcorn, purchased beforehand or popped during the party, is placed in a bowl and then put in the center of a large table. The players are grouped around the table, each with needle and thread. On signal, each player tries to thread as many pieces of popcorn as he can. After three or four minutes, the player with the longest string of popcorn wins. When the game is over, all of the popcorn strings are tied together, and this long string is then used to help decorate the Christmas tree.

In *Tangerine Bowling* each boy at the party is given an unbreakable Christmas-tree ornament and a piece of paper with a number on it. After taping their number to the ornament, the boys place the ornaments in a row on the floor. The girls then line up ten or twelve feet away and take turns bowling tangerines at the ornaments. When a girl hits an ornament, the boy whose number is on it becomes her partner for refreshments later on in the party.

In *The Night Before Christmas* the famous poem of the same name is used. Two or three of the best-known verses of the poem are duplicated, but many of the key words are left out. For example:

The _____ were nestled all snug in
  their _____,
While visions of _____ danced
  in their _____.
And Mama in her _____ and I in my
  _____,
Had just settled _____ for a long
  winter's _____.

Everyone is given a pencil and a copy of the verses with the blank spaces. On signal each person tries to fill in all the missing words. After five or ten minutes, the player or team with the most correct words wins.

Parties with Special Themes

It's not necessary to wait for holidays in order to have a party built around a particular theme. A *Rodeo* or *Gay Nineties Party,* for instance, can be planned for any time of the year to celebrate a birthday or anniversary, to raise money for charity or simply for any get-togethers of family or friends. While many of the parties suggested in this chapter can be enjoyed by children as well as by teen-agers and adults, the following section contains a group of nine parties with themes especially suitable for adults.

Rodeo Party

THEME: The party should have a Western flavor. If the weather permits, the party should be held outdoors—with a large Western-style barbecue and Western music.

Western themes are expressed in paper cutouts that can serve as wall and table decorations at a Rodeo Party.

INVITATIONS: Folded white construction paper decorated with ten-gallon hats, cowboy boots, horses, saddles or lariats make appropriate invitations for a *Rodeo Party.* Invitations should make clear that guests are to wear western-style clothing—levis, cowboy shirts, boots and hats. All aspects of the party should be as casual as the clothing.

REFRESHMENTS: Hearty Western style refreshments such as barbecued beef—if possible cooked outdoors over charcoal—chili relishes, sourdough bread or cornbread and cherry pie will be welcomed by all. The refreshments can be placed on a "chuckwagon"—a serving table with cardboard cutouts of spoked wheels taped to its legs.

DECORATIONS: Western decorations—lariats, saddles, and Indian blankets—can be informally arranged in the room or patio where the party is held. If authentic Western objects are not available, lariats fashioned from clothesline, toy six-shooters, cardboard cutouts of cowboys and pictures of Western scenes can be used.

GAMES: Active games and stunts in keeping with the Rodeo theme may be played. Teen-agers enjoy square dancing—a fitting *Rodeo Party* activity. Phonograph records should be available with both square dance music and calls. A pleasant pastime for any age is the singing of Western songs, especially if the host has taken the trouble to prepare songsheets for the guests. Singing is even more fun if someone at the party accompanies the group with a guitar.

Gay Nineties Party

THEME: The Gay Nineties is a period of history that provides a colorful theme for a party. Finding a proper costume is a game in itself. The women hunt in thrift shops, make or improvise the ankle-length dresses with their narrow waists and billowing leg-of-mutton sleeves, as well as the wide-brimmed plumed hats and feather boas that typify the period. Men may find it a bit more difficult to locate authentic clothing of the Nineties, but they can get by with padded suit shoulders, checked vests and bow ties. For a finishing touch, the men may part their hair in the middle and paste on artificial handlebar moustaches.

Skill with needle and thread can turn thrift-shop wear into Gay Nineties *costumes. Men can wear checked vests.*

INVITATIONS: Ideally, the message should be written in old-fashioned, fancy script letters and should specify that guests come in *Gay Nineties* dress.

REFRESHMENTS: Food may be set up on a simulated "free lunch" counter, with ingredients for sandwiches set out on plates so that guests can make their own.

DECORATIONS: An old-fashioned photographic session is a popular pastime at a *Gay Nineties Party.* One corner of the room is set up for the taking of simulated tintype photographs. (A Polaroid camera may be used.) Pictures are taken of the ladies seated and the men standing in exaggerated poses. All of the guests will get a good laugh at the display of photos.

GAMES: Old songs, like "East Side, West Side" and "After the Ball is Over" are just the thing for a *Gay Nineties Party.* Dancing to waltz and polka music also adds to the fun.

Hawaiian Luau

THEME: In Hawaii, the *Luau* is a dinner cooked and served on the beach. In the continental United States, this traditional Hawaiian feast makes a fine theme for a summer party on any beach, and it also works well as a lawn party.

INVITATIONS: Guests should be instructed to wear casual, colorful beach clothes and be told to be prepared to sit on the ground.

REFRESHMENTS: The authentic *Hawaiian Luau* features a young pig barbecued on a spit, but the continental version can include anything customarily grilled outdoors—steaks, hamburgers or pork chops. Any grilled dish can be given an Hawaiian flavor by adding sliced pineapple, baked bananas, chutney or chopped peanuts; food should be served with fruit punch.

DECORATIONS: To create a festive Hawaiian atmosphere, the host may wish to provide inexpensive paper leis for all the guests and flowers for the women to pin in their hair and the men to put in button holes.

GAMES: Any games suitable for a beach or lawn play are appropriate, especially various types of outdoor bowling—a popular game in Hawaii. In addition, a record player can provide Hawaiian music as the accompaniment for any girl or woman who might want to dance a Hawaiian hula.

Snow Party

THEME: Whenever there is snow on the ground, it's a good occasion for an active party held both outdoors and in. A nearby hill can be used for skiing, sledding and tobogganing; a pond or backyard swimming pool, for ice skating if the thermometer reads well below freezing.

INVITATIONS: Guests should be informed in the invitation what the outdoor activities will be, so that they can dress warmly and bring whatever equipment—skis, skates or sleds—is required for the party.

REFRESHMENTS: Lots of steaming hot food is the order of the day. Cocoa is an ideal beverage for children or teen-agers, while many adults enjoy hot, buttered rum.

GAMES: When guests come in for warmth and refreshments, they'll probably want to sit and relax; however, some indoor games may be necessary, especially for young children. Children may enjoy indoor "snowball" throwing contests in which white balloons or Styrofoam balls are substituted for the real thing.

Carnival Party

THEME: A *Carnival Party* is useful for fund-raising affairs. This type of party requires a spacious playroom, basement or patio.

INVITATIONS: Any type of invitation may be sent. However, if money is to be used, the message should state this clearly. Either a small fee (a penny, nickel or dime) may be charged for playing any game, or guests may be asked to purchase rolls of tickets to use in payment for playing games and buying refreshments.

REFRESHMENTS: One or two booths can be set aside for refreshments, such as frankfurters, hamburgers and soft drinks.

DECORATIONS: To create a carnival atmosphere, a variety of game and contest booths are set up around the walls. Their construction can be as simple or as elaborate as the host desires.

GAMES: Some ideas for games are *Beanbag Toss, Dart Shooting, Ring Toss* and *Penny Pitching.* Guests can play the games at random, or a competition can be set up between individuals or teams. In the latter case, the players should keep track of their scores on paper so that they can be checked later to determine a winner.

Father-and-Son Party

THEME: This type of party—a special day for father and son—is popular with youth groups, sports clubs and civic organizations.

INVITATIONS: An invitation can be sent to either the father or the son, but it should make clear that both are expected to attend together.

REFRESHMENTS: Any type of food—in quantities that will satisfy the hearty male appetite—is appreciated.

DECORATIONS: Decorations need not be elaborate but should be appropriately masculine—sports equipment or trophies, for instance.

GAMES: Games in which father and son perform as a team are popular—and avoid any embarrassment that might result if father and son compete against one another. Guest speakers, entertainers and movies also are popular entertainment at the *Father-and-Son Party.*

VARIATION: A similar kind of party can be held for *Mother-and-Daughter.* Decorations, games and entertainment are planned from a feminine point of view.

Cooperative Dinner Party

THEME: A *Cooperative Dinner Party* is usually planned by a close-knit group of friends, such as a small club, neighbors or members of a family. When the same group of people holds more than one *Cooperative Dinner Party,* it is customary to change the site from one home to another with each occasion.

INVITATIONS: The person at whose house the party is to be held asks each guest to furnish part of the meal. The invitation must state what each guest is to bring so that the various courses are not duplicated and will go well together.

REFRESHMENTS: One person or couple brings appetizers, another the salad and another the dessert; the hosts prepare the main course.

GAMES: Some party games and dancing may add to the enjoyment of the party.

VARIATIONS: The *Potluck Party* is more informal than the *Cooperative Dinner Party.* All guests are asked to bring any food of their choice to a large buffet—salad, dessert, meat or vegetable dish, casserole, bread, punch and the like. *Potluck Parties* are great fun, because any number of people can attend and the menu possibilities are unlimited! For the *International Party* guests are asked to bring their favorite foreign dishes, such as *paella, chop suey, shish kebab,* etc.

Hillbilly Shindig

THEME: Everything should reflect an authentic country atmosphere. Country music played on a phonograph enhances the *Hillbilly Shindig*.

INVITATIONS: Guests are invited to come in old, but colorful, clothes.

REFRESHMENTS: A menu of fried chicken, buttered ears of corn, cider and corn bread is perfect.

DECORATIONS: Decorations are carefully contrived to create a dilapidated effect. Tattered burlap curtains can be hung, for example, and old earthenware jugs scattered about.

GAMES: Relay Races between teams named the Hatfields and McCoys will add the flavor of a playful mountaineer feud to the party.

VARIATION: At the *Lil Abner Party,* the guests dress as their favorite characters in the popular comic strip. Prizes can be given for the most elaborate and/or most original costumes.

Mexican Fiesta

THEME: Everything is Mexican. Many of the guests, as well as the hosts, may wish to wear Mexican sombreros (hats) or serapes (shawls).

INVITATIONS: Construction paper cut into the shapes of sombreros, donkeys or maps of Mexico make interesting invitations.

REFRESHMENTS: Such Mexican refreshments as tacos, tortillas, enchiladas and chili are delicious and easy to prepare.

DECORATIONS: Real Mexican souvenirs or cardboard cut-outs of sombreros, cacti and burros can be displayed around the room. Colorful travel posters of Mexico may be taped to the walls. Mexican background music, played on a phonograph, adds to the atmosphere.

Serapes and sombreros as well as paper cutouts of cacti and burros help make a Mexican Fiesta *truly festive.*

GAMES: The traditional *Mexican Piñata Game* is great fun—especially if there are young children at the *Fiesta*. A piñata is hung from the ceiling. (A piñata is a paper and tinsel hollow animal figure, filled with candy, nuts and noisemakers.)

Candy and other inexpensive items—whistles, balloons and noisemakers—are appropriate stuffings for a piñata.

In turn, each child (or teen-ager or adult) is blindfolded, given a stick and told to try to break the piñata. Eventually, someone succeeds and showers the piñata's contents on the floor. Once the piñata is broken, all the children grab for loot—amidst excited squeals and giggles.

Children's Parties

Many kinds of parties are suitable for young children. Listed here are those that have long been popular with children between the ages of four and twelve. If a party for children between the ages of four and seven is planned, the host should keep in mind that youngsters of this age tend to get boisterous and bored with equal speed. The guest list should be kept small, the duration of the party short (two hours or less) and the activities simple. No more than two or three easy-to-play games are necessary. Most of the parties mentioned here are suitable for mixed groups but some (for instance, the *Pirate Party* and *Doll Party*) may be enjoyed more by one sex than the other.

Doll Party

- *Girls* • *4 to 8*

Invitations can be in the shape of a doll, and the message should ask that girl-guests come with their favorite doll. At the party, prizes are awarded for the prettiest doll, the best-dressed doll, the most unusual doll and enough other categories so that every doll wins at least one prize.

Games for both the girls and their dolls should be included—for example, *Doll Hide and Seek* in which girls try to find their hidden dolls. Another interesting activity for this type of party is for the guests to make yarn dolls out of pipe cleaners, bits of colored cotton and wool yarn. The materials should be laid out on a large work table, and an adult should be present to demonstrate how the dolls are made and to supervise the operation.

Pirate Party

- *Boys* • *4 to 12*

The invitations and decorations should include such pirate symbols as the Jolly Roger flat (a white skull and two crossed white bones on a black background), curved cutlasses, flintlock pistols, old-fashioned treasure chests and maps showing the location of buried treasure. Guests can be asked to wear pirate costumes, readily assembled from bits of old clothing and colorful scarves or rags.

"Pirate" games such as *Dueling with Cutlasses* (of cardboard) may be played, and no *Pirate Party* would be complete without a *Treasure Hunt*. Each child is given a map (or a portion of a map), on which clues have been written to guide them to particular places—a hollow tree, an odd-shaped rock or a fencepost—where other clues are waiting. The hunt is more exciting when the final clue leads to a spot where they must dig down a few inches to uncover the treasure chest. The chest may be a painted cigar box filled with such things as "junk" jewelry, play money, toys and candy bars. The lucky pirate, or band of pirates, who finds the treasure gets to keep it, of course.

Circus Party

- *Boys and Girls* • *4 to 12*

The ideal decorations for this kind of party are colorful circus posters. The best way to obtain them is to have children make them when they arrive at the party. Each child should be given some crayons and asked to make his own poster on one of the large blank sheets of sturdy paper hanging on the wall.

The adult who acts as the game leader should be dressed as a ringmaster in boots, pants, fancy jacket, top hat and whistle. Games and stunts should all be based on circus themes, such as tight-rope walking, animal training and acrobatic feats. Circus-music records and circus refreshments—frankfurters, ice cream, popcorn and soda—add to the atmosphere.

Deck-the-Tree Party

● *Boys and Girls*   ● *4 to 12*

A Christmas party that gives children an opportunity to do one of the things they love best—decorate the Christmas tree—is invariably a success. If the children are old enough, they can make their own decorations from a supply of colored paper, aluminum foil, pipe cleaners, transparent tape and small Styrofoam balls. For smaller children, a supply of inexpensive ornaments, tinsel and artificial snow should be available. Sturdy chairs are placed around the tree so that the children can reach the upper branches.

Once the decorating is finished, games with Christmas themes and carol singing make the party go quickly. The end of the party is a good time to give each child a small, gaily wrapped Christmas present to take home and place under his own tree.

Space Party

● *Boys and Girls*   ● *4 to 12*

Since space and space travel are fascinating subjects to children, a space party is sure to be enjoyed by all. Invitations in the shape of rockets may be sent. Guests are invited to dress as astronauts or as outerspace creatures from other planets. Decorations may include rocketships made of paper and cardboard tissue rolls. The games may be improvised to fit such themes as space exploration, Martians or moon-walking.

Indian Powwow Party

● *Boys*   ● *4 to 8*

Guests are invited to wear Indian costumes. Indoors, special wall decorations—cutouts of tepees, war bonnets, peace pipes, bows and arrows—help establish the Indian theme. An enjoyable indoor activity is to have the children sit in a semicircle on the floor in front of an adult, or older child, who reads them Indian stories and legends.

If the party is outdoors, a tepee may be made by draping a canvas tarpaulin or a large sheet of opaque plastic over a framework of long poles. Races and other active games with Indian themes—hunting, stalking and archery—are exciting activities for such a party.

Easter Egg Hunt Party

● *Boys and Girls*   ● *4 to 8*

Easter is a fine time for an indoor or outdoor party. Decorations might include colorful balloons, and cutouts of Easter bunnies, gaily decorated Easter eggs and flowers. The children may be asked to bring along painted Easter eggs, and more eggs can be decorated during the party. The host should supply a table with a bowl of hard-boiled eggs, dye and crayons.

The highlight of the party is the *Easter Egg Hunt* itself. If eggs have not been hidden around the room or in the yard before the party, the children can participate in egg-rolling contests and relays while this is being done.

Olympic Party

● *Boys and Girls*   ● *4 to 12*

Since the emphasis is on physical competition, an *Olympic Party* should be held outdoors, if at all possible. However, in case of bad weather, the host should have in mind some games that can be played indoors.

The differing capacities of boys and girls should be taken into account when planning the events. If there are running events, for example, the boys should either run separately over longer distances than the girls, or, if they run together, the girls should be given a head start. If there are big differences in the ages of guests, the younger children should not be expected to compete in the same events as older children. Scores may be kept on the basis of three points for finishing first in an event, two points for second and one point for third. At the end of the *Olympics,* the players with the three highest point-totals may receive simulated medals.

CHAPTER 11

Party Games for Teens and Adults

There are many games that are suitable for house parties and informal get-togethers of either teen-agers or adults. Most of them require little or no special equipment. Some, like the icebreakers and games for mixing, are most useful to introduce people at large parties and help them mingle freely and informally. Others, like the mental games, practical jokes and stunts, are better suited for small gatherings of friends. Most of these games can be played indoors in a large room, especially a living room or recreation room. Some, however, require an even larger area, such as a social hall or gymnasium. Still others can be played outdoors at a lawn party. As these games are appropriate for both sexes, there is little emphasis on physical skills or exercise. In fact, many of the games can be played while sitting.

The first group of games is classified as "icebreakers." The purpose of icebreakers is to encourage people in large groups to meet, mingle, chat and learn about one another. They are particularly useful at the beginning of a party or dance, when people first enter the room or the hall. They help overcome the tendency of guests to remain together in clusters with a small group of friends and acquaintances, never getting to know any "new" people.

Numerals indicate the number of players.

What's My Name?

● *20 to 50* ● *Slips of paper; pencil; pins*

PREPARATION: The names of famous men and women are printed on small slips of paper, and one of these slips is pinned to the back of each person entering the room. The players are not told the names.

ACTION: To determine his famous identity, each player circulates around the room, letting other players read the name on his back. He may then ask questions that will be answered only by a "yes" or "no." By asking general questions—"Am

I alive?" "Am I a man?" and the like—the player tries to gather enough information to take a guess at the name. When he guesses correctly, he may continue to play by answering the questions of other players until all of the guests guess their identities.

VARIATIONS: In *Guess Who?* the players are handed the slips of paper so that each one knows his identity immediately. The object of the game is then to go around the room and try to guess the identities of other players by the same sort of "yes" or "no" questions. In *Name Stealers,* the names are pinned to the players' backs. Each player tries to observe and write down as many names as he can in ten minutes while trying to conceal his own name. Backing up against walls or furniture is not allowed.

The Name Game

● *20 to 50*   ● *Writing paper; pencils*

PREPARATION: Each player is given a sheet of paper and a pencil. He then prints his full name down the center of the sheet from top to bottom. Nicknames are permitted.

ACTION: The player goes around the room, asking the names of the other players. Each time he hears a name that includes one of the letters from his own name, he prints that name (it can be either the first or last name) across his sheet in such a way that his name and the other name are joined by the common letter. The winner is the first player to match every letter in his name with the name of another player. Each name may be used only once.

Name Bingo

● *15 to 50*   ● *Writing paper; pencils*

PREPARATION: Each player is handed a sheet of paper that is marked off in five rows of five squares each, for a total of 25 squares. If there are fewer than 25 players, the sheet may be

Sally	John		Tom	Adam
	Anne	Sue		Joe
Kim		Joan		Dale
Helen	Dan		Peter	
Laura		Sam		Amy

marked with either four rows of four squares each, or three rows of three squares each.

ACTION: The game is played like *Bingo,* except that names are used instead of numbers. As the player moves around the room, he asks other players their names, writing each one in a square until all the squares are filled. When all the players have filled their sheets with names, the game leader or host calls out the names of players from a prepared list. As each name is called, the player looks at his sheet to see if he has written the name in one of the boxes. If he has, he draws an X through that box. The first player to fill an entire line of squares with X's, vertically, horizontally or diagonally, wins.

Rhyming Names

● *12 to 20*

PREPARATION: The leader asks each player to rise in turn and introduce himself with a rhyme that includes his or her first name.

ACTION: A heavy man named Jim might say: "I am Jim/They call me Slim." A bruiser named Pete could rhyme: "My name is Pete/I've got dainty feet." If a name is hard to rhyme, a couplet may be composed in which the name is used, but not rhymed, such as: "Samantha's my name/Teaching's my game."

Handshake Treasure

● *20 to 50*   ● *A quarter*

PREPARATION: The host announces that one of the players has a secret treasure—a quarter—which he will give to the fifteenth person who shakes hands with him.

ACTION: As nobody knows who has the treasure, the players circulate about and begin shaking hands with one another until the treasure-holder announces the winner.

VARIATION: In *Ten for Ten,* each player receives a dime and is instructed to give it to the tenth person who shakes hands with him.

Scattered Proverbs

● *12 to 20*   ● *Slips of paper; pencil*

PREPARATION: A number of familiar proverbs are printed on slips of paper, which are then cut into three parts. Some examples are: "A stitch/in time/saves nine" and "A rolling/stone gathers/no moss." Before the guests arrive, the cut-up slips are jumbled together and scattered around the room. They may be placed on shelves, beneath ashtrays, pinned to cushions or taped on walls.

ACTION: At a signal, each player gathers up all the slips he can find and tries to piece them together. Swapping is permitted. The winner is the one who finds the most in ten minutes.

Games for Mixing

A popular group of party games is the mixers, designed to pair off partners for dances and games. These are especially useful at informal teen-age affairs, where girls and boys often attend unescorted, and are also appropriate for adult parties attended by couples as well as single people. By making the changing of partners into a game or a series of games, the players are assured of meeting a number of new people.

Numerals indicate the number of players.

Multiplication Dance

● *20 to 50*

PREPARATION: The dance floor is cleared and one couple is designated to begin dancing when the music starts.

ACTION: The music is stopped at intervals of a minute or two. At the first interval, the original couple separates, with the male and female selecting new partners from those lining the dance floor. At the next interval, the two couples invite four new people to dance. This process is repeated at each interval until everyone in the room is dancing.

Balloon Grab

● *12 to 20*   ● *Small balloons for each girl*

PREPARATION: The balloons are inflated and tied with a piece of string, to which is attached a small slip of paper. Each female is given a balloon and is directed to write her name on the attached paper.

ACTION: The females form a circle and walk in a clockwise direction. The males form a larger circle outside and walk in a counter-clockwise direction. On signal, the females toss their balloons into the center. The males then rush in, and each grabs one of the balloons. The female whose name is written on the piece of paper attached to the balloon becomes his partner for the next dance.

Partner on a String

● *12 to 50*   ● *Ball of string*

PREPARATION: The group is divided, and all the females line up in a row. The game leader or host ties one end of a long string around each of their wrists. Then he deliberately goes about tangling the strings, handing an end to each of the males, who are lined up on the other side of the room.

ACTION: The males must locate their partners by untangling the jumbled strings—without letting go of their own strings. If *Partner on a String* is used more than once during the party, it's fun to reverse the procedure and have the females try to untangle the strings and find their way to the males.

Matching Numbers

- *20 to 50*   - *Slips of paper; pencil*

PREPARATION: Two sets of matching numbers are printed on separate slips of paper: two 1's, two 2's, two 3's, and so on. Females are given numbers from one set, and males are given numbers from the other.

ACTION: On signal, each male begins looking for the female whose number matches his. She then becomes his partner for the next game or for the dance.

VARIATIONS: There are a number of similar matching games that serve the same purpose. In *Famous Couples,* each female has a slip of paper on which is written the name of a famous woman; each male has a slip with the name of a famous man. The males move about the room trying to locate the female whose identity in history or literature is associated with his. For example: Anthony would look for Cleopatra; Rochester would seek out Jane Eyre; Romeo would search for Juliet.

Playing Card Match uses two decks of playing cards, one set distributed to the females and the other to the males. *Matching Pictures* uses pictures cut out of magazines and sliced in two. In *State Capitals,* the males receive slips with the names of states and the females are given the names of their capitals. *Matching Words* requires the players to match words that are usually paired together, like "bread" and "butter." *Split Proverbs* substitutes halves of well-known proverbs. For example, the male who receives the slip of paper with the words "out of sight" looks for a female who has the words "out of mind." In *Hum a Tune,* the players receive matching sets of slips with the names of popular tunes. The females hum their tunes, while each male tries to pick out the one written on his slip of paper. *Pantomime Partners* uses the names of occupations, such as golfer, painter or carpenter. All players move about doing a pantomime of their assigned occupations until the two with the same occupations recognize the pantomimes—and their partners.

In *Cinderella,* each female is required to remove one shoe. All the shoes are placed in a large box and are mixed up. Each male is then given a shoe and must find the female with the matching shoe.

Backward Choice

- *12 to 20*

PREPARATION: Males and females form two lines at opposite sides of the room or dance floor, facing away from each other. All obstacles between the two lines are cleared away.

ACTION: On signal, the two lines begin walking slowly backward toward each other. When they make contact, the male and female who bump into each other become partners.

Matching Mates

- *50 to 100*

PREPARATION: This simple matching game is effective with large groups of dancers and requires only an observant leader with either a loud voice or an amplification system.

ACTION: The leader notes what the dancers are wearing and tries to find something that many share in common. He will then call out something like, "All males with brown slacks, please invite a new partner to dance." A few moments later he might make a similar request of the females wearing pink dresses. Or he might single out those wearing wristwatches, eyeglasses or anything red. The idea is to make sure that everyone is included eventually.

Change Partners

- *20 to 50*

PREPARATION: A particular dance record is chosen, which may be played several times throughout the evening.

ACTION: The music is stopped five or six times, and each time the leader calls out, "Everyone change partners!" The dancers then separate, ask new partners to dance and resume dancing when the music begins again.

Broom Mixer

- *12 to 20*   - *Straw broom*

PREPARATION: As the dance begins, all the males—but one—have partners. The one without a partner dances alone with a broom held upright in his hands.

ACTION: The male with the broom dances around for a minute or two, then suddenly lowers the broom, props his foot against the sweeping end and lets the handle snap against the floor. The sound is the signal to stop the music and for all the dancers to change partners. The broom dancer, who knows when the music will stop, quickly finds himself a partner. When everyone else is paired off again, another male is left without a partner. He picks up the broom and the game begins again. It continues in this manner until at least four or five males have danced around the room with the broom.

Lemon Dance

- *12 to 20*   - *Several real or artificial lemons*

PREPARATION: As the couples begin dancing around the floor, lemons are given to the unattached males.

ACTION: The lemon-holders must go out on the dance floor and each cut in on one of the couples by handing the lemon to the male partner. The new lemon-holders must then cut in on other couples. This procedure continues until the music ends. Of course, the object is not to be one of the final lemon-holders.

VARIATION: In *Broom Cut-In,* the unattached males receive brooms instead of lemons. Each must dance with his broom until he cuts in on a couple. The male who is cut in on gets the broom and repeats the action.

Side by Side

- *12 to 20*

PREPARATION: One male is designated to dance alone, while the others choose partners.

ACTION: The leader stops the music at intervals and calls out, "Side by side!" The couples separate and pick new partners, with whom they

LONE DANCER

stand side by side until the music begins again. The male who has been dancing alone finds a partner if he can. When the music begins again, either he or another male will be without a partner and must dance alone until the music stops and the couples change partners.

VARIATION: In *Blind Choice,* the unattached male stands blindfolded in the center of the dance floor while the couples dance around him in a circle. At any moment the blindfolded male may raise an arm, point in any direction and call, "I claim you!" If he should point to a passing couple, the female of that twosome becomes the lone male's partner. They join the dancers while her ex-partner goes to the center, is blindfolded and repeats the pointing procedure. The trick for the dancers is to keep from being claimed.

Elimination Dances

The purpose of most dancing games is to get more people dancing. The most notable exceptions are the elimination dances, enjoyable novelties in which the objective is to reduce the number of dancers to one couple. The eliminations are actually informal contests, not based on dancing skill, in which the players compete for small, token prizes. Some of the eliminations require the players to perform some physical activity, while others are based strictly on chance, giving everyone an equal opportunity to win. These dances are enjoyed by adults as much as by teen-agers.

Numerals indicate the number of players.

Orange Dance

- *12 to 20* - *Oranges*

PREPARATION: Each of the couples is given an orange.

ACTION: The couples dance with an orange pressed between their foreheads and may not touch it with their hands. A couple is eliminated and must leave the floor if their orange drops. To add zest to the game, slow music is played at first; then faster music; finally, after about half of the couples are eliminated, a bumpy Latin rhythm is played. The last couple who continues to dance with an orange still in place wins the game.

Broom Dance

- *12 to 20* - *Straw broom*

PREPARATION: As the couples begin dancing, one of them is handed a broom.

ACTION: The couple dancing with the broom must try to give it to another couple as quickly as possible. The second couple must accept it and try to pass it on to another couple. The music is stopped abruptly from time to time by the host, and the couple then holding the broom is eliminated. The broom then goes to another couple and the dance begins again. As couples are eliminated, both the music and the action grow livelier; the last eliminations are usually quite hectic.

VARIATION: In *Pass the Hat,* the dance begins with a funny hat being placed on the head of one of the males. He must then get rid of the hat by placing it on another male's head. When the music stops, the hat-wearer and his partner are eliminated. The hat is then placed on the head of another male as the music resumes and the game proceeds, passing the hat as before. *Pass the Hat* can also be played with the hat being passed to either a male or female or, if there is a large group of dancers, with several hats being passed simultaneously.

Lucky Number Dance

- *20 to 50* - *Slips of paper; a glass jar*

PREPARATION: Each couple is given a slip of paper with a number written on it. Slips with matching sets of numbers are then placed in a container.

ACTION: Every minute or two, the leader stops the music, draws two or three numbers from the container and calls them out. The couples holding those numbers are eliminated. When there are only a few couples left, the leader calls out one number at a time to build up suspense. The last couple to remain on the floor is declared the winner.

VARIATION: *Lucky Card Dance* is played the same way, except that two decks of playing cards are used. The dancers receive cards from one deck, while the leader calls out the eliminations from the other deck.

Balloon Buster

- *12 to 20*   - *Balloons for each couple*

PREPARATION: The balloons are inflated. One is tied to the ankle of each male so that the balloon trails behind him by about a foot.

ACTION: As the couples dance, they try to maneuver close enough to other couples so that they can stamp on their balloons and burst them. At the same time, they try to dance out of the way of couples heading for their balloon. The couples may not separate or stop dancing. The last couple with an unburst balloon wins.

Heads or Tails

- *50 to 100*   - *Coin*

PREPARATION: A real or imaginary line is drawn down the center of the dance floor.

ACTION: The couples dance until the music is stopped, and then remain in place. The host asks a couple to call "heads or tails." Then he flips a coin and calls out the result. If the couple has guessed correctly, the couples on their half of the floor resume dancing and the couples on the other side are eliminated. If the couple guessed incorrectly, their half of the floor is eliminated, and the other side continues to dance. A few minutes later, the process is repeated with another couple being asked to guess on a toss of the coin. When there are only a few couples left, the leader may divide them evenly, each group on its own side of the floor. By repeating this action, a point is reached when two couples are left, dividing the floor, for the last coin toss.

Siege

- *20 to 50*

PREPARATION: Couples move about the floor as in an ordinary dance.

ACTION: The couples dance normally until the host stops the music and calls out a number

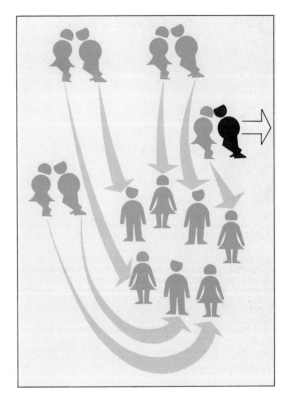

from 3 to 8. The prescribed number of dancers must then join hands, quickly forming a series of circles around the dance floor. Those who cannot join a circle are eliminated. The survivors take new partners and continue the dance until the leader stops the music and calls another number. The action is repeated several times until only one couple—the winner—is included in the final circle.

Stoop

- *10 to 50*

PREPARATION: Players divide into couples. Males and females form concentric circles—the females on the inside, the males on the outside. Males and females face each other.

ACTION: As the music plays, the females walk in a clockwise direction; the males, in a counter-clockwise direction. When the music suddenly stops, all rush to find their partners.

Then the couples join hands and stoop. The last couple to complete the action is eliminated. Then the circles are re-formed and the action is repeated. The contest continues until only the winning couple remains.

Statues

● *20 to 50*

PREPARATION: Couples move about the floor as in an ordinary dance.

ACTION: When the host stops the music and calls out "Freeze!," everyone must stop immedi- ately and stay motionless. They remain that way for about 15 seconds, and anyone detected moving during that period is eliminated along with his or her partner. Then the music is played again, a bit faster than before, and the process is repeated until only one couple remains.

VARIATION: In *Crazy Statues,* the couples freeze in the most absurd position they can think of when the leader calls out "Freeze!" They can lie down, squat, pose on one leg, drape over one another or choose any silly posture they please. The leader, or a committee of designated judges, goes around the floor and awards a prize to the couple with the most unusual pose.

Mental and Drama Games

One of the most enjoyable pastimes at small parties, where there are no more than 25 guests, is the mental game. It requires almost no physical activity, and usually can be played in a small room. All that is needed for this type of game is alertness, observation and a good memory. A good vocabulary may also be an advantage.

Numerals indicate the number of players.

Teakettle

● *5 to 20*

PREPARATION: One player leaves the room. The others then pick a set of words that sound the same but have different meanings, such as "four," "for," and "fore" or "pain" and "pane."

PLAY: When the absent player returns, the others take turns carrying on a conversation. Each of these players must use one of the pre-arranged sets of words in a sentence, but instead of pronouncing the word he must substitute the word "teakettle." Thus, if the key words are "bear" and "bare," the conversation might run something like this:
The first player says, "I went to the zoo today and saw a teakettle."
The next player replies, "Yes, but he wasn't really teakettle. In fact he was quite hairy."
The conversation continues until the player who was out of the room figures out the words that "teakettle" stands for. When he does, he an- nounces them. If he is correct, the last player to make a statement leaves the room and the game starts again.

Coffeepot

● *8 to 20*

PREPARATION: A player leaves the room while the others pick a secret verb, such as "kiss," "sniff," or "tickle."

PLAY: The player returns and tries to find out what the secret verb is by asking questions that may be answered only by "yes," "no," or "sometimes." In each question, he must substi- tute the word "coffeepot" for the verb. He might ask: "Do you coffeepot indoors?" or "Is it fun to coffeepot?" or "Is coffeepotting strenu- ous?" When he thinks he has a clue, he may take a guess at the verb. If he is correct, the last person to answer a question leaves the room while the others think of a new verb. If he is incorrect, the game continues until he takes two more guesses. If the third guess is incorrect, he is told the word and may select the next player to leave the room.

Botticelli

- *6 to 12*   - *A dictionary or encyclopedia—for settling disputes*

PREPARATION: Players scatter around the room in more or less of a circle formation. One player is the answer man—the others are questioners. The answer man picks a famous person—living or dead—and reveals his last initial. Questioning then begins, starting with the player on the answer man's left and moving clockwise around the room.

PLAY: The object, of course, is to guess the identity of the mystery person by asking questions of the answer man. Each player has one or two questions per turn, depending upon the answers he elicits. The first question refers directly to a figure whom the questioner has in mind; the second question, which must be answered "yes," or "no," provides a clue to the mystery person's identity. For example, if the mystery person is Bismarck, the first questioner, knowing only the initial B, might well ask: "Is he a famous German composer of the early nineteenth century."
The answer man must be able to provide the name of someone who fits the description in the question. He might answer: "No, it is not Beethoven."
If the answer man cannot supply a *proper answer,* the questioner identifies the person he had in mind and gets another turn. This time he can ask a question that supplies a clue, such as: "Is this person dead?"
The answer man replies, "Yes."
Now it is the turn of the second questioner, who has two clues: the mystery man's last name starts with B, and he is dead. His question might be: "Was he a nineteenth century English philosopher?"
The answer man must supply a name that suits the question, such as Jeremy Bentham. If he cannot, the questioner can ask a clue question, such as: "Was this person in the arts?"

If the questioners are shrewd enough, they will eventually narrow down the possible choices until someone guesses the right person. The player who makes the correct guess becomes the answer man for the next round. If no one guesses within a 15-minute time limit, the answer man tells the answer and picks a new mystery person, revealing only his last initial.

Chain Word

- *6 to 12*   - *Beanbag (or small pillow)*

PREPARATION: The players sit in a circle, and the player designated to start the game is given the beanbag.

PLAY: The first player says a word, such as "house," and tosses the beanbag to a player on the other side of the circle. This player must immediately say a word commonly used with that word, for example "detective." He then tosses the beanbag to another player, who must quickly say a word that goes with "detective." The word-calling and beanbag-tossing continue until a player cannot come up with a word. That player is then eliminated and the other players continue the game until one player is left.

VARIATION: In *Chain Rhyme,* the first player makes up a phrase, and the player to whom the beanbag is tossed must immediately reply with a rhyming phrase. Thus, a line like "No world without trees" might be answered by "No stew without peas." The players alternate to provide the first and second lines of the rhyme, and those who miss are eliminated.

Twenty Questions

- *2 to 12*

PREPARATION: One player is designated to begin the game and thinks of a person or an object that is also familiar to the other players.

RULES: Players are permitted to ask up to 20 questions to discover what the first player is thinking. The questions may be answered only with "yes," "no," or "sometimes." The first questions should establish broad categories: "Is this a person?" "Is this person alive?" "Is this person a man?" Gradually, the questions should become more specific to nail the subject down: "Was this man a President of the United States?" "Was he a Republican?" "Was he also a great general?" If the subject is named within the 20-question limit the person who guesses it begins a new game by thinking of another subject.

VARIATION: In *Reverse Twenty Questions,* one player leaves the room while the others agree on a subject. When the player returns, he questions the others, in turn, to guess the subject. If he succeeds within 20 questions, he continues as questioner in the next game. If he fails, he is succeeded by the last person questioned.

Who Could I Be?

● *6 to 12*

PREPARATION: The leader selects the name of a famous person.

ACTION: The game begins with the leader giving some basic fact about the person: "This person was an American male." The first person to volunteer is allowed one guess. If the guess is incorrect, the leader provides a second clue: "He lived during the nineteenth century." Another player is permitted a guess. The game continues, with more revealing clues, until someone guesses the name and begins a new game.

Animal, Vegetable or Mineral

● *2 to 12*

PREPARATION: The player who begins the game thinks of a subject and tells the other players that it is either animal (including humans and animal products, such as fur and eggs), vegetable (including all types of plants and their products, such as cereal and wood), or mineral (including glass, stone and metal).

ACTION: The other players take turns asking questions that can be answered "yes," "no," or "sometimes" until one of them guesses the subject correctly and starts the next game. There is no limit on the number of questions.

VARIATION: In *Reverse Animal, Vegetable or Mineral,* one player leaves the room while the others agree on a subject. The player returns, and the others inform him that the subject is animal, vegetable or mineral. The player then asks questions until he discovers the answer within an allotted ten-minute period. He is replaced by another player whether he succeeds or fails.

The Name Suggests

● *6 to 12*

PREPARATION: One player leaves the room while the others select the name of a famous person, living or dead. The player is then called back into the room.

ACTION: Instead of asking questions, the player calls out the name of a category, like "colors," "weather" or "emotions." In turn, the other players must then provide descriptive words or phrases that apply equally well both to the famous person and to the category named. For example, if Winston Churchill is the subject and trees the category, the answers might include: "sturdy," "short," or "English." The questioner then calls out another category, and gets another set of answers. The game continues until the questioner guesses the identity of the person.

Hidden Proverbs

● *6 to 12*

PREPARATION: One player leaves the room while the others agree on a well-known proverb, like "Too many cooks spoil the broth."

ACTION: The player comes back and begins the game by questioning the other players. He can ask them anything at all, but the others must use a word of the proverb in each of their answers. The first answer must contain the first word, the second answer the second word, and so on. If the questioner fails to piece the proverb together, the process begins all over again until he finally catches on. The player who says the last word then leaves the room, and the game begins again with a new proverb.

Highbrow Proverbs

● *6 to 12* ● *Writing paper; pencils*

PREPARATION: The players are divided into two teams. Each team is given a different list of proverbs, prepared in advance by the leader.

ACTION: Members of each team work together to translate each of the proverbs on its list into the most wordy and complicated language they can think of. This becomes the highbrow proverb that is then read aloud. Members of the other team then try to figure out the original proverb. The following examples show that a good vocabulary is valuable in this game: "A youthful person injured by the application of excessive heat grows timorous of the visible phenomenon of combustion" (originally "A burnt child dreads the fire") or "Extreme rapidity in performance creates inefficiency in utilization" (originally "Haste makes waste"). Each team takes turns reading its highbrow proverbs to the other team, while the leader keeps track of the time needed to unravel the proverbs. When all of the proverbs have been deciphered, the team with the faster total time is the winner.

Secret Questions

● *2* ● *Slips of paper*

PREPARATION: Each player is given a slip of paper on which is written an unusual question—the more unusual the better. Some samples might include: "Do you think Hitler is still alive?" "Have you ever tried ketchup with shish kebab?" or "Where can I buy a good pair of mukluks?"

ACTION: Without telling each other the question they have been given, the players engage each other in conversation. Eventually, each introduces his question as a seemingly normal part of the conversation. After an agreed-upon period of time—about 15 minutes—each player has three guesses at the other player's secret question. The winner is the one who picks out the correct question with the fewest guesses. To camouflage the secret question, players should try to use other unusual questions so as to throw their opponents off the track.

Six Guesses

● *12 to 20* ● *Small blackboard or slate; piece of chalk*

PREPARATION: One player leaves the room while the others select a word that is included in some familiar category, such as automobiles, states, animals or sports.

ACTION: When the player is called back, he is told the category and the number of letters in the selected word. He then takes the chalk and writes on the blackboard a series of numbers equalling the number of letters in the word. For example, if the word has eight letters, he writes the numbers 1, 2, 3, 4, 5, 6, 7, and 8 on the blackboard. The player then names any letter of the alphabet. If this letter appears in the secret word, the other players tell him which number, or numbers, corresponds with the letter's proper place within the word. The player then prints the letter above the number, or numbers. He is allowed to call six different letters, some of which may not appear in the word at all. When he has used up his guesses, he must then try to figure out the word from the letters he has written. If he succeeds, he goes out of the room to begin another game. If he fails, another player takes his place and leaves the room.

Word Lightning

● *6 to 12*

PREPARATION: The players sit in a circle. The game leader or host points to one of them and calls out a letter of the alphabet.

ACTION: The chosen player has exactly one minute to recite all the words he can think of that begin with the letter called. The leader keeps track of the time, while the other players call off the number of words. Proper names are not allowed, and the same word may not be repeated. The leader gives each player a turn; he uses a different letter for each player but avoids such difficult letters as "x" and "z." The player who compiles the longest list of words in the allotted minute wins the game. This game is not as simple as it sounds, because it is often surprisingly difficult to think of familiar words when under pressure.

VARIATION: In *Traveler,* instead of a letter of the alphabet, the leader uses the names of places—cities, states or countries. He may point to a player and say, "I'm traveling to California." The player then has five seconds to name three things beginning with the first letter of the destination, in this case "c." These might be "cabbage," "coat," "candy," "cloud," "cobalt," "cookie," "colt," etc. If he fails to name three within the time period, the player takes the leader's place. He then announces a new destination and, pointing to another player, begins the game again, proceeding as before.

Ghost

● *4 to 8*   ● *Dictionary*

PREPARATION: The players form a circle, and one player, chosen to start the game, calls out a letter of the alphabet.

ACTION: Each player, in turn, adds a letter to the preceding letter in order to form a word. However, he avoids being the one who adds the last letter to a word. So, if the first letter is "b," the second "o" and the third "r," (forming "bor"), the fourth player should not use "e," thus completing the word "bore." Instead, he could call out "i" and force another player to complete the word "boring." Players must have a specific word in mind; the trick is to think of word variations that can be passed on. If a participant believes that the player preceding

him does not have a real word in mind, he may challenge him. The game is then stopped while the leader looks up in a dictionary the word given by the challenged player. If there is no such word, the challenged player is penalized a letter and the game is started again. If the challenged player is upheld, the challenger is penalized and the game continues from that point. The player who completes a word is penalized with the letter "g." If he is penalized five times, he becomes the Ghost and is eliminated from the game—which continues until only one player remains.

Name Six

● *12 to 20*   ● *A small object, such as a ball or beanbag*

PREPARATION: The players stand in a circle facing in and begin passing the object from hand to hand around the circle.

ACTION: The host or game leader, who is not in the circle, calls out a letter of the alphabet. The person holding the object immediately passes the object to the person on his left and must then name six things beginning with that letter before the object can be passed completely around the circle and back to him. If he misses, he remains in the circle while the leader tries another player with a different letter. When all the players have had a chance, the leader may call on those who succeeded previously for a second round and request the other players to speed up the passing. The players who could not perform the feat drop out. The game continues, with the circle getting smaller each time, until only one player is able to list six things in the short time now available. This is an exciting game that calls for fast thinking.

VARIATIONS: *Name Four* is played the same way when there are fewer players—from six to ten. The players must name four things beginning with the designated letter. In *Name Ten,* which is played with circles of more than 20 players, ten things must be named before the object completes a full circuit.

Charades

A *Charade* is any game in which one or more players act out a title, slogan, name, or proverb, with a more or less formal presentation, for other players to guess. There are special signals employed by the actor in charades to help the audience guess the pantomimes. For example, before acting out individual words, the player indicates the subject by giving a visual clue:

Book Title:	He pretends to read a book
Song Title:	He pretends to sing
Saying or Quotation:	He holds up two fingers on each hand, as quotation marks
Movie Title:	"Turns" old-fashioned movie camera
Famous Name:	Places hand inside shirt, indicating famous person (like Napoleon)

The actor holds up a number of fingers to indicate the number of words in the title or saying. He then either acts out the entire title at once (to show this, he moves both hands in a sweeping circular gesture) or acts it out one word at a time (to show which word he is doing, he holds up the appropriate number of fingers for that word). He may even show a word one syllable at a time. (To do this he puts his fingers on his arm to show the number of syllables and which one he is pantomiming.) Other visual clues used in charades are holding up the thumb and forefinger of one hand to indicate a short word, like "a" or "the," or pulling the ear to indicate a "word that sounds like." An actor may also indicate, with a chopping motion of his hand, that the correct word is a shorter form of the word guessed, or, with a stretching motion of both hands, that the correct word is a longer form of the word guessed. Such signal giving is accepted as a legitimate part of the game and is done together with the actual pantomiming.

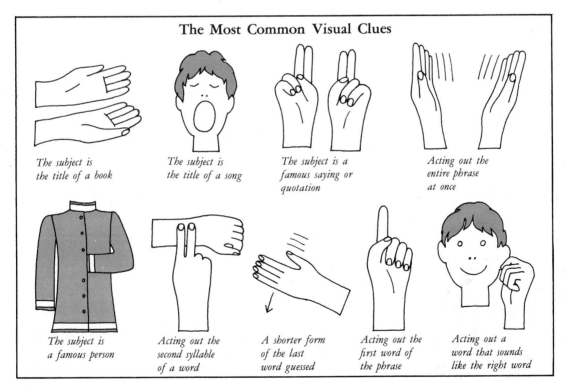

The Most Common Visual Clues

The subject is the title of a book

The subject is the title of a song

The subject is a famous saying or quotation

Acting out the entire phrase at once

The subject is a famous person

Acting out the second syllable of a word

A shorter form of the last word guessed

Acting out the first word of the phrase

Acting out a word that sounds like the right word

Relay Charades

- 10 to 20
- Slips of paper; pencil

Players divide into two teams. The leader writes out two separate, but similar, sets of charade subjects on slips of paper. A player from each team comes up, takes a piece of paper, and goes back to his team to act out the charade. As soon as a team guesses correctly, another player from that team goes up to get a new slip of paper and acts it out for his team. There should be as many charade subjects as there are players on each team, so that everyone has a chance to act. The first team to guess all of the subjects wins.

Individual Charades

- 2 to 20

One player thinks of a name, title, or saying and acts it out for the others to guess. There is no winner and no competition. Usually the player who guesses correctly is the next one to act out a charade.

Individual Pass Charades

- 4 to 20
- Writing paper; pencil

One player thinks of a good subject for a charade and writes it on a sheet of paper. Another player then volunteers to act it out for the others to guess. The person who thought it up may not, of course, take part in the guessing.

Circle Pass Charades

- 5 to 20
- Slips of paper; pencils

Players sit in a circle. Each player writes a subject for a charade on a piece of paper and passes it to his right. Then each player, in turn, steps into the circle and acts out what is written on his piece of paper for the others to guess. The player who succeeds in acting out his subject in the shortest period of time is the winner.

Speed Team Charades

- 10 to 20
- Slips of paper; pencils; two containers

Players divide into two equal teams. Each team makes up ten charade subjects, writes them on individual slips of paper, and puts them into a container. The teams exchange containers, so each team has the charade subjects prepared by the other team. Simultaneously, one member of each team takes a slip and acts it out for his own team. When a team guesses the charade, a new player from that team acts out the next subject, and so on. The first team to complete all ten charades is the winner. Teams may also alternate in acting out subjects, so that the team that made up the charade watches a player on the other team act out the subject for his teammates. Each actor is timed with a watch, and the team with the shorter cumulative time, after each of its players has acted, wins the game.

Team Charades

- 12 to 30
- Slips of paper; pencils

Players divide into three or more teams. Each team writes a charade on a slip of paper and passes it to another team. Each team in turn then briefly rehearses and puts on a "team charade," with the entire group taking part. The team (or teams) that did not make up the charade does the guessing.

The-Other-Half Charades

- 4 to 20
- Slips of paper; pencils

Players divide into two equal teams of males and females. The females think up a list of well-known women; the males do the same with well-known men. The names are then written on slips of paper and given to the opposite team. Each player acts out the name for his or her team to guess.

Alertness and Memory Games

This group of games does not require vocabulary skills, but depends instead on keen senses and a good memory. The players may be asked to identify objects by their touch, taste, smell or sound, as well as by their appearance. While many games in this category require a certain amount of preparation, they are worth the trouble because of the fun they provide for both teen-agers and adults. All of these games can be played equally well by both males and females.

Numerals indicate the number of players.

Something Smells

● *6 to 12* ● *Paper cups; small quantities of substances with distinctive odors: Crushed onions, cloves, ground coffee, toothpaste, soap, cologne, paint and turpentine*

PREPARATION: The game leader places a number of substances, each with a distinct odor, in paper cups; he places the cups on a table. The players are divided into two teams, and both teams leave the room.

ACTION: Members of each team are called back individually; they are each blindfolded and led to the table where the cups are set up. The game leader holds each cup close to the player's nose. Each player, in turn, tries to identify the various smells. Score is kept of how many smells are named correctly. When all of the players have had a chance to guess the smells, the team with the greatest number of correct identifications is declared the winner.

VARIATIONS: In *Gourmet Contest,* the leader prepares small quantities of different foods, drinks and seasonings. After being fed a tiny sample, the blindfolded players must guess what each one is. A few unusual entries—such as caviar or pomegranate seeds—make the game more interesting. *Sound Effects* requires the blindfolded players to identify a number of different objects by the sound they make. Some of the sounds can be produced by dropping things, such as a shoe, a basketball or a piece of silverware. Other sounds might range from someone brushing his teeth or his shoes to someone firing a popgun.

Feel

● *6 to 12* ● *Ten small, familiar objects, such as a comb, toothbrush, can opener or cigarette lighter; a large bag or pillowcase; paper and pencils*

PREPARATION: The objects, which should include one or two a little less familiar than the others—like an eggcup or a napkin ring, are placed in the bag.

ACTION: Each player is given a piece of paper and a pencil and is then allowed to put his hand into the sack for one minute. When the minute is up, he writes down all of the objects that he was able to identify. When all of the players are finished, the one with the largest number of correct identifications wins the game.

VARIATION: *What From?* is a more difficult version, in which parts of familiar objects are used. These might include a piece of a ballpoint pen, the cap from a toothpaste tube, an ornamental belt buckle, a Christmas tree light or similar things culled from desk drawers, medicine cabinets and workshelves.

What's Changed?

● *4 to 18*

PREPARATION: The players are asked to carefully look around the room. They then leave the room for a few minutes. While the players are gone, the leader makes a number of small changes in the room—moving a chair, switching pictures, turning on a lamp, removing a vase—and lists each such change on a piece of paper.

ACTION: When the players return, they are given five minutes to observe the room and to write down all the changes they detect. The leader then checks their lists against his, giving two points for every change correctly noted and deducting one point for every incorrect listing. The winner is the player with the highest score.

Smugglers and Inspectors

- *6 to 12* - *Box of toothpicks*

PREPARATION: Players are divided into two teams, the "smugglers" and the "inspectors." Each smuggler is given ten toothpicks. The inspectors leave the room while the smugglers hide their "smuggled goods"—the toothpicks— on their persons, in such a way that a small bit of the toothpick is visible. The toothpicks may be inserted into clothing, hair, jewelry or shoes.

ACTION: The smugglers stand in a line in the center of the room; the inspectors walk slowly down one side of the line, and then up the other side. As they walk, they reach out and extract any toothpick they see, but may not touch the smugglers in any other way. The inspectors are given three minutes to complete their inspection and may not retrace their steps. The seized toothpicks are then counted, and the inspectors get a point for every detected toothpick, while the smugglers get two points for every one undetected. The teams reverse roles, and the one with the higher combined score wins the game.

Know the Ads

- *6 to 12* - *Magazines; two large pieces of cardboard; paper and pencils*

PREPARATION: In advance, the leader goes through the old magazines and clips the slogans from advertisements of well-known products. (The name of the product should not appear on any of the slogans.) He pastes or tapes on each of the two large pieces of cardboard from six to ten different slogans—numbering each.

ACTION: The players are divided into two equal teams, and each team is given one of the cardboards and pencil and paper. Both teams try to write the products that go with the slogans on their board. After three minutes, the teams exchange cardboards and repeat the procedure. The team with more correct answers wins.

VARIATIONS: *TV Slogans* uses slogans—this time from products advertised on television. All players receive paper and pencils, and the leader reads aloud a list of from 15 to 20 slogans. Players try to write the name of the appropriate products, and the player with the most correct identifications wins. *Old Time Slogans* is a good game for those brought up before the age of television. The game leader writes down and numbers several famous slogans no longer in use, such as: "Ask the Man Who Owns One;" and "——— ——— Green has Gone to War." Players pass around the paper and then write on their own sheets, beside the appropriate numbers, the products to which the slogans refer. The player who identifies the greatest number wins the contest.

Know the Presidents

- *10 to 20* - *Set of pictures of Presidents of the United States*

PREPARATION: The pictures of the Presidents, with their names blocked out, are placed face up on a table or are taped to a wall. The Presidents are not shown in chronological sequence.

ACTION: Each player is given paper and pencil and asked to list the names of the Presidents in the order they are displayed. The winner is the one with the most correct names. This is a much more difficult game than it might appear, since the faces of all but a relatively small number of the Presidents are not familiar to most people.

VARIATION: Canadians might well play *Know the Prime Ministers* or *Know the Monarchs,* with pictures of the Canadian Prime Ministers or the Kings and Queens of Great Britain substituted for the Presidents.

Silly Milly

● *6 to 12*

PREPARATION: None required. The game leader or host may begin by telling the others: "I'm Silly Milly. I'm odd and silly, but not peculiar."

ACTION: The players try to guess why those particular words were used to describe Silly Milly. The leader provides additional clues on request: such as, "I like trees, but not mice" or "I like walls, but not windows." The secret, in this case, is that Silly Milly likes any word that contains a double letter. A player who detects this may ask a question like—"Do you eat herring but not sardines?"—to confirm his judgement. The game leader does not reveal the secret, even as the other players keep trying to unravel it. There is no winner or loser, and the players take turns being Silly Milly and concocting new secrets—such as, a preference for words with the letter "a" or dislike for words with the letter "r." The enormous range of possibilities can make this game quite simple or enormously complex—depending on the players.

Likes and Dislikes

● *6 to 12*   ● *Writing paper; pencils*

PREPARATION: Each player is given a sheet of paper, on which he writes his name, followed by a list of five likes and dislikes. These may cover his tastes in sports, fashion, politics, food, personalities or anything else.

ACTION: The leader collects the papers and reads them aloud, one at a time, without revealing the player's name. Participants try to figure out who wrote each set of likes and dislikes before the leader tells the name. The game continues until all the lists are read. There are no winners in this game, which is most enjoyable when the players know one another fairly well. The likes and dislikes should be genuine.

Novelty Tricks and Stunts

The gimmick, not the competition, is the important thing in this group of games. The novelty stunts are meant to be entertaining and they involve seemingly impossible challenges, unusual physical actions and offbeat word and picture games. Many of these stunts are really rehearsed exhibitions, rather than spontaneous contests. They are ideal for livening up parties during brief moments of inactivity between dances or games.

Numerals indicate the number of players.

The Strength of Superman

● *6 to 12*   ● *A newspaper*

PREPARATION: The host separates the pages of a newspaper so that everyone in the group has one sheet. He then tells them that only he, "Superman," has the strength to fold the sheet in half eight times.

ACTION: Those who accept the challenge try to fold their sheets in half eight times. Invariably they fail because of the doubled and redoubled thicknesses of paper. The host then takes a sheet, folds it in half, opens it, folds it again and repeats this action until he, indeed, folds the paper in half eight times.

VARIATION: *The Hypnotized Penny* is another seemingly simple chore that is actually impossible to perform. The leader tells the group that he is going to hypnotize a penny so that no one will be able to pick it up without losing his balance and falling. He then asks for a volunteer. The leader places the volunteer with his back to a wall, and with both heels touching the baseboard. He then puts the penny about 18 inches in front of the volunteer's toes and asks him to bend over and pick up the penny without moving his feet. It simply can't be done!

This Is My Hand

● *10 to 20*

PREPARATION: Players form a circle facing in with the game leader in the middle.

ACTION: The leader begins by touching his hand and saying, "This is my hand." The other players must immediately touch any other part of their bodies while repeating, "This is my hand." Anyone who touches his hand or uses a different phrase gets a penalty point. The game then continues with the leader touching another part of his body and describing it correctly. Again, the players must touch any part of their bodies, except the one mentioned, while repeating the leader's words. The first player to accumulate two penalty points takes the leader's place, and the game begins again.

VARIATION: In *Scrambled Anatomy,* a trickier version, the players stand in a circle. The leader goes up to each in turn, touches some part of his own body—such as his elbow—and says, "This is my ear." The player must then do exactly the opposite, touching his own ear and saying, "This is my elbow." If he fails, he replaces the leader. He then tries a similar ploy with the next player, perhaps touching his nose and saying, "This is my thumb."

Midget Man

● *6 to 12*

PREPARATION: The leader announces that he can slide himself under a closed door, and that anyone who doubts him should come forward.

ACTION: The challengers are asked to stand on the other side of a door in an adjoining room. The leader then closes the door and prints the word "myself" in large letters on a sheet of paper. He slides the paper under the door and then opens the door to let the chagrined challengers return.

VARIATION: In *Reverse Reader,* the leader claims that he can read anything backward as quickly and accurately as he can forward, and that he

will prove it by reading anything given him. When given a book, magazine or newspaper, he turns his back, so that he faces away from the challenger, and reads in a normal manner.

Pat and Rub

● *10 to 20*

PREPARATION: Players form a circle with the leader in the center.

ACTION: The leader tells the players to rub their stomachs with their right hands while patting the tops of their heads with their left hands. When he calls, "Change!" they must reverse the action, by patting their stomachs and rubbing their heads. Those who fail to switch over correctly are eliminated. To make the game more difficult, the leader may also call out, "Change hands!" The players must then move their left hands from head to stomach, and their right hands from stomach to head without disturbing the pat-and-rub pattern.

VARIATION: In *Crossed Wires,* the leader tells the players to grab their left ears with their right hands and stroke their noses with their left hands. At the commands of "Change!" and "Change hands!" the same rules apply as in *Pat and Rub.*

Professions

● *6 to 10*

PREPARATION: The players sit in a circle, and each chooses a different "profession" to demonstrate in pantomime. The leader stands in the center of the circle.

ACTION: One player begins a pantomime, while the leader performs a nonsensical pantomime of his own—like touching his thumbs to his ears and waggling his fingers. Suddenly, the leader begins doing the same pantomime as the player; this is a signal for the player to switch immediately to the leader's pantomime. When the leader shifts back, so does the player. They may switch back and forth several times as the leader tries to trap the player into performing the same pantomime he is doing. If the player falls into the leader's trap, he becomes the leader and begins the game again.

Walk the Straight and Narrow

● *6 to 10* ● *Binoculars*

PREPARATION: A straight line is drawn down the floor, from one end of the room to the other. If this is not possible, a cord may be stretched to form a line. Each player, in turn, is given a pair of binoculars.

ACTION: Each player walks the straight line across the room while looking down at the line through the wrong end of the binoculars. The heel and toe of both feet must touch the line with every step. This is much harder than it appears because of the distortion created by the reversed binoculars; the line appears much farther away than it actually is.

Smile

● *10 to 20*

PREPARATION: The players are divided into two teams, and line up facing each other. One team is designated as the smilers and the other as the non-smilers.

ACTION: The smilers simply smile, as broadly and as winningly as they can, at the non-smilers. The non-smilers, meanwhile, must keep straight faces for a full minute; if they fail, they must join the smilers. When the minute is up, the teams regroup and reverse their roles.

Spreading Gossip

● *6 to 20*

PREPARATION: The players and the leader sit in a circle, close together. The leader whispers into the ear of the player on his right a "news item" that he has made up and written on a piece of paper. It could be a make-believe wedding, divorce, funeral, accident or international event; it should contain some names, dates, places and other specific information.

ACTION: Each player, in turn, relays the information by whispering into the ear of the player on his right. When it reaches the player to the left of the leader, he stands up and tells the others the information he received. The leader then stands and reads the original message — which is often startlingly different. This is a fascinating game that can be repeated several times with different sets of "facts."

To Be Continued

● *4 to 10*

PREPARATION: The leader begins to tell an exciting ghost or adventure story to a seated group.

ACTION: At a tense moment in the narrative, the leader suddenly stops and points at one of the players. This player immediately picks up the story, making up new characters and incidents as he goes along. After a few minutes the leader points to another player, who picks up the story from where the first player leaves off. This continues until all of the players have a chance to contribute—the last player making up an exciting ending for the story.

Predicaments and Solutions

● *6 to 20* ● *Slips of paper; pencils*

PREPARATION: The players sit in a circle. They each have two slips of paper and a pencil. On one slip, they write a predicament, beginning with the words: "What would you do if" and completing the question with phrases like: "You had a flat tire on a lonely road at night?" or "You suddenly inherited a million dollars?" On the other slip, the player writes out a solution—real or fanciful—for his predicament.

ACTION: The players pass their predicaments to their right and their solutions to their left. Thus, each player finds himself with an unmatching predicament and solution. He reads both aloud to the group and passes them on in the same way as before. In this manner, each player receives and reads an entire series of unrelated predicaments and solutions—some of them making hysterical combinations.

Magic Telegram

● *6 to 12*   ● *Writing paper; pencils*

PREPARATION: The game leader reads any ten letters of the alphabet to the players.

ACTION: The players write down the ten letters, one under the other. In a set period of time, they must use each letter as the first word of a message. For example, "b-g-a-s-p-o-l-t-d-r" could become "Berry gardens always seem pleasant outdoor layouts to do recreation." Another possibility might be: "Beware! Ground artichokes supply poison. Open lid top; destroy

residue." Players read their results aloud for the amusement of the others.

Progressive Poems

● *6 to 12*   ● *Writing paper; pencils*

PREPARATION: Each player writes the first line of a poem at the top of a sheet of paper and folds the paper so that the line cannot be seen.

ACTION: On signal, each player passes his paper to the player on his right, telling him only the last word in the line. The next player, without peeking, writes another line rhyming with the first. He then refolds the paper to conceal his line and passes it to the right, telling only the last word of the line. The process continues until all papers return to their original owners. Each person, in turn, unfolds his paper and reads aloud the finished "poem."

Practical Jokes

The practical joke is a special kind of stunt in which the player is not usually aware that he has been made part of a game for the amusement of others. When properly performed, many practical jokes are harmless fun, enjoyed as much by the "victim" as by everyone else. However, it is important to avoid practical jokes that embarrass a person, hurt his feelings or hold him up to ridicule. The game leader or host should try to select an outgoing, good-natured "victim." If there is any doubt about the joke, the leader should try to put himself in the role of the "victim." Would he think it was funny? This provides a fair test of whether a practical joke is suitable or not. The jokes described here are quite harmless and should provide much amusement at both teen-age and adult get-togethers.

Numerals indicate the number of players.

The Stubborn Dime

● *4 to 6*   ● *A dime; glass of water*

PREPARATION: The host takes the dime, shows it to the players and announces that he can make it stick tightly to anyone's forehead. He then selects several volunteers to prove his statement.

ACTION: The leader, holding the dime with his thumb and forefinger, dips it into a glass of water and presses it firmly with his thumb

against the forehead of one of the players. The water causes the dime to stick momentarily, but a few shakes of the head soon dislodge it. The leader pretends to be surprised and tries again with another player. The result, of course, is the same. The leader may try again with another player or two before coming to the player whom he has selected for the practical joke. "Now I know what I was doing wrong," the leader says, "and this time I guarantee the dime will not fall off." Again, he dips the dime into the water and presses it against the player's forehead. This time he keeps a bit of his fingernail underneath the edge of the dime. When the leader takes away his thumb, he also removes the dime. The victim, unaware of this, shakes his head as the other players have done. When nothing happens, he shakes his head harder and harder until the laughter tells him that the joke—not the dime—is on him.

Pinchy-Winchy

- *6 to 12* - *Small amount of burnt cork or black grease; small mirror*

PREPARATION: The leader secretly smears the thumb of his right hand with either burnt cork or black grease. He then asks the players to sit in a circle.

ACTION: The leader begins by pinching the cheek of the player on his right, while saying, "Pinchy-winchy! Pass it along." Each player in turn pinches the cheek of the player on his right, and this process continues until everyone has been pinched three times. Only then does the leader produce the mirror and show his "victim" why everyone is laughing so hard. It's a good idea to have a moistened towel handy so that the results of the joke can be speedily removed.

VARIATION: In *Polaroid* the victim is asked to sit and pose while the leader takes a photograph of him with a Polaroid camera. The leader pretends to have trouble getting the pose he wants, and another player "volunteers" to help by moving the victim's head this way and that. He is actually dabbing the victim's face with burnt cork or black grease. The victim's first knowledge of the practical joke is when he sees the developed Polaroid print.

Obstacle Course

- *6 to 12* - *Several small, household objects*

PREPARATION: The host pretends to set up an obstacle course. He takes five or six small objects from around the house—soda bottles, potted plants, water pitchers, telephone books, kitchen pots or whatever else is convenient—and places them in a line across the floor of the room. He spaces each object approximately three feet apart. He now demonstrates to the group how easy it is to walk the line by carefully stepping over each object. When he has done so, he asks for volunteers from the group who believe they can duplicate this simple feat. A number of the partygoers come forward and easily walk the line. The host then asks which of them would be willing to try to duplicate the walk—this time wearing a blindfold over the eyes to block off all vision.

ACTION: The volunteer is allowed to practice the walk with his eyes open a couple of times. Afterwards, he is taken to the starting point and blindfolded. Then the leader quickly and quietly removes all of the obstacles. When the blindfolded player begins his walk, the leader and spectators applaud every high step as though he has successfully passed over another obstacle. The loudest applause is saved for the finish, when the player's blindfold is removed and he gets a look at the empty piece of floor he has so carefully crossed.

Who Could It Be?

- *6 to 12*

PREPARATION: This joke usually works best when played during the course of an actual guessing game, in which players leave the room and then return—trying to discover some piece of information by questioning the other players. This time, the player designated to leave the room is told that he must guess the name of another player.

ACTION: The victim is allowed to question all of the other players for clues to the mystery player's identity. What he doesn't know is that all of the players have been told to provide clues about the player on their right: Thus, every answer seems to point to another player, and it is impossible for the victim to make any sense out of his "clues."

Group Action Games

This group of party games differs from those already mentioned, because they involve all of the party guests in activities that require more physical activity. Many of these games are similar to outdoor and backyard games, but they may be played quite easily in a large area indoors. None present any real difficulty for the teen-ager or the adult.

Numerals indicate the number of players.

Gift on a String

- *12 to 20* - *Party favors for each player; roll of string*

PREPARATION: At a convenient time midway through the party, the host brings out a basket or box filled with inexpensive party favors. The players sit in a circle about eight feet from the container. A long string is attached to each favor. The leader deliberately tangles the strings together.

ACTION: Each player holds on to the edge of one string. On signal, he must find his way through the maze of tangled strings to get his party favor. The closer he gets to the container, the more difficult this feat becomes.

VARIATION: *Perfect Match* provides a novel and exciting addition to the above. The players find not only gifts but also partners for refreshments, a dance or whatever the host or hostess has in mind. Half of the tangled strings attached to the favors are of one color. These are given to the girls to unravel. The other half of the strings are another color and are given to the boys. The strings lead to two sets of favors, one set for girls, one set for boys. Two favors, one from each set, are wrapped in identical covering— perhaps a newspaper, saved Christmas paper or paper of distinctive color (bright orange, Kelly green) or pattern (zigzag, striped, checkered). The point is that when the boys and girls finally untangle the strings and claim their favors, the game is by no means over. Now each of the players is instructed to seek out the boy or girl who has an identically wrapped favor. When the two holders of the matching wrappings find each other, they become partners for whatever activity is to follow.

How Do You Like Your Neighbors?

- *20 to 50*

PREPARATION: Players sit in a large circle, with the game leader standing in the center. The game leader gives each player a number and tells him to remember it. The leader takes the last number for himself, so if there are 20 players in the circle, his number is 21.

ACTION: The leader calls out a number and asks: "How do you like your neighbors?" The player has two choices of reply. If he says, "Very well!" it is a signal for all the players to leave their chairs and find new seats on the other side of the circle. At the same time, the leader scrambles for a chair; if he is successful, the player without a seat becomes the leader. However, if the player answers, "Not very well!" the other players remain seated while the leader asks, "Who would you rather have?" The player then supplies two numbers at random. The players with those numbers rise and attempt to change places with the players on either side of the number-caller. At the same time, the leader tries to take over one of the four momentarily-vacant seats. The more jumbled the players and numbers become, the more fun the game.

Scavenger Hunt

- *20 to 50* - *Writing paper; pencil*

PREPARATION: The players divide into two or more equal-size teams, with one player on each team designated the captain. Each captain is then given a list of objects likely to be found in the possession of team members. These could be:

keys, pocket combs, ballpoint pens, eyeglasses, lipstick or some item of clothing or jewelry.

ACTION: The captains read off their lists to their team members, who try to locate each item and hand it to their captain. Bartering with members of other teams is permitted. The first captain to produce all of the items on his scavenger list wins the hunt for his team. When *Scavenger Hunt* is played without teams, the individual players are given lists of three objects. Each player must produce these objects, either by taking them off his own person or by bartering for them.

Monster Checkers

● 26 ● *24 party hats, 12 of one color, 12 of another; 32 pieces of cardboard—each one, one foot square*

PREPARATION: The room where this game is to be played must have a large clear space in the center. In this area the 32 squares of cardboard are laid down on the floor in the form of a huge checkerboard with one-foot-square spaces in between. Two players are selected to play checkers. They each choose a team of 12 boys and girls. The members of these two teams become the checkers, or "men," of the game. One side is given hats of one color to wear, perhaps red; the other team, hats of a contrasting color, say white. The red and white "men" now take their positions in rows—each standing on a cardboard square. The reds occupy the first three rows on one side; the whites the first three rows on the other.

ACTION: As the checker players toss for the first move, all the "men" crouch down in squat positions on their squares. The winner of the toss now directs one of his men to move to a certain empty square. His opponent does likewise with one of his men. The game continues as in normal checkers. When a jumping situation develops, one man literally leapfrogs over another, who then walks off the board. The game ends when one player is able to move one of his men into his opponent's backline.

Square Relay

● *20 to 40* ● *Four rubber balls; a chair for each player*

PREPARATION: The players divide into four teams of equal size. Each team sits in four lines of chairs, forming a large square. An easy chair or table is placed at the center of the square.

ACTION: The player at the left end of each line is given a rubber ball to hold. On a signal from the leader, each of the four ball holders passes his ball to the player on his right, who in turn passes it on until the ball reaches the player at the right end of each line. This player now jumps to his feet and, carrying the ball, runs around the piece of furniture in the center of the square. Meanwhile, the other players in his line each move one seat to the right, leaving the extreme left seat vacant. When each of the runners returns, he takes this vacant seat. He then immediately passes the ball to the player on his right, who in turn passes it on until it reaches the player at the right end. The procedure is repeated until all the players are back in their original seats. The team that accomplishes this first wins the race.

CHAPTER 12

Quizzes and Word Games

Quizzes and word games offer an intriguing form of family fun. Pitting one's knowledge against that of others in history, sports, literature and similar subjects can be an enjoyable and educational pastime. Anyone can make up quizzes. All it takes is a source of detailed information, such as an almanac or an encyclopedia.

Quizzes are most enjoyable when played as an oral contest between teams or between individuals. Usually each team or individual takes a turn at replying to a question—with one point awarded for each correct answer. Quizzes should be closely related to the contestants' knowledge level. Questions that are too easy or too hard soon cause players to become frustrated or bored. The following quizzes become more difficult as the chapter progresses.

Sports Terms Quiz

● *Teen to adult*

Sports are one of the most popular forms of entertainment and recreation today. Here are a number of sports terms. To what does each refer?

QUESTIONS:

1. Tee.	9. Christy.
2. T-formation.	10. Apprentice.
3. Lay-up.	11. Clay pigeon.
4. Shell.	12. Sulky.
5. Butterfly.	13. Spare.
6. Chukker.	14. Billy.
7. Puck.	15. Balk spot.
8. Shortstop.	16. Shuttlecock.

ANSWERS:
1. Golf. 2. Football. 3. Basketball. 4. Rowing. 5. Swimming. 6. Polo. 7. Hockey. 8. Baseball. 9. Skiing. 10. Horse racing. 11. Trap shooting. 12. Harness racing. 13. Bowling. 14. Field hockey. 15. Billiards or pool. 16. Badminton.

Sports Knowledge Quiz

● *Teen to adult*

Here is a difficult sports quiz, for the true fan who has followed all kinds of sports faithfully through the years.

QUESTIONS:
1. For what sports are the following cups awarded?
   a. Wightman.
   b. America's.
   c. Davis.
   d. Stanley.
   e. Ryder.

2. Who were the "four horsemen," and for what university did they play?

3. Looking back at sports history, what leading sports figures were known as:
   a. Little Miss Poker Face.
   b. The Galloping Ghost.
   c. The Yankee Clipper.
   d. The West Point Touchdown Twins.

4. In the box scores of a ball game, what do the following abbreviations stand for: AB; R; H; E; PO; A and RBI?

5. Football is divided into quarters. What are the following divided into?
   a. Ice hockey.
   b. Boxing.
   c. Polo.

6. Why is a football field sometimes referred to as a "gridiron"?

7. To what event does the phrase "the long count" refer?

8. In an eight-oar shell, is the "stroke" or the "bow" nearer to the coxswain?

9. How many players on a team in each of the following?
   a. Cricket.
   b. Water Polo.
   c. Rugby.
   d. Lacrosse.

10. What is the role of the "picador" in a bullfight?

11. Who first won the "grand slam" in golf, and what four tournaments comprised it?

12. What is a "cat rig"?

13. In reports of racing, one often reads the word "furlong." What does it mean?

14. With what sports are the following words or phrases associated, and what is the meaning of each?
   a. A service ace.
   b. An impost.
   c. A rabbit punch.
   d. A birdie.
   e. The hot corner.

15. What American has twice won the Olympic decathlon?

ANSWERS:

1. a. Women's tennis; b. Yachting; c. Tennis; d. Ice hockey; e. Golf.

2. The famous Notre Dame football backfield in the 20's: Crowley, Layden, Miller and Stuhldreher.

3. a. Helen Wills; b. Red Grange of Illinois; c. Joe DiMaggio; d. Doc Blanchard and Glenn Davis.

4. AB—times at bat; R—runs scored; H—safe hits; E—errors; PO—put-outs; A—assists in put-outs; RBI—runs batted in.

5. Ice hockey—periods; Boxing—rounds; Polo —chukkers.

6. In its early development, football had lines running not only sideways (marking five-yard lengths down the field) but lengthwise (so that the player who received the ball from center had to cross the scrimmage line no less than five yards to either side of where the ball was put in play.) At this time, with criss-crossing lines resembling a gridiron, the football field was nicknamed exactly that.

7. The famous Dempsey-Tunney heavyweight championship fight in 1927, in which the referee gave Tunney a "long count" because Dempsey did not move quickly enough to a neutral corner after flooring his opponent.

8. The "stroke" is nearest the coxswain.

9. a. Cricket—11; b. Water Polo—7; c. Rugby —15; d. Lacrosse—10.

10. The "picador" is a horseman with a lance, who excites and tires the bull by prodding him.

11. Bobby Jones, of Atlanta, Georgia, won the "grand slam"—comprised of the British Open, the British Amateur, the U.S. Open and the U.S. Amateur—in 1930.

12. A "cat rig" is a single sail on a mast placed far forward on the bow of a sailboat.

13. A "furlong" is one-eighth of a mile—or 220 yards.

14. a. In tennis, a service ace is an in-bounds serve that wins the point without the ball being touched by the opposing player; b. In horse racing, an impost is a weight carried by a horse as a method of handicapping him; c. In boxing, a rabbit punch is an illegal blow to the base of the skull; d. In golf, a birdie is one stroke under par (average); e. In baseball, the hot corner is third base.

15. Robert B. Mathias.

Who Wrote This Book?

● *Teen to adult*

Here are a number of well-known books or plays, most of them classics. Who wrote each of them?

QUESTIONS:
1. *Little Women.*
2. *Ivanhoe.*
3. *The Forsyte Saga.*
4. *War and Peace.*
5. *The Deerslayer.*
6. *Penrod.*
7. *The Adventures of Sherlock Holmes.*
8. *Two Years Before the Mast.*
9. *The Pickwick Papers.*
10. *Pilgrim's Progress.*
11. *Gone with the Wind.*
12. *David Copperfield.*
13. *Anthony Adverse.*
14. *Othello, the Moor of Venice.*
15. *Crusade in Europe.*
16. *In His Own Write.*

ANSWERS:
1. Louisa May Alcott. 2. Sir Walter Scott. 3. John Galsworthy. 4. Leo Tolstoy. 5. James Fenimore Cooper. 6. Booth Tarkington. 7. Arthur Conan Doyle. 8. Richard Henry Dana. 9. Charles Dickens. 10. John Bunyan. 11. Margaret Mitchell. 12. Charles Dickens. 13. Hervey Allen. 14. William Shakespeare. 15. Dwight D. Eisenhower. 16. John Lennon.

Famous Quotations

● *Teen to adult*

Written below are some famous lines from plays, poems, essays or other works of literature. The object of this quiz is to identify the author and the exact period of time in which he or she lived and wrote.

QUESTIONS:
1. "Drink to me only with thine eyes,
   And I will pledge with mine."
2. "East is East and West is West
   And never the twain shall meet."
3. "The woods are lovely, dark and deep,
   But I have promises to keep,
   And miles to go before I sleep,
   And miles to go before I sleep."
4. "If a man does not keep pace with his companions, perhaps it is because he hears a different drummer."
5. "This is the way the world ends
   Not with a bang but a whimper."
6. "These are the times that try men's souls. The summer soldier and the sunshine patriot will, in this crisis, shrink from the service of their country; but he that stands it now, deserves the love and thanks of man and woman."
7. "They also serve who only stand and wait."
8. "Power tends to corrupt and absolute power corrupts absolutely."
9. "Yes, Virginia, there is a Santa Claus."
10. "Men seldom make passes
    At girls who wear glasses."
11. "Breathes there the man, with soul so dead,
    Who never to himself hath said,
    This is my own, my native land!"
12. "Some are born great, some achieve greatness, and some have greatness thrust upon them."
13. "Oh wad some power the giftie gie us
    To see oursels as others see us!"
14. ". . . and therefore never send to know for whom the bell tolls; it tolls for thee."
15. "Oh death, where is thy sting? Oh grave, where is thy victory?"
16. "Once upon a midnight dreary,
    While I pondered, weak and weary."
17. "If a man can write a better book, preach a better sermon, or make a better mousetrap than his neighbor, though he builds his house in the woods, the world will make a beaten path to his door."
18. "And you, my father, there on the sad height,
    Curse, bless, me now with your fierce tears, I pray
    Do not go gentle into that good night.
    Rage, rage against the dying of the light."

ANSWERS:
1. Ben Jonson (1573–1637). 2. Rudyard Kipling (1865–1936). 3. Robert Frost (1875–1963). 4. Henry David Thoreau (1817–1862). 5. T. S. Eliot (1888–1965). 6. Thomas Paine (1737–1809). 7. John Milton (1608–1674). 8. Lord Acton (1834–1902). 9. Unsigned editorial in the New York *Sun,* September 21, 1897. 10. Dorothy Parker (1893–1967). 11. Sir Walter Scott (1771–1832). 12. Shakespeare (1564–1616): *Twelfth Night,* Act II. 13. Robert Burns (1759–1796). 14. John Donne (1573–1631). 15. *First Corinthians,* 15:55. 16. Edgar Allan Poe (1809–1849). 17. Ralph Waldo Emerson (1803–1882). 18. Dylan Thomas (1914–1953).

Famous Last Words

● *Teen to adult*

Here's a somewhat gruesome quiz—but one that will really challenge those who know their literature and history. The following were the last words of a number of world figures. Who said each of them?

QUESTIONS:
1. "I have such sweet thoughts."
2. "I must sleep now."
3. "Be sure you show my head to the mob. It will be a long time ere they see its like."
4. "It is well. I die hard but am not afraid to go."
5. "Let us cross the river and rest in the shade of the trees."
6. "What an artist the world is losing!"
7. "Let the tent be struck."
8. "Farewell, my children, forever; I am going to your father."
9. "We are over the mountain, we shall go better now."
10. "Wait till I have finished my problem."
11. "Now comes the mystery."
12. "All my possessions for a moment of time."

ANSWERS:
1. Prince Albert, Consort of Queen Victoria. 2. Poet, George Gordon (Lord) Byron. 3. Jacques Danton, the French revolutionary leader.
4. George Washington. 5. Stonewall Jackson, accidentally shot by his own troops during the Civil War. 6. Nero, the Roman Emperor, said to have killed himself to avoid capture. 7. Robert E. Lee, the famous Confederate general. 8. Marie Antoinette, before leaving for the guillotine. 9. Frederick the Great of Prussia. 10. Archimedes, to the Roman soldier who ordered him to his execution. 11. Henry Ward Beecher, famous American minister. 12. Queen Elizabeth I of England.

How Were They Known?

● *Teen to adult*

This quiz is guaranteed to be fun for the individual with an interest in biography. Many famous writers, artists and entertainers were not known to the public by their real names. By what names were the following famous personalities widely known?

QUESTIONS
1. An English novelist of Polish background, who wrote sea stories and whose real name was Josef Korzeniowski.
2. An American songwriter and entertainer, whose real name was Isidore Baline.
3. An English actor named William Pratt, who was an extremely kindly man but portrayed one of the most frightening characters in films—Frankenstein's monster. What was the "monster's" stage name?
4. A famous short story writer named William Sydney Porter, who was best known for his surprise endings.
5. A great American novelist born in Florida in 1835, whose legal name was Samuel Langhorne Clemens but who, as the author of *Tom Sawyer* and other famous books, was commonly known by another name.
6. An English mathematics teacher named Charles Dodgson, who was the author of two great books for children, one of which was *Through the Looking Glass.*
7. An American frontiersman and showman, born in 1846, who travelled around the world. His real name was William F. Cody.

8. A famous American dancer of stage and screen, who has been popular for over 40 years. His real name is Frederick Austerlitz.

ANSWERS:
1. Joseph Conrad. 2. Irving Berlin. 3. Boris Karloff. 4. O. Henry. 5. Mark Twain. 6. Lewis Carroll. 7. Buffalo Bill. 8. Fred Astaire.

The Line That Follows

● *Teen to adult*

In this quiz, players are expected to supply the line that follows in each of the famous quotations written below. (For an added challenge, players may cite the source of each quote.)

QUESTIONS:
1. "What is so rare as a day in June?"
2. "The stockings were hung by the chimney with care."
3. "To be, or not to be."
4. "Laugh and the world laughs with you."
5. "Shoot, if you must, this old gray head."
6. "I know not what course others may take."
7. "When I was a lad, I served a term."
8. "He hath loosed the fateful lightning of His terrible swift sword."
9. "Listen, my children, and you shall hear."
10. "I think that I shall never see."
11. "Let me live in my house by the side of the road."
12. "Here once the embattled farmers stood."

ANSWERS:
1. "Then, if ever, come perfect days."
2. "In hopes that St. Nicholas soon would be there."
3. "That is the question."
4. "Weep and you weep alone."
5. "But spare your country's flag, she said."
6. "But as for me, give me liberty or give me death."
7. "As office boy to an attorney's firm."
8. "His truth is marching on."
9. "Of the midnight ride of Paul Revere."
10. "A poem lovely as a tree."
11. "And be a friend of man."
12. "And fired the shot heard round the world."

American History Quiz

● *Teen to adult*

Here's a test of knowledge about American historical events and personalities.

QUESTIONS:
1. In September, 1793, the cornerstone of the Capitol in Washington, D.C., was laid by whom?
2. The first battle between armored vessels was fought between American ships in American waters. What was the battle and where was it fought?
3. In 1779, during the American Revolution, an American general tried to betray West Point for a position in the British Army. Who was this general, and what was the name of the British officer who was his accomplice?
4. What was the reason for Paul Revere's famous ride on the night of April 18, 1775?
5. In the early years of the republic, the American government paid over one million dollars for the right to trade in the Mediterranean Sea. To whom did it pay this tribute?
6. A man named John Wilkes Booth committed a heinous crime that shocked the American nation at the end of a tragic war. What was this crime?
7. Where was the Declaration of Independence signed?
8. Among the many foreigners who came to help George Washington and his troops during the American War of Independence were Pulaski, Von Steuben and a famous young Frenchman. Who was this Frenchman?
9. What was the real name of the American fighting ship known as *Old Ironsides?*
10. An American frontiersman was adopted by the Cherokee Indians in his youth, led the people of Texas in their struggle for independence and finally became governor of Tennessee. He also was the first U.S. Senator from Texas. Who was he?
11. What American invented the telegraph?
12. In a New England village, on April 19, 1775, there was a skirmish between colonial minutemen and British regulars which began

the American Revolution. What was the name of this famous encounter?

13. In Boston, there is an old bronze tablet with this inscription: "On this spot stood the famous Liberty Tree." Of what kind of tree was this inscription written?

14. In 1847, Brigham Young led a group of settlers who sought religious freedom westward over the Rocky Mountains. Who were these people, and where did they settle?

15. January 19 is a legal holiday in Southern states, because it marks the birthdate of the commander-in-chief of the Confederate army during the Civil War. Who was this man?

ANSWERS:

1. George Washington. 2. The fight between the *Monitor* and the *Merrimac* at Hampton Roads, Virginia, in 1862. 3. Benedict Arnold and Major John Andre. 4. To warn John Hancock and Samuel Adams, in hiding at Lexington, that British soldiers were coming to arrest them. 5. The Barbary pirates of Algiers and Tripoli. 6. The assassination of Abraham Lincoln. 7. Philadelphia, Pennsylvania. 8. The Marquis de Lafayette. 9. *The Constitution*. 10. General Sam Houston. 11. Samuel F. B. Morse. 12. The Battle of Lexington. 13. A huge elm tree, under which the patriots known as the Sons of Liberty held meetings before the Revolution. 14. The Mormons, and they settled in what was to become Salt Lake City, Utah. 15. General Robert E. Lee.

Know Your Occupations

● *Teen to adult*

The following quiz is a real puzzler. Name the occupation of the man or woman who uses each of these tools.

QUESTIONS:

1. Sextant.	7. Pipette.
2. Lathe.	8. Bushing.
3. Pestle.	9. Cant hook.
4. Spurs.	10. Binder.
5. Night stick.	11. Peel.
6. Niblick.	12. Burette.

13. Black snake.	15. Davit.
14. Vernier.	16. Baton.

ANSWERS:

1. A ship's navigator. 2. A carpenter or machinist. 3. A druggist. 4. A cowboy. 5. A policeman. 6. A golfer. 7. A chemist. 8. A machinist or auto mechanic. 9. A logger. 10. A farmer. 11. A baker. 12. A chemist. 13. A mule-skinner. 14. A surveyor. 15. A seaman. 16. A band leader or conductor.

Who Invented It?

● *Teen to adult*

Each of the following inventions has played an important part in modern industrial development. Who invented each of them?

QUESTIONS:

1. The telephone.
2. The phonograph.
3. The telegraph.
4. Dynamite.
5. The power loom.
6. The steamboat.
7. The reaper.
8. Vulcanized rubber.
9. Nylon.
10. The thermometer.
11. Penicillin.
12. The airplane.

ANSWERS:

1. Alexander Graham Bell. 2. Thomas A. Edison. 3. Samuel F. B. Morse. 4. Alfred Nobel. 5. Edmund Cartwright. 6. Robert Fulton. 7. Cyrus McCormick. 8. Charles Goodyear. 9. The Du Pont Company. 10. Galileo. 11. Sir Alexander Fleming. 12. Wilbur and Orville Wright.

What's in a Name?

● *Teen to adult*

Most cities have nicknames by which they are popularly known. What cities have each of the following nicknames?

QUESTIONS:
1. The City of the Seven Hills.
2. The Empire City.
3. The Windy City.
4. The Elm City.
5. The City of Brotherly Love.
6. The Queen of the Adriatic.
7. The City of the Golden Gate.
8. The Hub.
9. The City of Lights.
10. The Motor City.

ANSWERS:
1. Rome, Italy. 2. New York City. 3. Chicago, Illinois. 4. New Haven, Connecticut. 5. Philadelphia, Pennsylvania. 6. Venice, Italy. 7. San Francisco, California. 8. Boston, Massachusetts. 9. Paris, France. 10. Detroit, Michigan.

Know Your Canada

● *Teen to adult*

This quiz tests players on their knowledge of Canada, the "Land of the Maple Leaf."

QUESTIONS:
1. Canada's most northerly point is:
   a. Tuktoyaktuk.
   b. Cape Columbia.
   c. Middle Island.
   d. Norman Wells.
2. You are in Winnipeg, heading for Regina. The trip facing you is about:
   a. 100 miles.
   b. 200.
   c. 400.
   d. 600.
3. Canada's highest mountain peak is Mount:
   a. Eisenhower.
   b. Logan.
   c. Robson.
   d. Kennedy.
4. All the provinces touch at some point on salt water, with the exception of:
   a. One province.
   b. Two.
   c. Three.
   d. Four.

5. If you were to visit Heart's Delight and Heart's Content, you would be in:
   a. Newfoundland.
   b. Nova Scotia.
   c. British Columbia.
   d. Northwest Territories.
6. Only one of the following is not a pass through the Rocky Mountains:
   a. Crow's Nest.
   b. Yellowhead.
   c. Kicking Horse.
   d. Seven Persons.
7. The longest river system in Canada is the:
   a. St. Lawrence.
   b. Restigouche.
   c. Columbia.
   d. Mackenzie.
8. All but one of the following cities is its province's capital:
   a. Saint John.
   b. Victoria.
   c. Toronto.
   d. Quebec City.
9. The only one of the five Great Lakes which does not touch Canada is:
   a. Superior.
   b. Erie.
   c. Michigan.
   d. Ontario.
   e. Huron.
10. After Newfoundland, the most easterly Canadian province is:
    a. Nova Scotia.
    b. Prince Edward Island.
    c. Quebec.
    d. New Brunswick.
11. After the Great Lakes, Canada's largest lake is:
    a. Winnipeg.
    b. Great Slave.
    c. St. John.
    d. Great Bear.
12. The line of latitude forming 1300 miles of U.S.–Canadian border is the:
    a. 38th parallel.
    b. 49th parallel.
    c. 54th parallel.
    d. 60th parallel.

ANSWERS:
1. b. Cape Columbia on Ellesmere Island, 83 degrees north. 2. c. A few miles under 400. 3. b. Mount Logan in the Yukon is the highest, at 19,850 feet. 4. b. Two—Alberta and Saskatchewan are landlocked. 5. a. Both are Newfoundland fishing towns. 6. d. Seven Persons is a town in Alberta. 7. d. The Mackenzie system is 2,635 miles long—by far the longest. 8. a. Fredericton is the capital of New Brunswick. 9. c. Lake Michigan is entirely within the United States. 10. c. The strip of Quebec which south of Labrador puts it east of Nova Scotia. 11. d. Great Bear Lake is the largest, at 12,275 square miles. 12. b. The 49th parallel.

Animal Champions

● *Teen to adult*

This is an interesting quiz for animal lovers.

QUESTIONS:
1. What is the largest animal living today?
2. What is the largest animal that ever lived?
3. What is the largest land animal living in North America?
4. What is the largest bird in the world?
5. What is the longest snake in the world?
6. What bird has the greatest wingspread?
7. What animal lives the longest?
8. What mammal lives the longest?
9. What four-footed animal can run the fastest of any animal?
10. What is the largest of all deer?
11. What animal—next to man—is the most intelligent?
12. What animal produces the world's finest fleece (wool)?
13. What wild animal is most helpful to man?

ANSWERS:
1. The sulphur-bottom whale—estimated at over 150 tons. 2. The sulphur-bottom whale. 3. The bison—over 2,200 pounds. 4. The ostrich—over 300 pounds. 5. The reticulated python—over 30 feet. 6. The wandering albatross—as much as 11'6". 7. The turtle—as long as 152 years. 8. Man—as long as 114 years. 9. The cheetah—over 70 m.p.h. 10. The moose—up to 1,400 pounds. 11. The chimpanzee. 12. The vicuña, whose hairs are only half as thick as those of the finest sheep's wool. 13. The earthworm, because it constantly turns over the soil, thus greatly increasing the fertility of the land.

Bible Quiz

● *Teen to adult*

Apart from its religious significance, the Bible is recognized as one of the great literary works of man's past. Questions concerning famous biblical figures or events are presented below.

QUESTIONS:
1. What man in the Bible lived the longest?
2. Who wrestled with an angel?
3. Who were the five girls who ran out of oil?
4. What man was afflicted with boils?
5. Who saw the "handwriting on the wall"?
6. Why did Joseph's brothers go to Egypt?
7. Where did Noah's Ark find safe landing?
8. Who killed a giant with a slingshot?
9. Who threw a javelin at David?
10. What did Jesus do for a living?
11. Who blamed his sin on a woman?
12. Who was the strongest man in the Bible?
13. Did Jesus write any portion of the Bible?
14. Why was the child Jesus taken to Egypt by Mary and Joseph?
15. Who tried to walk on the Sea of Galilee?
16. What is the last word in the Bible?
17. What is the shortest verse in the Bible?
18. What animal was killed when the Prodigal Son returned home?
19. What man was thrown into a lions' den?
20. Which four books of the Bible are known as the Gospels?

ANSWERS:
1. Methuselah. 2. Jacob. 3. The foolish virgins. 4. Job. 5. Nebuchadnezzar. 6. For food. 7. Mount Ararat. 8. David. 9. King Saul. 10. Carpentry. 11. Adam. 12. Samson. 13. No. 14. To prevent his being killed by King Herod. 15. Peter. 16. "Amen." 17. "Jesus wept." 18. The fatted calf. 19. Daniel. 20. Matthew, Mark, Luke and John.

Popular Word Games

There are many popular word games which, like quizzes, may be played as paper-and-pencil contests, or as oral contests between individuals or teams. In some, players are tested as to the meaning of certain words; in some, the task is to build new words by adding letters; in some, the game is very much like a crossword puzzle, and in some, a spelling competition is involved. A variety of such word games follows.

What Does It Mean?

● *Teen to adult*

Players choose some interesting-looking words from the dictionary and then try to define them. A starting selection of words follows.

QUESTIONS:

1. Yawl.	9. Didapper.
2. Samisen.	10. Peplum.
3. Bolo.	11. Droshky.
4. Sarcophagus.	12. Cerebellum.
5. Cognomen.	13. Landau.
6. Doubloon.	14. Sanguine.
7. Sampan.	15. Samovar.
8. Abacus.	16. Maize.

ANSWERS:

1. A type of sailboat. 2. A Japanese, stringed musical instrument. 3. A machete-like knife used in the Philippines. 4. A stone coffin. 5. A family name, or sometimes a nickname. 6. An old Spanish coin. 7. An Oriental boat. 8. Beads strung on wires, used for counting. 9. A small diving bird. 10. A shawl-like garment. 11. A four-wheeled Russian carriage. 12. A section of the brain. 13. An enclosed, wheeled carriage. 14. Ruddy-complexioned, or optimistic. 15. A Russian vessel used to heat water for tea. 16. Corn grown by American Indians.

Mystic Initials

● *Teen to adult*

Professional titles, frequently used business or social phrases and the names of well-known organizations of many kinds are usually referred to by abbreviations consisting of their initials. In this quiz, participants should try to give the meaning of the following sets of familiar initials, some from the past and some more recent.

QUESTIONS:

1. C.O.D.	9. G.A.R.
2. O.E.O.	10. LL.D.
3. A.S.P.C.A.	11. T.G.I.F.
4. R.O.T.C.	12. S.N.A.F.U.
5. R.S.V.P.	13. H.E.W.
6. W.C.T.U.	14. M.D.
7. A.F.L.–C.I.O.	15. G.O.P.
8. S.D.S.	16. F.O.B.

ANSWERS:

1. Cash (or collect) on delivery. 2. Office of Economic Opportunity. 3. American Society for the Prevention of Cruelty to Animals. 4. Reserve Officers' Training Corps. 5. *Répondez s'il vous plaît* (please reply). 6. Women's Christian Temperance Union. 7. American Federation of Labor–Congress of Industrial Organizations. 8. Students for a Democratic Society. 9. Grand Army of the Republic. 10. Doctor of Laws. 11. Thank God It's Friday. 12. Situation Normal, All Fouled Up. 13. Health, Education and Welfare. 14. Doctor of Medicine. 15. Grand Old Party. 16. Free on Board.

Hidden Words

● *Teen to adult*

There are many games which involve changing the order of letters in words, or adding new letters, so as to form new words. Below is a sample. In this game, the task is to rearrange the letters in each word to make a new word in the shortest possible time.

QUESTIONS:

1. Canter.	11. Not.
2. Opus.	12. Pot.
3. Spine.	13. Pat.
4. Pate.	14. Deal.
5. But.	15. Pace.
6. Lewd.	16. Brake.
7. Dame.	17. Route.
8. Reset.	18. Vote.
9. Dial.	19. Scale.
10. Race.	20. Tang.

ANSWERS:

1. Trance. 2. Soup. 3. Snipe. 4. Tape. 5. Tub. 6. Weld. 7. Made. 8. Steer. 9. Laid. 10. Care. 11. Ton. 12. Top. 13. Tap. 14. Lead. 15. Cape. 16. Break. 17. Outer. 18. Veto. 19. Laces. 20. Gnat.

Juggling Letters

● *Teen to adult*

Here the task is to take a pair of different words and turn them into synonyms (words with the same meaning), or near synonyms, by taking a single letter from either word and placing it somewhere within the other word, without re-arranging any other letters. To illustrate: if the two words given are *ripe* and *tar,* then by taking the *e* from *ripe* and putting it into *tar,* the words *rip* and *tear* are obtained.

QUESTIONS:
1. Died — Ante.
2. Whiled — Spurn.
3. Grove — Rout.
4. Curt — Cave.
5. Pest — Cares.
6. Lice — Reline.
7. Salve — Savage.
8. Shred — Ban.
9. Our — Start.
10. Flat — Pump.
11. Lopes — Shills.

ANSWERS:

1. Dined — Ate. 2. Whirled — Spun. 3. Groove — Rut. 4. Cut — Carve. 5. Pet — Caress. 6. Lie — Recline. 7. Save — Salvage. 8. Shed — Barn. 9. Sour — Tart. 10. Fat — Plump. 11. Slopes — Hills.

Kangaroo Words

● *Teen to adult*

Here the trick is to find a word which contains within it, kangaroo-like, another word of the same, or nearly the same, meaning. Try to find the hidden synonym in each of the following words.

QUESTIONS:

1. Evacuate.	11. Perambulate.
2. Encourage.	12. Pinioned.
3. Prosecute.	13. Joviality.
4. Calumnies.	14. Container.
5. Rapscallion.	15. Regulates.
6. Indolent.	16. Splotches.
7. Prattle.	17. Slithered.
8. Diversified.	18. Perimeter.
9. Rampage.	19. Curtail.
10. Matches.	20. Respite.

ANSWERS:

1. Vacate. 2. Urge. 3. Sue. 4. Lies. 5. Rascal. 6. Idle. 7. Prate. 8. Divers. 9. Rage. 10. Mates. 11. Ramble. 12. Pinned. 13. Joy. 14. Can. 15. Rules. 16. Spots. 17. Slid. 18. Rim. 19. Cut. 20. Rest.

Twist a Word

● *Teen to adult*

The following contest is fairly difficult. A good way to play it is with teams competing against each other—to give several players the chance to work together on each problem. Several groups of descriptive words or phrases are given. For each group there is a single word that, by regrouping the letters, can form different words—each one a substitute for the one of the original descriptive words. Here's an example:
a. Airplane maneuvers — Loops.
b. One-masted vessel — Sloop.
c. Small ponds of water — Pools.

d. A cylinder for thread — Spool.

All of the words on the right are made from the same letters. In finding substitutes for the words or phrases below, the same rule must be observed; for each group of descriptive words, all of the substitute words must contain the same letters.

QUESTIONS:
1. a. Peril; hazard.
   b. Vegetable plot.
   c. Male goose.
   d. Moved within limits.
2. a. A tufted ornament.
   b. Grows rancid.
   c. Purloins.
   d. Small blackboards.
3. a. An expression of sorrow.
   b. Fireplace ledge.
   c. A long cloak.
   d. Pertaining to the mind.
4. a. Took an oath.
   b. A planter.
   c. Those in debt.
   d. Ill (comparative).
5. a. Animal's den.
   b. Metal track.
   c. Prevaricator.
   d. Seed covering.
6. a. Vipers.
   b. Totals again.
   c. Fears greatly.
   d. More sorrowful.
7. a. Football tosser.
   b. Not dense; scattered.
   c. Long-shafted weapons.
   d. Bowling term (plural).
8. a. Kind of cheese.
   b. Woman (slang).
   c. A meadow.
   d. Manufactured.
9. a. More pliant.
   b. Wooded area.
   c. To bring up.
   d. Talent; strong point (plural).
10. a. Fail to keep.
    b. Part of a shoe.
    c. Kind of gin drink.
    d. Name for a lion (plural).

ANSWERS:
1. a. Danger; b. Garden; c. Gander; d. Ranged.
2. a. Tassel; b. Stales; c. Steals; d. Slates.
3. a. Lament; b. Mantel; c. Mantle; d. Mental.
4. a. Swore; b. Sower; c. Owers; d. Worse.
5. a. Lair; b. Rail; c. Liar; d. Aril.
6. a. Adders; b. Readds; c. Dreads; d. Sadder.
7. a. Passer; b. Sparse; c. Spears; d. Spares.
8. a. Edam; b. Dame; c. Mead; d. Made.
9. a. Softer; b. Forest; c. Foster; d. Fortes.
10. a. Lose; b. Sole; c. Sloe; d. Leos.

Reverse the Word

● *Teen to adult*

This game is rather like *Hidden Words,* on page 292. Each player is given a set of sentences from each of which two words have been omitted. The second word should be the first word spelled in reverse. The game may also be played using combinations of three words with the same letters. Examples of such "triplets" are: live, evil, veil; spare, spear, pares; leap, pale, peal. In the following sentences, what are the two missing words in each sentence?

QUESTIONS:
1. I jumped into the _____, _____ the water was ice cold.
2. If you _____ the golf ball too hard when you're putting, you'll never make _____.
3. When the weather _____, track _____ are usually called off.
4. The cheese known as _____ is _____ in Holland.
5. I was hunting _____, but tripped on a tall _____.
6. By the time the first _____ shines, _____ are usually swarming through the garbage.
7. When you're painting the house, if you just _____ it on, it'll look _____.
8. From a _____ on the mountain, you can see the _____ of the houses.

ANSWERS:
1. Tub; but. 2. Rap; par. 3. Teems; meets.
4. Edam; made. 5. Deer; reed. 6. Star; rats.
7. Dab; bad. 8. Spot; tops.

CHAPTER 13

Teasers and Tests

Among the oldest forms of entertainment are riddles, tests and plays on words. Some exist purely for fun; others are adaptations of serious tests meant to gauge knowledge. In any case, all are presented here in the spirit of pure fun. They can be used as party games or after-dinner entertainment. The chapter opens with a round of riddles, some of them so outrageous that when they are told, groans will be mixed with laughter.

A Round of Riddles

QUESTION: Which days are the strongest?
ANSWER: Saturday and Sunday, because the others are *week*days.

QUESTION: What is the best paper for making kites?
ANSWER: *Fly paper.*

QUESTION: Where are the coldest seats in a theater?
ANSWER: In *Z-row.*

QUESTION: Why is a sick man improved when he makes a five-cent wager?
ANSWER: Because it makes him a *little better.*

QUESTION: If you were on a raft with a pack of cigarettes, but had no matches, how would you light your cigarette?
ANSWER: Throw one cigarette overboard to make the raft *a cigarette lighter.*

QUESTION: When is soup certain to run out of the bowl?
ANSWER: When there is a *leek* in it.

QUESTION: Why was the little drop of apple cider so furious?

ANSWER: Because all its friends were in the *jug.*

QUESTION: Why are the Irish the richest people in the world?
ANSWER: Because their capital is always *Dublin.*

QUESTION: When is a doctor most annoyed?
ANSWER: When he runs out of *patients.*

QUESTION: What should you do when you split your sides laughing?
ANSWER: Run till you get a *stitch* in them.

QUESTION: Why isn't a person's nose twelve inches long?
ANSWER: Because then it would be *a foot.*

QUESTION: What is it that is put on the table, cut and passed, but never eaten?
ANSWER: *A deck of cards.*

QUESTION: What has a foot on each end and one in the middle?
ANSWER: *A yardstick.*

QUESTION: Why is a dirty boy like flannel?
ANSWER: Because he *shrinks from washing.*

QUESTION: What has 18 legs and catches flies?
ANSWER: *A baseball team.*

QUESTION: Why is a room full of married persons like an empty room?

ANSWER: Because there is not a *single* person in the room.

QUESTION: Why is the center of a tree like a dog's tail?
ANSWER: Because it is farthest from the *bark*.

QUESTION: Why is a lollypop like a race horse?
ANSWER: Because the harder you *lick* it, the faster it *goes*.

QUESTION: What's the difference between a jeweler and a jailer?
ANSWER: A jeweler *sells watches,* and a jailer *watches cells.*

QUESTION: Would you rather an elephant attacked you or a gorilla?
ANSWER: I'd rather he attacked the *gorilla.*

QUESTION: Three large women were walking under a small umbrella, but none of them got wet. Why not?
ANSWER: Because it *wasn't raining.*

QUESTION: What is the surest way to keep water from coming into your house?
ANSWER: *Don't pay the water bill.*

QUESTION: When will water stop running downhill?
ANSWER: *When it gets to the bottom.*

QUESTION: What has eight legs and sings?
ANSWER: *A quartet.*

QUESTION: Why do white sheep eat so much more than black ones?
ANSWER: *Because there are so many more of them.*

QUESTION: What was the highest mountain before Mt. Everest was discovered?
ANSWER: *Mt. Everest.*

QUESTION: What does a hippopotamus have that no other animal has?
ANSWER: *Baby hippopotamuses.*

QUESTION: Is it all right to write a letter on an empty stomach?
ANSWER: Yes, but it's better to write it on *paper.*

QUESTION: If two is company and three is a crowd, what are four and five?
ANSWER: *Nine.*

QUESTION: Why is the letter A like noon?
ANSWER: Because it is in the middle of *day.*

QUESTION: Why is the letter D like a bad boy?
ANSWER: Because it makes *ma mad.*

QUESTION: What word can be pronounced quicker by adding a syllable to it?
ANSWER: The word *quick.*

QUESTION: What is the longest word in the English language?
ANSWER: The word *smiles,* because it has a *mile* between the first and last letters.

QUESTION: Who was the fastest runner in all of history?
ANSWER: Adam, because he was first in the *human race.*

QUESTION: At what time of day was Adam born?
ANSWER: A little before *Eve.*

QUESTION: Who was the greatest actor anywhere in the Bible?
ANSWER: Samson; he *brought down the house.*

QUESTION: What goes from New York to Chicago without moving?
ANSWER: *A highway.*

QUESTION: Why are fish so smart?
ANSWER: Because they are always found in *schools.*

Braintwisters

The following problems and puzzles provide a real challenge to a person's powers of creative thinking. In addition to testing brainpower, they're fun to do—either alone, or as a contest with others.

PROBLEM: A painter required three days to paint a room. How long would it take him, working at the same rate, to paint a room twice as long, twice as wide and twice as high?
ANSWER: Twelve days, because the walls would be four times as big.

PROBLEM: Express the number 100 by using the same figure six times.
ANSWER: $99 + 99/99$.

PROBLEM: When tomorrow is yesterday, today will be as near to Sunday as today was when yesterday was tomorrow. What day is it?
ANSWER: Sunday. A clue—Tuesday and Friday are each two days away from Sunday.

PROBLEM: From these letters, a single English word can be made. What is it? PNLLEEEESSSS.
ANSWER: Sleeplessness.

PROBLEM: Two motorcycle policemen paused behind a large billboard and lay in wait for speeding violators. One officer looked up the road, the other looked down it, so as to cover all territory. "Pat," said one without turning his head, "what are you smiling at?" How could he tell that Pat was smiling?
ANSWER: They were facing each other.

PROBLEM: If on February 28, you go to sleep at seven o'clock at night and you have set your alarm clock to awaken you at eight the next morning, assuming that you sleep soundly all the time, how many hours sleep will you get?
ANSWER: One hour. The alarm would have gone off at eight o'clock that night.

PROBLEM: Here is the beginning and ending of an everyday word. Can you fill in the middle five letters: U N D - - - - - U N D?
ANSWER: Underground.

PROBLEM: What is absolutely the closest relation that your mother's brother's brother-in-law could be to you?
ANSWER: Father.

PROBLEM: How is it possible for Jim to stand behind George and George to stand behind Jim—at the same time?
ANSWER: If they stand back-to-back.

PROBLEM: How can five people divide a sack of five apples equally, without cutting them up, and still have one apple remain in the sack?
ANSWER: Give the fifth person the sack with the apple still inside.

PROBLEM: You go into your kitchen and find that the sink is overflowing and water is rapidly covering the floor. A mop, a bucket, a dustpan and a covered floor drain were all within easy reach. What would you do first to prevent as much damage as possible?
ANSWER: Turn off the water.

PROBLEM: If a man-and-a-half can eat a pie-and-a-half in a minute-and-a-half, how many men would it take to eat 60 pies in 30 minutes?
ANSWER: If one-and-one-half men can eat one-and-one-half pies in one-and-one-half minutes, twice as many men can eat twice as many pies in the same time. If three men can eat three pies in one-and-one-half minutes, then one man can eat one pie in one-and-one-half minutes. So in 30 minutes one man can eat 30 divided-by-one-and-one-half, or 20 pies, and three men would be needed to eat 60 pies in 30 minutes.

Four-Minute Challenges

Here are some tricky challenges, using objects, to play around the family dinner table or at a party. The reader should try to figure them out first and then try them on his family and friends.

CHALLENGE: A dollar bill is placed flat on a table. An empty pop bottle is turned upside down so that its mouth rests on the center of the bill. Without tipping over the bottle and allowing nothing to touch the bottle other than the bill or the table, the dollar bill is removed from beneath the bottle.
SOLUTION: Using the thumb and index finger of each hand, the dollar bill is carefully rolled-up from one end, permitting the roll to push the bottle slowly off the bill, without tipping the bottle over.

CHALLENGE: Four rectangular cards of identical size are placed in a T-formation. A square is formed by moving only one card.
SOLUTION: The top card is moved upward until the opened space forms a square.

CHALLENGE: Three glasses are set on a table in a row. The glass on the left is rightside up; it is glass number one. The glass on the right is also rightside up; it is glass number three. The center glass is upside down; it is glass number two. Three moves are made. On each move, two glasses are picked up and turned over, but the same two glasses may not be turned in consecutive moves. After the three moves, all of the glasses are upside down. How is the trick performed?

SOLUTION: First move: glasses two and three are turned. Second move: glasses one and three are now turned. Third move: glasses two and three are once more turned, and all of the glasses are now upside down.

CHALLENGE: Here's how we'll settle who tips the waiter," says the challenger to his friend at lunch. He tears one paper match out of a matchfolder. "I'll toss it. If it lands on either side, I'll pay. If it stands on edge, you pay." Should the friend accept the bet?

SOLUTION: No. Just before tossing, the challenger will bend the match between thumb and forefinger so that it will land on its edge.

So You Think You're Clever

Here is a collection of word problems that test alertness and powers of logical thinking. Most are plays on words.

PROBLEM: I have two current coins in my hand. Together they total 55 cents. One is not a nickel. What are the coins?

ANSWER: A 50-cent piece and a nickel. The other is a nickel.

PROBLEM: A little Indian and a big Indian are walking down a path. The little Indian is the big Indian's son. The big Indian is not the little Indian's father. Who is the big Indian?

ANSWER: Mother.

PROBLEM: Which is correct: eight and eight are 15, or eight and eight is 15?

ANSWER: Neither, eight and eight are still 16.

PROBLEM: Is it legal for a man to marry his widow's sister?

ANSWER: Only dead men have widows.

PROBLEM: A monkey is at the bottom of a 30-foot well. Each day he jumps up three feet and slips back two. At that rate, when will the monkey reach the top of the well?

ANSWER: On the 28th day. At the end of the 27th day he had ascended 27 feet. On the 28th day, he reaches the top.

PROBLEM: There are ten black stockings and ten white stockings in a drawer. If you reach into the drawer in the dark, how many stockings must you take out before you are sure of having a pair that match?

ANSWER: Three: You might have a pair after taking out two, but the third one must match either the black or the white stocking you have already removed.

PROBLEM: Take two apples from three apples and what have you got?

ANSWER: Two apples, of course.

PROBLEM: The number of eggs in a basket doubles every minute. The basket is full of eggs in an hour. When was the basket half full?

ANSWER: In 59 minutes. If the basket is full in 60 minutes, it was half full a minute earlier, or at the end of 59 minutes.

PROBLEM: A shepherd has 17 sheep. All but nine died. How many did he have left?

ANSWER: Nine.

PROBLEM: A customer hands a cigar clerk a five-dollar bill for two dollars' worth of cigars. The cigar clerk has no change, but gets some next door from a drug clerk, who gives him five one-dollar bills for the five-dollar bill. The customer leaves with the cigars and three dollars in change. An hour later the drug clerk rushes in, saying the five-dollar bill was counterfeit. The cigar clerk gives him a good five-dollar bill. How much did the cigar clerk lose in all—in money and cigars?

ANSWER: Five dollars—two in merchandise and three in cash.

PROBLEM: What is the smallest number of ducks that could swim in this formation: two ducks in front of a duck, two ducks behind a duck and a duck between two ducks?

ANSWER: Three ducks in a straight line, one after the other.

PROBLEM: A boat will carry only 200 pounds. How may a man weighing 200 pounds and his two sons, each of whom weighs 100 pounds, use it to cross a river?

ANSWER: The two sons go first. One brings back the boat and the father rows over. Then the other son returns for his brother.

PROBLEM: The archaeologist who said he found a silver coin marked 649 B.C. was either lying or kidding. Why?

ANSWER: How did anyone know Christ was to be born in 649 years?

PROBLEM: Two trains, 100 miles apart, approach each other on the same track, the first at the rate of 60 miles an hour, the other at the rate of 40. A bee is going 25 miles an hour. What distance does it cover by the time the trains meet, if it started at the same time as the trains?

ANSWER: Twenty-five miles. The trains met in an hour, thus giving the bee one hour of flying time.

PROBLEM: Which would you prefer, a truckload of nickels, or half a truckload of dimes?

ANSWER: Since the dimes are smaller, and worth twice as much, you would be smart to take the half truckload.

PROBLEM: In which book of the Bible does it tell about Abel's slaying Cain?

ANSWER: None. Cain slew Abel.

Emergency Brain Teasers

The following group of brain teasers reconstruct some actual emergencies that required ingenious thinking and quick action. The problem section can be read to friends or family members to see how their solutions compare with the ones given here.

EMERGENCY: Mary was riding a frisky pony, and the bridle worked loose. The animal shook it off and started to gallop down the road, paying no attention to Mary's commands to stop. Mary stuck on and hoped for the best until a car loomed up ahead of her. Then she had to stop the pony. How did she do it?

SOLUTION: Mary simply clapped her hands tightly over the animal's eyes. The pony, unable to see where it was going, came to a quick stop.

EMERGENCY: One evening, as Tom was walking home from work, an insect flew into his ear. It started to crawl and buzz, sounding as if a jet plane was flying in his head. Tom tried to lift the insect out with his pinky finger, but the bug was too far in to be reached. He tried to shake it out, but that didn't work. Finally, Tom got a bright idea.

SOLUTION: As soon as he got home, Tom placed a flashlight close to his ear. The insect, attracted by the glow, immediately flew out.

EMERGENCY: While Jim was canoeing on a lake, a thunderstorm suddenly came up and overturned his boat. Jim swam to a rocky island, about a mile from his family's cottage, and there he found a small, abandoned shack. Inside were an old kerosene lamp and a few matches. All the wood on the island was too wet to burn, so the lamp was his only means of signaling for help. Unfortunately, the lamp held only about an inch of kerosene—not enough to reach its short wick. How did Jim get the lamp burning so he could summon help?

SOLUTION: Knowing that kerosene and water would not mix, Jim dipped the lamp in the lake and filled it with enough water so that the kerosene rose to the top, to cover the wick. The lamp was still burning an hour later when a motorboat reached him.

EMERGENCY: Ted became lost while driving in the country. Finally he saw a house, parked his car under a large tree nearby and started toward the house to make a phone call. Right after he got out of his car, a huge dog lunged at him from the opposite side of the tree. Fortunately the dog was chained, and Ted managed to get out of its reach. Finding no one at home at the house, Ted returned to his car. As he approached his car, the dog lunged again. The chain was so long that the snarling animal could cover both car doors. How did Ted escape the dog and get into his car?

SOLUTION: Ted moved slowly around the tree, keeping just out of the dog's reach. The vicious animal followed, winding its chain around the tree until it was too short to reach Ted's car.

A Different Kind of Test

Here's a set of tests that measure knowledge of human nature, familiarity with healthy living habits and basic facts about the environment in which we live. The reader should try them first himself and then on his family and friends. The correct answers follow each set of questions.

Are You a Good Judge of Character?

In sizing up people, we all fall back now and then on certain outward signs of inner character. You can check up on the accuracy of your character readings by marking each of the following common beliefs *true* or *false*.

QUESTIONS:
1. Long, slender hands mean the person has an artistic temperament.
2. Redheaded people are more temperamental than other people.
3. A slow learner remembers what he has learned better than a fast learner.
4. A person who does not look you in the eye is likely to be dishonest.
5. A receding chin denotes lack of will power.
6. Blondes are apt to be less trustworthy than are brunettes.
7. Fat people are usually good natured.
8. Ears pointed at the top warn of foxiness, selfishness or even dishonesty.
9. Wrinkles at the outer corners of the eyes show that a person has a sense of humor.
10. Curly hair is a symptom of great exuberance and vitality.
11. A high, bulging forehead is a sign of superior brainpower.
12. Cold hands are the sign of an affectionate disposition.

ANSWERS: Psychologists who use these questions to test candidates for personnel jobs say a score of seven correct answers means you're probably a pretty good judge of character. A score of six is passing. A score below five indicates you're substituting incorrect stereotypes for direct observation. And what are the correct answers? According to scientists who have checked these beliefs against actual fact, all are *false*.

What Do You Know About Eating?

We all have worried about certain food puzzlers at one time or another. Here's what some of the experts have learned about eating. Check your knowledge against theirs by answering *true* or *false*.

QUESTIONS:
1. Breakfast is your most important meal.
2. Hot meals warm you.
3. You should eat less in hot weather.
4. Some foods are sex stimulants.
5. We'd be better off if we ate five times daily.
6. The more you eat the more you want.
7. Exercising is a more efficient way to reduce than dieting.
8. Your disposition is worst just before meals.
9. It's almost impossible to overstuff a boy.
10. Food is a good cure for fatigue.
11. If most fat people ate what they say they eat, they'd be thin.
12. Bedtime snacks cause restless sleep.

ANSWERS:
1. *True.* Poor breakfasts are likely to mar health, efficiency and marital bliss. Surveys show that breakfast-skippers (or skimpers) are more subject to deficiency diseases, make more mistakes at work and make poorer grades as students. Sociologists blame many family fights, and even divorces, on poor or insufficient breakfasts.

2. *False.* Calories are what add body heat. On a zero day, the calories in ice cream will warm you as much as hot soup.

3. *False.* It's good practice to cut down on indigestibles. However, if you exercise a lot in summer and sit by the fireside all winter, you'll actually need more food in the hot months.

4. *False.* Just about every food from pork chops to peppers has been considered aphrodisiac. Actually, the only connection between food and sex is that a well-balanced diet stimulates the body in every function. Malnutrition dulls every interest—mental and physical.

5. *True.* Two extra snacks (not large meals) half-way between main meals—the routine of many school children, office workers and the British—provide quick-energy pickups, increase efficiency and make us less greedy at main meals.

6. *True.* When you overeat one day, you're hungrier the next. Huge meals stretch your stomach and throw your appetite out of proportion. Conversely, the less you eat the less you want—within limits, of course. After you become used to smaller intake you may wonder how you could have eaten so much previously.

7. *False.* You'd have to climb 20 flights of stairs to lose the calories in one slice of bread, or saw wood for 55 minutes to counteract one chocolate ice cream soda. Moreover, such strenuous exercise would only make you hungrier.

8. *True.* Studies show tempers reach their peak just before breakfast, lunch and dinner. That's one reason not to ask a favor until after a meal—as every salesman knows well.

9. *True.* A survey of 13- to 17-year-olds at St. Paul's School in Concord, N.H., showed they made good use of as many as 5000 calories a day—three times their basal energy requirements. So don't worry if a teen-ager seems to overstuff—provided it's not all sweets. .

10. *False.* Fatigue gives you an abnormal appetite. But never eat heavily when you're overtired. Instead of the quick pickup you're after, the meal is likely to lie undigested and may cause gastric complications.

11. *True.* Fat people who claim they eat "like birds" aren't deceitful; either they eat little compared with what they'd like to eat or they fool themselves. In recent clinical tests, a number of overweight people were put on a diet of what they said they ate. They proceeded to shed five pounds a day.

12. *False.* A light snack—a cup of soup or a glass of milk—before bedtime makes for a good rest. It draws blood into the digestive organs and away from the brain. Only if you overeat or choose heavy greasy foods are you in for trouble.

What Do You Know About Your Figure?

It is remarkable how little we know about our figures. Many of our ideas about the way we look, grow, gain weight, stand, walk or behave are not true. But science knows the right answers. Here's a chance to check your own.

QUESTIONS:

1. Fashion models have typical figures.
2. We stop growing at 21.
3. Our ancestors, the cave men, were bigger than we are.
4. A man can tell what his sweetheart's future figure will be by looking at her mother.
5. Thin people live longer than fat people.
6. Your type of figure has little relation to your general health.
7. The height, weight and age charts on public weighing machines are an accurate gauge as to what you should weigh.
8. A fine carriage is more important than an excellent figure.
9. Carrying a weight on the head develops a fine carriage.
10. Good posture consists of pushing the chest forward, and pulling the chin in and the shoulders back.
11. Childbearing ruins a woman's figure.

ANSWERS:

1. *False.* Most professional models are tall and slender. But a survey, based on the measurements of 10,240 women, revealed that the average woman on this continent is five inches shorter and more than 20 pounds heavier than typical fashion models.

2. *False.* We may grow even after the age of 25, attaining our maximum height at 35 or 40. After that we shrink about a quarter of an inch every ten years, owing in part to the drying up of the cartilages in the joints and spinal column.

3. *False.* Man's average height has increased nearly two inches since the Stone Age. Environment has a great influence on the size of the body. Where living conditions are comparatively easy and food plentiful, both men and women grow taller.

4. *Usually True.* Most children inherit the body types of their parents. There are exceptions, of course, but if your mother-in-law is youthful, slender and graceful, you may expect your wife to look just as charming when your 25th wedding anniversary rolls around.

5. *True.* Insurance companies hesitate to grant standard insurance to people who are more than moderately overweight. Your normal weight at the age of 25 should be your weight for the rest of your life.

6. *False.* The stout, stockily built person is more susceptible than a thin person to diseases of the heart and kidneys, high blood pressure and diabetes. The long, thin type is more susceptible to tuberculosis, digestive disturbances, constipation and chronic infections.

7. *False.* No tables of this kind are absolutely dependable; the human mechanism is far too complex. Many factors must be taken into consideration, such as your body type, bone and muscle structure and individual characteristics.

8. *True.* Even a poor figure looks well if carried with a buoyant air. The right use of the body actually changes its contours. Dowager's hump—that roll of fat at the base of the neck—a spare tire around the middle and a prominent "derrière" tend to disappear when the body is held easily erect and the muscles do their respective jobs properly.

9. *True.* Foreign women who carry baskets and jars on their heads usually have a beautiful straight body line. Perfect balance and coordination are needed to keep the burden from falling off.

10. *False.* Such a position is abnormal and creates strain. It may also make you sway-backed.

The correct position is to raise the chest, free the head, relax the shoulders and curl the hip section up under the upper body—without tension. Many people slouch under the misapprehension that it is restful. However, poor posture is actually a common cause of fatigue, since all the muscles involved are used incorrectly.

11. *False.* If adequate rest and suitable exercise are taken after having a baby, the figure will not be affected. Many movie actresses have had children and look as young and slim as ever. About one-third of all professional models are mothers, and photographers claim they are even lovelier than they were before.

What's Your Eye-Q?

Almost everyone is born with normal vision, yet many of us in time come to have serious eye defects. Many of these deficiencies could have been prevented. Care of the eyes begins at home, so test your knowledge about your eyes on the following statements.

QUESTIONS:

1. About the worst reading habit is using insufficient light.

2. If you have 20/20 vision, your eyes are considered perfect.

3. Cross-eyes in children will straighten themselves and become normal in time.

4. An oculist can sometimes trace eye trouble to the teeth.

5. You can have eye trouble without having anything permanently wrong with your eyes.

6. More men than women are color-blind.

7. The best way to get a cinder out of your eye is to blow your nose.

8. One quarter of your bodily energy is used in seeing.

ANSWERS:

1. *False.* Glare causes much greater eye fatigue and strain than insufficient light. It comes from shiny walls, glazed paper or a light shining directly into the eyes.

2. *False.* If you see at 20 feet what oculists think you should, your vision is 20/20, or "normal." You may actually be farsighted, and the muscles

of accommodation shape the eye lens so that you see "normally." But the result is a strain on the eyes.

3. *False.* This is a delusion of parents that leads to neglect. Cross-eyes should be treated as soon as discovered. Treatments include operations, wearing proper glasses and training weak eye muscles by means of eye exercises.

4. *True.* Eyes are sometimes disturbed by infection traceable to the teeth. Even blindness can result from badly infected teeth.

5. *True.* You may have difficulty seeing, your eyes may tire easily and feel strained, because of a general systemic disease or because of general fatigue or nervousness. Malnutrition also causes eye troubles.

6. *True.* The most common kind of color-blindness is hereditary. About one man in 25 has it; one woman in 250.

7. *False.* However, the theory behind the nose-blowing is good—that it will produce tears to wash out the cinder. Actually, the best thing is to close your eye and keep it shut for ten seconds. The flow of tears which follows will usually wash out the cinder.

8. *True.* According to the Mayo Clinic. This explains why the condition of your eyes can affect your general health.

Science or Superstition?

A great many people believe all the following statements—but they aren't all *true*. In fact, if you can pick those which are *true* and those which are *false* with not more than four mistakes, you know Mother Nature pretty well.

QUESTIONS:
1. Frogs drink through their skins.
2. Warts are caused by handling toads.
3. The 17-year cicada comes out of the ground only every 17 years.
4. Ants sometimes smell with their feet.
5. Moles are blind.
6. Eagles have been known to carry off babies.
7. The bite of a tarantula is fatal to man.
8. The growth of garden vegetables is affected by the moon.
9. The American cuckoo lays its eggs in the nests of other birds.
10. The dodo is a mythological bird.

ANSWERS:
1. *True.* Frogs absorb water through the skin; they can even "drink" from a piece of wet blotting paper.
2. *False.* Toads when in pain can exude a poison, irritating, for instance, to a dog's mouth, but not strong enough to affect the skin of the hand. True warts are caused, doctors now think, by filterable viruses.
3. *True.* The 17-year cicada (incorrectly called "locust") actually does spend 17 years (13 in some of the southern states) underground as a grub or larva, and about six weeks above ground as a winged adult. When the insects appear more often in any particular region, it is because there are different broods, maturing in different years.
4. *True.* Entomologists believe ants are able to follow the odor of a trail with their feet, and that they are also able to perceive odors with various joints of their antennae. However, absolute proof is lacking.
5. *False.* They can perceive the difference between light and darkness. It is doubtful if they can distinguish objects. Their eyes are small, weak and almost hidden by fur.
6. *False.* The Audubon Societies have checked many reports of this and found them false.
7. *False.* All spider bites contain some poison, but the only spider bites sometimes fatal are those of the black widow. The tarantula (or, to be scientifically exact, the bird-spider) seldom bites under any circumstances.
8. *False.* The reflected light of the moon cannot be utilized by plants for manufacturing food as the sunlight can, simply because it is too feeble. The phases of the moon have no effect upon either crops or weather.
9. *False.* The European cuckoo does so; the yellow-billed and black-billed cuckoos on this continent do not. The American bird that has this parasitic habit is the cow-bird.
10. *False.* The dodo was a huge, flightless relative of the pigeon. It inhabited certain islands of the Indian Ocean and became extinct in the 18th century.

Outdoor Fun

SECTION III

For Families

CHAPTER 14

Games for Trips and Outings

Whether the occasion is a camping trip, a seaside vacation, a weekend in ski country or just a few hours in a rural setting, the games in this chapter—from swimming relays to ice-skating contests to nature-appreciation pastimes played along the trail—add an extra dimension of enjoyment to a family outing. Although outings are great fun for all family members, long car rides to and from a vacation site are often frustrating experiences—particularly for the youngsters. Games played while traveling can bring fun and entertainment to an otherwise boring automobile trip. Thus, this chapter opens with a number of pastimes suitable for children—and often for adults as well—to play in the car. Many of these travel-time activities help sharpen a child's powers of observation as he competes to note license-plate numbers, road signs and landmarks—such as church steeples and smokestacks—along the highway.

License-Plate Spelling

● *Paper; crayons*

Each player chooses a three- or four-letter word and writes it on a slip of paper. Then, by taking letters from the license plates of oncoming or passing cars, he tries to spell out this word again. As a player sees a letter that is in his word, he crosses it out. The first player to cross out the entire word wins the game.

VARIATIONS: In *License Plate Alphabet,* players print the entire alphabet, one letter at a time, on a piece of paper. Taking turns, looking at oncoming and passing cars, they cross out the letters observed on the license plates. Since it is unlikely that any player will see every letter, from "a" to "z," the winner may be the player who crosses out the most letters in ten minutes. In *Number Race,* each player writes the numbers from zero to nine on a sheet of paper. Players take turns looking at license plates, and they cross out numbers as they are seen. The first contestant to cross out all ten digits wins the contest. In *Odd and Even Numbers,* two players compete by spotting the last number on on-coming license plates. One player gets a point for each odd last number he sees, and the other player gets a point for each even last number. The first player to reach a total of 30 is the winner.

How to Get There

● *A map including several states*

Each player selects a "destination"—a state far away from where the car is currently. Each player's destination-state is different from those of the other players. Looking at the license plates of oncoming or passing cars, they try to find all the states they might pass through to reach their particular destination. They may take any sort of winding, out-of-the-way route—provided that it actually carries them, in order, from state to state, as if they were really driving. The first player to reach his destination is the winner. This game works best on major highways where license plates of many states appear. Disputes are settled by referring to the map.

Paired Numbers

● *Paper; crayons*

There are two players: one has the numbers 0, 1, 2, 3, and 4, and the other has 5, 6, 7, 8, and 9. They take turns looking at license plates of oncoming or passing cars. Each player gets a point whenever he spots one of his numbers paired—such as 33, or 55. The first player to get five or ten points wins the game.

License Bingo

● *Paper; crayons*

Two or three contestants each make up a Bingo chart with nine boxes. Each box has two-digit numbers. The numbers ascend in value from left to right and descend in value from top to bottom. Another passenger observes the license plates of oncoming cars and calls out the first two digits of each license plate. When a player hears his number called, he crosses it out. The first player to cross out three numbers in a row—vertically, horizontally, or diagonally—is the winner.

How Far Away?

● *Paper; crayons*

In this game, the driver points out some distinctive landmark that may be seen at a considerable distance, such as the highest building in a distant town, an outcropping of land, the bend in a river or a mountain peak. Each player makes

a guess as to how many miles it is to this spot. The guesses are written down, and the distance is then clocked on the speedometer. The player whose guess is the closest to the actual distance is the winner. This game is most successful when the air is clear, so that landmarks that are fifteen or twenty miles away can be seen.

VARIATION: In *How Far Have We Gone?* the driver gives the players the signal to start estimating the distance being traveled. He makes a record of the actual mileage on the odometer. The players are not allowed to look at the odometer. After a fairly long time has elapsed, the driver consults the odometer to calculate exactly how far the car has traveled. He then asks the other players how far the car has gone and they each make an estimate: "Seven miles!" "Ten miles!" "Five miles!" The player with the closest guess wins the contest.

Three Trips

● *Paper; crayons; several copies of the same map*

Each player is given a copy of the same state or regional map. He is given three trips to take, each one with a pair of cities as a starting and ending point. He must calculate the distance covered for each trip, add the distances together and come up with a total for the three trips. Then the mileage charts are consulted and the correct figures added together for the total. The player with the closest total is the winner. This is a good exercise in arithmetic for older children.

Name the Car

This game may be played in two ways. Players may take turns trying to identify the make of an oncoming car, winning one point for each correct identification. Instead of taking turns, the game may be played with the first person to call out a guess winning one point if he is right—or losing one point if he is wrong. One person does not take part in the game but acts as judge to settle disputes.

Roadside Scavenger Hunt

● *Paper; pencils*

An adult makes up a list of all the different kinds of objects and people that are likely to be seen along a country road. Typical items might include:

a horse	a haystack
a cow	an apple tree
a barn	a tractor
a bicycle	a pond
a split rail fence	a house trailer
a river	a train
a field of corn	a cemetery

Each player is given one copy of the list and a pencil. Whenever a player spots one of the items on the list, he calls out its name and checks it off. The first player to see an object and call it out gets credit for it. The winner is the player who crosses off the most items in half an hour.

Highway Alphabet

The purpose of the game is to go through the alphabet by finding the letters on signs and billboards along the side of the road. There are two players: one takes the right side of the highway, and the other the left. They must spell out the alphabet in order, taking only one letter from each sign. The first player to go through the alphabet completely is the winner.

How Many Ways?

● *Paper; crayons; several copies of the same map*

Each player is given the same state or regional map. They are then given the names of two cities which are located fairly far apart on the map. Using crayons, players try to trace as many different routes as possible that connect the two cities—without duplicating a road in any of the routes.

Guess the Population

● *A road map*

When driving through a city or town, each person in the car tries to guess how many people live in the community. After everyone has guessed, the road map, which usually has population totals, is checked for the correct answer. The player whose guess was closest to the actual population wins the contest.

Find Seven Cities

● *Paper; crayons; several copies of the same map*

An adult makes up a list of seven cities and towns—all of which may be located on the map—and gives a copy to each player. Players try to find all seven of the communities on their respective maps. The first player to correctly locate and circle all seven wins the contest.

Sing-a-Song

Group singing is one of the best ways to relieve the boredom of long automobile trips. It is one activity in which the driver can join, and even children as young as two years old will enjoy participating. There are, of course, no winners or losers, but each person in the car should be given a chance to pick a song. It is generally a good idea if songs that are familiar to all passengers are picked: "I've Been Working on the Railroad" and "Row, Row, Row Your Boat" are good examples. From time to time, however, children and adults should be permitted to teach one another songs. Youngsters are generally quite fond of learning songs that were popular in the days when their parents and grandparents were young. Tunes from World War I and World War II usually make a hit. These might include such old favorites as "Smile, Smile, Smile," "Tipperary," "Praise the Lord and Pass the Ammunition" and "Over There."

Games for the Wilderness

With both camping in national parks and forests, and day-long forays into the countryside becoming favorite leisure-time activities for hundreds of thousands of families, there is now a new awakening to the great bounty of nature. To help make the natural world come alive for youngsters and adults alike, there are a number of games that make use of wilderness settings to test a family's knowledge of wild plants, animals and birds. These games, by imparting information and strengthening powers of observation, help create a deeper appreciation of the nation's natural heritage.

Memory Hike

● *Paper; pencils*

This game is played after a hike in the woods or a trip to the zoo, aquarium or botanical garden. During the outing, players are told to observe everything very carefully so that they can make a list of all they have seen. Just after the outing ends, perhaps back at the camping site or in the car, the leader hands out the paper and pencils and the players begin their lists. The player with the greatest number of correct observations wins. Large groups may be divided into teams, the members of each conferring on their lists.

VARIATION: *Hear, Smell, See* is played during a break in a hike. Each player is given pencil and paper and is asked to write down all the different sounds, smells and sights he observes. As time goes by, players become acutely aware of a tremendous number of things happening; things that are usually unnoticed and taken for granted such as the rustling of leaves in the wind, the reflection of the sun in a stream, insects crawling through the grass. After 15 minutes, the lists are read; each player gets a point for items noticed by others, two points for a unique observation.

Roadside Cribbage

As a hike begins each player picks up ten small stones or pebbles which he carries in one fist.

During the hike, the game leader points out some natural object—a kind of leaf, fern or flower—without identifying it. He calls on one hiker to name the item. If the identification is correct, that player can drop one of his pebbles. If not, the next hiker gets a chance to name the object. The game continues in this manner until one of the hikers has dropped all his pebbles.

Nature Trailing

The game leader clearly marks off an area no more than 200 yards in any direction from the camp site, beyond which the players may not go. One player then sets off by himself. As he walks he scuffs up fallen leaves, scrapes away moss on rocks, bends twigs and impresses his footprints in wet or sandy spots—in order to leave a trail that the others may follow. After ten minutes, the other players set out to find the trail blazer. They try to follow his trail, either individually or in groups. Meanwhile, the trail blazer finds a place to hide—in thick brush or in the branches of a tree. The first player to spot him is the winner.

Who Am I?

One person prepares a list of descriptive statements about familiar animals or birds. He reads these statements, one at a time, while the others try to guess the creature he is describing. The group is allowed only one guess per creature, so the players do not guess until they are fairly sure of its identity.

The descriptive statements are rather general at first but become more obvious after a while. Here are some examples:

1. I am a familiar fur-bearing animal.
2. I am larger than a squirrel and smaller than a cow.
3. I usually live in mixed woods and fields, and my home is in holes in the ground.
4. I have a very large bushy tail.
5. I eat many things, but live mainly on insects and rodents.
6. I have a gentle nature, usually move slowly, and am easily tamed. Some people make a pet of me. But first they send me to a veterinarian for an operation.
7. My color is black, with white stripes.
8. Although I am not dangerous, I am very unpopular with people because of my unusual method of defense.
   I am the common skunk.

1. I am a reptile. I keep my body encased in a kind of armor.
2. I pump air into my body by stretching and drawing back my neck and legs.
3. I usually live in the water, leaving it only to make a nest and lay eggs.
4. I may become as heavy as forty pounds.
5. I have a very long tail, with an alligator-like ridge along my back.
6. I have a large, powerful head and jaws.
7. I eat fish and wildfowl.
8. When I am full-grown, I can cut off your hand with a snap of my jaws.
   I am the snapping turtle.

Any general nature book or encyclopedia provides excellent source material for quizzes of this kind.

Find the Tree

Children divide into two equal teams; each team chooses the name of a tree found close by. (One group might pick oaks, for example, and the other beeches.) The teams line up opposite each other, a few yards apart. A parent or game leader calls out the name of one of the trees selected. If he calls out "Oaks!" the oak team members must run to oak trees for safety, with the beech team members trying to tag them. Whenever a member of the oaks is tagged before reaching a tree, the beech team gets a point. The game is repeated several times, with each team getting an equal number of tries at chasing. After ten minutes, the team with more points is declared the winner.

VARIATIONS: In *Safety Tree* there is one chaser. All the rest of the players are runners. Any trees of a particular type—oaks, beeches, maples, etc.—may be designated safety zones, and a player may temporarily avoid being tagged by touching such a tree. However, to force a runner from safety, a chaser may stand at least five feet from him and slowly count to three. A player who is tagged, or seeks safety by touching the wrong type of tree, automatically changes roles with the chaser. *Jumbled Safety Tree* is played in much the same way except that the game leader may change the designation of type of tree at any time. For example, if oak trees are considered safe, and too many players are touching oak, the game leader might suddenly shout "maples." At this all the runners have to scramble and look for maples.

Nature Scavenger Hunt

● *Large, strong bags*

One member of the family—or a Cub Scout, Boy Scout, or Girl Scout leader—makes up a list of things to be found in the surrounding countryside and brought in. These might include several kinds of rocks, leaves, seeds, fruit, twigs or insects. (Care should be taken not to list rare items, or any object that would have to be taken from living trees or plants.) Each player is given a copy of the list and a plastic bag. On signal, all go off into the woods and try to collect as many of the items as possible. The first player to bring in all the objects—or the player to bring in the most in 20 minutes—is the winner. This game can also be played on a team basis. A Boy Scout troop, for example, divides into three teams—the team with the most items winning.

VARIATIONS: In *Alphabet Nature Hunt* the players are asked to bring in 26 different items, each one starting with another letter of the alphabet. For example, a player might bring in an ant, for "a"; a birch leaf, for "b"; a chestnut for "c," and so on. As this contest is not easy, a time limit of 30 minutes may be established with the player who comes closest to fulfilling the assignment within that period declared the winner. *One Like It* is a similar game, except that a member of the family collects in advance a variety of items such as cocoons, leaves, twigs, seeds, etc. He holds them up, one at a time, and says to the players: "Bring me one like it." The first player to bring back a similar object wins a point. The player with the most points after 20 minutes wins. In *Bring and Name* the same routine is followed, except that three points are won by bringing in the required object and an additional point is given if the object is correctly identified. *What's Its Name?* is purely an identification game. The leader uses the same items as in *One Like It,* but the players are blindfolded and are asked to name the objects on the basis of touch alone. One point is given for each item correctly identified.

As they scramble in the underbrush, youngsters hunt for such items as fruits, nuts and certain kinds of leaves in the Nature Scavenger Hunt.

Water Games

One of the fastest growing forms of recreation is water sports and games. There are many enjoyable swimming games which may be played during a trip to the beach or at a swimming pool. Most of these involve simple, and often humorous, competition; some can even be adapted to the abilities of non-swimmers. In fact, by helping a child gain confidence in shallow water a parent may encourage him to learn to swim at an early age. A word of caution, however: There should be at least one person on hand with a Red Cross Life-Saving certificate. All water activities are potentially dangerous and require close adult supervision.

Plunging for Distance

Each player dives in turn from one end of the pool. He then glides underwater as far as possible without using his arms or legs and without lifting his head from the water. When the swimmer finally comes up for breath, the distance he has traveled is measured from the end of the pool to the ends of his outstretched arms. The distance is marked on the edge of the pool, and the player with the longest plunge wins.

Underwater Tag

The shallow portion of the pool is used for this game. One player is chosen as swimmer. He tries to tag the others who must duck under water and swim away to avoid being caught. Players are safe from being tagged only when they are out of the chaser's reach or are completely underwater. Although there may not be enough members of any one family to play this game successfully, there are usually plenty of parents and children around any beach or pool who can be drawn into play. Particular care should be taken to keep the action in the shallows, thus protecting players who are not good swimmers.

Shark

This is a game for good swimmers only. One player is chosen the shark and he swims about or treads water in the center of a pool. The other players stand in line, out of the water, on either side of the pool. Whenever a player chooses, he dives into the water and tries to cross over without being tagged by the shark. If the shark tags a player in the water, that player becomes the new shark for the next round of play—the old shark taking his place at poolside.

VARIATION: In *Elude the Shark,* players try to cross the pool as many times as possible in a five-minute period, without being tagged by the shark. The player who crosses most often gets to be the shark for the next round of play.

How Many Ways to Get There?

This game is played in waist-deep water. The object is to see how many methods can be used to get across a pool. Each player takes a turn, using a stroke not used by other players. At the beginning, players will use familiar strokes, like the crawl, the breast stroke, the back stroke and the side stroke. After a while, players begin to think up more original methods of locomotion. Whenever a player cannot employ a new means of travel, he drops out of the contest. The last player to cross, using a method not used before, wins the contest.

VARIATION: In *Follow the Leader,* the game leader stands at pool's edge and tells the others which stroke they should use while swimming. During the game, the leader asks for several different strokes, and players who do not follow his commands are eliminated. Finally only one swimmer, the winner, is left.

Rope Tug

● *Strong rope; large balloon*

Players divide into two teams of two or three players each. The teams line up facing each other, as in ordinary *Tug of War,* in waist-deep water. Each team takes one end of a heavy rope and, on signal, tries to pull the balloon, affixed to the center of the rope, over its own baseline.

VARIATION: In *Pull in the Water,* the teams line up on opposite sides of a swimming pool. Each team grips its end of the rope and, on signal, they pull with all their strength. Whichever team is pulled into the water loses the contest.

Water Rope Tag

● *Short length of rope*

One player is the rope carrier; the others are chasers. The rope is tied around the carrier's waist with two or three feet of rope trailing behind. On signal, the carrier begins swimming, the chasers in pursuit. Each chaser tries to grab hold of the free end of the rope, but no chaser may touch the carrier's body. The carrier may take whatever evasive action he wishes, so long as he stays in bounds previously agreed on. When a tag is made, the carrier and the chaser exchange roles.

Whale and Herring

One player is the whale; the others all are herring. Players stand in waist-deep water. The herring form a single-file line, each herring with his hands on the shoulders of the player in front. On signal, the whale starts toward the rear of the line; his aim is to tag the herring in the rear. To prevent this, the other herrings twist around as much as possible, still keeping their line intact. If the whale makes his tag, he hitches on to the line, becoming the last herring. The first herring in the line becomes the whale for the next round of play. The game continues until every player has been the whale at least once.

One player (center) acts as referee, while two couples vie to pull the balloon across a centerline in Rope Tug, *a water version of* Tug of War.

With a teammate on third, a batter hits the ball into the infield (top) during a game of Water Baseball. *The batter then swims toward first base (center) as her teammate strokes toward home with a fielder on her heels.*

Water Baseball

● *Three or four floats; rubber ball*

The bases are floats that are anchored in the water. The game can be played with only two bases (first and third) laid out in a triangle formation with home plate, or with three bases and home plate, laid out in diamond formation. The player at bat hits a light rubber ball (about four or five inches in diameter) with his fist or with both hands, *Volleyball* fashion. He is allowed only one swing. After the batter swings, he swims toward first base, while the fielders swim for the ball. A player is out if: the ball is thrown to a base before he reaches it; if he is tagged with the ball; if he hits a ball that is caught on the fly; if he hits a ball out of bounds. Each team is permitted three outs per inning, and runs are scored as in *Baseball* when a player safely swims in to home plate. Each team is permitted three outs per turn at bat, and a game may last four or five innings. Teams may have as few as three or four players per side.

VARIATION: In *Player at Bat,* one player hits the ball and tries to swim to one base and back before being put out. If he succeeds, he remains at bat for another turn; if not, he changes places with a player in the field. When all have had a turn, the one to have scored the most runs wins.

Water Horse and Rider

The action takes place in waist-deep water. Players form into pairs, and one player from each pair (usually the lighter one) mounts the shoulders of his partner. The object is for the riders of each competing pair to force the other riders to dismount by pushing or pulling them. No hitting or hair pulling is permitted. When a player falls, he splashes into the water—thus assuring that no one will be hurt. This game may be played as a straight contest between two pairs or as an elimination contest, with the winners of each round meeting in the next.

Novelty Swimming Races

Most swimmers are familiar with standard competition races that make use of recognized strokes or medleys of strokes. Novelty races, however, are performed more for pure and simple fun than for competition. These races may be conducted in a pool or a marked-off area of a pond or lake. The contestants, whether grown-ups or children, must all be competent swimmers, and, of course, at least one adult should act as life guard and referee.

Siamese Twin Race

● *Short lengths of rope*

Swimmers form into couples and stand behind a starting line at one side of the pool. The inside ankles of the couples are tied together. On signal, all couples join their inside hands and jump into the pool. They swim to the opposite side, using only the outside arms and legs for locomotion. The first couple to reach the opposite side wins.

VARIATION: In *Siamese Twin Relay,* teams of couples are formed. Each couple holds hands and, on signal, the first pair on each team swims across the pool and back, touching off the next couple in line. The first team to complete the action wins the relay.

Hoop Race

● *Several plastic Hula hoops; rope; large rocks*

Several floating plastic hoops are placed in the water, each at the same distance from the starting line. To prevent the hoops from moving, they are held by ropes anchored with rocks to the bottom. On signal, each contestant swims to the hoop assigned to him, and then he dives through the ring and swims back to the starting line. The first swimmer to complete the action, wins the race.

VARIATIONS: In the *Hoop Relay,* teams are formed; when one swimmer completes the action, he touches off the next on his team. In *Heads Up,* swimmers must come up through the hoops from underwater. This can be run as a race among individuals or as a relay.

Collecting Corks

● *A basket or bag full of corks*

Swimmers divide into two teams and line up on one edge of a pool. The game leader throws a basketful of corks out into fairly deep water. As the corks land, all the players jump in and swim for them. The team that accumulates more corks and brings them back to poolside wins. This contest can also be run on an individual basis between two players.

Treasure Diving

● *Small, brightly colored object; wristwatch or stopwatch*

Players divide into two teams and each team picks a captain. The captain of one team throws an object—small but heavy enough to sink—into the water. The object should also be brightly colored, so that it can be seen under water. One member of the opposing team then dives to find the treasure and bring it back. The captain uses a watch to determine the length of time it takes the diver to retrieve and return the treasure. Then the action is reversed, with the captain of the second team tossing the treasure into the water and a member of the first team diving after it. The contest goes on in this manner, with teams alternating between diving and throwing, until every member of each team has a turn in the water. The winning team is the one with the shortest total time.

VARIATION: In *Bottle-cap Diving,* soda bottle caps are thrown into a pool, and two swimmers at a time try to collect as many as possible before coming up for air.

Water Balloon Race

● *Several inflated balloons*

Swimmers line up behind a starting line at the shallow end of a pool. On signal, each player swims across the pool and back again, pushing an inflated balloon in front of him. As the balloon tends to bob about unpredictably in the water, the best swimmer is not always the winner.

VARIATION: *Water Balloon Relay* is played in the same way, except players line up in teams at one edge of the pool. When a player completes his round, he hands the balloon to the next player on his team, who repeats the action. The first team on which every player has completed the action wins the relay.

In the Water Balloon Race *players try to guide the bobbing spheres with their arm strokes. Should a balloon float off, the player must retrieve it.*

Holding umbrellas high, players in the Umbrella Race *swim across a pool, where teammates wait to take the umbrellas and swim back with them.*

Umbrella Race

● *Umbrella for each team*

Players form into teams of two swimmers each and line up at the shallow end of a pool. On signal, the first swimmer in each pair swims free-style to the opposite side of the pool. He then reaches up to the edge of the pool (or, in a lake, to a raft), takes a closed umbrella—placed there previously—ducks under and opens the umbrella, which is held above water. Then, holding the umbrella above his head, he swims back to the starting line. His partner reverses the action: He takes the umbrella, swims to the opposite edge of the pool, ducks under, closes the umbrella, places it at poolside and swims back to the starting line. The first pair to complete the action wins the *Umbrella Race.*

Waterball Carry

● *Plastic ball for each team*

Two teams stand beside each other and line up in single file at one end of the pool. A large plastic beach ball is given to the lead player on each team. On signal, each lead player places the ball between his knees and jumps into the pool. He swims to the opposite end of the pool and back again with the ball between his knees. He then hands the ball to the next player on his team, who repeats the action. Any swimmer who drops the ball must stop and place it back into position before resuming the relay. The first team to have all its members complete the action wins the race. The *Waterball Carry* can also be run as a contest between two or more individual swimmers.

Pebble Carry

- *A bag of pebbles*

Two teams line up in single file behind a starting line in waist-deep water. Each swimmer is given three small pebbles. On signal, the lead swimmers swim to the opposite side of the pool and back again to touch off the next players in line. The trick is that each swimmer must balance the three pebbles on the back of one hand. (This can be done most successfully if the dog paddle or the side stroke is employed—strokes in which one hand can be held in the air.) If the pebbles drop off, a swimmer must return to the starting line, get new ones and begin the race over again. The team that completes the action first wins.

Sing and Swim

This is an ordinary swimming race or relay, except that, at the beginning of the race, each player is assigned a song. Each swimmer must sing his song loud and clear as he swims the length of the pool—and back again, if the event is run as a relay. If a swimmer stops singing at any time—except for an occasional gurgle—he is disqualified. (In a relay, the swimmer must start over again.) The first singing swimmer to reach the finish line—or the first team to complete the action—wins the race.

Tunnel Race

Players form two teams, each of which stands single file in chest-deep water. All the players spread their legs wide apart. On signal, the lead player of each team turns, faces his teammates, does a surface dive and swims underwater through the legs of the other players. When he surfaces, he stands with his legs apart at the end of the line. The action continues until every player goes through the tunnel. The first team to finish wins the race.

Games for Winter Fun

Traditionally, winter has been the season of staying close to the fireside, with outdoor play activities reserved for only the very young and the most hearty. In recent years, however, there has been a boom in cold-weather sports and outdoor games, and more and more families are participating. The following games are in keeping with this new attitude that seeks to turn snow time into fun time.

Penny Race

- *20 to 50 pennies*

Ice skaters line up behind a starting line on a frozen pond or skating rink. A turning line is marked off about 100 feet away. The game leader tosses a handful of pennies on to the ice between the starting and turning lines. On signal, the skaters rush forward to the turning line, picking up as many pennies as they can along the way. (If the weather is quite cold, some of the pennies will have already frozen to the ice, and players will have to dislodge them with the blades of their skates.) As a player reaches the turning line, he races back to the starting line. The player who crosses the starting line first gets five points; all players receive one point for each penny they bring back. The skater with the highest point-total wins the race. Another way to run the race is to have each skater pick up one penny at a time and return it to the starting line. The player who collects the most in five minutes wins the contest.

Ice-Skating Balloon Race

- *Inflated balloons; hockey sticks*

Skaters line up behind a starting line, and a turning line is marked off about 100 feet away. Each player has a hockey stick and an inflated balloon. On signal, skaters race to the turning line and back, pushing their balloons in front of them. This is a difficult feat to accomplish, and victory does not always go to the best skater.

VARIATION: *Balloon Skating Relay* is played in much the same way except that two or three teams are formed. As each player completes the action, he passes his balloon on to the next.

Coasting for Distance

A starting line and a coasting line are marked off on the ice about 100 feet apart. On signal the skaters move off from the starting line, taking as powerful strides as they can to build up their momentum. At the coasting line, they stop skating and begin to coast—that is, they stop moving their legs and simply glide along as far as they can. The skater who covers the greatest distance wins the race.

VARIATION: *Elimination Distance Coasting* is good sport when large groups of people are participating. The event is divided into rounds. In the first round, a series of two-man coasting races take place. In the second round, the winners of the first compete in twos. The event goes on until, in the final round, only two players remain. The winner of this round is crowned champion coaster.

Snow Dodge Ball

Players divide into two equal-size groups. One group, the rim players, stand on the edge of a large circle stamped out in the snow. The others, the center players, stand inside the circle. The rim players make snowballs, and, one at a time, they throw them at the center players.

For their part, the center players try to dodge each oncoming snowball. When a center player is hit, he joins the rim players and awaits his turn to throw a snowball. The winner of each round is the last center player to be struck. At the end of a round, the center players take positions on the rim and the rim players move to the center.

Broom Carry

- *Two brooms*

Players divide into teams of two and stand behind a starting line on a frozen pond or skating rink. Each couple has an old broom; one member of the team sits on the brush end while his partner grips the handle. On signal, each broom holder skates forward to the turning line, pulling his sitting partner behind him. On reaching the turning line, the two players change positions and race back to the starting line. The first couple to complete the action wins the race.

VARIATION: In *Broom Carry Relay* two teams of couples line up behind the starting line. The action is the same as above, except, that as each couple returns to the starting line, they touch off the next couple on their team. The first team to have all players perform the action wins.

Squatting Race

- *Garbage can lids or aluminum discs*

Skaters form into pairs behind a starting line. A turning line is marked off 100 feet away. One player in each pair sits on an old garbage can lid or an aluminum disc of the sort made for snow coasting. The other player stands behind and holds the sitting player's shoulders. On signal, the standing player skates toward the turning line, pushing his partner along in front of him. On reaching the turning line, the two change roles and return to the starting line. The first pair to complete the action wins the race.

VARIATION: In *Squatting Relay* the action is the same except that teams of couples race.

A net player in Volleyball *jumps high to spike the ball to the opposing team, whose members are already setting themselves to make a return.*

CHAPTER 15

Backyard and
Neighborhood Sports

Competitive sports requiring skill and muscle control are enjoyed by virtually everyone, either as a player or spectator. Although strenuous team sports, such as baseball, basketball, football, soccer and hockey, are usually favorites of the young, there are many games—including volleyball, softball and tennis—that offer fun and recreation for the young, the middle-aged and even the elderly. Individual activities, such as skiing and ice skating as well as swimming, water-skiing and underwater exploration, are also growing in popularity and now attract millions of enthusiasts. Basic descriptions and rules for most of the better-known games and sports are given in this chapter. However, because highly competitive sports require more elaborate equipment, larger facilities and more participants than are ordinarily available in family or neighborhood play, only the more important points are explained here. Simple variations of major sports that have long been providing fun and exercise for smaller groups in backyards, playgrounds and streets are stressed. Touch football, for example, is more suitable for neighborhood play than tackle football, as the former requires fewer players, a smaller field and very little equipment.

Major sports and their variations form only a portion of this chapter. Here, also, are tips and guidelines that will help the average reader acquaint himself with such happy pursuits as pitching horseshoes, tossing quoits, pushing shuffleboard discs and whipping table-tennis balls over the net. In all instances, descriptions are applicable to right-handed players. Those who are left-handed merely reverse the instructions. Thus, for example, a diagram which shows a player holding a ball or racket in his right hand should be interpreted by "southpaws" as an instruction to hold the ball or racket in the left hand.

Archery

Modern *Archery* is a popular recreation enjoyed by both young and old, although it had its serious and practical beginnings thousands of years ago as man's principal means of obtaining food and clothing and of waging warfare. Today, in addition to informal, individual shooting, there are many organized tournaments sponsored by archery clubs throughout North America.

The two major forms of *Archery* competition are target shooting and field shooting. In the former type, targets are placed at a fixed distance. In field shooting, however, targets of varying size are placed at different distances on the course. Each player's score is computed by adding the values of the centerspot (or the bull's-eye) and the surrounding rings in which his arrows are lodged.

Obviously, *Archery* can be dangerous if safety rules are not carefully observed. In group competition, once the supervisor gives the commence-firing call, all archers remain behind the shooting line, moving forward only to retrieve their arrows after everyone has finished shooting. Adequate backstops must be used, and shooting should never be done where arrows flying past the target might hit bystanders or spectators.

For the family that takes up *Archery* as a hobby, outdoor space will probably be limited. Therefore, target shooting will have to be done at a fairly short distance—against a high fence or garage wall and with a large straw backstop protecting the area. Faulty equipment should never be used, and bows and arrows should be guarded carefully to prevent children or inexperienced persons from taking and using them.

EQUIPMENT: The bow, arrows and a target on a stand are basic equipment. It is also well to have a quiver to hold arrows, an arm-guard to

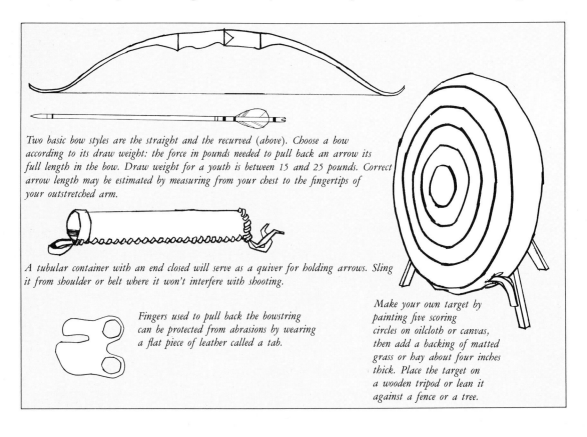

Two basic bow styles are the straight and the recurved (above). Choose a bow according to its draw weight: the force in pounds needed to pull back an arrow its full length in the bow. Draw weight for a youth is between 15 and 25 pounds. Correct arrow length may be estimated by measuring from your chest to the fingertips of your outstretched arm.

A tubular container with an end closed will serve as a quiver for holding arrows. Sling it from shoulder or belt where it won't interfere with shooting.

Fingers used to pull back the bowstring can be protected from abrasions by wearing a flat piece of leather called a tab.

Make your own target by painting five scoring circles on oilcloth or canvas, then add a backing of matted grass or hay about four inches thick. Place the target on a wooden tripod or lean it against a fence or a tree.

protect the forearm from a lash by the bowstring, a finger-guard (a flat piece of leather, also called a tab) to protect the arrow-holding fingers from abrasion, and a bow-sight, used to aim at the target. Modern bows are made of a combination of fiberglass and wood and also of metal. They are available in lengths of from four to six feet. Thickest at the center, they taper toward each end. The bow should be selected according to the height and strength of the archer: A man's usually requires a pull of from 35 to 40 pounds, a woman's between 20 and 30 and a child's or teen-ager's from 15 to 25.

Arrows are thin, perfectly straight pieces of wood, fiberglass or metal, varying from 20 to 30 inches in length and selected with the arm-reach of the archer in mind. Standard targets used in competition are circular, with a 48-inch diameter. The centerspot is colored gold and has a diameter of 9.6 inches. Surrounding concentric rings (red, blue, black and white) are each 4.8 inches wide. Their scoring values, beginning with the gold center and progressing outward,

In a proper shooting stance, stand sideways to the target, with feet spread at a comfortable distance. Draw the bowstring back to touch your jaw, lining up the arrow with the target.

are nine, seven, five, three and one. In international competition, however, the color rings are each divided in half so as to make ten scoring areas instead of five. The scoring values beginning with ten for the centerspot progress outward in receding order, through to one. In both scoring methods an arrow on the line between two areas and touching both scores the higher value.

STANCE AND GRIP: The archer takes his stance astride the shooting line with his left side turned toward the target. He holds the bow lightly with the thumb and fingers of the left hand so that the main pressure is against the palm just inside the base of the thumb. The arrow is placed on an arrow rest, a shelf or projection on the left-hand side of the bow. The archer places his three middle fingers on the bowstring, one on top of the nock and two beneath it. (The nock is a piece of slotted plastic on the butt end of an arrow into which the bowstring fits.)

DRAW, AIM AND RELEASE: Most archers include the use of a bow-sight as common practice in target and recreational shooting. A bow-sight can be as simple as a pin attached to the bow by a piece of adhesive tape or it can consist of movable bars, telescopic sights and other exotic aiming devices.

Once the sight is on the goal, the archer simultaneously presses the bow-arm forward and pulls the string-arm back so that the bow is brought to a full draw. He must keep the string-arm shoulder high and the bow exactly vertical. Most archers bring the bowstring back to touch the end of the nose and the center of the chin, anchoring the thumb and right forefinger under the chin. It is important that the "anchor," or grip on the bowstring and arrow, be the same each time if the target is to be hit consistently in the same place. To release the arrow, the fingers are relaxed and drawn back slightly. The string then springs forward, propelling the arrow. The archer should continue to press forward with his bow-arm and shoulder and to draw back with his right arm after releasing the string—holding the shooting position without body movement until the arrow hits the target.

The draw, aim and release are highly disciplined movements which should be practiced repeatedly until they can be accomplished successfully the same way each time.

VARIATIONS: In *Tournament Shooting,* a standard series of rounds and distances are used. The field for men is generally 100 yards long, with targets set at 80, 60, 50 and 40 yards from the shooting line. Women may use a shorter field, with targets at 50, 40 and 30 yards from the shooting line. Four archers usually are assigned to each target and draw numbers to determine the order of shooting. The various standard rounds include: the American Round (for men and women), the York Round (for men), the Professional Round and Field Round (for men and women), the Canadian Round (for men and women), the FITA International Rounds (used in Olympic competition) and others. As an example, the American Round requires shooting a total of 90 arrows: 30 arrows at 60 yards, 30 arrows at 50 yards, and 30 arrows at 40 yards. In addition, indoor shooting may be done, usually at a distance of 20 yards.

Archery Golf involves shooting on a golf course or a similar course laid out for archery. The target, a four-inch straw ball, is used in place of the cup. After each shot, the archer advances to the point where his arrow falls and then takes another shot at the target. Score is kept: The number of shots needed to hit each target are added, and finally the totals for nine or 18 "holes" are added. The contestant with the lowest score wins.

In *Clout Shooting,* arrows are shot over long distances at a 48-foot target laid flat on the ground. Men shoot 36 arrows at 180 yards, while women shoot the same number at 120 yards. The target is divided into concentric rings. A hit on the bull's-eye (clout) counts ten points, and other hits count five, three or one in order of closeness to the center.

In *Flight Shooting,* a large area is needed and contestants merely try to shoot for maximum distance.

Roving is a casual form of target shooting, in which hunters stroll through the countryside or wooded areas and shoot at inanimate targets of their choice, such as bushes or trees. Targets may also be improvised with paint or colored cloth. Sometimes toy balloons, cardboard cutouts of deer, pheasant, rabbits or similar objects are used as targets.

Badminton

Badminton is a lively net and racket game which may be played as singles or doubles, by all ages and both sexes, either indoors or out. Originally from India, it was popularized in England by British Army officers and brought to North America in the 1870s. Many schools and colleges offer badminton in the basic skills program of physical education. Since it requires only a small court and may be learned easily by beginners, it has become an extremely popular backyard family sport.

COURT AND EQUIPMENT: A court can be set up on any level ground with the net swung between two posts—each five feet, one inch high. The court is 44 feet by 20 feet for doubles; 44 feet by 17 feet for singles. For informal play, these boundaries can vary depending on the skills of the players and can be marked off with small stones or with string pegged into the ground. The racket resembles a tennis racket but is much lighter. Instead of a ball, a shuttlecock—or "bird"—is used. This is made from hard cork, or from plastic, with feathers attached and is so light that it floats in the air.

ACTION: The object of *Badminton* is to score points against the opposition by hitting the bird over the net in such a way that the opponent cannot return it. When an opponent cannot return a serve or fails to return it fair into his opponent's court, a point is scored in favor of the serving side. When a server fails to serve properly, or cannot return the bird which his opponent hits back, he (or his side, in a doubles game) loses the service. He does not lose the point, however, for in tournament play only the serving side makes points. First service is decided

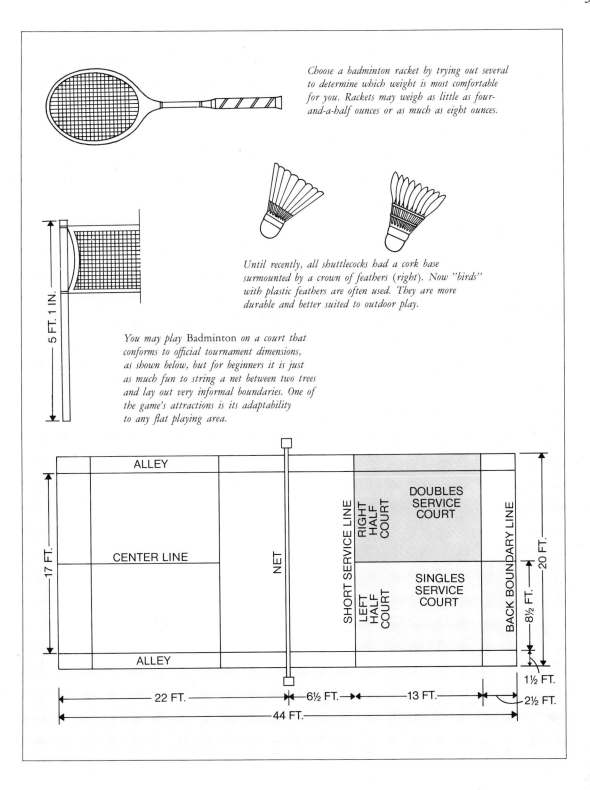

Choose a badminton racket by trying out several to determine which weight is most comfortable for you. Rackets may weigh as little as four-and-a-half ounces or as much as eight ounces.

Until recently, all shuttlecocks had a cork base surmounted by a crown of feathers (right). Now "birds" with plastic feathers are often used. They are more durable and better suited to outdoor play.

You may play Badminton on a court that conforms to official tournament dimensions, as shown below, but for beginners it is just as much fun to string a net between two trees and lay out very informal boundaries. One of the game's attractions is its adaptability to any flat playing area.

5 FT. 1 IN.

ALLEY

SHORT SERVICE LINE

RIGHT HALF COURT

DOUBLES SERVICE COURT

CENTER LINE

NET

BACK BOUNDARY LINE

17 FT.

20 FT.

LEFT HALF COURT

SINGLES SERVICE COURT

8½ FT.

ALLEY

1½ FT.

22 FT. — 6½ FT. — 13 FT. — 2½ FT.

44 FT.

Serve by hitting the bird with an underhand stroke
as it drops just below waist level. You are allowed
only one chance; if you fail, your opponent serves.

The smash, or kill, is a
hard downward blow, often in
response to a lob. It can be
a sure point-winner. The secret
is to keep your eye on the bird with
only a quick glance toward the
court you want to play it into.

The clear, or lob, is a defensive stroke made
either underhand or overhand. When your opponent is
playing a hard aggressive game, a lob can slow him
down if it forces him to the back boundary line.

Mastering the backhand stroke takes considerable
practice. Your right side should be facing the net, your
right foot forward. Strike the bird with a wrist
action when it is about a foot in front of you.

by the toss of a coin. In singles play, the server stands behind the serving line within the boundaries of the right-hand court, drops the bird, lets it fall below waist level and hits it with an underhand stroke diagonally into his opponent's right-hand court. If the serve is successful, or the resulting rally is won, the server moves to the left-hand court for the next serve.

In doubles play, the side that begins serving has only one player serve in their first inning. Thereafter the serve does not go directly from one team to the other with each fault. Both players on a team must have a chance at a series of serves from their own half-courts before service changes sides. For example, if A and B are opposing C and D, and B opens with the serve, B continues to serve until his side commits a fault. The service then moves to C, the player in the court diagonally opposite B. C serves until his side commits a fault. The serve does not then go to A, but rather to D, and only when C or D faults does the service cross the net, going first to A and then to B again. Also, in doubles play, the partners may divide the court, one taking the front and the other the back area or each covering one side.

SCORING: A service fault occurs when: the bird is served overhand; it touches ground on the server's side of the net; it does not land within the proper boundaries on the opposite side of the court, or it does not clear the net. If the bird touches the net on service but still goes over, it is considered a "let serve" and is played again. A receiver's fault occurs when: he fails to return a fair serve into boundaries of the opposing court; he strikes the bird twice in succession, or when he hits the net or reaches over it with his racket. When the receiving side commits a fault, a point is scored for the service. The receiving side cannot win a point until it gets the serve through a server fault. In men's *Badminton,* a game consists of 15 or 21 points; in women's, 11 points; in mixed play, 15 points.

STROKES AND STRATEGY: In serving, the bird is held lightly by the tips of the feathers between the thumb and index fingers of the left hand and batted with an easy underhand stroke. The racket is gripped for the forehand stroke as if the player were shaking hands with its handle— holding it at the extreme end, with the fingers well spread. For the backhand, some players use the same grip, while others turn the racket head a quarter-turn clockwise from the forehand position. In both cases, the hand, wrist and arm should be relaxed and the shuttlecock struck with a sharp flick of the wrist. Before all shots, the wrist should be held well back; after the stroke the arm should follow through.

Specific strokes include: service, a high, or lob shot, or a lower "drop" shot—always hit underhand; smash, in which the shuttlecock is struck with a strong wrist flick while high overhead in front of the body; lob, a high, deep shot, used as a defensive stroke; drive, a flat, low shot which may be sent to any area of the opponent's court, and drop, a soft shot which barely clears the net and begins to drop immediately.

Badminton strategy is based on being able to cover the entire court easily, without leaving an opponent an open area in which to place the bird and without giving him easy or soft shots which he may smash or drop out of reach. When receiving, it is a good idea for a player to be positioned about three feet behind the front service line near the center of the court and to return to this area after each shot. At the same time, the service and following volleys should alternate between long and short shots. Whenever possible, cross-court smashes or drives down the sidelines are employed to keep an opponent on the defensive.

VARIATION: *Aerial Tennis* is very much like *Badminton* but is played on a singles court that is 20 by 50 feet, and a doubles court that is 26 by 50 feet. The top of the net is seven feet from the ground with a service line ten feet from the back line. Instead of badminton rackets, short-handled wooden Ping-Pong paddles are used to hit the bird. In addition to playing this game as a regular singles or doubles match, it may be played as *Team Aerial Tennis* with several players on a side. The bird can be relayed from teammate to teammate before it clears the net.

Sponge Ball is another *Badminton*-type game in which a sphere, three-and-one-half inches in diameter, is cut from a sponge and it is used as the bird. It can be played with either badminton rackets or Ping-Pong paddles and the rules of *Badminton* apply.

Baseball

Baseball is often referred to as America's "national pastime," because the game has remained an object of the nation's affections for well over a century. Literally millions of fans crowd into stadiums around the country during the spring, summer and fall to see their favorite teams play. Uncounted millions watch the action on television—day after day, night after night. Still more millions of boys are organized into Little League, Babe Ruth League, Pony League and American Legion League competitions. It would be impossible even to guess how many "unorganized" games take place in the nation's parks and empty lots on any warm day, for there is hardly an American boy above the age of eight who does not know the fundamentals of the sport or who does not dream of feats of derring-do with bat, ball and glove.

FORMATION AND EQUIPMENT: *Baseball* is played by two teams of nine men each. When in the field, players take the following positions: pitcher, catcher, first baseman, second baseman, short stop, third baseman, right fielder, center fielder and left fielder. When at bat, each player in turn is simply referred to as the batter.

Baseball should be played on a large, level field. The diamond, or infield, with sides 90 feet long, is marked out at one end of the field. There is a base at each corner of the diamond. Behind the "home" corner of the diamond, facing the field itself, is a backstop, consisting of a metal frame covered with wire netting. Home plate is located on this corner of the field. This is usually a five-sided slab of hard rubber, flush with the ground. On either side of home plate there are batter's boxes—rectangular areas in which the right- or left-handed batter stands while trying to hit the ball being pitched over the plate. On each of the other bases, a canvas bag, fifteen inches square, is fastened to the ground. In the center of the diamond, 60 feet six inches from the home plate and on the axis between home and second base, is the pitcher's box or rubber. Beyond the diamond is the outfield. There is no set size for the outfield.

Baseball is played with a wooden bat and a hard leather-covered ball. All equipment is made according to specifications of size and weight stipulated by professional baseball leagues.

ACTION: The objective of the batting team is to hit pitched balls in such a way that the other team cannot field them before the batter has run around the "diamond" to score a run.

To begin, the first player of the batting team stands at home plate in the batter's box. He swings the bat at balls thrown in an overhand or sidearm motion by the pitcher. If the batter swings at a pitched ball and misses it completely, or if he fails to swing at a ball that passes directly over home plate at a height between his knee and shoulder, a "strike" is counted against him. If this happens three times, the batter is called out—providing that the catcher holds the ball after the third strike. Otherwise, if the ball is dropped, the batter may run to first base and is "safe" if he reaches it before the ball does or before the catcher tags him with the retrieved ball. When a pitched ball does not pass through the strike zone and is not swung at, it is considered a "ball." If the batter receives four balls, he is given a "walk," which means that he can go to first base and become a base-runner.

If the batter swings at a pitched ball and hits it outside of the foul lines of the field, it is a "foul" ball. Fouls are counted as strikes, until the batter has two strikes against him. However, a foul is not counted as the third strike unless the catcher—or some other fielder—catches it on the fly (in which case the batter is out). Any

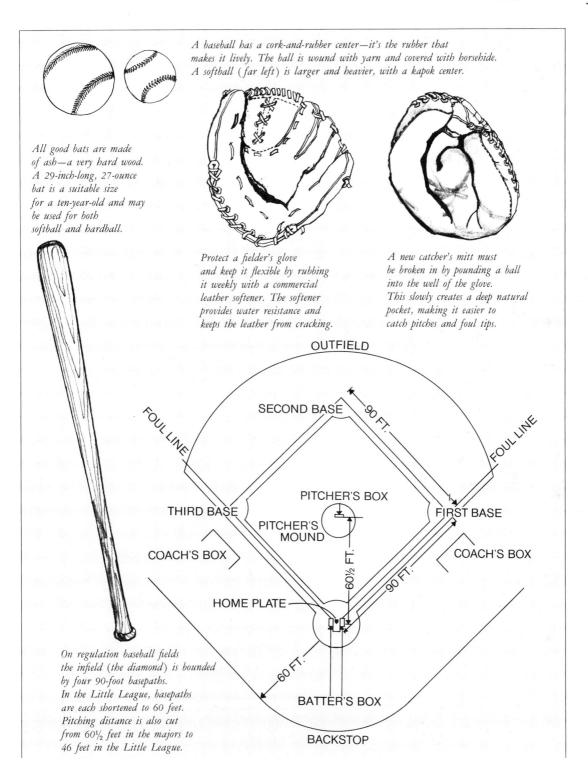

A baseball has a cork-and-rubber center—it's the rubber that
makes it lively. The ball is wound with yarn and covered with horsehide.
A softball (far left) is larger and heavier, with a kapok center.

All good bats are made
of ash—a very hard wood.
A 29-inch-long, 27-ounce
bat is a suitable size
for a ten-year-old and may
be used for both
softball and hardball.

Protect a fielder's glove
and keep it flexible by rubbing
it weekly with a commercial
leather softener. The softener
provides water resistance and
keeps the leather from cracking.

A new catcher's mitt must
be broken in by pounding a ball
into the well of the glove.
This slowly creates a deep natural
pocket, making it easier to
catch pitches and foul tips.

OUTFIELD

SECOND BASE

90 FT.

FOUL LINE

FOUL LINE

PITCHER'S BOX

THIRD BASE

PITCHER'S
MOUND

FIRST BASE

COACH'S BOX

60½ FT.

90 FT.

COACH'S BOX

HOME PLATE

60 FT.

On regulation baseball fields
the infield (the diamond) is bounded
by four 90-foot basepaths.
In the Little League, basepaths
are each shortened to 60 feet.
Pitching distance is also cut
from 60½ feet in the majors to
46 feet in the Little League.

BATTER'S BOX

BACKSTOP

foul ball caught on the fly counts as an out. An exception is a "foul tip," which is a foul ball that does not rise above ten feet. A foul tip caught by the catcher does not count as an out.

An official called an "umpire," who stands directly behind the catcher, decides whether a pitch is a ball or strike or whether a hit is foul or fair. In organized play, there are at least two other umpires—one stationed near first base and the other near third—who decide on such matters as whether a batter has reached base safely and whether a ball was caught fairly.

When a batter hits the ball and it flies or bounces forward, he runs toward first base. If the ball hits the ground within the foul line boundaries, it is a "fair" ball. It must then be retrieved by a player in the field, thrown to first base and caught by the first baseman before the batter reaches that base. When this happens, the batter is "out." If he reaches first base safely before the ball, it is called a "single." If he reaches second safely after hitting the ball, it is a "double," and if he reaches third, it is a "triple." If he is able to go completely around the bases and back to home plate after hitting the ball (usually by hitting the ball far into the outfield or into the stands), it is a "home run." If the batter hits the ball in the air and it is caught before it touches the ground, it is called a "fly" ball and he is automatically out.

After the first batter comes up and either is put out or reaches base safely, the next player in the batting order comes to bat. If the batter hits a fair ball and there is a player already on first base, that player must try to advance. If the ball is fielded and thrown to second base before the first base runner can reach it, it is a "force out"—the lead runner is called out while the batter occupies first base. If the ball can be thrown to second base and then to first before the batter can reach it, both players are out and it is a "double play." If a ball is caught on the fly, and then thrown to a base, before the runner who had been on that base and has started for the next can get back to it, it is also a double play. If a runner on the base paths

is hit by a batted ball, he is out. At any time the ball is in play, a base runner is permitted to "steal" to the next base by trying to run to it and not be touched by the ball. He is called out if he is tagged with the ball before reaching that base, or if he is tagged while trying to get back to the base he just left.

SCORING: A team remains at bat until it makes three outs—at which point it goes into the field. Then the opposing team comes to bat—remaining there until it has three outs. Both actions together constitute an "inning." There are usually nine innings in a game, although youngsters may play games with fewer innings. A game also may be "called" (considered completed) after five innings if bad weather or darkness interferes with play—and still have the score count. The team which scores more runs in a completed game wins.

There are many other complex rules for official play which govern such factors as the size of the gloves the fielders may use, the position of the pitcher, how the pitcher may release the ball and similar elements. In addition, there are many strategic plays which may be used by the team at bat. These are given to the batter, usually by a coach standing at third base, who uses hand signals. Finally, there is a system for keeping score of all the action in the game: Batters are credited with times at bat, runs scored, runs batted in, hits and stolen bases; players in the field are credited with putouts, assists and errors. Details on these additional aspects of *Baseball* may be found in the official playing guide for the sport, or in any of the many books that have been written about the game. As mentioned, *Baseball* requires at least 18 players for a game. (Often, there are equal numbers of players on the bench, waiting to come in as substitutes.) In addition, the game requires officials, special equipment and an extensive playing field. If all of these are not available, it is always possible to enjoy a simpler form of the sport. Several variations, such as *One Old Cat,* are described in Chapter One. There are others that may be played with a small number of participants and on a limited playing area.

VARIATIONS: *Softball* is played with equipment and rules that make it more suitable for informal recreation than regular *Baseball*. It is estimated that well over five million Americans play *Softball* today, including both young children and senior citizens—males and females. Besides being played for casual recreation, *Softball* is carried on in many organized leagues with state and national tournaments each year.

The playing field is similar to a regular baseball field, except that it is considerably shorter. (Baselines are 60 feet long, rather than 90 feet.) The distance from the pitcher's box to home plate is 38 feet for women and 46 feet for men. A softball is larger than a baseball, being from $11\frac{7}{8}$ to $12\frac{1}{8}$ inches in circumference, and between 6 and $6\frac{3}{4}$ ounces in weight. The bat should be no more than 34 inches long, and no more than two and one-eighth inches in diameter at its thickest point.

Although *Softball* was, at one time, played by a team of 10 players, the number has now been reduced to nine players—the same as on a regulation baseball team. Instead of nine innings, the regulation *Softball* game is played in seven innings. As in *Baseball,* a game that is called after five innings have been played is official. If the team that is second at bat is leading after four and one-half innings, the second half of the fifth inning of a called-game need not be played.

One of the major differences between *Softball* and regulation *Baseball* is in the style of pitching. The pitcher must face the batter directly, holding the ball with both hands in front of his body, and with both feet on the pitcher's rubber. He may then take only one step toward the batter, and deliver the ball with an underhand motion—following through with his hand and wrist past the line of the body before releasing the ball. One foot must be kept on the rubber until the ball is released. A highly skilled pitcher can dominate a game more completely in this sport than in *Baseball.* There are two varieties of softball—*Hard Pitch* and *Soft Pitch*. In the *Hard Pitch* game, the pitcher may throw the ball on a straight line to the batter;

in *Soft Pitch* the ball must arch high before crossing home plate. As *Soft Pitch* requires fewer skills from both batter and pitcher, it is to be recommended for young players just learning the basic rules and requirements of the game.

In *Rotation Baseball* several players take the field in the regular positions, while three players are batters. Usual rules governing pitching, hitting, fielding and running apply. There is one exception, however; Because there are not likely to be umpires, balls and strikes are not called.

The object of the game is to remain at bat and to score as many individual runs as possible. Once a batter is on base he waits to be driven home by the others, or he may be put out in an attempt to steal or be forced out by the next batter, as in *Baseball*. Whenever a player is put out, he must go into the field, where he takes the right-field position. The other fielders all move up one position: from right field to center field to left field, to third baseman to shortstop to second baseman to first baseman, and finally to pitcher and then to catcher. If the batter hits a fly ball which is caught by a fielder, that fielder comes to bat immediately; the others move up to fill his place and the batter goes to right field.

Speedball is played in many school gym periods, where it is advantageous to complete five innings in a relatively short period of time. Only four batters come to the plate in an inning. The inning is over for a team if the first three batters are put out or when the fourth batter either makes a run, is forced out, or is put out in any other manner. However, a run driven in by the fourth batter counts only if the batter reaches first base safely. In this game, as in regular *Baseball,* bases may be stolen starting with the motion of the pitcher's arm. Base runners may even try to steal home. When a player is given a walk on four pitched balls, his team is not charged with having had a player at bat.

Triangle Ball, often called *Punchball,* is easily played in schoolyards or on city streets. The field is reduced in size from *Baseball,* and there are only three bases: home plate, first and third base.

They make a triangle in which, depending on the space available, the distance from home plate to first base may be anywhere from 25 to 40 feet and the distance from first to third no more than 25 feet. A small rubber or tennis ball is used and instead of swinging a bat, the batter hits the ball with his fist. The pitcher may serve it to him on one bounce, or the batter simply may hold the ball in one hand, toss it in the air and hit it. Base running and scoring are the same as in regular *Baseball*. The game is quite fast and requires good ball handling.

If space is even more limited, *Two Base Punchball* may be played. The bases are home plate and a base where the pitcher's mound ordinarily is. The batter hits the ball and runs back and forth between home plate and this base. He gets one point for each round trip he makes before being tagged out by a player on the field.

Basketball

Invented in 1891 by Dr. James A. Naismith, Canadian-born athletic director of what is now Springfield College in Massachusetts, *Basketball* has become the most popular indoor sport in the United States and enjoys a growing following in many foreign lands as well. Dr. Naismith's aim was to devise a fast-action game that could be played indoors during the cold winter months, and in this he succeeded beyond his wildest expectations. *Basketball* is a game of rapid movement and quick ball handling, in which two teams of five players compete to move the ball down court and shoot it through the opposition's basket. The sport has the advantage of requiring only inexpensive equipment; it is also a highly adaptable game that can be played informally on almost any open space where a metal hoop can be mounted on a wall or hung from high posts. The basic rules, while simple enough to be grasped by an eight- or nine-year-old, can also form the foundation of a game that combines dazzling speed with intricate strategy—a form of *Basketball* well-known to college and professional fans alike.

FORMATION AND EQUIPMENT: There are five players on a team in boys' and men's play: a center (usually the tallest player); two forwards, who position themselves close to the opponents' defensive goal, and two guards, who play farther away from that basket. In women's play, there are six players on a team—three forwards and three guards. *Basketball* is normally played on a rectangular hardwood court with dimensions ranging from a maximum of 50 by 94 feet to a minimum of 42 by 74 feet for official play; however, smaller courts are frequently used for unofficial contests. A backboard is located two feet in from the end line at both ends of the court; a basket (a metal ring 18 inches in diameter with an open net suspended from it) is fixed to the board at a point ten feet above the floor. A free-throw or foul-shooting line is painted 15 feet in front of each backboard. The basketball is round, 29 to 30 inches in circumference, and usually made of a rubber bladder covered with a leather case.

ACTION: The basic objective in *Basketball* is for each team to move the ball down the court toward the basket and to score a two-point goal by throwing the ball through the basket from above. The game begins with a jump ball. The ball is tossed into the air in the center circle by an official, and the two opposing center players try to bat it to players on their own teams. The team that gains possession moves the ball down court and attempts to score. If successful, a member of the other team takes possession of the ball behind the end line; he passes the ball to one of his teammates in an attempt to move it down the court in the opposite direction and score. The ball may be moved down court by passing to a teammate and by dribbling—one player running with the ball while bouncing it on the floor. The offensive team can lose possession of the ball if a player takes more than one step with the ball without passing, dribbling or shooting, or if he kicks the ball or steps out of bounds. During down-court plays, the ball can also be captured by the opposition if they intercept a pass; if they capture a fumbled ball; if one of its players can

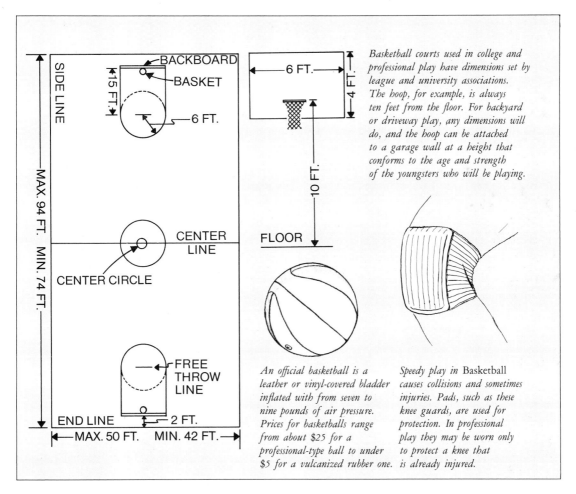

SIDE LINE

BACKBOARD
BASKET

15 FT.

6 FT.

MAX. 94 FT. MIN. 74 FT.

CENTER
LINE

CENTER CIRCLE

FREE
THROW
LINE

END LINE 2 FT.

MAX. 50 FT. MIN. 42 FT.

6 FT.

4 FT.

10 FT.

FLOOR

Basketball courts used in college and professional play have dimensions set by league and university associations. The hoop, for example, is always ten feet from the floor. For backyard or driveway play, any dimensions will do, and the hoop can be attached to a garage wall at a height that conforms to the age and strength of the youngsters who will be playing.

An official basketball is a leather or vinyl-covered bladder inflated with from seven to nine pounds of air pressure. Prices for basketballs range from about $25 for a professional-type ball to under $5 for a vulcanized rubber one.

Speedy play in Basketball *causes collisions and sometimes injuries. Pads, such as these knee guards, are used for protection. In professional play they may be worn only to protect a knee that is already injured.*

break into a dribble and steal the ball without coming into bodily contact with the dribbler, or if one of its players retrieves the rebound off the backboard from a shot that misses the basket.

The intercollegiate game is divided into two halves of 20 minutes each, with a 15-minute rest period at half-time. High school boys' teams play four quarters of eight minutes each, as do women, in official competition. However, if the score is tied at the end of regulation play, an overtime period of five minutes is scheduled in college games for men, two minutes for women and three minutes for high schoolers.

FOULS: Besides scoring two points for a regular basket, a team scores one point for each foul shot or "free throw," that it makes successfully. Free throws are awarded for a number of personal offenses, such as tripping, pushing, unnecessary roughness, holding, offensive charging or defensive blocking. If a foul is committed while a player is shooting, he is awarded two free throws, but if his shot scores, he only has one free throw. A player who commits five personal fouls in high school or college *Basketball* is expelled from the game. In professional *Basketball,* a player must go to the sidelines after he commits six fouls.

In addition to personal fouls, there are a number of technical fouls, such as: taking time out too often; coaching from the sidelines during play, or the failure of substitutes to report to the proper official. These usually result in the team's losing possession of the ball. Rules for play by girls and women vary at some points from those for men and boys, but the basic game is quite similar. Rules are revised each year by the Basketball Rules Committee, which is made up of representatives from a number of official athletic groups.

PASSING, DRIBBLING AND SHOOTING: Passing is one of the basic skills which facilitates successful performance in *Basketball*. There are several types of passes, such as: the chest pass, in which the player holds the ball close to his chest and then passes it with a strong pushing motion and wrist snap to a player on his team; the overhead pass, in which the ball is held overhead with both hands, and then released with a strong wrist snap; the shovel pass, in which the ball is held low— close to the floor—and passed underhand with a scooping motion, and the one-hand or shoulder pass, in which the ball is thrown like a baseball. Passes may travel directly through the air to another player or they may be bounced to him instead.

Dribbling is customarily done with one hand bouncing the ball out in front, where the ball can be readily controlled. The body is kept low, the head up, and the ball is pushed down and forward with a short bounce so that it does not come up higher than the waist. To avoid having an opponent take the ball away, a player tries to keep his body between the ball and his rivals.

One of the most familiar types of shots has been the two-hand set shot. Here, the shooter holds the ball about chin-high with both hands, and then brings it up with a strong thrusting forward movement, extending both the legs and arms. This shot has been largely replaced by the one-hand shot in which the player crouches slightly and then shoots the ball with only one hand (although the other hand may be used to guide or steady the ball for part of the shot).

The jump shot is usually employed from a dribble. The player comes to a stop, leaps high into the air and brings the ball overhead with his shooting hand behind it and the other hand

in front. At the jump's high point, he releases the ball with the shooting arm well-extended.

The lay-up shot is used when the player is close enough to the basket to leap directly up and bank the ball against the backboard or drop it directly over the hoop. One or both hands may be used in this shot.

In the hook-shot, the ball is brought to the side of the shooter that is away from the basket and thrown with a full sweeping motion of the shooting arm. This shot is often used by a center who is playing in the pivot position, close to the basket. Sometimes, he will stand with his back to the basket and then whirl to the right or left with a high, hooking shot. This type of shot is extremely difficult either to block or intercept.

DEFENSIVE PLAY: There are two major types of defense: man-to-man and zone. In man-to-man, each player is assigned one opponent to guard. He must always try to stay between this player and the basket to block his shot or prevent a drive for the basket. Depending on the style of play, defensive players may also switch the man for whom they are responsible.

Zone defense is based on a tightly guarded center area with the entire defensive territory divided into five smaller areas or zones. Each defensive player is responsible for one zone, although he may shift around in it. There are many variations of these defensive techniques, as well as a wide variety of offensive plays and movement patterns which make *Basketball* an extremely exciting game to watch.

VARIATIONS: For informal neighborhood *Basketball,* where space may be limited and there are not enough players to make up two full teams, a number of variations are available. The following are suggested in addition to the games described in Chapter One.

In *Guard Ball,* players divide into two equally matched teams. One team wears markings (handkerchiefs tied around arms, for instance) so that it is easy to tell members of one team from their opponents. The object of the game is for one team to pass the ball from player to player while preventing the other team from getting it. No individual player may hold the ball for more than five seconds. The regular rules of *Basketball* apply as far as passing, moving with the ball and guarding other players. When a rule is violated, the ball is given to the opposing team.

Since there is no set method of scoring, a winner is not usually declared. It is possible, however, to keep a time record, making the winner the team that is able to keep possession of the ball for the longest period. This game develops ball-handling skills and may be played either in a regular basketball court or in a clearly marked outdoor area.

Newcomb is played on a court about 25 by 50 feet with a seven-foot-high net dividing it into two equal parts. It is a good lead-up game for both *Basketball* and *Volleyball,* and either type of ball may be used.

The group is split into two equal teams, one on each side of the net. The object of the game is to catch the ball when it is thrown over the net and throw it back to the other side. The ball may not be passed from player to player but must be returned across the net by the player who catches it. A point is scored whenever a ball drops to the floor or if a team commits any of the following violations: hitting the net with the ball; throwing the ball under the net; relaying the ball from player to player, or throwing the ball outside the boundaries of the opponent's court.

Pin Basketball may be played when basketball hoops are not available. An area approximating that of a basketball court is used. A circle about three feet in diameter is drawn in the middle of both end lines. An Indian club is placed in each of these circles. (It may be attached to a square piece of wood to give it stability on bumpy ground.) A regular basketball is used, and the same rules apply for advancing the ball as in *Basketball.* The object of the game is for each team to knock down their opponent's Indian club and at the same time to prevent their own from being knocked over. The ball must hit the floor before hitting the club, and each hit scores two points. Players may not step

in the circles; the penalty for this or other violations (such as running with the ball) is a free throw from a line 12 feet away from the end circles.

In *One-Goal Basketball,* both teams shoot at the same basket. The only stipulation is that when a team gains possession of the ball (either when the other team scores, on an interception or on a rebound), it must take the ball out to a point about 30 feet away from the basket before putting it back into play. Two points are received for each basket; the game is 21 points. This game may be enjoyed in a very limited area with teams of only two or three players each. It is a particularly good game for driveways—with the hoop fastened above a garage door.

One Man Out is also played with one basket and as few as four players. One player is chosen to act as a guard against all the other players. The offensive players try to move the ball around and score, while the guard tries to intercept the ball or prevent them from scoring. Whenever a player scores a goal, he gets two points. When an offensive player misses a shot, he must change places with the guard. If the guard intercepts the ball, the last player to handle it becomes the guard. Each player is out to increase his own score, but the rule that a player must become the guard when he misses a shot discourages wild shots. The first player to reach a total of ten points is the winner.

Billiards

Billiards is a game played by two or more persons. It places a high premium on judgment, accuracy and disciplined movement—rather than physical endurance or speed. In all forms of the game, the basic object remains the same, to hit one ball—the cue ball—in such a way that it will bound into another ball—the object ball—and send it in a predetermined direction. Traditionally thought of as a game for "pool rooms," in recent years the game has become a fascinating and popular sport for family play. Part of the

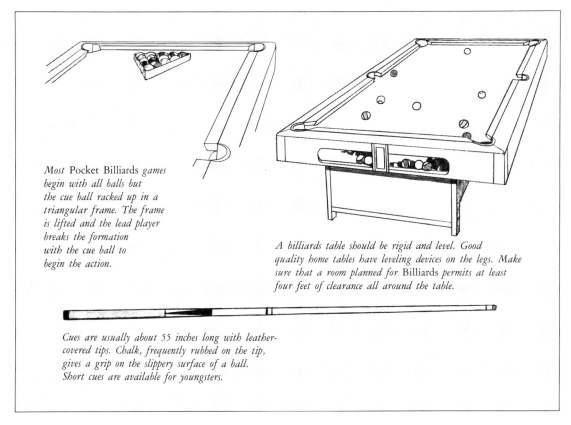

Most Pocket Billiards *games begin with all balls but the cue ball racked up in a triangular frame. The frame is lifted and the lead player breaks the formation with the cue ball to begin the action.*

A billiards table should be rigid and level. Good quality home tables have leveling devices on the legs. Make sure that a room planned for Billiards *permits at least four feet of clearance all around the table.*

Cues are usually about 55 inches long with leather-covered tips. Chalk, frequently rubbed on the tip, gives a grip on the slippery surface of a ball. Short cues are available for youngsters.

reason for this change of thought is the recent availability of relatively inexpensive equipment. Where once a table, even a stripped-down table, could not be bought for less than several hundred dollars, today tables are available for $150 new, and sometimes can be bought for even less secondhand.

Besides playing *Billiards* at home, families may now make use of community centers equipped with billiard tables and privately operated billiard parlors that are attractively designed and well lighted—a far cry from dim and dingy pool halls of the past.

EQUIPMENT: *Billiards* is played on heavy, green felt-covered tables that range in size from four by eight feet to five by ten feet. For one category of the game, called *Pocket Billiards* (also known as *Pool*), the table is equipped with six pockets—one in each corner and one in the middle of each long side. For the other basic form of the

game, *Carom Billiards,* there are no pockets. On both kinds of tables, a rubber railing surrounds the playing surface. Many tables are equipped for both forms of the game, the pockets being blocked off with inserts that create a solid railing around the table when the *Carom* game is played.

A number of colored billiard balls are used, the number and type depending on the specific game being played. These are struck with a billiard cue, a tapering stick averaging about 55 inches in length. The tip of the cue is covered with leather which is rubbed before a shot with a cube of chalk. The chalk prevents the tip from slipping when it hits the ball.

GRIP, STANCE AND AIM: The basic *Billiards* shot is made by gripping the cue about three or four inches from its thicker end with the right hand and placing the thin end of the shaft on a "bridge" formed with the extended left hand. This bridge is usually placed on the table five

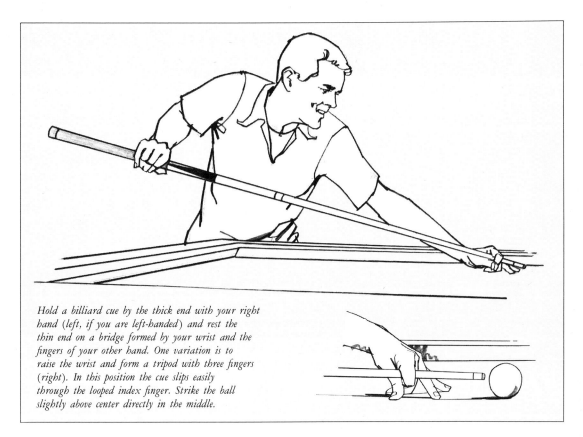

Hold a billiard cue by the thick end with your right hand (left, if you are left-handed) and rest the thin end on a bridge formed by your wrist and the fingers of your other hand. One variation is to raise the wrist and form a tripod with three fingers (right). In this position the cue slips easily through the looped index finger. Strike the ball slightly above center directly in the middle.

to seven inches from the cue ball. The player fashions the bridge by pressing his middle, ring and small fingers down on the table like a spread-out tripod; the cue goes over the thumb and through a loop made with the index finger. This position holds the cue tight enough to allow control, but still loose enough so that it can be stroked back and forth with ease.

The player faces the table in a comfortable stance, usually with his left foot forward, and he bends forward at the waist with his head directly above the cue stick. He sights along the cue as if he were a hunter sighting down the barrel of a rifle. Striking or "cueing" the ball is a highly developed art. Depending on how it is hit, the ball will behave in a variety of ways when it strikes an object ball or cushion. In most cases, a cue ball that is struck high in the center will follow the object ball after it has made contact. A cue ball that is hit low

in the center is called a "draw" shot, and it will return toward the player after hitting the object ball. A cue ball hit slightly left of center moves to the left after striking the object ball, and the reverse is true of a cue ball hit to the right of center. Controlling the cue ball in this way is called "English." The object of controlling the path taken by the cue ball is to determine the direction of the object ball once it is hit. The sharper the angle at which the object ball is hit, the more extreme the angle at which it will roll. The skilled player learns to judge the possibility of making shots that are extremely difficult. He also develops such control and precision that he is able to strike balls so that they travel to any desired point on the table.

THE GAME: *American Pyramid Pool*—often referred to as *Call Ball*—is probably the most popular *Billiards* game among beginners. It is the form of *Pocket Billiards* that requires the least skill, at the same time offering the opportunity to build up all of the skills that mark an advanced *Billiards* player. A white cue ball and 15 balls of different colors are used—each colored ball marked with a number from 1 to 15. The game is generally played by two, although three or four players can also participate. The numbered balls are arranged on the table in a triangle formation, with the apex of the triangle resting on the "foot spot," a dot printed on the green cloth. The cue ball is placed at any point behind the head or "balk" spot, a dot printed near the opposite end of the table. After the opening shot, or "break," the cue ball is played from wherever it lies.

The first player strikes the cue ball with sufficient force so that it hits the triangle and causes at least two object balls to touch a cushion or one object ball to roll into a pocket. If the player fails to do this, he gives up his turn and owes one ball to the table—that is, his score at that moment is minus one. When his turn comes up again, and if he successfully sinks a ball, he returns the ball to play by placing it on the foot spot. His score now stands at zero—he has "repaid" the ball. Should a player make the break successfully, he continues to shoot. Now he must call his shots, telling the others exactly which ball he proposes to pocket. If he fails to sink the called-ball, the turn goes to the next player, who also must call his shot.

A ball is pocketed successfully when it is called and sent into a pocket without the cue ball falling in behind it. An uncalled-ball sent into a pocket does not count and it is returned to play, unless the called-ball is sunk in the same shot. A player loses his turn, but incurs no penalty in the following instances: if he fails to hit the called-ball but hits another, if he pockets the cue ball along with the called-ball or if he pockets an uncalled-ball. A player incurs a penalty point and owes a ball to the table if any of the following happen: if he fails to hit the called-ball or any other ball with his cue ball; if he pockets the cue ball without pocketing another, or if he hits an object ball or cue ball off the table.

One point is given for every ball sunk successfully and, in a two-man game, the player who first gets eight points—that is, who sinks a majority of the object balls—wins the game. In a round with more players, the game ends when the person holding the third highest score cannot tie the second highest on the basis of the number of balls left on the table. The high-scoring player at that time wins.

VARIATIONS: In *Continuous Call Shot,* the players call not only the ball to be hit but also the pocket into which it will roll. Any ball pocketed that was not called is returned to the table. Players score one point for each successful pocketing, and the rules of *American Pyramid Pool* apply. There are a number of ways of scoring this game. It can be scored like *American Pyramid Pool,* with the first player in a two-man game to score eight points winning. A match can also be set at 21, 50, 75 or 100 points. In these high-score matches, whenever only one object ball remains in play, all balls pocketed are returned to the table and set up in triangle formation with the apex, or head ball, missing. The ball not set in the triangle remains where it lay on the table.

Rotation is a somewhat more demanding variety of *Pocket Billiards* in which the player must always pocket the lowest numbered ball on the table. To begin, balls are set in triangle formation with the number one ball at the apex, the two and three at the other corners. On the break, any ball sunk counts, but after that, the balls must be pocketed in numerical order. However, when another ball is pocketed along with the designated ball, both balls count. In scoring the game, the number on each ball is its point value. A player who pockets the four, seven and nine, for example, has 20 points. The winning total for *Rotation* is usually set at 61. As in *Pocket Billiards,* the player shooting continues to shoot until he misses or sinks the wrong ball.

In *Carom* or *Straight Rail Billiards,* there are no pockets, and the object is not to take balls out of play but to hit the cue ball in such a way that it follows a predetermined path and hits the other balls.

Three balls are used: one red and two white, with one of the latter distinguished by a black dot. The balls are placed in the following pattern: the red ball on the foot spot, the marked white ball on the balk spot and the other white ball (the cue ball) toward one of the long sides of the table and on a line with, and within six inches of, the marked white ball. The object is to hit the cue ball in such a way that it hits both of the other balls. On the opening shot of a match, the cue ball must hit the red ball first, and then the marked white ball. After that, the balls may be hit in any order. Cushion shots are usually employed—the first object ball being hit directly, then the cue ball bouncing off a cushion into the second object ball. However, if sufficient reverse spin is put on the cue ball, it may hit the first object ball and then roll directly into the second.

One point is scored for each successful shot. If a player misses both object balls, his opponent gets a point. A player continues to shoot so long as he makes successful shots; then his opponent takes over. A cue ball hit off the table is placed on the balk spot, and the striker is not charged any penalty. If a successful shot is made before the ball goes off the table, the striker receives the point and continues to shoot with his cue ball placed on the balk spot. A set number of points—25, 50 or 75—determines the winner.

In *Bank-Shot Billiards,* the cue ball must strike at least one cushion before hitting either object ball. If the cue ball hits an object ball before hitting a cushion, it is a foul and the player loses his turn. In *Cushion Billiards,* the cue ball must bound off a cushion at least once to complete the shot. The cushions may be touched before either object ball is hit, between hitting the two object balls or at both times.

Three-Cushion Billiards, as the name implies, requires that three cushions be hit before a shot is completed successfully. In most versions of the game, the three cushions must be hit before the second object ball is struck. This is a game for advanced players, and the winning total for a match is usually set at 10, 15 or 20 points.

Bowling

Bowling, a sport played by two or more persons, is believed to have begun more than a thousand years ago in Italy. It was played in England as early as the 12th century. During its long history, the game has been played both indoors and out on such surfaces as clay, cinders, grass and wood. In its earlier days, large stones were used for balls.

In North America, the modern form of *Bowling* which attracts millions of enthusiasts is *Tenpins.* It is played indoors on wooden alleys by two or more people or by competing teams. Every year, hundreds of local, state, provincial and national tournaments are held, sponsored by a variety of U.S., Canadian and international bowling organizations. Although tournament *Bowling* has a large following, the primary appeal of the game is as an amateur sport for all ages; children from the age of eight or nine, parents and grandparents all enjoy playing the game and competing with one another.

EQUIPMENT: Bowling alleys are far too expensive for all but a very few to build and maintain in their homes. Most people play in commercially operated establishments, but, in addition, many churches, Y's, social clubs, recreation agencies, hospitals, colleges and schools maintain alleys.

The standard bowling alley is 41 to 42 inches wide. It is 60 feet from the foul line to the number one pin, and there is an approach area behind the foul line of at least 15 feet. The surface of the alley must be of smooth, perfectly level wood. On either side of the alley are gutters which carry off poorly aimed balls; to the sides and above the gutters are rails used to return balls to the bowler. In almost all modern bowling alleys there are automatic machines which return the ball to the bowler.

The pins used in *Tenpin Bowling* are made of hard maple or laminated wood. They are 15 inches high and weigh between three and three and one-half pounds. A machine or, in a few cases, a "pin boy" sets up the pins in a triangle,

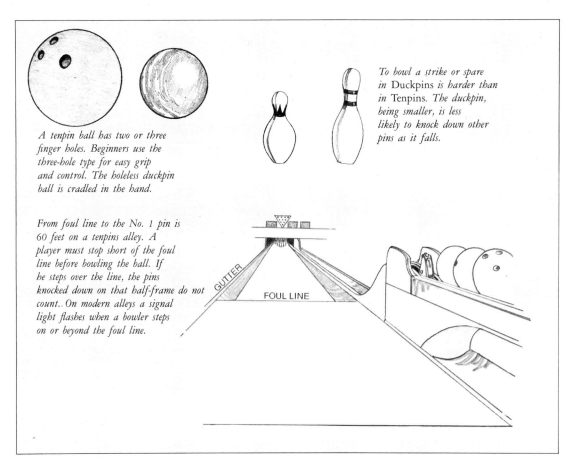

A tenpin ball has two or three finger holes. Beginners use the three-hole type for easy grip and control. The holeless duckpin ball is cradled in the hand.

From foul line to the No. 1 pin is 60 feet on a tenpins alley. A player must stop short of the foul line before bowling the ball. If he steps over the line, the pins knocked down on that half-frame do not count. On modern alleys a signal light flashes when a bowler steps on or beyond the foul line.

To bowl a strike or spare in Duckpins *is harder than in* Tenpins. *The duckpin, being smaller, is less likely to knock down other pins as it falls.*

GUTTER

FOUL LINE

the sides of which measure three feet each, with the apex toward the bowler. Pins are numbered from 1 to 10.

Bowling balls are made in different sizes and weights, but they cannot be larger than 27 inches in circumference or heavier than 16 pounds. Some balls have two holes, some three. The bowler holds his ball by inserting fingers in these holes. Most bowling alleys provide balls as part of their fee, but many enthusiasts own their own bowling balls. Bowling balls are available at sporting goods stores and at many large department stores; they sell for as little as $10.00. Before selecting a ball, either at a bowling alley or, more important, at a store, several balls of different sizes and weights should be held and swung to determine which one is the most comfortable.

Special, lightweight, rubber-soled shoes are used for *Bowling,* and most bowling alleys require that they be worn. These can usually be rented for a nominal fee at a bowling alley or bought at a sporting goods store.

ACTION: In *Tenpins,* the bowler stands as far behind the foul line as he wishes, takes as many steps as desired (being careful not to step beyond the foul line) and rolls the ball toward the pins. He is allowed to bowl two balls during one turn, (which, for scoring purposes, is called a "frame") unless he knocks down all of the pins with the first ball—a "strike." If a bowler knocks down all of the pins in one frame with his two balls, it is a "spare." Each player bowls in turn until all players have bowled ten frames. The score is then tabulated, and the bowler with the highest score wins.

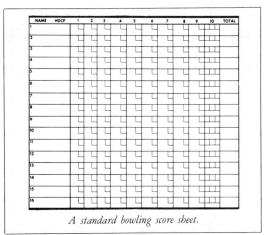

A standard bowling score sheet.

SCORING: In scoring a *Bowling* game, a sheet with rows divided into ten squares, one for each frame, is used. Each player is assigned a row of squares for tabulating his score. The small box in the upper right hand corner of each square is used to keep track of strikes (marked with an X) and spares (marked with a slash /). The total score for a frame is put in the main part of the square below the small box.

Basic scoring allows one point for each pin knocked down but much higher scores can be amassed by bowling strikes and spares. For example, if a strike (ten points) is made in one frame, the total number of pins knocked down by the player's next two balls are added to the first score and are counted again in the second frame. Thus, if a player knocks down nine pins in his second frame, the nine is added to the ten in the first frame giving him a score of 19 for frame one and nine for frame two—for a total score of 28 points at the end of his second turn. If a spare, (ten points) is made in one frame, the score made with the first ball of the next frame is added to the score of the spare and also is counted in its own frame. For example, if a player rolls a spare in frame one and knocks down three pins on his first roll in frame two, his total for frame one is 13. If he knocks down two more pins with his second roll in frame two, his total for that frame will be five, giving him a score of 18—13 plus five—at the end of his second frame.

To illustrate further, if a player bowls a strike followed by two more strikes, he gets the original ten plus 20 more in the first frame. Using the scoring system for strikes, each of the other two strikes are counted in successive frames. Thus, a perfect game in bowling is 300 points, achieved by rolling nothing but strikes, each one of which has a cumulative total of 30 points. A game ends after the 10th frame unless the bowler makes a strike or spare in the last frame. If this happens, he is permitted to bowl additional balls—two for a strike and one for a spare.

GRIP, APPROACH AND DELIVERY: If a two-hole ball is used, the thumb and middle finger are inserted into the holes, and the other fingers are spread out flat on the surface of the ball. If a three-hole ball is used, the thumb, second and third fingers are inserted, with the others on the ball.

A beginner should use the easiest possible approach and delivery. He stands, facing the pins, about eight feet behind the foul line. His knees are bent and his left foot is a few inches in front of the right, which rests on a line to the right of the number one pin. In two steps, moving first the right foot and then the left, the bowler advances to a point a few inches behind the foul line. As he moves, his body bends slightly forward while the arm holding the ball slowly swings back and then forward like a pendulum. The ball should be released at the end of the second step, at a point immediately beyond the foul line. As the ball is released the palm of the hand faces forward, directly at the pins, and the arm continues moving forward and up in a follow-through. Speed in the delivery is not essential; a ball rolled slowly can knock down as many pins as a ball rolled fast.

As the beginning bowler gains skill, he may vary his approach to suit his personal style. He may find, for example, that a three-, four- or five-step approach is more comfortable than the standard two-step method. He will also learn several ways to control the ball so that he can deliver it smoothly, directly toward the pins he is trying to hit. A straight ball, released about ten boards from the right gutter, will follow a straight line, moving diagonally down the alley to the pocket between the one and three pins. If bowled smoothly and with enough force, a straight ball will yield a strike. A hook ball, released near the right gutter with a quick twist of the wrist, will roll down the lane close to the gutter until it nears the end of the alley when it hooks over toward the one and three pins. A back-up ball spins from left to right, moving into the one-three pocket. A curve ball is delivered from the center of the alley and travels diagonally to the right and then curves gradually back into the one-three pocket. If pins left standing after one shot are on the left, the ball should be aimed at them on the diagonal starting from the right. If the pins are on the right, the ball is released on the left.

VARIATIONS: *Duckpins* can be played on a regular bowling alley, provided a line is drawn ten feet in front of the regular foul line. Any duckpin ball which drops beyond this second line is declared foul. The pins are smaller than bowling pins—only nine inches high. The balls are made of wood. They are exactly five inches in diameter and have no holes. Players bowl three balls in each frame and bowl two frames in one turn. If a player makes a strike with the first ball, he does not bowl again in that frame. As in *Tenpin Bowling,* he adds the score of the next two balls in the following frame to the score for the first as well as to the score for the second frame. A spare is credited if all pins are knocked down by the first two balls in a frame. The third ball is not used, and the score made by the first ball bowled in the next frame is added to the score for the first frame as well as to its own frame. The player with the highest score after ten frames is the winner.

Boccie is a form of *Bowling,* especially popular among Americans of Italian descent. The court is dirt, mixed with clay and sand. It is about 60 feet long and ten feet wide, and has wooden sides about one foot high. Eight special boccie balls, with diameters of four and one-half inches, and one smaller ball, the "Jack"—two and three-quarter inches in diameter—are needed. If boccie balls cannot be obtained duckpin balls, which are readily available at large sporting goods stores, may be used.

An even number of players (two, four or eight) divide into two teams. If eight are playing, two players from each team stand at opposite ends of the court ready to play alternate innings or frames. One team uses plain balls; the other uses balls marked with chalk or paint. A coin is tossed to determine which team begins. A player from the first team rolls the Jack ball from one end of the court to the other. With an underhand motion, he then rolls or throws one of the larger balls and tries to make it land as close as possible to the Jack ball. Then the members of the opposing team bowl in turn until someone's ball lands closer to the Jack ball than the first team's ball. When this happens, members of the first team bowl in turn, trying to get a ball closer to the Jack than the opposing team's closest ball. When all balls are bowled by both teams, the inning is complete. A player may legally hit the Jack ball or other balls with his ball. If the Jack ball is hit out of the court, it is replaced at the center of the far end. Other balls hit out of the court are out of play for the rest of the game.

Only the team with the ball closest to the Jack scores in each inning. It gets one point for each of its balls that is closer to the Jack than any of the opposing team's balls. Thus, if a team has four players it can score four points (if each of its balls is closer to the Jack than any opponent's ball), or three points or one. The winning team begins the next inning by throwing the Jack ball and bowling first. The first team to accumulate 21 points wins, provided it has at least two more points than the opposing team. (A game continues beyond 21 points if necessary.) The team that wins two out of three games takes the match.

Croquet

Croquet is a lawn game believed to have originated in France during the 13th or 14th Century; by the 15th Century it was being played

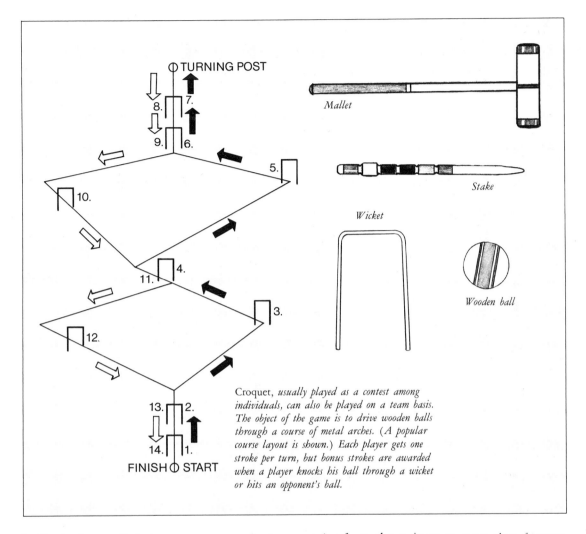

TURNING POST

Mallet

Stake

Wicket

Wooden ball

Croquet, *usually played as a contest among individuals, can also be played on a team basis. The object of the game is to drive wooden balls through a course of metal arches. (A popular course layout is shown.) Each player gets one stroke per turn, but bonus strokes are awarded when a player knocks his ball through a wicket or hits an opponent's ball.*

FINISH START

in England as well. It became very popular in North America in the late 1800s. *Croquet* is an ideal family game because it can be played with equal facility by the young and the old, the strong and the weak—in fact by everyone in sufficiently good health to swing a light mallet and old enough to understand simple rules. From two to ten players may participate. The object of the game is for each player to hit his ball through a course of metal arches—called "wickets"—and the first player to complete the course is the winner.

EQUIPMENT: Croquet sets can be purchased at most large sporting goods stores and range in

price from about $7.00 to more than $200.00. A set includes two 12- to 15-inch-high wooden stakes, nine wickets—ten inches high and five inches wide, five to ten wooden or hard rubber balls—each about three-and-one-half inches in diameter—and five to ten wooden mallets. The mallets have cylindrical heads about 12 inches long and three inches in diameter; each has a two-and-one-half-foot-long handle.

THE COURT: *Croquet* is played on a flat area of closely cut grass. The size of the court depends upon the space available, but it is best if the area is at least 25 by 50 feet. Tournament *Croquet* requires a court that is 30 by 70 feet. A stake is set into the ground at either end of the court, halfway between the sidelines. The nine wickets are then set into the lawn—forming a course through which the players hit the ball. Although there is an official pattern to this course, wide variations are permitted for home play. Normally, the first wicket is set in the ground close to the starting stake and the last wicket close to the turning stake. The other wickets may be set up in just about any pattern: the more convoluted the arrangement, the more difficult the course is to complete. In any case, each player must hit the ball through the wickets in their designated order.

ACTION: After the court is set up, each player chooses a mallet and ball. The balls are painted different colors for easy identification. Then the order of play is decided. In turn, each player stands at a point 15 feet away from one of the stakes and hits his ball toward it. The player whose ball lands closest to the stake goes first, and the others follow in an order determined by the closeness of their balls to the stake.

The players may act as individuals or divide into two teams. In either case the rules are very much the same, with players taking turns hitting their balls. For his first shot, each player places his ball a mallet's length in front of the home stake and then hits the ball toward the first wicket. If the ball passes through the wicket the player gets a second shot. If a ball passes through two wickets, the player is entitled to two more shots. The player continues to shoot until he fails to drive his ball through a wicket, and the turn passes to the next player.

It is often advantageous for a player to try to hit another player's ball. If player A, for example, hits an opponent's ball, he has the following options: He may place his ball against the ball he hit, and hit both at once so that they travel in any desired direction. He then has two shots to try to pass his ball through a wicket. On the other hand, player A may put his ball in back of his opponent's, place his foot on his own ball and tap B's ball away in any desired direction. After driving B's ball away, A has another shot. Finally, player A can decline to hit B's ball at all, and, instead, take two extra shots himself in an effort to move his own ball forward. A player may hit an opponent's ball only once—after which he is said to be "dead" on it—before passing his own ball through a wicket. Once he hits his ball through a wicket he may hit the same opponent's ball again. If A, for example, hits B's ball on the approach to wicket number three, he can exercise his options about driving B's ball away. After that, he must pass through wicket three before he may hit B's ball again.

If a player does not drive his ball through a wicket or hit another player's ball, he is not allowed any extra strokes and may not hit his ball again until the other players have had their turns. The first player to complete the course—pass through all the wickets, hit the turning stake, pass through the wickets on the return course and hit the home stake—wins the game.

Team play is very much the same as a game among individuals, except for one important difference: If a player passes through all the wickets but has not yet touched the home stake, he may elect to become a "rover." This means he may travel about freely trying to assist his partners (he may even hit his partners' balls through a wicket) and slow the opposition. A roving player may try to hit another player's ball on each turn if he desires. No ball is dead to him. He can, of course, take shots only when his turn comes up.

SKILLS: The basic skills required in *Croquet* are steadiness of hand, sharpness of eye and a sense of tactics. A player must know, for example, whether he will advance his own cause more by hitting an opponent's ball away or by taking two shots himself to move his ball forward. These are skills mostly acquired by practice. Unlike many other games in which a ball is hit by a bat or club or mallet, there is no set method of holding or swinging a croquet mallet. Players usually find that the easiest way to hit the ball is to hold the mallet with both hands, face the ball and swing in a manner similar to a putting

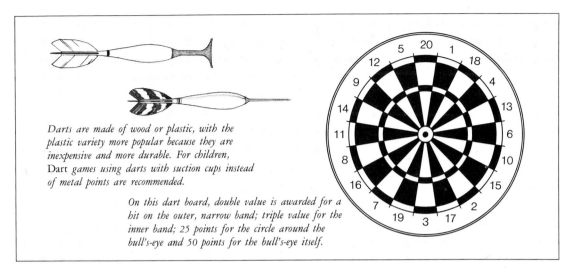

Darts are made of wood or plastic, with the plastic variety more popular because they are inexpensive and more durable. For children, Dart games using darts with suction cups instead of metal points are recommended.

On this dart board, double value is awarded for a hit on the outer, narrow band; triple value for the inner band; 25 points for the circle around the bull's-eye and 50 points for the bull's-eye itself.

shot in *Golf*. Often, however, they may find it helpful to stand over the ball by swinging the mallet between the legs.

Darts

Darts are a popular form of amusement in English pubs and in American recreation rooms. The game can also be played out of doors. Indoors or outdoors, *Darts* should never be played where people are likely to walk in front of or behind the target and should not be played by young children unless they are carefully supervised.

EQUIPMENT: There are two kinds of darts: ones with rubber suction heads and ones with pointed metal tips. The latter kind is more accurate and more commonly used.

There are different types of targets as well. Indoor targets are hung on a wall, the bull's-eye about five feet from the floor. The wall should be one that can take rough treatment, because some of the darts thrown will probably hit it rather than the target.

The most common indoor target is about 15 inches in diameter and consists of several concentric bands ranging in width from one and one-half to two inches. Each band is marked with a different point value—ranging from 20 for a bull's-eye (a direct hit in the center) to one for a dart landing in the outer band.

Another indoor board, the "clock-face," has 20 wedge-shaped segments. Each has a value from 1 to 20, and a dart that lands in a particular segment scores accordingly. However, should a dart land in the narrow circular band just inside the outer ring, the score is doubled; if it lands in the inner circular band, the score is tripled. A hit made in the band surrounding the bull's-eye scores 25 points. A bull's-eye itself is worth 50 points.

An outdoor target is about twice as large as an indoor target and has ten bands, each three inches wide. It should be set up about five feet from the ground either against an outdoor wall or nailed to a tree.

ACTION: From two to nine players participate. Players stand on a line, ten feet away from an indoor target and 20 feet away from an outdoor target. In turn, each player throws one or more darts at the target. If each player throws one dart, the score is tallied and the darts removed after everyone has had a turn. If each player throws more than one dart during his turn, he withdraws the darts after finishing his turn and marks down his score. In most informal *Dart* games, the first player to reach a set number—50, 100 or 150—is the winner.

Football

On the high school, college and professional levels, regulation *Tackle Football* is one of the most popular team sports in the United States. The regulation game, however, does not lend itself to family or informal neighborhood play. To stage it properly, a full complement of 22 players (11 per team) is necessary, as well as a lined field with a playing area 100 yards long and goalposts. In addition, uniforms and expensive protective equipment for each player are needed.

Because of the violent nature of the sport, with aggressive contact being an important element in both offensive and defensive play, injuries frequently occur. It is vital, therefore, to have careful supervision and medical aid available. Even such modified forms of *Tackle Football,* as *Six-Man Football* or *150-Pound Football,* in which the same basic skills of charging, blocking and tackling are used, cannot be played on a recreational basis as easily as many other team sports, and are dangerous even under proper supervision.

There are games based on *Tackle Football,* however, that can be played without elaborate uni-forms and equipment, with teams of smaller numbers and with the chances of injury greatly reduced. Foremost among these games is *Touch Football*—a game suitable for family and neighborhood play. It may be played by everyone, from eight-year-olds to people in their late middle years, providing they are in good health. Sometimes it is even played as a co-educational sport. The basic difference between this and the regulation game is that the ball carrier is stopped simply by being touched with both hands by an opponent, instead of being tackled. The basic skills of passing, kicking and running are very similar to those found in regulation *Tackle,* but *Touch Football* depends most on passing.

FIELD AND EQUIPMENT: When circumstances permit, the game should be played on a regulation-size field. However, it can be, and often is, played on a much shorter field. A regulation football is used, and gym suits, sweat suits or other informal clothing may be worn. It is a good idea, however, to have members of opposing teams wear jerseys of different colors so that identification is simple. Helmets, cleats and pads are not required, but because the game does

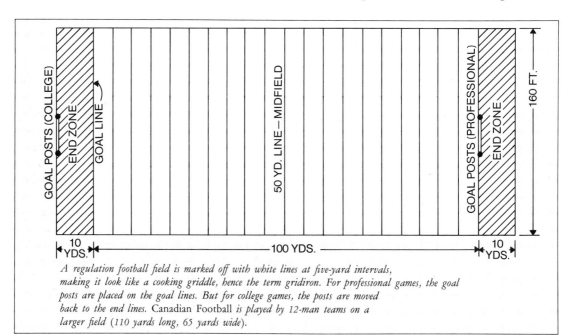

A regulation football field is marked off with white lines at five-yard intervals, making it look like a cooking griddle, hence the term gridiron. For professional games, the goal posts are placed on the goal lines. But for college games, the posts are moved back to the end lines. Canadian Football is played by 12-man teams on a larger field (110 yards long, 65 yards wide).

permit limited blocking, mouthguards are useful protective devices.

GLOSSARY OF TERMS: *Line of Scrimmage* is the line on which the forward motion of the football came to an end on the previous play. Linesmen from both teams line up here, and, from this point, the ball is put into motion again when the next play is called.

T-Formation for many years was the classic football formation and from it have been devised several variations. In the standard *T-formation,* the line is formed by two ends at either extreme, then two tackles, two guards, and, in the middle, the center, who passes the ball from the line to the backfield. Four players are in the backfield: the quarterback, who stands just behind the center and receives the ball; the right and left halfbacks, who stand behind, and respectively to the right and left of the quarterback, and the fullback, who is directly behind the quarterback. In play, when the quarterback receives the ball, he may pass it off to one of the other backs. In informal *Touch* play, the *T-formation* is usually modified to conform with the number of players in the game.

Downs are the four plays given to the offensive team to move the ball ten yards down the field toward the opposition's goal line. When a team succeeds in moving the ball the required distance within four downs, it receives a *First Down* and begins the cycle again.

Forward Pass is an offensive aerial play in which a backfield man receives the ball from behind the line of scrimmage and throws it to a teammate running down field.

Interception is a forward pass caught by a member of the opposition. When this happens, the defensive team moves over to the offense.

Lateral Pass is a pass in which the ball carrier throws the ball to a teammate who is behind him or to his side, but not in front of him.

Touchdown is a six-point score that occurs when the offensive team moves the ball into the opposition's end zone.

Extra Point is scored by a kick, usually a placement, made by a team after scoring a touchdown. The kicked ball must clear the crossbar between the goal posts and stay between the uprights to score the extra point. In college *Football,* the line of scrimmage for the conversion is at the opponent's three-yard line; in professional *Football,* at the two-yard line.

Field Goal, scored by a place-kick or drop-kick, is made by the offense from any point on the field. The ball must clear the crossbar of the opposition's goal and stay between the uprights to score three points.

Safety is a score made when a member of the offensive team is stopped with the ball behind his own goal line. This counts as two points for the defensive team.

Periods of Play: The game is divided into halves and again into quarters. In the regulation *Tackle* game, a quarter is 15 minutes of actual play. There is a rest period between halves that lasts 15 minutes. In *Touch Football,* period times vary according to local rules, but the most popular usage is to have four six-minute quarters with a six-minute rest period between halves.

Kickoff is the method of putting the ball into play in the first quarter, the second half and after each touchdown. The ball is place-kicked from the kicking team's 40-yard line or from just behind it. It is booted to the opposition which has the choice of catching the ball and running with it, or declaring it a dead ball and beginning their first down from the point where it came to rest. If a kickoff is declared dead after it falls behind the opposition's goal line, the offensive team takes the ball on its own 20-yard line.

Punt is a kick of the ball, usually made on a fourth down. It is employed when the offensive team thinks it cannot make a *First Down* in the single play left. The ball is snapped to a backfield man who kicks it as far down field as possible so that the opposition will take possession of the ball deep in its own territory.

End Zone is the section of the field at either end of the playing area. In regulation play, each end zone is 30 feet deep by 160 feet wide. Goal lines are at the front of the end zones. A ball carrier of the offensive team who passes the opposition's goal line scores a touchdown. Goalposts are at the back of the end zone in college play, and they are on the goal line in the professional game.

ACTION: The ball is put into play by the kicking team at the beginning of the game, the beginning of the second half and after a score is made by kicking it from their 40-yard line. If the ball goes past the goal line, it is put in play on the receiving team's 20-yard line. If it is caught and run back, the following rules apply: Players providing interference for the ball carrier may block their opponents, but they may not use their hands to hold them nor may they have both feet off the ground at once in a "flying block." The ball carrier is stopped and the ball is dead when a defensive player touches him simultaneously with both hands.

After its return of the kickoff, the offensive team must advance the ball ten yards in four downs from the original line of scrimmage, or surrender the ball to the opposition. The center lineman stands on the line of scrimmage and passes the ball between his legs to a backfield player who may then run with it, kick it or pass it forward, backwards or sidewards. Backfield players may not move toward the line of scrimmage until the ball is snapped by the center.

In *Six-Man Touch Football,* the offensive team must have at least three men on the line of scrimmage; the other three may be in the backfield. In *Nine-Man Touch Football* at least five offensive players are linemen.

During play, in *Touch,* any offensive player may receive a pass and any defensive player may intercept a pass. The defensive team moves onto the offense by gaining possession of the ball. This may occur in a number of ways: The ball may be intercepted during a forward pass try; the offensive team may lose possession after failing to advance ten yards in the alloted four downs; the ball may be fumbled (dropped) by the runner and captured by the opposition; the

ball may be received by the opposition after a touchdown, or the ball may be received on a punt when the offensive team believes it cannot make the required ten yards in the remaining number of downs.

PENALTIES: There are a number of penalties in *Touch Football* that can be declared against either the offense or defense. Tackling, tripping or roughing cost the offending team 15 yards. That is, if the offensive team is guilty of the foul, the line of scrimmage is moved back 15 yards; if the defensive team is guilty, the line is moved forward the same distance (toward the defensive team's goal). Illegal interference with a pass receiver (blocking him before he touches the ball) costs the defensive team ten yards. Five yards is charged to either side when a member of the team is offside—begins action before the ball is snapped by the center. A team which has been fouled may, if it wishes, refuse the penalty. For example, if the offensive team completes a 30 yard forward pass and during the play one of its members has been roughed by the defense, the offense will undoubtedly overlook the foul in favor of gaining the 30 yards (instead of 15). When a penalty is accepted, the down is played over again.

VARIATIONS: *Flag Football,* like *Touch Football,* is a modification of the regulation game. Played mostly by schools and colleges as an intramural game, the basic difference between *Flag* and *Touch* is that in the former, each player wears two "flags," or strips of cloth about two inches wide and 24 inches long. These are loosely attached behind his right and left hips, either with pieces of adhesive or by tucking the flags beneath his belt. In either case, the flags are easily removed, and this is the method of stopping the ball carrier, rather than tackling him or touching him with both hands. In some games, it is necessary to remove only one flag to stop the ball carrier; in other games, both flags must be removed.

Flag Football is even more informal than *Touch,* and players can make up their own rules before each game. Generally, however, the field is shorter (40 by 80 yards) than is required for regulation *Touch*. In the short-field game, two 30-yard lines are marked across the field. Instead of having to advance the ball ten yards in four downs, the offensive team must move it across a 30 yard marker in the alloted four downs to retain possession.

Street Football is the most informal of all football games. This is the kind of *Touch* game most often seen on city streets, in playgrounds and in parks. Eight or ten youngsters get together and form into two teams, making use of whatever open space is available to them. They mark off goal lines and divide the "field" into zones. Generally, players have no fixed positions, and a boy might be a lineman on one play and a backfield man on the next. Finer points, such as the requirement that the ball be snapped from between the center's legs, are more often ignored than not, and questions of penalties are usually decided by an argument rather than by a referee. The game may or may not be divided into periods, depending on the attitudes of the players; in fact, the game usually goes on until everybody is tired, bored or has to go home for lunch. Basic skills are perhaps learned more slowly in this kind of play, but for pre-teenage boys (and their fathers), *Street Football* may often be more fun than any other variety of the game because of its almost structureless form and its extreme casualness.

Handball

Handball is a game for two or four players, in which individuals or teams compete to hit a small rubber ball against a wall in such a way that it cannot be hit on the rebound and returned to the wall by the opposition. It is a game that requires speed, stamina and coordination. There are two major varieties of the sport: *One-Wall Handball* and *Four-Wall Handball,* with rules quite similar for both.

EQUIPMENT: Aside from a court, very little is needed to play *Handball*. The standard ball is of rubber and is not quite two inches thick.

Gloves, although not necessary, may be worn. (However, gloves in which the thumb and fingers are webbed together are illegal.) In informal games, an ordinary tennis ball can be substituted for a handball.

THE ONE-WALL COURT: This should be 34 feet long and 20 feet wide with a 16-foot-high-wall at one end of its length. A line, called the short line, is marked 16 feet from the wall and parallel to it. Nine feet behind the short line there are two marks—one by each sideline. These indicate a line in front of which players must stand while serving. This court is the optimum one, necessary for regulation play. For informal play, however, it is possible to use any wall—indoors or out—and mark off suitable boundaries.

THE ONE-WALL GAME: The server stands between the service marks and the short line. He bounces the ball once and hits it with his hand so that it will strike the wall and return to the ground between the short line and the service marks. The opposing player—or players—must return the ball by hitting it on the fly or after one bounce. A returned ball must strike the wall on the fly. The serve passes from one player (or one team) to the next if: the server steps in front of the short line twice in a row while making his serve; the server steps out of bounds twice; after striking the wall, the serve lands anywhere but between the short line and the service marks.

In doubles play, either player of a team may return the ball after the opposition hits it. The serving side continues to serve as long as it commits no service faults and it returns the ball fairly in exchanges. When a team loses the service, it does not lose a point, as points can only be made by the serving team. The action begins with the server standing in the service area and his teammate standing outside the court boundaries. The two opponents must stand behind the short line. After a served ball has crossed the shortline, the server's partner steps into the playing area. When the first player makes a fault or he or his teammate fail to successfully return in an exchange, service immediately moves to the opposition and both players on that side are given a turn. From this point on, teammates on both teams serve before the service changes sides. A game consists of 21 points.

THE FOUR-WALL COURT: This should be a room 46 feet long and 22 feet wide with walls that are 22 feet high. A line, the short line, is at the 23 foot mark, dividing the court in half, lengthwise. Five feet in back of this line is the service line. A foot-and-one-half from each side wall and parallel to them, there are lines which connect the short and service lines. These form two boxes—the service boxes.

THE FOUR-WALL GAME: The rules of the *Four-Wall* game are basically similar to those of the *Two-Wall* game. A major exception, however, is that, during an exchange, if the ball hits the front wall and then bounds off any other wall or the ceiling, it is still in play and may be hit on the fly or after one bounce. The server must always serve from one of the designated boxes, and, in a doubles game, the server's partner stands in the opposite service box with his back to the front wall until the serve is in play. For a service to be considered fair, the ball must bounce on the floor between the service lines and the short line, hit into the front wall and rebound behind the short line. A server has two chances to hit a fair serve on each point. A serve is not good if: the ball fails to land behind the short line; it hits the ceiling or back wall before bouncing on the floor; it hits the front wall and then both side walls before touching the floor. A serve that falls in front of the short line may be played if the opposition wishes to accept it. Players serve in the same order as in *One-Wall Handball*.

After a serve is in play, the opposing teams (or opposing players) take turns in returning the ball to the front wall after each rebound. In doubles play, either player on a team may hit the ball during a rally. Balls may be played as they rebound off any wall or the ceiling, but they must hit the front wall before striking any other. If a ball hit toward the front wall strikes an opponent, the serve is taken over. In doubles

play, if the ball strikes a teammate, a point or service is lost. If a returned ball is hit into the angle where the front wall and floor meet, it is a fault. (A point is lost or service switches sides.) Should a player block or hold an opponent and prevent him from making a return, it is a "hinder." If the hinder is intentional, it is a foul. (Either a point or service is lost.) If unintentional, the point is played over. The game is scored like *One-Wall Handball*.

POSITIONING, STROKES AND STRATEGY: In both forms of *Handball*, each player must learn how the ball rebounds when it hits the walls at different angles and speeds, so he can try to position himself in a spot where the opposition will be unable to return his shot. Footwork is extremely important. Players stand with the left foot slightly forward, their weight evenly balanced, their knees bent and their bodies in a slight crouch—a position which they are able to move out of quickly.

There are several standard strokes. The overarm is an action much like throwing a ball overhand; the sidearm is again similar to a sidearm throw; the underarm is a stroke in which the arm moves up and the ball is struck with the heel of the hand. This last stroke is generally used for a "kill"—a shot intended to hit the front wall at a point so low that its rebound will be too fast to be easily handled. The stroke that a player employs in any shot depends primarily on his positioning in terms of the ball. A ball may be legally hit with any portion of the palm or with a closed fist. A strong wrist snap puts speed on the ball, and after the ball has been struck, the hand follows through toward the point of aim. Learning an opponent's weaknesses and trying to make points by capitalizing on these weaknesses is the key to *Handball* strategy. It often helps to vary the pace of shots from fast strokes to easy lobs. A player should be aware of all chances to kill the ball or force his opponent into a position on the court from which it will be difficult for him to make a return. Generally, players try to keep themselves in the center of the court while—at the same time—forcing their opponents toward the edges.

Hockey

Hockey is one of the world's oldest games; the earliest form was played by the ancient Greeks and Egyptians. Its most common form is *Field Hockey,* a game played for many centuries in the British Isles where it was first introduced by invading Roman soldiers. In Scotland, it is called *Shinty* or *Shinny* and in Ireland, *Hurling* or *Hurley. Ice Hockey,* another common form of *Hockey,* originated in Canada more than 100 years ago. It is considered the unofficial national game of Canada, where, each year, an estimated, 100,000 Canadians play organized *Hockey.*

Field Hockey

Field Hockey is contested in many countries as a vigorous and exciting men's sport, but in North America it is played chiefly at girls' schools and women's colleges.

FORMATION: *Field Hockey* is played by two teams,

11 players to a team: five forwards in the front line, three halfbacks in the middle line, two fullbacks in the back line and a goalkeeper. It is an hour-long game divided into halves and is played on fields ranging in size from 150 by 270 feet to 180 by 300 feet. Three lines divide the field into fourths. There is a goal at either end of the field with posts 12 feet apart. A striking circle, beyond which no goal shot may be taken, is drawn 48 feet from the goal posts. All players wear shin pads, and the goalkeeper wears body padding and a face mask as well. Curved sticks are used to advance a leather-covered, cork-centered ball down the field and into the goal area.

ACTION: The game begins with a "bully," also known as a "face-off," in the center of the field. The center forwards face each other, holding their sticks just above the ground on opposite sides of the ball, which has been placed between them. At the official's signal, they touch the ground and then the opponent's stick, alternately, three times apiece. At the end of the

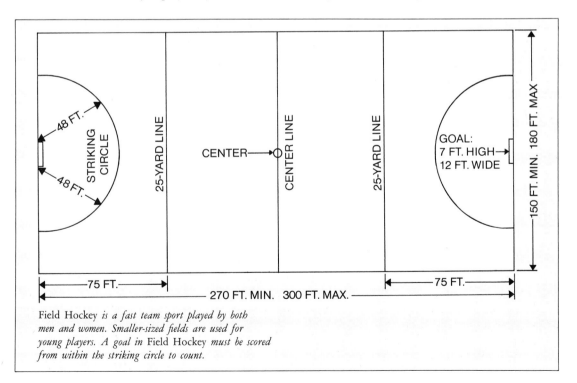

Field Hockey is a fast team sport played by both men and women. Smaller-sized fields are used for young players. A goal in Field Hockey must be scored from within the striking circle to count.

bully, both center forwards attempt to hit the ball to one of their own teammates in the front line. The forwards and the halfbacks move with the ball down the field—trying to work it past the opposing team and into position for a goal shot somewhere in front of the striking circle. The fullbacks remain in place to defend their goal, in case the opposing team should intercept the ball.

SHOTS: The most common moves in *Field Hockey* include the stop, in which the stick is held perpendicular to the ground to stop the ball before shooting; the dribble, in which the ball is propelled along in front with a quick series of hits or taps; the push, a short pass, usually to a player on the right; the flick, a quick pass to a player on the right or left by lifting the ball slightly off the ground; and the drive, a hard shot taken in an attempt to get the ball past an opponent or as a goal shot. Care should be taken in all shots never to raise the stick above shoulder height (a penalty known as "sticks"), or to hit directly into another player.

While *Field Hockey* is a game that requires knowledgeable coaching and repeated practice if it is to be played on a competitive level, it can also be enjoyed as a neighborhood recreational activity with careful adult supervision. A mother or older sister, who has played the game in college, would probably be able to lead the game most successfully.

VARIATION: *Slide-A-Puk* is an indoor variation of *Field Hockey* in which the players use a puck and ice hockey sticks. It may be played on basketball courts or other wood, concrete, or tile surfaces. The number of players on a team may range from five to 11, depending on the size of the playing area. The dividing lines and the goal areas are marked off with chalk.

Ice Hockey

Ice Hockey is a team sport with six players to a side. The object is for a team to score points by driving the puck into the opposition's goal.

Called the fastest game in the world because of its speedy skating and speedier shooting (the puck has been clocked at well over 100 miles per hour), *Ice Hockey* has great appeal for players and spectators alike.

FORMATION AND RINK: *Ice Hockey* is played indoors and out on natural and artificial ice. The regulation rink measures 200 feet long by 85 feet wide. It is enclosed by a wooden barrier or fence, termed the "boards." A goal is located at either end with the goal posts positioned at least 10 feet out from the end boards. The goals are cages of netting supported by metal posts. The rink is divided into three 60-foot-long zones: the defending zone (the end containing a goal being defended); the neutral zone (the area in the middle) and the offensive or attacking zone (the end containing the opponent's goal). One team's attacking zone is, of course, the other's defending zone. Each *Ice Hockey* team is composed of three forwards (left wing, center and right wing), two defensemen and a goaltender. Players wear special skates and protective padding. They hold long-handled L-shaped wooden sticks to carry, pass and shoot the puck—a small hard-rubber disc. Each game is divided into three periods of 20 minutes each with a rest time of 15 minutes between periods.

ACTION: The game (and each period) begins with a "face-off" in the center of the rink. The referee drops the puck between the two opposing centers, each of whom tries to secure the disc for his own team. Center rink face-offs are also held after goals are scored. Other face-offs occur following a stoppage of play for a penalty, an off-side or when the puck has gone over the boards and out of play. These face-offs, (not necessarily by the center players) are held in the region where play stops. After the face-off, the attacking team tries to keep control of the puck to make a goal, while the defending team tries to seize control and move over to the attack. A player with the puck may carry it (move it down rink, guided by the blade of his stick as he skates); pass it to a teammate, or shoot for a goal. No offensive player may precede the puck into the attacking zone.

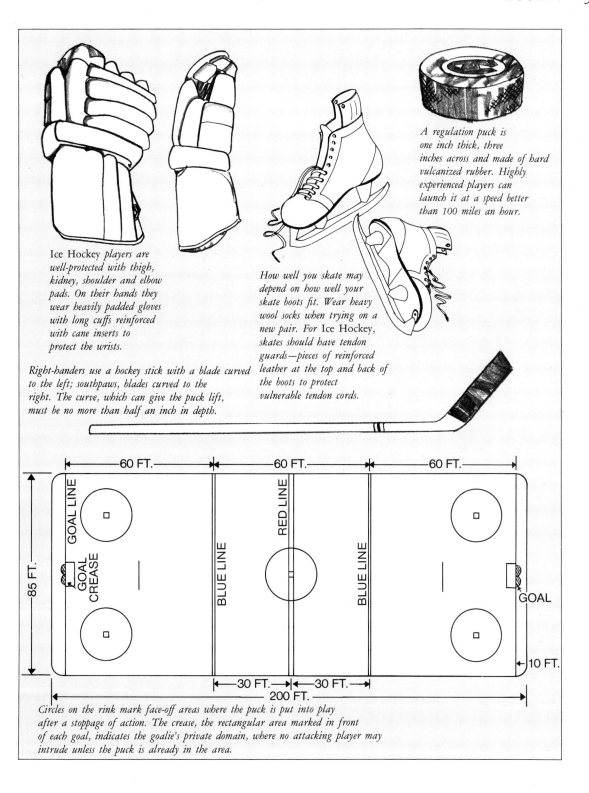

A regulation puck is one inch thick, three inches across and made of hard vulcanized rubber. Highly experienced players can launch it at a speed better than 100 miles an hour.

Ice Hockey *players are well-protected with thigh, kidney, shoulder and elbow pads. On their hands they wear heavily padded gloves with long cuffs reinforced with cane inserts to protect the wrists.*

How well you skate may depend on how well your skate boots fit. Wear heavy wool socks when trying on a new pair. For Ice Hockey, skates should have tendon guards—pieces of reinforced leather at the top and back of the boots to protect vulnerable tendon cords.

Right-handers use a hockey stick with a blade curved to the left; southpaws, blades curved to the right. The curve, which can give the puck lift, must be no more than half an inch in depth.

60 FT. — 60 FT. — 60 FT.

GOAL LINE

RED LINE

BLUE LINE

BLUE LINE

85 FT.

GOAL CREASE

GOAL

10 FT.

30 FT. — 30 FT.

200 FT.

Circles on the rink mark face-off areas where the puck is put into play after a stoppage of action. The crease, the rectangular area marked in front of each goal, indicates the goalie's private domain, where no attacking player may intrude unless the puck is already in the area.

PENALTIES: *Ice Hockey* is a rough-and-tumble game, and penalties are often called for such infractions of the rules as tripping, fighting and boarding (checking an opposing player into the boards). A penalty takes the form of banishing the offending player from the rink for periods of two minutes or more (depending on the seriousness of the infraction).

SCORING: One point is scored for each goal, and the team to make the higher score wins.

SAFETY: Because *Ice Hockey* is a fast and rough game, all players should wear the specially designed padded uniforms, gloves and helmets. The goaltender, in particular, should wear extra protective equipment, including a face mask.

Ice Hockey can be dangerous, and injuries do occur. If played as a neighborhood sport on a local ice rink, qualified adults should be in constant attendance to supervise play.

VARIATION: In *Roller Hockey,* players wear roller skates and play on a flat, concrete or blacktop area. (Even an indoor gymnasium may be used if plastic-wheeled skates are worn so as not to mar the floor.) Usually, a team consists of from three to five players. The players use regular *Ice Hockey* sticks and a puck. Instead of an actual cage, the goal may be painted or chalked-in at each end of the playing area. One of the "drawbacks" of *Roller Hockey* is that the puck does not slide along a concrete or blacktop surface as smoothly as it does on ice: often it skitters along the playing area or rolls erratically out of bounds. However, this "drawback" is part of the fun of play.

Horseshoes and Quoits

Like many of the other sports described in this book, *Horseshoes,* a game for two or four, was played in ancient times. It came to North America during the colonial period and has been a favorite pastime ever since. Today, it is played competitively by many clubs according to rules established by the National Horseshoe Pitchers' Association, and it is also played informally in parks, playgrounds and backyards.

COURT AND EQUIPMENT: The standard horseshoe court is 50 feet long and ten feet wide. Two one-inch-wide stakes are placed in the ground 40 feet apart. Each stake is in the center of a six-foot-square pitcher's box. The top of the stakes are ten inches above ground and lean forward one inch toward the center of the court. The horseshoes should be seven inches wide and seven and one-half inches long and should weigh two and one-half pounds. There are two horseshoes for each player.

ACTION: At the beginning of the match, players toss a coin to determine the order of play. The object of *Horseshoes* is to throw the shoe from the pitcher's box toward the opposite stake, so that the shoe encircles that stake or lands closer to it than an opponent's shoe. The player stands anywhere in the pitcher's box, provided that he is at least 18 inches away from the stake. The front of the pitcher's box is the foul line, and a player who steps over this line while pitching loses the value of the pitch.

If a shoe is tossed that encircles the stake (so that a ruler may be placed against its ends without touching the stake), it is called a ringer and is worth three points; a double ringer is worth six points. A shoe leaning against the stake counts only as a close shot. If each player gets one ringer, the two nullify each other—and the next closest shoe scores one point. A player with two ringers to his opponent's one gets only three points. If two opponents each get two ringers, there is no score. If a pitched shoe moves a previously pitched shoe, the new position is used for scoring.

In singles, the two players stand on the same side and, in turn, throw their two shoes at the far stake. At the end of each inning, they walk to the far stake, tally the score and pitch the shoes again in the opposite direction. In doubles, one opponent is at each end of the court, with his partner at the far end; scores are tallied each time the players on one end take two shots apiece. The first player, or team, to score 50 points wins the game; the winner of two out of three games wins the match.

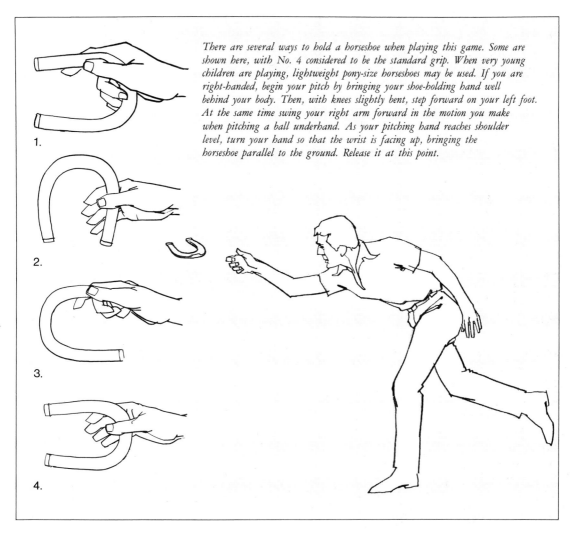

1.

2.

3.

4.

There are several ways to hold a horseshoe when playing this game. Some are shown here, with No. 4 considered to be the standard grip. When very young children are playing, lightweight pony-size horseshoes may be used. If you are right-handed, begin your pitch by bringing your shoe-holding hand well behind your body. Then, with knees slightly bent, step forward on your left foot. At the same time swing your right arm forward in the motion you make when pitching a ball underhand. As your pitching hand reaches shoulder level, turn your hand so that the wrist is facing up, bringing the horseshoe parallel to the ground. Release it at this point.

PITCHING TECHNIQUES: Skilled players develop their own pitching technique so they can control the course of the shoe through the air, thus getting a high percentage of ringers. A description of one of the most successful types of delivery follows: A player faces the opposite stake with his body erect and his feet close together. A right-handed player grips the rounded part of the shoe tightly with his right hand. Holding it at about chin height and supporting it lightly with his left hand, he straightens the right arm forward so that he can sight along the center of the shoe toward the opposite stake. He then swings his right arm down and back in a straight line, bending the knees at the same time. He steps forward with the left foot and brings the horseshoe straight forward with a smooth, pendulum-like motion. Just before releasing the shoe, he turns his wrist up and flicks it to the right so that the shoe is flat and parallel with the ground. Throughout the swing, the arm is kept close to the body— the entire motion resembling a softball pitch. The horseshoe should turn just enough in flight to reach the stake with the open end forward.

VARIATION: *Quoits* is very similar to *Horseshoes* but, instead of open-ended horseshoes, circular metal rings are used. The standard quoit weighs three pounds; it has a hole in the center that is four inches in diameter and a rim two and one-half inches wide. The court consists of two stakes hammered into the ground 54 feet apart; for children (as well as for beginning *Quoits* players), the stakes may be placed from 20 to 30 feet apart.

Players stand on a line beside, and just behind, the stake. No player may step ahead of the stake while pitching. Each player tosses two quoits, taking turns with his opponent. A ringer counts three points, a leaner (or "hobber") counts two and a quoit closer than an opponent's counts one. A ringer topping an opponent's ringer counts six points; a triple ringer counts nine points for the top ringer, and two leaners against a ringer count seven points for the leaners; the next nearer quoit scores one. Ties between two opponents' quoits are removed and do not score; the next nearer quoit scores one. The winner of the game is the player or team to reach 21 points first, and the winner of two out of three games takes the match.

Shuffleboard

The game of *Shuffleboard,* in which two or four players compete, is widely promoted in playgrounds and recreation centers, and especially in retirement communities, where it is enjoyed by many older persons. Although it is normally played on a specially designed concrete court, it can be staged on a driveway or even in a tile-floored playroom, with the court drawn in with paint or chalk.

COURT AND EQUIPMENT: The standard shuffleboard court measures 52 feet long by six feet wide. In the center, there is a 12-foot-long area marked by two "dead" lines. A large triangle is marked off six feet in from each end; it is subdivided into scoring areas with values of ten (at the apex), eight and seven. There is also a penalty area counting ten points off (10 OFF). The game is played with circular wooden disks and a wooden cue with a five-foot-long handle and a three-and-one-half-inch-long head. The head is curved to fit the disks, which are six inches in diameter and one inch thick.

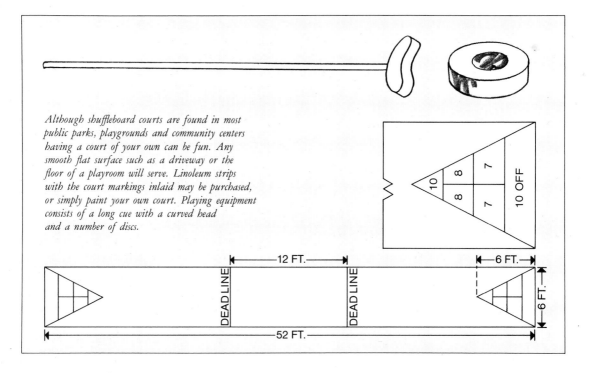

Although shuffleboard courts are found in most public parks, playgrounds and community centers having a court of your own can be fun. Any smooth flat surface such as a driveway or the floor of a playroom will serve. Linoleum strips with the court markings inlaid may be purchased, or simply paint your own court. Playing equipment consists of a long cue with a curved head and a number of discs.

ACTION: If two persons are playing, they take turns shooting their disks (which are customarily in sets of four red and four black) one at a time from the 10 OFF area at the same end of the court. The object is to slide them into one of the opposite scoring areas, to avoid landing in the opposite 10 OFF area, and to knock the opponent's disk either out of high-score areas or into the 10 OFF area. During play any disk is removed: that lands in the center of the court between the "dead" lines; that is less than eight inches beyond the base line, or that is more than halfway over the side line of the court. A disk that lands in the scoring triangle but on a dividing line stays there; however it does not count as a score.

After all eight shots have been taken, the round is scored—the disks counting ten, eight, seven or minus ten. The tally is written on the player's score sheet, and the game is continued from the opposite end of the court. The winning total usually is set at 50 points. If both players get over 50 in the round, the higher score wins. If there is a tie, a playoff determines the winner. When four players participate, the action is the same, with a player from each team at opposite ends of the court. The two teammates contribute to a single team score.

VARIATION: *Beanbag Shuffleboard* is a simpler version of the game which may be played on a level driveway, street, or paved terrace area. A shuffleboard court is outlined with chalk or paint. Dimensions may be whatever the area permits. Each player has four beanbags of a given color. Players take turns tossing their beanbags one at a time. In this game, if a beanbag lands on a dividing line, it is credited to the area in which most of it lies. Scores are totaled as in regular *Shuffleboard*—at the end of each round.

Soccer

Soccer—a sport in which 11-player teams compete to kick a ball through the opposition's goal—is one of the most popular team games and is played in various forms all over the world. In its early years, it was known as football. However, there were disagreements as to playing rules and two separate games were devised: rugby football, in which players are permitted to pick up the ball and run with it, and association football, a game based primarily on kicking the ball. The name of the latter game was shortened to "assoc" and finally to the term presently used, *Soccer*. In terms of worldwide competition, *Soccer* has more players and enthusiasts than any other sport; it is played mostly by boys and men, but there are some women's teams. Because *Soccer* is an extremely complex game to play (despite its simple basic formula), with difficult skills to master and a variety of rules and penalties, the standard game is best played as part of an organized competitive program. Players who know the rules, however, may form into smaller-than-regulation teams, using their own backyards, or parkland, and participate in a *Soccer* game simply for fun.

FORMATION: *Soccer* is played on a rectangular field ranging from 300 to 390 feet in length, and from 150 to 300 feet in width. (For young players or women, shorter fields may be used.) Goalposts eight feet high and 24 feet apart, connected by a crossbar at the top, are set in the center of the end lines. In front of each goal, an area 18 feet deep and 60 feet wide is marked out. Enclosing each goal area is a larger penalty area, 54 by 132 feet. The kickoff circle, 60 feet in diameter, is set in the middle of the field. The official *Soccer* ball is made of leather over a rubber bladder, and is slightly smaller in diameter than a basketball. A *Soccer* team consists of 11 players: three or four forwards, who advance the ball and are primarily offensive players; two or three halfbacks, who may play both offensive and defensive; four fullbacks, who are primarily defensive players and a goalkeeper, who is solely a defensive player.

ACTION: Professional and amateur *Soccer* consist of two 45-minute halves with a five-minute intermission. School *Soccer* may have four quarters of seven to ten minutes each. The action is continuous and moves rapidly up and down the field. The basic purpose of the game is for a team to advance the ball down the field by kicking, pushing or dribbling it (using any part of the body except the arms and hands), and to score a goal by kicking it between the opponent's goalposts—under the crossbar. Each goal counts one point. At the start of each half and after goals are scored, one team's center forward puts the ball into play. He place-kicks the ball toward the opposition's goal from the kick-off circle in the center of the field. The team with the higher score at the end of the regulation period is the winner. If the score is tied, there may be an overtime period of a set length, or with the first team to score winning in a "sudden death."

SHOTS: Since only the goalkeeper may use his hands to recover and throw the ball, other players learn to use their feet with great dexterity to control the ball. Various parts of the foot are used, including the heel and toe, the instep, and both the inside and outside of the foot. Players dribble the ball, moving it along with repeated short kicks made with the inside of a foot. They volley-kick the ball on the fly with either the foot or the knee. They learn to stop the ball by intercepting it in flight with the top part of the body, the lower part of the leg or the sole of the foot. They even use the head with surprising accuracy to block an opponent's shot or to butt the ball toward a teammate.

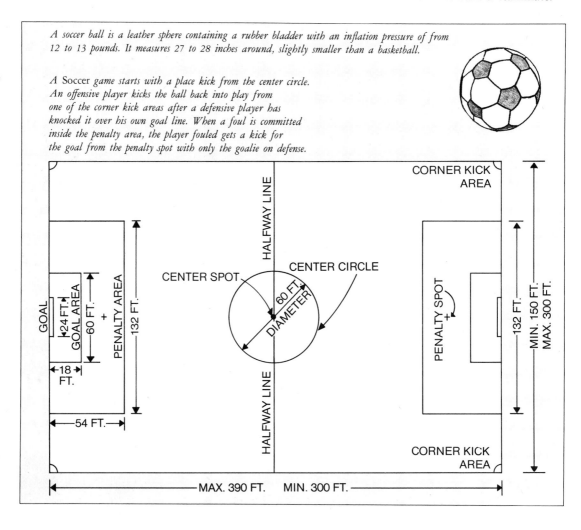

A soccer ball is a leather sphere containing a rubber bladder with an inflation pressure of from 12 to 13 pounds. It measures 27 to 28 inches around, slightly smaller than a basketball.

A Soccer game starts with a place kick from the center circle. An offensive player kicks the ball back into play from one of the corner kick areas after a defensive player has knocked it over his own goal line. When a foul is committed inside the penalty area, the player fouled gets a kick for the goal from the penalty spot with only the goalie on defense.

CORNER KICK AREA

HALFWAY LINE

CENTER SPOT

CENTER CIRCLE

60 FT. DIAMETER

GOAL

24 FT.

GOAL AREA

60 FT.

PENALTY AREA

132 FT.

18 FT.

54 FT.

PENALTY SPOT

132 FT.

MIN. 150 FT. MAX. 300 FT.

CORNER KICK AREA

MAX. 390 FT.   MIN. 300 FT.

OFF SIDES AND PENALTIES: When the ball goes over a side line, it is considered out of play. One of the players, standing outside of the side line and holding the ball over his head with both hands, uses the throw-in to put the ball back into play. When the ball is driven beyond the goal line (but not through the goal) by an offensive player, the goalkeeper or fullback returns it to play by a goal kick from the goal area. When a defense player happens to kick the ball over his own goal line, a corner kick—from the nearest corner of the field—is given to a player on the offensive team. In all of these plays, no opponent may stand within ten yards of the ball until it is kicked. This action—as well as charging from behind, roughness, being off-side or touching the ball with a hand (except for the goalkeeper)—constitutes a foul for which an opponent is given a free kick. A free kick is taken from the spot where the foul occurred, except when a foul takes place inside the penalty area. Then it is known as a penalty kick, and the player who was fouled kicks from a penalty spot 12 feet in front of the opponent's goal. Only the kicker and the goalkeeper can be in the penalty area when the kick is made.

VARIATIONS: *Square Soccer* is a simple version of *Soccer,* suitable for 14 to 20 players. A square court is laid out, at least 20 by 20 feet. Players divide into two equal teams, with one team lined up on two adjacent sides of the square and the other team on the other two sides. The object is to kick the ball through the opposing team, but not higher than the players' heads. The ball may be blocked by any part of the player's body except his hands. Players may go into the court to retrieve the ball but must go back to their places in line to kick. One point is scored when the ball is kicked through the opposing team, and the first team to score 10 points wins.

Pin Soccer may be played with as few as six players on a team in a court of limited size. The action is exactly the same as in regulation *Soccer,* with one team moving the ball down-field toward the opposite goal. Two Indian clubs or pieces of wood of approximately the same size are set up 16 inches apart, in the middle of each goal line. The purpose of the game is to knock down the opposing team's Indian clubs. Whenever a club is knocked down, one point is scored. The club is then set up again and the ball is put into play by the scored-upon team. When the ball is kicked out of bounds by one of the players, it is put into play by a member of the other team. The team with the highest score after a set period of time is the winner.

Table Tennis

Table Tennis, also known as *Ping-Pong,* is a miniature form of *Tennis* and may be played as singles, between two players, or as doubles, between two teams of two players each. It is played on a special table using small rackets or paddles and a light celluloid ball. A game of comparatively recent origin, *Table Tennis* has become extremely popular throughout the world. It is regarded as a major sport in England, Hungary and Czechoslovakia, and the Japanese and Chinese are among the leading *Table Tennis* players in world competition. Because it requires little space and can be played by adults and children alike, it is an ideal game for families to play indoors or out.

EQUIPMENT: The standard table is made of three-quarter-inch plywood. It is nine feet long and five feet wide and stands two and one-half feet off the floor. It is green, with a white line painted around the edges and lengthwise down the middle of the surface. Some tables are also made of metal and are collapsible.

The wooden paddles have an oval-shaped striking surface about five and one-quarter inches wide and six and one-quarter inches long. The striking surface is covered with textured rubber, cork or sandpaper. The ball is about two inches in diameter and extremely lightweight. A dark green net with white tape along the top is stretched across the center of the table crosswise. The net is from six to six and three-quarter inches high.

ACTION: The choice of who will first serve or receive the ball is determined by a toss. In singles, the server stands behind his end of the table and hits the ball so that it bounces once on his side, travels over the net and bounces again on the other side.

He loses the point: if he does not hit the ball; if the ball does not land on both sides of the table as described, or if his racket is over the end of the table or beyond the sidelines while serving. If the serve touches the net while passing over it and then lands in a fair position it is a "let" ball and is replayed. If it hits the net but does not land in a fair position on the opposite side, the server loses the point. If the serve is fair, the opponent must return the ball by hitting it after one bounce so that it travels directly over the net and lands in the opposite court. This action continues with the ball traveling back and forth until one player loses a point by: failing to return a good service or a good return; touching the net or table with his paddle or hand while the ball is in play, or by touching the ball, or letting the ball touch him, before it lands on the table. A let ball that touches the net and then lands correctly in the opposite court continues in play. When a point is scored, the server takes a new serve and starts the action again. Each player has five consecutive serves.

Play continues until the winning score of 21 points is reached; however, a game must be won by a margin of at least two points. For example, if the score reaches a tie of 20 all (or "deuce"), the game is continued—alternating the serve after each point—until one player is two points ahead. The player who takes two out of three games wins the match.

In doubles, the first server of the starting pair stands to the right of the center white line. The first five serves are hit from the right-hand side of his court, and must pass diagonally over the net to land in his opponents' right-hand court. Then the player who received the first five services serves diagonally across the court five times to the first server. (Thus, with Players A and B against Players C and D, A would serve to D, D to A, B to C, and C to B.) After the serve, partners on each team alternate in returning the ball until one team wins a point—as described above.

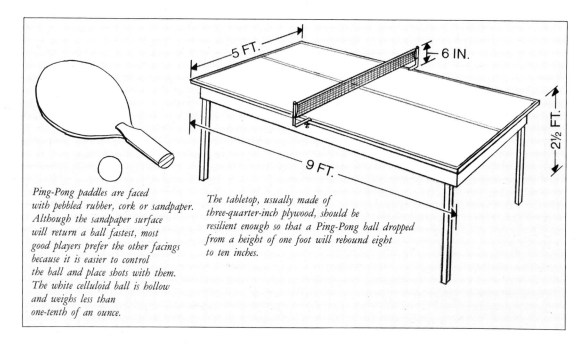

5 FT.   6 IN.   2½ FT.   9 FT.

Ping-Pong paddles are faced with pebbled rubber, cork or sandpaper. Although the sandpaper surface will return a ball fastest, most good players prefer the other facings because it is easier to control the ball and place shots with them. The white celluloid ball is hollow and weighs less than one-tenth of an ounce.

The tabletop, usually made of three-quarter-inch plywood, should be resilient enough so that a Ping-Pong ball dropped from a height of one foot will rebound eight to ten inches.

STROKES: Like *Tennis, Table Tennis* involves fore-hand and backhand strokes. When a right-handed player hits a forehand, his left side is toward the net, and his left foot is forward. The reverse is true of the backhand. The simplest and easiest shot in *Table Tennis* is the push shot: a direct, thrusting stroke, with the flat of the paddle parallel to the net, just as the ball is rising from a bounce. This shot is used by beginners in both offensive and defensive play. For more advanced defensive play, the most common shot is the chop, in which a player, standing several feet behind the table, returns a hard-hit drive with a stroke that begins high and well back and comes forward and down with the paddle face tilted slightly forward. This strong under-cutting movement gives the ball a backspin, and makes it difficult to return. The most common offensive shot is the topspin drive, in which the player, standing fairly far back, starts with the paddle low and swings forward and up. This causes the ball to drop after it crosses the net and to bounce forward at a sharp angle. Other offensive shots include the drop shot—a strong up-cutting motion causing the ball to stop dead just over the net—and the smash—a straight, forward and down stroke used on a high-bouncing ball.

Tennis

Tennis has been a popular sport in Europe and North America for many years. Originally en-joyed only by the nobility, it is played today by people of all classes, on every level of skill, in private tennis clubs and on public courts pro-vided by park and recreation departments.

COURT AND EQUIPMENT: *Tennis* is played as a singles game with one player pitted against one opponent, or as doubles with a team of two players facing another pair across the net. The game is played on outdoor and indoor courts. Outdoor courts may be of grass, clay, concrete, blacktop or composition surface. Indoor courts are usually of wood or composition. Courts used for singles play are 78 feet long by 27 feet wide.

There is an additional lane four and one-half feet wide on each side for doubles play. A net is stretched across the center of the court and is attached to two posts each three and one-half feet high. The height of the net is three feet. A line 21 feet away from the net on each side marks the right and left service courts.

Tennis balls are inflated rubber spheres covered with felt cloth. They are about two and one-half inches in diameter and weigh two ounces. Tennis rackets are made of wood, steel or aluminum with the oval head strung with nylon, silk, wire or gut. The size and weight of rackets vary according to whether they are being used by children or adults. Children should use rackets weighing about 12 to 13 ounces; adults should use rackets weighing 14 to 15 ounces.

ACTION: The basic object of *Tennis* is to hit the ball over the net, so that it lands within the opposite court's boundary lines. Whenever a player fails to do this, he loses the point. Before play begins, one player puts his racket head-down on the court and spins it. The other player calls "smooth" or "rough,"—referring to the weave of the string at the bottom or top of the racket-face. If the racket lands with the called-side up, the caller chooses either to serve or to take one side of the court; if not, the spinner has the choice. The first server serves a complete game, starting by hitting the ball, from the right side of the baseline, diagonally into his opponent's right service court. When a point is won or lost, the same player serves again—this time from the left side into his opponent's left service court, and so on, until the game is concluded. The two players then change courts, and the opponent serves a complete game. Following this, they change courts after every odd game for the duration of the set—that is, after the first, third, fifth, and seventh game, etc. Each player gets one point in the set for each game won, and the first player to win six games is the winner of the set. To take a set, a player must win by a margin of at least two games. Thus, a player might win a set by 6–4, or a greater margin. However, if there is a tie at 5–5, play continues until one player can reach a two-game advantage. In a

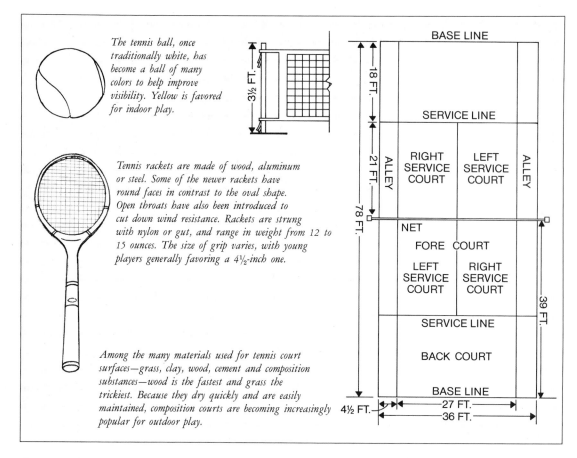

The tennis ball, once traditionally white, has become a ball of many colors to help improve visibility. Yellow is favored for indoor play.

Tennis rackets are made of wood, aluminum or steel. Some of the newer rackets have round faces in contrast to the oval shape. Open throats have also been introduced to cut down wind resistance. Rackets are strung with nylon or gut, and range in weight from 12 to 15 ounces. The size of grip varies, with young players generally favoring a 4½-inch one.

Among the many materials used for tennis court surfaces—grass, clay, wood, cement and composition substances—wood is the fastest and grass the trickiest. Because they dry quickly and are easily maintained, composition courts are becoming increasingly popular for outdoor play.

close match, the score may go as high as 10–8, 18–16 or even higher before the winner of the set is determined.

In order to short-cut such marathon sets, a sudden-death tie-breaking procedure has been introduced. This is a 13th game when a set is tied at six games all. The players engage in a special game that is won by the first player to score five points out of nine. A variation is a game that is won by the first player to score seven out of 12 points. The winner of this special 13th game also wins the set, seven games to six. The sudden-death tie-breaker was first tried out in the U.S. Open Tennis Championship in 1970 and is being used more and more not only in tournament play but also in *Tennis* games that are played purely for pleasure. However, some players still prefer the older system.

SCORING: It takes at least four points to win a *Tennis* game. These are counted as 15, 30, 40 and "game." The game starts at "love," or zero, and if it becomes tied at 40 the score is "deuce." To illustrate: If the server wins the first point, the score is 15–love. (The server's score is called first.) If the receiver wins the next two points, the score becomes 15–30. If the server then wins two points, and the receiver one, the score would be 40–all, or deuce. Starting at deuce, either player must win two points in a row before he can win the game. If the server wins the first point after deuce, the call is "advantage in," and if he wins the next, he wins the game. However, if he loses this second point, the score reverts to deuce. Should the receiver win the first point after deuce, the call is "advantage out," and if he wins the next, he wins the game. If he loses the point, the score goes back to deuce.

To serve, face at right angles to your opponent's service court, toss the ball high and bring your racket back and up so it meets the ball at the top of your reach. This will drive the ball sharply downward and puts the full weight of your body behind the drive.

A basic stroke is the forehand. Place your body with the left side at right angles to the net and swing your racket forward to meet the ball as it nears the top of its bounce—and always keep your eye on it.

To make the backhand stroke, turn your right side to the net and swing your racket across your body to meet the ball. Work on this stroke and avoid the temptation to run around a backhand shot so as to take it on your forehand.

Points are won in the following manner. If the first ball served is good (that is, if it bounces in the proper service court) it is in play. If this is the case, it then must be returned by the opponent after no more than one bounce. He must hit it back so that it bounces within the singles court of the server. However, upon the return of service, any player may "volley" the ball (that is, hit it on the fly) after it crosses the net.

A player loses the point if: (a) he fails to return the ball properly before it bounces twice; (b) he returns the ball so it does not land in the playing area; (c) he throws his racket to hit the ball; (d) he lets the ball hit him or his clothing during the exchange, or (e) he touches the net with his racket, any part of his body or his clothing. If the server fails to get the ball in the proper service court on the first try, he is allowed a second serve. If he fails again, he loses the point. A served ball that touches the net before going into the proper court is called a "let." It does not count, and the service is played again. A ball that touches the net and that lands in bounds during a rally, or exchange, after service, is good and remains in play.

STROKES AND STRATEGY: *Tennis* may be played on a very simple level of skill and still be enjoyed. The game, however, becomes increasingly fascinating as a player masters certain fundamental strokes.

The first of these is the serve in which the server stands behind the baseline with his left foot forward. He throws the ball high into the air with the left hand, at the same time bringing the racket back, up, over and down with the right hand. The ball should be hit at as high a point as the server can comfortably reach. As he hits the ball, he lets the momentum of the racket head pull it through, transferring his weight from the back foot to the forward left foot to finish the stroke.

Generally, in all rallies, or exchanges of ground strokes, players should stand slightly crouched and bent forward with the feet slightly spread

and the weight distributed evenly. Players must rely on both backhand and forehand shots. When a ball bounces to the left of a player, he stands with his right side toward the net, brings the racket back across the front of his body and then strokes it forward to hit the ball with a backhand shot. If the ball lands to the right of a player, he turns his left side to the net and brings the racket straight back and then forward, hitting the ball at waist level with a forehand shot. The forehand should first be learned without any cut or spin; then the player learns to hit the ball both with a topspin (an upward cut) and a slice (a downward cut). The stroke should involve the full arm, swinging through from the shoulder with the wrist fairly stiff. As in the forehand, the backhand should first be learned as a straight shot without a spin, then with topspin and finally with a slice.

Net Play includes other important methods of stroking. Net play is usually employed by experts who, immediately after serving, rush up to the net. Standing close to the net at an angle that blocks off the court for the opponent (who is normally forced by a hard service to make a weak or defensive return), they try to smash the ball with a hard overhead shot. If this cannot be done, they attempt to put the ball out of reach with a placement shot close to the opponent's side line or with a drop shot that lands close to the net. A player may volley—hit a ball before it bounces—from any position on the court. He would not normally volley from the back area, however, because a ball hit that far back would probably land out of bounds. When one player rushes the net to try to volley a return, the other player may lob the ball—a high, arching shot that travels over the opponent's head and lands close to the baseline.

DOUBLES PLAY: The scoring is the same as in singles play, with all four players alternating in service. (Thus, Player One of Team A serves the first game. Player One of Team B serves the next, then Player Two of Team A and finally Player Two of Team B.) Once the ball is put in play, either player of a team may hit it. Usually, one player plays up close to the net, slightly to one side, while the other player remains in the back court, covering the other side. However, players may be required to change places to return a difficult shot, or—after hitting a hard, well-placed drive—both players may rush to the net. Learning to play doubles well demands long practice with a partner; often outstanding singles players are not the best performers in doubles. In most amateur *Tennis*, singles is played by young enthusiasts, while middle-aged and older players tend to turn to doubles, which is somewhat less demanding physically.

VARIATIONS: *Deck Tennis* combines elements of *Volleyball* and *Quoits* as well as *Tennis*. It is often played on the decks of ocean liners, as well as in other confined spaces. It is played on a court 40 feet long by 12 feet wide for singles, and 40 by 18 for doubles. A net, four feet, eight inches high, divides the court.

The object of the game is to toss a rubber or rope quoit, six inches in diameter and one-half inch thick, back and forth across the net. It must be caught with one hand and returned immediately from the same spot to the opponent's court. A player loses the point when: he fails to catch a fair throw; he tosses a quoit that goes beyond the boundaries of the court; he tosses a quoit that is stopped by the net, or he makes an overhand throw. Only the server may score a point and he continues to serve as long as he wins the exchange. Fifteen points is usually considered a game, with the victor required to win by two points. The game may be played as singles, doubles, or with as many as nine players on a side. In the latter case, players rotate the serve and positions on the court as in *Volleyball* (see page 366).

Platform Paddle Tennis is enjoyed throughout the year, even in comparatively cold climates. It is staged on a wooden platform 60 by 30 feet, with backstops and side walls of wire mesh. A singles court, 44 feet long and 16 feet wide, is laid out on the platform. For doubles, there are two-foot-wide alleys on each side, making the doubles court 20 feet wide. Each service court is 12 feet long and eight feet wide. The net stands two feet, eight inches high at the ends, and two feet, six inches high at the center. A wooden paddle, from 15 to 17 inches long and weighing nine to 14 ounces, is used. A ball—about the size of a tennis ball and made of sponge rubber—is used in this game.

On a smaller scale, the game is very similar to regular *Tennis*. There are three exceptions: An adult player is allowed only one serve to put the ball in play (juniors get two); once the ball is in play, the entire court—including the doubles alleys—is used for adult singles (juniors using only the singles court); a ball that bounces once and then hits the backstop or side wall may be played before it bounces a second time, as in *Four-Wall Handball* (page 350).

Sidewalk Tennis is usually played on city streets and may also be played on driveways, playgrounds or other blacktop areas. The court consists of a rectangle 12 feet long by three feet wide, divided into four separate squares. There is no net; a line in the center simply divides the court.

The server stands anywhere in his back court, and serves a rubber ball or tennis ball. He bounces it once and then hits it with the palm of his hand into his opponent's service area. The opponent must let the serve bounce once before returning the ball. After this point, the ball may be volleyed, or it may be hit anywhere into the opponent's court. A point is won when a player fails to return a fair ball into the opposite court. Only the server scores, and he keeps serving as long as he wins points. The winning score is 11, but there must be a margin of two points to win. As in *Tennis*, the final score may go up as high as the 20s if the players are matched in ability. (In *Sidewalk Tennis*, however, there is no sudden death.)

In *Tether Ball* a ten-foot-high pole of wood or metal is set in concrete, and a two-inch-wide line is painted on it six feet from the ground. The tether ball is attached to the top of the pole by a cord seven and one-half feet long. The ball may be a tennis ball held in a net casing, or a somewhat larger and softer ball with a sewed-on tape holding the cord. The ball is hit with tennis rackets or, preferably, with paddle-tennis paddles. Using the pole as the center, a circle with a radius of three feet is drawn. A line is drawn which divides the circle in half and extends beyond it ten feet on each side. Two marks—the service marks—are drawn on this extension line, each six feet away from the pole.

The purpose of the game is to keep hitting the ball so that it goes around the pole, winding the cord until the ball is above the six-foot mark. One player serves, standing on his service spot, and strokes the ball forward and around the pole. His opponent returns it, trying to wind it around the pole in the opposite direction. Each player must stay on his side of the 20-foot line, outside the center circle. The action is fast and furious and continues until the ball is wound up above the mark on the pole. A player may not permit the cord to wind around his paddle or to wind around the pole below the six-foot mark; if he does, his opponent gets a free penalty shot.

Tether Ball is also played in a somewhat simplified version with the same type of pole, but using a rubber playground ball or volleyball. Players stand on either side of the pole—as close to it as they wish—and hit the ball in opposite directions with one or both hands. There is a tendency to catch the ball briefly before hitting it, but this is a foul that gives the other player a free hit in return.

Volleyball

Volleyball is a popular team sport played by both sexes, young and old. It is played in a wide variety of places indoors and out at beaches, parks, playgrounds, back yards, parking lots and gymnasiums. Since the rules for men's and women's play are the same, it is an excellent coeducational game.

COURT AND EQUIPMENT: The official volleyball court is 60 feet long and 30 feet wide and has an overhead clearance of at least 20 feet. A net 32 feet long and three feet wide is strung across the center of the court; its top is eight feet from the ground.

A volleyball is made of rubber or a rubber bladder covered with leather. Its circumference is between 26 and 27 inches, and it weighs from nine to ten ounces, about half the weight of a basketball.

ACTION: In regulation *Volleyball,* each team has six players. Each team forms a front line of three players and a rear line of three players on either side of the net. The object of the game is to hit the volleyball back and forth over the net. Each team tries to keep the ball from hitting the floor or ground on their side of the court and tries to make the ball land on the ground in the opposing team's court. The ball is usually batted with the hand, but it may also be struck by any part of the body above the knees. The ball may be batted by no more than three persons on a team before it goes over the net, and a player is not permitted to hit the ball twice in a row.

The ball is served by the player in the rear, right-hand position. He stands behind the end line, tosses the ball up and bats it with his fist or palm so that it goes into the opponent's court. On the serve, a ball that hits the net, even if it goes over, is a fault, and possession passes to the opposite team. During a volley, a ball that touches the net and goes over continues in play. If, during play, a player bats a ball that hits the net but does not go over the net, another player on the team may bat the ball over the net. No player may touch the net or step over the center line under the net.

Only the serving team scores. A player continues to serve as long as his team wins each volley. When the server's team faults, the serve goes to the opposite team. Players on the team that is about to serve each move one position in a clockwise direction. (The players in the front line move to the right, or back, and the players in the back line move to the left, or forward.) Thus, each time a team receives the service, a new person serves.

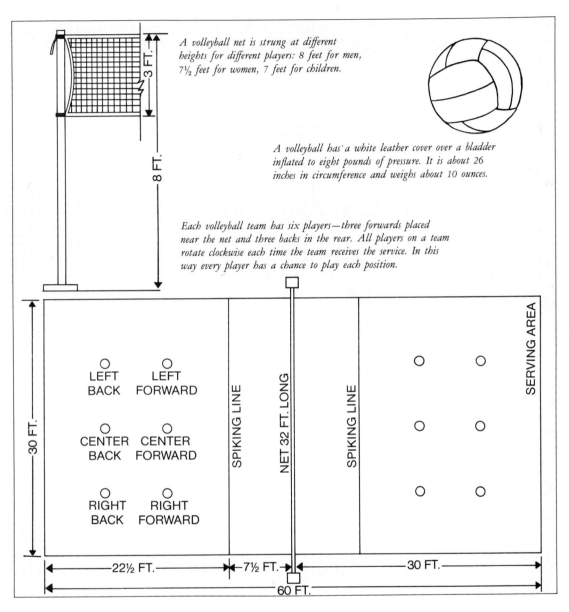

A volleyball net is strung at different heights for different players: 8 feet for men, 7½ feet for women, 7 feet for children.

3 FT.

8 FT.

A volleyball has a white leather cover over a bladder inflated to eight pounds of pressure. It is about 26 inches in circumference and weighs about 10 ounces.

Each volleyball team has six players—three forwards placed near the net and three backs in the rear. All players on a team rotate clockwise each time the team receives the service. In this way every player has a chance to play each position.

SERVING AREA

LEFT BACK   LEFT FORWARD

SPIKING LINE

NET 32 FT. LONG

SPIKING LINE

30 FT.

CENTER BACK   CENTER FORWARD

RIGHT BACK   RIGHT FORWARD

22½ FT. — 7½ FT. — 30 FT.

60 FT.

STRATEGY: The fundamental strategy in *Volleyball* is not for a player to hit any ball that comes to him directly over the net, but rather for one player to hit the ball to another on his team—preferably a player in the front line. In this way, the ball is "set up" so that the second player can "spike" it hard into the opponents' court with a smashing one- or two-handed overhead shot. In regulation *Volleyball*, a spiking line is drawn seven and one-half feet from the net. It does not affect front-line players, but the rear-line players may not cross it when trying to spike.

The winning score in *Volleyball* is normally 15 points. However, as in most games of this type, a two-point margin is required to win; a game tied at 14-all is continued until one team moves ahead by two points.

Games You

SECTION IV

Make Yourself

In a modification of Flying Envelope Toss, *two small players hold cups high as they compete to catch a soaring envelope launched by a playmate.*

Games You Make Yourself

Although the games that appear in this section are all made from such common items as paper, straws, file cards, and the like, their building does represent a challenge for children. Therefore, adult supervision is suggested, and with grownups helping, no game should take more than 30 minutes to construct. The fun of playing these games will be doubled by the child's pride in craftsmanship.

Numerals indicate the number of players. Spelled-out numbers suggest suitable age levels.

Flying Envelope Toss

● *3 to 8* ● *Six to twelve*

ACTION: Each player receives one triangle-shaped cup, cut from an envelope. The game leader holds 30 duplicate cups and tosses them in the air, one by one. Players take turns trying to catch the flying cups in their own cups, and each player's turn ends only when he fails to make a catch. A player may not touch a flying cup with his hands, but must use his cup as a scoop in which to catch the others. After each child has a turn, the child with the most cups wins.

CONSTRUCTION: All envelopes must be of the same size—three inch by seven inch works best. Each envelope makes two pyramid cups. The flap is cut off, and the envelope is cut into two squares. Each square is folded into a triangle shape which, when opened, forms a pyramid.

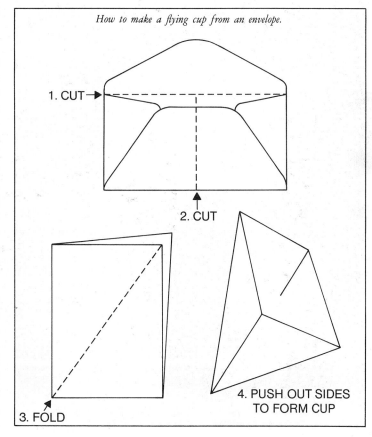

How to make a flying cup from an envelope.

1. CUT →

2. CUT

3. FOLD

4. PUSH OUT SIDES TO FORM CUP

A Ping-Pong ball rests on a spoon handle in this Catch 'n Cup *layout. A player presses down on the bowl to flip the ball into a cup.*

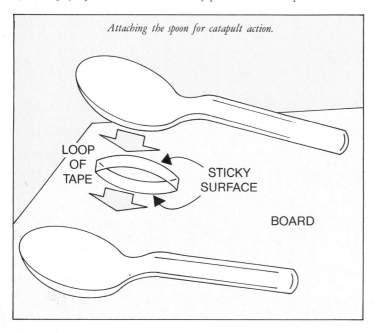

Attaching the spoon for catapult action.

LOOP
OF
TAPE

STICKY
SURFACE

BOARD

Catch 'n Cup

● *2 to 6*   ● *Six to adult*

ACTION: Each player in turn places a Ping-Pong ball at the handle end of one of the spoons and, by pressing down on the bowl, flips the ball—trying to make it land in a cup. The largest cups are worth three points; the medium size, two and the smallest, one. Each player gets three tries per turn. After each has nine tries, the player with the highest point-total wins.

CONSTRUCTION: Paper cups in three sizes are pasted at random on one half of a piece of 18-inch by 24-inch cardboard. Plastic spoons are taped at the other end with pieces of plastic tape. Each piece of tape is folded in half so that the sticky surface adheres to both the bowl of the spoon and the board.

Through the Rings

● *2 to 6*   ● *Six to adult*

ACTION: The object is to toss a Ping-Pong ball through one of the rings suspended from a wire hanger. As the sizes of the holes in the rings vary, so do the point values. A successful toss through the ring with the smallest hole counts six points, through the next smallest, five points and so on, down to one point. Each player gets three Ping-Pong balls and stands on a line six feet from the rings. After three throws, the next player gets a turn, and so on until each has a chance. The action is repeated three times until each player has a total of nine throws. The player with the highest point-total wins.

CONSTRUCTION: The rings are cut from colored construction paper and stapled to lengths of string. The strings are then tied to the crosspiece of a wire hanger. The hanger is suspended by string from a ceiling fixture to a height of about five feet from the floor. An adjustable compass is a most useful tool for drawing the rings.

Plate Balance

● *2 to 6* ● *Eight to adult*

ACTION: Players take turns trying to balance as many plates as they can on the straws. Each player continues his turn until he fails to balance a plate. He gets one point for each plate that is balanced. After a contestant finishes a turn, the board is cleared of plates for the next player. After every player has a turn the game ends, with the player who balances the most plates winning.

CONSTRUCTION: The materials needed are a piece of 18-inch by 24-inch corrugated cardboard; eight or nine paper plates and the same number of straws. Holes are punched in the cardboard for the straws, and glue is spread on an end of each straw to help it stand upright. The plates should be six inches in diameter and the straws should be set four inches apart. Some straws may be used full length, and some may be cut to different lengths.

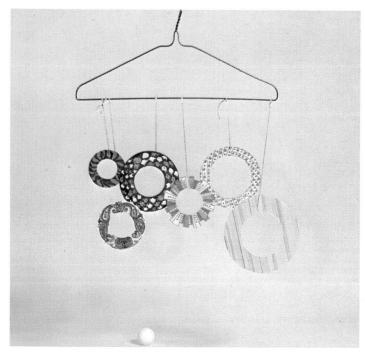

A Ping-Pong ball tossed through the smallest hole yields six points; through the largest hole, one point, in this Through the Rings *game.*

Although the paper plates teeter precariously, none falls from its paper-straw perch, making each one worth a point in the Plate Balance *game.*

*If the first stripe on the top ticket is green, the first player
must have a green wedge if he is to add a* Piece of Pie *to the whole.*

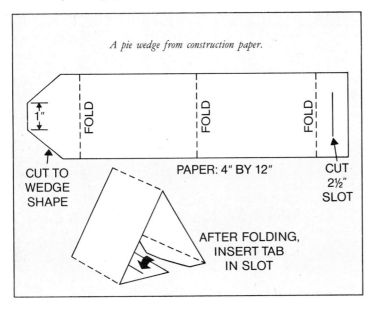

A pie wedge from construction paper.

FOLD

FOLD

FOLD

1"

CUT TO
WEDGE
SHAPE

PAPER: 4" BY 12"

CUT
2½"
SLOT

AFTER FOLDING,
INSERT TAB
IN SLOT

Piece of Pie

● *4, 6 or 8* ● *Eight to adult*

ACTION: Sixty-four paper wedges are distributed evenly among the players, and one multicolored striped card is placed in the center of the table. The other cards are placed in a stock to be drawn from as necessary. Play proceeds in turns: If the first player has a wedge corresponding in color to the stripe at the far left of the center card, he begins building the pie. If not, the player on his left tries to match a wedge with the same stripe. When one player does make the match, the next player must have a wedge with a color that corresponds to the second stripe from the left on the card, and so on. For each wedge contributed to the pie, a player gets a point. The player who completes a pie by contributing the eighth wedge gets eight points. Should no player be able to contribute a wedge on the basis of the color stripe shown on the card, another card is drawn from the stockpile. Whenever a pie is completed, another card is drawn from stock to make a new pie. As there are 64 wedges, it is possible to make a total of eight pies, but the game can end any time at the players' discretion. The player with the highest point-total wins the game.

CONSTRUCTION: To make the wedges, 32 pieces of eight-inch by 12-inch construction paper in five different colors are needed. These are cut in half to make 64 sheets, each four inches by 12 inches. The papers are then cut and folded into wedge shapes. Five sheets of white construction paper are used for the cards. From these, 20 cards are cut, each measuring one inch by four inches. Stripes of the same five colors used for the wedges are crayoned in random order on the cards.

String Along

● *4 to 8* ● *Six to nine*

ACTION: Each player has a piece of string about 20 inches long and a multicolored striped card. The game leader scatters the wedges around a room—on the floor, on shelves or under furniture. On signal, each player begins to string together the wedges according to the order of colors on his card from left to right. If a player, for example, has a card with yellow, red, green, blue, orange, red, blue, orange and yellow, he must string the wedges in that order— beginning with a yellow wedge and so forth. Players may not collect wedges in advance, but first must string one, then find another of the proper color. The first player to string all the wedges called for on his card wins. If after ten minutes no player has finished out his card, the one with the most wedges strung wins.

CONSTRUCTION: Materials used in *Piece of Pie* are also employed in this game. The only additional item needed for this game is the string. The game leader, however, might cut threading slots in the wedges beforehand.

Guided by the colored stripes on their cards, these young players look for the right wedges to thread during a game of String Along.

In Straw Balance, *players push straws of various lengths through the cylinder and try to rest their ends in corners of opposite holes.*

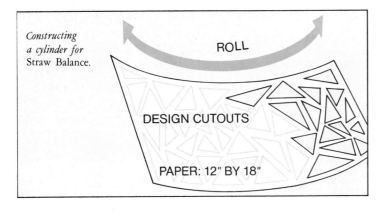

Constructing a cylinder for Straw Balance.

ROLL

DESIGN CUTOUTS

PAPER: 12" BY 18"

Straw Balance

● *2 to 6* ● *Eight to adult*

ACTION: The object is to push each straw through the six-inch-diameter cylinder so that it balances in two opposite triangular cutouts. There are three sizes of straws: The smallest, one-eighth inch longer than the diameter of the cylinder, is worth six points; the middle-size, one-fourth inch longer than the diameter, worth three points; the longest, three-eighths inch longer than the diameter, one point. Each player has 12 straws, four of each size. They take turns pushing the straws through, one straw per turn. If a player drops a straw or lets it touch another, he loses four points. After each player has had 12 turns, points are added—the player with the highest point-total winning the *Straw Balance* contest.

CONSTRUCTION: The materials needed are a piece of 12-by-18-inch construction paper; 24 to 72 straws (evenly divided into three colors); scissors and tape, glue or staples. The straws are cut to size. Triangles of various sizes are drawn at random on the construction paper and then cut out. The cylinder is formed by curving the 18-inch sides until the two 12-inch sides overlap slightly. These are then joined with tape, glue or staples. The exact diameter of the cylinder will depend on the amount of overlap, but it will be approximately six inches. It should be measured, however, so that the straws can be cut into the precise lengths needed.

Drop the Disc

● *2 to 4* ● *Eight to twelve*

ACTION: Players try to push down the colored discs from the tops of their straws to the bottoms with a pointer made from a straw. Each player is assigned all the discs of one color, and on signal, all contestants take their pointers and try to move a disc down. The first player to push a disc to the cardboard base wins the round. The game continues for nine rounds, and the player to win the most rounds also wins the game. Should a player touch a disc with his hand or bend a straw, he automatically loses the round.

CONSTRUCTION: Thirty-six holes are punched in an eight-inch-square piece of cardboard to accommodate the straws. The discs, nine of each color cut from colored construction paper, must fit tightly around the straws.

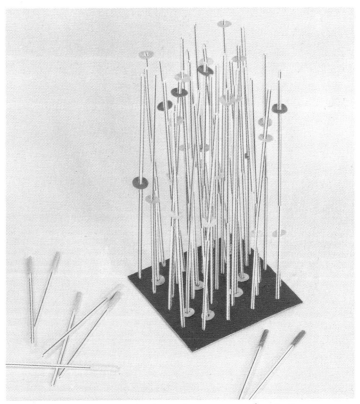

A Drop the Disc *winner is the player who, using pointers made of paper straws, pushes the greatest number of discs to the baseboard.*

Balance Board

● *2 to 8* ● *Seven to twelve*

ACTION: Each player, in turn, pulls on all the strings beneath the board—trying to make the macaroni stand up. After three rounds, the player who gets the most strands of macaroni to stand up away from the board wins.

CONSTRUCTION: Lengths of string, beaded with from four to ten pieces of macaroni, are drawn through holes in a piece of cardboard. The strings are tied together in a knot three inches below the board.

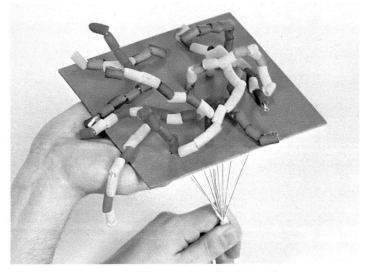

The Balance Board *player pulling on the knotted string is trying to force the threaded strands of macaroni to stand away from the board.*

Players get three minutes to match the ragged edges of the loose cup halves to their mates glued to a baseboard in the Cup Puzzle.

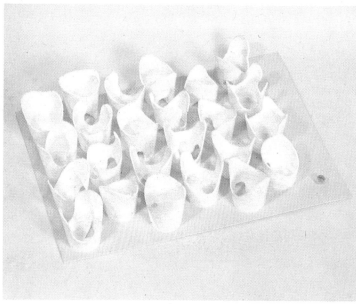

A little bit of luck, a keen eye and a steady hand are needed in Marble Maze *to tilt the board so that the marble goes through the cups.*

Cup Puzzle

● *2 to 4* ● *Eight to adult*

ACTION: The object is to match the lower and upper halves of the cups as quickly as possible. One point is scored for each cup reconstructed. When adults are playing, the time limit for each half-round is three minutes; for children this can be extended to four or five minutes. The game can be played between individuals or by two-man teams. After both sides have a chance, a round is complete. At the end of every round, the totals are added, the side with more points winning.

CONSTRUCTION: Twenty to 30 Styrofoam coffee cups are needed. Each is cut into two uneven pieces with free-form, jigsaw-like edges. Before play begins, the bottom halves are set on a table or glued to a board, and the top halves are scrambled.

Marble Maze

● *2 to 4* ● *Eight to adult*

ACTION: Players take turns trying to roll a marble into and out of the holes in each cup. The winner is the player who gets the marble into the most cups within three minutes. Should the marble fall off the board, the player loses the remainder of his time. A player receives one point for each cup the marble rolls into during the allotted time.

CONSTRUCTION: The bottom halves of the cups used for the *Cup Puzzle* may be used in this game. Holes are cut at the base of each cup, and the cups are glued firmly to a heavy cardboard, plywood or Masonite board. Edges can be tacked or glued around the board to keep the marble from falling off.

Carousel Twirl

● *2 to 6*   ● *Six to nine*

ACTION: Each player is assigned a color and receives 16 paper circles in that color. The game leader twirls the carousel. When it stops, the first player places one of his circles in the carousel pocket facing him. The game proceeds in this manner with players taking turns—each player having 16 turns in all. Players receive a point for every two of their circles placed in opposite pockets. Circles that fly out during play while the wheel is spinning are not counted. The player with the highest score wins.

CONSTRUCTION: Two paper plates, a straw and ten pieces of eight-inch by 11-inch construction paper are needed. The frame of the carousel is made by inserting each end of the straw into holes punched into the center of the plates. The plates are placed five inches apart on the straw. Ten pockets for the carousel are formed by cutting out five five-inch squares from the paper. These squares are folded in half and are glued or taped in place between the plates with the folds touching the straw. The colored circles, each about the size of a quarter, are cut from the remaining construction paper.

In Carousel Twirl, *a player places a disc in the segment facing him after each spin. The child with the most discs in opposite segments wins.*

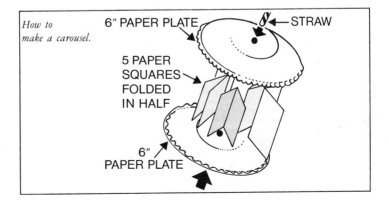

How to make a carousel.

6" PAPER PLATE — STRAW

5 PAPER SQUARES FOLDED IN HALF

6" PAPER PLATE

The winning trick in Tiltboard *is to tip the baseboard so that the marble completes the course without falling into any of the holes.*

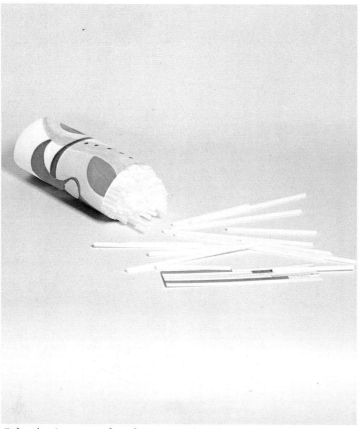

Before drawing a straw from the Honeycomb *a player guesses what its length will be. Then he draws a straw and measures it on the graph.*

Tiltboard

- *2 to 4* ● *Eight to adult*

ACTION: Each player in turn tries to tilt the board so that a marble moves from the starting point to the finish without falling into a hole. The player who comes closest to completing the course wins the game.

CONSTRUCTION: On a 12-inch by 18-inch piece of heavy cardboard, a maze of intricate tunnels is pasted. Traps, in the form of holes, are punched in strategic spots into the maze and through the baseboard.

Honeycomb

- *2 to 4* ● *Eight to twelve*

ACTION: Players take turns pulling straws from the honeycomb. Just before pulling, each player guesses the length of the straw and then measures it against the graph. If he guesses correctly, he keeps the straw; if not he returns it to the honeycomb. The next player then makes a choice. He can, if he knows where it is, pull out the same straw previously pulled. Having seen it, he is then able to make an educated guess as to its length. After each player has five turns, the one who collects the most straws wins.

CONSTRUCTION: Thirty straws are cut into ten different lengths and placed inside a paper cylinder made by rolling and taping a piece of eight-inch by ten-inch paper. A graph showing the exact lengths of the ten straws is drawn on a piece of paper.

Number Carpet

● *2 to 10* ● *Seven to eleven*

ACTION: Contestants pair off. The first two stand on opposite ends of the six-foot-long carpet, bend forward and hold hands. The next pair acts as scorekeepers. On signal, the two players try to pull one another across the carpet, in such a way that the opponent's feet land on minus-numbered areas rather than the plus-numbered areas. The contest goes on for a minute, and the scorekeepers, who mark down the numbered areas on which each player steps, tally up the totals. The player with the highest plus-score wins the round. Elimination rounds are held between winners until one player becomes the champion.

CONSTRUCTION: A three-by-six-foot carpet is cut from brown wrapping paper or corrugated cardboard. The numbered areas can be drawn on the carpet, or cutouts can be made from colored construction paper and pasted on the carpet.

VARIATION: In *Blind Man's Hop,* each contestant is given a minute to look at the carpet and fix in his mind the location of the plus and minus areas. Then he is blindfolded and told to hop across the carpet, stepping in as many plus areas as possible while avoiding the minus areas. Score is kept, with points subtracted for each minus area touched and added for each plus area touched. The player with the highest point-total wins the *Blind Man's Hop.*

Two youngsters pull and haul as each tries to force the other to lose balance and step on a minus-numbered area of Number Carpet.

If a player is lucky, a ball thrown into the top of Bag Stack *will drop through holes in the nest of bags and reach bottom.*

Bag Stack

● *2 to 8* ● *Six to twelve*

ACTION: Players stand three feet from the bag stack and take turns throwing a Ping-Pong ball into the top bag. If the ball falls into a hole in that bag's bottom and into the bag below, the player gets one point. If the ball falls through to the third bag, the player gets two points; if it falls to the fourth bag, he gets three points, and if it falls into the bottom bag, he gets four points. Players are able to determine at what level the ball comes to rest by looking into the peepholes cut into the sides of the bags. After five rounds of play, the scores are added, and the contestant with the highest total is declared the winner. Another way of scoring is to declare 25 points the winning total—the first player to reach this score winning the *Bag Stack* competition.

CONSTRUCTION: Five bags, all the same size, have three holes apiece cut in their bottoms. The holes are approximately two-and-one-half inches in diameter —a size somewhat larger than a Ping-Pong ball. The bags are stacked, one inside another, with three or four inches separating the bottoms. This allows sufficient space for the Ping-Pong ball to roll around freely. Sections of tape placed along the top edges of the bags hold the bags apart and the stack intact. Holes are cut into the stack's sides to permit viewing and to make it easier for players to retrieve the Ping-Pong balls.

Holey Moley
Marble Throw

● *2 to 8*   ● *Six to adult*

ACTION: Each player gets 20 marbles and, in turn, tries to roll them down the tube so that they fall into the plastic bag attached to its end. A marble that falls through one of the holes does not score. A point is given for every marble that reaches the bag. The high-scoring player wins.

CONSTRUCTION: Six pieces of construction paper are punched with holes slightly bigger than the size of a marble. The papers are taped together to form a long rectangle, which is then rolled into a tube held in shape with tape along the edges. A plastic bag is taped on one end of the tube. The tube can rest on two cardboard supports.

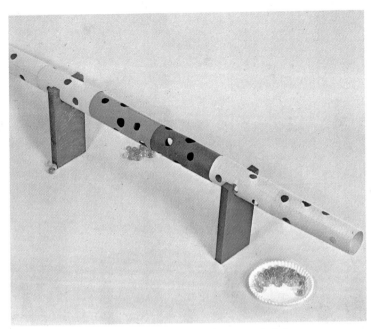

In Holey Moley *the object is to roll a marble from one end of the tube—past the holes—and into a collection bag at the opposite end.*

Clogged Drains

● *2 to 4*   ● *Five to nine*

ACTION: Each player is assigned a straw and given ten toothpicks. In two minutes, a player must work as many of his toothpicks as possible down his straw and into the cup. Since the straws are misshapen, this can be difficult. The player who gets the most toothpicks in the cup wins.

CONSTRUCTION: A hole is cut into the plastic lid of a coffee cup and four straws are stuffed through it. To make the game more difficult, the straws are bent and twisted and small cuts are made in them.

The player who works the greatest number of toothpicks through a twisted straw and into the cup wins the game of Clogged Drains.

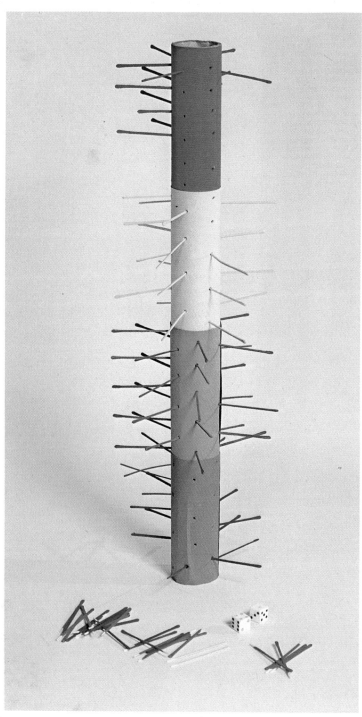

The colored markings that come up on a roll of the dice tell a player which toothpicks to place in the Porcupine Pole *and what his point-total is.*

Porcupine Pole

● *2 to 6*   ● *Ten to adult*

ACTION: The first player rolls the dice, hoping to come up with color combinations worth a high number of points. The markings on four sides of each die are colored: the side with the red markings worth eight points; the blue markings worth six; the yellow, four and the green, two. The two sides on each die that have black dots have no point value. If a player rolls a red and a blue, for example, his score is 14. He then places a red toothpick through the red portion of the porcupine pole and a blue toothpick through the blue. Play proceeds in this manner—each player getting a single role per turn. A player who can place a toothpick in the last available hole in a section gets double value. However, when a section is filled and a player rolls that color, he gets no points. The game continues until all holes are filled, and the player with the highest score wins.

CONSTRUCTION: The 16-inch pole can be made from a mailing tube. The four colors are painted on the pole in equal-size sections, and 36 holes are then punched in each section. The toothpicks are divided into four piles of 36 each; the toothpicks in each pile are then dipped in vegetable dye to give each pile a matching color from the tube. The dots on the dice are easily colored with crayons. Crayon can also be used to color the toothpicks, though this is likely to be a tedious task.

Surprise Drawing

● *2 to 4*   ● *Nine to adult*

ACTION: Two, three or four players are each given two sheets of paper with a piece of carbon paper between the two. The players are assigned a subject to draw, such as a funny man, a fat woman, a horse, a dog, or whatever. Instead of a pencil, each artist uses a knitting needle. When time is called, work stops. The top sheet and carbon are then turned back to reveal the finished art on the under sheet. Everyone, including the artists themselves, is likely to be surprised and amused by the results.

CONSTRUCTION: Several drawing pads are made simply by stapling together two sheets of white paper with a sheet of carbon paper in the middle.

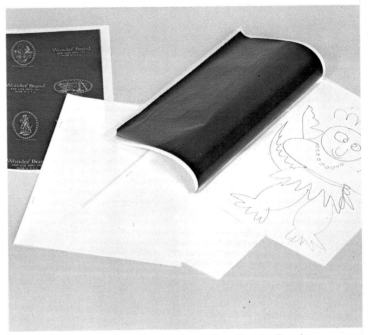

Because each player sketches with a knitting needle in Surprise Drawing, *no one knows how a picture will turn out until the carbon paper is lifted.*

Cylinder Poke

● *1 to 4*   ● *Three to six*

ACTION: The object is simply to poke the cutout shapes back into their places on the cylinders. For five- and six-year-olds, the game can be played competitively with one point awarded for each correct placement. There need be no contest for three- and four-year-olds; they simply enjoy fitting the pieces back in place.

CONSTRUCTION: Circles, squares and triangles are drawn on pieces of construction paper and then cut out. The cylinders are formed by gluing together two opposing sides of the cutout paper. The shapes are then attached to straws to make pokers.

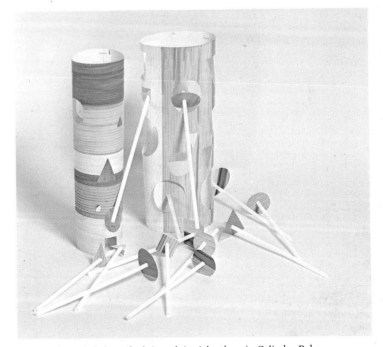

Pushing the varied shapes back into their right places in Cylinder Poke *is an activity that is both challenging and absorbing to the very young.*

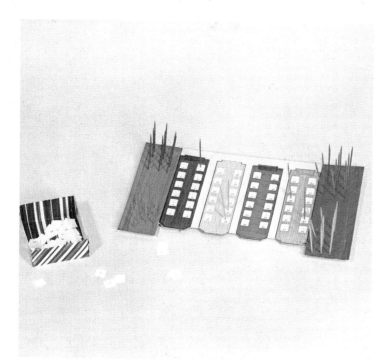

Colored toothpicks and numbered tickets are used by players to try to seat the most passengers in a four-car Commuter Special.

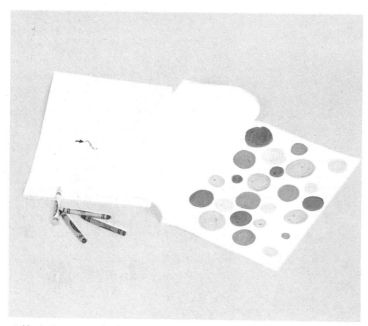

A blank sheet covers the dotted page in Follow the Dots, *and players try to remember, and mark, where their dots are located.*

Commuter Special

● *2 to 4*   ● *Eight to twelve*

ACTION: Tickets, numbered from 1 to 48, are placed face down in a box. Nearby are sets of 12 toothpicks—red, yellow, blue and green to match the colors of four commuter cars, each with 12 seats. The red car has seat numbers from 1 to 12; the yellow car, 13 to 24; the blue car, 25 to 36 and the green car, 37 to 48. In turn, each player chooses a toothpick of any color, then a ticket. If the ticket number corresponds to a seat in the car of the same color, that player places his toothpick in the appropriate seat, gets a point and takes another turn. If not, he returns the ticket, face down, to the pile, and the turn goes to the next player. The game ends when all toothpicks are placed in cars. The high scorer wins.

CONSTRUCTION: Four train cars, three by eight inches, are cut from separate pieces of cardboard; the tickets are cut from white construction paper. If colored toothpicks are not available, plain toothpicks can be colored or dyed.

Follow the Dots

● *2 to 4*   ● *Six to nine*

ACTION: Each player is given a crayon of the same color as some of the circles on the sheet of paper. All players look at the sheet and try to remember where the circles of their color are. Then the paper is covered with another nontransparent sheet. The first player makes a dot over the spot where he thinks a circle of his color is. The second player then draws a line from that dot to a point where he thinks a circle of his color might be. The third player does the same, and so on. When there are as many dots as there are circles below, the top sheet is lifted off. The player who places the most dots correctly wins.

CONSTRUCTION: Different sized circles are drawn and colored with as many colors as there are players. A sheet of heavy paper is laid over the sheet with the circles, and stapled to it along one edge.

Ring-a-Ding

● *2 to 6* ● *Four to six*

ACTION: All players have a basket apiece. As the leader throws the paper rings into the air, one at a time, the players try to catch the rings in the baskets. The player who catches the most rings wins.

CONSTRUCTION: Eight two-inch-by-18-inch strips of construction paper are needed for each basket. Six strips are crossed as if forming the spokes of a wheel and stapled together at the hub. The ends are then stapled to the seventh strip to form the basket edge. The eighth strip is stapled onto the basket to form a handle. The throwing rings, at least 30, are made by gluing or stapling together the ends of small strips of construction paper.

Two Ring-a-Ding *players scramble to catch the flying ring in their baskets. The player who snares the most rings wins the contest.*

Only the youngster who forms the most words in three minutes with these letters wins the Letter Toss. *But all players improve their spelling.*

Letter Toss

- *1 to 6*   - *Six to eight*

ACTION: The letters are distributed by the game leader. Each child gets at least ten, among which are several vowels. The child who forms the most words with his letters within three minutes wins the round.

CONSTRUCTION: Large letters are cut from construction paper. There should be a full alphabet plus four or five of each vowel for every two players.

VARIATIONS: *Letter Pick* is for four- and five-year-olds. Each gets the same letters and wins a point for each correct letter identification. In *Number Toss,* young children get cutout numbers, and the game leader asks them to form sequences, such as from one to five or from three to nine. Six- and seven-year-olds may be asked to do simple arithmetic problems.

Build a Word

- *2 to 6*   - *Ten to adult*

ACTION: Each player is dealt four cards from a 77-card deck. Each card has a single letter on it. The first player places any letter on the table. Then the other players, in turn, add a letter apiece—each one trying to form a word by adding his letter. As players add cards, they replenish their hands by drawing from the top of the stock. A player who completes a word gets one point for each letter in that word. The table is then cleared and the next player starts the word-building anew. A player who cannot complete a word may pass, or he may put on the table any letter in his hand. He must, however, have a word in mind and be able to identify that word if challenged. A player who fails to meet a challenge must subtract the number of letters on the table from his final score. If, however, a player makes a challenge which is answered, that player subtracts from his final score one point for each card on the table. The game ends when all cards from the stock are turned up. Each player subtracts from his total the number of cards remaining in his hand, and the contestant with the most points is declared the winner.

CONSTRUCTION: Three-by-five-inch file cards are used to make the cards. Two complete sets of the alphabet are written on 52 of the cards and five additional sets of the five vowels are written on the remaining 25 cards.

Flash-a-Card

- *1 to 4* • *Three to six*

ACTION: An adult leader holds up one card at a time and asks the children to shout, in turn, the name of the object shown on the card. The child who is able to make the most correct identifications is declared the winner of the contest.

CONSTRUCTION: Objects can be drawn on 50 file cards, or photographs from magazines can be stapled or pasted onto large file cards.

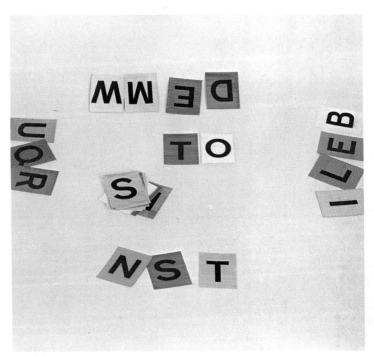

In Build a Word *players use the letter cards in their hands to spell words, each child placing a card per turn in the center of the table.*

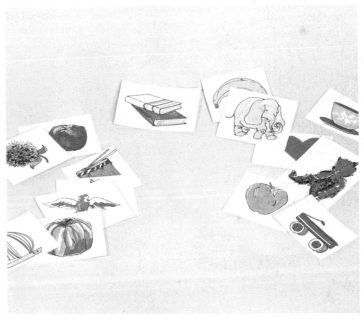

When each Flash-a-Card *is held up, the first child to identify the object pictured scores one point in this game for the very young.*

Bonus Puzzle *players receive cutout shapes which they try to match with identical shapes on the board. Points are given for successful matchings.*

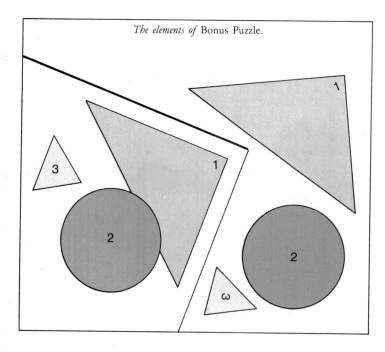

The elements of Bonus Puzzle.

Bonus Puzzle

● *2 to 4*   ● *Six to twelve*

ACTION: Players group around the board on which a number of geometric shapes are pasted. In some instances, smaller shapes are pasted on top of larger ones. Each shape has a point value written upon it. In turn, each player draws a numbered ticket from a pile. The number on the ticket corresponds to the point value of one of the shapes on the board and to a duplicate cutout shape from another pile. The player finds the cutout, places it on top of its twin on the board and receives the point value listed. If the shape he draws covers one or two other shapes on the board, he receives not only the points for his cutout but also the points for any shapes underneath. The game goes on in this manner, with players drawing tickets in turn, until all shapes are covered. The contestant with the most points wins. A player who draws a ticket for a shape already covered does not win points for that turn.

CONSTRUCTION: Exact duplicates of 35 to 40 geometric shapes are cut from colored construction paper. The pairs are then numbered consecutively from 1 to 35 or 40, and one of each pair is pasted on an 18-by-24-inch piece of cardboard. The pasted pieces can be arranged in any form, but several large pieces should have one or two smaller pieces pasted over them. Tickets are cut from white paper and numbered from 1 to 35 or 40.

Animal Puzzle

● *1 to 4* ● *Four to eight*

ACTION: The animal poster is put on the floor, and players take turns fitting puzzle pieces of the animals in place. One point is awarded for each piece properly placed or for putting the last piece of an animal in place.

CONSTRUCTION: Six or eight animals are drawn or traced on a piece of 18-by-24-inch paper. The same animals are then drawn and cut out of another sheet. The cutout animals are cut into jigsaw pieces. Animal pictures may also be taken from two copies of the same magazine.

In Animal Puzzle *the children try to fit the various pieces over matching portions on pictures of some members of the animal kingdom.*

Box Puzzle

● *1 to 4* ● *Seven to adult*

ACTION: Each player has 30 seconds (in the case of young children, one minute) to fit the cutout pieces of the box back into their proper places. The player who makes the most correct placements wins.

CONSTRUCTION: Gift paper with an intricate design is pasted on the bottom and sides of a cardboard box. The puzzle pieces are made by drawing circles, squares, rectangles, triangles and freeforms over the design and then cutting them out with a scissors. If gift paper is not available, designs can be painted or crayoned directly onto the box. When the game is to be played by young children, it is a good idea to keep both the design and the cutouts simple.

Each player has only 30 seconds—or one minute for children—to fit as many pieces of the Box Puzzle *as possible back into their places.*

*Using cards representing stories and roofs of buildings,
players of* Build a City *compete to finish the most structures.*

Build a City

● *2 to 6*   ● *Nine to adult*

ACTION: *Build a City* is played with a deck of 60 cards, some representing a story of a building; others, various kinds of rooftops. Each type of rooftop card has a different value, but all story cards are two points each. Every player is dealt four cards. Any player who holds a story card can begin play by putting it down. He thus earns three points: two for the value of the story card and one for starting a building. (Players always receive the number of points which the card they add is worth, plus one point for each story the building contains at the time.) The second player has three choices: He can add onto the first player's story card with another story card, thus earning four points (two for his story card and two for the stories in the building); he can roof the one story, thereby earning the points given for his rooftop card plus one point for the story underneath, or he can begin another building by placing a story card directly on the table, thereby earning three points. Once a building is roofed, it is finished. No player can add another card on top of the roof. Play proceeds in turns. When a player uses up the four cards dealt him, he is dealt four more. If a player holds an unfinished roof card, he should use it as quickly as possible. Such a card is valued at minus two points, and each story under it is counted as minus one point. At the end

CARD VALUES			
25	story cards	value	2 pts. ea.
16	house rooftop cards	value	5 pts. ea.
7	apartment rooftop cards	value	7 pts. ea.
5	unfinished rooftop cards	value	−2 pts. ea.
5	church steeples	value	8 pts. ea.
3	municipal building rooftops	value	3 pts. ea.
2	skyscraper tops	value	6 pts. ea.
2	gas-station rooftops	value	4 pts. ea.
1	fire-station top	value	10 pts.

of the game, when all possible cards are played, scores are tallied. The player with the highest score wins.

CONSTRUCTION: Sixty four-by-six-inch cards are cut from heavy paper and folded in half. They are painted with roof and story symbols, and the point values are written on them. Two one-fourth-inch slits are cut about two inches apart along the fold so that one card can be inserted on top of another.

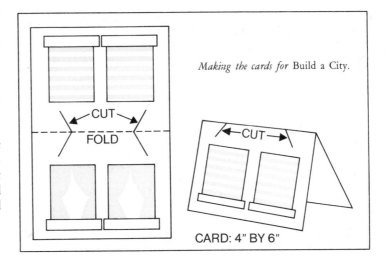

Making the cards for Build a City.

CARD: 4" BY 6"

Window Watch

● *1 to 4* ● *Three to four*

ACTION: The object is to identify what is drawn on the cards. An adult leader places one card at a time in a window. The game can be played with each child, in turn, identifying one picture or identifying one after another until he misses. A plus point may be given for each correct answer; a minus point for each incorrect identification. When all objects are identified, the player with the most plus points is declared the winner of the *Window Watch* contest.

CONSTRUCTION: Twenty-five two-by-three-inch windows are cut out of an 18-by-24-inch piece of cardboard. To hold the cards in place, a strip of paper is placed on one side of the cardboard below each row of windows and glued along its bottom edge. At least 25 cards, slightly larger than two by three inches, are cut from paper and an object easily recognized by children drawn on each one.

To win at Window Watch, *a contestant must identify more objects than his playmates as the items appear in the windows of the cardboard.*

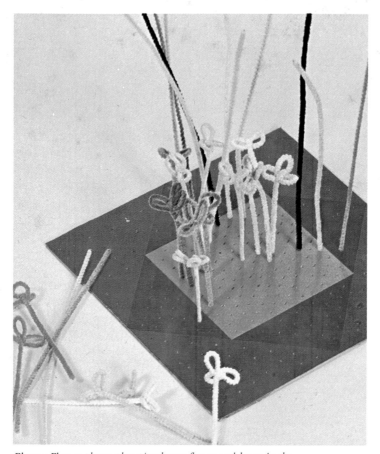

Plant a Flower *players place pipe-cleaner flowers and leaves in the board, each contestant trying not to touch the plants already in place.*

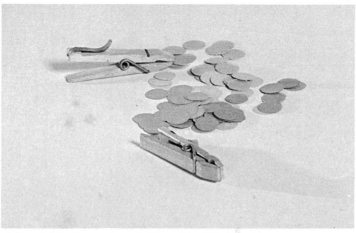

A hinged clothespin must be used with precision if it is to pick up one disc at a time without moving other discs in the game of Quick Sticks.

Plant a Flower

● *1 to 6* ● *Six to adult*

ACTION: In turn, each player places one pipe cleaner flower or leaf into the base. If it does not touch another flower or leaf already placed, he receives one point and is allowed another turn which, if successful, gives him a second point. Then the next player takes a turn. No player can make more than two points during one round. The game ends when as many flowers and leaves as possible are "planted" without touching one another. The player with the highest score wins.

CONSTRUCTION: The base is made from an eight-inch square of cardboard punctured with 64 holes, each an inch apart. Sixty-four pipe cleaners are needed to make the flowers. (They may be purchased at toy, hobby or department stores where they are much less expensive than the ones in tobacco shops.) Thirty-two pipe cleaners are shaped into three-petaled flowers, and 32 are kept long to symbolize leaves.

Quick Sticks

● *2 to 4* ● *Six to adult*

ACTION: A designated player sets up the game by dropping a handful of circles and a handful of toothpicks onto the playing surface. In turn, each player may use a comb or clothespin to pick up as many circles and tooth-picks as he can, one at a time, without moving any other pieces. Players forfeit their turns to the next contestant when they move a piece other than the one they are trying to withdraw. One point is counted for each pick or circle successfully removed. At the end of the game, the player with the highest score is declared the winner.

CONSTRUCTION: Only the circles require construction. Circles about the size of a quarter are drawn on heavy colored paper and cut out.

In and Out the Window

● *1 to 4*   ● *Six to eight*

ACTION: In turn, each player is blindfolded and given a five-foot length of yarn with a knot tied at one end. He then threads the yarn through five holes, receiving one point for each threaded hole within a window. Players may rethread holes already used, but rethreaded holes in the windows do not count for points. When all window holes are threaded, the player with the highest point-total wins the game.

CONSTRUCTION: Windows of various shapes and sizes are drawn on an 18-by-24-inch sheet of cardboard. Numerous small holes are then punched out with a knitting needle. (At least three holes should be punched in each window.) Instead of drawing windows onto the cardboard, pictures of real windows cut from magazines may be pasted within rectangles sketched on the board.

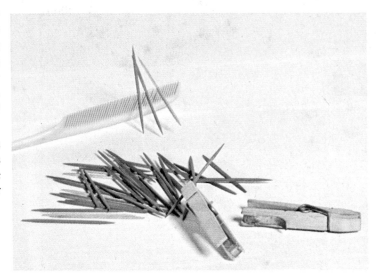

Toothpicks may also be used in Quick Sticks, *in which case they are picked up either by a clothespin or with a fine-toothed comb.*

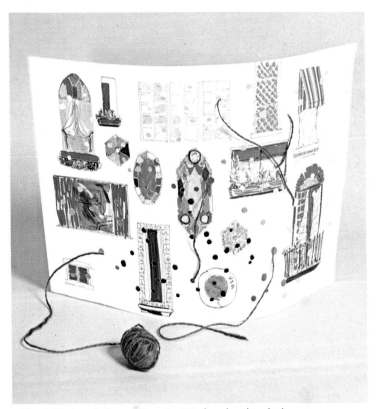

After looking at the In and Out the Window *board, each player is blindfolded and tries to thread yarn through only the window holes.*

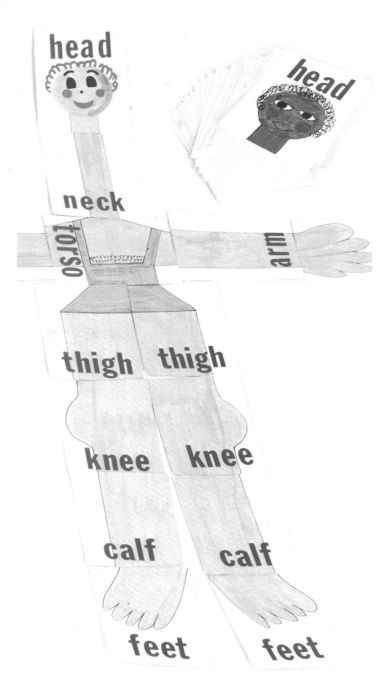

Each player gets a point for every card he contributes to help
Build a Body *and a bonus of 15 points for a card that completes a body.*

Build a Body

● *2 to 6*   ● *Six to ten*

ACTION: *Build a Body* is played with 60 cards divided into four sets. Each set of 15 is painted a different color and contains cards which form a body: a head card, neck card, torso card, two arm cards, two hand cards, two thigh cards, two knee cards, two calf cards, two foot cards. Each player is dealt four cards. Play proceeds in turns with the dealer going first. He places down any card. The second player must build directly onto that card (for instance, a neck card to a head card; a foot card to a calf card) with a card of the same color. If he cannot do this, he may start a second body. If he starts a second body, the third player may build onto either the first or the second body or start a third body. When all four bodies are started, players must build directly onto one of them with a card of matching color or forfeit a turn. If all players forfeit in a row, the dealer deals two more cards to each person. When a player has used all the cards in his hand, four more are dealt him. Players receive one point for each card placed, except for the card that completes a body—worth 15 points. When four bodies are finished, the player with the highest score wins.

CONSTRUCTION: Sixty cards, about four inches by six inches each, are cut from paper. Each set of 15 is painted a different color and each card marked with a part of the body.

Pine Cone

● *2 to 6*   ● *Eight to adult*

ACTION: Sixty hand-painted cards are cut in half, and 60 halves are put into slits in the pine cone. The other 60 halves are dealt to players. The object is to match the dealt cards with their other halves in the pine cone. Play proceeds in turns, with the first player putting one of his cards on the table and then trying to find its other half in the cone. If successful, he wins a point and puts the matched pieces aside. If he cannot find the card in the cone, he leaves his card on the table and receives a minus point. The next player may try to find the card in the cone that matches the first player's card. If successful (thereby earning a point), he may then try to match a card from his own hand—thus earning another point. If the second player does not match the first player's card, he receives a minus point and may not try to match a card from his own hand. The unmatched card is left on the table and subsequent players may try to match it. When all cards are matched, the player with the highest score is declared the winner.

CONSTRUCTION: Sixty two-inch-wide slits are cut into a piece of 12-by-18-inch paper. The 12-inch sides are glued together to form the pine cone. Sixty one-and-one-half-inch cards are cut from construction paper. They are painted with subtly different patterns and colors and then cut in half.

To earn a point, a player must match a card in his hand with its partially concealed mate that is stuck into the Pine Cone.

Games at a Glance

Planning activities for a party, an outing or even for a recuperating young-ster can often be a tedious chore. The tables that appear on the following pages are intended to relieve that tedium by providing tailored programs for a wide variety of occasions. These programs are presented in table form so that the essential information about each game—the number of players, the page on which its description will be found, the equipment needed, etc.—can be seen at a glance. These programs are intended as guides rather than rules. For example, in many instances where games for children or teen-agers are listed, adult supervision is recommended. This is not to say that youngsters are incapable of playing on their own. But a host or hostess may well find that with an adult on hand to settle disputes over rules, the games will go more smoothly. The suggested time periods should be viewed in very much the same light. If everybody is having fun playing a particular game, there is no need to end it just because the recommended time period has elapsed. On the other hand, if spirits flag after just a few minutes of play, the game should be quickly ended and the group can move on to the next activity in the program.

Although organized activity does require advanced planning, the rewards in fun make the effort worth while. If these *Games at a Glance* tables are con-sulted whenever there's a girls' club to entertain, a rainy day with children to get through, or an informal adult get-together to plan, the preliminary work will be eased and the fun greatly enhanced.

GAMES FOR AN INDOOR BIRTHDAY PARTY: THREE- TO SIX-YEAR-OLDS

GAMES	Page	Time period	No. of players	Adult leader	Equipment required	Play area
MULBERRY BUSH	116	10 min.	5 to 15	Yes	None	Playroom
SIMON SAYS	75	20 min.	5 to 15	Yes	None	Playroom
MAGIC STUNTS: 1. Temple Magic	130	10 min.	5 to 15	Yes	None	Playroom
2. Hindu Cane	131	10 min.	5 to 15	Yes	A cane	Playroom
3. Vanishing Coin	133	5 min.	5 to 15	Yes	Penny or nickel	Playroom
4. Heads or Tails	133	5 min.	5 to 15	Yes	Penny or nickel	Playroom
5. Rising Egg	139	5 min.	5 to 15	Yes	Glass of water, salt, hard-boiled egg	Playroom
6. Floating Needle	139	5 min.	5 to 15	Yes	Glass of water, two needles, candle, wax	Playroom

GAMES FOR AN OUTDOOR BIRTHDAY PARTY: THREE- TO SIX-YEAR-OLDS

GAMES	Page	Time period	No. of players	Adult leader	Equipment required	Play area
ENVELOPE TOSS	371	20 min.	5 to 15	Yes	Package of envelopes	Backyard
BLIND MAN'S BUFF	66	25 min.	5 to 15	Yes	Blindfold	Backyard
MAGIC CARPETS	74	20 min.	5 to 15	Yes	One sheet of cardboard per player	Backyard
WHERE IS THUMBKIN?	121	10 min.	5 to 15	Yes	None	Backyard
TWO LITTLE BLACKBIRDS	117	10 min.	5 to 15	Yes	None	Backyard

PLAYROOM GAMES FOR RAINY DAYS:
THREE- TO SIX-YEAR-OLDS

GAMES	Page	Time period	No. of players	Adult leader	Equipment required
DUCK WALK	52	5 min.	Any No.	Yes	None
FIVE JUMPS	50	20 min.	1 to 10	Yes	None
HIDE THE CLOCK	63	15 min.	1 to 10	Yes	Non-electric clock
STAY SOBER	70	10 min.	4 to 10	Yes	None
ONE LESS	74	20 min.	4 to 10	Yes	Small household objects
DOG AND BONE	76	20 min.	3 to 10	Yes	Book, blindfold, chairs
MULBERRY BUSH	116	10 min.	2 to 10	Yes	None
CLAPPING NAMES	114	10 min.	2 to 10	Yes	None
RING-A-DING	387	30 min.	2 to 10	Yes	Paper rings, baskets

GAMES FOR YOUNG CHILDREN TO PLAY IN THE PARK:
THREE- TO SIX-YEAR-OLDS

GAMES	Page	Time period	No. of players	Adult leader	Equipment required
SKIP TAG	16	20 min.	6 to 12	Yes	None
LEADER'S CHOICE	39	30 min.	3 to 7	Yes	A variety of balls
BEANBAG THROW	50	25 min.	2 to 10	Yes	Beanbag
FIVE JUMPS	50	15 min.	2 to 10	Yes	A ball of string
SIMON SAYS	75	15 min.	2 to 10	Yes	None
POISON PENNY	68	20 min.	4 to 10	Yes	Penny or other small object

GAMES FOR AN OUTDOOR BIRTHDAY PARTY:
SIX- TO EIGHT-YEAR-OLDS

GAMES	Page	Time period	No. of players	Adult leader	Equipment required	Play area
STEAL THE BACON	23	35 min.	8 to 20	Yes	A handkerchief or plastic bottle	Backyard
FETCH-AND-CARRY RELAY	37	20 min.	8 to 20	Yes	2 beanbags or potholders	Backyard
ICE-CREAM CONTEST	81	20 min.	8 to 20	Yes	2 blindfolds, 2 spoons, 2 dishes, ice cream	Backyard
GUESS THE CREATURE	107	30 min.	8 to 20	Yes	None	Backyard
HOW BIG?	100	25 min.	8 to 20	Yes	Pencils and paper for each player	Backyard

GAMES FOR AN INDOOR BIRTHDAY PARTY:
SIX- TO EIGHT-YEAR-OLDS

GAMES	Page	Time period	No. of players	Adult leader	Equipment required	Play area
MUSICAL CHAIRS	74	25 min.	5 to 20	Yes	Record player, one chair per player	Playroom
MAGIC MUSIC	65	20 min.	5 to 20	Yes	Any small common object	Playroom
WORD HUNT	96	10 min.	5 to 20	Yes	Pencils, paper	Playroom
WHAT IS IT?	125	30 min.	5 to 20	Yes	Paper, chalk or crayons for each player	Playroom
FOX AND FARMER	21	15 min.	5 to 20	Yes	None	Playroom
POTATO RACE	33	15 min.	5 to 20	Yes	6 potatoes, 2 spoons	Playroom
BLIND MAN'S BUFF	66	15 min.	5 to 20	Yes	A blindfold	Playroom

BEDROOM GAMES FOR RECUPERATING CHILDREN

GAMES	Page	Time period	No. of players	Equipment required	Adult leader
HANDKERCHIEF PUPPETS	110	20 min.	1	A few handkerchiefs	Yes
HOW BIG?	100	20 min.	1	Pencil, paper	No
CRAYON AND CHALK DRAWING	151	40 min.	1	Paper, crayons, chalk	No
WAR	163	20 min.	2	Deck of cards	No
FLASH A CARD	389	30 min.	2	Construction paper, crayons	Yes
CYLINDER POKE	385	40 min.	1	Scissors, straws, construction paper	Yes
FOUR-MINUTE CHALLENGES	297	20 min.	1	Paper, pencil	No
CLOCK SOLITAIRE	194	40 min.	1	Deck of cards	No

GAMES FOR YOUNG CHILDREN AND GRANDPARENTS TO PLAY TOGETHER

GAMES	Page	Time period	No. of players	Equipment required	Play area
GO BOOM	161	20 min.	2 to 4	Deck of cards	Living room or den
LOOK, SEE, LOOK	66	15 min.	2 to 6	None	Living room
HANDKERCHIEF PUPPETS	110	25 min.	2 to 6	Handkerchiefs for each participant	Living room
HIDE THE CLOCK	63	20 min.	2 to 6	Winding clock	Living room
MULTIPLE CLOCK SOLITAIRE	194	15 min.	1 to 10	Deck of cards for each player	Living room or den

GAMES FOR CITY SIDEWALKS:
SIX- TO TWELVE-YEAR-OLDS

GAMES	Page	Time period	No. of players	Adult leader	Equipment required
SHADOW TAG	14	15 min.	3 to 10	Yes	None
SQUIRREL IN THE TREE	20	20 min.	8 to 20	Yes	None
CROWS AND CRANES	21	30 min.	6 to 20	Yes	None
RING ON A STRING	68	20 min.	6 to 15	Yes	Ball of string, a ring
FOX, GUN, HUNTER	69	25 min.	6 to 15	Yes	None
BAG STACK	382	30 min.	2 to 8	Yes	Scissors, paper shopping bags, Ping-Pong ball
HOPSCOTCH	56	25 min.	2 to 6	No	Chalk, rubber heel or stone

GAMES TO PLAY ON A SCHOOL BUS:
SIX- TO TWELVE-YEAR-OLDS

GAMES	Page	Time period	No. of players	Referee	Equipment required
CLAPPING SONGS	114	10 min.	5 to 30	No	None
EENTSY-WEENTSY SPIDER	119	10 min.	5 to 30	No	None
IF YOU'RE HAPPY	121	10 min.	5 to 30	No	None
SPORTS-TERMS QUIZ	284	30 min.	5 to 30	No	None
HOW FAR AWAY?	307	25 min.	5 to 30	Yes	A pencil, paper
NAME THE CAR	307	20 min.	5 to 30	No	None
FIZZ	72	20 min.	5 to 30	Yes	None
PRINCE OF PARIS	72	25 min.	5 to 30	No	None

OUTDOOR GAMES TO PLAY ALONE:
SIX- TO TWELVE-YEAR-OLDS

GAMES	Page	Time period	Adult leader	Equipment required	Play area
HOPSCOTCH	56	25 min.	No	Chalk, rubber heel or stone	Driveway, sidewalk
FIVE TRIES	43	40 min.	No	Basketball and hoop	Driveway
BAG STACK	382	60 min.	Yes	Bags, scissors, Ping-Pong ball	Patio, garden
BOTTLE TENPINS	84	40 min.	No	Plastic or cardboard bottle	Backyard

INDOOR ACTIVITIES FOR THE INDIVIDUAL CHILD:
SIX- TO TWELVE-YEAR-OLDS

GAMES	Page	Time period	Adult leader	Equipment required	Play area
EASEL PAINTING	153	40 min.	Yes	An easel, paper, paints	Playroom
PAPIER-MÂCHÉ	153	60 min.	Yes	Newspaper, paste, paint	Playroom
A HOME-MADE XYLOPHONE	106	30 min.	Yes	Water, water glasses	Kitchen, playroom
MARBLE MAZE	378	40 min.	Yes	Scissors, string, wax paper, marbles	Playroom
WHAT DOES IT MEAN?	292	40 min.	No	Dictionary, pencils, paper	Playroom, den
CLOCK SOLITAIRE	194	15 min.	Yes	Deck of cards	Playroom, kitchen, living room or den
CEREAL-BOX SCULPTURE	154	60 min.	No	An oatmeal box, knife, paints	Playroom, kitchen

LIVING ROOM GAMES FOR TWO CHILDREN:
SIX- TO TWELVE-YEAR-OLDS

GAMES	Page	Time period	Adult leader	Equipment required
YOUR AGE, SIR	132	15 min.	No	Pencil, paper
FOUR KINGS	137	10 min.	No	Deck of cards
TICTACTOE	157	15 min.	No	Pencils, paper
HANGMAN	159	15 min.	No	Pencils, paper
WAR	163	25 min.	No	Deck of cards
I SEE BLUE	65	20 min.	No	None
HARE AND HOUND	78	15 min.	Yes	Blindfolds
CHECKERS	233	20 min.	No	A set of checkers and checkerboard
CHAIN OF FIGURES	155	25 min.	Yes	Sheet of paper, scissors

BACKYARD GAMES FOR TWO CHILDREN:
SIX- TO TWELVE-YEAR-OLDS

GAMES	Page	Time period	Adult leader	Equipment required
BEANBAG THROW	50	20 min.	No	Beanbag
CHINESE GET-UP	50	15 min.	No	None
ROOSTER FIGHT	53	10 min.	Yes	None
TWO-MAN TUG OF WAR	54	15 min.	Yes	Rope
ONE GOAL BASKETBALL	335	60 min.	No	Basketball and hoop
HAMMER CONTEST	82	10 min.	Yes	Hammer, nails, lumber

PLAYROOM GAMES FOR SMALL GROUPS:
SIX- TO TWELVE-YEAR-OLDS

GAMES	Page	Time period	No. of players	Adult leader	Equipment required
CUP PUZZLE	378	45 min.	2 to 8	No	Paper cups, cardboard
PRETZEL	77	15 min.	5 to 12	Yes	None
POISON PENNY	68	20 min.	5 to 12	No	Ball or record player, a penny
BLOCK DOMINOES	235	30 min.	2 to 9	No	Dominoes
CUTTING AND PASTING	151	30 min.	2 to 12	Yes	Paste, paper and cloth scraps, sheets of paper
CEREAL-BOX SCULPTURE	154	30 min.	2 to 8	Yes	Oatmeal boxes, knives, paints
OBSERVATION	65	20 min.	Any no.	Yes	15 to 20 small household objects

BACKYARD GAMES FOR SMALL GROUPS:
SIX- TO TWELVE-YEAR-OLDS

GAMES	Page	Time period	No. of players	Adult leader	Equipment required
SHADOW TAG	14	20 min.	4 to 8	Yes	None
CRAB WALK	52	15 min.	2 to 8	Yes	None
WRINGING THE DISHRAG	52	15 min.	2 to 8	Yes	None
FLYING ENVELOPE TOSS	371	40 min.	2 to 8	Yes	Pack of envelopes, scissors
PLAY WITH CLAY	150	40 min.	2 to 8	Yes	Clay
CATCH BALL	41	30 min.	3 to 8	Yes	Ball

OUTDOOR GAMES FOR LARGE GROUPS:
SIX- TO TWELVE-YEAR-OLDS

GAMES	Page	Time period	No. of players	Adult leader	Equipment required	Play area
SQUIRREL IN THE TREE	20	40 min.	14 to 35	Yes	None	Playlot or field
TEAM DODGE BALL	25	40 min.	12 to 40	Yes	Playground ball	Playlot or field
SACK RACE	30	30 min.	8 to 40	Yes	2 sacks	Playlot, backyard
KEEP AWAY	41	40 min.	8 to 30	Yes	Playground ball	Playlot or field
BLIND MAN'S BUFF	66	40 min.	8 to 40	Yes	Blindfold	Playlot, backyard

WEEKEND HOUSE-PARTY GAMES FOR CHILDREN:
SIX- TO TWELVE-YEAR-OLDS

GAMES	Page	Time period	No. of players	Adult leader	Equipment required	Play area
RED ROVER	14	40 min.	8 to 16	Yes	None	Large backyard or field
SKIP TAG	16	20 min.	5 to 10	Yes	None	Backyard or playroom
SACK RACE	30	30 min.	6 to 12	Yes	2 sacks	Large basement or backyard
BALL PASS	27	40 min.	5 to 16	Yes	A ball	Backyard
MUSICAL CHAIRS	74	40 min.	5 to 15	Yes	Chairs, records, record player	Playroom, patio or basement
PLAY WITH CLAY	150	40 min.	2 to 15	No	Clay	Playroom, patio or basement
GO FISH	161	40 min.	2 to 5	No	Deck of cards	Playroom

BACKYARD GAMES FOR YOUNGSTERS:
NINE- TO TWELVE-YEAR-OLDS

GAMES	Page	Time period	No. of players	Adult leader	Equipment required
BEAR IN THE CAGE	15	15 min.	5 to 15	No	None
CIRCLE DODGE BALL	25	30 min.	8 to 15	No	Playground ball
OVER AND UNDER RELAY	32	15 min.	6 to 16	No	Playground ball
FIVE TRIES	43	30 min.	8 to 12	No	Playground ball
SHOOT OUT THE CANDLE	82	20 min.	2 to 10	Yes	Water gun, candle
KNIFE AND PEANUT RACE	88	20 min.	4 to 10	Yes	Table knives, peanuts
TIN-CAN STILT RACE	91	20 min.	2 to 10	No	Tin cans, rope
TEAM AERIAL TENNIS	327	30 min. to hour	2 to 6	No	Badminton set

GAMES TO PLAY AROUND A CAMPFIRE:
NINE- TO TWELVE-YEAR-OLDS

GAMES	Page	Time period	No. of players	Adult leader	Equipment required
WHO AM I?	309	30 min.	Any No.	Yes	None
COMING ROUND THE MOUNTAIN	120	15 min.	Any No.	Yes	None
CIRCLE PASS CHARADES	274	30 min.	Any No.	Yes	None
FIND THE BELL	66	20 min.	Any No.	Yes	A bell
ADD AN ACTION	69	20 min.	Any No.	Yes	None
CHAIN WORD	269	30 min.	Any No.	Yes	A beanbag or pillow
GHOST	272	30 min.	Any No.	Yes	None

INDOOR GAMES FOR A GIRLS' CLUB:
NINE- TO TWELVE-YEAR-OLDS

GAMES	Page	Time period	No. of players	Adult leader	Equipment required	Play area
SKELETON STORIES	108	40 min.	6 to 20	Yes	None	Living room
BUTTON-SEWING RACE	88	20 min.	6 to 20	Yes	Buttons, 2 scraps of cloth, needles, thread	Living room
SOAP SCULPTURE	156	40 min.	6 to 20	Yes	Cakes of soap, kitchen knives, nail files, paper, pencils	Playroom or kitchen
FIND THE FORT	158	25 min.	6 to 20	Yes	Pencils for each player, paper	Playroom or living room
STRAW BALANCE	376	20 min.	6 to 20	Yes	Construction paper, tape, scissors, straws	Playroom

INDOOR GAMES FOR A BOYS' CLUB:
NINE- TO TWELVE-YEAR-OLDS

GAMES	Page	Time period	No. of players	Adult leader	Equipment required	Play area
BROOM HOCKEY	80	30 min.	8 to 20	Yes	2 brooms, a rag	Basement or playroom
PRETZEL	77	25 min.	8 to 20	Yes	None	Playroom
SCAVENGER HUNT	282	25 min.	8 to 20	Yes	None	Playroom
CIRCLE GEOGRAPHY	104	30 min.	8 to 20	Yes	World atlas	Playroom
BRAINTWISTERS	296	20 min.	8 to 20	Yes	Paper, pencils	Playroom
HEARTS	205	25 min.	3 to 7	No	A deck of cards	Basement or playroom

GAMES FOR A GIRLS' SLUMBER PARTY

GAMES	Page	Time period	No. of players	Adult leader	Equipment required	Play area
COFFEEPOT	268	40 min.	8 to 20	No	None	Living room, bedroom
SECRET QUESTIONS	271	20 min.	8 to 12	No	Pencils, paper	Living room, bedroom
NUMBER CARPET	381	30 min.	2 to 10	Yes	Long sheet of paper, paint	Living room, bedroom
DUNK IN THE OCEAN	201	40 min.	2 to 7	No	Deck of cards	Living room, bedroom
WHO WROTE THIS BOOK?	286	30 min.	2 to 10	No	None	Living room, bedroom
EMERGENCY BRAIN TEASERS	299	20 min.	2 to 10	No	None	Living room, bedroom
WORD HUNT	96	40 min.	2 to 10	No	Pencils, paper	Living room, bedroom

GAMES FOR A TEEN-AGERS' PICNIC

GAMES	Page	Time period	No. of players	Referee	Equipment required	Play area
SOCCER	357	60 min.	8 to 20	Yes	Soccer ball	Field
SCAVENGER HUNT	282	30 min.	8 to 20	Yes	Common household items, pencils, paper	Field
AMERICAN HISTORY QUIZ	288	30 min.	5 to 15	No	None	Any site
WHO INVENTED IT?	289	20 min.	5 to 15	No	None	Any site
WORD HUNT	96	30 min.	5 to 15	Yes	Pencils, paper	Any site
VOLLEYBALL	366	60 min.	6 to 14	Yes	Volleyball, net	Field

OUTDOOR GAMES FOR TEEN-AGERS

GAMES	Page	Time period	No. of players	Referee	Equipment required	Play area
SOFTBALL	331	90 min.	18	Yes	Softball and bat	Park or field
HORSESHOES	354	40 min.	2 to 4	Yes	Horseshoes and pegs	Park or field
VOLLEYBALL	366	40 min.	6 to 14	Yes	Volleyball and net	Park or field
CIRCLE PASS CHARADES	274	40 min.	5 to 20	No	None	Park or field
ELIMINATION DODGE BALL	25	30 min.	10 to 20	Yes	Playground ball	Park or field

GAMES TO PLAY AT A TEEN-AGE MIXER

GAMES	Page	Time period	No. of players	Referee	Equipment required	Play area
NAME BINGO	262	20 min.	16 to 50	Yes	Pencils, paper for each participant	Living room
MULTIPLICATION DANCE	263	20 min.	16 to 50	Yes	Record player	Living room
BROOM DANCE	266	15 min.	16 to 50	Yes	One broom, record player	Living room
SOMETHING SMELLS	275	25 min.	6 to 16	Yes	Paper cups, small quantities of foods with odors	Any room
NAME THE TUNE	123	20 min.	16 to 30	Yes	Record player, pencils, paper	Living room
PROP PLAYS	108	30 min.	16 to 30	Yes	8 to 10 common household items	Living room
CHARADES	273	30 min.	6 to 16	Yes	Pencils, paper	Living room

WEEKEND HOUSE-PARTY GAMES FOR TEEN-AGERS

GAMES	Page	Time period	No. of players	Referee	Equipment required	Play area
HORSESHOES	354	40 min.	2 or 4	Yes	Horseshoes and pegs	Backyard or field
ROTATION BASEBALL	331	60 min.	5 to 12	Yes	Softball and bat	Field, large backyard
HANDBALL	349	40 min.	2 or 4	Yes	A handball	Basement wall or any outside wall
VOLLEYBALL	366	60 min.	6 to 14	No	Volleyball and net	Backyard
SCAVENGER HUNT	282	40 min.	6 to 16	No	Common house-hold items, pencils, paper	Backyard, basement or playroom
BADMINTON	324	60 min.	2 or 4	No	Badminton set	Backyard
CHARADES	273	1 or 2 hours	4 to 16	No	Pencils, paper	Living room

GAMES FOR A FAMILY PICNIC

GAMES	Page	Time period	No. of players	Referee	Equipment required	Play area
CATCH BALL	41	30 min.	6 to 12	No	Ball	Field
NETBALL	41	40 min.	6 to 12	Yes	Playground ball, net	Field
TUG OF WAR	54	15 min.	6 to 12	Yes	Strong rope, handkerchiefs	Field
HARE AND HOUND	78	20 min.	2 to 6	Yes	Blindfold	Field
SHOOT OUT THE CANDLE	82	30 min.	2 to 12	Yes	Water gun, candle	Field
NATURE TRAILING	309	30 min.	4 to 12	Yes	No	Woods

FAMILY GAMES FOR
A DAY AT THE BEACH

GAMES	Page	Time period	No. of players	Referee	Play area
WHALE AND HERRING	313	30 min.	4 to 8	Yes	Pool, lake
HOW MANY WAYS TO GET THERE?	312	30 min.	4 to 8	Yes	Pool, lake
SPELLING BEE	97	25 min.	4 to 8	Yes	Beach, poolside
GOING TO CALIFORNIA	108	25 min.	4 to 8	Yes	Beach, poolside
A ROUND OF RIDDLES	295	20 min.	4 to 8	No	Beach, poolside
UNDERWATER TAG	312	25 min.	4 to 8	Yes	Pool, lake
PLUNGING FOR DISTANCE	312	15 min.	4 to 8	Yes	Pool, lake

AFTER-DINNER GAMES FOR FAMILY GATHERINGS

GAMES	Page	Time period	No. of players	Equipment required	Play area
CONCENTRATION	162	30 min.	2 or more	Deck of cards	Any room
ANIMAL CHAMPIONS	291	15 min.	2 or more	None	Any room
SPORTS-TERMS QUIZ	284	15 min.	2 or more	None	Any room
HIDDEN WORDS	292	25 min.	2 or more	Pencils, paper	Any room
ROUND OF RIDDLES	295	20 min.	2 or more	None	Any room
FOUR-MINUTE CHALLENGES	297	25 min.	2 or more	Pencils, paper	Any room
SO YOU THINK YOU'RE CLEVER	298	20 min.	2 or more	None	Any room
DOMINOES	234	30 min.	2 to 9	Domino set	Any room

GAMES TO PLAY ON A FAMILY CAMPING TRIP

GAMES	Page	Time period	No. of players	Equipment required	Play area
MEMORY HIKE	309	20 min.	4 to 10	Pencils, paper	Campsite
SAFETY TREE	310	20 min.	4 to 10	None	Campsite
ROADSIDE CRIBBAGE	309	40 min.	4 to 10	Pebbles	On the trail
UNDERWATER TAG	312	20 min.	7 to 20	None	Lake
FOLLOW THE LEADER	312	20 min.	4 to 10	None	Lake
ROPE TUG	313	20 min.	4 to 10	None	Lakeside or campsite
A ROUND OF RIDDLES	295	20 min.	2 to 10	None	Lakeside or campsite
SPORTS-TERMS QUIZ	284	10 min.	2 to 10	None	Lakeside or campsite
NATURE SCAVENGER HUNT	310	40 min.	4 to 20	Paper bags	Woods

FAMILY GAMES ON A SNOWY WINTER'S DAY

GAMES	Page	Time period	No. of players	Equipment required	Play area
COASTING FOR DISTANCE	319	40 min.	4 to 10	Ice skates	Skating rink
PENNY RACE	318	20 min.	4 to 10	Ice skates, pennies	Skating rink
SNOW DODGE BALL	319	30 min.	6 to 10	None	Backyard
INDIVIDUAL PASS CHARADES	274	40 min.	4 to 10	Pencils, paper	Fireside
GOURMET CONTEST	275	40 min.	4 to 10	Small quantities of different foods	Fireside
WALK THE STRAIGHT AND NARROW	279	30 min.	4 to 10	Binoculars	Playroom

GAMES TO PLAY ON
A FAMILY AUTOMOBILE TRIP

GAMES	Page	Time period	No. of players	Equipment required	Referee
PAIRED NUMBERS	307	20 min.	2	None	No
LICENSE BINGO	307	30 min.	2	Pencils, paper	Yes
HOW TO GET THERE	306	30 min.	2 to 4	Maps, pencils	No
HIGHWAY ALPHABET	308	20 min.	2	None	No
ROADSIDE SCAVENGER HUNT	308	30 min.	2 to 6	Pencils, paper	Yes
HOW MANY WAYS?	308	30 min.	2 to 4	Maps, crayons	Yes
WORD HUNT	96	15 min.	2 to 6	Pencils, paper	Yes
JUMBLED CITIES	104	15 min.	2 to 6	Pencils, paper	Yes
CIRCLE GEOGRAPHY	104	30 min.	2 to 6	None	No

YOUNG-ADULT PARTY GAMES

GAMES	Page	Time period	No. of players	Equipment required	Play area
NAME BINGO	262	20 min.	20 to 50	Pencils, paper	Any room
TEAKETTLE	268	25 min.	10 to 25	None	Any room
FEEL	275	20 min.	6 to 12	10 small familiar objects, such as a comb, toothbrush, lighter; paper, pencils	Any room
BOTTICELLI	269	40 min.	6 to 12	None	Any room
LIKES AND DISLIKES	277	15 min.	6 to 12	Pencils, paper	Any room
CHARADES	273	60 min.	6 to 16	Pencils, paper	Any room

WEEKEND HOUSE-PARTY GAMES FOR ADULTS

GAMES	Page	Time period	No. of players	Equipment required	Play area
VOLLEYBALL	366	40 min.	2 to 10	Volleyball and net	Field or large backyard
TABLE TENNIS	359	60 min.	2 to 4	Ping-Pong table, rackets and ball	Basement, playroom, garage
BADMINTON	324	40 min.	2 to 4	Badminton set	Backyard
CROQUET	342	40 min.	2 to 8	Croquet set	Level lawn
DARTS	345	30 min.	2 to 9	Darts, dartboard	Playroom, patio or basement
BOTTICELLI	269	40 min.	4 to 12	None	Living room, den
HIGHBROW PROVERBS	271	25 min.	6 to 12	Pencils, paper	Living room, den
ALL FIVES	236	1 hour or more	3 to 5	Domino set	Living room, den

GAMES FOR AN AFTER-THE-GAME BUFFET

GAMES	Page	Time period	No. of players	Equipment required	Play area
WHAT'S MY NAME	261	30 min.	10 to 25	Slips of paper, pencils	Dining room or living room
HIGHBROW PROVERBS	271	25–40 min.	10 to 25	None	Living room or playroom
A ROUND OF RIDDLES	295	20 min.	10 to 25	None	Living room or playroom

GAMES FOR A HOUSEWARMING PARTY

GAMES	Page	Time period	No. of players	Equipment required	Play area
RHYMING NAMES	262	20 min.	8 to 20	None	Any room
PARTNER ON A STRING	263	20 min.	12 to 20	Lengths of string	Any room
ORANGE DANCE	266	20 min.	12 to 20	Oranges, radio or phonograph	Playroom
STOOP	267	20 min.	12 to 20	None	Playroom
CHAIN RHYME	269	20 min.	12 to 20	None	Any room
SIX GUESSES	271	30 min.	8 to 20	Blackboard, chalk	Any room
TEAM CHARADES	274	40 min.	12 to 20	Pencils, paper	Any room
CRAZY STATUES	268	20 min.	12 to 20	None	Playroom

GAMES FOR AN ADULT'S BIRTHDAY PARTY

GAMES	Page	Time period	No. of players	Equipment required	Play area
COFFEEPOT	268	30 min.	8 to 20	None	Any room
NAME SIX	272	20 min.	12 to 20	Ball or beanbag	Any room
THE-OTHER-HALF CHARADES	274	30 min.	8 to 20	Pencils, paper	Any room
SOUND EFFECTS	275	20 min.	8 to 20	Variety of common household objects	Any room
PAT AND RUB	278	5 min.	8 to 20	None	Any room
ORANGE DANCE	266	20 min.	12 to 20	Oranges, radio or phonograph	Playroom
TO BE CONTINUED	279	40 min.	6 to 20	None	Any room
SPORTS-KNOWLEDGE QUIZ	284	20 min.	6 to 20	None	Any room

AFTER-DINNER PARTY GAMES FOR ADULTS

GAMES	Page	Time period	No. of players	Equipment required	Play area
CHARADES	273	60 min.	6 to 16	None	Living room
BOTTICELLI	269	30 min.	6 to 12	Paper, pencils	Living room
THE NAME SUGGESTS	270	30 min.	6 to 12	None	Living room
ALTERNATE SCHEDULE:					
HOW WERE THEY KNOWN?	287	30 min.	6 to 12	None	Living room
CASINO	192	60 min.	4	Cards	Living room
BRAINTWISTERS	296	30 min.	4 to 12	Pencils, paper	Living room

GAMES FOR THE ELDERLY

GAMES	Page	Time period	No. of players	Equipment required	Play area
MULTIPLE CLOCK SOLITAIRE	194	50 min.	1 to 10	A deck of playing cards for each person	Living room or den
CANASTA	189	60 min.	2 to 6	2 decks of cards, pencil, paper	Living room or den
BIBLE QUIZ	291	20 min.	2 to 10	None	Living room or den
GIN RUMMY	203	50 min.	2 to 6	Cards, paper, pencil	Living room or den
WHO WROTE THIS BOOK?	286	30 min.	2 to 10	None	Living room or den
FAMOUS QUOTATIONS	286	30 min.	2 to 10	None	Living room or den

Your Guide
to the Indexes

Where to find a listing of games for any and every occasion. The Master Index includes every game in the book. The 23 sub-indexes list games according to type and age group.

MASTER INDEX

Party Games for Children

Party Games for Teen-agers or Adults

Active Group Games for Children

Quiet Group Games for Children

Games for Two, Three or Four Children

Games for Two, Three or Four Teen-agers or Adults

Sports and Their Variations

Solitary Activities for Children

Solitary Activities for Teen-agers or Adults

Song and Dance Activities for Children

Song and Dance Activities for Teen-agers or Adults

Activities for Three- to Five-Year-Olds

Activities for the Elderly

Paper-and-Pencil Games for Children

Paper-and-Pencil Games for Teen-agers or Adults

Games and Puzzles That Test Mental Skill

Games of Knowledge

Guessing Games

Activities Involving Acting

Magic Tricks and Stunts

Card and Table Games

Games for the Mentally Retarded

Games for the Physically Handicapped

CONSULTING AUTHOR:

Richard Kraus, Professor of Recreation, Lehman College, City University of New York.

ADVISERS:

The Editors acknowledge their indebtedness to the following people and organizations: Michael Burns, United States Lawn Tennis Association, New York, N.Y.; Hawley T. Chester III, National Hockey League, New York, N.Y.; Nicholas P. Curran, National Basketball Association, New York, N.Y.; Monte Irvin, Baseball—Office of the Commissioner, New York, N.Y.; Mickey McConnell, Little League Baseball, Inc., Williamsport, Pa.; Alfred Spanjer, Bowling Products Group, AMF Incorporated, New York, N.Y.; Dave Staples, Professional Archers Association, Easton, Pa.; Clive Toye, New York Cosmos, North American Soccer League, New York, N.Y.; Christopher Waters, Field Hockey Association of America, New York, N.Y. William W. Lederer, Town of Greenburgh Recreation Commission, White Plains, N.Y.;

Cards for card-game illustrations supplied by Bicycle Playing Card Bureau. Whitman Checker Set, Dominoes and Backgammon Board, © Western Publishing Company, Inc. Nok-Hockey™ Game and Skittles Board, courtesy of Carrom Games. Parcheesi, Parcheesi® Backgammon Game, courtesy of Selchow & Righter Co. Additional assistance given by World Wide Games, Delaware, Ohio.

CONTRIBUTING ARTISTS:

Photography: Sid Avery, Irving Elkin, Robert Huntzinger, Kenneth P. Sneider, William Sonntag

Illustrations: Hal Ashmead, Bettan Prichard, Leonard Spiegel

Paper Game Designs: Angelo Perrone, Dinah James

ACKNOWLEDGMENTS:

A ROUND OF RIDDLES, pp. 295–296: From *Handbook of Indoor Games and Stunts* by Darwin A. Hindman, © 1955, Prentice-Hall, Inc., and from radio program *Doctor I.Q.* © 1954, Lee Segall. BRAINTWISTERS, pp. 296–297: From "Leisure Teasers." Reprinted by permission of the *American Mercury.* FOUR-MINUTE CHALLENGES, pp. 297–298: By Jules Leopold, from *This Week* magazine. SO YOU THINK YOU'RE CLEVER, pp. 298–299: By John Henry Cutler. Reprinted from *American Magazine.* EMERGENCY BRAIN TEASERS, p. 299: From "What Would You Have Done?" Reprinted with permission from *The Saturday Evening Post,* © 1948–1949, Curtis Publishing Co. ARE YOU A GOOD JUDGE OF CHARACTER? p. 300: By John Kord Lagemann, from *This Week* magazine. WHAT DO YOU KNOW ABOUT EATING? pp. 300–301: By Judith Chase Churchill. Reprinted by permission of Curtis Brown, Ltd. WHAT DO YOU KNOW ABOUT YOUR FIGURE? pp. 301–302: By Phoebe Radcliffe. Reprinted by permission. WHAT'S YOUR EYE-Q? pp. 302–303: By Joseph Samachson. Reprinted by permission.